W9-CZY-253

# THE
# AMERICAN
# MARKETPLACE

# THE AMERICAN MARKETPLACE

## Demographics and Spending Patterns

**4th edition**

**by the New Strategist Editors**

**New Strategist Publications, Inc.**
**Ithaca, New York**

New Strategist Publications, Inc.
P.O. Box 242, Ithaca, New York 14851
607/273-0913
www.newstrategist.com

ISBN 1-885070-19-5

Printed in the United States of America

# Table of Contents

**Introduction** ..................................................................................................... 1

## Chapter 1. Education Trends

*Highlights* ........................................................................................................ 3
Americans Are Well-Educated .......................................................................... 4
Hispanics Less Educated Than Whites or Blacks .......................................... 7
Educational Attainment Varies Widely by State ............................................ 9
More Than 4 Million First Graders ................................................................. 11
High School Enrollment Is on the Rise .......................................................... 14
Fewer High School Dropouts ........................................................................... 16
A Boom in High School Diplomas ................................................................... 18
SAT Scores Rising for All Minority Groups ................................................... 20
Among Affluent, Most Children Go to College .............................................. 22
College Enrollment Rate Has Soared ............................................................. 24
Most Older Students Are Part-Timers ............................................................ 27
One in Five College Students Is a Minority ................................................... 29
Women Earn Most Degrees ............................................................................. 34
College Enrollment Will Rise .......................................................................... 44
Most Couples Alike in Education .................................................................... 51
Adult Education Is Popular ............................................................................. 53

## Chapter 2. Health Trends

*Highlights* ........................................................................................................ 55
Americans Feel Good ....................................................................................... 56
Americans Eat More Fruits and Vegetables ................................................. 58
Vitamin Use Increases with Age ..................................................................... 61
Births to Remain below 4 Million until 2005 ............................................... 63
Newborns Show Diversity to Come ................................................................ 65
Men Are More Likely to Exercise Than women ............................................ 68
Sixteen Percent of Americans Do Not Have Health Insurance ................... 72
Vices on the Decline ........................................................................................ 74
Colds and Flu Are the Most Common Illnesses ........................................... 78
Many Americans Are Disabled ....................................................................... 82
Doctor Visits Number in the Millions ............................................................ 85
Hospital Stays Have Become Shorter ............................................................ 87
Millions Use Home Health Services ............................................................... 90
Number of AIDS Patients Continues to Grow ............................................... 93
Heart Disease and Cancer Are Biggest Killers ............................................. 96
Life Expectancy Continues to Rise ................................................................ 98

## Chapter 3. Income Trends

*Highlights* .................................................................................................... 101
Household Affluence Reaches Record High ................................................... 102
Richest Households Receive Growing Share of Income ................................ 104
Improving Fortunes for Young Adults ......................................................... 106
Married Couples Made Gains ....................................................................... 108
Black Incomes Are Growing the Fastest ....................................................... 110
Householders Aged 45 to 54 Have the Highest Incomes ............................. 112
Income Peaks in Middle-Age for Whites, Blacks, and Hispanics ................ 114
Median Income of Black Couples Tops $45,000 .......................................... 118
Median Income of Married Couples Exceeds $51,0000 ................................. 120
From Young Adults to Elderly, Incomes Vary Sharply by Household Type ... 122
Couples with Children Have Highest Incomes ............................................ 129
Single-Parent Families Have Low Incomes .................................................. 132
Many Women Who Live Alone Have Middle-Class Incomes ....................... 134
A College Degree Is Well Worth the Cost ..................................................... 137
Incomes Rise Faster for Women ................................................................... 139
Incomes Decline for Hispanic Men .............................................................. 142
One-Third of Men Aged 45 to 54 Have Incomes of $50,000 or More ......... 145
The 74-Cent Dollar ...................................................................................... 148
Education Boosts Earnings ........................................................................... 150
Few Women Earn More Than Men ............................................................... 153
Incomes Are Highest in the West ................................................................. 156
More Than 80 Percent of 15-to-64-Year-Olds Receive Wage or Salary Income ........... 159
Most Poor Are White .................................................................................... 161

## Chapter 4. Labor Force Trends

*Highlights* .................................................................................................... 165
Men Have Become Less Likely to Work ........................................................ 166
Two-Thirds of Americans Work .................................................................... 168
Labor Force Participation Varies by Race and Hispanic Origin ................... 170
Working Mothers Are the Norm .................................................................. 174
More Than Half the Couples Are Dual Earners ........................................... 177
More Part-Time Workers .............................................................................. 179
Most Working Women Are in White-Collar Occupations ............................ 181
Whites Most Likely to Be Managers and Professionals ............................... 185
Women's Jobs More Concentrated Than Men's ........................................... 190
Job Tenure Falls ........................................................................................... 193
Older Workers Most Likely to Be Self-Employed ........................................ 195
More Than 12 Million Alternative Workers ................................................. 197
More than 3 Million Americans Are Paid to Work at Home ........................ 199
Few Benefits for Part-Time Workers ............................................................ 201
Early Retirement Trend to End .................................................................... 204
Workers to Become More Diverse ................................................................ 206
White-Collar Jobs to Grow Fastest .............................................................. 209

Big Gain for Service Industries .................................................................................. 213
Workers with College Degrees Are in Greatest Demand .............................................. 216

## Chapter 5.  Living Arrangement Trends

*Highlights* ................................................................................................................ 219
People Living Alone Outnumber Married Couples with Children ............................ 220
Households Headed by 45-to-54-Year-Olds Are Growing Fastest ............................. 222
Households Vary by Age ............................................................................................ 224
Big Differences between Black and White Households .............................................. 227
Hispanic Households Are the Youngest ..................................................................... 230
Most Households Are Small ....................................................................................... 232
Half the Women Who Live Alone Are Aged 65 or Older .......................................... 234
More Than One-Third of Households Are in the South ............................................. 236
Most Black Children Live with Mother Only ............................................................ 240
Most Young Adults Live at Home .............................................................................. 242
Lifestyles of Men and Women Diverge in Old Age ................................................... 244
Most Married Couples Have Children at Home ......................................................... 246
Most Single Parents Are Women ............................................................................... 249
Many Unmarried Couples Are Older ......................................................................... 251
Most Americans Are Married ..................................................................................... 253
Most Blacks Are Not Married .................................................................................... 257

## Chapter 6.  Population Trends

*Highlights* ................................................................................................................ 261
More Women Than Men ............................................................................................ 262
Biggest Gainer Will Be the 55-to-59 Age Group ...................................................... 264
Diversity on the Rise ................................................................................................. 266
Aging Boomers Will Boost Fiftysomethings in Every Racial and Ethnic Group ....... 268
West to Grow Fastest ................................................................................................. 274
Minority Populations Are Larger in the South and West .......................................... 276
Nevada to Grow Fastest ............................................................................................ 279
Each State Has a Different Racial and Ethnic Mix .................................................... 282
A Metropolitan Nation .............................................................................................. 291
Americans Are Moving Less ...................................................................................... 295
Immigration Boosts Nation's Growth ........................................................................ 299
Immigrants Head to California ................................................................................... 301
Foreign-Born Americans Are Diverse ........................................................................ 303
Voting Rate Has Declined .......................................................................................... 307
Most Americans Have a Religion ............................................................................... 310
Attendance at Art Events Soars with Education ........................................................ 312

## Chapter 7.  Spending Trends

*Highlights* ................................................................................................................ 315
Little Change in Household Spending ........................................................................ 316
Older Householders Spend the Most .......................................................................... 320

Spending Rises with Income .............................................................................. 340
Couples with Children Spend the Most .......................................................... 360
Spending of Blacks and Hispanics Is above Average on Many Items ......... 374
Spending Is Highest in the West ...................................................................... 388
College Graduates Spend More ....................................................................... 401

## Chapter 8.  Wealth Trends

*Highlights* ......................................................................................................... 415
Net Worth Rises with Age ............................................................................... 416
Americans Have Few Financial Assets ........................................................... 418
Homes Are the Biggest Nonfinancial Asset ................................................... 421
Seventy-Five Percent of American Households Have Debt ........................... 424
Homeownership Is at Record High ................................................................. 427
Forty-Two Percent of Workers Are Covered by a Pension ........................... 430

**For More Information** ........................................................................................ 433

**Glossary** ............................................................................................................ 439

**Bibliography** ..................................................................................................... 443

**Index** ................................................................................................................. 446

# Tables

## Chapter 1. Education Trends

Educational Attainment of Men by Age, 1998 ............................................................. 5
Educational Attainment of Women by Age, 1998 ................................................ 6
Educational Attainment by Race and Hispanic Origin, 1998 ........................................... 8
Educational Attainment by State, 1998 ................................................. 10
School Enrollment by Grade Level, 1996 ................................................. 12
School Enrollment by Age, 1996 ................................................. 13
Projected Enrollment in Kindergarten Through 12th Grade, 1998 to 2008 .................. 15
High School Dropouts by Sex, Race, and Hispanic Origin, 1967 and 1996 .................. 17
Projections of High School Graduates, 1998 to 2008 ......................................... 19
SAT Scores by Race and Ethnicity, 1975–76 and 1994–95 ................................................. 21
Families with Children in College, 1996 ......................................... 23
College Enrollment Rates by Sex, 1960 to 1996 ......................................... 25
College Enrollment Rates by Race and Hispanic Origin, 1976 to 1996 .......................... 26
College Students by Age and Attendance Status, 1996 ......................................... 28
College Students by Race and Hispanic Origin, 1976 and 1995 ..................................... 30
Degrees Conferred by Race and Hispanic Origin, 1995–96 ................................................. 32
Associate's Degrees Conferred by Field of Study and Sex, 1995–96 ......................... 35
Bachelor's Degrees Conferred by Field of Study and Sex, 1995–96 .............................. 37
Master's Degrees Conferred by Field of Study and Sex, 1995–96 ................................. 39
Doctoral Degrees Conferred by Field of Study and Sex, 1995–96 ................................. 41
First-Professional Degrees Conferred by Field of Study and Sex, 1995–96 ................... 43
Projections of College Enrollment by Sex and Age, 1998 and 2008 ............................... 45
Projections of College Enrollment by Level of Degree, 1998 to 2008 .......................... 46
Projections of College Enrollment by Type of Institution, 1998 to 2008 ...................... 48
Projections of Degrees Conferred by Sex, 1998 to 2008 ................................................. 50
Education of Husband by Education of Wife, 1998 ......................................... 52
Adult Education by Age, 1995 ................................................. 54

## Chapter 2. Health Trends

Health Status, 1996 ................................................. 57
Food and Beverage Consumption, 1970 to 1996 ................................................. 59
Use of Vitamin and Mineral Supplements by Sex and Age, 1994–95 ........................... 62
Number of Births, 1990 to 2050 ................................................. 64
Births by Age, Race, and Hispanic Origin of Mother, 1997 ........................................... 66
Births by Race, Age and Marital Status of Mother, 1996 ................................................. 67
Vigorous Exercise by Sex and Age, 1994–95 ................................................. 69
Participation in Outdoor Recreational Activities, 1994–95 ............................................. 70
Health Insurance Coverage by Age, 1997 ................................................. 73
Cigarette Smoking by Sex and Age, 1965 to 1995 ................................................. 75

Alcohol Consumption by Age, 1994 ............................................................................ 76

Drug Use by Age and Type of Drug, 1996 ................................................................. 77

Acute Health Conditions by Age, 1995 ..................................................................... 79

People with Disabilities by Sex and Age, 1994–95 ............................................. 83

Adults with Disabilities by Type of Disability and Age, 1994–95 .................. 84

Physician Visits by Age and Sex, 1996 ..................................................................... 86

Hospital Care, 1980 and 1995 ..................................................................................... 88

Home Health Care Patients by Age, Sex, and Marital Status, 1996 ............... 91

Hospice Care Patients by Age, Sex, and Marital Status, 1996 .......................... 92

People with AIDS by Sex and Age at Diagnosis ................................................... 94

People with AIDS by Sex, Race, and Hispanic Origin ....................................... 95

Leading Causes of Death in the U.S., 1997 ............................................................ 97

Life Expectancy by Age and Sex, 1900 to 1997 ................................................... 99

## Chapter 3. Income Trends

Distribution of Households by Income, 1980 to 1997 ...................................... 103

Distribution of Aggregate Household Income, 1980 to 1997 ......................... 105

Median Household Income by Age of Householder, 1980 to 1997 .............. 107

Median Household Income by Type of Household, 1980 to 1997 ............... 109

Median Household Income by Race and
Hispanic Origin of Householder, 1980 to 1997 ................................................. 111

Household Income by Age of Householder, 1997: Total Households ......... 113

Household Income by Age of Householder, 1997: Black Households ......... 115

Household Income by Age of Householder, 1997: Hispanic Households ... 116

Household Income by Age of Householder, 1997: White Households ........ 117

Median Household Income by Type of Household,
Race, and Hispanic Origin, 1997 ............................................................................ 119

Household Income by Household Type, 1997: Total Households ................. 121

Household Income by Household Type, 1997: Householders Under Age 25 ........... 123

Household Income by Household Type, 1997: Householders Aged 25 to 34 ............. 124

Household Income by Household Type, 1997: Householders Aged 35 to 44 ............. 125

Household Income by Household Type, 1997: Householders Aged 45 to 54 ............. 126

Household Income by Household Type, 1997: Householders Aged 55 to 64 ............. 127

Household Income by Household Type, 1997: Householders Aged 65 or Older ...... 128

Household Income of Married Couples, 1997 ..................................................... 130

Household Income of Dual-Earner Married Couples, 1997 ........................... 131

Household Income of Female- and Male-Headed Families, 1997 ................. 133

Household Income of Men Who Live Alone, 1997 ........................................... 135

Household Income of Women Who Live Alone, 1997 ..................................... 136

Household Income by Education of Householder, 1997 .................................. 138

Median Income of Men by Age, 1980 to 1997 ................................................... 140

Median Income of Women by Age, 1980 to 1997 ............................................. 141

Median Income of Men by Race and Hispanic Origin, 1980 to 1997 ......... 143

Median Income of Women by Race and Hispanic Origin, 1980 to 1997 .... 144

Income of Men by Age, 1997: Total Men ............................................................ 146

Income of Women by Age, 1997: Total Women ................................................ 147

Median Income of Full-Time Workers by Age and Sex, 1997 ....................................... 149

Earnings Distribution of Men Aged 25 or Older by Education, 1997 ......................... 151

Earnings Distribution of Women Aged 25 or Older by Education, 1997 .................... 152

Median Weekly Earnings by Sex, 1998 .......................................................................... 154

Median Income by Metropolitan Status and Region of Residence, 1997 ................... 157

Median Income of Households by State, 1997 .............................................................. 158

Sources of Income, 1997 .................................................................................................. 160

People in Poverty by Age, Race, and Hispanic Origin, 1997 ....................................... 162

Families in Poverty by Race and Hispanic Origin of
Householder and Presence of Children, 1997 .............................................................. 163

## Chapter 4.  Labor Force Trends

Labor Force Participation by Sex and Age, 1970 to 1998 ............................................. 167

Employment Status by Sex and Age, 1998 .................................................................... 169

Employment Status of Blacks by Sex and Age, 1998 .................................................... 171

Employment Status of Hispanics by Sex and Age, 1998 .............................................. 172

Employment Status of Whites by Sex and Age, 1998 ................................................... 173

Labor Force Status of Women by Presence of Children, 1997 ..................................... 175

Labor Force Status of Parents with Children under Age 18, 1997 .............................. 176

Dual-Income Couples by Age, .................................................................................... 1998

Full-Time and Part-Time Workers by Sex, 1980 to 1998 ............................................. 180

Workers by Occupation and Sex, 1998 ......................................................................... 182

Women Workers by Occupation, 1983 and 1998 ......................................................... 183

Workers by Occupation, Race, and Hispanic Origin, 1998 ......................................... 186

Black and Hispanic Workers by Occupation, 1983 and 1998 ...................................... 187

Employment of Men by Industry and Occupation, 1998 ............................................ 191

Employment of Women by Industry and Occupation, 1998 ....................................... 192

Job Tenure by Age, 1983 and 1998 ................................................................................ 194

Self-Employed Workers by Age, 1998 ........................................................................... 196

Workers in Alternative Work Arrangements by Age, 1997 ......................................... 198

People Who Work at Home, 1997 .................................................................................. 200

Employee Benefits for Full- and Part-Time Workers by Size of Firm, 1996–97 ......... 202

Labor Force Projections by Sex and Age, 1996 to 2006 ............................................... 205

Labor Force Projections by Race and Hispanic Origin, 1996 to 2006 ......................... 207

Workers Entering and Leaving the Labor Force, 1996 to 2006 ................................... 208

Projections of Employment by Occupation, 1996 and 2006 ........................................ 210

Fastest-Growing Occupations, 1996 to 2006 ................................................................ 211

Occupations with Largest Job Gains, 1996 to 2006 ..................................................... 212

Projection of Employment by Industry, 1996 and 2006 .............................................. 214

Industries with Fastest Job Gains, 1996 to 2006 .......................................................... 215

Projections of Employment by Education, 1996 and 2006 .......................................... 217

## Chapter 5.  Living Arrangement Trends

Households by Type, 1990 and 1998 .............................................................................. 221

Households by Age of Householder, 1990 to 1998 ....................................................... 223

Households by Household Type and Age of Householder, 1998 ................................. 225

Households by Household Type, Race, and
Hispanic Origin of Householder, 1998 ........................................................................ 228
Households by Age, Race, and Hispanic Origin of Householder, 1998 ..................... 231
Households by Size, 1998 ............................................................................................ 233
People Living Alone by Age and Sex, 1998 ................................................................ 235
Households by Region, Race, and Hispanic Origin, 1998 .......................................... 237
Households by Metropolitan Status, 1998 .................................................................. 239
Living Arrangements of Children by Race and Hispanic Origin, 1980 and 1998 ...... 241
Living Arrangements of Young Adults, 1998 .............................................................. 243
Living Arrangements of People Aged 65 or Older, 1998 ............................................ 245
Married Couples with Children at Home by Age of
Householder and Age of Children, 1998 .................................................................... 247
Married Couples by Age of Householder and
Number of Children under Age 18 at Home, 1998 ...................................................... 248
Female- and Male-Headed Families with Children
under Age 18 at Home by Age of Householder, 1998 ................................................ 250
Characteristics of Cohabiting Couples, 1998 ............................................................. 252
Median Age at First Marriage by Sex, 1890 to 1998 .................................................. 254
Marital Status of Men by Age, 1998 ........................................................................... 255
Marital Status of Women by Age, 1998 ...................................................................... 256
Marital Status by Race, Hispanic Origin, and Age, 1998 ........................................... 258

## Chapter 6.  Population Trends

Population by Age and Sex, 1999 ................................................................................ 263
Population by Age, 1999 to 2005 ................................................................................ 265
Population by Race and Hispanic Origin, 1999 to 2005 ............................................. 267
Non-Hispanic Asians by Age, 1999 to 2005 ............................................................... 269
Non-Hispanic Blacks by Age, 1999 to 2005 ............................................................... 270
Hispanics by Age, 1999 to 2005 ................................................................................. 271
Non-Hispanic Native Americans by Age, 1999 to 2005 ............................................. 272
Non-Hispanic Whites by Age, 1999 to 2005 ............................................................... 273
Population by Region and Division, 1999 to 2005 ...................................................... 275
Population by Region, Race, and Hispanic Origin, 2000 ............................................ 277
Population by Region, Race, and Hispanic Origin, 2005 ............................................ 278
State Populations, 1999 to 2005 ................................................................................. 280
Population by State, Race, and Hispanic Origin, 2000 ............................................... 283
Distribution of State Populations by Race and Hispanic Origin, 2000 ....................... 285
Population by State, Race, and Hispanic Origin, 2005 ............................................... 287
Distribution of State Populations by Race and Hispanic Origin, 2005 ....................... 289
Population by Metropolitan Status, 1950 to 1990 ...................................................... 292
Populations of the Top 50 Metropolitan Areas, 1990 and 2000 ................................. 293
Geographic Mobility of the Population, 1950 to 1997 ................................................ 296
Number of Movers by Age, Housing Tenure, and Employment Status, 1996–97 ...... 297
Distribution of the Population by Mobility Status, 1996–97 ...................................... 298
Immigration to the U.S., 1901 to 1996 ....................................................................... 300
Immigrants by Country of Birth and State of Intended Residence, 1996 ................... 302

Foreign-Born Population by Country of Birth, 1998 ....................................................... 304

Characteristics of the Foreign-Born Population, 1997 .................................................... 305

Voting Rates by Age, 1972 to 1996 ................................................................................. 308

Reasons for Not Voting by Age, 1996 ............................................................................. 309

Religious Preference, 1976 to 1996 ................................................................................. 311

Attendance at Art Events, 1997 ....................................................................................... 313

Participation in the Arts, 1997 ......................................................................................... 314

## Chapter. 7.  Spending Trends

Spending Trends, 1987 to 1997 ....................................................................................... 317

Spending by Age of Householder, 1997 .......................................................................... 322

Indexed Spending by Age of Householder, 1997 ........................................................... 329

Market Shares by Age of Householder, 1997 ................................................................. 336

Spending by Household Income, 1997 ............................................................................ 342

Indexed Spending by Household Income, 1997 ............................................................. 349

Market Shares by Household Income, 1997 ................................................................... 356

Spending by Household Type, 1997 ................................................................................ 362

Indexed Spending by Household Type, 1997 ................................................................. 366

Market Shares by Household Type, 1997 ........................................................................ 370

Spending by Race and Hispanic Origin, 1997 ............................................................... 376

Indexed Spending by Race and Hispanic Origin, 1997 ................................................ 380

Market Shares by Race and Hispanic Origin, 1997 ...................................................... 384

Spending by Region, 1997 ............................................................................................... 389

Indexed Spending by Region, 1997 ................................................................................ 393

Market Shares by Region, 1997 ...................................................................................... 397

Spending by Education of Householder, 1997 ............................................................... 403

Indexed Spending by Education of Householder, 1997 ................................................ 407

Market Shares by Education, 1997 .................................................................................. 411

## Chapter 8.  Wealth Trends

Net Worth of Households, 1995 ....................................................................................... 417

Ownership of Financial Assets, 1995 .............................................................................. 419

Value of Nonfinancial Assets, 1995 ................................................................................ 422

Household with Debt, 1995 .............................................................................................. 425

Homeownership, 1998 ...................................................................................................... 428

Homeownership, 1982 to 1997 ........................................................................................ 429

Pension Coverage, 1997 ................................................................................................... 431

# Illustrations

## Chapter 1. Education Trends

The majority of blacks, whites, and Hispanics are high school graduates ..................... 7
Colorado has the largest proportion of college-educated residents ............................. 9
More than 90 percent of people under age 18 are students ........................................... 11
High school enrollment will rise while elementary declines ........................................ 14
Number of high school graduates will increase ......................................................... 18
College attendance rises with income ...................................................................... 22

## Chapter 2. Health Trends

Most women take vitamins ...................................................................................... 61
Those without health insurance are most likely to be aged 18 to 24 ............................. 72
Disability increases with age .................................................................................. 82
Older Americans visit doctors the most ................................................................... 85
Hospital stays are shortest in the West .................................................................... 87
One in three men diagnosed with AIDS is black ....................................................... 93

## Chapter 3. Income Trends

Big rise in affluence ............................................................................................. 102
Incomes of youngest householders still below 1980 level .......................................... 106
Income varies by household type ........................................................................... 108
Household income peaks in middle-age .................................................................. 112
Women's income can surpass men's ....................................................................... 134
Those with professional degrees have highest incomes ............................................ 137
Big gains for women ............................................................................................ 139
South has the lowest incomes ............................................................................... 156
Poverty rates high for blacks and Hispanics ........................................................... 161

## Chapter 4. Labor Force Trends

Rate is down for men, up for women ...................................................................... 166
Gap is biggest between Hispanic men and women ................................................... 170
Majority of mothers work ..................................................................................... 174
Dual earners dominate couples ............................................................................. 177
Self-employment rises with age ............................................................................ 195
More fiftysomethings at work ............................................................................... 204

## Chapter 5. Living Arrangement Trends

Three most common household types ..................................................................... 220
Fewer householders are aged 25 to 34 ................................................................... 222
Most households headed by people aged 25 to 64 are married couples ....................... 224
White households are the oldest ............................................................................ 230

Two-person households are most common ................................................................... 232
Women who live alone are older ............................................................................... 234
Most white children live with two parents ............................................................... 240
Older women are more likely than older men to live alone ........................................ 244
More than one in four cohabiting couples are same-sex partners ............................... 251

## Chapter 6.  Population Trends

Women increasingly outnumber men with age ............................................................ 262
Asians to grow fastest ................................................................................................ 266
Northeast will be growing slowly ............................................................................... 274
West has smallest share of non-Hispanic whites ......................................................... 276
West has fastest-growing states .................................................................................. 279
Mobility is down ........................................................................................................ 295
California is the top state for immigration ................................................................. 301
Young adults are less likely to vote ............................................................................ 307

## Chapter 7.  Spending Trends

Spending peaks in middle-age ..................................................................................... 320
Nearly one-half of spending is done by the most affluent households ........................ 340
Spending is below average for single parents .............................................................. 360
Blacks and Hispanics spend much more than average
on meats, poultry, fish, and eggs .............................................................................. 374
College graduates spend like yuppies ......................................................................... 401

## Chapter 6.  Wealth Trends

Median net worth peaks in 55-to-64 age group ........................................................... 416
Nonfinancial assets are greater than financial assets ................................................. 418
Credit card debt is most common ............................................................................... 424
Homeownership rate peaks in 55-to-64 age group ....................................................... 427

# Introduction

If there's one thing Americans have in abundance, it is numbers. Billions of statistics await our perusal only a mouse-click away. Harder to come by these days is insight—an understanding of the trends behind the statistics. After all, it is the story behind the statistics—not the numbers alone—that is most important to researchers. Stories reveal the big picture about how Americans live. By knowing the stories behind the statistics, researchers can identify important consumer segments, determine their wants and needs, and reach them with a compelling message.

This, the fourth edition of *The American Marketplace,* cuts through the statistical clutter and tells the American story. It examines our lifestyles in rich detail, from the proportion of immigrants who settle in California to the proportion of babies born out of wedlock, from the net worth of baby boomers to the amount of money people spend on entertainment. It also looks into the future, with projections of populations, occupations, and industries.

Since we published the first edition of *The American Marketplace* in 1992 (titled *The Official Guide to the American Marketplace*), dramatic technological change has reshaped the demographic reference industry. The government's detailed demographic data, once widely available to all in printed reports, is now accessible only to Internet users or in unpublished tables obtained by calling the appropriate government agency with a specific request. The government's web sites, which house enormous spreadsheets of data, are of great value to researchers with the time and skills to first download and then extract the important nuggets of information. The shift from printed reports to web sites—while convenient for number-crunchers—has made demographic analysis a bigger chore. For researchers, it has become more time-consuming than ever to get no-nonsense answers to their questions about the demographics of Americans and how those ever-changing demographics are remaking our society.

*The American Marketplace* has the answers. It has the numbers and the stories behind them. Thumbing through its pages, you can gain more insight into the consumer marketplace than you could by spending all afternoon surfing databases on the Internet. By having it on your bookshelf, you can get the answers to your questions even faster than you could with the fastest modem.

### How to Use This Book

*The American Marketplace* is designed for easy use. It is divided into eight chapters, organized alphabetically: Education, Health, Income, Labor Force, Living Arrangements, Population, Spending, and Wealth.

Most of the tables in this book are based on data collected and published by the federal government, in particular the Bureau of the Census, the Bureau of Labor Statistics, the National Center for Education Statistics, and the National Center for Health Statistics. The federal government continues to be the best source of up-to-date, reliable information on the changing characteristics of Americans. While most of the data we publish are produced by the government, the tables in *The American Marketplace* are not simply reprints of government spreadsheets—as is the case in many other reference books. Instead, each of the book's tables is individually compiled and created by New Strategist's editors, with calculations designed to reveal the stories behind the statistics.

Each chapter of *The American Marketplace* includes the demographic and lifestyle data most important to businesses. A page of text accompanies most of the tables, analyzing the data and highlighting future trends. If you want more statistical detail than the tables provide, you can plumb the original source of the data, listed at the bottom of each table.

The book contains a lengthy table list to help you locate the information you need. For a more detailed search, use the index at the back of the book. Also there is the glossary, which defines the terms commonly used in the tables and text. A list of telephone and web site contacts also appears at the end of the book, allowing researchers to access government specialists and web sites.

*The American Marketplace* will help you cut through the clutter, track the trends, and prosper in the years ahead.

# 1

# Education Trends

◆ **The U.S. has the best-educated population in the world.**
More than one in four men and one in five women are college graduates.

◆ **Blacks are closing the gap with whites in educational attainment.**
Eighty-four percent of whites aged 25 or older are high school graduates, compared with 75 percent of blacks and 55 percent of Hispanics.

◆ **School enrollment is on the rise.**
Between 1996 and 2006, enrollment in the nation's elementary and secondary schools will rise 6 percent. The biggest increase will occur at the secondary level.

◆ **The SAT scores of minority groups have been rising since 1975–76.**
Among blacks, verbal scores were up 24 points between 1975–76 and 1994–95, while math scores rose 34 points.

◆ **As family income rises, children are more likely to go to college.**
Among families with incomes of $75,000 or more who have children aged 18 to 24, 61 percent have a child in college full-time.

◆ **College enrollment rates have increased for whites, blacks, and Hispanics in the past two decades.**
The college enrollment rate grew from 49 to 66 percent for whites between 1976 and 1996, and from 42 to 55 percent for blacks.

◆ **Women earn over one-half of bachelor's and master's degrees.**
As more women gain educational credentials in the years ahead, their earnings will rise, narrowing the gap between men's and women's incomes.

# Americans Are Well-Educated

**Half the American population has some college experience.**

The educational attainment of Americans has increased dramatically over the past three decades. Just 30 years ago, over half the Americans had not even graduated from high school. Then the parents of the baby-boom generation encouraged their children to finish high school and go on to college. The well-educated baby-boom generation has lifted the educational level of the population as a whole.

Overall, 83 percent of men aged 25 or older are high school graduates. The proportion ranges from 68 percent among men aged 65 or older to 87 percent among men aged 25 to 54. The share of men with a college degree peaks among those aged 45 to 54, 32 percent of whom have a bachelor's degree. Only 20 percent of men aged 65 or older are college graduates.

At 83 percent, the proportion of women with a high school diploma is identical to that of men. The proportion ranges from 67 percent among women aged 65 or older to 89 percent among women aged 25 to 44. Women are less likely than men to be college graduates, however, with 22 percent of women holding a bachelor's degree. The women most likely to have completed college are those aged 25 to 34, at 29 percent. Among 25-to-34-year-olds, women are more likely than men to have a bachelor's degree.

♦ The educational level of Americans aged 65 or older will rise sharply as baby boomers reach old age. This development will increase the sophistication of older consumers, changing the ways businesses market to this segment of the population.

# Educational Attainment of Men by Age, 1998

*(number and percent distribution of men aged 25 or older by highest level of education and age, 1998; numbers in thousands)*

|  | total | 25 to 34 | 35 to 44 | 45 to 54 | 55 to 64 | 65 or older |
|---|---|---|---|---|---|---|
| **Total men** | **82,376** | **19,526** | **22,055** | **16,599** | **10,673** | **13,524** |
| Not a high school graduate | 14,175 | 2,579 | 2,873 | 2,230 | 2,109 | 4,386 |
| High school graduate | 26,575 | 6,592 | 7,538 | 4,701 | 3,661 | 4,084 |
| Some college, no degree | 14,122 | 3,657 | 3,895 | 2,995 | 1,589 | 1,986 |
| Associate's degree | 5,670 | 1,576 | 1,820 | 1,388 | 493 | 393 |
| Bachelor's degree | 14,090 | 3,931 | 3,971 | 3,091 | 1,550 | 1,549 |
| Master's degree | 4,640 | 821 | 1,174 | 1,341 | 744 | 560 |
| Professional degree | 1,749 | 242 | 474 | 451 | 266 | 317 |
| Doctoral degree | 1,353 | 131 | 311 | 401 | 260 | 250 |
| High school graduate or more | 68,199 | 16,950 | 19,183 | 14,368 | 8,563 | 9,139 |
| Some college or more | 41,624 | 10,358 | 11,645 | 9,667 | 4,902 | 5,055 |
| Bachelor's degree or more | 21,832 | 5,125 | 5,930 | 5,284 | 2,820 | 2,676 |
| **Total men** | **100.0%** | **100.0%** | **100.0%** | **100.0%** | **100.0%** | **100.0%** |
| Not a high school graduate | 17.2 | 13.2 | 13.0 | 13.4 | 19.8 | 32.4 |
| High school graduate | 32.3 | 33.8 | 34.2 | 28.3 | 34.3 | 30.2 |
| Some college, no degree | 17.1 | 18.7 | 17.7 | 18.0 | 14.9 | 14.7 |
| Associate's degree | 6.9 | 8.1 | 8.3 | 8.4 | 4.6 | 2.9 |
| Bachelor's degree | 17.1 | 20.1 | 18.0 | 18.6 | 14.5 | 11.5 |
| Master's degree | 5.6 | 4.2 | 5.3 | 8.1 | 7.0 | 4.1 |
| Professional degree | 2.1 | 1.2 | 2.1 | 2.7 | 2.5 | 2.3 |
| Doctoral degree | 1.6 | 0.7 | 1.4 | 2.4 | 2.4 | 1.8 |
| High school graduate or more | 82.8 | 86.8 | 87.0 | 86.6 | 80.2 | 67.6 |
| Some college or more | 50.5 | 53.0 | 52.8 | 58.2 | 45.9 | 37.4 |
| Bachelor's degree or more | 26.5 | 26.2 | 26.9 | 31.8 | 26.4 | 19.8 |

*Source: Bureau of the Census,* Educational Attainment in the United States: March 1998, *detailed tables from Current Population Report P20-513, 1998; calculations by New Strategist*

# Educational Attainment of Women by Age, 1998

*(number and percent distribution of women aged 25 or older by highest level of education and age, 1998; numbers in thousands)*

| | total | 25 to 34 | 35 to 44 | 45 to 54 | 55 to 64 | 65 or older |
|---|---|---|---|---|---|---|
| **Total women** | **89,835** | **19,828** | **22,407** | **17,459** | **11,582** | **18,558** |
| Not a high school graduate | 15,381 | 2,176 | 2,453 | 2,108 | 2,449 | 6,191 |
| High school graduate | 31,599 | 5,977 | 7,599 | 6,242 | 4,649 | 7,131 |
| Some college, no degree | 15,516 | 4,128 | 4,252 | 3,070 | 1,737 | 2,328 |
| Associate's degree | 7,198 | 1,858 | 2,326 | 1,520 | 670 | 825 |
| Bachelor's degree | 14,215 | 4,436 | 4,185 | 2,858 | 1,340 | 1,396 |
| Master's degree | 4,592 | 943 | 1,204 | 1,300 | 601 | 544 |
| Professional degree | 820 | 234 | 226 | 185 | 78 | 96 |
| Doctoral degree | 515 | 75 | 160 | 175 | 58 | 47 |
| High school graduate or more | 74,455 | 17,651 | 19,952 | 15,350 | 9,133 | 12,367 |
| Some college or more | 42,856 | 11,674 | 12,353 | 9,108 | 4,484 | 5,236 |
| Bachelor's degree or more | 20,142 | 5,688 | 5,775 | 4,518 | 2,077 | 2,083 |
| **Total women** | **100.0%** | **100.0%** | **100.0%** | **100.0%** | **100.0%** | **100.0%** |
| Not a high school graduate | 17.1 | 11.0 | 10.9 | 12.1 | 21.1 | 33.4 |
| High school graduate | 35.2 | 30.1 | 33.9 | 35.8 | 40.1 | 38.4 |
| Some college, no degree | 17.3 | 20.8 | 19.0 | 17.6 | 15.0 | 12.5 |
| Associate's degree | 8.0 | 9.4 | 10.4 | 8.7 | 5.8 | 4.4 |
| Bachelor's degree | 15.8 | 22.4 | 18.7 | 16.4 | 11.6 | 7.5 |
| Master's degree | 5.1 | 4.8 | 5.4 | 7.4 | 5.2 | 2.9 |
| Professional degree | 0.9 | 1.2 | 1.0 | 1.1 | 0.7 | 0.5 |
| Doctoral degree | 0.6 | 0.4 | 0.7 | 1.0 | 0.5 | 0.3 |
| High school graduate or more | 82.9 | 89.0 | 89.0 | 87.9 | 78.9 | 66.6 |
| Some college or more | 47.7 | 58.9 | 55.1 | 52.2 | 38.7 | 28.2 |
| Bachelor's degree or more | 22.4 | 28.7 | 25.8 | 25.9 | 17.9 | 11.2 |

*Source: Bureau of the Census,* Educational Attainment in the United States: March 1998, *detailed tables from Current Population Report P20-513, 1998; calculations by New Strategist*

# Hispanics Less Educated Than Whites or Blacks

## Only about 55 percent of Hispanics have a high school diploma.

Whites and blacks under age 45 are almost equally likely to be high school graduates, while Hispanics lag far behind in educational attainment. Eighty-eight percent of white men aged 35 to 44 have a high school diploma, for example, as do 82 percent of black men in the age group. But only 59 percent of Hispanic men aged 35 to 44 are high school graduates. Among women aged 35 to 44, 90 percent of whites and 86 percent of blacks are high school graduates, compared with only 61 percent of Hispanic women in the age group.

At the college level, the gap between blacks and whites widens. While 26 percent of white men aged 25 or older are college graduates, only 13 percent of black men and 11 percent of Hispanic men are college graduates. Among women, 22 percent of whites hold a college degree compared with 14 percent of blacks and 10 percent of Hispanics.

♦ Because immigrants with little education account for a large share of the nation's Hispanics, they lower educational attainment levels for the Hispanic population as a whole.

### The majority of blacks, whites, and Hispanics are high school graduates

*(percent of people aged 25 or older who are high school graduates, by sex, race, and Hispanic origin, 1998)*

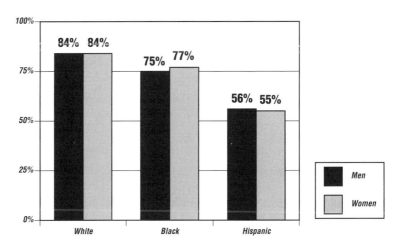

# Educational Attainment by Race and Hispanic Origin, 1998

*(percent of people aged 25 or older who are high school or college graduates, by sex, age, race, and Hispanic origin, 1998)*

| | high school graduate or more | | | | bachelor's degree or more | | | |
|---|---|---|---|---|---|---|---|---|
| | *total* | *white* | *black* | *Hispanic* | *total* | *white* | *black* | *Hispanic* |
| **Total men** | **82.8%** | **83.6%** | **75.2%** | **55.7%** | **26.5%** | **27.3%** | **13.9%** | **11.1%** |
| Aged 25 to 34 | 86.8 | 86.5 | 87.1 | 59.9 | 26.2 | 26.8 | 15.0 | 9.8 |
| Aged 35 to 44 | 87.0 | 87.6 | 81.5 | 60.1 | 26.9 | 27.8 | 14.1 | 13.0 |
| Aged 45 to 54 | 86.6 | 87.6 | 77.0 | 54.3 | 31.9 | 32.9 | 18.2 | 12.5 |
| Aged 55 to 64 | 80.2 | 81.9 | 63.0 | 49.2 | 26.4 | 27.1 | 12.4 | 11.6 |
| Aged 65 or older | 67.6 | 69.8 | 41.9 | 32.0 | 19.8 | 20.8 | 6.0 | 6.8 |
| **Total women** | **82.9** | **83.8** | **76.7** | **55.3** | **22.4** | **22.8** | **15.4** | **10.9** |
| Aged 25 to 34 | 88.6 | 89.5 | 86.9 | 63.7 | 26.6 | 30.1 | 15.6 | 12.3 |
| Aged 35 to 44 | 89.3 | 89.6 | 85.9 | 60.4 | 26.7 | 26.7 | 16.5 | 12.5 |
| Aged 45 to 54 | 84.5 | 89.1 | 82.0 | 55.5 | 22.8 | 26.2 | 19.5 | 11.7 |
| Aged 55 to 64 | 74.0 | 81.1 | 64.7 | 46.3 | 13.8 | 17.7 | 15.5 | 8.2 |
| Aged 65 or older | 66.6 | 69.0 | 44.4 | 27.7 | 11.2 | 11.5 | 7.7 | 4.5 |

*Source: Bureau of the Census,* Educational Attainment in the United States: March 1998, *detailed tables from Current Population Report P20-513, 1998; calculations by New Strategist*

# Educational Attainment Varies Widely by State

## In some states, more than 30 percent of adults are college graduates, while in other states the proportion is below 20 percent.

The proportion of Americans aged 25 or older who have a high school diploma ranges from a low of 76 percent in West Virginia to a high of 92 percent in Washington, a difference of 16 percentage points. The proportion of residents with a college degree is lowest in Arkansas and West Virginia, at 16 percent. In Colorado, the share of college graduates is more than twice as large. It is no surprise that the states with the least-educated populations are also some of the poorest, while those with the best-educated populations are some of the richest. Educated people typically make much more money than those with less education.

♦ The educational level of the workforce is one factor behind business location decisions. Better-educated populations attract business investment, increasing employment opportunities for people who live there.

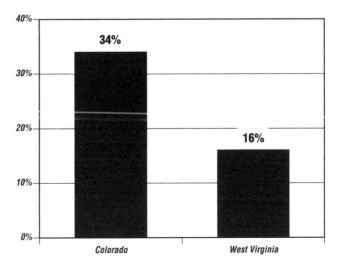

### Colorado has the largest proportion of college-educated residents

*(percent of people with a college degree in the states with the highest and lowest proportion, 1998)*

# Educational Attainment by State, 1998

*(percent of people aged 25 or older who are high school or college graduates, by state, 1998)*

| | high school graduate | college graduate | | high school graduate | college graduate |
|---|---|---|---|---|---|
| **Total U.S.** | **82.8%** | **24.4%** | Missouri | 82.9% | 22.4% |
| Alabama | 78.8 | 20.6 | Montana | 89.1 | 23.9 |
| Alaska | 90.6 | 24.2 | Nebraska | 87.7 | 20.9 |
| Arizona | 81.9 | 21.9 | Nevada | 89.1 | 20.6 |
| Arkansas | 76.8 | 16.2 | New Hampshire | 84.0 | 26.6 |
| California | 80.1 | 26.4 | New Jersey | 86.5 | 30.1 |
| Colorado | 89.6 | 34.0 | New Mexico | 79.6 | 23.1 |
| Connecticut | 83.7 | 31.4 | New York | 81.5 | 26.8 |
| Delaware | 85.2 | 25.1 | North Carolina | 81.4 | 23.3 |
| District of Columbia | 83.8 | 36.5 | North Dakota | 84.3 | 22.5 |
| Florida | 81.9 | 22.5 | Ohio | 86.2 | 21.5 |
| Georgia | 80.0 | 20.7 | Oklahoma | 84.6 | 20.5 |
| Hawaii | 84.6 | 24.0 | Oregon | 85.5 | 27.7 |
| Idaho | 82.7 | 20.3 | Pennsylvania | 84.1 | 22.1 |
| Illinois | 84.2 | 25.8 | Rhode Island | 80.7 | 27.8 |
| Indiana | 83.5 | 17.7 | South Carolina | 78.6 | 21.3 |
| Iowa | 87.7 | 20.3 | South Dakota | 86.3 | 21.8 |
| Kansas | 89.2 | 28.5 | Tennessee | 76.9 | 16.9 |
| Kentucky | 77.9 | 20.1 | Texas | 78.3 | 23.3 |
| Louisiana | 78.6 | 19.5 | Utah | 89.3 | 27.6 |
| Maine | 86.7 | 19.2 | Vermont | 86.7 | 27.1 |
| Maryland | 84.7 | 31.8 | Virginia | 82.6 | 30.3 |
| Massachusetts | 85.6 | 31.0 | Washington | 92.0 | 28.1 |
| Michigan | 85.4 | 22.1 | West Virginia | 76.4 | 16.3 |
| Minnesota | 89.4 | 31.0 | Wisconsin | 88.0 | 22.3 |
| Mississippi | 77.3 | 19.5 | Wyoming | 90.0 | 19.8 |

*Source: Bureau of the Census,* Educational Attainment in the United States: March 1998, *detailed tables from Current Population Report P20-513, 1998*

# More Than 4 Million First Graders

## Enrollment surpasses 4 million in 1st, 6th, and 9th grades.

The baby boomlet of the late 1980s and early 1990s is boosting school enrollment. More than 4.2 million children were in first grade in 1996, with another 4 million right behind them in kindergarten.

Overall, 28 percent of Americans aged three or older are in school. The proportion of the population enrolled in school has grown during the past few decades in both the younger and older age groups. The proportion of three- and four-year-olds enrolled in nursery school more than doubled between 1970 and 1996, from 21 to 48 percent. The proportion of 18- and 19-year-olds in school, most of them in college, has grown from 48 to 62 percent. Many older Americans are back in the classroom as well. In 1996, nearly 3 million people aged 35 or older were enrolled in school.

♦ With some public schools now opening their doors to four-year-olds, and with education becoming increasingly important to earnings, the percentage of younger and older Americans enrolled in school will continue to rise in the years ahead.

### More than 90 percent of people under age 18 are students

*(percent of people aged 3 or older enrolled in school by age, 1996)*

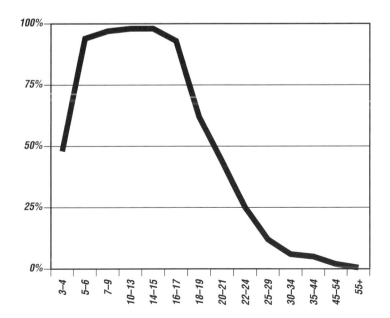

# School Enrollment by Grade Level, 1996

*(number and percent distribution of people attending elementary and secondary school by grade, fall 1996; numbers in thousands)*

|  | number | percent |
|---|---|---|
| **Total students** | **50,858** | **100.0%** |
| **Total elementary** | **35,548** | **69.9** |
| Kindergarten | 4,034 | 7.9 |
| 1st grade | 4,209 | 8.3 |
| 2nd grade | 3,942 | 7.8 |
| 3rd grade | 3,889 | 7.6 |
| 4th grade | 3,880 | 7.6 |
| 5th grade | 3,972 | 7.8 |
| 6th grade | 4,013 | 7.9 |
| 7th grade | 3,835 | 7.5 |
| 8th grade | 3,774 | 7.4 |
| **Total secondary** | **15,310** | **30.1** |
| 9th grade | 4,052 | 8.0 |
| 10th grade | 3,934 | 7.7 |
| 11th grade | 3,662 | 7.2 |
| 12th grade | 3,662 | 7.2 |

*Source: Bureau of the Census,* School Enrollment—Social and Economic Characteristics of Students: October 1996, *detailed tables from Current Population Report, P20-500, 1998; calculations by New Strategist*

# School Enrollment by Age, 1996

*(number and percent of people aged 3 or older enrolled in school by age, fall 1996; numbers in thousands)*

|  | number | percent |
|---|---|---|
| **Total people enrolled** | **70,297** | **27.8%** |
| Aged 3 and 4 | 3,959 | 48.3 |
| Aged 5 and 6 | 7,893 | 94.0 |
| Aged 7 to 9 | 11,577 | 97.2 |
| Aged 10 to 13 | 15,359 | 98.1 |
| Aged 14 and 15 | 7,598 | 97.9 |
| Aged 16 and 17 | 7,220 | 92.8 |
| Aged 18 and 19 | 4,539 | 61.5 |
| Aged 20 and 21 | 3,017 | 44.4 |
| Aged 22 to 24 | 2,605 | 24.8 |
| Aged 25 to 29 | 2,265 | 11.9 |
| Aged 30 to 34 | 1,286 | 6.1 |
| Aged 35 to 44 | 1,935 | 4.5 |
| Aged 45 to 54 | 790 | 2.4 |
| Aged 55 or older | 254 | 0.5 |

*Source: Bureau of the Census,* School Enrollment—Social and Economic Characteristics of Students: October 1996, *detailed tables from Current Population Report P20-500, 1998; calculations by New Strategist*

# High School Enrollment Is on the Rise

**The number of students in 9th through 12th grade should increase 11 percent between 1998 and 2008.**

Between 1998 and 2008, enrollment in the nation's elementary and secondary schools will rise 3 percent overall, but the entire gain will be in the 9th through 12th grades.

Enrollment in kindergarten through 8th grade is projected to decline slightly, falling 0.2 percent as the baby boomlet of the late 1980s and early 1990s ages out of the elementary grades. Enrollment in 9th through 12th grades, in contrast, is projected to rise 11 percent between 1998 and 2008 as the children of the boomlet grow up. The number of high school students is projected to climb from 14.6 million to 16.2 million during those years.

◆ With about 4 million births a year in the United States, elementary and secondary school enrollment will stabilize at more than 50 million for years to come.

### High school enrollment will rise while elementary declines

*(percent change in number of people enrolled in kindergarten through 12th grade, by grade level, 1998 to 2008)*

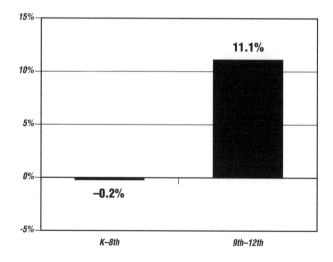

# Projected Enrollment in Kindergarten Through 12th Grade, 1998 to 2008

*(number of people enrolled in kindergarten through 12th grade by control of institution, fall 1998 to fall 2008; percent change, 1998–2008; numbers in thousands)*

|  | total | | | public | | | private | | |
|---|---|---|---|---|---|---|---|---|---|
|  | *total* | *K–8th* | *9th–12th* | *total* | *K–8th* | *9th–12th* | *total* | *K–8th* | *9th–12th* |
| 1998 | 52,718 | 38,110 | 14,608 | 46,792 | 33,522 | 13,270 | 5,927 | 4,588 | 1,339 |
| 1999 | 53,112 | 38,338 | 14,774 | 47,143 | 33,722 | 13,420 | 5,970 | 4,616 | 1,354 |
| 2000 | 53,445 | 38,543 | 14,902 | 47,439 | 33,903 | 13,537 | 6,006 | 4,640 | 1,366 |
| 2001 | 53,736 | 38,716 | 15,020 | 47,698 | 34,055 | 13,643 | 6,038 | 4,661 | 1,376 |
| 2002 | 53,987 | 38,795 | 15,192 | 47,924 | 34,124 | 13,800 | 6,063 | 4,671 | 1,392 |
| 2003 | 54,153 | 38,795 | 15,358 | 48,075 | 34,124 | 13,951 | 6,078 | 4,671 | 1,407 |
| 2004 | 54,308 | 38,606 | 15,702 | 48,221 | 33,958 | 14,263 | 6,087 | 4,648 | 1,439 |
| 2005 | 54,426 | 38,376 | 16,050 | 48,335 | 33,756 | 14,579 | 6,091 | 4,620 | 1,471 |
| 2006 | 54,457 | 38,181 | 16,276 | 48,368 | 33,584 | 14,785 | 6,088 | 4,597 | 1,491 |
| 2007 | 54,425 | 38,073 | 16,352 | 48,342 | 33,489 | 14,854 | 6,082 | 4,584 | 1,498 |
| 2008 | 54,268 | 38,034 | 16,234 | 48,201 | 33,455 | 14,746 | 6,067 | 4,579 | 1,488 |

**Percent change**

| 1998 to 2008 | 2.9% | –0.2% | 11.1% | 3.0% | –0.2% | 11.1% | 2.4% | –0.2% | 11.1% |
|---|---|---|---|---|---|---|---|---|---|

*Source: National Center for Education Statistics, Projections of Education Statistics to 2008, NCES 98-016, 1998; calculations by New Strategist*

# Fewer High School Dropouts

**High school dropout rates have fallen sharply among blacks during the past three decades.**

Among 16-to-24-year-olds in 1996, only 11 percent were neither high school graduates nor currently enrolled in school, down from 17 percent in 1967. Dropout rates have fallen for both men and women, and women's dropout rate now is below that of men.

Dropout rates remain stubbornly high for Hispanics. While just 7 percent of whites aged 16 to 24 were high school dropouts in 1996, fully 29 percent of Hispanics in the age group were dropouts. The Hispanic dropout rate has declined only 5 percentage points since 1972.

♦ The massive migration of poorly educated Hispanics into the United States during the past few decades explains why the dropout rate for Hispanics remains so high. The rate is not likely to fall until the immigrant share of the Hispanic population declines.

# High School Dropouts by Sex, Race, and Hispanic Origin, 1967 and 1996

*(percent of people aged 16 to 24 who were not enrolled in school and were not high school graduates by sex, race, and Hispanic origin, 1967 and 1996; percentage point change, 1967–96)*

|  | 1996 | 1967 | percentage point change 1967–96 |
|---|---|---|---|
| **Total people** | **11.1%** | **17.0%** | **–5.9** |
| White, non-Hispanic | 7.3 | 15.4 | –8.1 |
| Black, non-Hispanic | 13.0 | 28.6 | –15.6 |
| Hispanic* | 29.4 | 34.3 | –4.9 |
| **Total men** | **11.4** | **16.5** | **–5.1** |
| White, non-Hispanic | 7.3 | 14.7 | –7.4 |
| Black, non-Hispanic | 13.5 | 30.6 | –17.1 |
| Hispanic* | 30.3 | 33.7 | –3.4 |
| **Total women** | **10.9** | **17.3** | **–6.4** |
| White, non-Hispanic | 7.3 | 16.1 | –8.8 |
| Black, non-Hispanic | 12.5 | 26.9 | –14.4 |
| Hispanic* | 28.3 | 34.9 | –6.6 |

*\* The earliest available statistics for Hispanics are from 1972.*
*Source: National Center for Education Statistics,* Digest of Education Statistics 1997, *NCES 98-015, 1997; calculations by New Strategist*

# A Boom in High School Diplomas

**The number of people graduating from high school will climb 17 percent between 1998 and 2008.**

As the children born during the late 1980s and early 1990s enter the nation's high schools, the number of high school graduates will climb from 2.7 million in 1998 to 3.1 million in 2008. The annual crop of graduates is projected to rise steadily during the entire 10-year period. The number of graduates from private schools is projected to grow at about the same rate as that from public schools, and should remain at about 10 percent of total graduates.

◆ The projected rise in high school graduates is good news for the nation's colleges, which have been scrambling for students while the small Generation X graduated from high school.

### Number of high school graduates will increase

*(number of people graduating from high school, 1998 to 2008; in millions)*

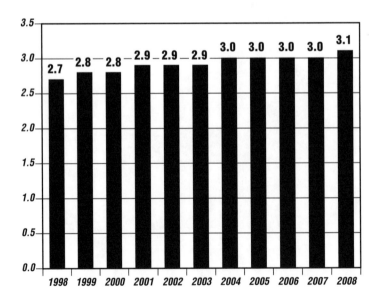

# Projections of High School Graduates, 1998 to 2008

*(number of people graduating from high school by control of institution, 1998–2008; percent change 1998–2008; numbers in thousands)*

|  | total | public | private |
|---|---|---|---|
| 1998 | 2,653 | 2,378 | 275 |
| 1999 | 2,751 | 2,465 | 285 |
| 2000 | 2,847 | 2,552 | 295 |
| 2001 | 2,875 | 2,576 | 298 |
| 2002 | 2,887 | 2,587 | 299 |
| 2003 | 2,909 | 2,607 | 302 |
| 2004 | 2,972 | 2,664 | 308 |
| 2005 | 2,976 | 2,667 | 309 |
| 2006 | 2,985 | 2,675 | 310 |
| 2007 | 3,044 | 2,728 | 316 |
| 2008 | 3,093 | 2,772 | 321 |
| **Percent change** | | | |
| 1998 to 2008 | 16.6% | 16.6% | 16.7% |

*Source: National Center for Education Statistics,* Projections of Education Statistics to 2008, *NCES 98-016, 1998; calculations by New Strategist*

# SAT Scores Rising for All Minority Groups

**The much-talked-about decline in SAT scores over the past few decades is a more complex story than it seems. For many test takers, scores are rising.**

The growing diversity of test takers has been driving down average scores. In 1994–95, more than 1 million prospective college students took the Scholastic Aptitude Test (SAT), up from just 11,000 in 1941, when the test was first administered. As increasing numbers of students took the test, average scores were pushed down. But a closer look reveals rising scores for most groups.

The SAT scores of minority groups have been rising since 1975–76. Among blacks, verbal scores were up 24 points between 1975–76 and 1994–95, while math scores were 34 points higher. Whites are the only racial group whose scores have declined—and only on the verbal section of the exam.

◆ Overall, SAT scores are likely to show slow improvement in the years ahead as minority scores continue to rise.

# SAT Scores by Race and Ethnicity, 1975–76 and 1994–95

*(average Scholastic Assessment Test scores by race and ethnicity of student, 1975–76 and 1994–95; change in score, 1975–76 to 1994–95)*

|  | 1994–95 | 1975–76 | change |
|---|---|---|---|
| **Verbal SAT** | | | |
| **Total students** | 428 | 431 | –3 |
| White | 448 | 451 | –3 |
| Black | 356 | 332 | 24 |
| Mexican-American | 376 | 371 | 5 |
| Puerto Rican | 372 | 364 | 8 |
| Asian-American | 418 | 414 | 4 |
| American Indian | 403 | 388 | 15 |
| Other | 432 | 410 | 22 |
| **Mathematical SAT** | | | |
| **Total students** | 482 | 472 | 10 |
| White | 498 | 493 | 5 |
| Black | 388 | 354 | 34 |
| Mexican-American | 426 | 410 | 16 |
| Puerto Rican | 411 | 401 | 10 |
| Asian-American | 538 | 518 | 20 |
| American Indian | 447 | 420 | 27 |
| Other | 486 | 458 | 28 |

*Source: National Center for Education Statistics,* Digest of Education Statistics *1997, NCES 98-015, 1997; calculations by New Strategist*

# Among Affluent, Most Children Go to College

## As family income rises, children are more likely to go to college.

It's no surprise that family income is one of the best predictors of whether children have the opportunity to go to college. Among all families with children aged 18 to 24, 41 percent have a child in college full-time. This proportion rises steadily with income, to the 61 percent majority of families with incomes of $75,000 or more.

Among families with children aged 18 to 24 whose incomes are below $20,000, just 24 percent have a child in college full-time.

◆ Children of the affluent can devote full attention to their studies because their parents are paying the bills. Many children from less affluent families must attend school part-time because they have to work.

### College attendance rises with income

*(among families with children aged 18 to 24, percentage of children who attend college full-time, by household income, 1996)*

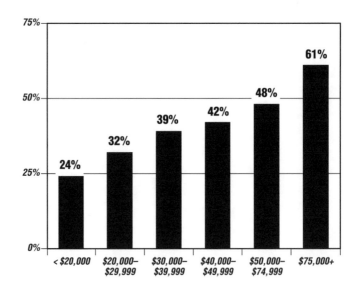

# Families with Children in College, 1996

*(total number of families, number with children aged 18 to 24, and number and percent with children aged 18 to 24 attending college full-time, by household income, 1996; numbers in thousands)*

| | total | with children aged 18–24 | with one or more children attending college full-time | | |
|---|---|---|---|---|---|
| | | | number | percent of total families | percent of families with children 18–24 |
| **Total families** | **71,088** | **10,265** | **4,244** | **6.0%** | **41.3%** |
| Under $20,000 | 15,207 | 1,812 | 430 | 2.8 | 23.7 |
| $20,000 to $29,999 | 10,074 | 1,284 | 406 | 4.0 | 31.6 |
| $30,000 to $39,999 | 9,225 | 1,213 | 478 | 5.2 | 39.4 |
| $40,000 to $49,999 | 6,882 | 986 | 414 | 6.0 | 42.0 |
| $50,000 to $74,999 | 12,050 | 1,992 | 958 | 8.0 | 48.1 |
| $75,000 or more | 9,834 | 1,855 | 1,126 | 11.5 | 60.7 |

*Source: Bureau of the Census,* School Enrollment–Social and Economic Characteristics of Students: October 1996, *Current Population Reports, P20-500, 1998; calculations by New Strategist*

# College Enrollment Rate Has Soared

## Rate is up because Americans are trying to improve their lives.

The rate at which high school graduates enroll in college has soared over the past few decades, despite the rising cost of attending college. Once a privilege reserved for the nation's elite, the college experience now belongs to the majority of young adults.

Among women aged 16 to 24 who graduated from high school in 1996, 70 percent enrolled in college within 12 months. This figure is up sharply from just 38 percent in 1960. Among men, rates increased from 54 to 60 percent between 1960 and 1996.

College enrollment rates have increased for whites, blacks, and Hispanics in the past two decades. For whites, the rate has grown from 49 percent in 1976 to 66 percent in 1996. For blacks, the rate increased from 42 to 55 percent during those years. The Hispanic rate has also grown, from 49 percent in 1976 to 51 percent in 1995.

♦ Many of those who start college never finish—which is why fewer than half the nation's young adults have a college diploma even though more than half enroll in college. Because even a few years of college can make a big difference in earning power, however, the rise in enrollment rates is good news.

# College Enrollment Rates by Sex, 1960 to 1996

*(percent of people aged 16 to 24 graduating from high school in the previous 12 months who were enrolled in college as of October of each year, by sex; percentage point difference in enrollment rates of men and women, 1960–96)*

|  | men | women | percentage point difference |
|---|---|---|---|
| 1996 | 60.1% | 69.7% | –9.6 |
| 1995 | 62.6 | 61.4 | 1.2 |
| 1994 | 60.6 | 63.2 | –2.6 |
| 1993 | 59.7 | 65.4 | –5.7 |
| 1992 | 59.6 | 63.8 | –4.2 |
| 1991 | 57.6 | 67.1 | –9.5 |
| 1990 | 57.8 | 62.0 | –4.2 |
| 1989 | 57.6 | 61.6 | –4.0 |
| 1988 | 57.0 | 60.8 | –3.8 |
| 1987 | 58.4 | 55.3 | 3.1 |
| 1986 | 55.9 | 51.9 | 4.0 |
| 1985 | 58.6 | 56.9 | 1.7 |
| 1980 | 46.7 | 51.8 | –5.1 |
| 1975 | 52.6 | 49.0 | 3.6 |
| 1970 | 55.2 | 48.5 | 6.7 |
| 1965 | 57.3 | 45.3 | 12.0 |
| 1960 | 54.0 | 37.9 | 16.1 |

*Source: National Center for Education Statistics,* Digest of Education Statistics 1997, *NCES 98-015, 1997; calculations by New Strategist*

# College Enrollment Rates by Race and Hispanic Origin, 1976 to 1996

*(percent of people aged 16 to 24 graduating from high school in the previous 12 months who were enrolled in college as of October of each year, by race and Hispanic origin, 1976–96)*

|      | white | black | Hispanic* |
|------|-------|-------|-----------|
| 1996 | 65.8% | 55.3% | –         |
| 1995 | 62.6  | 51.4  | 51.1%     |
| 1994 | 63.6  | 50.9  | 55.1      |
| 1993 | 62.8  | 55.6  | 55.4      |
| 1992 | 63.4  | 47.9  | 58.1      |
| 1991 | 64.6  | 45.6  | 53.1      |
| 1990 | 61.5  | 46.3  | 53.3      |
| 1989 | 60.4  | 52.8  | 53.2      |
| 1988 | 60.7  | 45.0  | 48.6      |
| 1987 | 56.6  | 51.9  | 45.0      |
| 1986 | 56.0  | 36.5  | 43.0      |
| 1985 | 59.4  | 42.3  | 46.6      |
| 1980 | 49.9  | 41.8  | 49.9      |
| 1976 | 48.9  | 41.9  | 48.9      |

*\* Three-year rolling average due to small sample size.*
*Source: National Center for Education Statistics,* Digest of Education Statistics 1997, *NCES 98-015*

# Most Older Students Are Part-Timers

## With families to support, older students cannot afford to go to school full-time.

As the number of older college students has grown, so has the number of students attending college part-time. Many older students have families to support and cannot afford the luxury of full-time study. Instead, they juggle jobs and classes by attending school part-time. In 1996, 35 percent of college students were part-timers.

Most students under age 25 attend school full-time. Eighty-nine percent of college students aged 18 or 19 are full-time students, as are 86 percent of those aged 20 to 21. This figure stands at 76 percent among 22-to-24-year-olds, and drops to 50 percent among students aged 25 to 29.

Among full-time students, 77 percent are under age 25. Among part-time students, 74 percent are aged 25 or older.

♦ College students represent two very different markets, a younger market of full-time students and an older market of students juggling jobs, families, and classes.

# College Students by Age and Attendance Status, 1996

*(number of people aged 15 or older enrolled in institutions of higher education by age and attendance status, 1996; numbers in thousands)*

| | total | full-time number | full-time percent | part-time number | part-time percent |
|---|---|---|---|---|---|
| **Total people** | **15,226** | **9,839** | **64.6%** | **5,388** | **35.4%** |
| Aged 15 to 17 | 237 | 192 | 81.0 | 44 | 18.6 |
| Aged 18 to 19 | 3,309 | 2,956 | 89.3 | 353 | 10.7 |
| Aged 20 to 21 | 2,907 | 2,502 | 86.1 | 405 | 13.9 |
| Aged 22 to 24 | 2,551 | 1,935 | 75.9 | 616 | 24.1 |
| Aged 25 to 29 | 2,215 | 1,102 | 49.8 | 1,112 | 50.2 |
| Aged 30 to 34 | 1,228 | 458 | 37.3 | 770 | 62.7 |
| Aged 35 to 39 | 1,068 | 333 | 31.2 | 735 | 68.8 |
| Aged 40 to 44 | 742 | 161 | 21.7 | 579 | 78.0 |
| Aged 45 to 49 | 501 | 119 | 23.8 | 383 | 76.4 |
| Aged 50 to 54 | 243 | 54 | 22.2 | 189 | 77.8 |
| Aged 55 to 59 | 92 | 12 | 13.0 | 80 | 87.0 |
| Aged 60 to 64 | 68 | 5 | 7.4 | 62 | 91.2 |
| Aged 65 or older | 65 | 8 | 12.3 | 58 | 89.2 |

*Source: Bureau of the Census,* School Enrollment—Social and Economic Characteristics of Students: October 1996, *detailed tables from Current Population Report P20-500, 1998; calculations by New Strategist*

# One in Five College Students Is a Minority

**Among the nation's 14 million college students, 3.5 million are black, Hispanic, Asian, or another minority.**

Non-Hispanic whites accounted for 72 percent of college students in 1995, according to the National Center for Education Statistics. Non-Hispanic blacks were just over 10 percent of college students, slightly lower than the black share of the total population. Eight percent of college students were Hispanic, while 6 percent were Asian. Foreign students (called nonresident aliens) accounted for 3 percent of college students, but were a much larger share of those earning graduate degrees.

Non-Hispanic whites were awarded 76 percent of all bachelor's degrees in 1995–96. Blacks earned 8 percent, and Hispanics, 5 percent. The minority share of degrees awarded is lower at the master's and doctoral levels, while the share of nonresident aliens is much higher. At the master's level, nonresident aliens accounted for 12 percent of degrees awarded in 1995–96. At the doctoral level, they accounted for 26 percent of degrees.

◆ Blacks and Hispanics are underrepresented in college because of the steep cost of higher education. Expanding financial aid would boost minority enrollment.

# College Students by Race and Hispanic Origin, 1976 and 1995

*(number and percent distribution of people enrolled in institutions of higher education by race, Hispanic origin, and level of enrollment, fall 1976 and fall 1995; percent change in number and percentage point change in distribution, 1976–95; numbers in thousands)*

| | number | | percent change | percent distribution | | percentage point change |
|---|---|---|---|---|---|---|
| | 1995 | 1976 | 1976–95 | 1995 | 1976 | 1976–95 |
| **Total enrollment** | **14,262** | **10,986** | **29.8%** | **100.0%** | **100.0%** | – |
| White, non-Hispanic | 10,311 | 9,076 | 13.6 | 72.3 | 82.6 | −10.3 |
| Total minority | 3,496 | 1,691 | 106.8 | 24.5 | 15.4 | 9.1 |
| Black, non-Hispanic | 1,474 | 1,033 | 42.7 | 10.3 | 9.4 | 0.9 |
| Hispanic | 1,094 | 384 | 185.0 | 7.7 | 3.5 | 4.2 |
| Asian | 797 | 198 | 302.9 | 5.6 | 1.8 | 3.8 |
| Native American | 131 | 76 | 72.5 | 0.9 | 0.7 | 0.2 |
| Nonresident alien | 454 | 219 | 107.8 | 3.2 | 2.0 | 1.2 |
| **Undergraduate enrollment** | **12,232** | **9,419** | **29.9** | **100.0** | **100.0** | – |
| White, non-Hispanic | 8,806 | 7,741 | 13.8 | 72.0 | 82.2 | −10.2 |
| Total minority | 3,159 | 1,535 | 105.7 | 25.8 | 16.3 | 9.5 |
| Black, non-Hispanic | 1,334 | 943 | 41.4 | 10.9 | 10.0 | 0.9 |
| Hispanic | 1,012 | 353 | 186.8 | 8.3 | 3.7 | 4.5 |
| Asian | 692 | 169 | 308.9 | 5.7 | 1.8 | 3.9 |
| Native American | 121 | 70 | 73.2 | 1.0 | 0.7 | 0.2 |
| Nonresident alien | 268 | 143 | 86.9 | 2.2 | 1.5 | 0.7 |
| **Graduate enrollment** | **1,733** | **1,323** | **31.0** | **100.0** | **100.0** | – |
| White, non-Hispanic | 1,282 | 1,116 | 14.9 | 74.0 | 84.4 | −10.3 |
| Total minority | 271 | 135 | 101.3 | 15.6 | 10.2 | 5.5 |
| Black, non-Hispanic | 119 | 79 | 51.1 | 6.8 | 5.9 | 0.9 |
| Hispanic | 68 | 26 | 157.6 | 3.9 | 2.0 | 1.9 |
| Asian | 76 | 25 | 208.6 | 4.4 | 1.9 | 2.5 |
| Native American | 9 | 5 | 66.7 | 0.5 | 0.4 | 0.1 |
| Nonresident alien | 180 | 72 | 147.9 | 10.4 | 5.5 | 4.9 |

*(continued)*

*(continued from previous page)*

| | number | | percent change | percent distribution | | percentage point change |
|---|---|---|---|---|---|---|
| | 1995 | 1976 | 1976–95 | 1995 | 1976 | 1976–95 |
| **First-professional** | | | | | | |
| **enrollment** | **298** | **244** | **21.9%** | **100.0%** | **100.0%** | – |
| White, non-Hispanic | 223 | 220 | 1.5 | 75.0 | 90.1 | –15.1 |
| Total minority | 67 | 21 | 217.5 | 22.5 | 8.6 | 13.9 |
| Black, non-Hispanic | 21 | 11 | 91.1 | 7.2 | 4.6 | 2.6 |
| Hispanic | 14 | 5 | 206.7 | 4.6 | 1.8 | 2.8 |
| Asian | 30 | 4 | 622.0 | 9.9 | 1.7 | 8.3 |
| Native American | 2 | 1 | 61.5 | 0.7 | 0.5 | 0.2 |
| Nonresident alien | 7 | 3 | 135.5 | 2.5 | 1.3 | 1.2 |

*Note: (–) means not applicable.*
*Source: National Center for Education Statistics,* Digest of Education Statistics 1997, *NCES 98-015, 1997; calculations by New Strategist*

# Degrees Conferred by Race and Hispanic Origin, 1995–96

*(number and percent distribution of degrees conferred by institutions of higher education by level of degree, race, and Hispanic origin of degree holder, 1995–96)*

|  | number | percent |
|---|---|---|
| **Associate's degrees** | **555,216** | **100.0%** |
| White, non-Hispanic | 417,158 | 75.1 |
| Black, non-Hispanic | 50,927 | 9.2 |
| Hispanic | 37,430 | 6.7 |
| Asian | 22,644 | 4.1 |
| Native American | 5,458 | 1.0 |
| Unknown | 11,399 | 2.1 |
| Nonresident alien | 10,131 | 1.8 |
| **Bachelor's degrees** | **1,164,792** | **100.0** |
| White, non-Hispanic | 883,875 | 75.9 |
| Black, non-Hispanic | 89,284 | 7.7 |
| Hispanic | 56,900 | 4.9 |
| Asian | 62,824 | 5.4 |
| Native American | 6,809 | 0.6 |
| Unknown | 27,401 | 2.4 |
| Nonresident alien | 37,690 | 3.2 |
| **Master's degrees** | **406,301** | **100.0** |
| White, non-Hispanic | 282,338 | 69.5 |
| Black, non-Hispanic | 24,494 | 6.0 |
| Hispanic | 13,668 | 3.4 |
| Asian | 17,181 | 4.2 |
| Native American | 1,692 | 0.4 |
| Unknown | 19,017 | 4.7 |
| Nonresident alien | 47,910 | 11.8 |
| **Doctoral degrees** | **44,652** | **100.0** |
| White, non-Hispanic | 26,363 | 59.0 |
| Black, non-Hispanic | 1,563 | 3.5 |
| Hispanic | 950 | 2.1 |
| Asian | 2,492 | 5.6 |
| Native American | 153 | 0.3 |
| Unknown | 1,681 | 3.8 |
| Nonresident alien | 11,450 | 25.6 |

*(continued)*

*(continued from previous page)*

|  | number | percent |
|---|---|---|
| **First-professional degrees** | **76,734** | **100.0%** |
| White, non-Hispanic | 58,166 | 75.8 |
| Black, non-Hispanic | 4,913 | 6.4 |
| Hispanic | 3,394 | 4.4 |
| Asian | 6,495 | 8.5 |
| Native American | 453 | 0.6 |
| Unknown | 1,690 | 2.2 |
| Nonresident alien | 1,622 | 2.1 |

*Source: National Center for Education Statistics,* Degrees and Other Awards Conferred by Degree-granting Institutions: 1995–96, *NCES 98-256, 1998; calculations by New Strategist*

# Women Earn Most Degrees

## Women earn over half the bachelor's and master's degrees.

As women pursue careers, they are eager for credentials that can command a premium wage. Women are now a significant presence in all degree programs and all fields of study. They earned 61 percent of associate's degrees in 1995–96, 55 percent of bachelor's degrees, and 56 percent of master's degrees.

Women's share of degrees is relatively small in engineering, where they earned only 18 percent of bachelor's and 17 percent of master's degrees in 1995–96. But in other traditionally male fields, such as mathematics, women earned 46 percent of bachelor's degrees and 39 percent of master's degrees.

Women earned 40 percent of doctorates in 1995–96. While they earned only 13 percent of doctorates in engineering and 20 percent of those in mathematics, they earned the majority of doctoral degrees in education, English, foreign languages, health professions, psychology, and library science.

Women earned 42 percent of professional degrees in 1995–96. They earned the 66 percent majority of degrees in both pharmacy and veterinary medicine, as well as 41 percent of those in medicine and 44 percent of law degrees.

♦ The share of doctors, lawyers, and other professionals who are women should expand rapidly in the next few decades as young women now earning degrees replace older men retiring from these professions.

♦ As a growing share of women gain educational credentials in the years ahead, women's earnings will rise, narrowing the gap between men's and women's incomes.

# Associate's Degrees Conferred by Field of Study and Sex, 1995–96

*(number of associate's degrees conferred by field of study and sex, and women's share of total degrees by field, 1995–96)*

| | total | men | women | percent women |
|---|---|---|---|---|
| **Total degrees** | **555,216** | **219,514** | **335,702** | **60.5%** |
| Agricultural business and production | 3,846 | 2,574 | 1,272 | 33.1 |
| Agricultural sciences | 877 | 476 | 401 | 45.7 |
| Architecture and related programs | 256 | 40 | 216 | 84.4 |
| Area, ethnic, and cultural studies | 111 | 28 | 83 | 74.8 |
| Biological sciences/life sciences | 2,037 | 817 | 1,220 | 59.9 |
| Business management and administrative services | 93,487 | 25,932 | 67,555 | 72.3 |
| Communications | 2,187 | 1,077 | 1,110 | 50.8 |
| Communications technologies | 1,757 | 1,169 | 588 | 33.5 |
| Computer and information sciences | 9,658 | 4,954 | 4,704 | 48.7 |
| Conservation and renewable natural resources | 1,459 | 1,168 | 291 | 19.9 |
| Construction trades | 2,141 | 2,035 | 106 | 5.0 |
| Education | 9,750 | 3,109 | 6,641 | 68.1 |
| Engineering | 2,197 | 1,914 | 283 | 12.9 |
| Engineering-related technologies | 33,002 | 28,871 | 4,131 | 12.5 |
| English language and literature | 1,310 | 471 | 839 | 64.0 |
| Foreign languages and literature | 607 | 163 | 444 | 73.1 |
| Health professions and related sciences | 101,872 | 17,295 | 84,577 | 83.0 |
| Home economics | 940 | 75 | 865 | 92.0 |
| Law and legal studies | 9,106 | 1,119 | 7,987 | 87.7 |
| Liberal/general studies and humanities | 174,970 | 67,994 | 106,976 | 61.1 |
| Library science | 94 | 13 | 81 | 86.2 |
| Marketing operations/marketing and distribution | 5,960 | 1,424 | 4,536 | 76.1 |
| Mathematics | 758 | 463 | 295 | 38.9 |
| Mechanics and repairers | 12,524 | 11,723 | 801 | 6.4 |
| Military technologies | 556 | 514 | 42 | 7.6 |
| Multi/interdisciplinary studies | 8,611 | 4,212 | 4,399 | 51.1 |
| Parks, recreation, leisure and fitness | 936 | 545 | 391 | 41.8 |
| Personal and miscellaneous services | 7,721 | 4,967 | 2,754 | 35.7 |
| Philosophy and religion | 83 | 45 | 38 | 45.8 |
| Physical sciences | 1,749 | 961 | 788 | 45.1 |
| Precision production trades | 10,217 | 8,119 | 2,098 | 20.5 |
| Protective services | 19,196 | 13,427 | 5,769 | 30.1 |

*(continued)*

*(continued from previous page)*

| | total | men | women | percent women |
|---|---|---|---|---|
| Psychology | 1,583 | 406 | 1,177 | 74.4% |
| Public administration and services | 4,218 | 765 | 3,453 | 81.9 |
| Science technologies | 863 | 497 | 366 | 42.4 |
| Social sciences and history | 4,021 | 1,488 | 2,533 | 63.0 |
| Theological studies/religious vocations | 608 | 314 | 294 | 48.4 |
| Transportation and material moving | 1,571 | 1,325 | 246 | 15.7 |
| Visual and performing arts | 13,534 | 5,806 | 7,728 | 57.1 |
| Vocational home economics | 7,252 | 682 | 6,570 | 90.6 |
| Undesignated fields | 1,591 | 537 | 1,054 | 66.2 |

*Source: National Center for Education Statistics,* Degrees and Other Awards Conferred by Degree-granting Institutions: 1995–96, *NCES 98-256, 1998; calculations by New Strategist*

# Bachelor's Degrees Conferred by Field of Study and Sex, 1995–96

*(number of bachelor's degrees conferred by field of study and sex, and women's share of total degrees by field, 1995–96)*

| | total | men | women | percent women |
|---|---|---|---|---|
| **Total degrees** | **1,164,792** | **522,454** | **642,338** | **55.1%** |
| Agricultural business and production | 4,848 | 3,506 | 1,342 | 27.7 |
| Agricultural sciences | 7,457 | 4,256 | 3,201 | 42.9 |
| Architecture and related programs | 8,352 | 5,340 | 3,012 | 36.1 |
| Area, ethnic, and cultural studies | 5,786 | 1,984 | 3,802 | 65.7 |
| Biological sciences/life sciences | 60,994 | 28,849 | 32,145 | 52.7 |
| Business management and administrative services | 222,149 | 114,671 | 107,478 | 48.4 |
| Communications | 47,320 | 19,391 | 27,929 | 59.0 |
| Communications technologies | 683 | 369 | 314 | 46.0 |
| Computer and information sciences | 24,098 | 17,468 | 6,630 | 27.5 |
| Conservation and renewable natural resources | 9,126 | 5,773 | 3,353 | 36.7 |
| Construction trades | 80 | 76 | 4 | 5.0 |
| Education | 105,509 | 26,233 | 79,276 | 75.1 |
| Engineering | 62,114 | 51,069 | 11,045 | 17.8 |
| Engineering-related technologies | 15,189 | 13,763 | 1,426 | 9.4 |
| English language and literature | 50,698 | 17,253 | 33,445 | 66.0 |
| Foreign languages and literature | 13,952 | 4,219 | 9,733 | 69.8 |
| Health professions and related sciences | 84,036 | 15,432 | 68,604 | 81.6 |
| Home economics | 15,328 | 1,682 | 13,646 | 89.0 |
| Law and legal studies | 2,052 | 556 | 1,496 | 72.9 |
| Liberal/general studies and humanities | 33,997 | 13,379 | 20,618 | 60.6 |
| Library science | 58 | 8 | 50 | 86.2 |
| Marketing operations/marketing and distribution | 4,697 | 2,004 | 2,693 | 57.3 |
| Mathematics | 13,143 | 7,134 | 6,009 | 45.7 |
| Mechanics and repairers | 54 | 48 | 6 | 11.1 |
| Military technologies | 7 | 7 | – | 0.0 |
| Multi/interdisciplinary studies | 26,515 | 9,286 | 17,229 | 65.0 |
| Parks, recreation, leisure and fitness | 13,983 | 7,090 | 6,893 | 49.3 |
| Personal and miscellaneous services | 256 | 167 | 89 | 34.8 |
| Philosophy and religion | 7,388 | 4,859 | 2,529 | 34.2 |
| Physical sciences | 19,518 | 12,517 | 7,001 | 35.9 |
| Precision production trades | 401 | 305 | 96 | 23.9 |
| Protective services | 24,810 | 15,274 | 9,536 | 38.4 |

*(continued)*

*(continued from previous page)*

| | total | men | women | percent women |
|---|---|---|---|---|
| Psychology | 73,291 | 19,817 | 53,474 | 73.0% |
| Public administration and services | 19,849 | 4,205 | 15,644 | 78.8 |
| Science technologies | 129 | 61 | 68 | 52.7 |
| Social sciences and history | 126,479 | 65,872 | 60,607 | 47.9 |
| Theological studies/religious vocations | 5,358 | 4,044 | 1,314 | 24.5 |
| Transportation and material moving | 3,561 | 3,143 | 418 | 11.7 |
| Visual and performing arts | 49,296 | 20,126 | 29,170 | 59.2 |
| Vocational home economics | 475 | 203 | 272 | 57.3 |
| Undesignated fields | 1,756 | 1,015 | 741 | 42.2 |

*Note: (–) means no degrees were awarded.*
*Source: National Center for Education Statistics,* Degrees and Other Awards Conferred by Degree-granting *Institutions: 1995–96, NCES 98-256, 1998; calculations by New Strategist*

# Master's Degrees Conferred by Field of Study and Sex, 1995–96

*(number of master's degrees conferred by field of study and sex, and women's share of total degrees by field, 1995–96)*

| | total | men | women | percent women |
|---|---|---|---|---|
| **Total degrees** | **406,301** | **179,081** | **227,220** | **55.9%** |
| Agricultural business and production | 648 | 411 | 237 | 36.6 |
| Agricultural sciences | 1,601 | 895 | 706 | 44.1 |
| Architecture and related programs | 3,993 | 2,361 | 1,632 | 40.9 |
| Area, ethnic, and cultural studies | 1,713 | 798 | 915 | 53.4 |
| Biological sciences/life sciences | 6,157 | 2,902 | 3,255 | 52.9 |
| Business management and administrative services | 93,320 | 58,333 | 34,987 | 37.5 |
| Communications | 5,080 | 1,900 | 3,180 | 62.6 |
| Communications technologies | 524 | 271 | 253 | 48.3 |
| Computer and information sciences | 10,151 | 7,444 | 2,707 | 26.7 |
| Conservation and renewable natural resources | 2,320 | 1,344 | 976 | 42.1 |
| Construction trades | – | – | – | – |
| Education | 106,253 | 25,214 | 81,039 | 76.3 |
| Engineering | 27,441 | 22,735 | 4,706 | 17.1 |
| Engineering-related technologies | 1,125 | 906 | 219 | 19.5 |
| English language and literature | 7,893 | 2,814 | 5,079 | 64.3 |
| Foreign languages and literature | 3,124 | 1,017 | 2,107 | 67.4 |
| Health professions and related sciences | 33,398 | 7,021 | 26,377 | 79.0 |
| Home economics | 2,885 | 494 | 2,391 | 82.9 |
| Law and legal studies | 2,751 | 1,751 | 1,000 | 36.4 |
| Liberal/general studies and humanities | 2,778 | 961 | 1,817 | 65.4 |
| Library science | 5,099 | 1,071 | 4,028 | 79.0 |
| Marketing operations/marketing and distribution | 662 | 352 | 310 | 46.8 |
| Mathematics | 4,031 | 2,465 | 1,566 | 38.8 |
| Mechanics and repairers | – | – | – | – |
| Military technologies | 136 | 132 | 4 | 2.9 |
| Multi/interdisciplinary studies | 2,347 | 1,082 | 1,265 | 53.9 |
| Parks, recreation, leisure and fitness | 1,751 | 911 | 840 | 48.0 |
| Personal and miscellaneous services | – | – | – | – |
| Philosophy and religion | 1,302 | 845 | 457 | 35.1 |
| Physical sciences | 5,823 | 3,952 | 1,871 | 32.1 |
| Precision production trades | 8 | 6 | 2 | 25.0 |
| Protective services | 1,812 | 1,151 | 661 | 36.5 |

*(continued)*

*(continued from previous page)*

| | total | men | women | percent women |
|---|---|---|---|---|
| Psychology | 13,792 | 3,813 | 9,979 | 72.4% |
| Public administration and services | 24,229 | 6,927 | 17,302 | 71.4 |
| Science technologies | 24 | 14 | 10 | 41.7 |
| Social sciences and history | 15,012 | 8,093 | 6,919 | 46.1 |
| Theological studies/religious vocations | 5,107 | 3,056 | 2,051 | 40.2 |
| Transportation and material moving | 919 | 856 | 63 | 6.9 |
| Visual and performing arts | 10,280 | 4,361 | 5,919 | 57.6 |
| Vocational home economics | 32 | 2 | 30 | 93.8 |
| Undesignated fields | 780 | 420 | 360 | 46.2 |

*Note: (–) means no degrees were awarded.*
*Source: National Center for Education Statistics,* Degrees and Other Awards Conferred by Degree-granting Institutions: 1995–96, *NCES 98-256, 1998; calculations by New Strategist*

# Doctoral Degrees Conferred by Field of Study and Sex, 1995–96

*(number of doctoral degrees conferred by field of study and sex, and women's share of total degrees by field, 1995–96)*

| | total | men | women | percent women |
|---|---|---|---|---|
| **Total degrees** | **44,652** | **26,841** | **17,811** | **39.9%** |
| Agricultural business and production | 236 | 182 | 54 | 22.9 |
| Agricultural sciences | 744 | 540 | 204 | 27.4 |
| Architecture and related programs | 141 | 96 | 45 | 31.9 |
| Area, ethnic, and cultural studies | 184 | 94 | 90 | 48.9 |
| Biological sciences/life sciences | 4,780 | 2,773 | 2,007 | 42.0 |
| Business management and administrative services | 1,367 | 974 | 393 | 28.7 |
| Communications | 338 | 184 | 154 | 45.6 |
| Communications technologies | 7 | 6 | 1 | 14.3 |
| Computer and information sciences | 867 | 741 | 126 | 14.5 |
| Conservation and renewable natural resources | 291 | 213 | 78 | 26.8 |
| Construction trades | – | – | – | – |
| Education | 6,676 | 2,525 | 4,151 | 62.2 |
| Engineering | 6,369 | 5,570 | 799 | 12.5 |
| Engineering-related technologies | 11 | 10 | 1 | 9.1 |
| English language and literature | 1,535 | 590 | 945 | 61.6 |
| Foreign languages and literature | 876 | 387 | 489 | 55.8 |
| Health professions and related sciences | 2,119 | 919 | 1,200 | 56.6 |
| Home economics | 409 | 113 | 296 | 72.4 |
| Law and legal studies | 91 | 59 | 32 | 35.2 |
| Liberal/general studies and humanities | 75 | 33 | 42 | 56.0 |
| Library science | 53 | 10 | 43 | 81.1 |
| Marketing operations/marketing and distribution | 1 | – | 1 | 100.0 |
| Mathematics | 1,209 | 962 | 247 | 20.4 |
| Mechanics and repairers | – | – | – | |
| Military technologies | – | – | – | – |
| Multi/interdisciplinary studies | 441 | 218 | 223 | 50.6 |
| Parks, recreation, leisure and fitness | 104 | 65 | 39 | 37.5 |
| Personal and miscellaneous services | – | – | – | |
| Philosophy and religion | 549 | 385 | 164 | 29.9 |
| Physical sciences | 4,563 | 3,508 | 1,055 | 23.1 |
| Precision production trades | – | – | – | – |
| Protective services | 38 | 22 | 16 | 42.1 |

*(continued)*

*(continued from previous page)*

| | total | men | women | percent women |
|---|---|---|---|---|
| Psychology | 3,711 | 1,259 | 2,452 | 66.1% |
| Public administration and services | 499 | 220 | 279 | 55.9 |
| Science technologies | 8 | 7 | 1 | 12.5 |
| Social sciences and history | 3,760 | 2,339 | 1,421 | 37.8 |
| Theological studies/religious vocations | 1,521 | 1,304 | 217 | 14.3 |
| Transportation and material moving | – | – | – | – |
| Visual and performing arts | 1,067 | 524 | 543 | 50.9 |
| Vocational home economics | 5 | 4 | 1 | 20.0 |
| Undesignated fields | 7 | 5 | 2 | 28.6 |

*Note: (–) means no degrees were awarded.*
*Source: National Center for Education Statistics,* Degrees and Other Awards Conferred by Degree-granting Institutions: 1995–96, *NCES 98-256, 1998; calculations by New Strategist*

# First-Professional Degrees Conferred by Field of Study and Sex, 1995–96

*(number of first-professional degrees conferred by field of study and sex, and women's share of total degrees by field, 1995–96)*

| | total | men | women | percent women |
|---|---|---|---|---|
| **Total degrees** | **76,734** | **44,748** | **31,986** | **41.7%** |
| Chiropractic (D.C., D.C.M.) | 3,379 | 2,470 | 909 | 26.9 |
| Dentistry (D.D.S., D.M.D.) | 3,697 | 2,374 | 1,323 | 35.8 |
| Medicine (M.D.) | 15,341 | 9,061 | 6,280 | 40.9 |
| Optometry (O.D.) | 1,231 | 568 | 663 | 53.9 |
| Osteopathic medicine (D.O.) | 1,895 | 1,232 | 663 | 35.0 |
| Pharmacy (Pharm.D.) | 2,555 | 873 | 1,682 | 65.8 |
| Podiatry (Pod.D., D.P., D.P.M.) | 650 | 453 | 197 | 30.3 |
| Veterinary medicine (D.V.M.) | 2,109 | 715 | 1,394 | 66.1 |
| Law (LL.B., J.D.) | 39,828 | 22,508 | 17,320 | 43.5 |
| Divinity/ministry (B.D., M.Div.) | 5,594 | 4,136 | 1,458 | 26.1 |
| Rabbinical and Talmudic Studies (M.H.L./Rav) | 285 | 264 | 21 | 7.4 |

*Note: Numbers will not add to total because "other" is not shown.*
*Source: National Center for Education Statistics,* Degrees and Other Awards Conferred by Degree-granting Institutions: 1995–96, *NCES 98-256, 1998; calculations by New Strategist*

# College Enrollment Will Rise

**As the children of baby boomers reach college age, the number of college students will climb.**

By 2008, the number of people enrolled in college will top 16 million, a gain of 13 percent since 1996. During those years, students of traditional college age, 18 to 21, will grow from 40 to 45 percent of total college enrollment as the children of boomers go to school. Women will remain the majority of college students through 2008, according to the National Center for Education Statistics.

Because of the rise in the number of college students aged 18 to 21, undergraduate enrollment will grow faster than graduate-level enrollment between 1996 and 2008. Similarly, the number of full-time students will grow faster than the number of part-time students. Public institutions, which account for 78 percent of college enrollment, will see their student population grow by 1 million between 1996 and 2008. Private colleges will gain just over 300,000 additional students.

The number of degrees awarded by institutions of higher education is projected to rise 9 percent during the next decade, with associate's degrees gaining the most—11 percent. The number of first-professional degrees awarded (such as degrees in law and medicine) is projected to decline 4 percent.

♦ Saving for college and paying college bills will be central concerns of baby boomers during the next decade. Institutions of higher education have the opportunity to distance themselves from their competitors by creating unique ways to help boomers pay the bills.

# Projections of College Enrollment by Sex and Age, 1996 and 2008

*(number and percent distribution of people enrolled in institutions of higher education by sex and age, 1996 and 2008; percent change in number, 1996–2008; numbers in thousands)*

| | 1996 | | 2008 | | percent change 1996–2008 |
|---|---|---|---|---|---|
| | number | percent | number | percent | |
| **Total people** | **14,334** | **100.0%** | **16,240** | **100.0%** | **13.3%** |
| Aged 14 to 17 | 184 | 1.3 | 255 | 1.6 | 38.6 |
| Aged 18 to 19 | 3,036 | 21.2 | 3,874 | 23.9 | 27.6 |
| Aged 20 to 21 | 2,647 | 18.5 | 3,257 | 20.1 | 23.0 |
| Aged 22 to 24 | 2,225 | 15.5 | 2,561 | 15.8 | 15.1 |
| Aged 25 to 29 | 2,066 | 14.4 | 2,152 | 13.3 | 4.2 |
| Aged 30 to 34 | 1,242 | 8.7 | 1,249 | 7.7 | 0.6 |
| Aged 35 or older | 2,934 | 20.5 | 2,893 | 17.8 | −1.4 |
| **Total men** | **6,304** | **100.0** | **6,939** | **100.0** | **10.1** |
| Aged 14 to 17 | 93 | 1.5 | 111 | 1.6 | 19.4 |
| Aged 18 to 19 | 1,368 | 21.7 | 1,672 | 24.1 | 22.2 |
| Aged 20 to 21 | 1,238 | 19.6 | 1,461 | 21.1 | 18.0 |
| Aged 22 to 24 | 1,080 | 17.1 | 1,233 | 17.8 | 14.2 |
| Aged 25 to 29 | 962 | 15.3 | 1,007 | 14.5 | 4.7 |
| Aged 30 to 34 | 563 | 8.9 | 527 | 7.6 | −6.4 |
| Aged 35 or older | 1,001 | 15.9 | 929 | 13.4 | −7.2 |
| **Total women** | **8,030** | **100.0** | **9,300** | **100.0** | **15.8** |
| Aged 14 to 17 | 91 | 1.1 | 145 | 1.6 | 59.3 |
| Aged 18 to 19 | 1,669 | 20.8 | 1,202 | 23.7 | 31.9 |
| Aged 20 to 21 | 1,409 | 17.5 | 1,796 | 19.3 | 27.5 |
| Aged 22 to 24 | 1,145 | 14.3 | 1,328 | 14.3 | 16.0 |
| Aged 25 to 29 | 1,104 | 13.7 | 1,145 | 12.3 | 3.7 |
| Aged 30 to 34 | 679 | 8.5 | 723 | 7.8 | 6.5 |
| Aged 35 or older | 1,934 | 24.1 | 1,964 | 21.1 | 1.6 |

*Source: National Center for Education Statistics,* Projections of Education Statistics to 2008, *NCES 98-016, 1998; calculations by New Strategist*

# Projections of College Enrollment by Level of Degree, 1998 to 2008

*(number of people enrolled in institutions of higher education by level of degree, sex, and attendance status; 1998–2008; percent change, 1998–2008; numbers in thousands)*

| | | men | | women | |
|---|---|---|---|---|---|
| | total | full-time | part-time | full-time | part-time |
| **Undergraduate enrollment** | | | | | |
| 1998 | 12,600 | 3,272 | 2,144 | 4,129 | 3,055 |
| 1999 | 12,773 | 3,329 | 2,152 | 4,225 | 3,066 |
| 2000 | 12,915 | 3,383 | 2,164 | 4,297 | 3,071 |
| 2001 | 13,026 | 3,429 | 2,168 | 4,355 | 3,075 |
| 2002 | 13,087 | 3,451 | 2,177 | 4,382 | 3,077 |
| 2003 | 13,211 | 3,491 | 2,186 | 4,450 | 3,084 |
| 2004 | 13,360 | 3,531 | 2,202 | 4,530 | 3,098 |
| 2005 | 13,511 | 3,568 | 2,215 | 4,617 | 3,111 |
| 2006 | 13,685 | 3,616 | 2,229 | 4,716 | 3,123 |
| 2007 | 13,850 | 3,665 | 2,246 | 4,804 | 3,136 |
| 2008 | 14,045 | 3,730 | 2,265 | 4,901 | 3,149 |
| **Percent change** | | | | | |
| 1998 to 2008 | 11.5% | 14.0% | 5.6% | 18.7% | 3.1% |
| **Graduate enrollment** | | | | | |
| 1998 | 1,716 | 310 | 442 | 329 | 635 |
| 1999 | 1,714 | 305 | 443 | 329 | 637 |
| 2000 | 1,706 | 301 | 443 | 326 | 636 |
| 2001 | 1,698 | 299 | 440 | 326 | 633 |
| 2002 | 1,699 | 300 | 439 | 328 | 632 |
| 2003 | 1,703 | 301 | 438 | 333 | 631 |
| 2004 | 1,715 | 304 | 439 | 340 | 632 |
| 2005 | 1,728 | 307 | 439 | 348 | 634 |
| 2006 | 1,737 | 309 | 439 | 354 | 635 |
| 2007 | 1,746 | 312 | 439 | 360 | 635 |
| 2008 | 1,752 | 315 | 439 | 364 | 634 |
| **Percent change** | | | | | |
| 1998 to 2008 | 2.1% | 1.6% | –0.7% | 10.6% | –0.2% |

*(continued)*

*(continued from previous page)*

| | total | men | | women | |
|---|---|---|---|---|---|
| | | *full-time* | *part-time* | *full-time* | *part-time* |
| **First-professional enrollment** | | | | | |
| 1998 | 273 | 136 | 20 | 104 | 13 |
| 1999 | 271 | 134 | 20 | 104 | 13 |
| 2000 | 269 | 132 | 20 | 103 | 13 |
| 2001 | 267 | 131 | 20 | 103 | 13 |
| 2002 | 268 | 132 | 20 | 104 | 13 |
| 2003 | 270 | 132 | 20 | 105 | 13 |
| 2004 | 274 | 134 | 20 | 108 | 13 |
| 2005 | 278 | 135 | 20 | 110 | 13 |
| 2006 | 281 | 136 | 20 | 112 | 13 |
| 2007 | 284 | 137 | 20 | 114 | 13 |
| 2008 | 286 | 138 | 20 | 115 | 13 |
| **Percent change** | | | | | |
| 1998 to 2008 | 4.8% | 1.5% | 0.0% | 10.6% | 0.0% |

*Source: National Center for Education Statistics,* Projections of Education Statistics to 2008, *NCES 98-016, 1998; calculations by New Strategist*

# Projections of College Enrollment by Type of Institution, 1998 to 2008

*(number of people enrolled in institutions of higher education by type of institution, sex, attendance status, and control of institution; 1998–2008; percent change, 1998–2008; numbers in thousands)*

| | total | men | women | attendance status full-time | part-time | control public | private |
|---|---|---|---|---|---|---|---|
| **Total institutions** | | | | | | | |
| 1998 | 14,590 | 6,324 | 8,266 | 8,280 | 6,310 | 11,395 | 3,194 |
| 1999 | 14,758 | 6,383 | 8,375 | 8,426 | 6,332 | 11,525 | 3,233 |
| 2000 | 14,889 | 6,442 | 8,447 | 8,543 | 6,346 | 11,626 | 3,263 |
| 2001 | 14,992 | 6,487 | 8,505 | 8,643 | 6,349 | 11,705 | 3,287 |
| 2002 | 15,053 | 6,518 | 8,536 | 8,696 | 6,358 | 11,751 | 3,303 |
| 2003 | 15,185 | 6,568 | 8,616 | 8,813 | 6,372 | 11,849 | 3,335 |
| 2004 | 15,349 | 6,628 | 8,721 | 8,946 | 6,403 | 11,975 | 3,374 |
| 2005 | 15,516 | 6,684 | 8,833 | 9,085 | 6,432 | 12,101 | 3,415 |
| 2006 | 15,703 | 6,749 | 8,954 | 9,243 | 6,460 | 12,242 | 3,461 |
| 2007 | 15,880 | 6,819 | 9,062 | 9,391 | 6,489 | 12,378 | 3,502 |
| 2008 | 16,083 | 6,906 | 9,177 | 9,562 | 6,520 | 12,534 | 3,549 |
| **Percent change** | | | | | | | |
| 1998 to 2008 | 10.2% | 9.2% | 11.0% | 15.5% | 3.3% | 10.0% | 11.1% |
| | | | | | | | |
| **Two-year institutions** | | | | | | | |
| 1998 | 5,660 | 2,359 | 3,301 | 2,090 | 3,569 | 5,426 | 234 |
| 1999 | 5,712 | 2,379 | 3,333 | 2,130 | 3,582 | 5,475 | 237 |
| 2000 | 5,751 | 2,400 | 3,351 | 2,156 | 3,595 | 5,512 | 239 |
| 2001 | 5,779 | 2,413 | 3,367 | 2,180 | 3,600 | 5,539 | 241 |
| 2002 | 5,794 | 2,422 | 3,372 | 2,187 | 3,607 | 5,553 | 242 |
| 2003 | 5,831 | 2,437 | 3,394 | 2,213 | 3,618 | 5,587 | 244 |
| 2004 | 5,887 | 2,460 | 3,427 | 2,248 | 3,639 | 5,640 | 247 |
| 2005 | 5,938 | 2,478 | 3,459 | 2,281 | 3,657 | 5,688 | 250 |
| 2006 | 5,995 | 2,500 | 3,495 | 2,319 | 3,676 | 5,742 | 253 |
| 2007 | 6,054 | 2,526 | 3,529 | 2,357 | 3,697 | 5,798 | 256 |
| 2008 | 6,124 | 2,559 | 3,566 | 2,403 | 3,721 | 5,864 | 260 |
| **Percent change** | | | | | | | |
| 1998 to 2008 | 8.2% | 8.5% | 8.0% | 15.0% | 4.3% | 8.1% | 11.1% |

*(continued)*

*(continued from previous page)*

| | total | men | women | attendance status | | control | |
|---|---|---|---|---|---|---|---|
| | | | | full-time | part-time | public | private |
| **Four-year institutions** | | | | | | | |
| 1998 | 8,930 | 3,964 | 4,966 | 6,190 | 2,741 | 5,969 | 2,961 |
| 1999 | 9,046 | 4,004 | 5,042 | 6,296 | 2,750 | 6,049 | 2,996 |
| 2000 | 9,138 | 4,043 | 5,095 | 6,386 | 2,752 | 6,114 | 3,024 |
| 2001 | 9,213 | 4,075 | 5,138 | 6,463 | 2,749 | 6,166 | 3,046 |
| 2002 | 9,259 | 4,096 | 5,163 | 6,509 | 2,750 | 6,198 | 3,061 |
| 2003 | 9,354 | 4,132 | 5,222 | 6,600 | 2,753 | 6,262 | 3,092 |
| 2004 | 9,462 | 4,168 | 5,294 | 6,698 | 2,764 | 6,335 | 3,127 |
| 2005 | 9,578 | 4,205 | 5,373 | 6,804 | 2,774 | 6,413 | 3,165 |
| 2006 | 9,708 | 4,249 | 5,459 | 6,924 | 2,783 | 6,500 | 3,207 |
| 2007 | 9,826 | 4,293 | 5,533 | 7,034 | 2,792 | 6,580 | 3,246 |
| 2008 | 9,958 | 4,347 | 5,611 | 7,159 | 2,800 | 6,670 | 3,288 |
| **Percent change** | | | | | | | |
| 1998 to 2008 | 11.5% | 9.7% | 13.0% | 15.7% | 2.2% | 11.7% | 11.0% |

*Source: National Center for Education Statistics,* Projections of Education Statistics to 2008, *NCES 98-016, 1998; calculations by New Strategist*

# Projections of Degrees Conferred by Sex, 1998 to 2008

*(number of degrees conferred by sex and level of degree, 1998 and 2008; percent change in number, 1998–2008)*

|  | 1998 | 2008 | percent change 1998–2008 |
|---|---|---|---|
| **Total degrees** | **2,221,600** | **2,419,500** | **8.9%** |
| Associate's degree | 520,000 | 579,000 | 11.3 |
| Bachelor's degree | 1,172,000 | 1,270,000 | 8.4 |
| Master's degree | 406,000 | 446,000 | 9.9 |
| Doctoral degree | 45,200 | 49,500 | 9.5 |
| First-professional degree | 78,400 | 75,000 | –4.3 |
| **Men, total degrees** | **988,300** | **1,016,400** | **2.8** |
| Associate's degree | 209,000 | 216,000 | 3.3 |
| Bachelor's degree | 523,000 | 530,000 | 1.3 |
| Master's degree | 183,000 | 203,000 | 10.9 |
| Doctoral degree | 27,200 | 26,600 | –2.2 |
| First-professional degree | 46,100 | 40,800 | –11.5 |
| **Women, total degrees** | **1,233,300** | **1,402,100** | **13.7** |
| Associate's degree | 311,000 | 363,000 | 16.7 |
| Bachelor's degree | 649,000 | 739,000 | 13.9 |
| Master's degree | 223,000 | 243,000 | 9.0 |
| Doctoral degree | 18,000 | 22,900 | 27.2 |
| First-professional degree | 32,300 | 34,200 | 5.9 |

*Source: National Center for Education Statistics,* Projections of Education Statistics to 2008, *NCES 98-016, 1998; calculations by New Strategist*

# Most Couples Alike in Education

**In one-half of the nation's 55 million married couples, both partners have the same level of educational attainment.**

When comparing the educational level of husbands and wives, the largest single group is husbands and wives who have graduated from high school but have not gone to college. This group accounts for 19 percent of all couples. The second-largest group is husbands and wives who both have bachelor's degrees or higher levels of education, accounting for 17 percent of all couples. Couples in which both husband and wife are high school drop-outs account for 8 percent of couples. For another 10 percent of couples, both husband and wife have attended college but lack a bachelor's degree.

Overall, 29 percent of husbands have a bachelor's degree, compared with 24 percent of wives. Only 8 percent of wives have a bachelor's degree while their husbands do not.

♦ As the well-educated baby-boom generation ages, the proportion of couples in which both husband and wife are college graduates will increase sharply, as will the share of married couples in which the wife is better-educated than the husband.

# Education of Husband by Education of Wife, 1998

*(number and percent distribution of husbands and wives aged 18 or older by education of husband and wife, 1998; numbers in thousands)*

| | | education of wife | | | |
| Education of husband | total wives | not a high school graduate | high school graduate only | some college or associate's degree | bachelor's degree or more |
| --- | --- | --- | --- | --- | --- |
| **Total husbands** | **55,303** | **7,495** | **20,272** | **14,186** | **13,350** |
| Not a high school graduate | 8,779 | 4,635 | 3,052 | 889 | 203 |
| High school graduate only | 17,522 | 1,994 | 10,353 | 3,717 | 1,457 |
| Some college/assoc. degree | 13,243 | 650 | 4,508 | 5,611 | 2,472 |
| Bachelor's degree or more | 15,759 | 215 | 2,357 | 3,969 | 9,218 |
| **Total husbands** | **100.0%** | **13.6%** | **36.7%** | **25.7%** | **24.1%** |
| Not a high school graduate | 15.9 | 8.4 | 5.5 | 1.6 | 0.4 |
| High school graduate only | 31.7 | 3.6 | 18.7 | 6.7 | 2.6 |
| Some college/assoc. degree | 23.9 | 1.2 | 8.2 | 10.1 | 4.5 |
| Bachelor's degree or more | 28.5 | 0.4 | 4.3 | 7.2 | 16.7 |

*Source: Bureau of the Census,* Educational Attainment in the United States: March 1998, *detailed tables from Current Population Report P20-513, 1998; calculations by New Strategist*

# Adult Education Is Popular

**Professional advancement is the primary reason for participation in adult education.**

Fully 40 percent of adults took some type of educational course in 1995. Nearly half the adults qunder age 55 participated in adult education.

Among the core working-age population (aged 25 to 54), the most frequently cited reason for participating in adult education is job advancement. Among people aged 55 to 64, about half cite job advancement and half cite personal reasons. Among those aged 65 or older, the great majority participate for personal reasons.

Young people aged 17 to 24 are the ones most likely to take a course to train for a new job (21 percent). Among this age group, a substantial proportion of 39 percent also takes courses for personal reasons.

♦ Boomers and younger generations value education not only for its professional benefits, but also for the way it broadens their perspectives on the world. Enrollment in adult education among older Americans should increase as these generations age.

# Adult Education by Age, 1995

*(number and percent of people aged 17 or older not attending elementary or secondary school full-time who have been enrolled in any educational activity in the past 12 months, and percent distribution by reason for taking course, by age, 1995; numbers in thousands)*

| | | participants in adult education | | | | | |
| | | total | | reason for taking course | | | |
| | total | number | percent | personal/ social | advance on the job | train for a new job | complete degree or diploma |
|---|---|---|---|---|---|---|---|
| **Total people** | **189,543** | **76,261** | **40%** | **44%** | **54%** | **11%** | **10%** |
| Aged 17 to 24 | 22,407 | 10,539 | 47 | 39 | 33 | 21 | 19 |
| Aged 25 to 34 | 40,326 | 19,508 | 48 | 41 | 56 | 14 | 8 |
| Aged 35 to 44 | 42,304 | 20,814 | 49 | 40 | 64 | 10 | 9 |
| Aged 45 to 54 | 31,807 | 14,592 | 46 | 39 | 65 | 7 | 10 |
| Aged 55 to 64 | 21,824 | 6,117 | 28 | 52 | 54 | 4 | 6 |
| Aged 65 or older | 30,876 | 4,691 | 15 | 86 | 14 | 1 | 3 |

*Note: Percent distribution by reason will not add to 100 because some participants took more than one course or had more than one reason for participating.*
*Source: Bureau of the Census,* Statistical Abstract of the United States: 1998

# 2

# Health Trends

♦ **The food preferences of Americans have changed dramatically over the past two decades.**
Americans are eating more yogurt, poultry, broccoli, and cheese, and less beef, eggs, sugar, ice cream, and whole milk.

♦ **The number of births peaked in 1990.**
The 4,158,000 babies born in 1990 were the most since the end of the baby boom in the early 1960s.

♦ **Half of Americans exercise vigorously at least twice a week.**
Americans' most popular recreational activities include walking, swimming, fishing, and bicycling.

♦ **Most Americans have health insurance, but millions do not.**
Only 1 percent of the nation's elderly are without health care coverage, compared with 15 percent of children.

♦ **Americans are less likely to smoke, drink, or use drugs today than a few decades ago.**
But half of 30-to-44-year-olds have smoked marijuana and one in five has used cocaine.

♦ **Americans born in 1997 can expect to live to age 76.5.**
Most of the gains in life expectancy during this century have been due to declining death rates among infants and children.

# Americans Feel Good

**The majority rate their health as excellent or good.**

Overall, 31 percent of adults say their health is excellent, ranging from 36 percent of 18-to-29-year-olds to 17 percent of people aged 70 or older. While the proportion of Americans who rate their health as excellent declines with age, even in the oldest age group only about one-third say their health is no better than fair or poor. Sixty-three percent of the oldest Americans say their health is good or excellent.

The higher their education, the better people feel. Fully 46 percent of college graduates say their health is excellent, compared with just 14 percent of people who did not graduate from high school. One reason for the poorer health of the less-educated is that older Americans are the ones with the least education.

Men and women are about equally likely to report good or excellent health. In contrast, whites are much more likely than blacks to say their health is excellent, 32 versus 22 percent. Many blacks have low incomes, which is often associated with poor health.

♦ As the population ages, the proportion of Americans who feel excellent may decline, while the proportion of those who feel only fair or poor could grow.

# Health Status, 1996

## "Would you say your own health, in general, is excellent, good, fair, or poor?"

(percent of people aged 18 or older responding by sex, race, age, and education, 1996)

|  | excellent | good | fair | poor |
|---|---|---|---|---|
| **Total people** | **31%** | **49%** | **16%** | **4%** |
| Men | 31 | 49 | 17 | 3 |
| Women | 30 | 48 | 15 | 5 |
| Black | 22 | 50 | 23 | 5 |
| White | 32 | 49 | 14 | 4 |
| Aged 18 to 29 | 36 | 49 | 14 | 1 |
| Aged 30 to 39 | 35 | 52 | 10 | 2 |
| Aged 40 to 49 | 32 | 50 | 15 | 3 |
| Aged 50 to 59 | 30 | 44 | 19 | 7 |
| Aged 60 to 69 | 23 | 49 | 18 | 9 |
| Aged 70 or older | 17 | 46 | 29 | 8 |
| Not a high school graduate | 14 | 40 | 33 | 12 |
| High school graduate | 29 | 52 | 16 | 3 |
| Bachelor's degree | 46 | 46 | 6 | 1 |
| Graduate degree | 46 | 44 | 8 | 1 |

Note: Numbers may not add to 100 because no answer is not included.
Source: 1996 General Social Survey, National Opinion Research Center, University of Chicago; calculations by New Strategist

# Americans Eat More Fruits and Vegetables

## But they still indulge in high-fat foods and sweets.

In 1996, Americans ate more yogurt, poultry, broccoli, cheese, and low-fat milk than they did in 1970. They ate less beef, eggs, sugar, ice cream, and whole milk. They drank less coffee and more bottled water.

These changes in eating habits are due partly to the deluge of nutritional advice directed at the public over the past few decades. Food consumption trends also reflect changing tastes. A growing preference for spicy foods, for example, has boosted consumption of onions by 77 percent.

Many eating trends run counter to the advice of nutritionists, however. Consumption of soft drinks was 114 percent greater in 1996 than in 1970, for example. People are eating less sugar but more corn sweetener. They are eating more fresh fruits and vegetables, but also more fats and oils.

◆ The trend away from red meat and high-fat foods is likely to continue as medical research confirms the health benefits of a low-fat diet.

# Food and Beverage Consumption, 1970 to 1996

*(number of pounds of selected foods and gallons of selected beverages consumed per capita, 1970 and 1996; percent change in consumption, 1970–96)*

|  | 1996 | 1970 | percent change 1970–96 |
|---|---|---|---|
| Red meat | 112.0 | 131.7 | –15.0% |
| Beef | 64.2 | 79.6 | –19.3 |
| Pork | 46.0 | 48.0 | –4.2 |
| Fish and shellfish | 14.7 | 11.7 | 25.6 |
| Fresh and frozen | 9.9 | 6.9 | 43.5 |
| Canned | 4.5 | 4.4 | 2.3 |
| Poultry | 64.3 | 33.8 | 90.2 |
| Chicken | 49.8 | 27.4 | 81.8 |
| Turkey | 14.6 | 6.4 | 128.1 |
| Eggs (number) | 236.2 | 308.9 | –23.5 |
| Milk and milk products | 575.6 | 563.8 | 2.1 |
| Plain whole milk | 72.1 | 213.5 | –66.2 |
| Plain low-fat milk | 69.1 | 29.8 | 131.9 |
| Plain skim milk | 55.7 | 11.6 | 380.2 |
| Yogurt | 4.8 | 0.8 | 500.0 |
| Cheese | 27.7 | 11.4 | 143.0 |
| Cheddar | 9.2 | 5.8 | 58.6 |
| Mozzarella | 8.5 | 1.2 | 608.3 |
| Swiss | 1.1 | 0.9 | 22.2 |
| Ice cream | 15.9 | 17.8 | –10.7 |
| Fats and oils | 65.6 | 52.6 | 24.7 |
| Butter | 4.3 | 5.4 | –20.4 |
| Margarine | 9.1 | 10.8 | –15.7 |
| Salad and cooking oils | 26.0 | 15.4 | 68.8 |
| Flour and cereal products | 198.5 | 135.3 | 46.7 |
| Caloric sweeteners | 152.0 | 122.3 | 24.3 |
| Sugar | 66.2 | 101.8 | –35.0 |
| Corn sweeteners | 84.5 | 19.1 | 342.4 |
| Fresh fruits | 129.2 | 101.2 | 27.7 |
| Bananas | 28.0 | 17.4 | 60.9 |
| Apples | 19.3 | 17.0 | 13.5 |

*(continued)*

*(continued from previous page)*

| | 1995 | 1970 | percent change 1970–96 |
|---|---|---|---|
| Grapes | 6.9 | 2.9 | 137.9% |
| Pears | 3.1 | 1.9 | 63.2 |
| Strawberries | 4.4 | 1.7 | 158.8 |
| Watermelons | 17.4 | 13.5 | 28.9 |
| Cantaloups | 10.6 | 7.2 | 47.2 |
| Oranges | 12.8 | 16.2 | −21.0 |
| Fresh vegetables | 178.7 | 85.4 | 109.3 |
| Broccoli | 4.1 | 0.5 | 720.0 |
| Carrots | 10.2 | 6.0 | 70.0 |
| Corn | 8.3 | 7.8 | 6.4 |
| Head lettuce | 23.3 | 22.4 | 4.0 |
| Onions | 17.9 | 10.1 | 77.2 |
| Potatoes | 48.8 | 61.8 | −21.0 |
| Tomatoes | 16.6 | 12.1 | 37.2 |
| Nonalcoholic beverages | 136.9 | 101.5 | 34.9 |
| Tea | 8.0 | 6.8 | 17.6 |
| Coffee | 23.1 | 33.4 | −30.8 |
| Bottled water | 12.4 | 2.4* | 383.3 |
| Soft drinks | 51.9 | 24.3 | 113.6 |
| Diet | 11.7 | 2.1 | 457.1 |
| Regular | 40.2 | 22.2 | 81.1 |
| Fruit juices | 8.7 | 5.7 | 52.6 |
| Fruit drinks, cocktails, and ades | 7.4 | 5.8** | 34.5 |
| Alcoholic beverages | 36.1 | 35.7 | 1.1 |
| Beer | 31.6 | 30.6 | 3.3 |
| Wine | 2.7 | 2.2 | 22.7 |
| Distilled spirits | 1.8 | 3.0 | −40.0 |

* Data for 1980.
** Data for 1990.
*Source: Bureau of the Census,* Statistical Abstract of the United States: 1996 *and* Statistical Abstract of the United States: 1998*; calculations by New Strategist*

# Vitamin Use Increases with Age

## People aged 30 or older are most likely to take vitamins.

Health concerns increase with age, so it is no surprise that the use of vitamin and mineral supplements is most common among older Americans. Among women, supplement use peaks in the 50-to-59 age group at 62 percent. For men, it peaks among those in their sixties at 46 percent.

Females are more likely than men to use vitamin and mineral supplements at all ages, with the exception of children. Boys aged 6 to 11 are more likely to take vitamin and mineral supplements than girls in that age group.

People under age 50 are more likely to take a multivitamin rather than single supplements. Among women aged 40 or older, single supplements are more widely used than multivitamins.

♦ Older Americans seeking to treat or prevent specific health problems are responsible for a substantial portion of vitamin and mineral sales in the U.S. As younger generations age, their use of vitamins and minerals is likely to increase.

### Most women take vitamins

*(percent of women who take vitamins, by age, 1994–95)*

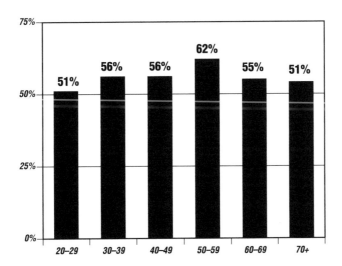

# Use of Vitamin and Mineral Supplements by Sex and Age, 1994–95

*(percent of people aged 6 or older using selected vitamin/mineral supplements by sex and age, 1994–95)*

| | total | multivitamin | multivitamin with iron or other minerals | single vitamins/ minerals |
|---|---|---|---|---|
| **Total people** | **47.0%** | **21.9%** | **15.8%** | **14.6%** |
| **Males** | | | | |
| Aged 6 to 11 | 46.9 | 24.7 | 17.7 | 4.1 |
| Aged 12 to 19 | 31.3 | 16.2 | 6.4 | 9.3 |
| Aged 20 to 29 | 36.6 | 20.4 | 8.7 | 9.9 |
| Aged 30 to 39 | 41.1 | 21.5 | 13.9 | 10.4 |
| Aged 40 to 49 | 42.0 | 21.2 | 11.4 | 14.3 |
| Aged 50 to 59 | 45.0 | 22.4 | 11.3 | 19.0 |
| Aged 60 to 69 | 45.5 | 20.9 | 13.7 | 19.0 |
| Aged 70 or older | 44.8 | 20.0 | 12.9 | 20.6 |
| **Females** | | | | |
| Aged 6 to 11 | 40.6 | 20.2 | 14.1 | 5.2 |
| Aged 12 to 19 | 40.6 | 17.5 | 11.2 | 11.3 |
| Aged 20 to 29 | 51.0 | 23.2 | 21.0 | 12.9 |
| Aged 30 to 39 | 56.0 | 21.9 | 24.6 | 16.4 |
| Aged 40 to 49 | 56.2 | 23.0 | 19.2 | 24.4 |
| Aged 50 to 59 | 61.8 | 27.5 | 20.2 | 29.5 |
| Aged 60 to 69 | 55.0 | 20.9 | 17.9 | 27.4 |
| Aged 70 or older | 53.6 | 23.4 | 15.6 | 23.4 |

*Source: USDA, ARS Food Surveys Research Group,* 1994 and 1995 Continuing Survey of Food Intakes by Individuals, *Internet web site <http://www.barc.usda.gov/bhnrc>*

# Births to Remain below 4 Million until 2005

## Births peaked in 1990, at nearly 4.2 million.

The 4,158,000 babies born in 1990 were the most since the end of the baby boom in the early 1960s. The children born in 1990 entered first grade in 1996, boosting the U.S. elementary and secondary school population to a record high. The school-aged population will continue to expand through 2006 as the children of the birth boom fill the elementary and secondary grades.

After peaking in 1990, the number of births drifted downward, stabilizing at about 3.9 million through 1998. The Bureau of the Census projects that the annual number of births will remain at this level through the turn of the century, then rise again as the children of the most recent birth boom begin to have children.

♦ Many of the nation's already-crowded schools should budget for expansion because the nation's forecasters see no substantial decline in the school-aged population.

# Number of Births, 1990 to 2050

(annual number of births, 1990 to 1997, and projected to 2050; numbers in thousands)

| year | births |
|------|--------|
| 1990 | 4,158 |
| 1991 | 4,111 |
| 1992 | 4,065 |
| 1993 | 4,000 |
| 1994 | 3,953 |
| 1995 | 3,900 |
| 1996 | 3,891 |
| 1997 | 3,895 |
| 1998 | 3,899 |
| 1999 | 3,896 |
| 2000 | 3,899 |
| 2005 | 4,001 |
| 2010 | 4,243 |
| 2015 | 4,450 |
| 2020 | 4,579 |
| 2025 | 4,679 |
| 2030 | 4,822 |
| 2035 | 5,022 |
| 2040 | 5,248 |
| 2045 | 5,465 |
| 2050 | 5,672 |

Source: National Center for Health Statistics, Births and Deaths: Preliminary Data for 1997, National Vital Statistics Report, Vol. 47, No. 4, 1998; and Bureau of the Census, Population Projections of the United States by Age, Sex, Race and Hispanic Origin: 1995 to 2050, Current Population Reports, P25-1130, 1996

# Newborns Show Diversity to Come

## Today's young adults are ushering in dramatic social change.

Despite frequent stories in the media about older mothers, most babies are born to women in their twenties. In 1997, 52 percent of newborns had mothers aged 20 to 29. These young adults are not only far more racially diverse than older Americans, but they are also less likely to be married when giving birth.

Only 60 percent of the 3.9 million newborns of 1997 had non-Hispanic white mothers. The other 40 percent were born to Hispanic, black, Asian, or Native American women. As these children grow up, they will create an increasingly multicultural society. Eventually, no single racial or ethnic group will dominate the U.S. population.

Many future adults will have little experience with a two-parent family. Fully 32 percent of newborns in 1996 were born to unmarried women. The proportion of babies born out of wedlock surged during the past two decades, rising from just 11 percent in 1970. Among blacks, 70 percent of babies are born out of wedlock. The share among Hispanics is 41 percent, and among whites, 26 percent.

♦ Marketing to today's new parents requires not only an understanding of diverse cultures, but also a willingness to embrace nontraditional lifestyles.

# Births by Age, Race, and Hispanic Origin of Mother, 1997

*(number and percent distribution of births by age, race, and Hispanic origin of mother, 1997)*

| | total | white | black | Asian | Native American | Hispanic | non-Hispanic white |
|---|---|---|---|---|---|---|---|
| | | | race | | | Hispanic origin | |
| **Total births** | **3,894,970** | **3,085,477** | **600,898** | **170,110** | **38,486** | **711,753** | **2,343,636** |
| Under age 15 | 10,852 | 5,388 | 5,074 | 191 | 198 | 3,210 | 2,286 |
| Aged 15 to 19 | 489,211 | 342,029 | 130,401 | 8,972 | 7,810 | 120,220 | 221,777 |
| Aged 20 to 24 | 946,357 | 724,288 | 182,630 | 27,159 | 12,281 | 216,675 | 504,003 |
| Aged 25 to 29 | 1,074,559 | 876,178 | 135,939 | 53,289 | 9,153 | 188,943 | 678,532 |
| Aged 30 to 34 | 887,892 | 737,416 | 93,641 | 51,042 | 5,793 | 121,152 | 605,148 |
| Aged 35 to 39 | 408,111 | 336,982 | 44,316 | 24,131 | 2,682 | 51,025 | 280,414 |
| Aged 40 to 44 | 74,778 | 60,646 | 8,572 | 5,019 | 541 | 10,116 | 49,397 |
| Aged 45 to 49 | 3,209 | 2,549 | 325 | 307 | 28 | 411 | 2,078 |

**Percent distribution by race and Hispanic origin**

| | total | white | black | Asian | Native American | Hispanic | non-Hispanic white |
|---|---|---|---|---|---|---|---|
| **Total births** | **100.0%** | **79.2%** | **15.4%** | **4.4%** | **1.0%** | **18.3%** | **60.2%** |
| Under age 15 | 100.0 | 49.6 | 46.8 | 1.8 | 1.8 | 29.6 | 21.1 |
| Aged 15 to 19 | 100.0 | 69.9 | 26.7 | 1.8 | 1.6 | 24.6 | 45.3 |
| Aged 20 to 24 | 100.0 | 76.5 | 19.3 | 2.9 | 1.3 | 22.9 | 53.3 |
| Aged 25 to 29 | 100.0 | 81.5 | 12.7 | 5.0 | 0.9 | 17.6 | 63.1 |
| Aged 30 to 34 | 100.0 | 83.1 | 10.5 | 5.7 | 0.7 | 13.6 | 68.2 |
| Aged 35 to 39 | 100.0 | 82.6 | 10.9 | 5.9 | 0.7 | 12.5 | 68.7 |
| Aged 40 to 44 | 100.0 | 81.1 | 11.5 | 6.7 | 0.7 | 13.5 | 66.1 |
| Aged 45 to 49 | 100.0 | 79.4 | 10.1 | 9.6 | 0.9 | 12.8 | 64.8 |

**Percent distribution by age**

| | total | white | black | Asian | Native American | Hispanic | non-Hispanic white |
|---|---|---|---|---|---|---|---|
| **Total births** | **100.0%** | **100.0%** | **100.0%** | **100.0%** | **100.0%** | **100.0%** | **100.0%** |
| Under age 15 | 0.3 | 0.2 | 0.8 | 0.1 | 0.5 | 0.5 | 0.1 |
| Aged 15 to 19 | 12.6 | 11.1 | 21.7 | 5.3 | 20.3 | 16.9 | 9.5 |
| Aged 20 to 24 | 24.3 | 23.5 | 30.4 | 16.0 | 31.9 | 30.4 | 21.5 |
| Aged 25 to 29 | 27.6 | 28.4 | 22.6 | 31.3 | 23.8 | 26.5 | 29.0 |
| Aged 30 to 34 | 22.8 | 23.9 | 15.6 | 30.0 | 15.1 | 17.0 | 25.8 |
| Aged 35 to 39 | 10.5 | 10.9 | 7.4 | 14.2 | 7.0 | 7.2 | 12.0 |
| Aged 40 to 44 | 1.9 | 2.0 | 1.4 | 3.0 | 1.4 | 1.4 | 2.1 |
| Aged 45 to 49 | 0.1 | 0.1 | 0.1 | 0.2 | 0.1 | 0.1 | 0.1 |

*Note: Numbers will not add to total because Hispanics may be of any race.*
*Source: National Center for Health Statistics,* Births and Deaths: Preliminary Data for 1997, *National Vital Statistics Reports, Vol. 47, No. 4, 1998; calculations by New Strategist*

# Births by Race, Age, and Marital Status of Mother, 1996

*(total number of births and number and percent to unmarried women, by race, Hispanic origin, and age of mother, 1996)*

|  | total | births to unmarried women | |
|---|---|---|---|
|  |  | number | percent |
| **Total births** | **3,891,494** | **1,260,306** | **32.4%** |
| Under age 15 | 11,148 | 10,460 | 93.8 |
| Aged 15 to 19 | 491,577 | 373,289 | 75.9 |
| Aged 20 to 24 | 945,210 | 431,462 | 45.6 |
| Aged 25 to 29 | 1,071,287 | 235,651 | 22.0 |
| Aged 30 to 34 | 897,913 | 133,048 | 14.8 |
| Aged 35 to 39 | 399,510 | 62,656 | 15.7 |
| Aged 40 or older | 74,849 | 13,740 | 18.4 |
| **Births to whites** | **3,093,057** | **795,432** | **25.7** |
| Under age 15 | 5,526 | 4,959 | 89.7 |
| Aged 15 to 19 | 344,685 | 236,815 | 68.7 |
| Aged 20 to 24 | 726,669 | 272,673 | 37.5 |
| Aged 25 to 29 | 878,449 | 148,498 | 16.9 |
| Aged 30 to 34 | 747,436 | 83,108 | 11.1 |
| Aged 35 to 39 | 329,782 | 40,109 | 12.2 |
| Aged 40 or older | 60,510 | 9,270 | 15.3 |
| **Births to blacks** | **594,781** | **415,213** | **69.8** |
| Under age 15 | 5,193 | 5,147 | 99.1 |
| Aged 15 to 19 | 130,596 | 124,602 | 95.4 |
| Aged 20 to 24 | 179,361 | 142,903 | 79.7 |
| Aged 25 to 29 | 133,204 | 76,489 | 57.4 |
| Aged 30 to 34 | 94,295 | 43,057 | 45.7 |
| Aged 35 to 39 | 43,716 | 19,353 | 44.3 |
| Aged 40 or older | 8,416 | 3,662 | 43.5 |
| **Births to Hispanics** | **701,339** | **285,501** | **40.7** |
| Under age 15 | 3,056 | 2,639 | 86.4 |
| Aged 15 to 19 | 118,878 | 80,501 | 67.7 |
| Aged 20 to 24 | 214,173 | 96,904 | 45.2 |
| Aged 25 to 29 | 185,478 | 57,872 | 31.2 |
| Aged 30 to 34 | 119,690 | 31,160 | 26.0 |
| Aged 35 to 39 | 49,812 | 13,392 | 26.9 |
| Aged 40 or older | 10,252 | 3,033 | 29.6 |

*Note: Numbers will not add to total because Hispanics may be of any race and not all races are shown.*
*Source: National Center for Health Statistics,* Report of Final Natality Statistics, 1996, *Monthly Vital Statistics Report, Vol. 46, No. 11(S), 1998; calculations by New Strategist*

# Men Are More Likely to Exercise Than Women

## Young men are most likely to exercise daily.

Thirty-two percent of men aged 18 to 29 exercise vigorously on a daily basis, the highest exercise rate found among adults. In contrast, among women it is the 50-to-69-year-olds who are most likely to exercise vigorously every day—15 percent reported doing so in 1994–95. Overall, 25 percent of men, but only 13 percent of women, exercise vigorously on a daily basis.

Men and women aged 70 or older are the ones most likely to say they exercise rarely or never—57 percent of men and 72 percent of women. They are not alone, however. Among adults of all ages, 28 percent of men and 44 percent of women exercise rarely or never.

Walking is the most popular recreational activity, with 67 percent of Americans aged 16 or older saying they have walked for exercise at least once in the past year. Many of the most popular recreational activities do not require much exertion, including sightseeing, picnicking, attending outdoor sports events, boating, and fishing. Only 29 percent of Americans have been bicycling in the past year, just 15 percent have been golfing, 11 percent have played tennis, and fewer than 1 percent have been snowboarding.

◆ The aging population will boost the popularity of some fitness activities, while making others less popular. A big gainer is likely to be fitness walking.

◆ As baby-boom women age into their fifties and gain more free time, look for a surge in the number of women who exercise vigorously on a daily basis.

# Vigorous Exercise by Sex and Age, 1994–95

*(percent of people aged 20 or older by age and frequency of vigorous exercise, 1994–95)*

| | daily | 5 to 6 times per week | 2 to 4 times per week | once a week | 1 to 3 times per month | rarely or never |
|---|---|---|---|---|---|---|
| **Total people** | **18.5%** | **6.8%** | **23.9%** | **8.2%** | **5.8%** | **36.5%** |
| **Total men** | **24.6** | **7.9** | **25.7** | **8.3** | **4.9** | **28.2** |
| Aged 20 to 29 | 31.8 | 9.2 | 29.5 | 8.8 | 4.8 | 15.6 |
| Aged 30 to 39 | 23.5 | 9.8 | 29.2 | 10.0 | 6.3 | 21.2 |
| Aged 40 to 49 | 22.6 | 8.3 | 27.1 | 9.1 | 5.4 | 26.8 |
| Aged 50 to 59 | 20.2 | 7.5 | 23.3 | 9.0 | 4.8 | 34.7 |
| Aged 60 to 69 | 26.9 | 6.0 | 19.6 | 4.8 | 3.6 | 38.5 |
| Aged 70 or older | 18.9 | 2.5 | 14.9 | 3.9 | 1.9 | 57.1 |
| **Total women** | **12.9** | **5.8** | **22.3** | **8.0** | **6.5** | **44.2** |
| Aged 20 to 29 | 12.0 | 5.7 | 28.0 | 10.4 | 7.5 | 36.2 |
| Aged 30 to 39 | 12.4 | 7.1 | 28.1 | 10.4 | 9.1 | 32.9 |
| Aged 40 to 49 | 12.3 | 6.1 | 23.1 | 9.6 | 7.5 | 40.8 |
| Aged 50 to 59 | 15.1 | 8.3 | 20.0 | 6.4 | 5.5 | 44.5 |
| Aged 60 to 69 | 15.5 | 3.5 | 16.6 | 5.2 | 4.5 | 54.5 |
| Aged 70 or older | 11.2 | 2.6 | 9.3 | 2.2 | 1.9 | 71.9 |

*Source: USDA, ARS Food Surveys Research Group,* 1994 and 1995 Diet and Health Knowledge Survey, *Internet web site <http://www.barc.usda.gov/bhnrc>*

# Participation in Outdoor Recreational Activities, 1994–95

*(number and percent of people aged 16 or older who participated in selected recreational activities at least once in the past 12 months, 1994–95; ranked by percentage participating)*

|  | number (millions) | percent |
|---|---|---|
| Walking | 133.6 | 66.7% |
| Sightseeing | 113.4 | 56.6 |
| Picnicking | 98.4 | 49.1 |
| Attending outdoor sports event | 95.2 | 47.5 |
| Swimming (pool) | 88.5 | 44.2 |
| Swimming (nonpool) | 78.1 | 39.0 |
| Wildlife viewing | 62.5 | 31.2 |
| Boating (any) | 60.1 | 30.0 |
| Fishing (any) | 58.3 | 29.1 |
| Bicycling | 57.4 | 28.6 |
| Studying nature near water | 55.3 | 27.6 |
| Birdwatching | 54.1 | 27.0 |
| Camping (any) | 53.7 | 26.8 |
| Running, jogging | 52.5 | 26.2 |
| Outdoor team sports | 49.5 | 24.7 |
| Freshwater fishing | 48.9 | 24.4 |
| Hiking | 47.7 | 23.8 |
| Motor boating | 46.9 | 23.4 |
| Camping (developed area) | 41.5 | 20.7 |
| Attending outdoor concert | 41.5 | 20.7 |
| Golf | 29.6 | 14.8 |
| Volleyball | 28.8 | 14.4 |
| Camping (primitive area) | 28.0 | 14.0 |
| Off-road driving | 27.8 | 13.9 |
| Fish viewing | 27.4 | 13.7 |
| Softball | 26.2 | 13.1 |
| Basketball | 25.6 | 12.8 |
| Tennis | 21.2 | 10.6 |
| Sledding | 20.4 | 10.2 |
| Saltwater fishing | 19.0 | 9.5 |
| Hunting (any) | 18.8 | 9.4 |
| Water skiing | 17.8 | 8.9 |
| Downhill skiing | 16.8 | 8.4 |
| Backpacking | 15.2 | 7.6 |

*(continued)*

*(continued from previous page)*

|  | number (millions) | percent |
|---|---|---|
| Floating, rafting | 15.2 | 7.6% |
| Snorkeling | 14.4 | 7.2 |
| Big-game hunting | 14.2 | 7.1 |
| Horseback riding | 14.2 | 7.1 |
| Football | 13.6 | 6.8 |
| Baseball | 13.6 | 6.8 |
| Canoeing | 13.2 | 6.6 |
| Small-game hunting | 13.0 | 6.5 |
| Ice skating | 10.4 | 5.2 |
| Sailing | 9.6 | 4.8 |
| Soccer | 9.4 | 4.7 |
| Caving | 9.4 | 4.7 |
| Personal watercraft | 9.4 | 4.7 |
| Mountain climbing | 9.0 | 4.5 |
| Rowing | 8.4 | 4.2 |
| Rock climbing | 7.4 | 3.7 |
| Snowmobiling | 7.0 | 3.5 |
| Cross-country skiing | 6.6 | 3.3 |
| Orienteering | 4.8 | 2.4 |
| Migratory bird hunting | 4.2 | 2.1 |
| Surfing | 2.6 | 1.3 |
| Windsurfing | 2.2 | 1.1 |
| Snowboarding | 1.6 | 0.8 |
| Kayaking | 1.4 | 0.7 |

*Source: USDA Forest Service,* 1994–95 National Survey of Recreation and the Environment; *calculations by New Strategist*

# Sixteen Percent of Americans Do Not Have Health Insurance

**The majority of Americans have health care coverage, but 43 million do not.**

Young adults are most likely to be without health insurance. Thirty percent of 18-to-24-year-olds do not have coverage, nor do 23 percent of 25-to-34-year-olds.

Because the federal government's Medicare program covers the elderly, those most likely to have health insurance are Americans aged 65 or older. Only 1 percent of the oldest Americans are without health care coverage. In contrast, 15 percent of the children under age 18 do not have health insurance, accounting for fully 25 percent of the nation's uninsured.

♦ The proportion of Americans who lack health insurance has been rising because a growing share of workers are employed by businesses that do not offer coverage.

### Those without health insurance are most likely to be aged 18 to 24

*(percent of people without health insurance by age, 1997)*

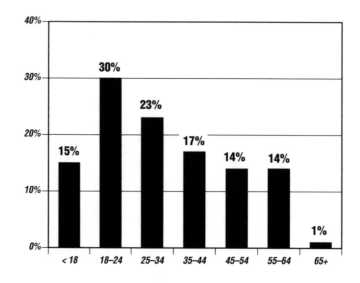

# Health Insurance Coverage by Age, 1997

*(number and percent distribution of people by age and health insurance coverage status, 1997; numbers in thousands)*

| | | | | | | | | | |
|---|---|---|---|---|---|---|---|---|---|
| | | | private health insurance | | government health insurance | | | | |
| | | | | employment | | | | | not |
| | total | total | total | based | total | Medicaid | Medicare | military | covered |
| **Total** | | | | | | | | | |
| **people** | **269,094** | **225,646** | **188,532** | **165,091** | **66,685** | **28,956** | **35,590** | **8,527** | **43,448** |
| Under 18 | 71,682 | 60,939 | 47,968 | 44,869 | 16,800 | 14,683 | 395 | 2,163 | 10,743 |
| 18 to 24 | 25,201 | 17,619 | 15,256 | 12,638 | 3,283 | 2,555 | 155 | 692 | 7,582 |
| 25 to 34 | 39,354 | 30,192 | 27,138 | 25,496 | 3,956 | 2,842 | 365 | 1,011 | 9,163 |
| 35 to 44 | 44,462 | 36,763 | 33,673 | 31,560 | 4,257 | 2,700 | 878 | 1,161 | 7,699 |
| 45 to 54 | 34,057 | 29,319 | 27,063 | 25,099 | 3,677 | 1,766 | 1,133 | 1,281 | 4,738 |
| 55 to 64 | 22,255 | 19,065 | 16,748 | 14,466 | 3,771 | 1,509 | 1,794 | 1,095 | 3,190 |
| 65 or older | 32,082 | 31,749 | 20,687 | 10,963 | 30,942 | 2,901 | 30,870 | 1,125 | 333 |
| **Percent distribution by type of coverage** | | | | | | | | | |
| **Total people** | **100.0%** | **83.9%** | **70.1%** | **61.4%** | **24.8%** | **10.8%** | **13.2%** | **3.2%** | **16.1%** |
| Under 18 | 100.0 | 85.0 | 66.9 | 62.6 | 23.4 | 20.5 | 0.6 | 3.0 | 15.0 |
| 18 to 24 | 100.0 | 69.9 | 60.5 | 50.1 | 13.0 | 10.1 | 0.6 | 2.7 | 30.1 |
| 25 to 34 | 100.0 | 76.7 | 69.0 | 64.8 | 10.1 | 7.2 | 0.9 | 2.6 | 23.3 |
| 35 to 44 | 100.0 | 82.7 | 75.7 | 71.0 | 9.6 | 6.1 | 2.0 | 2.6 | 17.3 |
| 45 to 54 | 100.0 | 86.1 | 79.5 | 73.7 | 10.8 | 5.2 | 3.3 | 3.8 | 13.9 |
| 55 to 64 | 100.0 | 85.7 | 75.3 | 65.0 | 16.9 | 6.8 | 8.1 | 4.9 | 14.3 |
| 65 or older | 100.0 | 99.0 | 64.5 | 34.2 | 96.4 | 9.0 | 96.2 | 3.5 | 1.0 |
| **Percent distribution by age** | | | | | | | | | |
| **Total people** | **100.0%** | **100.0%** | **100.0%** | **100.0%** | **100.0%** | **100.0%** | **100.0%** | **100.0%** | **100.0%** |
| Under 18 | 26.6 | 27.0 | 25.4 | 27.2 | 25.2 | 50.7 | 1.1 | 25.4 | 24.7 |
| 18 to 24 | 9.4 | 7.8 | 8.1 | 7.7 | 4.9 | 8.8 | 0.4 | 8.1 | 17.5 |
| 25 to 34 | 14.6 | 13.4 | 14.4 | 15.4 | 5.9 | 9.8 | 1.0 | 11.9 | 21.1 |
| 35 to 44 | 16.5 | 16.3 | 17.9 | 19.1 | 6.4 | 9.3 | 2.5 | 13.6 | 17.7 |
| 45 to 54 | 12.7 | 13.0 | 14.4 | 15.2 | 5.5 | 6.1 | 3.2 | 15.0 | 10.9 |
| 55 to 64 | 8.3 | 8.4 | 8.9 | 8.8 | 5.7 | 5.2 | 5.0 | 12.8 | 7.3 |
| 65 or older | 11.9 | 14.1 | 11.0 | 6.6 | 46.4 | 10.0 | 86.7 | 13.2 | 0.8 |

*Note: Numbers may not add to total because some people have more than one type of health insurance coverage.*
*Source: Bureau of the Census, unpublished tables from the 1998 Current Population Survey; calculations by New Strategist*

# Vices on the Decline

**Americans are less likely to smoke, drink, or use drugs than they were a few decades ago.**

The proportion of Americans who smoke cigarettes fell by nearly 18 percentage points between 1965 and 1995, from 42 to 25 percent. In 1995, only 27 percent of men smoked cigarettes, down from 52 percent in 1965. Among women, smokers have declined from 34 to 23 percent.

A far higher proportion of Americans drink alcoholic beverages. In 1994, 69 percent said they drank alcohol at least occasionally, while 31 percent said they abstained. Drinking is most common among young adults and declines with age. Fully 81 percent of people aged 18 to 29 say they drink, compared with fewer than half of Americans aged 70 or older.

Although the media have focused attention on the small rise in drug use over the past few years, the proportion of Americans who use drugs is down sharply from the levels of the 1970s. Overall, only 6 percent of people aged 12 or older are current drug users, although 35 percent have ever used drugs. Those most likely to be current drug users are people aged 18 to 20, with 20 percent doing so. Those most likely ever to have used drugs, however, are people aged 30 to 44. Over half of people in this age group have smoked marijuana, and one in five has used cocaine.

♦ The proportions of people who smoke cigarettes, drink alcohol, and use drugs should continue to decline as the population ages.

# Cigarette Smoking by Sex and Age, 1965 to 1995

*(percent of people aged 18 or older who currently smoke cigarettes by sex and age, 1965 and 1995; percentage point change, 1965–95)*

|  | 1995 | 1965 | percentage point change 1965–95 |
|---|---|---|---|
| **Total people** | **24.7%** | **42.4%** | **−17.7** |
| **Total men** | **27.0** | **51.9** | **−24.9** |
| Aged 18 to 24 | 27.8 | 54.1 | −26.3 |
| Aged 25 to 34 | 29.5 | 60.7 | −31.2 |
| Aged 35 to 44 | 31.5 | 58.2 | −26.7 |
| Aged 45 to 64 | 27.1 | 51.9 | −24.8 |
| Aged 65 or older | 14.9 | 28.5 | −13.6 |
| **Total women** | **22.6** | **33.9** | **−11.3** |
| Aged 18 to 24 | 21.8 | 38.1 | −16.3 |
| Aged 25 to 34 | 26.4 | 43.7 | −17.3 |
| Aged 35 to 44 | 27.1 | 43.7 | −16.6 |
| Aged 45 to 64 | 24.0 | 32.0 | −8.0 |
| Aged 65 or older | 11.5 | 9.6 | 1.9 |

*Source: National Center for Health Statistics,* Health, United States, 1998; *calculations by New Strategist*

# Alcohol Consumption by Age, 1994

**"Do you ever have occasion to use any alcoholic beverages such as liquor, wine, or beer, or are you a total abstainer?"**

*(percent of people aged 18 or older who currently drink alcohol or abstain, by age, 1994)*

|  | currently use | abstain |
|---|---|---|
| **Total people** | **69.1%** | **30.9%** |
| Aged 18 to 29 | 80.6 | 19.4 |
| Aged 30 to 39 | 79.6 | 20.4 |
| Aged 40 to 49 | 67.4 | 32.6 |
| Aged 50 to 59 | 63.5 | 36.5 |
| Aged 60 to 69 | 67.3 | 32.7 |
| Aged 70 to 79 | 43.1 | 56.9 |
| Aged 80 or older | 40.0 | 60.0 |

*Source: 1994 General Social Survey, National Opinion Research Center, University of Chicago; calculations by New Strategist*

# Drug Use by Age and Type of Drug, 1996

*(percent of people aged 12 or older who ever used or currently use any illicit drug, marijuana, or cocaine, by age, 1996)*

| | any illicit drug | | marijuana | | cocaine | |
|---|---|---|---|---|---|---|
| | current user | ever used | current user | ever used | current user | ever used |
| **Total people** | **6.1%** | **34.8%** | **4.7%** | **32.0%** | **0.8%** | **10.3%** |
| Aged 12 to 13 | 2.2 | 7.5 | 1.2 | 3.6 | 0.0 | 0.2 |
| Aged 14 to 15 | 8.8 | 22.6 | 6.7 | 15.7 | 0.3 | 1.3 |
| Aged 16 to 17 | 15.6 | 35.1 | 13.1 | 30.4 | 1.4 | 4.2 |
| Aged 18 to 20 | 20.0 | 45.2 | 17.1 | 41.6 | 2.2 | 8.5 |
| Aged 21 to 25 | 12.9 | 49.7 | 10.9 | 45.5 | 1.9 | 11.2 |
| Aged 26 to 29 | 9.1 | 48.9 | 7.3 | 46.4 | 1.3 | 17.3 |
| Aged 30 to 34 | 7.9 | 56.1 | 5.7 | 53.5 | 1.7 | 23.5 |
| Aged 35 to 39 | 6.4 | 53.6 | 5.5 | 51.0 | 1.5 | 22.1 |
| Aged 40 to 44 | 5.0 | 53.2 | 3.0 | 50.3 | 0.7 | 21.1 |
| Aged 45 to 49 | 4.0 | 42.3 | 2.9 | 40.1 | 0.2 | 9.4 |
| Aged 50 or older | 0.8 | 10.1 | 0.3 | 8.5 | – | 0.8 |

*Note: Current users are those who used the drug at least once during the month prior to the survey; (–) means sample is too small to make a reliable estimate.*
*Source: U.S. Substance Abuse and Mental Health Services Administrations,* National Household Survey on Drug Abuse, 1997; *Internet web site <http://www.samhsa.gov>*

# Colds and Flu Are the Most Common Illnesses

**Americans experienced more than 60 million colds and more than 100 million bouts with the flu in 1995.**

Acute conditions are most likely to strike young adults and children, while chronic conditions are most likely to affect older Americans.

The incidence of most acute illnesses declines with age. Not only do older people have more immunities than children, but they are less likely to be around others who are sick. Over one-half of the 60 million colds that were bad enough to keep people in bed for at least half a day or send them to a doctor were experienced by people under age 25. Fully 83 percent of flu victims in 1995 were under age 45.

In contrast to acute illnesses, the prevalence of most chronic conditions increases with age. The most common chronic conditions among Americans of all ages are chronic sinusitis, arthritis, high blood pressure, hay fever, and hearing impairments. People aged 65 or older account for 47 percent of those with arthritis, 40 percent of those with hearing impairments, and 42 percent of those with heart conditions. They also account for 60 percent of those with prostate disease, 68 percent of those with cerebrovascular disease, and 57 percent of people with emphysema.

◆ As the baby-boom generation enters its fifties and sixties during the next decades, the number of chronic conditions—such as arthritis and high blood pressure— will surge.

# Acute Health Conditions by Age, 1995

*(total number of acute conditions by type, and percent distribution of conditions by age, 1995; numbers in thousands)*

|  | total number | total percent | < 5 | 5 to 17 | 18 to 24 | 25 to 44 | 45 to 64 | 65+ |
|---|---|---|---|---|---|---|---|---|
| **Total acute conditions** | **456,874** | **100.0%** | **16.2%** | **26.1%** | **8.6%** | **28.5%** | **13.5%** | **7.1%** |
| **Infective and parasitic diseases** | **52,605** | **100.0** | **20.0** | **37.9** | **8.7** | **21.3** | **8.5** | **3.5** |
| Common childhood diseases | 3,105 | 100.0 | 49.8 | 41.4 | 4.8 | 3.9 | – | – |
| Intestinal viruses | 12,447 | 100.0 | 19.1 | 35.1 | 9.4 | 26.1 | 8.2 | 2.2 |
| Viral infections | 16,875 | 100.0 | 19.9 | 38.4 | 7.0 | 19.7 | 10.6 | 4.6 |
| **Respiratory conditions** | **223,037** | **100.0** | **14.5** | **27.7** | **8.9** | **30.0** | **13.4** | **5.5** |
| Common cold | 60,564 | 100.0 | 18.0 | 27.5 | 9.0 | 25.5 | 13.8 | 6.3 |
| Influenza | 108,009 | 100.0 | 10.1 | 27.7 | 9.9 | 34.8 | 13.4 | 4.1 |
| Acute bronchitis | 13,250 | 100.0 | 19.4 | 19.4 | 8.3 | 27.8 | 12.5 | 12.6 |
| Pneumonia | 5,113 | 100.0 | 17.5 | 20.9 | 1.6 | 22.9 | 23.6 | 13.4 |
| **Digestive system conditions** | **15,828** | **100.0** | **15.0** | **23.2** | **9.9** | **26.5** | **14.6** | **10.8** |
| Dental conditions | 3,503 | 100.0 | 26.8 | 5.6 | 4.9 | 47.9 | 12.6 | 2.3 |
| Indigestion, nausea, and vomiting | 7,323 | 100.0 | 6.2 | 41.1 | 13.9 | 18.5 | 13.7 | 6.7 |
| **Injuries** | **64,619** | **100.0** | **8.5** | **23.6** | **9.7** | **30.1** | **18.6** | **9.6** |
| Fractures and dislocations | 8,200 | 100.0 | 3.3 | 26.6 | 9.1 | 34.0 | 17.5 | 9.5 |
| Sprains and strains | 12,961 | 100.0 | 1.1 | 23.1 | 12.2 | 34.9 | 22.2 | 6.5 |
| Open wounds and lacerations | 12,417 | 100.0 | 13.2 | 26.0 | 10.7 | 29.8 | 14.4 | 5.9 |
| Contusions and superficial injuries | 12,295 | 100.0 | 6.1 | 29.4 | 6.8 | 30.0 | 16.7 | 11.0 |
| **Selected other acute conditions** |  |  |  |  |  |  |  |  |
| Eye conditions | 2,431 | 100.0 | 10.8 | 16.5 | 5.5 | 31.2 | 12.7 | 23.3 |
| Acute ear infections | 23,568 | 100.0 | 54.1 | 27.9 | 2.0 | 11.5 | 4.0 | 0.5 |
| Acute urinary conditions | 7,089 | 100.0 | 4.4 | 13.5 | 10.7 | 31.9 | 19.5 | 20.0 |
| Skin conditions | 5,474 | 100.0 | 11.9 | 25.2 | 7.2 | 30.9 | 11.1 | 13.7 |
| Acute musculoskeletal conditions | 7,866 | 100.0 | – | 9.6 | 3.4 | 46.3 | 24.7 | 16.0 |
| Headache, excluding migraine | 4,128 | 100.0 | 3.7 | 38.4 | 12.0 | 29.7 | 9.5 | 6.8 |
| Fever, unspecified | 6,282 | 100.0 | 45.6 | 39.0 | 3.3 | 7.7 | 1.2 | 3.2 |

*Note: The acute conditions shown here are those that caused people to seek medical attention or to restrict their activity for at least half a day. (–) means not applicable or sample is too small to make a reliable estimate.*
*Source: National Center for Health Statistics,* Current Estimates from the National Health Interview Survey, 1995, *Series 10, No. 199, 1998; calculations by New Strategist*

# Chronic Health Conditions by Age, 1995

*(total number of chronic conditions by type, and percent distribution of conditions by age, 1995; numbers in thousands)*

| | total | | | | | aged 65 or older | | |
|---|---|---|---|---|---|---|---|---|
| | number | percent | < 18 | 18 to 44 | 45 to 64 | total | 65 to 74 | 75+ |
| **Skin and musculoskeletal conditions** | | | | | | | | |
| Arthritis | 32,663 | 100.0% | 0.5% | 15.5% | 36.9% | 47.2% | 25.3% | 21.8% |
| Gout, including gouty arthritis | 2,478 | 100.0 | – | 17.0 | 47.7 | 35.3 | 22.7 | 12.6 |
| Intervertebral disc disorders | 5,927 | 100.0 | 0.6 | 41.9 | 40.5 | 17.0 | 9.4 | 7.6 |
| Bone spur or tendinitis, unspecified | 2,750 | 100.0 | 1.3 | 34.1 | 48.2 | 16.3 | 8.5 | 7.8 |
| Disorders of bone or cartilage | 1,793 | 100.0 | 9.7 | 18.1 | 31.9 | 40.3 | 21.9 | 18.5 |
| Bunions | 3,262 | 100.0 | 2.4 | 29.5 | 37.8 | 29.7 | 16.0 | 13.6 |
| Bursitis, unclassified | 5,372 | 100.0 | 0.7 | 33.8 | 37.5 | 28.0 | 18.5 | 9.5 |
| Sebaceous skin cyst | 1,288 | 100.0 | 5.2 | 56.8 | 28.9 | 9.2 | 3.3 | 5.8 |
| Acne | 5,339 | 100.0 | 34.9 | 58.8 | 6.0 | 0.3 | 0.3 | – |
| Psoriasis | 2,489 | 100.0 | 8.2 | 38.2 | 34.7 | 18.9 | 11.9 | 7.0 |
| Dermatitis | 9,333 | 100.0 | 26.6 | 43.9 | 19.8 | 9.6 | 5.8 | 3.7 |
| Dry, itching skin, unclassified | 6,440 | 100.0 | 14.9 | 37.3 | 24.2 | 23.2 | 12.7 | 10.6 |
| Ingrown nails | 5,371 | 100.0 | 10.5 | 40.3 | 27.9 | 21.3 | 10.8 | 10.5 |
| Corns and calluses | 4,347 | 100.0 | 2.1 | 32.1 | 34.1 | 31.7 | 14.1 | 17.6 |
| **Impairments** | | | | | | | | |
| Visual impairment | 8,511 | 100.0 | 5.8 | 36.7 | 29.3 | 28.1 | 11.8 | 16.3 |
| Color blindness | 2,966 | 100.0 | 7.2 | 48.2 | 31.9 | 12.7 | 4.8 | 7.9 |
| Cataracts | 6,256 | 100.0 | 0.2 | 4.0 | 15.9 | 79.8 | 31.1 | 48.8 |
| Glaucoma | 2,478 | 100.0 | – | 7.9 | 25.7 | 66.5 | 30.5 | 36.0 |
| Hearing impairment | 22,465 | 100.0 | 4.7 | 22.2 | 33.3 | 39.8 | 19.4 | 20.3 |
| Tinnitus | 6,805 | 100.0 | 1.4 | 25.6 | 41.6 | 31.4 | 19.7 | 11.7 |
| Speech impairment | 2,747 | 100.0 | 46.5 | 27.5 | 17.1 | 8.9 | 5.4 | 3.5 |
| Absence of extremities | 1,195 | 100.0 | 1.9 | 40.1 | 37.9 | 20.1 | 17.1 | 3.0 |
| Paralysis of extremities | 1,509 | 100.0 | 11.7 | 28.2 | 24.8 | 35.4 | 22.5 | 12.9 |
| Deformity/orthopedic impairment | 31,784 | 100.0 | 6.6 | 47.2 | 28.6 | 17.6 | 9.7 | 7.9 |
| **Digestive conditions** | | | | | | | | |
| Ulcer | 4,297 | 100.0 | 2.0 | 44.6 | 34.6 | 18.8 | 13.1 | 5.7 |
| Hernia of abdominal cavity | 4,664 | 100.0 | 3.0 | 24.1 | 35.9 | 37.0 | 21.6 | 15.4 |
| Gastritis or duodenitis | 3,663 | 100.0 | 3.8 | 35.5 | 31.8 | 29.0 | 14.8 | 14.1 |
| Frequent indigestion | 7,196 | 100.0 | 3.2 | 48.3 | 29.6 | 18.9 | 10.9 | 8.0 |
| Enteritis or colitis | 2,409 | 100.0 | 5.9 | 39.1 | 34.9 | 20.1 | 11.6 | 8.5 |

*(continued)*

*(continued from previous page)*

| | total | | < 18 | 18 to 44 | 45 to 64 | aged 65 or older | | |
|---|---|---|---|---|---|---|---|---|
| | *number* | *percent* | | | | *total* | *65 to 74* | *75+* |
| Spastic colon | 2,437 | 100.0% | 4.5% | 45.5% | 32.4% | 17.6% | 11.3% | 6.3% |
| Diverticula of intestines | 2,121 | 100.0 | – | 10.8 | 28.1 | 61.1 | 38.0 | 23.1 |
| Frequent constipation | 3,644 | 100.0 | 8.8 | 33.6 | 24.3 | 33.3 | 11.4 | 21.9 |
| **Genitourinary, nervous, endocrine, metabolic, and blood conditions** | | | | | | | | |
| Goiter or other thyroid disorders | 4,521 | 100.0 | 1.8 | 30.9 | 34.4 | 32.8 | 19.5 | 13.3 |
| Diabetes | 8,693 | 100.0 | 2.1 | 14.2 | 27.6 | 45.8 | 28.2 | 17.5 |
| Anemias | 4,177 | 100.0 | 12.2 | 49.2 | 23.3 | 15.4 | 5.4 | 10.0 |
| Epilepsy | 1,443 | 100.0 | 19.8 | 43.2 | 22.9 | 14.1 | 10.4 | 3.7 |
| Migraine headache | 11,897 | 100.0 | 7.6 | 61.9 | 25.2 | 5.3 | 4.1 | 1.3 |
| Neuralgia or neuritis, unspecified | 373 | 100.0 | – | 24.7 | 22.3 | 53.1 | 32.7 | 20.4 |
| Kidney trouble | 3,022 | 100.0 | 6.2 | 45.4 | 26.3 | 22.0 | 15.1 | 7.0 |
| Bladder disorders | 4,135 | 100.0 | 4.8 | 33.7 | 24.7 | 36.8 | 16.7 | 20.0 |
| Diseases of prostate | 2,591 | 100.0 | – | 6.6 | 33.6 | 59.8 | 39.7 | 20.1 |
| Diseases of female genital organs | 5,362 | 100.0 | 3.1 | 62.9 | 27.2 | 6.8 | 4.9 | 1.8 |
| **Circulatory conditions** | | | | | | | | |
| Rheumatic fever | 2,166 | 100.0 | 3.2 | 34.9 | 37.9 | 23.9 | 14.5 | 9.3 |
| Heart disease | 21,114 | 100.0 | 6.2 | 18.3 | 29.6 | 45.9 | 23.4 | 22.4 |
| High blood pressure | 29,954 | 100.0 | 0.1 | 19.0 | 38.4 | 42.4 | 24.2 | 18.2 |
| Cerebrovascular disease | 3,314 | 100.0 | 1.6 | 7.4 | 23.3 | 67.7 | 28.9 | 38.8 |
| Hardening of the arteries | 1,845 | 100.0 | – | 3.7 | 26.1 | 70.1 | 28.8 | 41.4 |
| Varicose veins of lower extremities | 7,396 | 100.0 | – | 33.1 | 32.3 | 34.6 | 19.3 | 15.3 |
| Hemorrhoids | 9,077 | 100.0 | 0.7 | 43.7 | 36.2 | 19.3 | 11.0 | 8.3 |
| **Respiratory conditions** | | | | | | | | |
| Chronic bronchitis | 14,533 | 100.0 | 26.1 | 37.3 | 22.7 | 13.9 | 8.4 | 5.5 |
| Asthma | 14,878 | 100.0 | 35.6 | 37.5 | 18.5 | 8.4 | 5.7 | 2.7 |
| Hay fever or allergic rhinitis | 25,730 | 100.0 | 18.2 | 49.7 | 23.2 | 8.9 | 5.8 | 3.1 |
| Chronic sinusitis | 37,003 | 100.0 | 14.4 | 47.5 | 25.0 | 13.0 | 7.8 | 5.2 |
| Deviated nasal septum | 1,705 | 100.0 | 3.9 | 51.7 | 31.0 | 13.4 | 9.1 | 4.2 |
| Chronic disease of tonsils/adenoids | 2,706 | 100.0 | 48.3 | 40.5 | 9.1 | 2.1 | 2.1 | – |
| Emphysema | 1,870 | 100.0 | – | 6.8 | 35.9 | 57.3 | 35.4 | 21.9 |

*Note: Chronic conditions are those that last at least three months or belong to a group of conditions that are considered to be chronic regardless of when they begin. (–) means sample is too small to make a reliable estimate.*
*Source: National Center for Health Statistics,* Current Estimates from the National Health Interview Survey, 1995, *Series 10, No. 199, 1998; calculations by New Strategist*

# Many Americans Are Disabled

## One in five adults has a disability.

Fifty-four million Americans have a disability, and 26 million of them are severely disabled. Not surprisingly, those most likely to be disabled are the oldest Americans. Over half of people aged 80 or older are severely disabled. A severe disability is defined as using a wheelchair or other mobility aid for at least six months, being unable to perform one or more functional activities such as climbing stairs, or needing daily assistance to function.

The most common disabilities among Americans aged 15 or older are difficulty lifting, climbing stairs, and walking. Among people aged 80 or older, one in four has trouble seeing or hearing. Nearly half in this age group have trouble climbing stairs or walking. Nineteen percent have a mental disability. Despite the rise in disability with age, only 34 percent of the oldest Americans need personal assistance to help them manage their daily lives.

♦ As the enormous baby-boom generation ages, the number of Americans with disabilities will grow rapidly even if the disability rate remains the same. Expect the disabled to become increasingly vocal as boomers join their ranks.

### Disability increases with age

*(percent of people who have a disability by age, 1994–95)*

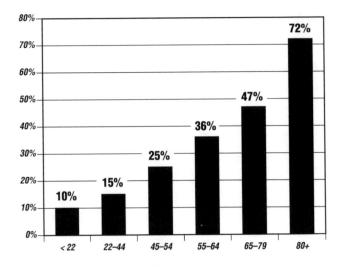

# People with Disabilities by Sex and Age, 1994–95

*(total number of people, percent with a disability and percent severely disabled, by sex and age, 1994–95; numbers in thousands)*

| | | disabled | | | |
| | | total | | severely | |
| | total | number | percent | number | percent |
|---|---|---|---|---|---|
| **Total people** | **261,748** | **53,920** | **20.6%** | **25,913** | **9.9%** |
| Under age 22 | 84,527 | 8,453 | 10.0 | 1,437 | 1.7 |
| Aged 22 to 44 | 95,002 | 14,155 | 14.9 | 6,080 | 6.4 |
| Aged 45 to 54 | 30,316 | 7,427 | 24.5 | 3,486 | 11.5 |
| Aged 55 to 64 | 20,647 | 7,495 | 36.3 | 4,522 | 21.9 |
| Aged 65 to 79 | 24,470 | 11,574 | 47.3 | 6,803 | 27.8 |
| Aged 80 or older | 6,786 | 4,852 | 71.5 | 3,631 | 53.5 |
| **Total males** | **127,908** | **25,326** | **19.8** | **10,616** | **8.3** |
| Under age 22 | 43,131 | 5,176 | 12.0 | 906 | 2.1 |
| Aged 22 to 44 | 47,090 | 6,640 | 14.1 | 2,637 | 5.6 |
| Aged 45 to 54 | 14,825 | 3,558 | 24.0 | 1,527 | 10.3 |
| Aged 55 to 64 | 9,798 | 3,459 | 35.3 | 1,881 | 19.2 |
| Aged 65 to 79 | 10,693 | 4,940 | 46.2 | 2,652 | 24.8 |
| Aged 80 or older | 2,371 | 1,572 | 66.3 | 1,065 | 44.9 |
| **Total females** | **133,840** | **28,508** | **21.3** | **15,392** | **11.5** |
| Under age 22 | 41,369 | 3,310 | 8.0 | 579 | 1.4 |
| Aged 22 to 44 | 47,912 | 7,474 | 15.6 | 3,450 | 7.2 |
| Aged 45 to 54 | 15,491 | 3,857 | 24.9 | 1,936 | 12.5 |
| Aged 55 to 64 | 10,849 | 4,036 | 37.2 | 2,647 | 24.4 |
| Aged 65 to 79 | 13,777 | 6,627 | 48.1 | 4,147 | 30.1 |
| Aged 80 or older | 4,415 | 3,280 | 74.3 | 2,565 | 58.1 |

*Note: Persons were considered to have a disability if they used a wheelchair; used a cane, crutches, or walker for at least six months; had difficulty with a functional activity or activity of daily living such as doing light housework or dressing; or had a learning disability, or developmental, mental, or emotional condition. In addition, people aged 16 to 67 were considered to have a disability if they had a condition that limited the kind or amount of work they could do at a job. People were classified as having a severe disability if they used a wheelchair or other mobility aid for at least six months; were unable to perform one or more functional activities or needed assistance with an activity of daily living; were prevented from working or doing housework; or had a selected condition such as autism or Alzheimer's disease. Persons under age 65 who received Medicare or SSI were considered to have a severe disability.*
*Source: Bureau of the Census, Internet web site <http://www.census.gov>; calculations by New Strategist*

# Adults with Disabilities by Type of Disability and Age, 1994–95

*(total number of people aged 15 or older and percent with a disability, by type of disability and age, 1994–95; numbers in thousands)*

|  | 15 or older | 15 to 21 | 22 to 44 | 45 to 54 | 55 to 64 | 65 to 79 | 80 or older |
|---|---|---|---|---|---|---|---|
| **Total people** | 202,367 | 25,146 | 95,002 | 30,316 | 20,647 | 24,471 | 6,785 |
| **With any disability** | **24.0%** | **12.1%** | **14.9%** | **24.5%** | **36.3%** | **47.3%** | **71.5%** |
| Severe | 12.5 | 3.2 | 6.4 | 11.5 | 21.9 | 27.8 | 53.5 |
| Not severe | 11.5 | 8.9 | 8.5 | 13.0 | 14.4 | 19.5 | 18.1 |
| With a mental disability | 4.8 | 4.9 | 3.8 | 4.4 | 4.5 | 5.7 | 18.8 |
| Uses wheelchair | 0.9 | 0.3 | 0.3 | 0.4 | 1.3 | 2.1 | 6.9 |
| Used cane/crutch/walker for six or more months | 2.6 | 0.2 | 0.5 | 1.4 | 3.3 | 7.8 | 24.3 |
| Difficulty with or unable to perform one or more functional activities | 16.4 | 3.7 | 7.8 | 16.1 | 26.2 | 41.2 | 67.8 |
| Seeing words and letters | 5.8 | 0.7 | 1.6 | 4.2 | 6.0 | 10.0 | 25.2 |
| Hearing normal conversation | 6.2 | 1.0 | 2.0 | 4.1 | 6.5 | 12.5 | 28.2 |
| Having speech understood | 1.0 | 1.0 | 0.6 | 0.7 | 1.3 | 2.0 | 4.5 |
| Lifting, carrying 10 pounds | 7.9 | 1.1 | 3.2 | 7.4 | 12.9 | 20.9 | 39.6 |
| Climbing stairs without resting | 8.9 | 1.2 | 3.1 | 7.8 | 15.3 | 25.2 | 45.3 |
| Walking three city blocks | 9.1 | 1.3 | 3.3 | 7.7 | 15.5 | 25.2 | 48.5 |
| Difficulty with or unable to perform one or more ADLs | 4.0 | 0.6 | 1.5 | 3.1 | 6.0 | 10.5 | 27.5 |
| Getting around inside the home | 1.7 | 0.3 | 0.5 | 1.0 | 2.3 | 4.6 | 14.7 |
| Getting in and out of bed or chair | 2.7 | 0.4 | 1.0 | 2.2 | 4.1 | 6.9 | 18.0 |
| Bathing | 2.2 | 0.3 | 0.7 | 1.3 | 3.0 | 5.8 | 19.4 |
| Dressing | 1.6 | 0.3 | 0.6 | 1.0 | 2.4 | 3.8 | 12.2 |
| Eating | 0.5 | 0.2 | 0.2 | 0.3 | 0.8 | 1.4 | 3.4 |
| Getting to/using toilet | 0.9 | 0.3 | 0.3 | 0.5 | 1.3 | 2.5 | 8.9 |
| Difficulty with or unable to perform one or more IADLs | 6.1 | 1.5 | 2.5 | 4.5 | 8.1 | 15.3 | 40.4 |
| Going outside alone | 4.0 | 0.7 | 1.2 | 2.6 | 5.5 | 10.8 | 31.4 |
| Keeping track of money and bills | 1.9 | 0.9 | 0.9 | 1.3 | 1.7 | 3.8 | 15.8 |
| Preparing meals | 2.1 | 0.6 | 0.8 | 1.1 | 2.2 | 5.0 | 17.8 |
| Doing light housework | 3.4 | 0.6 | 1.3 | 2.3 | 4.7 | 8.6 | 23.7 |
| Taking prescribed medicines | 1.5 | 0.8 | 0.6 | 1.0 | 1.3 | 3.4 | 12.8 |
| Using the telephone | 1.3 | 0.5 | 0.4 | 0.6 | 1.3 | 3.6 | 13.3 |
| Needs personal assistance with an ADL or an IADL | 4.7 | 1.3 | 1.9 | 3.3 | 6.1 | 11.5 | 34.1 |

*Note: An ADL is an activity of daily living; an IADL is an instrumental activity of daily living.*
*Source: Bureau of the Census, Internet web site <http://www.census.gov>*

# Doctor Visits Number in the Millions

## Americans visited doctors more than 734 million times in 1996.

The average American visits a doctor 2.8 times a year. Women see doctors more often than men—3.2 times a year versus men's 2.3—and account for 59 percent of all doctor visits.

Boys under age 15 visit doctors more often than girls, but at all other ages women see doctors more often than men. Pregnancy is one reason for the higher physician visit rate among women. Women of childbearing age—25 to 44—accounted for the largest share (17 percent) of doctor visits in 1996. Americans aged 75 or older see doctors much more frequently than younger people, an average of 6.3 times a year, compared with only once or twice for young adults.

◆ As the population ages, doctor visits will increase. The future cost of medical care will rise significantly unless less-expensive practitioners such as nurses or physician's assistants begin to provide more care.

### Older Americans visit doctors the most

*(average annual number of physician visits per person by age, 1996)*

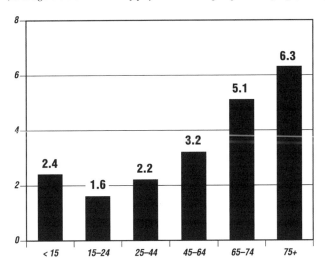

# Physician Visits by Age and Sex, 1996

*(total number, percent distribution, and number of physician visits per person per year, by age and sex, 1996; numbers in thousands)*

|  | total | percent distribution | visits per year |
|---|---|---|---|
| **Total visits** | **734,493** | **100.0%** | **2.8** |
| Under age 15 | 140,851 | 19.2 | 2.4 |
| Aged 15 to 24 | 59,086 | 8.0 | 1.6 |
| Aged 25 to 44 | 184,449 | 25.1 | 2.2 |
| Aged 45 to 64 | 170,229 | 23.2 | 3.2 |
| Aged 65 to 74 | 93,879 | 12.8 | 5.1 |
| Aged 75 or older | 85,999 | 11.7 | 6.3 |
| **Total males** | **299,984** | **40.8** | **2.3** |
| Under age 15 | 73,071 | 9.9 | 2.4 |
| Aged 15 to 24 | 20,177 | 2.7 | 1.1 |
| Aged 25 to 44 | 60,459 | 8.2 | 1.5 |
| Aged 45 to 64 | 70,240 | 9.6 | 2.7 |
| Aged 65 to 74 | 40,547 | 5.5 | 5.0 |
| Aged 75 or older | 35,490 | 4.8 | 6.8 |
| **Total females** | **434,510** | **59.2** | **3.2** |
| Under age 15 | 67,781 | 9.2 | 2.3 |
| Aged 15 to 24 | 38,909 | 5.3 | 2.2 |
| Aged 25 to 44 | 123,989 | 16.9 | 2.9 |
| Aged 45 to 64 | 99,989 | 13.6 | 3.6 |
| Aged 65 to 74 | 53,333 | 7.3 | 5.3 |
| Aged 75 or older | 50,509 | 6.9 | 6.0 |

*Source: National Center for Health Statistics,* National Ambulatory Medical Care Survey: 1996 Summary, *Advance Data, No. 295, 1997*

# Hospital Stays Have Become Shorter

## The average hospital stay was 5.2 days in 1995, down from 7.1 days in 1980.

As insurance companies try to cut costs, hospital stays have shortened and hospital discharges and days of hospital care have fallen sharply. The consequence has been turmoil in the hospital industry as health care institutions cope with declining revenues.

The hospital discharge rate per 1,000 persons fell 34 percent between 1980 and 1995, while the number of days of hospital care dropped an even larger 52 percent. Behind these declines is the growing use of outpatient surgery. Declines in days of hospital care, discharges, and length of stay have occurred for both men and women, in all age groups, and in every region of the country.

Hospital discharges, days of hospital care, and length of stay are all greater for Americans aged 75 or older than for younger people. But length of stay fell the most for the oldest Americans, from 11.4 days in 1980 to just 7.1 days in 1995.

◆ The public is protesting shorter hospital stays, resulting in legislation designed to limit the power of insurance companies to dictate hospital care. Because of public outcry, the average length of hospital stays is likely to stabilize.

### Hospital stays are shortest in the West

*(average length of hospital stay in days by region, 1995)*

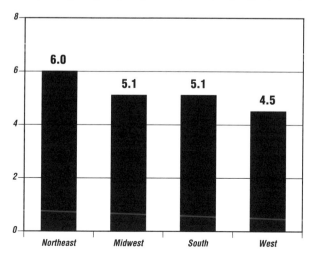

# Hospital Care, 1980 and 1995

*(hospital discharges and days of care per 1,000 persons, and average length of stay in days, for nonfederal short-stay hospitals by sex, age, and region, 1980 and 1995; percent change in rate of discharge and days of care, and change in length of stay, 1980–95)*

|  | 1995 | 1980 | percent change 1980–95 |
|---|---|---|---|
| **Hospital discharges** | | | |
| **(per 1,000 persons)** | **104.7** | **158.5** | **–33.9%** |
| Females | 117.4 | 177.0 | –33.7 |
| Males | 92.3 | 140.3 | –34.2 |
| Under age 15 | 41.7 | 71.6 | –41.8 |
| Aged 15 to 44 | 89.8 | 150.1 | –40.2 |
| Aged 45 to 64 | 118.2 | 194.8 | –39.3 |
| Aged 65 to 74 | 257.6 | 315.8 | –18.4 |
| Aged 75 or older | 455.2 | 489.3 | –7.0 |
| Northeast | 120.0 | 147.6 | –18.7 |
| Midwest | 99.5 | 175.4 | –43.3 |
| South | 110.9 | 165.1 | –32.8 |
| West | 86.0 | 136.9 | –37.2 |
| **Days of hospital care** | | | |
| **(per 1,000 persons)** | **544.3** | **1,129.0** | **–51.8** |
| Females | 556.7 | 1,187.1 | –53.1 |
| Males | 533.1 | 1,076.0 | –50.5 |
| Under age 15 | 185.6 | 315.7 | –41.2 |
| Aged 15 to 44 | 346.0 | 786.8 | –56.0 |
| Aged 45 to 64 | 655.6 | 1,596.9 | –58.9 |
| Aged 65 to 74 | 1,669.0 | 3,147.0 | –47.0 |
| Aged 75 or older | 3,220.1 | 5,578.7 | –42.3 |
| Northeast | 722.1 | 1,204.7 | –40.1 |
| Midwest | 502.9 | 1,296.2 | –61.2 |
| South | 564.9 | 1,105.5 | –48.9 |
| West | 385.2 | 836.2 | –53.9 |

*(continued)*

*(continued from previous page)*

| | 1995 | 1980 | change<br>1980–95 |
|---|---|---|---|
| **Average length** | | | |
| **of stay (in days)** | **5.2** | **7.1** | **–1.9** |
| Females | 4.7 | 6.7 | –2.0 |
| Males | 5.8 | 7.7 | –1.9 |
| | | | |
| Under age 15 | 4.5 | 4.4 | 0.1 |
| Aged 15 to 44 | 3.9 | 5.2 | –1.3 |
| Aged 45 to 64 | 5.5 | 8.2 | –2.7 |
| Aged 65 to 74 | 6.5 | 10.0 | –3.5 |
| Aged 75 or older | 7.1 | 11.4 | –4.3 |
| | | | |
| Northeast | 6.0 | 8.2 | –2.2 |
| Midwest | 5.1 | 7.4 | –2.3 |
| South | 5.1 | 6.7 | –1.6 |
| West | 4.5 | 6.1 | –1.6 |

*Source: National Center for Health Statistics,* Health, United States, 1996–97; *calculations by New Strategist*

# Millions Use Home Health Services

**More than 2 million Americans received home health care services in 1996.**

As hospital stays have shortened, the need for home health care services has grown. Among the 2.4 million Americans receiving home health care in 1996, 72 percent were aged 65 or older, two-thirds were women, and over half had never married or were widowed. Home health care services are particularly important to people living alone, such as widows and the never married, because there is no one at home to help them manage after an illness.

The number of Americans being cared for through hospice programs stood at 59,400 in 1996. Hospice programs help the terminally ill spend their final days in comfort. As with home health care, most patients in hospice care are aged 65 or older—78 percent in 1996.

♦ If the costs of home health and hospice care can be controlled, these alternatives to hospital stays are likely to surge in popularity over the next few decades.

# Home Health Care Patients by Age, Sex, and Marital Status, 1996

*(number and percent distribution of current home health care patients by age at admission, sex, and marital status, 1996)*

|  | number | percent distribution |
|---|---|---|
| **Total patients** | **2,427,500** | **100.0%** |
| Under age 45 | 347,400 | 14.3 |
| Aged 45 to 54 | 130,200 | 5.4 |
| Aged 55 to 64 | 187,600 | 7.7 |
| Aged 65 or older | 1,753,400 | 72.2 |
| Aged 65 to 69 | 213,600 | 8.8 |
| Aged 70 to 74 | 314,300 | 12.9 |
| Aged 75 to 79 | 416,200 | 17.1 |
| Aged 80 to 84 | 404,300 | 16.7 |
| Aged 85 or older | 404,900 | 16.7 |
| Female | 1,628,500 | 67.1 |
| Male | 798,700 | 32.9 |
| Never married | 455,100 | 18.7 |
| Married | 703,000 | 29.0 |
| Divorced or separated | 100,100 | 4.1 |
| Widowed | 857,600 | 35.3 |
| Unknown | 311,600 | 12.8 |

*Source: National Center for Health Statistics,* An Overview of Home Health and Hospice Care Patients: 1996 National Home and Hospice Care Survey, *Advance Data, No. 297, 1998*

# Hospice Care Patients by Age, Sex, and Marital Status, 1996

*(number and percent distribution of current hospice care patients by age, sex, and marital status, 1996)*

|  | number | percent distribution |
|---|---|---|
| **Total patients** | **59,400** | **100.0%** |
| Under age 45 | 4,300 | 7.3 |
| Aged 45 to 54 | 2,700 | 4.5 |
| Aged 55 to 64 | 6,100 | 10.3 |
| Aged 65 or older | 46,100 | 77.7 |
| Aged 65 to 69 | 5,000 | 8.4 |
| Aged 70 to 74 | 9,600 | 16.2 |
| Aged 75 to 79 | 9,800 | 16.6 |
| Aged 80 to 84 | 9,100 | 15.2 |
| Aged 85 or older | 12,700 | 21.3 |
| Female | 32,700 | 55.1 |
| Male | 26,600 | 44.9 |
| Never married | 5,000 | 8.5 |
| Married | 25,900 | 43.7 |
| Divorced or separated | 5,500 | 9.3 |
| Widowed | 19,100 | 32.2 |
| Unknown | 3,800 | 6.3 |

*Source: National Center for Health Statistics,* An Overview of Home Health and Hospice Care Patients: 1996 National Home and Hospice Care Survey, *Advance Data, No. 297, 1998*

# Number of AIDS Patients Continues to Grow

**The AIDS toll approached 600,000 as of June 1997.**

Although drug treatments for AIDS are improving, the number of Americans with AIDS mounts each year. Through June 1997, 592,000 Americans had been diagnosed with AIDS. Men account for the great majority (84 percent) of AIDS cases. The 30-to-39 age group is the one in which AIDS is most typically diagnosed, accounting for 45 percent of cases. The 40-to-49 age group accounts for another 25 percent of cases.

Among men, a slim majority of those with AIDS are non-Hispanic whites—52 percent as of 1997. Blacks account for 32 percent of AIDS cases among men, a share much higher than blacks' share of the total population. Among women with AIDS, blacks are the 58 percent majority. Blacks also account for the majority of AIDS cases occurring among children under age 13.

♦ Because of the way in which HIV is acquired, and because of its long incubation period, AIDS will continue to be a disease that primarily strikes adults in the 30-to-49 age group.

### One in three men diagnosed with AIDS is black

*(percent distribution of men diagnosed with AIDS by race and Hispanic origin, through June 1997)*

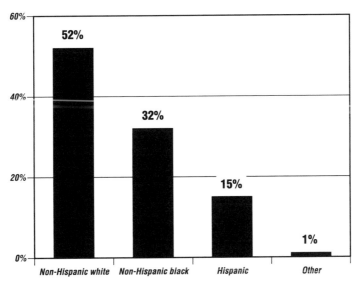

# People with AIDS by Sex and Age at Diagnosis

*(total number and percent distribution of cumulative AIDS cases, by sex and age at diagnosis, through June 1997)*

|  | number | percent |
|---|---|---|
| **Total cases** | **592,144** | **100.0%** |
| **Males** | | |
| **Total, aged 13 or older** | **496,642** | **100.0** |
| Aged 13 to 19 | 1,769 | 0.4 |
| Aged 20 to 29 | 83,548 | 16.8 |
| Aged 30 to 39 | 227,984 | 45.9 |
| Aged 40 to 49 | 130,444 | 26.3 |
| Aged 50 to 59 | 39,074 | 7.9 |
| Aged 60 or older | 13,823 | 2.8 |
| **Females** | | |
| **Total, aged 13 or older** | **87,976** | **100.0** |
| Aged 13 to 19 | 1,055 | 1.2 |
| Aged 20 to 29 | 19,820 | 22.5 |
| Aged 30 to 39 | 40,442 | 46.0 |
| Aged 40 to 49 | 18,690 | 21.2 |
| Aged 50 to 59 | 5,130 | 5.8 |
| Aged 60 or older | 2,839 | 3.2 |
| **Children** | | |
| **Total, under age 13** | **7,526** | **100.0** |
| Under age 1 | 3,029 | 40.2 |
| Aged 1 to 12 | 4,497 | 59.8 |

*Source: National Center for Health Statistics,* Health, United States, 1998*; calculations by New Strategist*

# People with AIDS by Sex, Race, and Hispanic Origin

*(number and percent distribution of cumulative AIDS cases, by sex, race, and Hispanic origin, through June 1997)*

|  | number | percent |
|---|---|---|
| **Total cases** | **592,144** | **100.0%** |
| **Males** | | |
| **Total, aged 13 or older** | **496,642** | **100.0** |
| White, non-Hispanic | 256,246 | 51.6 |
| Black, non-Hispanic | 160,859 | 32.4 |
| Hispanic | 73,718 | 14.8 |
| Native American | 1,390 | 0.3 |
| Asian | 3,831 | 0.8 |
| **Females** | | |
| **Total, aged 13 or older** | **87,976** | **100.0** |
| White, non-Hispanic | 21,311 | 24.2 |
| Black, non-Hispanic | 51,352 | 58.4 |
| Hispanic | 14,470 | 16.4 |
| Native American | 261 | 0.3 |
| Asian | 476 | 0.5 |
| **Children** | | |
| **Total, under age 13** | **7,526** | **100.0** |
| White, non-Hispanic | 1,399 | 18.6 |
| Black, non-Hispanic | 4,579 | 60.8 |
| Hispanic | 1,465 | 19.5 |
| Native American | 26 | 0.3 |
| Asian | 41 | 0.5 |

*Source: National Center for Health Statistics,* Health, United States, 1998; *calculations by New Strategist*

# Heart Disease and Cancer Are Biggest Killers

**In 1997, more than half of all deaths in the United States were caused by heart disease or cancer.**

Heart disease and cancer each kill more than 500,000 Americans a year. Chronic diseases such as these are by far the leading causes of death in the United States. Accidents are responsible for just 4 percent of deaths.

AIDS, which became a top-10 cause of death in 1990, fell off the list in 1997—thanks to improved drug treatments for the disease. AIDS now ranks 14th among causes of death, killing 16,685 Americans in 1997. This number is down sharply from the more than 42,000 deaths in 1995.

◆ Although medical science has made considerable progress in combating heart disease, it will remain the number one cause of death for years to come.

# Leading Causes of Death in the U.S., 1997

*(number and percent distribution of deaths for the 10 leading causes of death, 1997)*

|  |  | number | percent |
|---|---|---|---|
|  | **All causes** | **2,314,729** | **100.0%** |
| 1. | Diseases of heart | 725,790 | 31.4 |
| 2. | Malignant neoplasms | 537,390 | 23.2 |
| 3. | Cerebrovascular diseases | 159,877 | 6.9 |
| 4. | Chronic obstructive pulmonary diseases and allied conditions | 110,637 | 4.8 |
| 5. | Accidents and adverse effects | 92,191 | 4.0 |
| 6. | Pneumonia and influenza | 88,383 | 3.8 |
| 7. | Diabetes mellitus | 62,332 | 2.7 |
| 8. | Suicide | 29,725 | 1.3 |
| 9. | Nephritis, nephrotic syndrome, and nephrosis | 25,570 | 1.1 |
| 10. | Chronic liver disease and cirrhosis | 24,765 | 1.1 |
|  | All other causes | 458,069 | 19.8 |

*Source: National Center for Health Statistics,* Births and Deaths: Preliminary Data for 1997, *National Vital Statistics Reports, Vol. 47, No. 4, 1998; calculations by New Strategist*

# Life Expectancy Continues to Rise

**Americans born in 1997 can expect to live 76.5 years.**

Since 1900, life expectancy at birth has climbed almost 30 years, from 47 to nearly 77. Life expectancy for males has increased 27 years, while the gain for females has been an even greater 31 years. At the turn of the century, newborn girls could expect to outlive newborn boys by just two years. Today, female life expectancy exceeds that of males by 5.6 years. Most research points to biological rather than social causes for this difference in life expectancy.

Most of the gains in life expectancy during this century have been due to declining death rates among infants and children. But life expectancy has grown even at older ages as medical science combats heart disease and other chronic ailments. Life expectancy at age 65 has increased from 11.9 to 17.6 years. Again, the gain for women has been greater than that for men. At the turn of the century, women aged 65 or older outlived their male counterparts by just half a year, on average. Today's 65-year-old woman can expect to live 19.0 more years, 3.2 years longer than a 65-year-old man.

♦ The costs of extending life at very old ages are enormous, raising ethical questions about the equitable distribution of society's medical resources. Those questions will have to be addressed as the baby-boom generation ages.

# Life Expectancy by Age and Sex, 1900 to 1997

*(years of life remaining at birth and age 65 by sex, 1900 to 1997; change in years of life remaining, 1900–97)*

|  | total | males | females |
|---|---|---|---|
| **At birth** | | | |
| 1997 | 76.5 | 73.6 | 79.2 |
| 1990 | 75.4 | 71.8 | 78.8 |
| 1980 | 73.7 | 70.0 | 77.4 |
| 1970 | 70.8 | 67.1 | 74.7 |
| 1960 | 69.7 | 66.6 | 73.1 |
| 1950 | 68.2 | 65.6 | 71.1 |
| 1900 | 47.3 | 46.3 | 48.3 |
| Change 1900 to 1997 | 29.2 | 27.3 | 30.9 |
| **At age 65** | | | |
| 1997 | 17.6 | 15.8 | 19.0 |
| 1990 | 17.2 | 15.1 | 18.9 |
| 1980 | 16.4 | 14.1 | 18.3 |
| 1970 | 15.2 | 13.1 | 17.0 |
| 1960 | 14.3 | 12.8 | 15.8 |
| 1950 | 13.9 | 12.8 | 15.0 |
| 1900 | 11.9 | 11.5 | 12.2 |
| Change 1900 to 1997 | 5.7 | 4.3 | 6.8 |

*Source: National Center for Health Statistics,* Health United States, 1996–97; *and* Births and Deaths: Preliminary Data for 1997, *National Vital Statistics Reports, Vol. 47, No. 4, 1998; calculations by New Strategist*

CHAPTER
# 3

# Income Trends

♦ **Nearly 1 in 10 households has an income of $100,000 or more.**
The U.S. is enjoying record levels of affluence now that the baby-boom generation is in its peak-earning years.

♦ **Americans' economic fortunes are closely tied to their living arrangements.**
Married couples are by far the most affluent household type, with a median income of $51,681 in 1997.

♦ **The median income of householders with a bachelor's degree was $63,292 in 1997.**
The higher the education, the greater the financial rewards—nearly half the householders with professional degrees had household incomes of $100,000 or more.

♦ **Since 1980, men's median income has grown 3 percent, while women's has gained 43 percent, after adjusting for inflation.**
Women's income has grown rapidly over the past two decades because more women are working full-time.

♦ **The median income of black men rose 16 percent between 1980 and 1997, after adjusting for inflation.**
Non-Hispanic white men saw their income grow only 2 percent during those years, while the income of Hispanic men fell 14 percent.

♦ **Whites account for most of the nation's 36 million poor.**
Childhood poverty will remain a chronic problem until single parents become a smaller share of families.

# Household Affluence Reaches Record High

**Nearly 1 in 10 households has an income of $100,000 or more.**

The share of households with incomes of $100,000 or more reached 9.4 percent in 1997, far above the 7.7 percent of 1990 and nearly double the 4.8 percent of 1980. The share of households with incomes of $50,000 or more is 37 percent—also a record high, surpassing the old record of 35 percent set in 1989.

At the other end of the income scale, the share of households with incomes below $25,000 stood at 34 percent in 1997, well below the 39 percent of 1980. The middle class—if defined as households with incomes between $25,000 and $50,000—really is disappearing, falling from 34 percent of households in 1980 to 30 percent in 1997.

◆ The United States is likely to enjoy at least 10 years of record-level affluence as the two-income couples of the baby-boom generation fill the peak-earning age groups.

◆ When boomers begin to retire en masse, beginning in about 2010, affluence will decline as boomer income shifts from paychecks to retirement savings.

## Big rise in affluence

*(percent of households with incomes of $100,000 or more, 1980 to 1997; in 1997 dollars)*

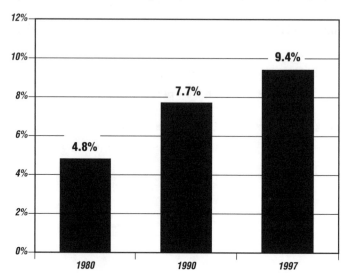

# Distribution of Households by Income, 1980 to 1997

*(number and percent distribution of households by income, 1980 to 1997; in 1997 dollars; households in thousands as of the following year)*

|  | total households | total | under $15,000 | $15,000–$24,999 | $25,000–$34,999 | $35,000–$49,999 | $50,000–$74,999 | $75,000–$99,999 | $100,000 or more |
|---|---|---|---|---|---|---|---|---|---|
| 1997 | 102,528 | 100.0% | 19.1% | 14.9% | 13.3% | 16.3% | 18.1% | 9.0% | 9.4% |
| 1996 | 101,018 | 100.0 | 19.9 | 15.1 | 13.6 | 16.1 | 18.2 | 8.4 | 8.7 |
| 1995 | 99,627 | 100.0 | 19.8 | 15.3 | 14.0 | 16.7 | 17.7 | 8.3 | 8.2 |
| 1994 | 98,990 | 100.0 | 20.7 | 15.6 | 13.8 | 16.5 | 17.1 | 8.2 | 8.1 |
| 1993 | 97,107 | 100.0 | 21.1 | 15.5 | 14.1 | 16.3 | 17.3 | 7.9 | 7.8 |
| 1992 | 96,426 | 100.0 | 21.0 | 15.2 | 14.1 | 16.6 | 17.9 | 7.9 | 7.2 |
| 1991 | 95,699 | 100.0 | 20.2 | 15.3 | 13.9 | 17.1 | 17.8 | 8.3 | 7.3 |
| 1990 | 94,312 | 100.0 | 19.5 | 14.8 | 13.8 | 17.7 | 18.2 | 8.3 | 7.7 |
| 1989 | 93,347 | 100.0 | 18.8 | 14.8 | 13.7 | 17.1 | 18.7 | 8.8 | 8.2 |
| 1988 | 92,830 | 100.0 | 19.5 | 14.8 | 13.3 | 17.1 | 18.8 | 8.7 | 7.8 |
| 1987 | 91,124 | 100.0 | 19.6 | 14.6 | 13.5 | 17.4 | 18.6 | 8.8 | 7.4 |
| 1986 | 89,479 | 100.0 | 20.0 | 14.9 | 13.3 | 17.6 | 18.7 | 8.3 | 7.2 |
| 1985 | 88,458 | 100.0 | 20.5 | 15.1 | 14.1 | 17.9 | 17.9 | 8.2 | 6.2 |
| 1984 | 86,789 | 100.0 | 20.5 | 15.9 | 14.0 | 17.9 | 18.0 | 7.6 | 6.0 |
| 1983 | 85,290 | 100.0 | 21.0 | 16.3 | 14.5 | 18.0 | 17.6 | 7.2 | 5.4 |
| 1982 | 83,918 | 100.0 | 21.3 | 16.0 | 14.8 | 18.0 | 17.7 | 7.1 | 5.1 |
| 1981 | 83,527 | 100.0 | 21.0 | 16.5 | 14.0 | 18.5 | 18.2 | 7.2 | 4.7 |
| 1980 | 82,368 | 100.0 | 20.6 | 15.8 | 14.0 | 19.2 | 18.4 | 7.2 | 4.8 |

*Source: Bureau of the Census,* Money Income in the United States: 1997, *Current Population Reports, P60-200, 1998; calculations by New Strategist*

# Richest Households Receive Growing Share of Income

**The poorest households receive a smaller share of income today than they did in 1980.**

If you add up all the money going to American households, including earnings, interest, dividends, Social Security benefits, and so on, the result is called "aggregate household income." Year-to-year changes in how this aggregate is divided among the nation's households can reveal trends in income inequality. The numbers on the next page show how much aggregate income each one-fifth of households receives, from poorest to richest. They also show how much accrues to the 5 percent of households with the highest incomes.

Since 1980, incomes have become more unequal. The percentage of aggregate income the richest 5 percent of households receive rose from 15.8 percent in 1980 to a peak of 21.7 percent in 1997. The percentage the bottom one-fifth of households received fell from 4.3 to 3.6 percent during those years.

♦ A rise or fall in the amount of income accruing to each one-fifth of households reveals trends in the distribution of income, not the economic well-being of individual households. Households headed by young adults typically start out at the bottom, for example, then rise through the income distribution as entry-level workers gain job experience and earn bigger paychecks.

# Distribution of Aggregate Household Income, 1980 to 1997

*(total number of households and percent of income received by each fifth and top 5 percent of households, 1980–97; households in thousands as of the following year)*

|  | total households | total | bottom fifth | second fifth | third fifth | fourth fifth | top fifth | top 5 percent |
|---|---|---|---|---|---|---|---|---|
| 1997 | 102,528 | 100.0% | 3.6% | 8.9% | 15.0% | 23.2% | 49.4% | 21.7% |
| 1996 | 101,018 | 100.0 | 3.7 | 9.0 | 15.1 | 23.3 | 49.0 | 21.4 |
| 1995 | 99,627 | 100.0 | 3.7 | 9.1 | 15.2 | 23.3 | 48.7 | 21.0 |
| 1994 | 98,990 | 100.0 | 3.6 | 8.9 | 15.0 | 23.4 | 49.1 | 21.2 |
| 1993 | 97,107 | 100.0 | 3.6 | 9.0 | 15.1 | 23.5 | 48.9 | 21.0 |
| 1992 | 96,426 | 100.0 | 3.8 | 9.4 | 15.8 | 24.2 | 46.9 | 18.6 |
| 1991 | 95,699 | 100.0 | 3.8 | 9.6 | 15.9 | 24.2 | 46.5 | 18.1 |
| 1990 | 94,312 | 100.0 | 3.9 | 9.6 | 15.9 | 24.0 | 46.6 | 18.6 |
| 1989 | 93,347 | 100.0 | 3.8 | 9.5 | 15.8 | 24.0 | 46.8 | 18.9 |
| 1988 | 92,830 | 100.0 | 3.8 | 9.6 | 16.0 | 24.3 | 46.3 | 18.3 |
| 1987 | 91,124 | 100.0 | 3.8 | 9.6 | 16.1 | 24.3 | 46.2 | 18.2 |
| 1986 | 89,479 | 100.0 | 3.9 | 9.7 | 16.2 | 24.5 | 45.7 | 17.5 |
| 1985 | 88,458 | 100.0 | 4.0 | 9.7 | 16.3 | 24.6 | 45.3 | 17.0 |
| 1984 | 86,789 | 100.0 | 4.1 | 9.9 | 16.4 | 24.7 | 44.9 | 16.5 |
| 1983 | 85,290 | 100.0 | 4.1 | 10.0 | 16.5 | 24.7 | 44.7 | 16.4 |
| 1982 | 83,918 | 100.0 | 4.1 | 10.1 | 16.6 | 24.7 | 44.5 | 16.2 |
| 1981 | 83,527 | 100.0 | 4.2 | 10.2 | 16.8 | 25.0 | 43.8 | 15.6 |
| 1980 | 82,368 | 100.0 | 4.3 | 10.3 | 16.9 | 24.9 | 43.7 | 15.8 |

*Source: Bureau of the Census,* Money Income in the United States: 1997, *Current Population Reports, P60-200, 1997*

# Improving Fortunes for Young Adults

## The income of householders under age 35 has grown since 1990.

After watching their income decline during the 1980s, young adults have enjoyed real income growth during the 1990s. The median income of households headed by people under age 35 increased 2 percent after adjusting for inflation, while the median income of households headed by people aged 35 to 44 fell by the same percentage. Households headed by people aged 45 to 54 had stable incomes during the decade, while the median income of householders aged 55 to 64 rose 4 percent.

Between 1980 and 1997, the median income of householders aged 65 or older surged 21 percent as a more affluent generation moved into the age group. Most of that growth occurred in the 1980s. As interest rates declined in the 1990s, growth in the median income of elderly householders came to a halt.

♦ The low unemployment rates of the mid-1990s boosted the incomes of young adults, driving up wages for entry-level workers. As long as workers remain in short supply, the fortunes of young adults should continue to improve.

### Incomes of youngest householders still below 1980 level

*(percent change in median income of households by age of householder, 1980–97; in 1997 dollars)*

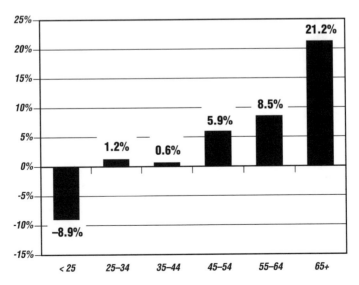

# Median Household Income
# by Age of Householder, 1980 to 1997

*(median household income by age of householder, 1980–97; percent change for selected years; in 1997 dollars)*

|  | total households | under 25 | 25 to 34 | 35 to 44 | 45 to 54 | 55 to 64 | 65 or older |
|---|---|---|---|---|---|---|---|
| 1997 | $37,005 | $22,583 | $38,174 | $46,359 | $51,875 | $41,356 | $20,761 |
| 1996 | 36,306 | 21,930 | 36,711 | 45,439 | 51,630 | 40,729 | 19,894 |
| 1995 | 35,887 | 22,094 | 36,545 | 45,775 | 50,612 | 40,101 | 20,111 |
| 1994 | 34,942 | 20,945 | 35,902 | 45,125 | 51,183 | 38,156 | 19,597 |
| 1993 | 34,700 | 21,474 | 34,745 | 45,387 | 51,323 | 37,180 | 19,717 |
| 1992 | 35,047 | 20,206 | 35,737 | 45,591 | 50,834 | 38,887 | 19,602 |
| 1991 | 35,501 | 21,580 | 36,345 | 46,369 | 51,557 | 39,246 | 20,004 |
| 1990 | 36,770 | 22,107 | 37,281 | 47,353 | 51,480 | 39,744 | 20,698 |
| 1989 | 37,415 | 24,157 | 38,602 | 48,713 | 53,746 | 39,891 | 20,413 |
| 1988 | 36,937 | 23,119 | 38,542 | 49,594 | 51,844 | 39,213 | 20,246 |
| 1987 | 36,820 | 23,237 | 38,099 | 49,711 | 52,565 | 38,938 | 20,406 |
| 1986 | 36,460 | 22,420 | 37,925 | 48,014 | 52,221 | 39,211 | 20,275 |
| 1985 | 35,229 | 22,448 | 37,418 | 46,339 | 49,557 | 38,122 | 19,770 |
| 1984 | 34,626 | 21,670 | 36,665 | 46,009 | 48,684 | 37,219 | 19,771 |
| 1983 | 33,655 | 21,597 | 35,043 | 44,603 | 48,911 | 36,706 | 18,883 |
| 1982 | 33,864 | 23,195 | 35,728 | 44,272 | 46,983 | 37,061 | 18,536 |
| 1981 | 33,978 | 23,589 | 36,541 | 45,218 | 48,175 | 37,481 | 17,641 |
| 1980 | 34,538 | 24,789 | 37,711 | 46,077 | 48,991 | 38,120 | 17,125 |

**Percent change**

| | | | | | | | |
|---|---|---|---|---|---|---|---|
| 1990–1997 | 0.6% | 2.2% | 2.4% | –2.1% | 0.8% | 4.1% | 0.3% |
| 1980–1997 | 7.1 | –8.9 | 1.2 | 0.6 | 5.9 | 8.5 | 21.2 |

*Source: Bureau of the Census, Internet web site <http://www.census.gov>; calculations by New Strategist*

# Married Couples Made Gains

**The median income of married couples rose 5 percent during the 1990s, after adjusting for inflation.**

Since 1980, the median income of married couples has grown 14 percent, after adjusting for inflation. While substantial, this growth was surpassed by that of women living alone, whose median income rose 19 percent between 1980 and 1997. Behind the rising incomes of couples and women living alone is the growing economic power of women. Even female-headed families have seen a 9 percent gain in median income since 1980.

In contrast, the incomes of households headed by men have fallen behind inflation. Male-headed families saw their median income fall 5.5 percent during the 1990s, while the median income of men who live alone fell 3 percent.

◆ The incomes of married couples will continue to grow faster than those of other household types as the baby-boom generation fills the peak-earning age groups during the next few years.

### Income varies by household type

*(median income of households by household type, 1997)*

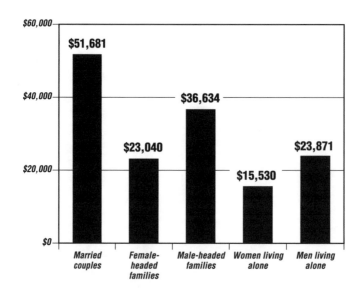

# Median Household Income by Type of Household, 1980 to 1997

*(median household income by type of household, 1980–97; percent change for selected years; income in 1997 dollars)*

| | total households | family households | | | | nonfamily households | | |
|---|---|---|---|---|---|---|---|---|
| | | total | married couples | female hh, no spouse present | male hh, no spouse present | total | women living alone | men living alone |
| 1997 | $37,005 | $45,347 | $51,681 | $23,040 | $36,634 | $21,705 | $15,530 | $23,871 |
| 1996 | 36,306 | 44,071 | 51,002 | 22,059 | 36,476 | 21,454 | 14,962 | 24,602 |
| 1995 | 35,887 | 43,415 | 49,634 | 22,483 | 35,316 | 20,988 | 15,093 | 23,786 |
| 1994 | 34,942 | 42,659 | 48,779 | 21,521 | 33,001 | 20,520 | 14,546 | 22,977 |
| 1993 | 34,700 | 41,634 | 47,905 | 20,598 | 33,154 | 20,971 | 14,434 | 23,738 |
| 1992 | 35,047 | 42,317 | 48,008 | 21,010 | 34,674 | 20,283 | 14,795 | 22,856 |
| 1991 | 35,502 | 42,898 | 48,403 | 21,170 | 36,543 | 20,950 | 15,124 | 23,873 |
| 1990 | 36,770 | 43,848 | 49,115 | 22,189 | 38,746 | 21,723 | 15,409 | 24,516 |
| 1989 | 37,415 | 44,827 | 50,045 | 22,500 | 39,266 | 22,153 | 15,778 | 25,391 |
| 1988 | 36,937 | 44,081 | 49,433 | 21,777 | 38,859 | 21,908 | 15,768 | 24,806 |
| 1987 | 36,820 | 44,147 | 49,383 | 21,871 | 37,730 | 20,979 | 15,143 | 24,010 |
| 1986 | 36,460 | 43,556 | 48,144 | 20,995 | 38,517 | 20,720 | 14,609 | 24,116 |
| 1985 | 35,229 | 41,799 | 46,481 | 21,354 | 36,327 | 20,582 | 14,579 | 24,332 |
| 1984 | 34,626 | 41,169 | 45,858 | 20,812 | 37,925 | 20,062 | 14,890 | 23,483 |
| 1983 | 33,655 | 39,936 | 44,039 | 19,722 | 36,873 | 19,353 | 14,730 | 22,754 |
| 1982 | 33,864 | 39,645 | 43,763 | 19,950 | 35,619 | 19,173 | 13,695 | 23,197 |
| 1981 | 33,978 | 40,173 | 44,723 | 20,380 | 36,593 | 18,499 | 13,191 | 22,867 |
| 1980 | 34,538 | 41,270 | 45,205 | 21,120 | 36,615 | 18,441 | 13,047 | 22,480 |
| **Percent change** | | | | | | | | |
| 1990–1997 | 0.6% | 3.4% | 5.2% | 3.8% | –5.5% | –0.1% | 0.8% | –2.6% |
| 1980–1997 | 7.1 | 9.9 | 14.3 | 9.1 | 0.1 | 17.7 | 19.0 | 6.2 |

*Source: Bureau of the Census, Internet web site <http://www.census.gov>; calculations by New Strategist*

# Black Incomes Are Growing the Fastest

**The median income of black households rose 9 percent between 1990 and 1997, after adjusting for inflation.**

Black households continue to outpace others in income growth. Since 1980, the median income of black households has grown 19 percent, after adjusting for inflation. This is far above the 9 percent growth for non-Hispanic white households. The median income of non-Hispanic white households rose 3 percent between 1990 and 1997, while that of Hispanic households fell 3 percent. The median income of Hispanic households has not grown at all since 1980.

Despite the rise in the incomes of blacks, their household median is just 62 percent of that for non-Hispanic whites. This figure is up from 57 percent in 1980, however. The median income of Hispanic households fell relative to the median for non-Hispanic whites between 1980 and 1997, from 72 to 66 percent.

♦ The gap between black and white household incomes is largely due to the difference in the composition of black and white households. Black households are much less likely than white households to be headed by married couples—the most affluent household type.

♦ Hispanic household income has been falling because of the influx of Hispanic immigrants, most of whom have low earnings.

# Median Household Income by Race and Hispanic Origin of Householder, 1980 to 1997

*(median household income by race and Hispanic origin of householder, 1980–97; percent change in median for selected years; in 1997 dollars)*

| | total households | white | black | Hispanic | non-Hispanic white |
|---|---|---|---|---|---|
| 1997 | $37,005 | $38,972 | $25,050 | $26,628 | $40,577 |
| 1996 | 36,306 | 38,014 | 24,021 | 25,477 | 39,677 |
| 1995 | 35,887 | 37,667 | 23,583 | 24,075 | 39,154 |
| 1994 | 34,942 | 36,852 | 22,772 | 25,365 | 38,041 |
| 1993 | 34,700 | 36,610 | 21,696 | 25,420 | 37,957 |
| 1992 | 35,047 | 36,846 | 21,455 | 25,850 | 38,083 |
| 1991 | 35,501 | 37,201 | 22,162 | 26,739 | 38,090 |
| 1990 | 36,770 | 38,352 | 22,934 | 27,421 | 39,229 |
| 1989 | 37,415 | 39,356 | 23,406 | 28,374 | 40,203 |
| 1988 | 36,937 | 39,048 | 22,260 | 27,621 | 40,124 |
| 1987 | 36,820 | 38,794 | 22,142 | 27,319 | 39,861 |
| 1986 | 36,460 | 38,331 | 22,083 | 26,875 | 39,202 |
| 1985 | 35,229 | 37,154 | 22,105 | 26,051 | 37,989 |
| 1984 | 34,626 | 36,529 | 20,809 | 26,248 | 37,287 |
| 1983 | 33,655 | 35,294 | 20,029 | 25,632 | – |
| 1982 | 33,864 | 35,453 | 20,093 | 25,482 | 36,047 |
| 1981 | 33,978 | 35,900 | 20,145 | 27,255 | 36,418 |
| 1980 | 34,538 | 36,437 | 20,992 | 26,622 | 37,083 |

**Percent change**

| | | | | | |
|---|---|---|---|---|---|
| 1990–1997 | 0.6% | 1.6% | 9.2% | –2.9% | 3.4% |
| 1980–1997 | 7.1 | 7.0 | 19.3 | 0.0 | 9.4 |

*Note: (–) means data not available.*
*Source: Bureau of the Census,* Money Income in the United States: 1997, *Current Population Reports, P60-200, 1998; calculations by New Strategist*

# Householders Aged 45 to 54 Have the Highest Incomes

## Median household income peaks at $51,875 in the 45-to-54 age group.

Incomes are greatest for householders aged 45 to 54 because, at that age, workers typically are at the height of their career. More than one in six households headed by a 45-to-54-year-old had an income of $100,000 or more in 1997. Householders aged 65 or older have the lowest incomes, a median of $20,761 in 1997. The median income of householders under age 25 was $22,583 in 1997.

Nearly 10 million households had incomes of $100,000 or more in 1997. More than 3 million of those households were headed by 45-to-54-year-olds, while another 2.6 million were headed by 35-to-44-year-olds. A smaller 1.7 million households with householders aged 55 to 64 had incomes of $100,000 or more, but this age group ranks second in the proportion of households with affluent incomes—13 percent are in the $100,000-plus category versus 11 percent of householders aged 35 to 44.

◆ As baby boomers enter their late fifties and early sixties during the next decade, the number of affluent householders in the 55-to-64 age group will surge.

### Household income peaks in middle age

*(median income of households by age of householder, 1997)*

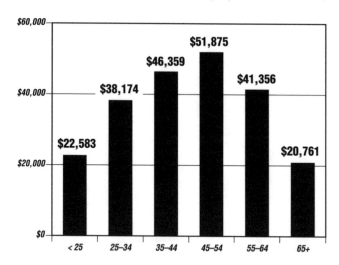

# Household Income by Age of Householder, 1997:
# Total Households

*(number and percent distribution of households by household income and age of householder, 1997; households in thousands as of 1998)*

| | total | under 25 | 25 to 34 | 35 to 44 | 45 to 54 | 55 to 64 | 65 or older |
|---|---|---|---|---|---|---|---|
| **Total households** | **102,528** | **5,435** | **19,033** | **23,943** | **19,547** | **13,072** | **21,497** |
| Under $25,000 | 34,865 | 2,959 | 5,620 | 5,569 | 4,141 | 4,021 | 12,554 |
| $25,000 to $49,999 | 30,284 | 1,762 | 6,767 | 7,319 | 5,181 | 3,708 | 5,548 |
| $50,000 to $74,999 | 18,530 | 460 | 4,062 | 5,580 | 4,406 | 2,300 | 1,723 |
| $75,000 to $99,999 | 9,186 | 129 | 1,530 | 2,846 | 2,625 | 1,297 | 758 |
| $100,000 or more | 9,661 | 125 | 1,054 | 2,629 | 3,193 | 1,747 | 913 |
| Median income | $37,005 | $22,583 | $38,174 | $46,359 | $51,875 | $41,356 | $20,761 |
| **Total households** | **100.0%** | **100.0%** | **100.0%** | **100.0%** | **100.0%** | **100.0%** | **100.0%** |
| Under $25,000 | 34.0 | 54.4 | 29.5 | 23.3 | 21.2 | 30.8 | 58.4 |
| $25,000 to $49,999 | 29.5 | 32.4 | 35.6 | 30.6 | 26.5 | 28.4 | 25.8 |
| $50,000 to $74,999 | 18.1 | 8.5 | 21.3 | 23.3 | 22.5 | 17.6 | 8.0 |
| $75,000 to $99,999 | 9.0 | 2.4 | 8.0 | 11.9 | 13.4 | 9.9 | 3.5 |
| $100,000 or more | 9.4 | 2.3 | 5.5 | 11.0 | 16.3 | 13.4 | 4.2 |

*Source: Bureau of the Census,* Money Income in the United States: 1997, *Current Population Reports, P60-200, 1998; calculations by New Strategist*

# Income Peaks in Middle-Age for Whites, Blacks, and Hispanics

**Median household income peaks at ages 45 to 54 for all racial and ethnic groups.**

Among whites, the median income of households headed by householders aged 45 to 54 was nearly $55,000 in 1997. One in six white householders in this age group had an income of $100,000 or more. Among blacks, median household income peaked at $33,761 in the 45-to-54 age group, with 6 percent having incomes of $100,000 or more. Incomes peak for Hispanics at $32,074 among 45-to-54-year-olds, with 8 percent of households in the age group having an income of $100,000 or more.

Among whites, blacks, and Hispanics, the poorest households are those headed by someone aged 65 or older. Black households with heads in this age group had a median income of just $14,241 in 1997.

The median income of black households is far below that of whites because white households are much more likely to be headed by married couples—the most affluent household type. Hispanic household incomes are low because many Hispanics are recent immigrants with low earnings.

♦ With the enormous baby-boom generation now in the peak-earning age groups, the number of households with affluent incomes should continue to rise within each racial and ethnic group during the next few years.

# Household Income by Age of Householder, 1997:
# Black Households

*(number and percent distribution of black households by household income and age of house-holder, 1997; households in thousands as of 1998)*

| | total | under 25 | 25 to 34 | 35 to 44 | 45 to 54 | 55 to 64 | 65 or older |
|---|---|---|---|---|---|---|---|
| **Total households** | **12,474** | **935** | **2,752** | **3,096** | **2,371** | **1,441** | **1,878** |
| Under $25,000 | 6,225 | 644 | 1,323 | 1,356 | 866 | 694 | 1,342 |
| $25,000 to $49,999 | 3,625 | 181 | 879 | 1,039 | 717 | 440 | 368 |
| $50,000 to $74,999 | 1,637 | 70 | 424 | 436 | 448 | 165 | 96 |
| $75,000 to $99,999 | 570 | 20 | 80 | 169 | 198 | 68 | 32 |
| $100,000 or more | 415 | 17 | 48 | 95 | 145 | 72 | 39 |
| | | | | | | | |
| Median income | $25,050 | $15,056 | $26,149 | $27,710 | $33,761 | $27,350 | $14,241 |
| | | | | | | | |
| **Total households** | **100.0%** | **100.0%** | **100.0%** | **100.0%** | **100.0%** | **100.0%** | **100.0%** |
| Under $25,000 | 49.9 | 68.9 | 48.1 | 43.8 | 36.5 | 48.2 | 71.5 |
| $25,000 to $49,999 | 29.1 | 19.4 | 31.9 | 33.6 | 30.2 | 30.5 | 19.6 |
| $50,000 to $74,999 | 13.1 | 7.5 | 15.4 | 14.1 | 18.9 | 11.5 | 5.1 |
| $75,000 to $99,999 | 4.6 | 2.1 | 2.9 | 5.5 | 8.4 | 4.7 | 1.7 |
| $100,000 or more | 3.3 | 1.8 | 1.7 | 3.1 | 6.1 | 5.0 | 2.1 |

*Source: Bureau of the Census, Internet web site <http://www.bls.census.gov/cps/ads/1998/sdata.htm>; calculations by New Strategist*

# Household Income by Age of Householder, 1997: Hispanic Households

*(number and percent distribution of Hispanic households by household income and age of householder, 1997; households in thousands as of 1998)*

| | total | under 25 | 25 to 34 | 35 to 44 | 45 to 54 | 55 to 64 | 65 or older |
|---|---|---|---|---|---|---|---|
| **Total households** | **8,590** | **780** | **2,303** | **2,316** | **1,386** | **889** | **916** |
| Under $25,000 | 4,048 | 505 | 1,012 | 929 | 531 | 418 | 651 |
| $25,000 to $49,999 | 2,718 | 226 | 831 | 780 | 463 | 232 | 189 |
| $50,000 to $74,999 | 1,046 | 36 | 290 | 346 | 204 | 130 | 40 |
| $75,000 to $99,999 | 429 | 8 | 114 | 149 | 82 | 59 | 15 |
| $100,000 or more | 351 | 3 | 55 | 117 | 105 | 51 | 20 |
| Median income | $26,628 | $19,341 | $27,519 | $31,148 | $32,074 | $27,648 | $14,168 |
| **Total households** | **100.0%** | **100.0%** | **100.0%** | **100.0%** | **100.0%** | **100.0%** | **100.0%** |
| Under $25,000 | 47.1 | 64.7 | 43.9 | 40.1 | 38.3 | 47.0 | 71.1 |
| $25,000 to $49,999 | 31.6 | 29.0 | 36.1 | 33.7 | 33.4 | 26.1 | 20.6 |
| $50,000 to $74,999 | 12.2 | 4.6 | 12.6 | 14.9 | 14.7 | 14.6 | 4.4 |
| $75,000 to $99,999 | 5.0 | 1.0 | 5.0 | 6.4 | 5.9 | 6.6 | 1.6 |
| $100,000 or more | 4.1 | 0.4 | 2.4 | 5.1 | 7.6 | 5.7 | 2.2 |

*Source: Bureau of the Census, Internet web site <http://www.bls.census.gov/cps/ads/1998/sdata.htm>; calculations by New Strategist*

# Household Income by Age of Householder, 1997:
# White Households

*(number and percent distribution of white households by household income and age of house-holder, 1997; households in thousands as of 1998)*

| | total | under 25 | 25 to 34 | 35 to 44 | 45 to 54 | 55 to 64 | 65 or older |
|---|---|---|---|---|---|---|---|
| **Total households** | **86,106** | **4,242** | **15,344** | **19,761** | **16,400** | **11,163** | **19,196** |
| Under $25,000 | 27,454 | 2,166 | 4,015 | 3,970 | 3,098 | 3,202 | 11,000 |
| $25,000 to $49,999 | 25,520 | 1,503 | 5,606 | 5,968 | 4,227 | 3,135 | 5,083 |
| $50,000 to $74,999 | 16,190 | 367 | 3,464 | 4,886 | 3,830 | 2,060 | 1,583 |
| $75,000 to $99,999 | 8,183 | 106 | 1,353 | 2,542 | 2,316 | 1,187 | 682 |
| $100,000 or more | 8,762 | 101 | 907 | 2,396 | 2,930 | 1,580 | 848 |
| Median income | $38,972 | $24,423 | $40,477 | $49,695 | $54,879 | $43,053 | $21,374 |
| **Total households** | **100.0%** | **100.0%** | **100.0%** | **100.0%** | **100.0%** | **100.0%** | **100.0%** |
| Under $25,000 | 31.9 | 51.1 | 26.2 | 20.1 | 18.9 | 28.7 | 57.3 |
| $25,000 to $49,999 | 29.6 | 35.4 | 36.5 | 30.2 | 25.8 | 28.1 | 26.5 |
| $50,000 to $74,999 | 18.8 | 8.7 | 22.6 | 24.7 | 23.4 | 18.5 | 8.2 |
| $75,000 to $99,999 | 9.5 | 2.5 | 8.8 | 12.9 | 14.1 | 10.6 | 3.6 |
| $100,000 or more | 10.2 | 2.4 | 5.9 | 12.1 | 17.9 | 14.2 | 4.4 |

*Source: Bureau of the Census, Internet web site <http://www.bls.census.gov/cps/ads/1998/sdata.htm>; calculations by New Strategist*

# Median Income of Black Couples Tops $45,000

**Black married couples have a median income nearly twice as high as that of the average black household.**

The median income of black households is only 64 percent as high as that of white households, but the median income of black couples is 87 percent as high as that of their white counterparts. Black couples had a median household income of $45,372 in 1997, versus $52,199 for white couples. The median income of all black households is much lower ($25,050) because so many black households are female-headed families.

Female-headed families have low incomes regardless of race or Hispanic origin. Among these households, blacks and Hispanics have the lowest incomes. Black female-headed families had a median income of $17,962 in 1997. Hispanic female-headed families had an even lower income of $16,393, while white female-headed families had a significantly higher income of $25,670.

Within each racial and ethnic group, women who live alone have the lowest household incomes. Hispanic women who live alone have the lowest median income of all—just $9,666 in 1997.

♦ Because black households are much less likely than white households to be headed by married couples, the median income of black households will remain below that of whites for the foreseeable future.

# Median Household Income by Type of Household, Race, and Hispanic Origin, 1997

*(median household income by type of household, race, and Hispanic origin of householder, 1997)*

|  | total | white | black | Hispanic |
|---|---|---|---|---|
| **Total households** | **$37,005** | **$38,972** | **$25,050** | **$26,628** |
| **Family households** | **45,347** | **47,454** | **29,915** | **29,253** |
| Married couples | 51,681 | 52,199 | 45,372 | 34,317 |
| Female householder, no spouse present | 23,040 | 25,670 | 17,962 | 16,393 |
| Male householder, no spouse present | 36,634 | 38,511 | 28,593 | 28,249 |
| **Nonfamily households** | **21,705** | **22,380** | **17,073** | **16,807** |
| Female householder | 17,613 | 17,997 | 15,341 | 11,485 |
| Living alone | 15,530 | 15,818 | 13,738 | 9,666 |
| Male householder | 27,592 | 30,009 | 19,459 | 21,059 |
| Living alone | 23,871 | 25,415 | 17,139 | 16,524 |

*Source: Bureau of the Census,* Money Income in the United States: 1997, *Current Population Reports, P60-200, 1998*

# Median Income of Married Couples Exceeds $51,000

## Married couples are by far the most affluent household type.

Many married couples are dual earners, which accounts for their higher incomes. More than one in seven couples had an income of $100,000 or more in 1997. More than one in four had an income of $75,000 or more.

Married couples are the only household type whose median income is above the all-household average of $37,005. Female-headed families have a median income of $23,040, while male-headed families have an income of $36,634.

Women who live alone have the lowest household incomes, a median of just over $15,530 in 1997. Most women who live alone are older widows, which accounts for their low incomes. Men who live alone have much higher incomes (a median of $23,871) than their female counterparts because most men who live alone are under age 45 and in the labor force.

♦ The incomes of women who live alone are likely to rise in the decades ahead as baby-boom women with pensions of their own become widows in old age.

# Household Income by Household Type, 1997: Total Households

*(number and percent distribution of households by household income and type of household, 1997; households in thousands as of 1998)*

| | | family households | | | | | nonfamily households | | | |
|---|---|---|---|---|---|---|---|---|---|---|
| | total | total | married couples | female hh, no spouse present | male hh, no spouse present | total | female householders | | male householders | |
| | | | | | | | total | living alone | total | living alone |
| Total households | 102,528 | 70,880 | 54,317 | 12,652 | 3,911 | 31,648 | 17,516 | 15,317 | 14,133 | 11,010 |
| Under $25,000 | 34,865 | 17,326 | 9,442 | 6,746 | 1,138 | 17,542 | 11,150 | 10,602 | 6,390 | 5,714 |
| $25,000 to $49,999 | 30,284 | 21,658 | 16,454 | 3,784 | 1,420 | 8,626 | 4,131 | 3,349 | 4,495 | 3,398 |
| $50,000 to $74,999 | 18,531 | 15,380 | 13,205 | 1,370 | 805 | 3,151 | 1,306 | 885 | 1,844 | 1,136 |
| $75,000 to $99,999 | 9,186 | 8,001 | 7,240 | 433 | 328 | 1,186 | 504 | 238 | 683 | 381 |
| $100,000 or more | 9,661 | 8,517 | 7,976 | 321 | 220 | 1,145 | 424 | 241 | 720 | 380 |
| Median income | $37,005 | $45,347 | $51,681 | $23,040 | $36,634 | $21,705 | $17,613 | $15,530 | $27,592 | $23,871 |
| Total households | 100.0% | 100.0% | 100.0% | 100.0% | 100.0% | 100.0% | 100.0% | 100.0% | 100.0% | 100.0% |
| Under $25,000 | 34.0 | 24.4 | 17.4 | 53.3 | 29.1 | 55.4 | 63.7 | 69.2 | 45.2 | 51.9 |
| $25,000 to $49,999 | 29.5 | 30.6 | 30.3 | 29.9 | 36.3 | 27.3 | 23.6 | 21.9 | 31.8 | 30.9 |
| $50,000 to $74,999 | 18.1 | 21.7 | 24.3 | 10.8 | 20.6 | 10.0 | 7.5 | 5.8 | 13.0 | 10.3 |
| $75,000 to $99,999 | 9.0 | 11.3 | 13.3 | 3.4 | 8.4 | 3.7 | 2.9 | 1.6 | 4.8 | 3.5 |
| $100,000 or more | 9.4 | 12.0 | 14.7 | 2.5 | 5.6 | 3.6 | 2.4 | 1.6 | 5.1 | 3.5 |

*Source: Bureau of the Census, Money Income in the United States: 1997, Current Population Reports, P60-200, 1998; calculations by New Strategist*

# From Young Adults to Elderly, Incomes Vary Sharply by Household Type

**In most age groups, married couples have the highest incomes, while female-headed families and women who live alone have the lowest.**

Only 25 percent of households headed by people under age 25 are married couples, which is one reason for the low incomes of this age group. In contrast, households headed by 45-to-54-year-olds have the highest incomes, partly because most are married couples. Households headed by couples aged 45 to 54 are the nation's income elite. In 1997, the median income of these couples surpassed $66,000.

While female-headed families and women who live alone typically have low incomes, this is not the case in every age group. Among householders aged 25 to 54, the median income of women who live alone surpasses $25,000. Women aged 25 to 34 who live alone have a higher median income than their male counterparts.

◆ The economic power of baby-boom women is evident in the relatively high incomes of middle-aged women who head their own families or who live alone. As boomer women age into their sixties, the economic power of older women will surge.

# Household Income by Household Type, 1997: Householders Under Age 25

*(number and percent distribution of households headed by householders under age 25, by household income and type of household, 1997; households in thousands as of 1998)*

| | | family households | | | | | nonfamily households | | | |
| | | | | | | | female householders | | male householders | |
| | total | total | married couples | female hh, no spouse present | male hh, no spouse present | total | total | living alone | total | living alone |
|---|---|---|---|---|---|---|---|---|---|---|
| Total households | 5,435 | 3,019 | 1,373 | 1,095 | 551 | 2,417 | 1,081 | 528 | 1,336 | 723 |
| Under $25,000 | 2,960 | 1,627 | 594 | 810 | 223 | 1,331 | 633 | 448 | 698 | 529 |
| $25,000 to $49,999 | 1,762 | 973 | 600 | 197 | 176 | 790 | 330 | 70 | 459 | 176 |
| $50,000 to $74,999 | 462 | 284 | 134 | 51 | 99 | 176 | 62 | 6 | 115 | 18 |
| $75,000 to $99,999 | 129 | 77 | 34 | 13 | 30 | 52 | 25 | – | 25 | – |
| $100,000 or more | 125 | 56 | 11 | 24 | 21 | 68 | 30 | 3 | 38 | – |
| Median income | $22,583 | $22,819 | $27,756 | $13,307 | $29,419 | $22,405 | $21,246 | $11,730 | $23,586 | $15,341 |
| Total households | 100.0% | 100.0% | 100.0% | 100.0% | 100.0% | 100.0% | 100.0% | 100.0% | 100.0% | 100.0% |
| Under $25,000 | 54.5 | 53.9 | 43.3 | 74.0 | 40.5 | 55.1 | 58.6 | 84.8 | 52.2 | 73.2 |
| $25,000 to $49,999 | 32.4 | 32.2 | 43.7 | 18.0 | 31.9 | 32.7 | 30.5 | 13.3 | 34.4 | 24.3 |
| $50,000 to $74,999 | 8.5 | 9.4 | 9.8 | 4.7 | 18.0 | 7.3 | 5.7 | 1.1 | 8.6 | 2.5 |
| $75,000 to $99,999 | 2.4 | 2.6 | 2.5 | 1.2 | 5.4 | 2.2 | 2.3 | – | 1.9 | – |
| $100,000 or more | 2.3 | 1.9 | 0.8 | 2.2 | 3.8 | 2.8 | 2.8 | 0.6 | 2.8 | – |

*Note: (–) means sample is too small to make a reliable estimate.*
*Source: Bureau of the Census, Internet web site <http://www.bls.census.gov/ads/1998/sdata.htm>; calculations by New Strategist*

# Household Income by Household Type, 1997: Householders Aged 25 to 34

*(number and percent distribution of households headed by householders aged 25 to 34, by household income and type of household, 1997; households in thousands as of 1998)*

| | | family households | | | | nonfamily households | | | | |
| | total | total | married couples | female hh, no spouse present | male hh, no spouse present | total | female householders total | female householders living alone | male householders total | male householders living alone |
|---|---|---|---|---|---|---|---|---|---|---|
| Total households | 19,033 | 13,639 | 9,886 | 2,887 | 866 | 5,395 | 2,070 | 1,457 | 3,325 | 2,222 |
| Under $25,000 | 5,621 | 3,793 | 1,588 | 1,955 | 250 | 1,828 | 717 | 620 | 1,112 | 947 |
| $25,000 to $49,999 | 6,768 | 4,602 | 3,596 | 674 | 332 | 2,167 | 886 | 675 | 1,280 | 902 |
| $50,000 to $74,999 | 4,062 | 3,210 | 2,848 | 173 | 189 | 854 | 280 | 109 | 572 | 248 |
| $75,000 to $99,999 | 1,531 | 1,179 | 1,065 | 51 | 63 | 350 | 122 | 28 | 229 | 89 |
| $100,000 or more | 1,054 | 857 | 792 | 32 | 33 | 197 | 65 | 26 | 132 | 37 |
| Median income | $38,174 | $40,808 | $48,331 | $16,388 | $36,333 | $32,766 | $32,184 | $27,739 | $33,258 | $27,124 |
| Total households | 100.0% | 100.0% | 100.0% | 100.0% | 100.0% | 100.0% | 100.0% | 100.0% | 100.0% | 100.0% |
| Under $25,000 | 29.5 | 27.8 | 16.1 | 67.7 | 28.9 | 33.9 | 34.6 | 42.6 | 33.4 | 42.6 |
| $25,000 to $49,999 | 35.6 | 33.7 | 36.4 | 23.3 | 38.3 | 40.2 | 42.8 | 46.3 | 38.5 | 40.6 |
| $50,000 to $74,999 | 21.3 | 23.5 | 28.8 | 6.0 | 21.8 | 15.8 | 13.5 | 7.5 | 17.2 | 11.2 |
| $75,000 to $99,999 | 8.0 | 8.6 | 10.8 | 1.8 | 7.3 | 6.5 | 5.9 | 1.9 | 6.9 | 4.0 |
| $100,000 or more | 5.5 | 6.3 | 8.0 | 1.1 | 3.8 | 3.7 | 3.1 | 1.8 | 4.0 | 1.7 |

*Source: Bureau of the Census, Internet web site <http://www.bls.census.gov/ads/1998/sdata.htm>; calculations by New Strategist*

# Household Income by Household Type, 1997: Householders Aged 35 to 44

*(number and percent distribution of households headed by householders aged 35 to 44, by household income and type of household, 1997; households in thousands as of 1998)*

| | | family households | | | | nonfamily households | | | | |
| --- | --- | --- | --- | --- | --- | --- | --- | --- | --- | --- |
| | | | | | | | female householders | | male householders | |
| | total | total | married couples | female hh, no spouse present | male hh, no spouse present | total | total | living alone | total | living alone |
| Total households | **23,943** | **18,872** | **14,180** | **3,637** | **1,055** | **5,072** | **1,863** | **1,498** | **3,208** | **2,555** |
| Under $25,000 | 5,572 | 3,662 | 1,509 | 1,887 | 266 | 1,906 | 711 | 647 | 1,194 | 1,075 |
| $25,000 to $49,999 | 7,319 | 5,449 | 3,826 | 1,165 | 458 | 1,873 | 689 | 575 | 1,183 | 951 |
| $50,000 to $74,999 | 5,580 | 4,841 | 4,240 | 398 | 203 | 737 | 265 | 178 | 470 | 326 |
| $75,000 to $99,999 | 2,846 | 2,551 | 2,374 | 106 | 71 | 299 | 118 | 66 | 178 | 114 |
| $100,000 or more | 2,629 | 2,368 | 2,233 | 79 | 56 | 261 | 77 | 33 | 184 | 89 |
| Median income | $46,359 | $51,107 | $59,237 | $23,814 | $35,931 | $31,749 | $30,689 | $27,792 | $32,420 | $29,761 |
| Total households | **100.0%** | **100.0%** | **100.0%** | **100.0%** | **100.0%** | **100.0%** | **100.0%** | **100.0%** | **100.0%** | **100.0%** |
| Under $25,000 | 23.3 | 19.4 | 10.6 | 51.9 | 25.2 | 37.6 | 38.2 | 43.2 | 37.2 | 42.1 |
| $25,000 to $49,999 | 30.6 | 28.9 | 27.0 | 32.0 | 43.4 | 36.9 | 37.0 | 38.4 | 36.9 | 37.2 |
| $50,000 to $74,999 | 23.3 | 25.7 | 29.9 | 10.9 | 19.2 | 14.5 | 14.2 | 11.9 | 14.7 | 12.8 |
| $75,000 to $99,999 | 11.9 | 13.5 | 16.7 | 2.9 | 6.7 | 5.9 | 6.3 | 4.4 | 5.5 | 4.5 |
| $100,000 or more | 11.0 | 12.5 | 15.7 | 2.2 | 5.3 | 5.1 | 4.1 | 2.2 | 5.7 | 3.5 |

*Source: Bureau of the Census, Internet web site <http://www.bls.census.gov/ads/1998/sdata.htm>; calculations by New Strategist*

# Household Income by Household Type, 1997: Householders Aged 45 to 54

*(number and percent distribution of households headed by householders aged 45 to 54, by household income and type of household, 1997; households in thousands as of 1998)*

| | | family households | | | | nonfamily households | | | | |
| --- | --- | --- | --- | --- | --- | --- | --- | --- | --- | --- |
| | | | | | | | female householders | | male householders | |
| | total | total | married couples | female hh, no spouse present | male hh, no spouse present | total | total | living alone | total | living alone |
| Total households | 19,547 | 14,694 | 11,734 | 2,260 | 700 | 4,853 | 2,421 | 2,109 | 2,432 | 2,011 |
| Under $25,000 | 4,142 | 2,066 | 1,046 | 832 | 188 | 2,077 | 1,105 | 1,047 | 972 | 871 |
| $25,000 to $49,999 | 5,181 | 3,705 | 2,719 | 796 | 190 | 1,476 | 778 | 686 | 701 | 595 |
| $50,000 to $74,999 | 4,406 | 3,660 | 3,079 | 403 | 178 | 744 | 328 | 255 | 415 | 329 |
| $75,000 to $99,999 | 2,624 | 2,372 | 2,152 | 136 | 84 | 253 | 108 | 53 | 145 | 97 |
| $100,000 or more | 3,193 | 2,889 | 2,738 | 91 | 60 | 304 | 105 | 65 | 199 | 118 |
| Median income | $51,875 | $59,985 | $66,192 | $32,297 | $45,321 | $30,112 | $27,385 | $25,181 | $32,658 | $30,554 |
| Total households | 100.0% | 100.0% | 100.0% | 100.0% | 100.0% | 100.0% | 100.0% | 100.0% | 100.0% | 100.0% |
| Under $25,000 | 21.2 | 14.1 | 8.9 | 36.8 | 26.9 | 42.8 | 45.6 | 49.6 | 40.0 | 43.3 |
| $25,000 to $49,999 | 26.5 | 25.2 | 23.2 | 35.2 | 27.1 | 30.4 | 32.1 | 32.5 | 28.8 | 29.6 |
| $50,000 to $74,999 | 22.5 | 24.9 | 26.2 | 17.8 | 25.4 | 15.3 | 13.5 | 12.1 | 17.1 | 16.4 |
| $75,000 to $99,999 | 13.4 | 16.1 | 18.3 | 6.0 | 12.0 | 5.2 | 4.5 | 2.5 | 6.0 | 4.8 |
| $100,000 or more | 16.3 | 19.7 | 23.3 | 4.0 | 8.6 | 6.3 | 4.3 | 3.1 | 8.2 | 5.9 |

*Source: Bureau of the Census, Internet web site <http://www.bls.census.gov/ads/1998/sdata.htm>; calculations by New Strategist*

# Household Income by Household Type, 1997: Householders Aged 55 to 64

*(number and percent distribution of households headed by householders aged 55 to 64, by household income and type of household, 1997; households in thousands as of 1998)*

| | total | family households | | | | nonfamily households | | | | |
| | | total | married couples | female hh, no spouse present | male hh, no spouse present | total | female householders | | male householders | |
| | | | | | | | total | living alone | total | living alone |
|---|---|---|---|---|---|---|---|---|---|---|---|
| **Total households** | **13,072** | **9,387** | **7,936** | **1,099** | **352** | **3,685** | **2,337** | **2,148** | **1,348** | **1,153** |
| Under $25,000 | 4,020 | 1,856 | 1,291 | 475 | 90 | 2,166 | 1,477 | 1,412 | 690 | 624 |
| $25,000 to $49,999 | 3,709 | 2,787 | 2,291 | 374 | 122 | 923 | 565 | 517 | 359 | 310 |
| $50,000 to $74,999 | 2,299 | 1,983 | 1,747 | 156 | 80 | 317 | 166 | 142 | 152 | 113 |
| $75,000 to $99,999 | 1,296 | 1,179 | 1,088 | 57 | 34 | 120 | 71 | 34 | 50 | 31 |
| $100,000 or more | 1,747 | 1,587 | 1,519 | 40 | 28 | 160 | 61 | 39 | 99 | 75 |
| Median income | $41,356 | $50,204 | $53,527 | $28,959 | $41,613 | $19,968 | $18,561 | $17,594 | $23,537 | $21,307 |
| **Total households** | **100.0%** | **100.0%** | **100.0%** | **100.0%** | **100.0%** | **100.0%** | **100.0%** | **100.0%** | **100.0%** | **100.0%** |
| Under $25,000 | 30.8 | 19.8 | 16.3 | 43.2 | 25.6 | 58.8 | 63.2 | 65.7 | 51.2 | 54.1 |
| $25,000 to $49,999 | 28.4 | 29.7 | 28.9 | 34.0 | 34.7 | 25.0 | 24.2 | 24.1 | 26.6 | 26.9 |
| $50,000 to $74,999 | 17.6 | 21.1 | 22.0 | 14.2 | 22.7 | 8.6 | 7.1 | 6.6 | 11.3 | 9.8 |
| $75,000 to $99,999 | 9.9 | 12.6 | 13.7 | 5.2 | 9.7 | 3.3 | 3.0 | 1.6 | 3.7 | 2.7 |
| $100,000 or more | 13.4 | 16.9 | 19.1 | 3.6 | 8.0 | 4.3 | 2.6 | 1.8 | 7.3 | 6.5 |

*Source: Bureau of the Census, Internet web site <http://www.bls.census.gov/ads/1998/sdata.htm>; calculations by New Strategist*

# Household Income by Household Type, 1997: Householders Aged 65 or Older

*(number and percent distribution of households headed by householders aged 65 or older, by household income and type of household, 1997; households in thousands as of 1998)*

| | | family households | | | | nonfamily households | | | | |
| | | | | | | | female householders | | male householders | |
| | total | total | married couples | female hh, no spouse present | male hh, no spouse present | total | total | living alone | total | living alone |
|---|---|---|---|---|---|---|---|---|---|---|
| **Total households** | **21,497** | **11,270** | **9,208** | **1,676** | **386** | **10,227** | **7,744** | **7,577** | **2,483** | **2,345** |
| Under $25,000 | 12,556 | 4,321 | 3,412 | 787 | 122 | 8,232 | 6,508 | 6,427 | 1,724 | 1,668 |
| $25,000 to $49,999 | 5,547 | 4,154 | 3,429 | 583 | 142 | 1,398 | 882 | 826 | 514 | 465 |
| $50,000 to $74,999 | 1,724 | 1,398 | 1,155 | 185 | 58 | 324 | 204 | 193 | 118 | 103 |
| $75,000 to $99,999 | 757 | 640 | 529 | 67 | 44 | 117 | 61 | 55 | 56 | 50 |
| $100,000 or more | 913 | 758 | 682 | 54 | 22 | 155 | 86 | 76 | 69 | 61 |
| Median income | $20,761 | $30,637 | $31,239 | $26,528 | $34,109 | $12,944 | $12,069 | $11,937 | $17,086 | $16,634 |
| **Total households** | **100.0%** | **100.0%** | **100.0%** | **100.0%** | **100.0%** | **100.0%** | **100.0%** | **100.0%** | **100.0%** | **100.0%** |
| Under $25,000 | 58.4 | 38.3 | 37.1 | 47.0 | 31.6 | 80.5 | 84.0 | 84.8 | 69.4 | 71.1 |
| $25,000 to $49,999 | 25.8 | 36.9 | 37.2 | 34.8 | 36.8 | 13.7 | 11.4 | 10.9 | 20.7 | 19.8 |
| $50,000 to $74,999 | 8.0 | 12.4 | 12.5 | 11.0 | 15.0 | 3.2 | 2.6 | 2.5 | 4.8 | 4.4 |
| $75,000 to $99,999 | 3.5 | 5.7 | 5.7 | 4.0 | 11.4 | 1.1 | 0.8 | 0.7 | 2.3 | 2.1 |
| $100,000 or more | 4.2 | 6.7 | 7.4 | 3.2 | 5.7 | 1.5 | 1.1 | 1.0 | 2.8 | 2.6 |

*Source: Bureau of the Census, Internet web site <http://www.bls.census.gov/ads/1998/sdata.htm>; calculations by New Strategist*

# Couples with Children Have Highest Incomes

## The median income for couples with school-aged children exceeded $58,000 in 1997.

The median income of all married couples stood at $51,591 in 1997. Among couples with children under age 18 at home, median income was an even higher $54,395. In 30 percent of the nation's couples, both husband and wife work full-time. These couples had a median income of $69,507, 35 percent higher than that of all married couples.

Among all married couples, those with school-aged children have the highest incomes because they are likely to be in their peak-earning years. Couples without children at home have the lowest incomes because many are older and retired.

Among couples in which both husband and wife work full-time, those without children at home have the highest incomes—a median of $73,280 in 1997. One in four had incomes of $100,000 or more. Many are empty-nesters in the peak-earning age groups.

♦ The proportion of married couples in which both husband and wife work full-time will rise as baby boomers' children grow up and more women take on full-time jobs.

♦ The growing number of dual-earner married couples in their peak earning years will be a powerful boost to the economy. The affluence of married couples will continue to rise for at least another decade.

# Household Income of Married Couples, 1997

*(number and percent distribution of married-couple households by income and presence and age of children under age 18 at home, 1997; households in thousands as of 1998)*

| | total couples | no children | with one or more children | | | |
|---|---|---|---|---|---|---|
| | | | total | all under 6 | some under 6, some 6 to 17 | all 6 to 17 |
| **Total couples** | **54,321** | **27,892** | **26,430** | **6,790** | **5,810** | **13,830** |
| Under $25,000 | 9,487 | 5,749 | 3,738 | 1,247 | 1,008 | 1,484 |
| $25,000 to $49,999 | 16,476 | 8,562 | 7,913 | 2,143 | 2,007 | 3,762 |
| $50,000 to $74,999 | 13,200 | 5,975 | 7,224 | 1,778 | 1,443 | 4,004 |
| $75,000 to $99,999 | 7,223 | 3,546 | 3,676 | 783 | 675 | 2,217 |
| $100,000 or more | 7,937 | 4,058 | 3,879 | 840 | 678 | 2,361 |
| Median income | $51,591 | $48,588 | $54,395 | $50,059 | $48,580 | $58,871 |
| | | | | | | |
| **Total couples** | **100.0%** | **100.0%** | **100.0%** | **100.0%** | **100.0%** | **100.0%** |
| Under $25,000 | 17.5 | 20.6 | 14.1 | 18.4 | 17.3 | 10.7 |
| $25,000 to $49,999 | 30.3 | 30.7 | 29.9 | 31.6 | 34.5 | 27.2 |
| $50,000 to $74,999 | 24.3 | 21.4 | 27.3 | 26.2 | 24.8 | 29.0 |
| $75,000 to $99,999 | 13.3 | 12.7 | 13.9 | 11.5 | 11.6 | 16.0 |
| $100,000 or more | 14.6 | 14.5 | 14.7 | 12.4 | 11.7 | 17.1 |

*Source: Bureau of the Census, Money Income in the United States: 1997, Current Population Reports, P60-200, 1998; calculations by New Strategist*

# Household Income of Dual-Earner Married Couples, 1997

*(number and percent distribution of married-couple households in which both husband and wife work full-time, year-round by income and presence and age of children under age 18 at home, 1997; households in thousands as of 1998)*

| | total couples | no children | with one or more children | | | |
|---|---|---|---|---|---|---|
| | | | total | all under 6 | some under 6, some 6 to 17 | all 6 to 17 |
| **Total couples** | **16,244** | **7,392** | **8,852** | **2,047** | **1,594** | **5,211** |
| Under $25,000 | 412 | 174 | 237 | 87 | 54 | 97 |
| $25,000 to $49,999 | 3,475 | 1,417 | 2,058 | 539 | 442 | 1,077 |
| $50,000 to $74,999 | 5,296 | 2,214 | 3,082 | 676 | 604 | 1,802 |
| $75,000 to $99,999 | 3,540 | 1,773 | 1,767 | 358 | 274 | 1,134 |
| $100,000 or more | 3,521 | 1,814 | 1,707 | 386 | 221 | 1,101 |
| Median income | $69,507 | $73,280 | $66,477 | $63,918 | $61,358 | $69,239 |
| **Total couples** | **100.0%** | **100.0%** | **100.0%** | **100.0%** | **100.0%** | **100.0%** |
| Under $25,000 | 2.5 | 2.4 | 2.7 | 4.3 | 3.4 | 1.9 |
| $25,000 to $49,999 | 21.4 | 19.2 | 23.2 | 26.3 | 27.7 | 20.7 |
| $50,000 to $74,999 | 32.6 | 30.0 | 34.8 | 33.0 | 37.9 | 34.6 |
| $75,000 to $99,999 | 21.8 | 24.0 | 20.0 | 17.5 | 17.2 | 21.8 |
| $100,000 or more | 21.7 | 24.5 | 19.3 | 18.9 | 13.9 | 21.1 |

*Source: Bureau of the Census,* Money Income in the United States: 1997, *Current Population Reports, P60-200, 1998; calculations by New Strategist*

# Single-Parent Families Have Low Incomes

**Single-parent families headed by men have much higher incomes than those with female heads.**

Seventy percent of families headed by women comprise a single parent with children under age 18. Among families headed by men, 56 percent are of the single-parent variety. The remaining male- and female-headed families represent a variety of family types such as women living with their grown children, sisters sharing an apartment, or middle-aged sons whose mothers live with them.

The incomes of these families are as disparate as their living arrangements. The poorest are single-parent families headed by women, whose median income was just $17,256 in 1997. Single-parent families headed by men had a much higher median of $28,668.

Female-headed families without children under age 18 had a median income of $31,038 in 1997. Their male counterparts had a median income of $41,483. Many of these households include at least two adults with earnings, boosting their incomes.

◆ Families headed by women are likely to see growing incomes in the years ahead as women's earnings rise.

# Household Income of Female- and Male-Headed Families, 1997

*(number and percent distribution of female- and male-headed families with no spouse present, by household income and presence of children under age 18 at home, 1997; families in thousands as of 1998)*

| | female-headed families | | | male-headed families | | |
|---|---|---|---|---|---|---|
| | *total* | *no children* | *one or more children* | *total* | *no children* | *one or more children* |
| **Total households** | **12,652** | **3,830** | **8,822** | **3,911** | **1,735** | **2,175** |
| Under $25,000 | 7,278 | 1,482 | 5,796 | 1,353 | 446 | 909 |
| $25,000 to $49,999 | 3,560 | 1,393 | 2,167 | 1,400 | 600 | 799 |
| $50,000 to $74,999 | 1,197 | 656 | 536 | 719 | 394 | 324 |
| $75,000 to $99,999 | 361 | 175 | 186 | 245 | 167 | 78 |
| $100,000 or more | 258 | 123 | 135 | 196 | 128 | 68 |
| Median income | $21,023 | $31,038 | $17,256 | $32,960 | $41,483 | $28,668 |
| **Total households** | **100.0%** | **100.0%** | **100.0%** | **100.0%** | **100.0%** | **100.0%** |
| Under $25,000 | 57.5 | 38.7 | 65.7 | 34.6 | 25.7 | 41.8 |
| $25,000 to $49,999 | 28.1 | 36.4 | 24.6 | 35.8 | 34.6 | 36.7 |
| $50,000 to $74,999 | 9.5 | 17.1 | 6.1 | 18.4 | 22.7 | 14.9 |
| $75,000 to $99,999 | 2.9 | 4.6 | 2.1 | 6.3 | 9.6 | 3.6 |
| $100,000 or more | 2.0 | 3.2 | 1.5 | 5.0 | 7.4 | 3.1 |

*Source: Bureau of the Census, unpublished tables from the 1996 Current Population Survey, Internet web site <http://www.bls.census.gov/cps/ads/1998/sdata.htm>; calculations by New Strategist*

# Many Women Who Live Alone Have Middle-Class Incomes

**Among 25-to-34-year-olds who live alone, women have higher incomes than men.**

Women living alone account for 58 percent of the nation's 26 million single-person households. Their median income was just $15,530 in 1997. Men who live alone had a higher median income of $23,871. This income difference can be explained almost entirely by the differing ages of men and women who live alone. Most women who live alone are older widows with low incomes, whereas most men who live alone are under age 55 and in the workforce.

The incomes of men and women aged 25 to 44 who live alone are about the same. The median income of women aged 25 to 34 who live alone was $27,739 in 1997, higher than the $27,124 of their male counterparts. The median income of men aged 35 to 44 who live alone ($29,761) was not much greater than that of their female counterparts ($27,792).

◆ The incomes of men and women who live alone will continue to converge as women's incomes grow.

◆ The incomes of elderly men and women who live alone should rise as today's poorer elderly population is replaced by the more affluent cohort now entering its sixties.

### Women's income can surpass men's

*(median income of people who live alone, by age and sex, 1997)*

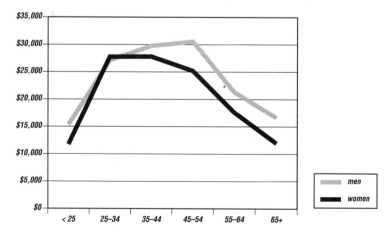

# Household Income of Men Who Live Alone, 1997

*(number and percent distribution of male-headed single-person households by household income and age of householder, 1997; households in thousands as of 1998)*

| | total | 15 to 24 | 25 to 34 | 35 to 44 | 45 to 54 | 55 to 64 | 65 or older |
|---|---|---|---|---|---|---|---|
| **Total households** | **11,010** | **723** | **2,222** | **2,555** | **2,011** | **1,153** | **2,345** |
| Under $25,000 | 5,714 | 529 | 947 | 1,075 | 871 | 624 | 1,668 |
| $25,000 to $49,999 | 3,399 | 176 | 902 | 951 | 595 | 310 | 465 |
| $50,000 to $74,999 | 1,136 | 18 | 248 | 326 | 329 | 113 | 103 |
| $75,000 to $99,999 | 381 | – | 89 | 114 | 97 | 31 | 50 |
| $100,000 or more | 380 | – | 37 | 89 | 118 | 75 | 61 |
| Median income | $23,871 | $15,341 | $27,124 | $29,761 | $30,554 | $21,307 | $16,634 |
| **Total households** | **100.0%** | **100.0%** | **100.0%** | **100.0%** | **100.0%** | **100.0%** | **100.0%** |
| Under $25,000 | 51.9 | 73.2 | 42.6 | 42.1 | 43.3 | 54.1 | 71.1 |
| $25,000 to $49,999 | 30.9 | 24.3 | 40.6 | 37.2 | 29.6 | 26.9 | 19.8 |
| $50,000 to $74,999 | 10.3 | 2.5 | 11.2 | 12.8 | 16.4 | 9.8 | 4.4 |
| $75,000 to $99,999 | 3.5 | – | 4.0 | 4.5 | 4.8 | 2.7 | 2.1 |
| $100,000 or more | 3.5 | – | 1.7 | 3.5 | 5.9 | 6.5 | 2.6 |

*Note: (–) means sample is too small to make a reliable estimate.*
*Source: Bureau of the Census, Internet web site <http://www.bls.census.gov/cps/ads/1998/sdata.htm>; calculations by New Strategist*

# Household Income of Women Who Live Alone, 1997

*(number and percent distribution of female-headed single-person households by household income and age of householder, 1997; households in thousands as of 1998)*

| | total | 15 to 24 | 25 to 34 | 35 to 44 | 45 to 54 | 55 to 64 | 65 or older |
|---|---|---|---|---|---|---|---|
| **Total households** | **15,317** | **528** | **1,457** | **1,498** | **2,109** | **2,148** | **7,577** |
| Under $25,000 | 10,602 | 448 | 620 | 647 | 1,047 | 1,412 | 6,427 |
| $25,000 to $49,999 | 3,349 | 70 | 675 | 575 | 686 | 517 | 826 |
| $50,000 to $74,999 | 885 | 6 | 109 | 178 | 255 | 142 | 193 |
| $75,000 to $99,999 | 238 | – | 28 | 66 | 53 | 34 | 55 |
| $100,000 or more | 241 | 3 | 26 | 33 | 65 | 39 | 76 |
| Median income | $15,530 | $11,730 | $27,739 | $27,792 | $25,181 | $17,594 | $11,937 |
| **Total households** | **100.0%** | **100.0%** | **100.0%** | **100.0%** | **100.0%** | **100.0%** | **100.0%** |
| Under $25,000 | 69.2 | 84.8 | 42.6 | 43.2 | 49.6 | 65.7 | 84.8 |
| $25,000 to $49,999 | 21.9 | 13.3 | 46.3 | 38.4 | 32.5 | 24.1 | 10.9 |
| $50,000 to $74,999 | 5.8 | 1.1 | 7.5 | 11.9 | 12.1 | 6.6 | 2.5 |
| $75,000 to $99,999 | 1.6 | – | 1.9 | 4.4 | 2.5 | 1.6 | 0.7 |
| $100,000 or more | 1.6 | 0.6 | 1.8 | 2.2 | 3.1 | 1.8 | 1.0 |

*Note: (–) means sample is too small to make a reliable estimate.*
*Source: Bureau of the Census, Internet web site <http://www.bls.census.gov/cps/ads/1998/sdata.htm>; calculations by New Strategist*

# A College Degree Is Well Worth the Cost

## The median income of households headed by college graduates is 66 percent higher than that of the average household.

The higher the educational degree, the greater the financial reward. At the top are householders with professional degrees, such as doctors or lawyers. Their median household income was $92,228 in 1997. Forty-six percent of this group had a household income of $100,000 or more.

The median household income of householders with a bachelor's degree was $63,292 in 1997, versus a median of $38,190 for the average household. Households headed by householders who went no further than high school had a median income of $33,779, below the national average. The median household income of householders who did not graduate from high school was less than $20,000.

◆ As the incomes of college graduates soar, those without a college degree will find themselves at an increasing disadvantage in earning power.

### Those with professional degrees have highest incomes

*(median income of households by education of householder, 1997)*

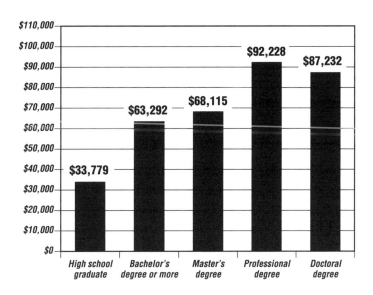

# Household Income by Education of Householder, 1997

*(number and percent distribution of householders aged 25 or older by household income and educational attainment of householder, 1997; households in thousands as of 1998)*

| | total | less than 9th grade | 9th to 12th grade, no diploma | high school graduate | some college, no degree | assoc. degree | bachelor's degree or more | | | | |
|---|---|---|---|---|---|---|---|---|---|---|---|
| | | | | | | | total | bachelor's degree | master's degree | prof. degree | doctoral degree |
| **Total households** | **97,093** | **7,369** | **9,686** | **30,739** | **17,225** | **7,263** | **24,811** | **16,098** | **5,735** | **1,693** | **1,285** |
| Under $25,000 | 31,907 | 5,231 | 5,802 | 11,156 | 4,943 | 1,706 | 3,068 | 2,261 | 599 | 114 | 95 |
| $25,000 to $49,999 | 28,523 | 1,533 | 2,543 | 10,420 | 5,712 | 2,297 | 6,018 | 4,185 | 1,335 | 301 | 198 |
| $50,000 to $74,999 | 18,070 | 375 | 898 | 5,755 | 3,533 | 1,742 | 5,768 | 4,020 | 1,257 | 261 | 231 |
| $75,000 to $99,999 | 9,057 | 114 | 267 | 2,064 | 1,738 | 828 | 4,047 | 2,612 | 979 | 239 | 217 |
| $100,000 or more | 9,537 | 117 | 176 | 1,345 | 1,300 | 690 | 5,909 | 3,021 | 1,565 | 778 | 545 |
| Median income | $38,190 | $15,541 | $19,851 | $33,779 | $40,015 | $45,258 | $63,292 | $59,048 | $68,115 | $92,228 | $87,232 |
| **Total households** | **100.0%** | **100.0%** | **100.0%** | **100.0%** | **100.0%** | **100.0%** | **100.0%** | **100.0%** | **100.%0%** | **100.0%** | **100.0%** |
| Under $25,000 | 32.9 | 71.0 | 59.9 | 36.3 | 28.7 | 23.5 | 12.4 | 14.0 | 10.4 | 6.7 | 7.4 |
| $25,000 to $49,999 | 29.4 | 20.8 | 26.3 | 33.9 | 33.2 | 31.6 | 24.3 | 26.0 | 23.3 | 17.8 | 15.4 |
| $50,000 to $74,999 | 18.6 | 5.1 | 9.3 | 18.7 | 20.5 | 24.0 | 23.2 | 25.0 | 21.9 | 15.4 | 18.0 |
| $75,000 to $99,999 | 9.3 | 1.5 | 2.8 | 6.7 | 10.1 | 11.4 | 16.3 | 16.2 | 17.1 | 14.1 | 16.9 |
| $100,000 or more | 9.8 | 1.6 | 1.8 | 4.4 | 7.5 | 9.5 | 23.8 | 18.8 | 27.3 | 46.0 | 42.4 |

*Source: Bureau of the Census, Money Income in the United States: 1997, Current Population Reports, P60-200, 1998; calculations by New Strategist*

# Incomes Rise Faster for Women

**Since 1980, men's median income has increased 3 percent, while women's has grown 43 percent, after adjusting for inflation.**

Women's incomes are growing faster than men's as well-educated baby-boom and younger women enter the workforce. Women's median income stood at a record high of $13,703 in 1997. Men's median of $25,212 in 1997 was about $500 below the record-level of 1989, after adjusting for inflation.

Men's incomes are far higher than women's because men are more likely to work full-time. Incomes peak for men aged 45 to 54 at a median of $37,624. Incomes peak for women at $20,534 in the 45-to-54 age group (including both full- and part-time workers). Women aged 45 to 54 have seen their incomes grow the most since 1980—up 64 percent after adjusting for inflation.

♦ Women will continue to close the income gap with men, but their median income is unlikely to ever equal that of men because many choose to work part-time while their children are young.

## Big gains for women

*(percent change in median income of people aged 15 or older, by sex, 1980–97; in 1997 dollars)*

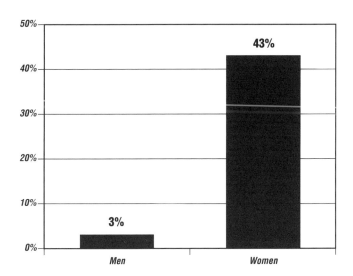

# Median Income of Men by Age, 1980 to 1997

*(number of men aged 15 or older with income and median income of those with income, by age, 1980–97; in 1997 dollars; men in thousands as of the following year)*

| | number with income | income total | under 25 | 25 to 34 | 35 to 44 | 45 to 54 | 55 to 64 | 65+ |
|---|---|---|---|---|---|---|---|---|
| 1997 | 94,168 | $25,212 | $7,468 | $25,996 | $32,851 | $37,624 | $31,157 | $17,768 |
| 1996 | 93,439 | 24,381 | 7,120 | 25,757 | 32,905 | 37,063 | 30,203 | 17,067 |
| 1995 | 92,066 | 23,761 | 7,280 | 24,864 | 33,090 | 37,477 | 30,520 | 17,360 |
| 1994 | 91,254 | 23,523 | 7,633 | 24,482 | 33,256 | 37,832 | 29,322 | 16,516 |
| 1993 | 90,194 | 23,439 | 7,141 | 24,355 | 33,702 | 36,825 | 27,923 | 16,642 |
| 1992 | 90,175 | 23,400 | 7,204 | 24,592 | 33,737 | 36,814 | 29,303 | 16,699 |
| 1991 | 88,653 | 24,121 | 7,402 | 25,448 | 34,529 | 37,449 | 30,002 | 16,918 |
| 1990 | 88,220 | 24,920 | 7,760 | 26,271 | 36,561 | 38,077 | 30,459 | 17,417 |
| 1989 | 87,454 | 25,749 | 8,171 | 27,656 | 38,102 | 40,076 | 31,617 | 16,965 |
| 1988 | 86,584 | 25,653 | 7,927 | 28,195 | 38,728 | 40,129 | 30,726 | 16,920 |
| 1987 | 85,713 | 25,129 | 7,710 | 28,154 | 38,206 | 40,248 | 30,917 | 16,851 |
| 1986 | 84,471 | 25,062 | 7,737 | 28,061 | 38,327 | 40,646 | 30,803 | 16,905 |
| 1985 | 83,631 | 24,330 | 7,451 | 27,837 | 37,825 | 38,551 | 30,216 | 16,259 |
| 1984 | 82,183 | 24,098 | 7,274 | 27,949 | 37,948 | 37,984 | 30,164 | 16,143 |
| 1983 | 80,909 | 23,577 | 6,903 | 27,080 | 36,161 | 37,249 | 30,124 | 15,699 |
| 1982 | 79,722 | 23,420 | 7,432 | 27,560 | 36,346 | 36,168 | 29,931 | 15,425 |
| 1981 | 79,688 | 24,000 | 5,472 | 28,666 | 37,617 | 37,448 | 30,933 | 14,497 |
| 1980 | 78,661 | 24,436 | 8,965 | 30,384 | 39,076 | 38,953 | 31,035 | 14,312 |
| **Percent change** | | | | | | | | |
| 1990–1997 | 6.7% | 1.2% | −3.8% | −1.0% | −10.1% | −1.2% | 2.3% | 2.0% |
| 1980–1997 | 19.7 | 3.2 | −16.7 | −14.4 | −15.9 | −3.4 | 0.4 | 24.1 |

*Source: Bureau of the Census, Internet web site <http://www.census.gov>; calculations by New Strategist*

# Median Income of Women by Age, 1980 to 1997

*(number of women aged 15 or older with income and median income of those with income, by age, 1980–97; in 1997 dollars; women in thousands as of the following year)*

| | number with income | income | | | | | | |
| | | total | under 25 | 25 to 34 | 35 to 44 | 45 to 54 | 55 to 64 | 65+ |
|---|---|---|---|---|---|---|---|---|
| 1997 | 97,447 | $13,703 | $6,342 | $17,647 | $18,706 | $20,534 | $14,376 | $10,062 |
| 1996 | 96,558 | 13,109 | 6,016 | 16,760 | 18,870 | 19,483 | 13,622 | 9,847 |
| 1995 | 96,007 | 12,775 | 5,592 | 16,384 | 18,322 | 18,665 | 13,039 | 9,852 |
| 1994 | 95,147 | 12,418 | 5,965 | 16,119 | 17,533 | 18,466 | 11,769 | 9,693 |
| 1993 | 94,417 | 12,269 | 5,944 | 15,537 | 17,598 | 18,132 | 12,028 | 9,440 |
| 1992 | 93,517 | 12,257 | 5,914 | 15,594 | 17,637 | 18,134 | 11,592 | 9,361 |
| 1991 | 92,569 | 12,345 | 6,124 | 15,277 | 17,824 | 17,351 | 11,669 | 9,650 |
| 1990 | 92,245 | 12,366 | 6,020 | 15,459 | 17,811 | 17,474 | 11,543 | 9,878 |
| 1989 | 91,399 | 12,457 | 6,134 | 15,831 | 17,869 | 17,012 | 11,860 | 9,908 |
| 1988 | 90,593 | 12,053 | 6,085 | 15,690 | 17,021 | 16,308 | 11,365 | 9,637 |
| 1987 | 89,661 | 11,720 | 6,228 | 15,512 | 16,947 | 15,913 | 10,654 | 9,743 |
| 1986 | 87,822 | 11,144 | 5,922 | 15,098 | 16,202 | 15,201 | 10,803 | 9,409 |
| 1985 | 86,531 | 10,765 | 5,655 | 14,736 | 15,327 | 14,348 | 10,700 | 9,417 |
| 1984 | 85,555 | 10,609 | 5,575 | 14,508 | 14,769 | 13,753 | 10,561 | 9,299 |
| 1983 | 83,830 | 10,183 | 5,571 | 13,702 | 14,277 | 13,222 | 9,877 | 9,022 |
| 1982 | 82,505 | 9,884 | 5,628 | 13,384 | 13,181 | 12,595 | 9,917 | 9,007 |
| 1981 | 82,139 | 9,723 | 3,556 | 13,535 | 13,121 | 12,523 | 9,575 | 8,383 |
| 1980 | 80,826 | 9,595 | 6,092 | 13,599 | 12,608 | 12,487 | 9,607 | 8,241 |
| **Percent change** | | | | | | | | |
| 1990–1997 | 5.6% | 10.8% | 5.3% | 14.2% | 5.0% | 17.5% | 24.5% | 1.9% |
| 1980–1997 | 20.6 | 42.8 | 4.1 | 29.8 | 48.4 | 64.4 | 49.6 | 22.1 |

*Source: Bureau of the Census, Internet web site <http://www.census.gov>; calculations by New Strategist*

# Incomes Decline for Hispanic Men

**The median income of Hispanic men fell 14 percent between 1980 and 1997, after adjusting for inflation.**

Black men saw their incomes rise 16 percent between 1980 and 1997, after adjusting for inflation. Non-Hispanic white men had an income gain of 3 percent during those years. In 1980, the income of black men was just 59 percent as high as the income of non-Hispanic white men. By 1997, it was 66 percent as high as that of non-Hispanic whites.

Black, white, and Hispanic women saw their incomes grow between 1980 and 1997. Median income rose the most for non-Hispanic white women, who logged a 48 percent gain. Black women were not far behind with a 46 percent rise in median income. Hispanic women saw a 19 percent increase in median income between 1980 and 1997.

The median income of non-Hispanic white women was just 52 percent as high as that of non-Hispanic white men in 1997. For blacks, the ratio was 72 percent and for Hispanics, 63 percent. Women's median income is well below that of men largely because women are more likely to work part-time.

◆ The incomes of Hispanic men and women have not grown as much as those of blacks or non-Hispanic whites because of the enormous Hispanic immigration during the past two decades. Many Hispanic immigrants have low incomes, depressing the income statistics for all Hispanics.

# Median Income of Men by Race and Hispanic Origin, 1980 to 1997

*(median income of men aged 15 or older with income, by race and Hispanic origin; percent change, 1980–97; in 1997 dollars)*

|  | total | white | black | Hispanic | non-Hispanic white |
|---|---|---|---|---|---|
| 1997 | $ 25,212 | $26,115 | $18,096 | $16,216 | $27,559 |
| 1996 | 24,381 | 25,521 | 16,869 | 15,791 | 26,893 |
| 1995 | 23,761 | 25,165 | 16,857 | 15,629 | 26,835 |
| 1994 | 23,523 | 24,550 | 16,225 | 15,703 | 26,124 |
| 1993 | 23,439 | 24,415 | 16,222 | 15,205 | 25,737 |
| 1992 | 23,400 | 24,488 | 14,945 | 15,338 | 25,624 |
| 1991 | 24,121 | 25,212 | 15,275 | 16,283 | 26,130 |
| 1990 | 24,920 | 25,997 | 15,802 | 16,541 | 26,964 |
| 1989 | 25,749 | 27,004 | 16,321 | 17,344 | 28,036 |
| 1988 | 25,653 | 27,079 | 16,340 | 17,678 | 28,088 |
| 1987 | 25,129 | 26,710 | 15,845 | 17,279 | 27,825 |
| 1986 | 25,062 | 26,447 | 15,848 | 16,888 | 27,636 |
| 1985 | 24,330 | 25,523 | 16,062 | 17,055 | 26,390 |
| 1984 | 24,098 | 25,437 | 14,595 | 17,148 | 26,194 |
| 1983 | 23,625 | 24,855 | 14,535 | 17,470 | 25,578 |
| 1982 | 23,420 | 24,760 | 14,838 | 17,579 | 25,393 |
| 1981 | 24,000 | 25,466 | 15,143 | 18,175 | 26,136 |
| 1980 | 24,436 | 25,992 | 15,619 | 18,837 | 26,680 |
| **Percent change** | | | | | |
| 1990–1997 | 1.2% | 0.5% | 14.5% | –2.0% | 2.2% |
| 1980–1997 | 3.2 | 0.5 | 15.9 | –13.9 | 3.3 |

*Source: Bureau of the Census,* Money Income in the United States: 1997, *Current Population Reports, P60-200, 1998; calculations by New Strategist*

# Median Income of Women by Race and Hispanic Origin, 1980 to 1997

*(median income of women aged 15 or older with income, by race and Hispanic origin; percent change, 1980–97; in 1997 dollars)*

| | total | white | black | Hispanic | non-Hispanic white |
|---|---|---|---|---|---|
| 1997 | $13,703 | $13,792 | $13,048 | $10,260 | $14,389 |
| 1996 | 13,109 | 13,258 | 12,042 | 9,702 | 13,824 |
| 1995 | 12,775 | 12,971 | 11,544 | 9,403 | 13,488 |
| 1994 | 12,418 | 12,595 | 11,419 | 9,328 | 12,936 |
| 1993 | 12,269 | 12,513 | 10,561 | 8,997 | 12,883 |
| 1992 | 12,257 | 12,541 | 10,167 | 9,504 | 12,872 |
| 1991 | 12,345 | 12,634 | 10,389 | 9,443 | 12,964 |
| 1990 | 12,366 | 12,669 | 10,227 | 9,249 | 12,994 |
| 1989 | 12,457 | 12,700 | 10,193 | 9,898 | 12,960 |
| 1988 | 12,053 | 12,350 | 9,971 | 9,483 | 12,639 |
| 1987 | 11,720 | 12,019 | 9,818 | 9,367 | 12,289 |
| 1986 | 11,144 | 11,364 | 9,615 | 9,281 | 11,556 |
| 1985 | 10,765 | 10,974 | 9,363 | 8,980 | 11,095 |
| 1984 | 10,609 | 10,734 | 9,522 | 9,006 | 10,906 |
| 1983 | 10,321 | 10,502 | 8,974 | 8,655 | 10,734 |
| 1982 | 9,884 | 10,018 | 8,836 | 8,629 | 10,317 |
| 1981 | 9,723 | 9,831 | 8,734 | 9,014 | 10,008 |
| 1980 | 9,595 | 9,648 | 8,932 | 8,591 | 9,712 |
| **Percent change** | | | | | |
| 1990–1997 | 10.8% | 8.9% | 27.6% | 10.9% | 10.7% |
| 1980–1997 | 42.8 | 43.0 | 46.1 | 19.4 | 48.2 |

*Source: Bureau of the Census,* Money Income in the United States: 1997, *Current Population Reports, P60-200, 1998; calculations by New Strategist*

# One-Third of Men Aged 45 to 54
# Have Incomes of $50,000 or More

**Among women aged 45 to 54, 12 percent have incomes that high.**

The incomes of both men and women peak in the 45-to-54 age group. Men aged 45 to 54 had a median income of $37,624 in 1997 while women had a median income of $20,534. The gap between women's and men's incomes is so large because the statistics include both full- and part-time workers, and women are much more likely than men to work part-time.

Thirty-four percent of men aged 45 to 54 had an income of $50,000 or more in 1997, as did 27 percent of those younger (aged 35 to 44) and older (55 to 64). Incomes are lowest for men under age 25, with a median of just $7,468 in 1997. Many men in this age group are college students who work part-time.

Although women are much less likely to have high incomes than men, a substantial number are doing well. More than 6 million women had incomes of $50,000 or more in 1997; 60 percent of the high earners were aged 35 to 54. Older women have much lower incomes than their male counterparts because fewer of them are covered by pensions. Women aged 65 or older had a median income of just $10,062 in 1997, versus a median of $17,768 for men.

◆ As boomer women age into their late fifties and early sixties during the next 10 years, the incomes of women aged 55 to 64 should grow rapidly.

◆ The income gap between older men and women should narrow as working women with their own pensions replace older women with no work experience.

# Income of Men by Age, 1997: Total Men

*(number and percent distribution of men aged 15 or older by income and age, and median income of those with income, 1997; men in thousands as of 1998)*

| | total | under 25 | 25 to 34 | 35 to 44 | 45 to 54 | 55 to 64 | 65 or older |
|---|---|---|---|---|---|---|---|
| **Total men** | **101,123** | **18,747** | **19,526** | **22,054** | **16,598** | **10,673** | **13,524** |
| **With income** | **94,168** | **13,905** | **18,936** | **21,456** | **16,203** | **10,361** | **13,308** |
| Under $15,000 | 28,871 | 10,152 | 4,309 | 3,814 | 2,567 | 2,494 | 5,535 |
| $15,000 to $24,999 | 17,800 | 2,330 | 4,561 | 3,446 | 2,289 | 1,671 | 3,504 |
| $25,000 to $49,000 | 29,107 | 1,257 | 7,418 | 8,411 | 5,802 | 3,385 | 2,831 |
| $50,000 to $74,999 | 10,938 | 91 | 1,859 | 3,556 | 3,262 | 1,391 | 782 |
| $75,000 or more | 7,451 | 77 | 788 | 2,229 | 2,281 | 1,420 | 659 |
| Median income | $25,212 | $7,468 | $25,996 | $32,851 | $37,624 | $31,157 | $17,768 |
| **Total men with income** | **100.0%** | **100.0%** | **100.0%** | **100.0%** | **100.0%** | **100.0%** | **100.0%** |
| Under $15,000 | 30.7 | 73.0 | 22.8 | 17.8 | 15.8 | 24.1 | 41.6 |
| $15,000 to $24,999 | 18.9 | 16.8 | 24.1 | 16.1 | 14.1 | 16.1 | 26.3 |
| $25,000 to $49,000 | 30.9 | 9.0 | 39.2 | 39.2 | 35.8 | 32.7 | 21.3 |
| $50,000 to $74,999 | 11.6 | 0.7 | 9.8 | 16.6 | 20.1 | 13.4 | 5.9 |
| $75,000 or more | 7.9 | 0.6 | 4.2 | 10.4 | 14.1 | 13.7 | 5.0 |

*Source: Bureau of the Census,* Money Income in the United States: 1997, *Current Population Reports, P60-200, 1998; calculations by New Strategist*

# Income of Women by Age, 1997: Total Women

*(number and percent distribution of women aged 15 or older by income and age, and median income of those with income, 1997; women in thousands as of 1998)*

|  | total | under 25 | 25 to 34 | 35 to 44 | 45 to 54 | 55 to 64 | 65 or older |
|---|---|---|---|---|---|---|---|
| **Total women** | **108,168** | **18,333** | **19,828** | **22,407** | **17,459** | **11,582** | **18,558** |
| **With income** | **97,447** | **13,626** | **18,081** | **20,809** | **16,231** | **10,607** | **18,093** |
| Under $15,000 | 51,656 | 10,954 | 7,756 | 8,627 | 6,082 | 5,455 | 12,782 |
| $15,000 to $24,999 | 19,472 | 1,856 | 4,573 | 4,426 | 3,554 | 2,073 | 2,992 |
| $25,000 to $49,000 | 20,019 | 709 | 4,761 | 5,899 | 4,713 | 2,209 | 1,728 |
| $50,000 to $74,999 | 4,350 | 91 | 715 | 1,276 | 1,311 | 592 | 362 |
| $75,000 or more | 1,948 | 16 | 274 | 583 | 570 | 277 | 230 |
| Median income | $13,703 | $6,342 | $17,647 | $18,706 | $20,534 | $14,376 | $10,062 |
| **Total women with income** | **100.0%** | **100.0%** | **100.0%** | **100.0%** | **100.0%** | **100.0%** | **100.0%** |
| Under $15,000 | 53.0 | 80.4 | 42.9 | 41.5 | 37.5 | 51.4 | 70.6 |
| $15,000 to $24,999 | 20.0 | 13.6 | 25.3 | 21.3 | 21.9 | 19.5 | 16.5 |
| $25,000 to $49,000 | 20.5 | 5.2 | 26.3 | 28.3 | 29.0 | 20.8 | 9.6 |
| $50,000 to $74,999 | 4.5 | 0.7 | 4.0 | 6.1 | 8.1 | 5.6 | 2.0 |
| $75,000 or more | 2.0 | 0.1 | 1.5 | 2.8 | 3.5 | 2.6 | 1.3 |

*Source: Bureau of the Census,* Money Income in the United States: 1997, *Current Population Reports, P60-200, 1998; calculations by New Strategist*

# The 74-Cent Dollar

## The "59-cent dollar" has been replaced by the "74-cent dollar" as women's incomes grow faster than men's.

The "59-cent dollar" is a phrase that has long been used to symbolize women's low earnings relative to men's. But women are catching up. Among full-time workers, women's incomes are now 74 percent as high as men's.

Women who worked full-time had a median income of $26,029 in 1997. Men who worked full-time had a median income of $35,248. Younger women earn much higher incomes relative to men than older women do. The ratio is higher because young women and men are educational equals and have about the same number of years on the job. Older women, on the other hand, are not only less educated than older men, but most have less job experience because many did not work when their children were young.

◆ The "74-cent dollar" will grow over the next decade as well-educated and career-oriented younger women replace older, "just-a-job" women.

# Median Income of Full-Time Workers by Age and Sex, 1997

*(median income of people aged 15 or older working full-time, year-round by age and sex, and women's income as a percent of men's, 1997)*

| | men | women | women's income as a percent of men's |
|---|---|---|---|
| **Total people** | **$35,248** | **$26,029** | **74%** |
| Under age 25 | 17,651 | 16,290 | 92 |
| Aged 25 to 34 | 30,145 | 25,144 | 83 |
| Aged 35 to 44 | 37,413 | 27,524 | 74 |
| Aged 45 to 54 | 42,370 | 29,364 | 69 |
| Aged 55 to 64 | 41,096 | 26,661 | 65 |
| Aged 65 or older | 45,648 | 30,359 | 67 |

*Source: Bureau of the Census,* Money Income in the United States: 1997, *Current Population Reports, P60-200, 1998; calculations by New Strategist*

# Education Boosts Earnings

## Although college costs have soared, the payback is enormous.

Men with bachelor's degrees earned a median of $46,736 in 1997. Those who went no further than high school earned just $27,005. Women with bachelor's degrees earned a median of $30,882 in 1997, compared with just $16,225 earned by those who went no further than high school. Women's earnings are much lower than men's because these statistics include both full- and part-time workers, and women are much more likely than men to work part-time.

The highest-paid men are those with professional degrees, such as doctors and lawyers. Their personal earnings amounted to more than $71,000 in 1997. One-third earned more than $100,000. The highest-paid women, also those with professional degrees, earned a median of $45,650 in 1997.

♦ Educational credentials will become more important in the years ahead as the economy continues to reward highly trained workers. A master's degree may be a necessity for a middle-class lifestyle in the 21st century.

♦ Because people tend to marry those with similar backgrounds, highly educated men are likely to marry highly educated women. This union creates an affluent dual-income couple, adding to the nation's economic elite.

# Earnings Distribution of Men Aged 25 or Older by Education, 1997

*(number and percent distribution of men aged 25 or older by earnings and educational attainment, and median earnings of those with earnings, 1997; men in thousands as of 1998)*

| | total | less than 9th grade | 9th to 12th grade, no degree | high school graduate, inc. GED | some college, no degree | associate's degree | bachelor's degree or more | | | | |
|---|---|---|---|---|---|---|---|---|---|---|---|
| | | | | | | | total | bachelor's degree | master's degree | professional degree | doctoral degree |
| **Total men** | **82,376** | **6,159** | **8,018** | **26,575** | **14,122** | **5,670** | **21,832** | **14,090** | **4,640** | **1,749** | **1,353** |
| **With earnings** | **64,293** | **2,993** | **5,103** | **20,615** | **11,540** | **5,003** | **19,039** | **12,338** | **3,996** | **1,547** | **1,158** |
| Under $25,000 | 23,898 | 2,320 | 3,213 | 8,970 | 4,113 | 1,617 | 3,668 | 2,689 | 666 | 185 | 130 |
| $25,000 to $49,999 | 24,753 | 571 | 1,535 | 8,991 | 5,005 | 2,235 | 6,415 | 4,659 | 1,163 | 352 | 241 |
| $50,000 to $74,999 | 9,676 | 54 | 261 | 2,089 | 1,723 | 870 | 4,678 | 2,943 | 1,168 | 256 | 312 |
| $75,000 to $99,999 | 2,896 | 23 | 38 | 327 | 402 | 166 | 1,938 | 1,041 | 484 | 215 | 197 |
| $100,000 or more | 3,070 | 25 | 55 | 239 | 297 | 117 | 2,338 | 1,008 | 512 | 538 | 280 |
| Median earnings | $31,262 | $14,826 | $20,314 | $27,005 | $31,174 | $33,218 | $46,736 | $41,579 | $51,813 | $71,459 | $65,593 |
| **Total men with earnings** | **100.0%** | **100.0%** | **100.0%** | **100.0%** | **100.0%** | **100.0%** | **100.0%** | **100.0%** | **100.0%** | **100.0%** | **100.0%** |
| Under $25,000 | 37.2 | 77.5 | 63.0 | 43.5 | 35.6 | 32.3 | 19.3 | 21.8 | 16.7 | 12.0 | 11.2 |
| $25,000 to $49,999 | 38.5 | 19.1 | 30.1 | 43.6 | 43.4 | 44.7 | 33.7 | 37.8 | 29.1 | 22.8 | 20.8 |
| $50,000 to $74,999 | 15.0 | 1.8 | 5.1 | 10.1 | 14.9 | 17.4 | 24.6 | 23.9 | 29.2 | 16.5 | 26.9 |
| $75,000 to $99,999 | 4.5 | 0.8 | 0.7 | 1.6 | 3.5 | 3.3 | 10.2 | 8.4 | 12.1 | 13.9 | 17.0 |
| $100,000 or more | 4.8 | 0.8 | 1.1 | 1.2 | 2.6 | 2.3 | 12.3 | 8.2 | 12.8 | 34.8 | 24.2 |

*Source: Bureau of the Census, unpublished tables from the 1998 Current Population Survey, Internet web site <http://www.bls.census.gov/cps/ads/1998/sdata.htm>; calculations by New Strategist*

# Earnings Distribution of Women Aged 25 or Older by Education, 1997

*(number and percent distribution of women aged 25 or older by earnings and educational attainment, and median earnings of those with earnings, 1997; women in thousands as of 1998)*

| | total | less than 9th grade | 9th to 12th grade, no degree | high school graduate, inc. GED | some college, no degree | associate's degree | bachelor's degree or more | | | | |
| --- | --- | --- | --- | --- | --- | --- | --- | --- | --- | --- | --- |
| | | | | | | | total | bachelor's degree | master's degree | professional degree | doctoral degree |
| Total women | 89,835 | 6,623 | 8,758 | 31,599 | 15,516 | 7,198 | 20,142 | 14,215 | 4,592 | 820 | 515 |
| With earnings | 56,134 | 1,624 | 3,574 | 18,794 | 10,702 | 5,502 | 15,938 | 11,108 | 3,726 | 663 | 441 |
| Under $25,000 | 35,037 | 1,526 | 3,190 | 14,202 | 7,040 | 3,088 | 5,992 | 4,707 | 1,042 | 149 | 91 |
| $25,000 to $49,999 | 16,625 | 94 | 355 | 4,141 | 3,111 | 2,061 | 6,863 | 4,761 | 1,729 | 215 | 157 |
| $50,000 to $74,999 | 3,263 | 1 | 20 | 339 | 436 | 289 | 2,179 | 1,206 | 735 | 116 | 120 |
| $75,000 to $99,999 | 659 | 2 | – | 52 | 76 | 31 | 498 | 277 | 122 | 57 | 40 |
| $100,000 or more | 548 | – | 6 | 63 | 37 | 31 | 411 | 159 | 98 | 121 | 33 |
| Median earnings | $19,891 | $10,007 | $10,775 | $16,225 | $19,332 | $22,220 | $30,882 | $28,328 | $36,428 | $45,650 | $45,910 |
| Total women with earnings | 100.0% | 100.0% | 100.0% | 100.0% | 100.0% | 100.0% | 100.0% | 100.0% | 100.0% | 100.0% | 100.0% |
| Under $25,000 | 62.4 | 94.0 | 89.3 | 75.6 | 65.8 | 56.1 | 37.6 | 42.4 | 28.0 | 22.5 | 20.6 |
| $25,000 to $49,999 | 29.6 | 5.8 | 9.9 | 22.0 | 29.1 | 37.5 | 43.1 | 42.9 | 46.4 | 32.4 | 35.6 |
| $50,000 to $74,999 | 5.8 | 0.1 | 0.6 | 1.8 | 4.1 | 5.3 | 13.7 | 10.9 | 19.7 | 17.5 | 27.2 |
| $75,000 to $99,999 | 1.2 | 0.1 | – | 0.3 | 0.7 | 0.6 | 3.1 | 2.5 | 3.3 | 8.6 | 9.1 |
| $100,000 or more | 1.0 | – | 0.2 | 0.3 | 0.3 | 0.6 | 2.6 | 1.4 | 2.6 | 18.3 | 7.5 |

*Note: (–) means sample is too small to make a reliable estimate*

*Source: Bureau of the Census, unpublished tables from the 1998 Current Population Survey, Internet web site <http://www.bls.census.gov/cps/ads/1998/sdata.htm>; calculations by New Strategist*

# Few Women Earn More Than Men

## Among legal assistants, however, women earn more.

Men who work full-time earned a median of $598 a week in 1998. Women earned a median of $456—or 76 percent of what men earned. Although a substantial gap exists between men's and women's earnings, women have been closing the gap. In many occupations, women now make almost as much as men.

While women in precision production occupations earn only 65 percent as much as their male counterparts, women therapists earn 99 percent as much as men in the profession. Women legal assistants earn 4 percent more than their male counterparts. Other occupations in which women earn at least 90 percent as much as men include registered nurses, secretaries, health service occupations, and financial records processing.

A big earnings gap exists in many executive, administrative, and managerial jobs. Among educational administrators, women earn only 65 percent as much as men. Women's earnings are less than 70 percent of men's among officials and administrators in public administration, financial managers, and marketing managers.

♦ One reason for the earnings gap is that the average male worker has been on the job longer than the average female worker. As women gain job experience, the earnings gap will continue to shrink.

# Median Weekly Earnings by Sex, 1998

*(median weekly earnings of full–time wage and salary workers aged 16 or older by selected occupation and sex, and women's earnings as a percent of men's, 1998)*

| | men | women | women's earnings as a percent of men's |
|---|---|---|---|
| **Total workers** | **$598** | **$456** | **76.3%** |
| Managerial and professional specialty | 905 | 655 | 72.4 |
| Executive, administrative, and managerial | 915 | 626 | 68.4 |
| Officials and administrators, public administration | 957 | 663 | 69.3 |
| Financial managers | 1,017 | 703 | 69.1 |
| Personnel and labor relations managers | 947 | 747 | 78.9 |
| Purchasing managers | 965 | 724 | 75.0 |
| Managers, marketing, advertising, and public relations | 1,128 | 759 | 67.3 |
| Administrators, education and related fields | 1,111 | 730 | 65.7 |
| Managers, medicine and health | 869 | 679 | 78.1 |
| Managers, property and real estate | 638 | 518 | 81.2 |
| Professional specialty | 895 | 682 | 76.2 |
| Engineers | 1,011 | 831 | 82.2 |
| Mathematical and computer scientists | 986 | 859 | 87.1 |
| Natural scientists | 908 | 732 | 80.6 |
| Physicians | 1,255 | 966 | 77.0 |
| Registered nurses | 774 | 734 | 94.8 |
| Pharmacists | 1,146 | 985 | 86.0 |
| Therapists | 713 | 709 | 99.4 |
| Teachers, college and university | 998 | 769 | 77.1 |
| Teachers, except college and university | 746 | 644 | 86.3 |
| Psychologists | 740 | 621 | 83.9 |
| Social, recreation, and religious workers | 593 | 531 | 89.5 |
| Lawyers and judges | 1,348 | 946 | 70.2 |
| Writers, artists, entertainers, and athletes | 713 | 591 | 82.9 |
| Technical, sales, and administrative support | 606 | 419 | 69.1 |
| Health technologists and technicians | 588 | 486 | 82.7 |
| Engineering and related technologists and technicians | 668 | 529 | 79.2 |
| Science technicians | 623 | 463 | 74.3 |
| Technicians, except health, engineering, and science | 870 | 609 | 70.0 |
| Computer programmers | 884 | 715 | 80.9 |
| Legal assistants | 561 | 581 | 103.4 |

*(continued)*

*(continued from previous page)*

| | men | women | women's earnings as a percent of men's |
|---|---|---|---|
| Sales occupations | $622 | $372 | 59.8% |
| Supervisors and proprietors | 649 | 449 | 69.2 |
| Sales representatives, finance and business services | 772 | 566 | 73.3 |
| Sales representatives, commodities, except retail | 765 | 603 | 78.8 |
| Sales workers, retail and personal services | 412 | 272 | 66.0 |
| Administrative support, including clerical | 518 | 418 | 80.7 |
| Supervisors | 679 | 556 | 81.9 |
| Computer equipment operators | 591 | 477 | 80.7 |
| Secretaries, stenographers, and typists | 484 | 436 | 90.1 |
| Information clerks | 453 | 363 | 80.1 |
| Records processing occupations, except financial | 419 | 416 | 99.3 |
| Financial records processing | 466 | 426 | 91.4 |
| Service occupations | 389 | 296 | 76.1 |
| Police and detectives | 662 | 583 | 88.1 |
| Food preparation and service occupations | 303 | 271 | 89.4 |
| Health service occupations | 342 | 315 | 92.1 |
| Cleaning and building service occupations | 358 | 288 | 80.4 |
| Personal service occupations | 368 | 301 | 81.8 |
| Precision production, craft, and repair | 587 | 408 | 69.5 |
| Mechanics and repairers | 599 | 519 | 86.6 |
| Construction trades | 545 | 408 | 74.9 |
| Precision production occupations | 611 | 392 | 64.2 |
| Operators, fabricators, and laborers | 456 | 327 | 71.7 |
| Machine operators, assemblers, and inspectors | 472 | 328 | 69.5 |
| Transportation and material moving occupations | 519 | 373 | 71.9 |
| Truck drivers | 520 | 371 | 71.3 |
| Bus drivers | 476 | 352 | 73.9 |
| Handlers, equipment cleaners, helpers, and laborers | 362 | 311 | 85.9 |
| Farming, forestry, and fishing | 307 | 272 | 88.6 |

*Source: Bureau of Labor Statistics,* Employment and Earnings, *January 1999; calculations by New Strategist*

# Incomes Are Highest in the West

**Metropolitan residents have higher incomes than those in nonmetropolitan areas.**

Suburban households in the nation's largest metropolitan areas have the highest incomes, a median of $47,981 in 1997—30 percent higher than the national median. Many suburban householders are middle-aged married couples in their peak earning years. Nonmetropolitan households have the lowest incomes, a median of $30,057, or just 81 percent of the national average. The elderly—many of them having low incomes because they are retired—head a larger share of households in nonmetropolitan areas. But cost of living differences between urban and rural areas make it difficult to measure people's standard of living by income alone.

Households in the Northeast, Midwest, and West have above-average incomes, while those in the South are below average. Among the 50 states, Alaska has the highest household income, a median of $50,992 in 1997. But the cost of living in Alaska is also high, making it questionable whether households there are actually any better off than those elsewhere in the United States. West Virginia has the lowest median household income, just $26,657 in 1997.

◆ The changing structure of the economy may result in smaller income differences by region and metropolitan residence. Because of increased telecommuting, place of residence may not determine income level in the future as much as it does today.

## South has the lowest incomes

*(median income of households by region, 1997)*

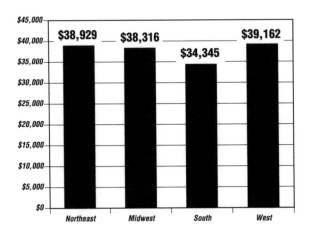

# Median Income by Metropolitan Status and Region of Residence, 1997

*(number of households and median household income by metropolitan status and region of residence, 1997; households in thousands as of 1998)*

|  | number of households | median income |
|---|---|---|
| **Total households** | 102,528 | $37,005 |
| **Metropolitan status** | | |
| Inside metropolitan areas | 82,122 | 39,381 |
| 1 million or more | 54,667 | 41,502 |
| Inside central cities | 20,310 | 31,789 |
| Outside central cities | 34,357 | 47,981 |
| Under 1 million | 27,455 | 35,409 |
| Inside central cities | 11,597 | 31,168 |
| Outside central cities | 15,858 | 38,581 |
| Outside metropolitan areas | 20,406 | 30,057 |
| **Region** | | |
| Northeast | 19,810 | 38,929 |
| Midwest | 24,236 | 38,316 |
| South | 36,578 | 34,345 |
| West | 21,905 | 39,162 |

*Source: Bureau of the Census,* Money Income in the United States: 1997, *Current Population Reports, P60-200, 1998*

# Median Income of Households by State, 1997

*(median income of households by state, 1997)*

| | median income | | median income |
|---|---|---|---|
| Alabama | $31,468 | Montana | $29,277 |
| Alaska | 50,992 | Nebraska | 34,743 |
| Arizona | 32,552 | Nevada | 39,139 |
| Arkansas | 26,954 | New Hampshire | 40,655 |
| California | 39,699 | New Jersey | 48,289 |
| Colorado | 42,562 | New Mexico | 27,874 |
| Connecticut | 43,535 | New York | 36,010 |
| Delaware | 41,622 | North Carolina | 36,129 |
| District of Columbia | 32,280 | North Dakota | 31,927 |
| Florida | 31,900 | Ohio | 35,493 |
| Georgia | 34,953 | Oklahoma | 29,709 |
| Hawaii | 41,832 | Oregon | 36,777 |
| Idaho | 34,455 | Pennsylvania | 36,609 |
| Illinois | 40,873 | Rhode Island | 36,316 |
| Indiana | 37,421 | South Carolina | 34,861 |
| Iowa | 33,877 | South Dakota | 29,949 |
| Kansas | 34,902 | Tennessee | 31,066 |
| Kentucky | 33,305 | Texas | 34,453 |
| Louisiana | 32,108 | Utah | 40,332 |
| Maine | 34,132 | Vermont | 34,077 |
| Maryland | 45,844 | Virginia | 41,534 |
| Massachusetts | 41,212 | Washington | 41,040 |
| Michigan | 39,434 | West Virginia | 26,657 |
| Minnesota | 42,248 | Wisconsin | 40,257 |
| Mississippi | 27,894 | Wyoming | 32,543 |
| Missouri | 35,802 | | |

*Source: Bureau of the Census,* Money Income in the United States: 1997, *Current Population Reports, P60-200, 1998*

# More Than 80 Percent of 15-to-64-Year-Olds Receive Wage or Salary Income

## Wages and salaries are the most important source of income for the largest proportion of Americans.

Among the 160 million Americans of working age who had any income in 1997, fully 82 percent earned money from wages or salaries. The average amount those with wage or salary income received was $28,648.

For Americans aged 65 or older, the most important source of income is Social Security. Ninety-two percent of the elderly receive Social Security checks, averaging $8,690 per person in 1997.

Interest is another widely received source of income. More than 102 million people received interest income in 1997, although the average amount received was small—$1,869. Interest is a larger source of income for the elderly, who received an average of $3,971 in interest in 1997.

♦ Many of the nation's older Americans are dependent on Social Security for the bulk of their retirement income. As Social Security benefits are scaled back in the years ahead, future retirees will need to rely on other sources of income to make ends meet.

# Sources of Income, 1997

*(number and percent of people aged 15 or older with income and average income for those with income, by selected sources of income and age, 1997; people in thousands as of 1998)*

| | total | | | aged 15 to 64 | | | aged 65 or older | | |
|---|---|---|---|---|---|---|---|---|---|
| | number | percent | average | number | percent | average | number | percent | average |
| **Total people** | **191,615** | **100.0%** | **$27,022** | **160,214** | **100.0%** | **$28,439** | **31,401** | **100.0%** | **$19,788** |
| Earnings | 144,429 | 75.4 | 28,754 | 139,506 | 87.1 | 29,007 | 4,923 | 15.7 | 21,588 |
| Wages and salary | 136,132 | 71.0 | 28,415 | 131,957 | 82.4 | 28,648 | 4,174 | 13.3 | 21,044 |
| Nonfarm self-employment | 11,477 | 6.0 | 23,180 | 10,743 | 6.7 | 23,281 | 734 | 2.3 | 21,709 |
| Social Security | 37,743 | 19.7 | 8,359 | 8,902 | 5.6 | 7,287 | 28,841 | 91.8 | 8,690 |
| Public assistance | 3,758 | 2.0 | 3,240 | 3,652 | 2.3 | 3,283 | 107 | 0.3 | 1,748 |
| Veteran benefits | 2,353 | 1.2 | 7,047 | 1,240 | 0.8 | 7,688 | 1,113 | 3.5 | 6,332 |
| Survivor benefits | 2,405 | 1.3 | 10,004 | 871 | 0.5 | 13,063 | 1,534 | 4.9 | 8,268 |
| Disability benefits | 1,508 | 0.8 | 10,213 | 1,289 | 0.8 | 10,151 | 219 | 0.7 | 10,577 |
| Pensions | 14,611 | 7.6 | 12,220 | 4,399 | 2.7 | 15,445 | 10,212 | 32.5 | 10,831 |
| Company or union | 8,902 | 4.6 | 8,964 | 2,333 | 1.5 | 12,377 | 6,569 | 20.9 | 7,752 |
| IRA, KEOGH, or 401K | 308 | 0.2 | 9,756 | 135 | 0.1 | 11,559 | 172 | 0.5 | 8,344 |
| Interest | 102,933 | 53.7 | 1,869 | 83,604 | 52.2 | 1,383 | 19,329 | 61.6 | 3,971 |
| Dividends | 32,885 | 17.2 | 2,883 | 26,535 | 16.6 | 2,428 | 6,350 | 20.2 | 4,786 |
| Rents, royalties, estates, or trusts | 12,592 | 6.6 | 4,316 | 9,560 | 6.0 | 3,968 | 3,032 | 9.7 | 5,414 |
| Education | 7,817 | 4.1 | 3,732 | 7,789 | 4.9 | 3,733 | 28 | 0.1 | – |
| Child support | 5,034 | 2.6 | 3,643 | 5,031 | 3.1 | 3,645 | 3 | 0.0 | – |
| Alimony | 409 | 0.2 | 9,923 | 366 | 0.2 | 10,158 | 43 | 0.1 | – |

*Note: (–) means sample is too small to make a reliable estimate.*
*Source: Bureau of the Census, Money Income in the United States: 1997, Current Population Reports, P60-200, 1998; calculations by New Strategist*

# Most Poor Are White

## Although blacks are more likely to be poor, whites account for the majority of people living in poverty.

Among the nation's 36 million poor in 1997, 69 percent were white while 26 percent were black. But blacks are more likely to be poor than whites, 27 versus 11 percent. The poverty rate stands at 27 percent for Hispanics as well.

Children under age 18 are more likely to be poor than any other age group. Overall, 20 percent of the nation's children are poor. But among blacks and Hispanics, the figure is 37 percent. Only 9 percent of whites aged 65 or older are poor, compared to 26 percent of blacks and 24 percent of Hispanics in the age group.

Seven million families in the United States are poor. Again, white families account for the majority of poor families, although black families are more likely to be poor (8 percent of white families versus 24 percent of black families). Single-parent families have the highest poverty rates. More than half of those headed by Hispanic women are poor, as are 47 percent of black single-parent families. The poverty rate for single-parent families headed by whites is 38 percent.

◆ Childhood poverty will remain a chronic problem until single parents become a smaller share of families.

## Poverty rates high for blacks and Hispanics

*(percent of people living in poverty, by race and Hispanic origin, 1997)*

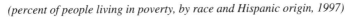

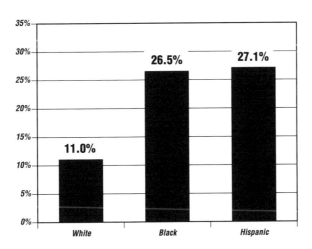

# People in Poverty by Age, Race and Hispanic Origin, 1997

*(number and percent of people in poverty by age, race, and Hispanic origin, 1997; people in thousands as of 1998)*

|  | total | white | black | Hispanic |
|---|---|---|---|---|
| **Total people** | **35,574** | **24,396** | **9,116** | **8,308** |
| Under age 18 | 14,113 | 8,990 | 4,225 | 3,972 |
| Aged 18 to 24 | 4,416 | 3,131 | 1,041 | 979 |
| Aged 25 to 34 | 4,759 | 3,327 | 1,106 | 1,201 |
| Aged 35 to 44 | 4,251 | 2,928 | 1,063 | 992 |
| Aged 45 to 54 | 2,439 | 1,817 | 489 | 427 |
| Aged 55 to 59 | 1,092 | 778 | 270 | 191 |
| Aged 60 to 64 | 1,127 | 857 | 222 | 161 |
| Aged 65 or older | 3,376 | 2,569 | 700 | 384 |
| **Total people** | **13.3%** | **11.0%** | **26.5%** | **27.1%** |
| Under age 18 | 19.9 | 16.1 | 37.2 | 36.8 |
| Aged 18 to 24 | 17.5 | 15.5 | 28.0 | 25.8 |
| Aged 25 to 34 | 12.1 | 10.5 | 20.9 | 21.9 |
| Aged 35 to 44 | 9.6 | 8.0 | 19.3 | 21.5 |
| Aged 45 to 54 | 7.2 | 6.3 | 13.3 | 15.8 |
| Aged 55 to 59 | 9.0 | 7.4 | 22.2 | 20.5 |
| Aged 60 to 64 | 11.2 | 9.9 | 22.1 | 22.9 |
| Aged 65 or older | 10.5 | 9.0 | 26.0 | 23.8 |

*Note: Numbers will not add to total because Hispanics may be of any race and not all races are shown.*
*Source: Bureau of the Census,* Poverty in the United States, *Current Population Reports, P60-201, 1998*

# Families in Poverty by Race and Hispanic Origin of Householder and Presence of Children, 1997

*(number and percent of families in poverty by type of family, presence of children under age 18 at home, and race and Hispanic origin of householder, 1997; families in thousands as of 1998)*

|  | total | white | black | Hispanic |
|---|---|---|---|---|
| **Total families** | **7,324** | **4,990** | **1,985** | **1,721** |
| With children under 18 | 5,884 | 3,895 | 1,721 | 1,492 |
| Married couples | 2,821 | 2,312 | 312 | 836 |
| With children under 18 | 1,863 | 1,516 | 205 | 692 |
| Female householders, |  |  |  |  |
| no spouse present | 3,995 | 2,305 | 1,563 | 767 |
| With children under 18 | 3,614 | 2,069 | 1,436 | 701 |
| Male householders, |  |  |  |  |
| no spouse present | 508 | 373 | 110 | 118 |
| With children under 18 | 407 | 310 | 80 | 99 |
| **Total families** | **10.3%** | **8.4%** | **23.6%** | **24.7%** |
| With children under 18 | 15.7 | 13.0 | 30.5 | 30.4 |
| Married couples | 5.2 | 4.8 | 8.0 | 17.4 |
| With children under 18 | 7.1 | 6.7 | 9.0 | 21.0 |
| Female householders, |  |  |  |  |
| no spouse present | 31.6 | 27.7 | 39.8 | 47.6 |
| With children under 18 | 41.0 | 37.6 | 46.9 | 54.2 |
| Male householders, |  |  |  |  |
| no spouse present | 13.0 | 11.9 | 19.6 | 21.7 |
| With children under 18 | 18.7 | 17.5 | 25.6 | 30.5 |

*Note: Numbers will not add to total because Hispanics may be of any race and because all races are not shown.*
*Source: Bureau of the Census,* Poverty in the United States*, Current Population Reports, P60-201, 1998*

# 4

# Labor Force Trends

♦ **Sixty-seven percent of Americans aged 16 or older are in the labor force, a record high.**

Behind this increase is the rise of working women, whose labor force participation rate grew more than 16 percentage points between 1970 and 1998.

♦ **Seventy-two percent of women with children under age 18 are in the labor force.**

Among those in the labor force, 73 percent have full-time jobs.

♦ **Three out of 10 workers are managers or professionals.**

Overall, 48 percent of men and 72 percent of women are white-collar workers.

♦ **Twenty-two percent of black workers are in service occupations, while 35 percent of Hispanics are blue-collar workers.**

The proportion of blacks and Hispanics in managerial and professional specialty occupations is growing.

♦ **Job tenure fell between 1983 and 1998.**

The biggest decline in job tenure has been among workers aged 55 to 64.

♦ **Non-Hispanic white men will decline as a proportion of all workers.**

By 2006, non-Hispanic white men will account for only 38 percent of workers.

♦ **Computer scientists, computer engineers, and system analysts will double between 1996 and 2006.**

Workers with bachelor's degrees will be in greatest demand.

# Men Have Become Less Likely to Work

## Women are far more likely to work today than in 1970.

In 1998, 60 percent of women aged 16 or older were in the labor force, up from only 43 percent in 1970. In contrast, men's labor force participation rate fell from 80 to 75 percent during those years.

Women's labor force participation rate has grown in all but the oldest age group since 1970. The biggest gain has been among women aged 25 to 34. In 1970, just 45 percent of women in that age group were in the labor force, but by 1998, the proportion surpassed 76 percent as mothers with young children went to work.

Among men, the labor force participation rate has fallen in every age group, with the biggest drop (15 percentage points) among men aged 55 to 64. In 1970, 83 percent of men in this age group were in the labor force. By 1998, only 68 percent were working as early retirement grew in popularity. The decline in labor force participation among younger men can be attributed to working women. With most wives earning a paycheck, some men can afford to go back to school or stay home for a few years and care for their children.

♦ The labor force participation rate will stabilize in the future. Additional gains in women's labor force participation will be minimal, since most women are already at work. The decline in men's rate will come to a halt as fewer employers offer early retirement incentives.

### Rate is down for men, up for women

*(percent of people aged 16 or older in the civilian labor force, by sex, 1970 and 1998)*

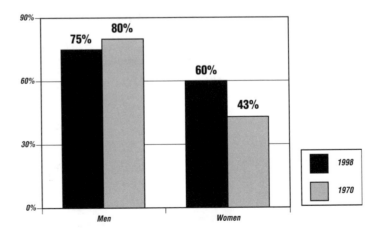

# Labor Force Participation by Sex and Age, 1970 to 1998

*(civilian labor force participation rate for people aged 16 or older by sex and age, 1970 to 1998; percentage point change, 1970–98)*

|  | *1998* | *1990* | *1980* | *1970* | *percentage point change, 1970–98* |
|---|---|---|---|---|---|
| **Total men** | **74.9%** | **76.1%** | **77.4%** | **79.7%** | **–4.8** |
| Aged 16 to 19 | 53.3 | 55.7 | 60.5 | 56.1 | –2.8 |
| Aged 20 to 24 | 82.0 | 84.3 | 85.9 | 83.3 | –1.3 |
| Aged 25 to 34 | 93.2 | 94.2 | 95.2 | 96.4 | –3.2 |
| Aged 35 to 44 | 92.6 | 94.4 | 95.5 | 96.9 | –4.3 |
| Aged 45 to 54 | 89.2 | 90.7 | 91.2 | 94.3 | –5.1 |
| Aged 55 to 64 | 68.1 | 67.7 | 72.1 | 83.0 | –14.9 |
| Aged 65 or older | 16.5 | 16.4 | 19.0 | 26.8 | –10.3 |
| **Total women** | **59.8** | **57.5** | **51.5** | **43.3** | **16.5** |
| Aged 16 to 19 | 52.3 | 51.8 | 52.9 | 44.0 | 8.3 |
| Aged 20 to 24 | 73.0 | 71.6 | 68.9 | 57.7 | 15.3 |
| Aged 25 to 34 | 76.3 | 73.6 | 65.5 | 45.0 | 31.3 |
| Aged 35 to 44 | 77.1 | 76.5 | 65.5 | 51.1 | 26.0 |
| Aged 45 to 54 | 76.2 | 71.2 | 59.9 | 54.4 | 21.8 |
| Aged 55 to 64 | 51.2 | 45.3 | 41.3 | 43.0 | 8.2 |
| Aged 65 or older | 8.6 | 8.7 | 8.1 | 9.7 | –1.1 |

*Source: Bureau of Labor Statistics,* Employment and Earnings, *January 1999 and January 1991; and* Handbook of Labor Statistics, *Bulletin 2340, 1989; calculations by New Strategist*

# Two-Thirds of Americans Work

**Sixty-seven percent of Americans aged 16 or older are in the labor force, up from 59 percent in 1960.**

Never before have so many Americans been in the labor force, both numerically and proportionately. Of the nation's 205 million people aged 16 or older, 138 million are in the civilian labor force. The labor force participation rate is at a record high because working women have become the norm. Of the nation's 138 million workers, 46 percent are women.

Men's and women's labor force participation rates are similar among 16-to-19-year-olds, of whom slightly more than half are in the labor force. Men's participation rate rises to a peak of 93 percent in the 25-to-44 age group. Women's rate peaks at 77 percent in the 35-to-44 age group. Both men's and women's participation rates fall sharply in the 55-to-64 age group as early retirement drains workers from the labor force. Few people aged 65 or older work.

◆ Women's labor force participation rate will rise more slowly in the years ahead because most women are already in the labor force.

◆ Men's labor force participation rate is likely to stabilize because fewer employers can afford generous retirement benefits for older workers.

# Employment Status by Sex and Age, 1998

*(number and percent of people aged 16 or older in the civilian labor force by sex, age, and employment status, 1998; numbers in thousands)*

| | civilian noninstitutional population | civilian labor force | | | unemployed | |
| | | total | percent of population | employed | number | percent of labor force |
|---|---|---|---|---|---|---|
| **Total people** | **205,220** | **137,673** | **67.1%** | **131,463** | **6,210** | **4.5%** |
| Aged 16 to 19 | 15,644 | 8,256 | 52.8 | 7,051 | 1,205 | 14.6 |
| Aged 20 to 24 | 17,593 | 13,638 | 77.5 | 12,557 | 1,081 | 7.9 |
| Aged 25 to 34 | 38,778 | 32,813 | 84.6 | 31,394 | 1,419 | 4.3 |
| Aged 35 to 44 | 44,299 | 37,536 | 84.7 | 36,278 | 1,258 | 3.4 |
| Aged 45 to 54 | 34,373 | 28,368 | 82.5 | 27,587 | 782 | 2.8 |
| Aged 55 to 64 | 22,296 | 13,215 | 59.3 | 12,872 | 343 | 2.6 |
| Aged 65 or older | 32,237 | 3,847 | 11.9 | 3,725 | 122 | 3.2 |
| **Total men** | **98,758** | **73,959** | **74.9** | **70,693** | **3,266** | **4.4** |
| Aged 16 to 19 | 7,968 | 4,244 | 53.3 | 3,558 | 686 | 16.2 |
| Aged 20 to 24 | 8,804 | 7,221 | 82.0 | 6,638 | 583 | 8.1 |
| Aged 25 to 34 | 19,094 | 17,796 | 93.2 | 17,097 | 699 | 3.9 |
| Aged 35 to 44 | 21,857 | 20,242 | 92.6 | 19,634 | 609 | 3.0 |
| Aged 45 to 54 | 16,773 | 14,963 | 89.2 | 14,544 | 420 | 2.8 |
| Aged 55 to 64 | 10,649 | 7,253 | 68.1 | 7,052 | 201 | 2.8 |
| Aged 65 or older | 13,613 | 2,240 | 16.5 | 2,171 | 69 | 3.1 |
| **Total women** | **106,462** | **63,714** | **59.8** | **60,771** | **2,944** | **4.6** |
| Aged 16 to 19 | 7,676 | 4,012 | 52.3 | 3,493 | 519 | 12.9 |
| Aged 20 to 24 | 8,790 | 6,418 | 73.0 | 5,919 | 498 | 7.8 |
| Aged 25 to 34 | 19,683 | 15,017 | 76.3 | 14,298 | 720 | 4.8 |
| Aged 35 to 44 | 22,442 | 17,294 | 77.1 | 16,644 | 650 | 3.8 |
| Aged 45 to 54 | 17,600 | 13,405 | 76.2 | 13,043 | 362 | 2.7 |
| Aged 55 to 64 | 11,646 | 5,962 | 51.2 | 5,820 | 141 | 2.4 |
| Aged 65 or older | 18,625 | 1,607 | 8.6 | 1,554 | 53 | 3.3 |

*Note: The civilian labor force equals the number of employed plus the number of unemployed. The civilian population equals the number of Americans in the labor force plus the number of those not in the labor force.*
*Source: Bureau of Labor Statistics,* Employment and Earnings, *January 1999*

# Labor Force Participation Varies by Race and Hispanic Origin

## Participation ranges from a high of 80 percent among Hispanic men to a low of 56 percent among Hispanic women.

The gap in the labor force participation rate between men and women is greatest for Hispanics. With 80 percent of Hispanic men and only 56 percent of Hispanic women in the labor force, the 24 percentage point gap is far larger than the one between white or black men and women. Sixty-nine percent of black men and 63 percent of black women are in the labor force—a gap of just 6 percentage points. Among whites, the gap is 17 percentage points, with a labor force participation rate of 76 percent for men and 59 percent for women.

Black and white women have similar labor force participation rates, except in the youngest age groups, where blacks are less likely to work than whites. Black men have a much lower labor force participation rate than white men in all age groups. Only 41 percent of black men aged 16 to 19 are in the labor force versus 57 percent of their white counterparts. Black men are almost twice as likely as white men to be unemployed. Fully 30 percent of black men aged 16 to 19 could not find a job in 1998, versus 14 percent of white men in the age group.

◆ Despite the booming economy, many blacks and Hispanics have trouble finding jobs. One reason for their employment difficulties is that many live in central cities while job growth has been in the suburbs.

### Gap is biggest between Hispanic men and women

*(labor force participation rate by race and Hispanic origin, by sex, 1998)*

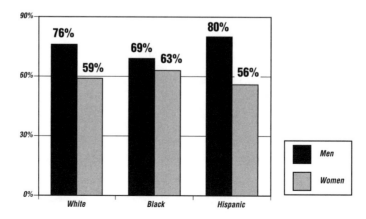

# Employment Status of Blacks by Sex and Age, 1998

*(number and percent of blacks aged 16 or older in the civilian labor force by sex, age, and employment status, 1998; numbers in thousands)*

| | civilian noninstitutional population | civilian labor force | | | unemployed | |
|---|---|---|---|---|---|---|
| | | total | percent of population | employed | number | percent of labor force |
| **Total black men** | **10,927** | **7,542** | **69.0%** | **6,871** | **671** | **8.9%** |
| Aged 16 to 19 | 1,201 | 488 | 40.7 | 341 | 147 | 30.1 |
| Aged 20 to 24 | 1,166 | 837 | 71.8 | 686 | 151 | 18.0 |
| Aged 25 to 34 | 2,335 | 2,034 | 87.1 | 1,886 | 148 | 7.3 |
| Aged 35 to 44 | 2,520 | 2,142 | 85.0 | 2,008 | 133 | 6.2 |
| Aged 45 to 54 | 1,682 | 1,343 | 79.9 | 1,284 | 60 | 4.4 |
| Aged 55 to 64 | 956 | 548 | 57.3 | 524 | 24 | 4.5 |
| Aged 65 or older | 1,068 | 150 | 14.0 | 142 | 8 | 5.2 |
| **Total black women** | **13,446** | **8,441** | **62.8** | **7,685** | **756** | **9.0** |
| Aged 16 to 19 | 1,243 | 528 | 42.5 | 395 | 134 | 25.3 |
| Aged 20 to 24 | 1,380 | 960 | 69.6 | 810 | 150 | 15.7 |
| Aged 25 to 34 | 2,886 | 2,298 | 79.6 | 2,081 | 218 | 9.5 |
| Aged 35 to 44 | 2,991 | 2,390 | 79.9 | 2,230 | 160 | 6.7 |
| Aged 45 to 54 | 2,053 | 1,520 | 74.0 | 1,455 | 65 | 4.3 |
| Aged 55 to 64 | 1,268 | 615 | 48.5 | 594 | 21 | 3.4 |
| Aged 65 or older | 1,626 | 128 | 7.9 | 120 | 8 | 6.1 |

*Note: The civilian labor force equals the number of employed plus the number of unemployed. The civilian population equals the number of Americans in the labor force plus the number of those not in the labor force.*
*Source: Bureau of Labor Statistics,* Employment and Earnings, *January 1999*

# Employment Status of Hispanics by Sex and Age, 1998

*(number and percent of Hispanics aged 16 or older in the civilian labor force by sex, age, and employment status, 1998; numbers in thousands)*

| | civilian noninstitutional population | civilian labor force | | | unemployed | |
|---|---|---|---|---|---|---|
| | | total | percent of population | employed | number | percent of labor force |
| **Total Hispanic men** | **10,734** | **8,571** | **79.8%** | **8,018** | **552** | **6.4%** |
| Aged 16 to 19 | 1,161 | 565 | 48.7 | 449 | 117 | 20.6 |
| Aged 20 to 24 | 1,462 | 1,288 | 88.1 | 1,173 | 115 | 8.9 |
| Aged 25 to 34 | 2,907 | 2,733 | 94.0 | 2,592 | 142 | 5.2 |
| Aged 35 to 44 | 2,377 | 2,173 | 91.4 | 2,077 | 97 | 4.5 |
| Aged 45 to 54 | 1,342 | 1,164 | 86.7 | 1,115 | 49 | 4.2 |
| Aged 55 to 64 | 771 | 541 | 70.2 | 512 | 29 | 5.3 |
| Aged 65 or older | 714 | 106 | 14.9 | 101 | 5 | 5.0 |
| **Total Hispanic women** | **10,335** | **5,746** | **55.6** | **5,273** | **473** | **8.2** |
| Aged 16 to 19 | 1,044 | 442 | 42.4 | 345 | 98 | 22.1 |
| Aged 20 to 24 | 1,269 | 789 | 62.2 | 710 | 80 | 10.1 |
| Aged 25 to 34 | 2,539 | 1,639 | 64.5 | 1,521 | 118 | 7.2 |
| Aged 35 to 44 | 2,259 | 1,533 | 67.9 | 1,428 | 106 | 6.9 |
| Aged 45 to 54 | 1,433 | 927 | 64.7 | 879 | 48 | 5.1 |
| Aged 55 to 64 | 844 | 353 | 41.9 | 334 | 19 | 5.4 |
| Aged 65 or older | 948 | 62 | 6.6 | 57 | 5 | 8.8 |

*Note: The civilian labor force equals the number of employed plus the number of unemployed. The civilian population equals the number of Americans in the labor force plus the number of those not in the labor force.*
*Source: Bureau of Labor Statistics, Employment and Earnings, January 1999*

# Employment Status of Whites by Sex and Age, 1998

*(number and percent of whites aged 16 or older in the civilian labor force by sex, age, and employment status, 1998; numbers in thousands)*

| | civilian noninstitutional population | civilian labor force | | | unemployed | |
| | | total | percent of population | employed | number | percent of labor force |
| --- | --- | --- | --- | --- | --- | --- |
| **Total white men** | **83,352** | **63,034** | **75.6%** | **60,604** | **2,431** | **3.9%** |
| Aged 16 to 19 | 6,386 | 3,614 | 56.6 | 3,103 | 510 | 14.1 |
| Aged 20 to 24 | 7,170 | 6,063 | 84.6 | 5,659 | 405 | 6.7 |
| Aged 25 to 34 | 15,644 | 14,770 | 94.4 | 14,259 | 512 | 3.5 |
| Aged 35 to 44 | 18,310 | 17,157 | 93.7 | 16,715 | 441 | 2.6 |
| Aged 45 to 54 | 14,400 | 13,003 | 90.3 | 12,661 | 342 | 2.6 |
| Aged 55 to 64 | 9,286 | 6,415 | 69.1 | 6,251 | 164 | 2.6 |
| Aged 65 or older | 12,155 | 2,013 | 16.6 | 1,955 | 58 | 2.9 |
| **Total white women** | **88,126** | **52,380** | **59.4** | **50,327** | **2,053** | **3.9** |
| Aged 16 to 19 | 6,053 | 3,351 | 55.4 | 2,986 | 365 | 10.9 |
| Aged 20 to 24 | 6,969 | 5,180 | 74.3 | 4,853 | 327 | 6.3 |
| Aged 25 to 34 | 15,642 | 11,937 | 76.3 | 11,470 | 467 | 3.9 |
| Aged 35 to 44 | 18,300 | 14,064 | 76.9 | 13,604 | 460 | 3.3 |
| Aged 45 to 54 | 14,732 | 11,279 | 76.6 | 11,001 | 279 | 2.5 |
| Aged 55 to 64 | 9,944 | 5,133 | 51.6 | 5,021 | 112 | 2.2 |
| Aged 65 or older | 16,486 | 1,435 | 8.7 | 1,392 | 43 | 3.0 |

*Note: The civilian labor force equals the number of employed plus the number of unemployed. The civilian population equals the number of Americans in the labor force plus the number of those not in the labor force. Source: Bureau of Labor Statistics,* Employment and Earnings, *January 1999*

# Working Mothers Are the Norm

**Seventy-two percent of women with children under age 18 were in the labor force in 1997.**

Working mothers, once an anomaly, are now the norm. Even among women with children under age 1, the 58 percent majority are in the labor force. Most of those at work have full-time jobs.

The labor force participation rate is higher for mothers of school-aged children than for those with preschoolers. Fully 78 percent of mothers with children aged 6 to 17 are in the labor force, and 76 percent work full-time. Among mothers with children under age 6, 65 percent are in the labor force, and 70 percent work full-time.

Sixty-five percent of the nation's married couples with children under age 18 are dual-earners, with both mother and father in the labor force. In just 28 percent of couples, only the father is employed. Even among couples with preschoolers, the 58 percent majority are dual-earners.

◆ Whether it is good or bad for children if their mother works is now a moot point. With the majority of mothers—even those with infants—at work, businesses offering simplicity and convenience will prosper.

## Majority of mothers work

*(percent of women with children under age 18 in the labor force, by age of children, 1997)*

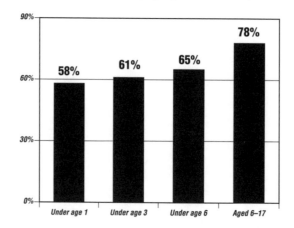

# Labor Force Status of Women by Presence of Children, 1997

*(labor force status of women by presence and age of own children under age 18, 1997; numbers in thousands)*

| | civilian population | | | employed | | | percent of total women who work full-time |
| | | civilian labor force | | | percent of employed who work | | |
| | total | number | percent | total | full-time | part-time | full-time |
|---|---|---|---|---|---|---|---|
| **Total women** | **105,418** | **63,143** | **59.9.%** | **59,940** | **73.5.%** | **26.5.%** | **41.8.%** |
| No children under age 18 | 69,980 | 37,677 | 53.8 | 35,873 | 73.7 | 26.3 | 37.8 |
| With children under age 18 | 35,438 | 25,466 | 71.9 | 24,067 | 73.2 | 26.8 | 49.7 |
| Children aged 6 to 17, | | | | | | | |
| none younger | 19,175 | 14,935 | 77.9 | 14,273 | 75.8 | 24.2 | 56.4 |
| Children under age 6 | 16,263 | 10,531 | 64.8 | 9,794 | 69.6 | 30.4 | 41.9 |
| Children under age 3 | 9,347 | 5,738 | 61.4 | 5,306 | 67.1 | 32.9 | 38.1 |
| Children under age 1 | 3,170 | 1,836 | 57.9 | 1,692 | 67.7 | 32.2 | 36.2 |

*Source: Bureau of Labor Statistics, Internet web site <http://www.bls.gov/news.release/famee.t05.htm> and <http://www.bls.gov/news.release/famee.t06htm>; calculations by New Strategist*

# Labor Force Status of Parents with Children Under Age 18, 1997

*(percent distribution of people aged 16 or older with children under age 18 by family type, labor force status, and age of own children under age 18, 1997; numbers in thousands)*

| | total | with children under age 18 aged 6 to 17, none younger | under age 6 |
|---|---|---|---|
| **Married couples** | **100.0%** | **100.0%** | **100.0%** |
| One or both parents employed | 96.9 | 96.7 | 97.1 |
| Mother employed | 68.7 | 74.8 | 61.4 |
| Both parents employed | 64.5 | 69.8 | 58.2 |
| Mother employed not father | 4.2 | 5.1 | 3.3 |
| Father employed, not mother | 28.2 | 21.9 | 35.6 |
| Neither parent employed | 3.1 | 3.3 | 2.9 |
| **Female-headed families, no spouse present** | **100.0** | **100.0** | **100.0** |
| Mother employed | 69.2 | 74.9 | 60.9 |
| Mother not employed | 30.8 | 25.1 | 39.1 |
| **Male-headed families, no spouse present** | **100.0** | **100.0** | **100.0** |
| Father employed | 85.8 | 86.8 | 84.6 |
| Father not employed | 14.2 | 13.2 | 15.4 |

*Source: Bureau of Labor Statistics, Internet web site <http://www.bls.gov/news.release/famee.t04.htm>*

# More Than Half the Couples Are Dual Earners

## In just one-fifth of married couples is only the husband in the labor force.

Dual incomes are the norm among married couples in the U.S. Both husband and wife are in the labor force in 56 percent of married couples. In another 21 percent, the husband is the only worker. Not far behind are the 17 percent of couples in which neither spouse is in the labor force. The wife is the sole worker in 6 percent of couples.

More than 70 percent of couples aged 25 to 54 are dual earners. This lifestyle accounts for a 44 percent minority among couples aged 55 to 64. The wife is the only one employed in a substantial 14 percent of couples aged 55 to 64. In these homes, typically, the older husband is retired while the younger wife is still at work. In 75 percent of couples aged 65 or older, neither husband nor wife is working.

◆ As boomers age into their sixties and begin to retire, the number of couples in which neither spouse is in the labor force will surpass the number in which only the husband is employed.

### Dual earners dominate couples

*(percent distribution of married couples by labor force status of husband and wife, 1998)*

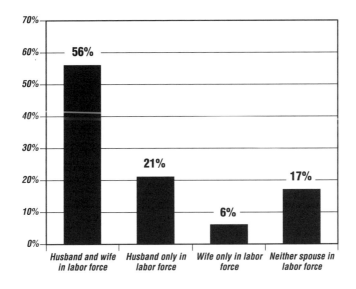

# Dual-Income Couples by Age, 1998

*(number and percent distribution of married couples by labor force status of husband and wife, 1998; numbers in thousands)*

| | total married couples | husband and wife in labor force | husband only in labor force | wife only in labor force | husband and wife not in labor force |
|---|---|---|---|---|---|
| **Total couples** | **54,317** | **30,591** | **11,582** | **3,087** | **9,057** |
| Under age 25 | 1,373 | 889 | 429 | 24 | 30 |
| Aged 25 to 34 | 9,886 | 6,998 | 2,585 | 204 | 98 |
| Aged 35 to 44 | 14,180 | 10,111 | 3,422 | 416 | 232 |
| Aged 45 to 54 | 11,734 | 8,368 | 2,452 | 555 | 359 |
| Aged 55 to 64 | 7,936 | 3,560 | 1,791 | 1,107 | 1,480 |
| Aged 65 or older | 9,209 | 666 | 902 | 782 | 6,857 |
| **Total couples** | **100.0%** | **56.3%** | **21.3%** | **5.7%** | **16.7%** |
| Under age 25 | 100.0 | 64.7 | 31.2 | 1.7 | 2.2 |
| Aged 25 to 34 | 100.0 | 70.8 | 26.1 | 2.1 | 1.0 |
| Aged 35 to 44 | 100.0 | 71.3 | 24.1 | 2.9 | 1.6 |
| Aged 45 to 54 | 100.0 | 71.3 | 20.9 | 4.7 | 3.1 |
| Aged 55 to 64 | 100.0 | 44.9 | 22.6 | 13.9 | 18.6 |
| Aged 65 or older | 100.0 | 7.2 | 9.8 | 8.5 | 74.5 |

*Source: Bureau of the Census, detailed tables for* Household and Family Characteristics: March 1998, *Current Population Reports, P20-515, 1998; calculations by New Strategist*

# More Part-Time Workers

## The number of Americans who work part-time has grown 36 percent since 1980.

Twenty-six percent of working women worked part-time in 1998. This proportion has barely changed since 1980. Because the population of working women has expanded during those years, however, the number of women who work part-time has grown more than 4 million.

Eleven percent of men work part-time, up about 1 percentage point since 1980. The number of men who work part-time rose more than 2 million between 1980 and 1998. Working wives are behind the slight rise in the share of men who work part-time. As more women go to work, more men can reduce their work hours to pursue other activities, such as going to school or caring for children.

♦ If health care and other benefits were available to more part-time workers, the proportion of people who work part-time would expand.

# Full-Time and Part-Time Workers by Sex, 1980 to 1998

*(number and percent of people aged 16 or older in the civilian labor force by sex and full- and part-time status, 1980 to 1998; numbers in thousands)*

| | total | *usually work full-time* total | *usually work full-time* percent of labor force | *usually work part-time* total | *usually work part-time* percent of labor force |
|---|---|---|---|---|---|
| **Total labor force** | | | | | |
| **1998** | **137,673** | **113,118** | **82.2%** | **24,554** | **17.8%** |
| 1990 | 124,788 | 103,535 | 83.0 | 21,252 | 17.0 |
| 1980 | 106,940 | 88,831 | 83.1 | 18,109 | 16.9 |
| **Men in labor force** | | | | | |
| 1998 | 73,959 | 65,895 | 89.1 | 8,064 | 10.9 |
| 1990 | 68,233 | 61,246 | 89.8 | 6,987 | 10.2 |
| 1980 | 61,454 | 55,420 | 90.2 | 6,034 | 9.8 |
| **Women in labor force** | | | | | |
| 1998 | 63,714 | 47,223 | 74.1 | 16,491 | 25.9 |
| 1990 | 56,553 | 42,288 | 74.8 | 14,265 | 25.2 |
| 1980 | 45,485 | 33,409 | 73.5 | 12,076 | 26.5 |

*Note: The unemployed are distributed by full- or part-time work depending on whether they are looking for full- or part-time work. Part-time employment is less than 35 hours per week.*
*Source: Bureau of Labor Statistics,* Employment and Earnings, *January 1991 and January 1999; and* Handbook of Labor Statistics, *Bulletin 2340, 1989; calculations by New Strategist*

# Most Working Women Are in White-Collar Occupations

## Nearly one-third of women workers are managers or professionals.

Overall, 48 percent of men are white-collar workers (a category that includes managers and professionals, and technical, sales, and administrative support workers). Another 38 percent of men are blue-collar workers (a category that includes precision production, craft, and repair workers; and operators, fabricators, and laborers). Ten percent of men are service workers, while 4 percent are in farming, forestry, or fishing.

Among women, fully 72 percent are white-collar workers, while 18 percent are service workers. Only 9 percent of women have blue-collar jobs, and just 1 percent are in farming, forestry, or fishing.

Women account for more than 50 percent of workers in many occupations, including financial managers, educational administrators, registered nurses, therapists, legal assistants, computer equipment operators, and bus drivers. Between 1983 and 1998, women's share of all workers grew 2.5 percentage points. Women's share of some occupations grew much more than that, with the biggest gains for managers of medicine and health (up 22 percentage points, from 57 to 79 percent of those employed in the occupation), personnel and labor relations managers (also up 22 percentage points, from 44 to 66 percent), and educational administrators (up 21 percentage points, from 41 to 62 percent).

♦ While women have made inroads on most occupations, they continue to be underrepresented in such important jobs as engineer (only 11 percent are women), physician (27 percent), and college teacher (42 percent).

# Workers by Occupation and Sex, 1998

*(number and percent distribution of employed people aged 16 or older in the civilian labor force, by occupation and sex, 1998; numbers in thousands)*

|  | total | men | women |
|---|---|---|---|
| **Total employed** | **131,463** | **70,693** | **60,771** |
| Managerial and professional specialty | 38,937 | 19,867 | 19,070 |
| Executive, administrative, and managerial | 19,054 | 10,585 | 8,469 |
| Professional specialty | 19,883 | 9,282 | 10,602 |
| Technical, sales, and administrative support | 38,521 | 13,792 | 24,728 |
| Technicians and related support | 4,261 | 1,976 | 2,285 |
| Sales occupations | 15,850 | 7,875 | 7,975 |
| Administrative support, including clerical | 18,410 | 3,941 | 14,469 |
| Service occupations | 17,836 | 7,222 | 10,614 |
| Private household | 847 | 46 | 801 |
| Protective services | 2,417 | 1,986 | 431 |
| Services, except private household and protective | 14,572 | 5,190 | 9,382 |
| Precision production, craft, and repair | 14,411 | 13,208 | 1,203 |
| Operators, fabricators, and laborers | 18,256 | 13,769 | 4,487 |
| Machine operators, assemblers, and inspectors | 7,791 | 4,882 | 2,909 |
| Transportation and material moving occupations | 5,363 | 4,818 | 545 |
| Handlers, equipment cleaners, helpers, and laborers | 5,102 | 4,069 | 1,033 |
| Farming, forestry, and fishing | 3,502 | 2,835 | 668 |
| **Total employed** | **100.0%** | **100.0%** | **100.0%** |
| Managerial and professional specialty | 29.6 | 28.1 | 31.4 |
| Executive, administrative, and managerial | 14.5 | 15.0 | 13.9 |
| Professional specialty | 15.1 | 13.1 | 17.4 |
| Technical, sales, and administrative support | 29.3 | 19.5 | 40.7 |
| Technicians and related support | 3.2 | 2.8 | 3.8 |
| Sales occupations | 12.1 | 11.1 | 13.1 |
| Administrative support, including clerical | 14.0 | 5.6 | 23.8 |
| Service occupations | 13.6 | 10.2 | 17.5 |
| Private household | 0.6 | 0.1 | 1.3 |
| Protective services | 1.8 | 2.8 | 0.7 |
| Services, except private household and protective | 11.1 | 7.3 | 15.4 |
| Precision production, craft, and repair | 11.0 | 18.7 | 2.0 |
| Operators, fabricators, and laborers | 13.9 | 19.5 | 7.4 |
| Machine operators, assemblers, and inspectors | 5.9 | 6.9 | 4.8 |
| Transportation and material moving occupations | 4.1 | 6.8 | 0.9 |
| Handlers, equipment cleaners, helpers, and laborers | 3.9 | 5.8 | 1.7 |
| Farming, forestry, and fishing | 2.7 | 4.0 | 1.1 |

*Source: Bureau of Labor Statistics,* Employment and Earnings, *January 1999; calculations by New Strategist*

# Women Workers by Occupation, 1983 and 1998

*(women as a percent of total employed people aged 16 or older in selected occupations, 1983 and 1998, and percentage point change, 1983–98)*

| | *1998* | *1983* | *percentage point change 1983–98* |
|---|---|---|---|
| **Total, aged 16 or older** | **46.2%** | **43.7%** | **2.5** |
| Managerial and professional specialty | 49.0 | 40.9 | 8.1 |
| Executive, administrative, and managerial | 44.4 | 32.4 | 12.0 |
| Officials and administrators, public admin. | 48.5 | 38.5 | 10.0 |
| Financial managers | 53.3 | 38.6 | 14.7 |
| Personnel and labor relations managers | 65.9 | 43.9 | 22.0 |
| Purchasing managers | 39.4 | 23.6 | 15.8 |
| Managers, marketing, advertising, and public relations | 38.5 | 21.8 | 16.7 |
| Administrators, education and related fields | 62.2 | 41.4 | 20.8 |
| Managers, medicine and health | 79.2 | 57.0 | 22.2 |
| Managers, property and real estate | 52.2 | 42.8 | 9.4 |
| Professional specialty | 53.3 | 48.1 | 5.2 |
| Architects | 17.5 | 12.7 | 4.8 |
| Engineers | 11.1 | 5.8 | 5.3 |
| Mathematical and computer scientists | 28.9 | 29.6 | –0.7 |
| Natural scientists | 30.9 | 20.5 | 10.4 |
| Physicians | 26.6 | 15.8 | 10.8 |
| Dentists | 19.8 | 6.7 | 13.1 |
| Registered nurses | 92.5 | 95.8 | –3.3 |
| Pharmacists | 44.0 | 26.7 | 17.3 |
| Dietitians | 86.0 | 90.8 | –4.8 |
| Therapists | 75.4 | 76.3 | –0.9 |
| Teachers, college and university | 42.3 | 39.3 | 3.0 |
| Teachers, except college and university | 75.3 | 70.9 | 4.4 |
| Librarians, archivists, and curators | 80.8 | 84.4 | –3.6 |
| Economists | 46.3 | 37.9 | 8.4 |
| Psychologists | 62.1 | 57.1 | 5.0 |
| Social, recreation, and religious workers | 55.1 | 43.1 | 12.0 |
| Lawyers and judges | 28.6 | 15.8 | 12.8 |
| Writers, artists, entertainers, and athletes | 51.4 | 42.7 | 8.7 |
| Technical, sales and administrative support | 64.2 | 64.6 | –0.4 |
| Health technologists and technicians | 81.6 | 84.3 | –2.7 |
| Engineering and related technologists and technicians | 20.8 | 18.4 | 2.4 |
| Science technicians | 43.3 | 29.1 | 14.2 |

*(continued)*

*(continued from previous page)*

| | 1998 | 1983 | percentage point change 1983–98 |
|---|---|---|---|
| Technicians, except health, engineering and science | 42.8% | 35.3% | 7.5 |
| Airplane pilots and navigators | 3.4 | 2.1 | 1.3 |
| Computer programmers | 28.5 | 32.5 | –4.0 |
| Legal assistants | 82.0 | 74.0 | 8.0 |
| Sales occupations | 50.3 | 47.5 | 2.8 |
| Supervisors and proprietors | 40.1 | 28.4 | 11.7 |
| Sales representatives, finance and business services | 43.6 | 37.2 | 6.4 |
| Sales representatives, commodities, except retail | 26.0 | 15.1 | 10.9 |
| Sales workers, retail and personal services | 65.4 | 69.7 | –4.3 |
| Administrative support, including clerical | 78.6 | 79.9 | –1.3 |
| Supervisors, administrative support | 60.1 | 53.4 | 6.7 |
| Computer equipment operators | 54.7 | 63.9 | –9.2 |
| Secretaries, stenographers, and typists | 97.6 | 98.2 | –0.6 |
| Information clerks | 89.0 | 88.9 | 0.1 |
| Record-processing occupations, except financial | 79.2 | 82.4 | –3.2 |
| Financial record processing | 92.1 | 89.4 | 2.7 |
| Service occupations | 59.5 | 60.1 | –0.6 |
| Private household | 94.6 | 96.1 | –1.5 |
| Firefighting and fire prevention | 2.5 | 1.0 | 1.5 |
| Police and detectives | 16.3 | 9.4 | 6.9 |
| Food preparation and service occupations | 56.5 | 63.3 | –6.8 |
| Health service occupations | 88.5 | 89.2 | –0.7 |
| Cleaning and building service occupations | 44.5 | 38.8 | 5.7 |
| Personal service occupations | 81.5 | 79.2 | 2.3 |
| Precision production, craft, and repair | 8.3 | 8.1 | 0.2 |
| Mechanics and repairers | 4.0 | 3.0 | 1.0 |
| Construction trades | 2.0 | 1.8 | 0.2 |
| Precision production occupations | 23.0 | 21.5 | 1.5 |
| Operators, fabricators, and laborers | 24.6 | 26.6 | –2.0 |
| Machine operators, assemblers, and inspectors | 37.3 | 42.1 | –4.8 |
| Transportation and material moving occupations | 10.2 | 7.8 | 2.4 |
| Truck drivers | 5.3 | 3.1 | 2.2 |
| Bus drivers | 50.4 | 45.5 | 4.9 |
| Taxicab drivers and chauffeurs | 10.5 | 10.4 | 0.1 |
| Handlers, equipment cleaners, helpers, and laborers | 20.3 | 16.8 | 3.5 |
| Farming, forestry, and fishing | 19.1 | 16.0 | 3.1 |

*Source: Bureau of Labor Statistics,* Employment and Earnings, *January 1999; calculations by New Strategist*

# Whites Most Likely to Be Managers and Professionals

## Hispanics are most likely to be blue-collar workers.

Among employed whites, 31 percent are managers or professionals. The proportion is only 20 percent among blacks and 15 percent among Hispanics. The proportion of workers in technical, sales, or administrative support positions is more similar by race and Hispanic origin, with 29 percent of both whites and blacks and 24 percent of Hispanics holding these jobs.

Blacks and Hispanics are more likely to be service workers than whites, with at least 22 percent of blacks, 20 percent of Hispanics, and only 14 percent of whites in service occupations. Blue-collar work (precision production, craft, and repair; and operators, fabricators, and laborers) is much more common among Hispanics, 35 percent of whom have blue-collar jobs. The proportions are 28 percent among blacks and 25 percent among whites.

Blacks account for 11 percent of all employed workers, while Hispanics account for 10 percent. In many occupations, blacks and Hispanics account for a much larger share of workers. Eighteen percent of dietitians are black, as are 19 percent of police and detectives. Seventeen percent of machine operators, assemblers, and inspectors are Hispanic, as are 14 percent of construction workers.

♦ Although blacks and Hispanics lag behind whites in upper-level white-collar jobs, they are slowly catching up. Blacks accounted for 7 percent of executives, administrators, and managers in 1998, up from 5 percent in 1983. Hispanics were 5 percent of all executives, administrators, and managers in 1998, up from 3 percent in 1983.

# Workers by Occupation, Race, and Hispanic Origin, 1998

*(number and percent distribution of employed people aged 16 or older in the civilian labor force, by occupation, race, and Hispanic origin, 1998; numbers in thousands)*

|  | total | white | black | Hispanic |
|---|---|---|---|---|
| **Total employed** | **131,463** | **110,931** | **14,556** | **13,291** |
| Managerial and professional specialty | 38,937 | 34,063 | 2,947 | 1,933 |
| Executive, administrative, and managerial | 19,054 | 16,903 | 1,368 | 1,028 |
| Professional specialty | 19,883 | 17,160 | 1,579 | 905 |
| Technical, sales, and administrative support | 38,521 | 32,490 | 4,264 | 3,186 |
| Technicians and related support | 4,261 | 3,557 | 441 | 283 |
| Sales occupations | 15,850 | 13,704 | 1,415 | 1,245 |
| Administrative support, including clerical | 18,410 | 15,229 | 2,408 | 1,657 |
| Service occupations | 17,836 | 13,807 | 3,148 | 2,670 |
| Private household | 847 | 704 | 116 | 262 |
| Protective services | 2,417 | 1,892 | 463 | 204 |
| Services, except private household and protective | 14,572 | 11,211 | 2,569 | 2,204 |
| Precision production, craft, and repair | 14,411 | 12,729 | 1,158 | 1,793 |
| Operators, fabricators, and laborers | 18,256 | 14,609 | 2,866 | 2,917 |
| Machine operators, assemblers, and inspectors | 7,791 | 6,146 | 1,200 | 1,340 |
| Transportation and material moving occupations | 5,363 | 4,351 | 872 | 640 |
| Handlers, equipment cleaners, helpers, and laborers | 5,102 | 4,112 | 795 | 938 |
| Farming, forestry, and fishing | 3,502 | 3,233 | 172 | 792 |
| **Total employed** | **100.0%** | **100.0%** | **100.0%** | **100.0%** |
| Managerial and professional specialty | 29.6 | 30.7 | 20.2 | 14.5 |
| Executive, administrative, and managerial | 14.5 | 15.2 | 9.4 | 7.7 |
| Professional specialty | 15.1 | 15.5 | 10.8 | 6.8 |
| Technical, sales, and administrative support | 29.3 | 29.3 | 29.3 | 24.0 |
| Technicians and related support | 3.2 | 3.2 | 3.0 | 2.1 |
| Sales occupations | 12.1 | 12.4 | 9.7 | 9.4 |
| Administrative support, including clerical | 14.0 | 13.7 | 16.5 | 12.5 |
| Service occupations | 13.6 | 12.4 | 21.6 | 20.1 |
| Private household | 0.6 | 0.6 | 0.8 | 2.0 |
| Protective services | 1.8 | 1.7 | 3.2 | 1.5 |
| Services, except private household and protective | 11.1 | 10.1 | 17.6 | 16.6 |
| Precision production, craft, and repair | 11.0 | 11.5 | 8.0 | 13.5 |
| Operators, fabricators, and laborers | 13.9 | 13.2 | 19.7 | 21.9 |
| Machine operators, assemblers, and inspectors | 5.9 | 5.5 | 8.2 | 10.1 |
| Transportation and material moving occupations | 4.1 | 3.9 | 6.0 | 4.8 |
| Handlers, equipment cleaners, helpers, and laborers | 3.9 | 3.7 | 5.5 | 7.1 |
| Farming, forestry, and fishing | 2.7 | 2.9 | 1.2 | 6.0 |

*Note: Numbers will not add to total because Hispanics may be of any race and because not all races are shown.*
*Source: Bureau of Labor Statistics,* Employment and Earnings, *January 1999; calculations by New Strategist*

# Black and Hispanic Workers by Occupation, 1983 and 1998

*(blacks and Hispanics as a percent of total employed people aged 16 or older in selected occupations, 1983 and 1998; percentage point change, 1983–98)*

| | black | | | Hispanic | | |
|---|---|---|---|---|---|---|
| | 1998 | 1983 | percentage point change, 1983–98 | 1998 | 1983 | percentage point change, 1983–98 |
| **Total, aged 16 or older** | **11.1%** | **9.3%** | **1.8** | **10.1%** | **5.3%** | **4.8** |
| Managerial and professional specialty | 7.6 | 5.6 | 2.0 | 5.0 | 2.6 | 2.4 |
| Executive, administrative, and managerial | 7.2 | 4.7 | 2.5 | 5.4 | 2.8 | 2.6 |
| Officials and admins., public admin. | 12.1 | 8.3 | 3.8 | 4.5 | 3.8 | 0.7 |
| Financial managers | 6.8 | 3.5 | 3.3 | 4.4 | 3.1 | 1.3 |
| Personnel and labor relations managers | 7.7 | 4.9 | 2.8 | 4.3 | 2.6 | 1.7 |
| Purchasing managers | 5.0 | 5.1 | –0.1 | 5.5 | 1.4 | 4.1 |
| Managers, marketing, advertising, p.r. | 3.8 | 2.7 | 1.1 | 3.4 | 1.7 | 1.7 |
| Administrators, education, related fields | 10.6 | 11.3 | –0.7 | 4.2 | 2.4 | 1.8 |
| Managers, medicine and health | 6.8 | 5.0 | 1.8 | 5.3 | 2.0 | 3.3 |
| Managers, properties and real estate | 7.1 | 5.5 | 1.6 | 9.4 | 5.2 | 4.2 |
| Professional specialty | 7.9 | 6.4 | 1.5 | 4.6 | 2.5 | 2.1 |
| Architects | 2.0 | 1.6 | 0.4 | 5.2 | 1.5 | 3.7 |
| Engineers | 4.1 | 2.7 | 1.4 | 3.8 | 2.2 | 1.6 |
| Mathematical and computer scientists | 7.2 | 5.4 | 1.8 | 4.2 | 2.6 | 1.6 |
| Natural scientists | 3.9 | 2.6 | 1.3 | 3.0 | 2.1 | 0.9 |
| Physicians | 4.9 | 3.2 | 1.7 | 4.8 | 4.5 | 0.3 |
| Dentists | 2.8 | 2.4 | 0.4 | 2.0 | 1.0 | 1.0 |
| Registered nurses | 9.3 | 6.7 | 2.6 | 3.2 | 1.8 | 1.4 |
| Pharmacists | 4.1 | 3.8 | 0.3 | 5.1 | 2.6 | 2.5 |
| Dietitians | 18.2 | 21.0 | –2.8 | 4.3 | 3.7 | 0.6 |
| Therapists | 7.3 | 7.6 | –0.3 | 3.8 | 2.7 | 1.1 |
| Teachers, college and university | 10.0 | 4.4 | 5.6 | 5.4 | 1.8 | 3.6 |
| Teachers, except college and university | 14.4 | 9.1 | 5.3 | 8.0 | 2.7 | 5.3 |
| Librarians, archivists, and curators | 5.9 | 7.8 | –1.9 | 5.4 | 1.6 | 3.8 |
| Economists | 3.6 | 6.3 | –2.7 | 6.5 | 2.7 | 3.8 |
| Psychologists | 10.2 | 8.6 | 1.6 | 4.0 | 1.1 | 2.9 |
| Social, recreation, and religious workers | 17.5 | 12.1 | 5.4 | 5.9 | 3.8 | 2.1 |
| Lawyers and judges | 4.3 | 2.7 | 1.6 | 3.0 | 1.0 | 2.0 |
| Writers, artists, entertainers, and athletes | 6.2 | 4.8 | 1.4 | 5.6 | 2.9 | 2.7 |

*(continued)*

*(continued from previous page)*

| | black | | | Hispanic | | |
|---|---|---|---|---|---|---|
| | **1998** | **1983** | **percentage point change, 1983–98** | **1998** | **1983** | **percentage point change, 1983–98** |
| Technical, sales, and administrative support | 11.1% | 7.6% | 3.5 | 8.3% | 4.3% | 4.0 |
| Health technologists and technicians | 13.9 | 12.7 | 1.2 | 7.0 | 3.1 | 3.9 |
| Engineering/related technologists/technicians | 8.6 | 6.1 | 2.5 | 7.6 | 3.5 | 4.1 |
| Science technicians | 8.8 | 6.6 | 2.2 | 5.8 | 2.8 | 3.0 |
| Technicians, excl. health, engineering, science | 7.2 | 5.0 | 2.2 | 5.6 | 2.7 | 2.9 |
| Airplane pilots and navigators | 1.9 | – | – | 2.5 | 1.6 | 0.9 |
| Computer programmers | 6.4 | 4.4 | 2.0 | 4.9 | 2.1 | 2.8 |
| Legal assistants | 8.1 | 4.3 | 3.8 | 7.2 | 3.6 | 3.6 |
| Sales occupations | 8.9 | 4.7 | 4.2 | 7.9 | 3.7 | 4.2 |
| Supervisors and proprietors | 6.5 | 3.6 | 2.9 | 6.3 | 3.4 | 2.9 |
| Sales reps., finance and business svcs. | 7.6 | 2.7 | 4.9 | 4.8 | 2.2 | 2.6 |
| Sales reps., commodities, except retail | 2.9 | 2.1 | 0.8 | 5.4 | 2.2 | 3.2 |
| Sales workers, retail and personal services | 12.5 | 6.7 | 5.8 | 10.7 | 4.8 | 5.9 |
| Admin. support occupations, incl. clerical | 13.1 | 9.6 | 3.5 | 9.0 | 5.0 | 4.0 |
| Supervisors, administrative support | 15.1 | 9.3 | 5.8 | 5.9 | 5.0 | 0.9 |
| Computer equipment operators | 14.1 | 12.5 | 1.6 | 7.1 | 6.0 | 1.1 |
| Secretaries, stenographers, and typists | 9.6 | 7.3 | 2.3 | 7.0 | 4.5 | 2.5 |
| Information clerks | 11.5 | 8.5 | 3.0 | 10.7 | 5.5 | 5.2 |
| Record processing, except financial | 14.5 | 13.9 | 0.6 | 10.6 | 4.8 | 5.8 |
| Financial record processing | 7.7 | 4.6 | 3.1 | 6.5 | 3.7 | 2.8 |
| Service occupations | 17.6 | 16.6 | 1.0 | 15.0 | 6.8 | 8.2 |
| Private household | 13.7 | 27.8 | −14.1 | 30.9 | 8.5 | 22.4 |
| Firefighting and fire prevention | 10.9 | 6.7 | 4.2 | 5.3 | 4.1 | 1.2 |
| Police and detectives | 19.4 | 13.1 | 6.3 | 8.8 | 4.0 | 4.8 |
| Food preparation and service occupations | 11.8 | 10.5 | 1.3 | 17.0 | 6.8 | 10.2 |
| Health service occupations | 30.1 | 23.5 | 6.6 | 10.0 | 4.8 | 5.2 |
| Cleaning and building service occupations | 22.8 | 24.4 | −1.6 | 20.5 | 9.2 | 11.3 |
| Personal service occupations | 13.5 | 11.1 | 2.4 | 9.8 | 6.0 | 3.8 |
| Precision production, craft, and repair | 8.0 | 6.8 | 1.2 | 12.4 | 6.2 | 6.2 |
| Mechanics and repairers | 7.9 | 6.8 | 1.1 | 10.4 | 5.3 | 5.1 |
| Construction trades | 7.1 | 6.6 | 0.5 | 14.0 | 6.0 | 8.0 |
| Precision production occupations | 9.5 | 7.3 | 2.2 | 12.7 | 7.4 | 5.3 |

*(continued)*

*(continued from previous page)*

| | black | | | Hispanic | | |
|---|---|---|---|---|---|---|
| | **1998** | **1983** | **percentage point change, 1983–98** | **1998** | **1983** | **percentage point change, 1983–98** |
| Operators, fabricators, and laborers | 15.7% | 14.0% | 1.7 | 16.0% | 8.3% | 7.7 |
| Machine operators, assemblers, inspectors | 15.4 | 14.0 | 1.4 | 17.2 | 9.4 | 7.8 |
| Transportation/material moving occupations | 16.3 | 13.0 | 3.3 | 11.9 | 5.9 | 6.0 |
| Truck drivers | 14.9 | 12.3 | 2.6 | 12.0 | 5.7 | 6.3 |
| Bus drivers | 20.3 | 22.2 | –1.9 | 11.2 | 7.0 | 4.2 |
| Taxicab drivers and chauffeurs | 26.5 | 19.6 | 6.9 | 15.0 | 8.6 | 6.4 |
| Handlers, equipment cleaners, helpers, and laborers | 15.6 | 15.1 | 0.5 | 18.4 | 8.6 | 9.8 |
| Farming, forestry, and fishing | 4.9 | 7.5 | –2.6 | 22.6 | 8.2 | 14.4 |

*Note: (–) means less than 0.5 percent.*
*Source: Bureau of Labor Statistics,* Employment and Earnings, *January 1999; calculations by New Strategist*

# Women's Jobs More Concentrated Than Men's

**Both men and women are most likely to be managers and professionals in the service industries, however.**

Among both women and men, the largest share of workers by industry and occupation are managers or professionals in the service industries—13 percent of employed men and 21 percent of employed women. The service industries are wide-ranging and include hotels and motels, beauty shops, advertising agencies, computer operations, repair shops, amusement parks, health clubs, hospitals, law firms, public and private schools, social service agencies, and accounting firms. Service industry managers and professionals include nurses, teachers, lawyers, and people running Internet start-ups.

No other industry/occupation combination accounts for more than 1 in 10 working men. Among working women, 14 percent are technical, sales, or administrative support workers in the service industries; 13 percent are technical, sales, or administrative support workers in wholesale trade; and 12 percent are service workers in the service industries.

◆ The distribution of working women by occupation and industry could become less concentrated as well-educated younger women get jobs in industries and occupations traditionally dominated by men.

# Employment of Men by Industry and Occupation, 1998

*(number and percent distribution of employed men aged 16 or older by industry and occupation, 1998; numbers in thousands)*

| | total | managerial and prof. specialty | technical, sales, admin. support | service | precision prod., craft & repair | oper- ators, fabri- cators | farming, forestry, fishing |
|---|---|---|---|---|---|---|---|
| **Total employed men** | **70,693** | **19,867** | **13,793** | **7,221** | **13,208** | **13,769** | **2,836** |
| Agriculture | 2,553 | 133 | 32 | 12 | 38 | 73 | 2,266 |
| Mining | 535 | 135 | 36 | 6 | 205 | 151 | 1 |
| Construction | 7,721 | 1,255 | 132 | 19 | 4,809 | 1,484 | 21 |
| Manufacturing | 14,138 | 3,544 | 1,660 | 213 | 3,319 | 5,330 | 72 |
| Transportation/public utilities | 6,598 | 1,248 | 1,386 | 137 | 1,214 | 2,601 | 12 |
| Wholesale/retail trade | 14,367 | 1,735 | 6,068 | 2,460 | 1,323 | 2,734 | 47 |
| Finance/insurance/real estate | 3,552 | 1,337 | 1,746 | 226 | 167 | 32 | 46 |
| Services | 17,906 | 9,252 | 2,311 | 2,746 | 1,963 | 1,283 | 351 |
| Public administration | 3,323 | 1,228 | 422 | 1,402 | 170 | 81 | 20 |
| **Total employed men** | **100.0%** | **28.1%** | **19.5%** | **10.2%** | **18.7%** | **19.5%** | **4.0%** |
| Agriculture | 3.6 | 0.2 | 0.0 | 0.0 | 0.1 | 0.1 | 3.2 |
| Mining | 0.8 | 0.2 | 0.1 | 0.0 | 0.3 | 0.2 | 0.0 |
| Construction | 10.9 | 1.8 | 0.2 | 0.0 | 6.8 | 2.1 | 0.0 |
| Manufacturing | 20.0 | 5.0 | 2.3 | 0.3 | 4.7 | 7.5 | 0.1 |
| Transportation/public utilities | 9.3 | 1.8 | 2.0 | 0.2 | 1.7 | 3.7 | 0.0 |
| Wholesale/retail trade | 20.3 | 2.5 | 8.6 | 3.5 | 1.9 | 3.9 | 0.1 |
| Finance/insurance/real estate | 5.0 | 1.9 | 2.5 | 0.3 | 0.2 | 0.0 | 0.1 |
| Services | 25.3 | 13.1 | 3.3 | 3.9 | 2.8 | 1.8 | 0.5 |
| Public administration | 4.7 | 1.7 | 0.6 | 2.0 | 0.2 | 0.1 | 0.0 |

*Source: Bureau of Labor Statistics,* Employment and Earnings, *January 1999; calculations by New Strategist*

# Employment of Women by Industry and Occupation, 1998

*(number and percent distribution of employed women aged 16 or older by industry and occupation, 1998; numbers in thousands)*

| | total | managerial and prof. specialty | technical, sales, admin. support | service | precision prod., craft & repair | oper- ators, fabri- cators | farming, forestry, fishing |
|---|---|---|---|---|---|---|---|
| **Total employed women** | **60,771** | **19,071** | **24,729** | **10,614** | **1,203** | **4,484** | **667** |
| Agriculture | 825 | 81 | 178 | 9 | – | 8 | 548 |
| Mining | 85 | 29 | 49 | 2 | 2 | 3 | – |
| Construction | 798 | 268 | 385 | 9 | 80 | 54 | 1 |
| Manufacturing | 6,595 | 1,470 | 1,733 | 78 | 638 | 2,672 | 4 |
| Transportation/public utilities | 2,709 | 620 | 1,559 | 159 | 71 | 299 | 1 |
| Wholesale/retail trade | 12,836 | 1,393 | 7,717 | 2,722 | 199 | 749 | 55 |
| Finance/insurance/real estate | 5,053 | 1,509 | 3,423 | 97 | 10 | 10 | 3 |
| Services | 29,306 | 12,632 | 8,544 | 7,218 | 191 | 672 | 48 |
| Public administration | 2,564 | 1,069 | 1,141 | 320 | 12 | 17 | 7 |
| **Total employed women** | **100.0%** | **31.4%** | **40.7%** | **17.5%** | **2.0%** | **7.4%** | **1.1%** |
| Agriculture | 1.4 | 0.1 | 0.3 | 0.0 | – | 0.0 | 0.9 |
| Mining | 0.1 | 0.0 | 0.1 | 0.0 | 0.0 | 0.0 | – |
| Construction | 1.3 | 0.4 | 0.6 | 0.0 | 0.1 | 0.1 | 0.0 |
| Manufacturing | 10.9 | 2.4 | 2.9 | 0.1 | 1.0 | 4.4 | 0.0 |
| Transportation/public utilities | 4.5 | 1.0 | 2.6 | 0.3 | 0.1 | 0.5 | 0.0 |
| Wholesale/retail trade | 21.1 | 2.3 | 12.7 | 4.5 | 0.3 | 1.2 | 0.1 |
| Finance/insurance/real estate | 8.3 | 2.5 | 5.6 | 0.2 | 0.0 | 0.0 | 0.0 |
| Services | 48.2 | 20.8 | 14.1 | 11.9 | 0.3 | 1.1 | 0.1 |
| Public administration | 4.2 | 1.8 | 1.9 | 0.5 | 0.0 | 0.0 | 0.0 |

*Note: (–) means sample is too small to make a reliable estimate.*
*Source: Bureau of Labor Statistics,* Employment and Earnings, *January 1999; calculations by New Strategist*

# Job Tenure Falls

## Decline was greatest among 55-to-64-year-olds.

As layoffs become commonplace and corporate loyalty wanes, job tenure—the number of years workers have been with their current employer—is on the decline. Since 1983, median job tenure has fallen from 5.0 to 4.7 years. The biggest decline has been among workers aged 55 to 64. In 1983, workers in this age group had been with their current employer a median of 12.2 years. By 1998, the figure was 10.1 years. Job tenure fell nearly two years for workers aged 65 or older, and by more than one year for those aged 45 to 54.

Job tenure declines when workers voluntarily switch jobs or when they are laid off and forced to find new jobs. The fact that job tenure has declined most among older workers points toward involuntary layoffs as the biggest factor.

♦ For many companies, laying off older, highly paid workers and replacing them with younger workers at a lower salary can boost the bottom line. With the baby-boom generation fast becoming the nation's older workers, expect to hear more complaints about this practice in the future.

# Job Tenure by Age, 1983 and 1998

*(median number of years workers aged 25 or older have been with their current employer by age; 1983 and 1998; change in years, 1983–98)*

| | 1998 | 1983 | change in years 1983–98 |
|---|---|---|---|
| **Total workers** | **4.7** | **5.0** | **–0.3** |
| Aged 25 to 34 | 2.7 | 3.0 | –0.3 |
| Aged 35 to 44 | 5.0 | 5.2 | –0.2 |
| Aged 45 to 54 | 8.1 | 9.5 | –1.4 |
| Aged 55 to 64 | 10.1 | 12.2 | –2.1 |
| Aged 65 or older | 7.8 | 9.6 | –1.8 |

*Source: Bureau of Labor Statistics, Internet web site <http://www.bls.gov/news.release/tenure.t01.htm>; calculations by New Strategist*

# Older Workers Most Likely to Be Self-Employed

## Nearly 9 million Americans were self-employed in 1998.

Of the 128 million Americans employed in nonagricultural industries, only 9 million are self-employed—or 7 percent. This figure underestimates the number of people who work for themselves because it excludes those who have a business on the side that is not their primary source of income. It also excludes sole proprietorships that are incorporated.

Self-employment rises with age, from fewer than 1 percent of workers aged 16 to 19 to 19 percent of workers aged 65 or older. Many older self-employed workers are retired from a primary career and have started a business to supplement their retirement income. Although workers aged 65 or older are most likely to be self-employed, they account for only 7 percent of the self-employed because few people aged 65 or older work.

♦ Self-employment is likely to become more common in the years ahead as the baby-boom generation ages, and as technology allows people to do more on their own.

### Self-employment rises with age

*(percent of workers employed in nonagricultural industries who are self-employed, by age, 1998)*

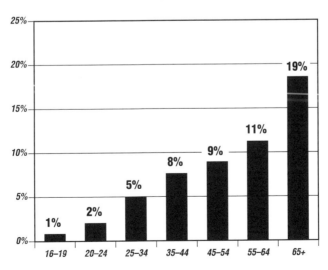

# Self-Employed Workers by Age, 1998

*(number of workers aged 16 or older employed in nonagricultural industries, number and percent who are self-employed, and percent distribution of self-employed by age, 1998; numbers in thousands)*

| | total workers | self-employed number | self-employed percent of total | self-employed percent distribution |
|---|---|---|---|---|
| **Total aged 16 or older** | **128,084** | **8,962** | **7.0%** | **100.0%** |
| Aged 16 to 19 | 6,791 | 57 | 0.8 | 0.6 |
| Aged 20 to 24 | 12,218 | 242 | 2.0 | 2.7 |
| Aged 25 to 34 | 30,677 | 1,513 | 4.9 | 16.9 |
| Aged 35 to 44 | 35,486 | 2,710 | 7.6 | 30.2 |
| Aged 45 to 54 | 26,991 | 2,403 | 8.9 | 26.8 |
| Aged 55 to 64 | 12,477 | 1,399 | 11.2 | 15.6 |
| Aged 65 or older | 3,448 | 639 | 18.5 | 7.1 |

*Source: Bureau of Labor Statistics,* Employment and Earnings, *January 1999; calculations by New Strategist*

# More Than 12 Million Alternative Workers

## Ten percent of working Americans do not have traditional jobs.

Nontraditional workers are defined as independent contractors, on-call workers (such as substitute teachers), workers for temporary-help agencies, or workers provided by contract firms (such as lawn service companies). These workers are considered alternative because they are not employees of the organization for which they perform their services, nor do they necessarily work standard schedules.

Two out of three alternative workers are independent contractors—freelancers, consultants, and others who obtain customers on their own for whom they provide a product or service. The likelihood of being an independent contractor increases with age to a peak of 16 percent among workers aged 65 or older. The likelihood of being an on-call worker, such as a substitute teacher or construction worker, is greatest among the youngest and oldest workers, at more than 3 percent. Temp work is slightly more prevalent among the young, while contract work varies little by age.

Most independent contractors prefer their alternative work. But other types of alternative workers would prefer a more traditional job, according to the Bureau of Labor Statistics.

◆ As the large baby-boom generation ages into its fifties and sixties, the number of independent contractors will surge.

# Workers in Alternative Work Arrangements by Age, 1997

*(number of employed workers aged 16 or older, and number and percent of employed workers in alternative work arrangements, by age, 1997; numbers in thousands)*

| | | alternative workers | | | | |
| --- | --- | --- | --- | --- | --- | --- |
| | total | total | independent contractors | on-call workers | temporary-help agency workers | workers provided by contract firms |
| **Total employed** | 126,742 | 12,561 | 8,456 | 1,996 | 1,300 | 809 |
| Aged 16 to 19 | 6,031 | 354 | 66 | 193 | 79 | 16 |
| Aged 20 to 24 | 11,958 | 723 | 206 | 237 | 214 | 66 |
| Aged 25 to 34 | 31,647 | 2,668 | 1,549 | 448 | 394 | 277 |
| Aged 35 to 44 | 35,282 | 3,670 | 2,631 | 508 | 279 | 252 |
| Aged 45 to 54 | 26,146 | 2,851 | 2,237 | 288 | 211 | 115 |
| Aged 55 to 64 | 12,032 | 1,515 | 1,173 | 193 | 87 | 62 |
| Aged 65 or older | 3,646 | 783 | 595 | 129 | 37 | 22 |
| **Total employed** | 100.0% | 9.9% | 6.7% | 1.6% | 1.0% | 0.6% |
| Aged 16 to 19 | 100.0 | 5.9 | 1.1 | 3.2 | 1.3 | 0.3 |
| Aged 20 to 24 | 100.0 | 6.0 | 1.7 | 2.0 | 1.8 | 0.6 |
| Aged 25 to 34 | 100.0 | 8.4 | 4.9 | 1.4 | 1.2 | 0.9 |
| Aged 35 to 44 | 100.0 | 10.4 | 7.5 | 1.4 | 0.8 | 0.7 |
| Aged 45 to 54 | 100.0 | 10.9 | 8.6 | 1.1 | 0.8 | 0.4 |
| Aged 55 to 64 | 100.0 | 12.6 | 9.7 | 1.6 | 0.7 | 0.5 |
| Aged 65 or older | 100.0 | 21.5 | 16.3 | 3.5 | 1.0 | 0.6 |

*Note: Independent contractors are workers who obtain customers on their own to provide a product or service, including the self-employed. On-call workers are in a pool of workers who are called to work only as needed, such as substitute teachers and construction workers supplied by a union hiring hall. Temporary-help agency workers are those who said they are paid by a temporary-help agency. Workers provided by contract firms are those employed by a company that provides employees or their services to others under contract, such as security, landscaping, and computer programming.*
*Source: Bureau of Labor Statistics,* Contingent and Alternative Employment Arrangements, *February 1997, Internet web site <http://stats.bls.gov/newsrels.htm>; calculations by New Strategist*

# More Than 3 Million Americans Are Paid to Work at Home

## The number of employees paid to work at home is growing rapidly.

Twenty-one million people employed in nonagricultural industries spend at least a few hours a week working at home. Most are wage and salary workers who are not paid for the time they spend working at home—they are the ones lugging a briefcase full of papers home with them to finish a project after hours.

A growing minority of people who work at home are paid for doing so, however. Seventeen percent of people who work at home are wage and salary workers paid by their employer for the time they log. These home workers numbered 3.6 million in 1997, up from 1.9 million in 1991, according to the Bureau of Labor Statistics. Another 19 percent of home workers are the home-based self-employed.

Most of the workers who are paid to work at home are in white-collar occupations, including nearly 2 million in managerial or professional specialty occupations. Sales and administrative support workers paid to work at home number more than 1 million. Among the major industry groups, the services industry was the only one that paid more than 1 million wage and salary workers to work at home. Whites are more than twice as likely as blacks and Hispanics to work at home for pay.

♦ The number of workers paid to work at home will continue to grow rapidly as employers awaken to the potential savings in overhead costs.

# People Who Work at Home, 1997

*(number and percent of people aged 16 or older employed in nonagricultural industries who work at home on their primary job, by sex, occupation, industry, race, Hispanic origin, and pay status, 1997; numbers in thousands)*

| | total who work at home | | wage and salary workers who work at home for pay | | home-based self-employed | |
|---|---|---|---|---|---|---|
| | number | percent of total workers | number | percent of home workers | number | percent of home workers |
| Total aged 16 or older | 21,478 | 17.8% | 3,644 | 17.0% | 4,125 | 19.2% |
| Men | 11,202 | 17.3 | 1,683 | 15.0 | 2,157 | 19.3 |
| Women | 10,275 | 18.3 | 1,960 | 19.1 | 1,968 | 19.2 |
| **Occupation** | | | | | | |
| Managerial and professional specialty | 13,120 | 36.7 | 1,836 | 14.0 | 1,714 | 13.1 |
| Executive, administrative, and managerial | 5,940 | 34.0 | 867 | 14.6 | 1,014 | 17.1 |
| Professional specialty | 7,180 | 39.2 | 969 | 13.5 | 700 | 9.7 |
| Technical, sales, and administrative support | 5,457 | 15.0 | 1,363 | 25.0 | 1,016 | 18.6 |
| Technicians and related support | 417 | 10.6 | 112 | 26.9 | 36 | 8.6 |
| Sales occupations | 3,356 | 22.4 | 640 | 19.1 | 722 | 21.5 |
| Administrative support, including clerical | 1,684 | 9.7 | 611 | 36.3 | 259 | 15.4 |
| Service occupations | 1,250 | 7.2 | 256 | 20.5 | 616 | 49.3 |
| Precision production, craft, and repair | 1,145 | 8.2 | 116 | 10.1 | 564 | 49.2 |
| Operators, fabricators, and laborers | 506 | 2.9 | 73 | 14.4 | 215 | 42.5 |
| **Industry** | | | | | | |
| Mining | 73 | 12.3 | – | – | – | – |
| Construction | 1,330 | 16.2 | 136 | 10.2 | 726 | 54.6 |
| Manufacturing | 2,318 | 11.5 | 517 | 22.3 | 193 | 8.3 |
| Transportation and public utilities | 963 | 10.9 | 205 | 21.3 | 132 | 13.7 |
| Wholesale trade | 1,202 | 24.4 | 343 | 28.5 | 185 | 15.4 |
| Retail trade | 1,964 | 9.2 | 289 | 14.7 | 532 | 27.1 |
| Finance, insurance, and real estate | 2,008 | 25.7 | 330 | 16.4 | 291 | 14.5 |
| Services | 10,954 | 25.1 | 1,616 | 14.8 | 2,054 | 18.8 |
| Public administration | 666 | 12.3 | 196 | 29.4 | – | – |
| **Race and Hispanic origin** | | | | | | |
| White | 19,646 | 19.2 | 3,345 | 17.0 | 3,868 | 19.7 |
| Black | 1,117 | 8.5 | 185 | 16.6 | 135 | 12.1 |
| Hispanic | 830 | 7.2 | 145 | 17.5 | 156 | 18.8 |

*Note: Numbers will not add to total because wage and salary workers who work at home but are not paid for doing so are not shown. (–) means data are not available.*
*Source: Bureau of Labor Statistics,* Work at Home in 1997, *USDL 98-93, Internet web site <http://stats.bls .gov/>; calculations by New Strategist*

# Few Benefits for Part-Time Workers

**A minority of part-time workers receive paid vacations, health insurance, or retirement benefits.**

Not surprisingly, large firms offer a broader range of employee benefits than small firms, according to the Bureau of Labor Statistics. But neither large nor small firms offer much to their part-time workers. Most large firms—those with at least 100 workers—offer paid vacations (95 percent), health insurance (76 percent), and retirement plans (79 percent). Among small firms, most offer paid vacations (86 percent) and health insurance (64 percent), while only 46 percent have any kind of retirement plan. Nonproduction bonuses are the only benefit more common at small companies than at large ones—perhaps to make up for the lack of other benefits.

At large firms, a 44 percent minority of part-time employees receive paid vacations, only 21 percent receive health insurance, and just 34 percent have retirement plans. The proportions are even lower for part-time workers at small firms. Nonproduction bonuses are the only benefit more widely available to part-timers at small firms (26 percent) than at large firms (17 percent).

◆ More Americans would choose part-time work if benefits for part-timers were more widely available.

# Employee Benefits for Full- and Part-Time Workers by Size of Firm, 1996–97

*(percent of employees in private, nonfarm industries offered selected employee benefits, by size of firm and full- or part-time employment status, 1996–97)*

| | medium and large firms | | small firms | |
|---|---|---|---|---|
| | full-time | part-time | full-time | part-time |
| **Paid time off** | | | | |
| Holidays | 89% | 40% | 80% | 24% |
| Vacations | 95 | 44 | 86 | 30 |
| Personal leave | 20 | 9 | 14 | 5 |
| Funeral leave | 81 | 34 | 51 | 16 |
| Jury duty leave | 87 | 37 | 59 | 23 |
| Military leave | 47 | 9 | 18 | 5 |
| Family leave | 2 | – | 2 | 1 |
| **Unpaid time off** | | | | |
| Family leave | 93 | 54 | – | – |
| **Disability benefits** | | | | |
| Paid sick leave | 56 | 18 | 50 | 10 |
| Short-term disability coverage | 55 | 18 | 29 | 13 |
| Long-term disability insurance | 43 | 4 | 22 | 2 |
| **Insurance** | | | | |
| Medical care | 76 | 21 | 64 | 6 |
| Dental care | 59 | 16 | 31 | 4 |
| Vision care | 26 | 9 | – | – |
| Life | 87 | 18 | 62 | 7 |
| **Retirement** | | | | |
| Any retirement plan* | 79 | 34 | 46 | 13 |
| Defined benefit plans | 50 | 17 | 15 | 4 |
| Defined contribution plans | 57 | 23 | 38 | 10 |
| Savings and thrift | 39 | 13 | 23 | 4 |
| Deferred profit sharing | 13 | 7 | 12 | 5 |
| Employee stock ownership | 4 | – | 1 | – |
| Money purchase pension | 8 | – | 4 | 2 |
| **Tax-deferred savings arrangements** | | | | |
| With employer contributions | 46 | 15 | 24 | 5 |
| Without employer contributions | 9 | 4 | 4 | 2 |

*(continued)*

*(continued from previous page)*

| | medium and large firms | | small firms | |
|---|---|---|---|---|
| | *full-time* | *part-time* | *full-time* | *part-time* |
| **Income continuation plans** | | | | |
| Severance pay | 36% | 10% | 15% | 2% |
| Supplemental unemployment benefits | 5 | – | – | – |
| **Family benefits** | | | | |
| Child care | 10 | 7 | 2 | 2 |
| Adoption assistance | 10 | 3 | 1 | – |
| Long-term care insurance | 7 | 3 | 1 | – |
| Flexible workplace | 2 | – | 1 | 1 |
| **Health promotion programs** | | | | |
| Wellness | 36 | 17 | 8 | 6 |
| Employee assistance | 61 | 36 | 14 | 9 |
| Fitness center | 21 | 11 | 4 | 3 |
| **Miscellaneous benefits** | | | | |
| Job-related travel accident insurance | 42 | 18 | 12 | 4 |
| Nonproduction bonuses | 42 | 17 | 44 | 26 |
| Subsidized commuting | 6 | 2 | 1 | – |
| Educational assistance, total | – | 34 | – | – |
|   Job related | 67 | – | 38 | 13 |
|   Not job related | 20 | – | 5 | 2 |
| Section 125 cafeteria benefits | 52 | 15 | 23 | 4 |
| Flexible benefit plans | 13 | 3 | 4 | 1 |
| Reimbursement plans | 32 | 11 | 12 | 3 |
| Premium conversion plans | 7 | 1 | 7 | 1 |

*\* Includes defined benefit and defined contribution plans. Some employees participate in both types, but are counted just once in any retirement plan.*
*Note: Data for small firms—those employing fewer than 100 workers—are for 1996; data for medium and large firms—those employing 100 or more workers—are for 1997. (–) means data not available.*
*Source: Bureau of Labor Statistics,* Employee Benefits in Medium and Large Private Establishments, *1997; and* Employee Benefits in Small Private Establishments, *1996, Internet web site <http://stats.bls.gov/ebshome.htm>*

# Early Retirement Trend to End

## The number of working men and women aged 55 to 59 is projected to rise substantially between 1996 and 2006

Among men aged 55 to 59, labor force participation will rise from 78 to 79 percent between 1996 and 2006. This small increase signals that the decades-long trend toward early retirement is coming to an end. With the nation's businesses trimming costs, early retirement incentives will no longer be available to older workers.

The labor force participation rate of women will continue to rise in all but the youngest age group during the next decade. The rate is projected to decline among women under age 20 as more go to college.

The number of older workers is projected to expand as the baby-boom generation enters its fifties. The number of working women aged 55 to 59 should rise an enormous 74 percent between 1996 and 2006. The number of working men in the age group should increase 58 percent.

◆ While it will become less common for workers to retire in their fifties, many will retire before age 65.

### More fiftysomethings at work

*(percent change in number of men in the civilian labor force, by age, 1996–2006)*

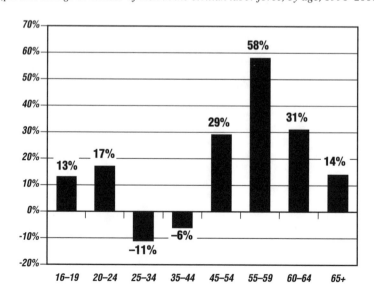

# Labor Force Projections by Sex and Age, 1996 to 2006

*(number and percent of people aged 16 or older in the civilian labor force by sex and age, 1996 and 2006; percent change in number and percentage point change in rate 1996–2006; numbers in thousands)*

| | number | | | participation rate | | |
|---|---|---|---|---|---|---|
| | *1996* | *2006* | *percent change 1996–2006* | *1996* | *2006* | *percentage point change 1996–2006* |
| **Total labor force** | **133,943** | **148,847** | **11.1%** | **66.8%** | **67.1%** | **0.3** |
| **Total men in labor force** | **72,087** | **78,226** | **8.5** | **74.9** | **73.1** | **−1.8** |
| Aged 16 to 19 | 4,043 | 4,551 | 12.6 | 53.2 | 51.5 | −1.7 |
| Aged 20 to 24 | 7,104 | 8,297 | 16.8 | 82.5 | 81.1 | −1.4 |
| Aged 25 to 34 | 18,431 | 16,469 | −10.6 | 93.2 | 92.5 | −0.7 |
| Aged 35 to 44 | 19,602 | 18,478 | −5.7 | 92.4 | 90.7 | −1.7 |
| Aged 45 to 54 | 13,967 | 17,961 | 28.6 | 89.1 | 87.7 | −1.4 |
| Aged 55 to 59 | 4,184 | 6,622 | 58.3 | 77.9 | 78.7 | 0.8 |
| Aged 60 to 64 | 2,510 | 3,297 | 31.4 | 54.3 | 54.0 | −0.3 |
| Aged 65 or older | 2,247 | 2,551 | 13.5 | 16.9 | 17.3 | 0.4 |
| **Total women in labor force** | **61,857** | **70,620** | **14.2** | **59.3** | **61.4** | **2.1** |
| Aged 16 to 19 | 3,763 | 4,373 | 16.2 | 51.3 | 51.0 | −0.3 |
| Aged 20 to 24 | 6,273 | 7,197 | 14.7 | 71.3 | 71.8 | 0.5 |
| Aged 25 to 34 | 15,403 | 14,373 | −6.7 | 75.2 | 77.6 | 2.4 |
| Aged 35 to 44 | 16,954 | 16,977 | 0.1 | 77.5 | 80.2 | 2.7 |
| Aged 45 to 54 | 12,430 | 17,196 | 38.3 | 75.4 | 79.9 | 4.5 |
| Aged 55 to 59 | 3,474 | 6,047 | 74.1 | 59.8 | 66.6 | 6.8 |
| Aged 60 to 64 | 1,978 | 2,787 | 40.9 | 38.2 | 41.3 | 3.1 |
| Aged 65 or older | 1,581 | 1,670 | 5.6 | 8.6 | 8.7 | 0.1 |

*Source: Bureau of Labor Statistics,* Monthly Labor Review, *November 1997*

# Workers to Become More Diverse

## Non-Hispanic whites will decline as a share of workers.

Between 1996 and 2006, the civilian labor force will grow 11 percent, to 149 million, according to projections by the Bureau of Labor Statistics. The number of minority workers will grow much faster than that of non-Hispanic white workers. Asian workers will see a 41 percent gain, climbing to more than 8 million. Hispanic workers will grow 36 percent, to 17 million. Black workers will expand 14 percent and number slightly fewer than Hispanic workers in 2006. In that year, minorities will account for more than one in four workers.

Non-Hispanic white men will account for only 38 percent of the labor force in 2006, down from 41 percent in 1996. As older workers retire and are replaced by more diverse younger workers, non-Hispanic white men will account for 39 percent of those leaving the labor force and for a smaller 31 percent of those joining the labor force.

Non-Hispanic white women will account for another 31 percent of workers entering the labor force between 1996 and 2006. Blacks will account for 16 percent, Hispanics 15 percent, and Asians 8 percent.

◆ Businesses that have not already done so need to prepare for a diverse workplace. It will be especially important to recruit and retain women and minority workers.

# Labor Force Projections by Race and Hispanic Origin, 1996 to 2006

*(number and percent distribution of people aged 16 or older in the civilian labor force by race and Hispanic origin, 1996 and 2006; percent change in number and percentage point change in distribution, 1996–2006; numbers in thousands)*

| | number | | | participation rate | | |
|---|---|---|---|---|---|---|
| | *1996* | *2006* | *percent change 1996–2006* | *1996* | *2006* | *percentage point change 1996–2006* |
| **Total in labor force** | **133,943** | **148,847** | **11.1%** | **100.0%** | **100.0%** | – |
| **Race** | | | | | | |
| White | 113,108 | 123,581 | 9.3 | 84.4 | 83.0 | –1.4 |
| Black | 15,134 | 17,225 | 13.8 | 11.3 | 11.6 | 0.3 |
| Asian and other | 5,703 | 8,041 | 41.0 | 4.3 | 5.4 | 1.1 |
| **Hispanic origin** | | | | | | |
| Non-Hispanic | 121,169 | 131,446 | 8.5 | 90.5 | 88.3 | –2.2 |
| White, non-Hispanic | 100,915 | 108,166 | 7.2 | 75.3 | 72.7 | –2.7 |
| Hispanic | 12,774 | 17,401 | 36.2 | 9.5 | 11.7 | 2.2 |

*Source: Bureau of Labor Statistics,* Monthly Labor Review, *November 1997*

# Workers Entering and Leaving the Labor Force, 1996 to 2006

*(number and percent of people aged 16 or older in the civilian labor force, 1996 and 2006; number and percent distribution of labor force entrants and leavers, 1996 to 2006; by sex, race, and Hispanic origin; numbers in thousands)*

| | total labor force, 1996 | entrants 1996–2006 | leavers 1996–2006 | total labor force, 2006 |
|---|---|---|---|---|
| **TOTAL NUMBER** | **133,944** | **39,670** | **24,768** | **148,847** |
| Men | 72,087 | 19,978 | 13,839 | 78,226 |
| Women | 61,857 | 19,692 | 10,929 | 70,620 |
| **White, non-Hispanic** | **100,915** | **24,214** | **16,963** | **108,166** |
| Men | 54,451 | 12,132 | 9,728 | 56,856 |
| Women | 46,464 | 12,082 | 7,236 | 51,310 |
| **Black, non-Hispanic** | **14,795** | **6,191** | **5,003** | **15,983** |
| Men | 7,091 | 2,807 | 2,550 | 7,347 |
| Women | 7,704 | 3,384 | 2,453 | 8,636 |
| **Asian and other, non-Hispanic** | **5,459** | **3,346** | **1,508** | **7,296** |
| Men | 2,899 | 1,674 | 785 | 3,788 |
| Women | 2,561 | 1,671 | 724 | 3,508 |
| **Hispanic** | **12,774** | **5,920** | **1,293** | **17,401** |
| Men | 7,646 | 3,365 | 776 | 10,235 |
| Women | 5,128 | 2,555 | 516 | 7,166 |
| **TOTAL PERCENT** | **100.0%** | **100.0%** | **100.0%** | **100.0%** |
| Men | 53.8 | 50.4 | 55.9 | 52.6 |
| Women | 46.2 | 49.6 | 44.1 | 47.4 |
| **White, non-Hispanic** | **75.3** | **61.0** | **68.5** | **72.7** |
| Men | 40.7 | 30.6 | 39.3 | 38.2 |
| Women | 34.7 | 30.5 | 29.2 | 34.5 |
| **Black, non-Hispanic** | **11.0** | **15.6** | **20.2** | **10.7** |
| Men | 5.3 | 7.1 | 10.3 | 4.9 |
| Women | 5.8 | 8.5 | 9.9 | 5.8 |
| **Asian and other, non-Hispanic** | **4.1** | **8.4** | **6.1** | **4.9** |
| Men | 2.2 | 4.2 | 3.2 | 2.5 |
| Women | 1.9 | 4.2 | 2.9 | 2.4 |
| **Hispanic** | **9.5** | **14.9** | **5.2** | **11.7** |
| Men | 5.7 | 8.5 | 3.1 | 6.9 |
| Women | 3.8 | 6.4 | 2.1 | 4.8 |

*Source: Bureau of Labor Statistics,* Monthly Labor Review, *November 1997*

# White-Collar Jobs to Grow Fastest

## Computer specialists will be in greatest demand.

Employment in professional specialty and technical jobs will grow the fastest overall between 1996 and 2006, according to projections by the Bureau of Labor Statistics. Professional specialty jobs are projected to grow 27 percent during those years, while technical jobs should gain 20 percent. In contrast, precision production jobs will grow only 7 percent more numerous.

A look at the occupations projected to grow the fastest shows computer specialists to be in great demand. The number of database administrators, computer support specialists, computer engineers, and system analysts should more than double in the 10 years between 1996 and 2006. Other fast-growing occupations include health care jobs such as physical therapy assistants and home health aides.

Some of the occupations expected to gain the greatest number of jobs between 1996 and 2006 are far from glamorous. Number one on the list is cashier, with the number of cashiers projected to increase more than half a million. Other big gainers are retail salespersons, truck drivers, teacher aides, and receptionists.

♦ One problem for the future economy is how to fill the many low-paying service jobs that are begging for workers. A potential source of workers is immigration.

# Projections of Employment by Occupation, 1996 and 2006

*(number of people aged 16 or older employed by major occupational group, 1996 and 2006; percent change, 1996–2006; numbers in thousands)*

|  | 1996 | 2006 | percent change 1996–2006 |
|---|---|---|---|
| **Total employed** | **132,353** | **150,927** | **14.0%** |
| Executive, administrative, and managerial | 13,542 | 15,866 | 17.2 |
| Professional specialty | 18,173 | 22,998 | 26.6 |
| Technicians and related support | 4,618 | 5,558 | 20.4 |
| Marketing and sales | 14,633 | 16,897 | 15.5 |
| Administrative support, including clerical | 24,019 | 25,825 | 7.5 |
| Service | 21,294 | 25,147 | 18.1 |
| Agriculture, forestry, fishing | 3,785 | 3,823 | 1.0 |
| Precision production, craft, and repair | 14,446 | 15,448 | 6.9 |
| Operators, fabricators, and laborers | 17,843 | 19,365 | 8.5 |

*Source: Bureau of Labor Statistics,* Monthly Labor Review, *November 1997*

# Fastest-Growing Occupations, 1996 to 2006

*(number of people aged 16 or older employed in occupations with the largest percentage increase in employment, 1996–2006; numerical and percent change in employment, 1996–2006; ranked by percent change; numbers in thousands)*

| | | | change, 1996–2006 | |
| --- | --- | --- | --- | --- |
| | *1996* | *2006* | *number* | *percent* |
| Database administrators, computer support specialists, and all other computer scientists | 212 | 461 | 249 | 117.5% |
| Computer engineers | 216 | 451 | 235 | 108.8 |
| System analysts | 506 | 1025 | 519 | 102.6 |
| Personal and home care aides | 202 | 374 | 172 | 85.1 |
| Physical and corrective therapy assistants and aides | 84 | 151 | 66 | 79.0 |
| Home health aides | 495 | 873 | 378 | 76.4 |
| Medical assistants | 225 | 391 | 166 | 73.8 |
| Desktop publishing specialists | 30 | 53 | 22 | 74.0 |
| Physical therapists | 115 | 196 | 81 | 71.0 |
| Occupational therapy assistants and aides | 16 | 26 | 11 | 69.0 |

*Source: Bureau of Labor Statistics,* Monthly Labor Review, *November 1997*

# Occupations with Largest Job Gains, 1996 to 2006

*(number of people aged 16 or older employed in occupations with the largest job gains, 1996–2006; numerical and percent change in employment, 1996–2006; ranked by numerical change; numbers in thousands)*

| | 1996 | 2006 | change, 1996–2006 number | change, 1996–2006 percent |
|---|---|---|---|---|
| Cashiers | 3,146 | 3,677 | 530 | 16.8% |
| System analysts | 506 | 1,025 | 520 | 102.7 |
| General managers and top executives | 3,210 | 3,677 | 467 | 14.5 |
| Registered nurses | 1,971 | 2,382 | 411 | 20.9 |
| Salespersons, retail | 4,072 | 4,481 | 408 | 10.0 |
| Truck drivers | 2,719 | 3,123 | 404 | 14.9 |
| Home health aides | 495 | 873 | 378 | 76.4 |
| Teacher aides and educational assistants | 981 | 1,352 | 370 | 37.8 |
| Nursing aides, orderlies, and attendants | 1,312 | 1,645 | 333 | 25.4 |
| Receptionists and information clerks | 1,074 | 1,392 | 318 | 29.6 |
| Teachers, secondary school | 1,406 | 1,718 | 312 | 22.1 |

*Source: Bureau of Labor Statistics,* Monthly Labor Review, *November 1997*

# Big Gain for Service Industries

**Employment in the service industries will grow twice as fast as total employment between 1996 and 2006.**

The number of jobs in the service industries will expand 33.5 percent between 1996 and 2006. According to the Bureau of Labor Statistics, the specific services projected to grow the fastest include computer and data processing, health care, management and public relations, water and sanitation, and amusement and recreation.

Goods-producing jobs are projected to increase only 0.1 percent between 1996 and 2006, and will account for 16 percent of all jobs in the year 2006. Manufacturing employment is projected to fall 2 percent and mining employment will lose a substantial 23 percent.

The number of agricultural workers should fall 0.7 percent between 1996 and 2006, while private household workers will decline 16.5 percent. The number of nonagricultural self-employed will climb 13 percent, slightly below overall growth in employment.

♦ These projections are based on current trends. Unforeseen technological breakthroughs or major new government programs could shift growth from one industry to another during the next decade.

# Projections of Employment by Industry, 1996 and 2006

*(number of people aged 16 or older employed by major industry, 1996 and 2006; percent change, 1996–2006; numbers in thousands)*

| | 1996 | 2006 | percent change 1996–2006 |
|---|---|---|---|
| **Total employed** | **132,352** | **150,927** | **14.0%** |
| Nonfarm wage and salary employment | 118,731 | 136,318 | 14.8 |
| Goods-producing | 24,431 | 24,451 | 0.1 |
| Mining | 574 | 443 | −22.8 |
| Construction | 5,400 | 5,900 | 9.3 |
| Manufacturing | 18,457 | 18,108 | −1.9 |
| Durable | 10,766 | 10,514 | −2.3 |
| Nondurable | 7,691 | 7,593 | −1.3 |
| Service-producing | 94,300 | 111,867 | 18.6 |
| Transportation, communications, utilities | 6,260 | 7,111 | 13.6 |
| Wholesale trade | 6,483 | 7,228 | 11.5 |
| Retail trade | 21,625 | 23,875 | 10.4 |
| Finance, insurance, and real estate | 6,899 | 7,651 | 10.9 |
| Services | 33,586 | 44,852 | 33.5 |
| Federal government | 2,757 | 2,670 | −3.2 |
| State and local government | 16,690 | 18,480 | 10.7 |
| Agriculture | 3,642 | 3,618 | −0.7 |
| Private household wage and salary | 928 | 775 | −16.5 |
| Nonagricultural self-employed, unpaid family workers | 9,051 | 10,216 | 12.9 |

*Source: Bureau of Labor Statistics,* Monthly Labor Review, *November 1997*

# Industries with Fastest Job Gains, 1996 to 2006

*(number of people aged 16 or older employed in industries with the fastest job gains, 1996–2006; numerical and percent change in employment, 1996–2006; ranked by percent change; numbers in thousands)*

| | 1996 | 2006 | change, 1996–2006 | |
| --- | --- | --- | --- | --- |
| | | | number | percent |
| Computer and data processing services | 1,208 | 2,509 | 1,301 | 107.7% |
| Health services, not elsewhere classified | 1,172 | 1,968 | 796 | 67.9 |
| Management and public relations | 873 | 1,400 | 527 | 60.4 |
| Miscellaneous transportation services | 204 | 327 | 123 | 60.3 |
| Residential care | 672 | 1,070 | 398 | 59.2 |
| Personnel supply services | 2,646 | 4,039 | 1,393 | 52.6 |
| Water and sanitation | 231 | 349 | 118 | 51.1 |
| Individual and miscellaneous social services | 846 | 1,266 | 420 | 49.6 |
| Offices of health practitioners | 2,751 | 4,046 | 1,295 | 47.1 |
| Amusement and recreation services | 1,109 | 1,565 | 456 | 41.1 |

*Source: Bureau of Labor Statistics,* Monthly Labor Review, *November 1997*

# Workers with College Degrees Are in Greatest Demand

## Demand is also great for workers with only short-term on-the-job training.

Between 1996 and 2006, employment will grow the fastest for workers with bachelor's degrees. Jobs that demand a bachelor's degree will increase 25 percent during those years, compared with a 14 percent gain for all jobs. Workers with associate's degrees will also be in great demand, with job growth projected at 22 percent between 1996 and 2006. The slowest growth is projected for jobs requiring postsecondary vocational training, long-term on-the-job training, and moderate-term on-the-job training.

Although the fastest job growth is projected for jobs requiring a bachelor's or associate's degree, the largest job gains are forecast for workers with only short-term on-the-job training. With cashiers, truck drivers, and home health aides among the top 10 occupations in projected job gains, this explains why more than 21 million additional workers with short-term on-the-job training will be needed by 2006.

♦ As the labor force becomes increasingly educated, the biggest problem for employers will be attracting workers to entry-level jobs. Easing immigration restrictions is one way around this problem.

# Projections of Employment by Education, 1996 and 2006

*(number of people aged 16 or older employed by highest level of educational attainment or job training, 1996 and 2006, and percent change, 1996–2006; job openings by education and training, 1996–2006; numbers in thousands)*

| | 1996 | 2006 | percent change 1996–2006 | job openings, 1996–2006* |
|---|---|---|---|---|
| **Total employed** | **132,353** | **150,927** | **14.0%** | **50,563** |
| First professional degree | 1,707 | 2,015 | 18.0 | 582 |
| Doctoral degree | 1,016 | 1,209 | 19.0 | 460 |
| Master's degree | 1,371 | 1,577 | 15.0 | 430 |
| Work experience plus bachelor's or higher degree | 8,971 | 10,568 | 17.8 | 3,481 |
| Bachelor's degree | 15,821 | 19,838 | 25.4 | 7,343 |
| Associate degree | 4,122 | 5,036 | 22.2 | 1,614 |
| Postsecondary vocational training | 8,091 | 8,689 | 7.4 | 2,329 |
| Work experience in a related occupation | 9,966 | 11,177 | 12.2 | 3,285 |
| Long-term on-the-job training | 12,373 | 13,497 | 9.1 | 3,988 |
| Moderate-term on-the-job training | 16,792 | 18,260 | 8.7 | 5,628 |
| Short-term on-the-job training | 52,125 | 59,062 | 13.3 | 21,422 |

*\* Total job openings are the sum of employment increases and net replacements.*
*Source: Bureau of Labor Statistics, Internet web site <http://www.bls.gov/news.release/ecopro.table5htm>*

# 5

# Living Arrangement Trends

♦ **Single-person households now outnumber married couples with children.**
The second most common household type in 1998, single-person households, are likely to become the most common household type in a few years.

♦ **Between 1990 and 1998, the number of households headed by 45-to-54-year-olds grew 36 percent.**
In contrast, the number of households headed by 25-to-34-year-olds fell 7 percent.

♦ **Fifty-eight percent of American households are home to only one or two people.**
Overall, 2.62 people lived in the average U.S. household in 1998.

♦ **Fifty-one percent of black children live with only their mother, while just 36 percent live with both parents.**
An increasing proportion of all children—black, white, and Hispanic—live with only their mothers, and a shrinking proportion live with two parents.

♦ **Eighty percent of men and 73 percent of women aged 18 or 19 live with their parents.**
Entry-level wages have fallen sharply over the past 15 years, forcing young adults to live with their parents until they can afford independence.

♦ **Nearly 6 million American households are headed by unmarried couples.**
Seventy-two percent of cohabiting couples are heterosexual partners, while 28 percent are same-sex couples.

♦ **Men are more likely than women to be married—58 versus 55 percent in 1998.**
Men are also more likely to never marry than women—31 versus 25 percent.

# People Living Alone Outnumber Married Couples with Children

**Single-person households outnumber married couples with children by 1 million.**

People who live alone have become the second most common household type in the United States, accounting for more than one in four households. The only households more common than men or women who live alone are married couples without children under age 18 at home, accounting for 28 percent of the total.

While the number of married couples with children rose just 3 percent between 1990 and 1998, the number of female-headed families increased 16 percent. Male-headed families grew an even faster 36 percent during those years, with single-parent families headed by men growing 56 percent—although their number remains small.

Nonfamily households have grown 16 percent since 1990, with those headed by men growing faster than ones headed by women.

◆ The number of people who live alone will continue to grow rapidly in the years ahead as the baby-boom generation enters old age. Single-person households are likely to become the most common household type in the United States.

## Three most common household types

*(number of households by type for the three most common household types, 1998; numbers in millions)*

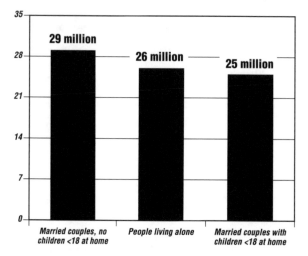

29 million — Married couples, no children <18 at home

26 million — People living alone

25 million — Married couples with children <18 at home

# Households by Type, 1990 and 1998

*(number and percent distribution of households by household type and presence of own children under age 18, 1990 and 1998; percent change 1990–98; numbers in thousands)*

|  | 1998 | | 1990 | | percent change 1990–98 |
|---|---|---|---|---|---|
|  | *number* | *percent* | *number* | *percent* |  |
| **Total households** | **102,528** | **100.0%** | **93,347** | **100.0%** | **9.8%** |
| Family households | 70,880 | 69.1 | 66,090 | 70.8 | 7.2 |
| Married couples | 54,317 | 53.0 | 52,317 | 56.0 | 3.8 |
| With children <18 | 25,269 | 24.6 | 24,537 | 26.3 | 3.0 |
| Without children <18 | 29,048 | 28.3 | 27,780 | 29.8 | 4.6 |
| Female householder, | | | | | |
| no spouse present | 12,652 | 12.3 | 10,890 | 11.7 | 16.2 |
| With children <18 | 7,693 | 7.5 | 6,599 | 7.1 | 16.6 |
| Without children <18 | 4,960 | 4.8 | 4,291 | 4.6 | 15.6 |
| Male householder, | | | | | |
| no spouse present | 3,911 | 3.8 | 2,884 | 3.1 | 35.6 |
| With children <18 | 1,798 | 1.8 | 1,153 | 1.2 | 55.9 |
| Without children <18 | 2,113 | 2.1 | 1,731 | 1.9 | 22.1 |
| **Nonfamily households** | **31,648** | **30.9** | **27,257** | **29.2** | **16.1** |
| Female householder | 17,516 | 17.1 | 15,651 | 16.8 | 11.9 |
| Living alone | 15,317 | 14.9 | 13,950 | 14.9 | 9.8 |
| Male householder | 14,133 | 13.8 | 11,606 | 12.4 | 21.8 |
| Living alone | 11,010 | 10.7 | 9,049 | 9.7 | 21.7 |

*Source: Bureau of the Census, unpublished data from the 1998 Current Population Survey, Internet web site <http://www.bls.census.gov/cps>; calculations by New Strategist*

# Households Headed by 45-to-54-Year-Olds Are Growing Fastest

## The number of households headed by 25-to-34-year-olds is declining.

Between 1990 and 1998, the number of households headed by 45-to-54-year-olds grew 36 percent, much faster than the 10 percent gain for all households. Behind this rapid growth was the aging of the baby-boom generation into its late forties and early fifties.

In contrast, the number of households headed by 25-to-34-year-olds fell 7 percent as the small Generation X entered the age group. Between 1990 and 1998, the number of householders aged 25 to 34 declined by more than 1 million.

♦ The number of households headed by people aged 65 or older will grow slowly during the next decade as the small generation born during the Depression ages.

### Fewer householders are aged 25 to 34

*(percent change in number of households by age of householder, 1990 to 1998)*

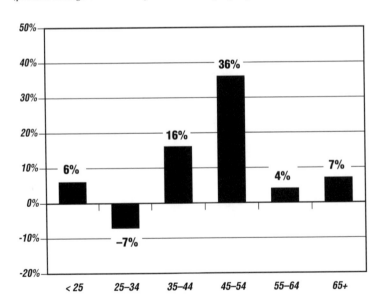

# Households by Age of Householder, 1990 to 1998

*(number of households by age of householder, 1990 to 1998; percent change 1990–98; numbers in thousands)*

|  | 1998 | 1990 | percent change 1990–98 |
|---|---|---|---|
| **Total households** | **102,528** | **93,347** | **9.8%** |
| Under age 25 | 5,435 | 5,121 | 6.1 |
| Aged 25 to 34 | 19,033 | 20,472 | −7.0 |
| Aged 35 to 44 | 23,943 | 20,554 | 16.5 |
| Aged 45 to 54 | 19,547 | 14,415 | 35.6 |
| Aged 55 to 64 | 13,072 | 12,529 | 4.3 |
| Aged 65 or older | 21,497 | 20,156 | 6.7 |

*Source: Bureau of the Census, unpublished data from the 1998 Current Population Survey, Internet web site <http://www.bls.census.gov/cps>; calculations by New Strategist*

# Households Vary by Age

**The households of young adults are different from those of middle-aged and older Americans.**

Married couples are far less common among the youngest and oldest householders than they are among the middle-aged. Only 25 percent of households headed by people under age 25 are married couples. Among the elderly, married couples head a 43 percent minority of households. In contrast, couples account for the majority of households headed by people aged 25 to 64.

Female-headed families are most common among the youngest householders, at 20 percent. Women who live alone are most common among the oldest householders, at 35 percent. Female-headed families account for just 12 percent of households headed by 45-to-54-year-olds and for fewer than 10 percent of households among 55-to-64-year-olds. Nonfamily households bottom out at 21 percent in the 35-to-44 age group. Householders aged 35 to 44 are least likely to live alone.

◆ With the baby-boom generation now in middle-age, household composition is much more stable than it was in the 1970s and 1980s.

### Most households headed by people aged 25 to 64 are married couples

*(percent of households headed by married couples, by age of householder, 1998)*

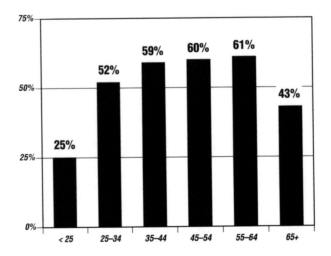

# Households by Household Type and Age of Householder, 1998

*(number and percent distribution of households by household type and age of householder, 1998; numbers in thousands)*

| | total | under 25 | 25 to 34 | 35 to 44 | 45 to 54 | 55 to 64 | 65 or older |
|---|---|---|---|---|---|---|---|
| **NUMBER** | | | | | | | |
| **Total households** | **102,528** | **5,435** | **19,033** | **23,943** | **19,547** | **13,072** | **21,497** |
| **Family households** | **70,880** | **3,019** | **13,639** | **18,872** | **14,694** | **9,387** | **11,270** |
| Married couples | 54,317 | 1,373 | 9,886 | 14,180 | 11,734 | 7,936 | 9,208 |
| Female householder, | | | | | | | |
| no spouse present | 12,652 | 1,095 | 2,887 | 3,637 | 2,260 | 1,099 | 1,676 |
| Male householder, | | | | | | | |
| no spouse present | 3,911 | 551 | 866 | 1,055 | 700 | 352 | 386 |
| **Nonfamily households** | **31,648** | **2,417** | **5,395** | **5,072** | **4,853** | **3,685** | **10,227** |
| Female householder | 17,516 | 1,081 | 2,070 | 1,863 | 2,421 | 2,337 | 7,744 |
| Living alone | 15,317 | 528 | 1,457 | 1,498 | 2,109 | 2,148 | 7,577 |
| Male householder | 14,133 | 1,336 | 3,325 | 3,208 | 2,432 | 1,348 | 2,483 |
| Living alone | 11,010 | 723 | 2,222 | 2,555 | 2,011 | 1,153 | 2,345 |
| **PERCENT DISTRIBUTION** | | | | | | | |
| **BY HOUSEHOLD TYPE** | | | | | | | |
| **Total households** | **100.0%** | **100.0%** | **100.0%** | **100.0%** | **100.0%** | **100.0%** | **100.0%** |
| **Family households** | **69.1** | **55.5** | **71.7** | **78.8** | **75.2** | **71.8** | **52.4** |
| Married couples | 53.0 | 25.3 | 51.9 | 59.2 | 60.0 | 60.7 | 42.8 |
| Female householder, | | | | | | | |
| no spouse present | 12.3 | 20.1 | 15.2 | 15.2 | 11.6 | 8.4 | 7.8 |
| Male householder, | | | | | | | |
| no spouse present | 3.8 | 10.1 | 4.5 | 4.4 | 3.6 | 2.7 | 1.8 |
| **Nonfamily households** | **30.9** | **44.5** | **28.3** | **21.2** | **24.8** | **28.2** | **47.6** |
| Female householder | 17.1 | 19.9 | 10.9 | 7.8 | 12.4 | 17.9 | 36.0 |
| Living alone | 14.9 | 9.7 | 7.7 | 6.3 | 10.8 | 16.4 | 35.2 |
| Male householder | 13.8 | 24.6 | 17.5 | 13.4 | 12.4 | 10.3 | 11.6 |
| Living alone | 10.7 | 13.3 | 11.7 | 10.7 | 10.3 | 8.8 | 10.9 |

*(continued)*

*(continued from previous page)*

| PERCENT DISTRIBUTION BY AGE | total | under 25 | 25 to 34 | 35 to 44 | 45 to 54 | 55 to 64 | 65 or older |
|---|---|---|---|---|---|---|---|
| **Total households** | **100.0%** | **5.3%** | **18.6%** | **23.4%** | **19.1%** | **12.7%** | **21.0%** |
| **Family households** | **100.0** | **4.3** | **19.2** | **26.6** | **20.7** | **13.2** | **15.9** |
| Married couples | 100.0 | 2.5 | 18.2 | 26.1 | 21.6 | 14.6 | 17.0 |
| Female householder, no spouse present | 100.0 | 8.7 | 22.8 | 28.7 | 17.9 | 8.7 | 13.2 |
| Male householder, no spouse present | 100.0 | 14.1 | 22.1 | 27.0 | 17.9 | 9.0 | 9.9 |
| **Nonfamily households** | **100.0** | **7.6** | **17.0** | **16.0** | **15.3** | **11.6** | **32.3** |
| Female householder | 100.0 | 6.2 | 11.8 | 10.6 | 13.8 | 13.3 | 44.2 |
| Living alone | 100.0 | 3.4 | 9.5 | 9.8 | 13.8 | 14.0 | 49.5 |
| Male householder | 100.0 | 9.5 | 23.5 | 22.7 | 17.2 | 9.5 | 17.6 |
| Living alone | 100.0 | 6.6 | 20.2 | 23.2 | 18.3 | 10.5 | 21.3 |

*Source: Bureau of the Census, unpublished data from the 1998 Current Population Survey, Internet web site <http://www.bls.census.gov/cps>; calculations by New Strategist*

# Big Differences between Black and White Households

**Married couples head more than one-half of white households, but fewer than one-third of black households.**

Female-headed families are just as numerous as married couples among black households, each accounting for a 31 percent share of total black households. In contrast, only 10 percent of white households are female-headed families, while the 56 percent majority are married couples. Married couples also account for 56 percent of Hispanic households, while female-headed families represent 19 percent of the total.

Hispanics are less likely to live in nonfamily households than both whites and blacks. Only 7 percent of Hispanic women live alone, far below the 15 percent share among whites and 16 percent share among blacks. Hispanic men are also less likely to live alone than white and black men.

◆ Businesses targeting nuclear families should examine household statistics carefully. Although black households outnumber Hispanic households by a considerable margin (12.5 million versus 8.6 million), Hispanic married couples significantly outnumber black couples (4.8 million versus 3.9 million).

# Households by Household Type, Race, and Hispanic Origin of Householder, 1998

*(number and percent distribution of households by household type, race, and Hispanic origin of householder, 1998; numbers in thousands)*

|  | total | white | black | Hispanic |
|---|---|---|---|---|
| **NUMBER** | | | | |
| **Total households** | **102,528** | **86,106** | **12,474** | **8,590** |
| **Family households** | **70,880** | **59,511** | **8,409** | **6,961** |
| Married couples | 54,317 | 48,066 | 3,921 | 4,804 |
| Female householder, | | | | |
| no spouse present | 12,652 | 8,308 | 3,926 | 1,612 |
| Male householder, | | | | |
| no spouse present | 3,911 | 3,137 | 562 | 545 |
| **Nonfamily households** | **31,649** | **26,596** | **4,066** | **1,629** |
| Female householder | 17,516 | 14,871 | 2,190 | 754 |
| Living alone | 15,317 | 12,980 | 1,982 | 617 |
| Male householder | 14,133 | 11,725 | 1,876 | 875 |
| Living alone | 11,010 | 9,018 | 1,594 | 623 |
| **PERCENT DISTRIBUTION** | | | | |
| **BY HOUSEHOLD TYPE** | | | | |
| **Total households** | **100.0%** | **100.0%** | **100.0%** | **100.0%** |
| **Family households** | **69.1** | **69.1** | **67.4** | **81.0** |
| Married couples | 53.0 | 55.8 | 31.4 | 55.9 |
| Female householder, | | | | |
| no spouse present | 12.3 | 9.6 | 31.5 | 18.8 |
| Male householder, | | | | |
| no spouse present | 3.8 | 3.6 | 4.5 | 6.3 |
| **Nonfamily households** | **30.9** | **30.9** | **32.6** | **19.0** |
| Female householder | 17.1 | 17.3 | 17.6 | 8.8 |
| Living alone | 14.9 | 15.1 | 15.9 | 7.2 |
| Male householder | 13.8 | 13.6 | 15.0 | 10.2 |
| Living alone | 10.7 | 10.5 | 12.8 | 7.3 |

*(continued)*

*(continued from previous page)*

### PERCENT DISTRIBUTION BY RACE AND HISPANIC ORIGIN

| | *total* | *white* | *black* | *Hispanic* |
|---|---|---|---|---|
| **Total households** | **100.0%** | **84.0%** | **12.2%** | **8.4%** |
| **Family households** | **100.0** | **84.0** | **11.9** | **9.8** |
| Married couples | 100.0 | 88.5 | 7.2 | 8.8 |
| Female householder, no spouse present | 100.0 | 65.7 | 31.0 | 12.7 |
| Male householder, no spouse present | 100.0 | 80.2 | 14.4 | 13.9 |
| **Nonfamily households** | **100.0** | **84.0** | **12.8** | **5.1** |
| Female householder | 100.0 | 84.9 | 12.5 | 4.3 |
| Living alone | 100.0 | 84.7 | 12.9 | 4.0 |
| Male householder | 100.0 | 83.0 | 13.3 | 6.2 |
| Living alone | 100.0 | 81.9 | 14.5 | 5.7 |

*Note: Numbers will not add to total because Hispanics may be of any race and not all races are shown.*
*Source: Bureau of the Census, unpublished data from the 1998 Current Population Survey, Internet web site <http://www.bls.census.gov/cps>; calculations by New Strategist*

# Hispanic Households Are the Youngest

## More than one-third of Hispanic households are headed by young adults.

Thirty-six percent of Hispanic households are headed by people under age 35. This compares with only 23 percent of white households. The Hispanic population is far more youthful than the white population, which accounts for these differences in the ages of householders. Among black households, 30 percent are headed by people under age 35.

The differences between white and Hispanic households are just as extreme at the other end of the age spectrum. While 22 percent of white households are headed by people aged 65 or older, only 11 percent of Hispanic households are headed by the elderly. Among blacks, people aged 65 or older head 15 percent of households.

♦ In the years ahead, the generation gap between whites and Hispanics could lead to political conflict over the equitable distribution of the nation's economic resources.

### White households are the oldest

*(percent of households headed by people aged 65 or older, by race and Hispanic origin, 1998)*

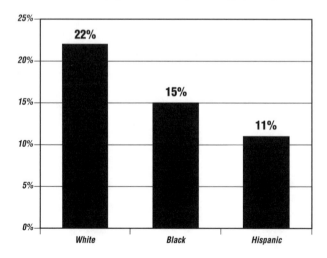

# Households by Age, Race, and Hispanic Origin of Householder, 1998

*(number and percent distribution of households by age, race, and Hispanic origin of householder, 1998; numbers in thousands)*

| | total | white | black | Hispanic |
|---|---|---|---|---|
| **Number** | | | | |
| **Total households** | **102,528** | **86,106** | **12,474** | **8,590** |
| Under age 25 | 5,435 | 4,242 | 935 | 780 |
| Aged 25 to 34 | 19,033 | 15,344 | 2,752 | 2,303 |
| Aged 35 to 44 | 23,943 | 19,761 | 3,096 | 2,316 |
| Aged 45 to 54 | 19,547 | 16,400 | 2,371 | 1,386 |
| Aged 55 to 64 | 13,072 | 11,163 | 1,441 | 889 |
| Aged 65 or older | 21,497 | 19,196 | 1,878 | 916 |
| | | | | |
| **Percent distribution by age** | | | | |
| **Total households** | **100.0%** | **100.0%** | **100.0%** | **100.0%** |
| Under age 25 | 5.3 | 4.9 | 7.5 | 9.1 |
| Aged 25 to 34 | 18.6 | 17.8 | 22.1 | 26.8 |
| Aged 35 to 44 | 23.4 | 22.9 | 24.8 | 27.0 |
| Aged 45 to 54 | 19.1 | 19.0 | 19.0 | 16.1 |
| Aged 55 to 64 | 12.7 | 13.0 | 11.6 | 10.3 |
| Aged 65 or older | 21.0 | 22.3 | 15.1 | 10.7 |
| | | | | |
| **Percent distribution by race and Hispanic origin** | | | | |
| **Total households** | **100.0%** | **84.0%** | **12.2%** | **8.4%** |
| Under age 25 | 100.0 | 78.0 | 17.2 | 14.4 |
| Aged 25 to 34 | 100.0 | 80.6 | 14.5 | 12.1 |
| Aged 35 to 44 | 100.0 | 82.5 | 12.9 | 9.7 |
| Aged 45 to 54 | 100.0 | 83.9 | 12.1 | 7.1 |
| Aged 55 to 64 | 100.0 | 85.4 | 11.0 | 6.8 |
| Aged 65 or older | 100.0 | 89.3 | 8.7 | 4.3 |

*Note: Numbers will not add to total because Hispanics may be of any race and not all races are shown.*
*Source: Bureau of the Census, unpublished data from the 1998 Current Population Survey, Internet web site <http://www.bls.census.gov/cps>; calculations by New Strategist*

# Most Households Are Small

**Fifty-eight percent of American households are home to only one or two people.**

Two-person households are the most common, accounting for 32 percent of the nation's 103 million households. Single-person households represent 26 percent of the total. Three- and four-person households together account for another one-third of households. Only 10 percent of households have five or more people. Overall, the average household in the U.S. was home to 2.62 people in 1998.

♦ Household size, which has been shrinking for years, should remain stable while the baby-boom generation is raising children. But as boomers become widowed in old age, household size could shrink again as the number of single-person households climbs.

### Two-person households are most common

*(percent distribution of households by size, 1998)*

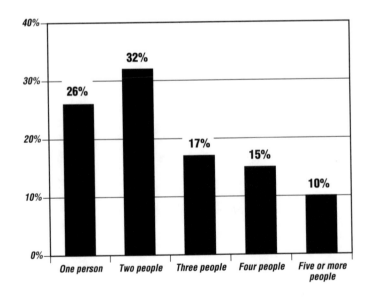

# Households by Size, 1998

*(number and percent distribution of households by size, 1998; numbers in thousands)*

|  | *number* | *percent* |
|---|---|---|
| **Total households** | **102,528** | **100.0%** |
| One person | 26,327 | 25.7 |
| Two people | 32,965 | 32.2 |
| Three people | 17,331 | 16.9 |
| Four people | 15,358 | 15.0 |
| Five people | 7,048 | 6.9 |
| Six people | 2,232 | 2.2 |
| Seven or more people | 1,267 | 1.2 |
| Average number of people per household | 2.62 | – |

*Source: Bureau of the Census, detailed tables from* Household and Family Characteristics: March 1998, *Current Population Reports, P20-515, 1998; calculations by New Strategist*

# Half the Women Who Live Alone Are Aged 65 Or Older

## Nearly two out of three are aged 55 or older.

Among the nation's single-person households, 58 percent are headed by women and 50 percent are headed by people aged 55 or older.

There are sharp differences in the ages of men and women who live alone. Most men who live alone are under age 55, while most women who live alone are aged 55 or older. Among men who live alone, the largest share is in the 35-to-44 age group (23 percent). Among women who live alone, the largest share is aged 65 or older (49 percent). Most men live alone before marriage or after divorce. Most women live alone following the death of a spouse.

♦ People who live alone account for 26 percent of all households, one of the most important segments of the household market. But because the average man who lives alone is at a different lifestage than the average woman who lives alone, they should be targeted separately.

### Women who live alone are older

*(percent distribution of women who live alone by age, 1998)*

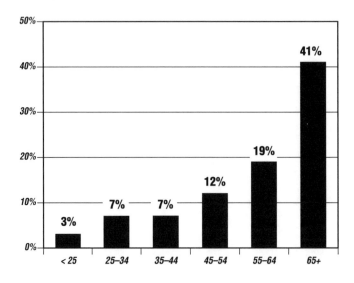

# People Living Alone by Age and Sex, 1998

*(number and percent of people aged 15 or older living alone by age and sex, 1998; numbers in thousands)*

|  | men | | | women | | |
|  |  | living alone | |  | living alone | |
|  | total | number | percent | total | number | percent |
|---|---|---|---|---|---|---|
| **Total people** | **101,123** | **11,010** | **10.9%** | **108,168** | **15,317** | **14.2%** |
| Under age 25 | 18,747 | 723 | 3.9 | 18,333 | 528 | 2.9 |
| Aged 25 to 34 | 19,526 | 2,222 | 11.4 | 19,828 | 1,456 | 7.3 |
| Aged 35 to 44 | 22,055 | 2,555 | 11.6 | 22,407 | 1,499 | 6.7 |
| Aged 45 to 54 | 16,599 | 2,012 | 12.1 | 17,459 | 2,108 | 12.1 |
| Aged 55 to 64 | 10,673 | 1,153 | 10.8 | 11,582 | 2,148 | 18.5 |
| Aged 65 or older | 13,524 | 2,345 | 17.3 | 18,559 | 7,578 | 40.8 |

*Source: Bureau of the Census, unpublished tables from the 1998 Current Population Survey, Internet web site <http://www.bls.census.gov/cps>; calculations by New Strategist*

# More Than One-Third of Households Are in the South

## The Northeast is home to the smallest number of households.

Thirty-six percent of the nation's households are in the South, making it by far the most populous region. Only 19 percent of households are in the Northeast, fewer than the 21 percent in the West. The Midwest is the second most populous region, home to one in four households.

The majority of black households are in the South, while the South and West combined are home to three out of four Hispanic households. Overall, nearly one in five households in the South is headed by a black householder, while 16 percent of households in the West are headed by Hispanics.

♦ The concentration of black and Hispanic households in certain regions makes it easier for marketers to target these consumers.

# Households by Region, Race, and Hispanic Origin, 1998

*(number and percent distribution of households by region, race, and Hispanic origin of house-holder, 1998; numbers in thousands)*

|  | total | white | black | Hispanic |
|---|---|---|---|---|
| **Total households** | **102,528** | **86,106** | **12,474** | **8,590** |
| Northeast | 19,810 | 16,926 | 2,286 | 1,468 |
| Midwest | 24,236 | 21,465 | 2,288 | 644 |
| South | 36,578 | 28,948 | 6,814 | 2,939 |
| West | 21,905 | 18,767 | 1,086 | 3,539 |
| **Percent distribution by region** | | | | |
| **Total households** | **100.0%** | **100.0%** | **100.0%** | **100.0%** |
| Northeast | 19.3 | 19.7 | 18.3 | 17.1 |
| Midwest | 23.6 | 24.9 | 18.3 | 7.5 |
| South | 35.7 | 33.6 | 54.6 | 34.2 |
| West | 21.4 | 21.8 | 8.7 | 41.2 |
| **Percent distribution by race and Hispanic origin** | | | | |
| **Total households** | **100.0%** | **84.0%** | **12.2%** | **8.4%** |
| Northeast | 100.0 | 85.4 | 11.5 | 7.4 |
| Midwest | 100.0 | 88.6 | 9.4 | 2.7 |
| South | 100.0 | 79.1 | 18.6 | 8.0 |
| West | 100.0 | 85.7 | 5.0 | 16.2 |

*Note: Numbers will not add to total because Hispanics may be of any race and not all races are shown.*
*Source: Bureau of the Census, detailed tables from* Household and Family Characteristics: March 1998, *Current Population Reports, P20-515, 1998; calculations by New Strategist*

# Half of Nation's Households Are in Suburbs

**Only one in five households is outside a metropolitan area.**

Of the nation's 103 million households, 80 percent are located in metropolitan areas, defined as counties with a city of 50,000 or more population plus any adjacent counties with economic ties to the core county. Only 20 percent of households are located in nonmetropolitan areas.

The suburbs are home to nearly one-half of households, with one in three households living in the suburbs of large metropolitan areas with populations of 1 million or more. Slightly fewer than one-third of American households are in the nation's central cities.

♦ Advances in telecommunications are allowing people to live where they want rather than where they must. This could stem the growth of the largest metropolitan areas since many Americans prefer to live in smaller towns and cities.

# Households by Metropolitan Status, 1998

*(number and percent distribution of households by metropolitan status and size of metropolitan area, 1998; numbers in thousands)*

|  | number | percent |
|---|---|---|
| **Total households** | **102,528** | **100.0%** |
| Households in metropolitan areas | 82,122 | 80.1 |
| Central cities | 31,907 | 31.1 |
| Suburbs | 50,215 | 49.0 |
| Households in nonmetropolitan areas | 20,406 | 19.9 |
| **Size of metropolitan area** |  |  |
| **Total households in metropolitan areas** | **82,122** | **80.1** |
| In metropolitan areas of 2,500,000 or more | 36,623 | 35.7 |
| Central cities | 13,541 | 13.2 |
| Suburbs | 23,082 | 22.5 |
| In metropolitan areas of 1,000,000 to 2,499,999 | 18,044 | 17.6 |
| Central cities | 6,769 | 6.6 |
| Suburbs | 11,275 | 11.0 |
| In metropolitan areas of 250,000 to 999,999 | 19,611 | 19.1 |
| Central cities | 7,895 | 7.7 |
| Suburbs | 11,716 | 11.4 |
| In metropolitan areas of under 250,000 | 7,843 | 7.6 |
| Central cities | 3,702 | 3.6 |
| Suburbs | 4,142 | 4.0 |

*Source: Bureau of the Census, detailed tables from* Household and Family Characteristics: March 1998, *Current Population Reports, P20-515, 1998; calculations by New Strategist*

# Most Black Children Live with Mother Only

## Fifty-one percent of black children live with only their mother, up from 44 percent in 1980

Among whites, 74 percent of children live with both parents. Just 18 percent live with their mother only, up from 14 percent in 1980. Among Hispanic children, 64 percent live with both parents, while 27 percent live with only their mother—up from 20 percent in 1980.

Few children live with only their father: 5 percent of white and 4 percent of Hispanic and black children. Nine percent of black children, 5 percent of Hispanic children, and 3 percent of white children live with someone other than their mother or father, often a grandmother.

♦ While the living arrangements of black children differ from those of white or Hispanic children, the trends are the same for all three groups. An increasing proportion of children live with only their mothers, and a shrinking proportion live with two parents.

### Most white children live with two parents

*(percent of children under age 18 who live with two parents, by race and Hispanic origin, 1998)*

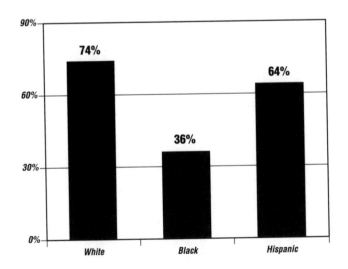

# Living Arrangements of Children by Race and Hispanic Origin, 1980 and 1998

*(number and percent distribution of children under age 18 by living arrangement, race, and Hispanic origin of child, 1980 and 1998; numbers in thousands)*

|  | 1998 | | 1980 | |
|---|---|---|---|---|
|  | *number* | *percent* | *number* | *percent* |
| **Total children** | **71,377** | **100.0%** | **63,427** | **100.0%** |
| Two parents | 48,642 | 68.1 | 48,624 | 76.7 |
| Mother only | 16,634 | 23.3 | 11,406 | 18.0 |
| Father only | 3,143 | 4.4 | 1,060 | 1.7 |
| Other | 2,959 | 4.1 | 2,337 | 3.7 |
| **White children** | **56,124** | **100.0** | **52,242** | **100.0** |
| Two parents | 41,547 | 74.0 | 43,200 | 82.7 |
| Mother only | 10,210 | 18.2 | 7,059 | 13.5 |
| Father only | 2,562 | 4.6 | 842 | 1.6 |
| Other | 1,799 | 3.2 | 1,141 | 2.2 |
| **Black children** | **11,414** | **100.0** | **9,375** | **100.0** |
| Two parents | 4,137 | 36.2 | 3,956 | 42.2 |
| Mother only | 5,830 | 51.1 | 4,117 | 43.9 |
| Father only | 424 | 3.7 | 180 | 1.9 |
| Other | 1,015 | 8.9 | 1,122 | 12.0 |
| **Hispanic children** | **10,863** | **100.0** | **5,459** | **100.0** |
| Two parents | 6,909 | 63.6 | 4,116 | 75.4 |
| Mother only | 2,915 | 26.8 | 1,069 | 19.6 |
| Father only | 482 | 4.4 | 83 | 1.5 |
| Other | 551 | 5.1 | 191 | 3.5 |

*Note: Numbers will not add to total because Hispanics may be of any race and not all races are shown.*
*Source: Bureau of the Census, Marital Status and Living Arrangements: March 1998, Current Population Reports, P20-514, 1998; calculations by New Strategist*

# Most Young Adults Live at Home

**Seventy-seven percent of the nation's 18- and 19-year-olds still live with their parents.**

Young men are far more likely to live at home than young women.

Eighty percent of men and 73 percent of women aged 18 or 19 live with their parents. Among those aged 20 to 24, 50 percent of men and 37 percent of women still live at home. These statistics count young adults who live in college dormitories as living at home. The proportion of young adults who live at home has been rising during the past few years not only because more are going to college, but also because a growing share cannot yet afford the expense of setting up an independent household.

Only 13 percent of men aged 20 to 24 live with a spouse. A larger 26 percent share lives alone or with nonrelatives. Among women in the age group, 24 percent live with a spouse while 23 percent live alone or with nonrelatives. Women are more likely than men to live with a spouse because they marry at a younger age, on average.

Among 25-to-29-year-olds, the majority of women live with a spouse. Among men, the proportion is 41 percent. Twenty percent of men and 12 percent of women in this age group still live at home.

◆ Young adults are more likely to live at home than they once were out of necessity. Entry-level wages have fallen sharply over the past 15 years, forcing young adults to live with their parents until they can afford independence.

# Living Arrangements of Young Adults, 1998

*(number and percent distribution of people aged 18 to 29 by living arrangement and sex, 1998; numbers in thousands)*

| | number | | | percent | | |
|---|---|---|---|---|---|---|
| | *total* | *men* | *women* | *total* | *men* | *women* |
| **Aged 18 and 19** | **7,587** | **3,807** | **3,780** | **100.0%** | **100.0%** | **100.0%** |
| Living with parents | 5,796 | 3,030 | 2,766 | 76.4 | 79.6 | 73.2 |
| Living with spouse | 242 | 62 | 180 | 3.2 | 1.6 | 4.8 |
| Living with other relatives | 698 | 354 | 344 | 9.2 | 9.3 | 9.1 |
| Living alone or with nonrelatives | 851 | 361 | 490 | 11.2 | 9.5 | 13.0 |
| **Aged 20 to 24** | **17,614** | **8,826** | **8,788** | **100.0** | **100.0** | **100.0** |
| Living with parents | 7,575 | 4,368 | 3,207 | 43.0 | 49.5 | 36.5 |
| Living with spouse | 3,314 | 1,179 | 2,135 | 18.8 | 13.4 | 24.3 |
| Living with other relatives | 2,383 | 995 | 1,388 | 13.5 | 11.3 | 15.8 |
| Living alone or with nonrelatives | 4,342 | 2,284 | 2,058 | 24.7 | 25.9 | 23.4 |
| **Aged 25 to 29** | **18,996** | **9,450** | **9,546** | **100.0** | **100.0** | **100.0** |
| Living with parents | 3,013 | 1,848 | 1,165 | 15.9 | 19.6 | 12.2 |
| Living with spouse | 8,816 | 3,914 | 4,902 | 46.4 | 41.4 | 51.4 |
| Living with other relatives | 2,525 | 932 | 1,593 | 13.3 | 9.9 | 16.7 |
| Living alone or with nonrelatives | 4,642 | 2,756 | 1,886 | 24.4 | 29.2 | 19.8 |

*Source: Bureau of the Census,* Marital Status and Living Arrangements: March 1998, *Current Population Reports, P20-514, 1998; and unpublished tables from the 1998 Current Population Survey, Internet web site <http://www.census.gov/cps>; calculations by New Strategist*

# Lifestyles of Men And Women Diverge in Old Age

## Older men are much more likely to live with a spouse.

Among men aged 65 or older, 73 percent live with a spouse. Among women in the age group, the proportion is just 41 percent. This difference is due to the fact that, on average, women marry men who are slightly older than they are and that men die at a younger age than women.

Equal shares of women aged 65 or older live alone and live with a spouse, 41 percent in 1998. Among men in the age group, only 17 percent live alone. Elderly women are twice as likely as elderly men to live with other relatives, 17 versus 7 percent. Often, the other relative with whom they live is a son or daughter who helps care for them.

♦ The different lifestyles of older men and women divide the market into two distinct segments: older women who live alone and older couples. These two segments will continue to dominate the elderly market for years to come.

### Older women are more likely than older men to live alone

*(percent of people aged 65 or older who live with a spouse or alone, by sex, 1998)*

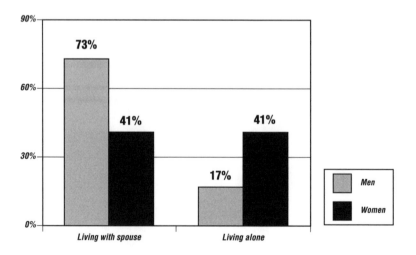

# Living Arrangements of People Aged 65 or Older, 1998

*(number and percent distribution of people aged 65 or older by living arrangement and sex, 1998; numbers in thousands)*

|  | *total* | *men* | *women* |
|---|---|---|---|
| **Total people** | **32,084** | **13,525** | **18,559** |
| Living with spouse | 17,382 | 9,821 | 7,561 |
| Living alone | 9,922 | 2,345 | 7,577 |
| Living with other relatives | 4,067 | 952 | 3,115 |
| Living with nonrelatives | 713 | 407 | 306 |
| **Total people** | **100.0%** | **100.0%** | **100.0%** |
| Living with spouse | 54.2 | 72.6 | 40.7 |
| Living alone | 30.9 | 17.3 | 40.8 |
| Living with other relatives | 12.7 | 7.0 | 16.8 |
| Living with nonrelatives | 2.2 | 3.0 | 1.6 |

*Source: Bureau of the Census,* Marital Status and Living Arrangements: March 1998, *Current Populations Reports, P20-514, 1998; and unpublished data from the 1998 Current Population Survey, Internet web site <http://www.bls.census.gov/cps>; calculations by New Strategist*

# Most Married Couples Have Children at Home

## The couples most likely to have children at home are aged 35 to 44.

With young adults increasingly likely to live at home, parenting duties are extending into later life. The majority of married couples under age 55 have children in their home. Even among couples in the 55-to-64 age group, a substantial 29 percent have children living with them.

The majority of married couples under age 45 have children under age 18 at home. In the 45-to-64 age group, the share with children under age 18 at home falls to a minority, but more than one couple in five has grown children living with them.

The couples most likely to have preschoolers at home are under age 35. Those most likely to have teens at home are aged 40 to 44. Half the couples in this age group are living with teens.

◆ The number of married couples with adult children at home will rise as boomers age and their children become young adults.

# Married Couples with Children at Home by Age of Householder and Age of Children, 1998

*(number and percent distribution of total married couples and couples with own children at home, by age of householder and age of children, 1998; numbers in thousands)*

| | | | with children | | | | |
|---|---|---|---|---|---|---|---|
| | | | | under age 18 | | | |
| | *total* | *of any age* | *aged 18 or older* | *total* | *12 to 17* | *6 to 11* | *under 6* |
| **Total couples** | **54,317** | **31,288** | **6,019** | **25,269** | **11,406** | **12,285** | **11,773** |
| Under age 20 | 86 | 56 | – | 56 | 1 | – | 55 |
| Aged 20 to 24 | 1,287 | 760 | 5 | 755 | 12 | 99 | 731 |
| Aged 25 to 29 | 3,967 | 2,543 | 8 | 2,535 | 104 | 984 | 2,227 |
| Aged 30 to 34 | 5,919 | 4,712 | 10 | 4,702 | 873 | 2,376 | 3,566 |
| Aged 35 to 39 | 6,941 | 6,047 | 80 | 5,967 | 2,436 | 3,670 | 3,045 |
| Aged 40 to 44 | 7,239 | 6,098 | 473 | 5,625 | 3,636 | 3,093 | 1,477 |
| Aged 45 to 54 | 11,734 | 7,550 | 2,615 | 4,935 | 3,819 | 1,872 | 593 |
| Aged 55 to 64 | 7,936 | 2,332 | 1,741 | 591 | 468 | 153 | 55 |
| Aged 65 or older | 9,209 | 1,191 | 1,087 | 104 | 56 | 38 | 23 |
| **Total couples** | **100.0%** | **57.6%** | **11.1%** | **46.5%** | **20.0%** | **22.6%** | **21.7%** |
| Under age 20 | 100.0 | 65.1 | – | 65.1 | 1.2 | – | 63.0 |
| Aged 20 to 24 | 100.0 | 59.1 | 0.4 | 58.7 | 0.9 | 7.7 | 56.8 |
| Aged 25 to 29 | 100.0 | 64.1 | 0.2 | 63.9 | 2.6 | 24.8 | 56.1 |
| Aged 30 to 34 | 100.0 | 79.6 | 0.2 | 79.4 | 14.7 | 40.1 | 60.2 |
| Aged 35 to 39 | 100.0 | 87.1 | 1.2 | 85.0 | 35.1 | 52.9 | 43.9 |
| Aged 40 to 44 | 100.0 | 84.2 | 6.5 | 77.7 | 50.2 | 42.7 | 20.4 |
| Aged 45 to 54 | 100.0 | 64.3 | 22.3 | 42.1 | 32.5 | 15.0 | 5.1 |
| Aged 55 to 64 | 100.0 | 29.4 | 21.9 | 7.4 | 5.9 | 1.9 | 0.7 |
| Aged 65 or older | 100.0 | 12.9 | 11.8 | 1.1 | 0.6 | 0.4 | 0.2 |

*Note: (–) means sample is too small to make a reliable estimate.*
*Source: Bureau of the Census, detailed tables from* Household *and* Family Characteristics: March 1998, *Current Population Reports, P20-515, 1998; calculations by New Strategist*

# Married Couples by Age of Householder and Number of Children Under Age 18 at Home, 1998

*(number and percent distribution of married couples by age of householder and number of own children under age 18 living at home, 1998; numbers in thousands)*

| | total | no children < 18 | with children < 18 total | one | two | three or more |
|---|---|---|---|---|---|---|
| **Total couples** | **54,317** | **29,048** | **25,269** | **9,507** | **10,241** | **5,521** |
| Under age 25 | 1,373 | 562 | 811 | 471 | 240 | 99 |
| Aged 25 to 29 | 3,967 | 1,432 | 2,535 | 1,033 | 1,041 | 461 |
| Aged 30 to 34 | 5,919 | 1,217 | 4,702 | 1,533 | 1,949 | 1,219 |
| Aged 35 to 39 | 6,941 | 974 | 5,967 | 1,495 | 2,758 | 1,714 |
| Aged 40 to 44 | 7,239 | 1,614 | 5,625 | 1,885 | 2,426 | 1,315 |
| Aged 45 to 54 | 11,734 | 6,799 | 4,935 | 2,581 | 1,690 | 663 |
| Aged 55 to 64 | 7,936 | 7,345 | 591 | 444 | 108 | 40 |
| Aged 65 or older | 9,209 | 9,105 | 104 | 66 | 28 | 9 |
| **Total couples** | **100.0%** | **53.5%** | **46.5%** | **17.5%** | **18.9%** | **10.2%** |
| Under age 25 | 100.0 | 40.9 | 59.1 | 34.3 | 17.5 | 7.2 |
| Aged 25 to 29 | 100.0 | 36.1 | 63.9 | 26.0 | 26.2 | 11.6 |
| Aged 30 to 34 | 100.0 | 20.6 | 79.4 | 25.9 | 32.9 | 20.6 |
| Aged 35 to 39 | 100.0 | 14.0 | 85.0 | 21.5 | 39.7 | 24.7 |
| Aged 40 to 44 | 100.0 | 22.3 | 77.7 | 26.0 | 33.5 | 18.2 |
| Aged 45 to 54 | 100.0 | 57.9 | 42.1 | 21.0 | 14.4 | 5.7 |
| Aged 55 to 64 | 100.0 | 92.6 | 7.4 | 5.6 | 1.4 | 0.5 |
| Aged 65 or older | 100.0 | 98.9 | 1.1 | 0.7 | 0.3 | 0.1 |

*Source: Bureau of the Census, detailed tables from* Household and Family Characteristics: March 1998, *Current Population Reports, P20-515, 1998; calculations by New Strategist*

# Most Single Parents Are Women

**Of the nation's 9 million single-parent families, 81 percent are headed by women.**

Not all male- and female-headed families are single-parent families. Many such householders are men and women heading households in which other relatives live, such as an elderly parent, a sister, or a nephew. The 61 percent majority of the nation's 12.7 million female-headed families are single parents with children under age 18. In contrast, a 45 percent minority of male-headed families are single-parent families.

Most of the female-headed families with a householder under age 50 include children under age 18. Most of the male-headed families with a householder between the ages of 25 and 49 include children.

◆ As the children of baby boomers grow up and leave home, the number of single-parent families should stabilize or even decline.

# Female- and Male-Headed Families with Children under Age 18 at Home by Age of Householder, 1998

*(total number of female- and male-headed families, and number and percent with own children under age 18 at home, by age of householder, 1998; numbers in thousands)*

| | total | with children under 18 | |
| --- | --- | --- | --- |
| | | number | percent |
| **Female-headed families** | **12,652** | **7,693** | **60.8%** |
| Aged 15 to 19 | 152 | 76 | 50.0 |
| Aged 20 to 24 | 943 | 790 | 83.8 |
| Aged 25 to 29 | 1,305 | 1,204 | 92.3 |
| Aged 30 to 34 | 1,582 | 1,489 | 94.1 |
| Aged 35 to 39 | 1,818 | 1,684 | 92.6 |
| Aged 40 to 44 | 1,819 | 1,357 | 74.6 |
| Aged 45 to 49 | 1,367 | 740 | 54.1 |
| Aged 50 to 54 | 893 | 226 | 25.3 |
| Aged 55 to 59 | 679 | 95 | 14.0 |
| Aged 60 to 64 | 420 | 10 | 2.4 |
| Aged 65 or older | 1,676 | 22 | 1.3 |
| **Male-headed families** | **3,911** | **1,798** | **46.0** |
| Aged 15 to 19 | 167 | 18 | 10.8 |
| Aged 20 to 24 | 384 | 168 | 43.8 |
| Aged 25 to 29 | 462 | 251 | 54.3 |
| Aged 30 to 34 | 404 | 238 | 58.9 |
| Aged 35 to 39 | 493 | 332 | 67.3 |
| Aged 40 to 44 | 562 | 362 | 64.4 |
| Aged 45 to 49 | 405 | 231 | 57.0 |
| Aged 50 to 54 | 296 | 118 | 39.9 |
| Aged 55 to 59 | 213 | 50 | 23.5 |
| Aged 60 to 64 | 139 | 15 | 10.8 |
| Aged 65 or older | 386 | 14 | 3.6 |

*Source: Bureau of the Census, detailed tables from* Household and Family Characteristics: March 1998; *Current Population Reports, P20–515, 1998; calculations by New Strategist*

# Many Unmarried Couples Are Older

## More than 1 million cohabiting couples are aged 45 or older.

Unmarried couples include young adults as well as middle-aged and older Americans. Only 20 percent of cohabiting couples are under age 25. Fifty-seven percent are aged 25 to 44, and 23 percent are aged 45 or older.

More than 70 percent of cohabiting couples are heterosexual partners, while 28 percent are homosexual couples. Among same-sex couples, 52 percent are men.

◆ Baby boomers were the first to make cohabitation common. As boomers age, the number of cohabitors aged 45 and older will soar.

### More than one in four cohabiting couples are same-sex partners

*(percent distribution of cohabiting couples by sex of partner, 1998)*

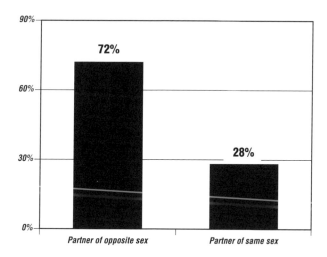

# Characteristics of Cohabiting Couples, 1998

*(number and percent distribution of households with two unrelated adults, by sex of partner and age of householder, 1998; numbers in thousands)*

| | total | | male householder | | female householder | |
|---|---|---|---|---|---|---|
| | *number* | *percent* | *number* | *percent* | *number* | *percent* |
| **Total cohabiting couples** | **5,911** | **100.0%** | **3,217** | **100.0%** | **2,694** | **100.0%** |
| **Partner of opposite sex** | 4,236 | 71.7 | 2,352 | 73.1 | 1,885 | 70.0 |
| Under age 25 | 776 | 13.1 | 408 | 12.7 | 369 | 13.7 |
| Aged 25 to 34 | 1,618 | 27.4 | 891 | 27.7 | 727 | 27.0 |
| Aged 35 to 44 | 857 | 14.5 | 514 | 16.0 | 343 | 12.7 |
| Aged 45 to 64 | 797 | 13.5 | 441 | 13.7 | 356 | 13.2 |
| Aged 65 or older | 188 | 3.2 | 98 | 3.0 | 90 | 3.3 |
| **Partner of same sex** | 1,674 | 28.3 | 865 | 26.9 | 810 | 30.1 |
| Under age 25 | 407 | 6.9 | 204 | 6.3 | 203 | 7.5 |
| Aged 25 to 34 | 571 | 9.7 | 309 | 9.6 | 262 | 9.7 |
| Aged 35 to 44 | 339 | 5.7 | 181 | 5.6 | 158 | 5.9 |
| Aged 45 to 64 | 263 | 4.4 | 140 | 4.4 | 123 | 4.6 |
| Aged 65 or older | 95 | 1.6 | 31 | 1.0 | 64 | 2.4 |

*Source: Bureau of the Census,* Marital Status and Living Arrangements: March 1998; *Current Population Reports, P20-514, 1998; calculations by New Strategist*

# Most Americans Are Married

## Men are more likely to be married than women—58 versus 55 percent in 1997.

Men are also more likely than women to never have been married—31 percent of men compared with 25 percent of women. Despite reports about never-married women in their thirties having trouble finding husbands, the reverse is more likely to be the case. Never-married men outnumber never-married women up to age 65.

The proportion of young adults who have not yet married has been growing for decades as men and women postpone marriage. The median age at first marriage is 26.7 years for men and 25.0 years for women. For women, this is a record high. By age 30, most men are married, with the proportion peaking at 80 percent for those aged 55 to 64. Among women, the married proportion peaks at 73 percent for those aged 40 to 44.

A substantial 18 percent of women aged 45 to 54 are currently divorced. This figure, while high, greatly understates the experience of divorce among baby boomers because it does not include the many women in the age group who have divorced and are now remarried.

Men are likely to be married for the rest of their lives, while women are likely to be widowed in old age. Overall, 10 percent of women are currently widowed, compared with 2.5 percent of men. Women are more likely to be widowed than men because they tend to marry men who are older, and because men's life expectancy is lower than women's. Most women aged 75 or older are widows, while the proportion of men who are widowers never rises above 42 percent.

♦ With so many young adults going to college, the median age at first marriage is likely to remain high as men and women postpone marriage until they have established a career.

# Median Age at First Marriage by Sex, 1890 to 1998

*(median age at first marriage by sex, 1890 to 1998)*

| | men | women |
|---|---|---|
| 1998 | 26.7 | 25.0 |
| 1997 | 26.8 | 25.0 |
| 1996 | 27.1 | 24.8 |
| 1995 | 26.9 | 24.5 |
| 1994 | 26.7 | 24.5 |
| 1993 | 26.5 | 24.5 |
| 1992 | 26.5 | 24.4 |
| 1991 | 26.3 | 24.1 |
| 1990 | 26.1 | 23.9 |
| 1980 | 24.7 | 22.0 |
| 1970 | 23.2 | 20.8 |
| 1960 | 22.8 | 20.3 |
| 1950 | 22.8 | 20.3 |
| 1940 | 24.3 | 21.5 |
| 1930 | 24.3 | 21.3 |
| 1920 | 24.6 | 21.2 |
| 1910 | 25.1 | 21.6 |
| 1900 | 25.9 | 21.9 |
| 1890 | 26.1 | 22.0 |
| **Change in age** | | |
| 1950–1998 | 3.9 | 4.7 |
| 1890–1998 | 0.6 | 3.0 |

*Source: Bureau of the Census,* Marital Status and Living Arrangements: March 1998, *Current Population Report P20-514, 1998; calculations by New Strategist*

# Marital Status of Men by Age, 1998

*(number and percent distribution of men aged 15 or older by age and marital status, 1998; numbers in thousands)*

| | total men | never married | married | divorced | widowed |
|---|---|---|---|---|---|
| **Total number** | **101,123** | **31,591** | **58,633** | **8,331** | **2,569** |
| Aged 15 to 19 | 9,921 | 9,778 | 121 | 19 | 3 |
| Aged 20 to 24 | 8,826 | 7,360 | 1,332 | 133 | – |
| Aged 25 to 29 | 9,450 | 4,822 | 4,219 | 398 | 10 |
| Aged 30 to 34 | 10,076 | 2,939 | 6,345 | 773 | 20 |
| Aged 35 to 39 | 11,299 | 2,444 | 7,598 | 1,213 | 44 |
| Aged 40 to 44 | 10,756 | 1,676 | 7,633 | 1,397 | 50 |
| Aged 45 to 54 | 16,598 | 1,481 | 12,665 | 2,303 | 150 |
| Aged 55 to 64 | 10,673 | 572 | 8,559 | 1,266 | 275 |
| Aged 65 to 74 | 7,992 | 328 | 6,331 | 626 | 707 |
| Aged 75 to 84 | 4,527 | 145 | 3,327 | 166 | 888 |
| Aged 85 or older | 1,006 | 45 | 502 | 36 | 423 |
| **Total percent** | **100.0%** | **31.2%** | **58.0%** | **8.2%** | **2.5%** |
| Aged 15 to 19 | 100.0 | 98.6 | 1.2 | 0.2 | 0.0 |
| Aged 20 to 24 | 100.0 | 83.4 | 15.1 | 1.5 | – |
| Aged 25 to 29 | 100.0 | 51.0 | 44.6 | 4.2 | 0.1 |
| Aged 30 to 34 | 100.0 | 29.2 | 63.0 | 7.7 | 0.2 |
| Aged 35 to 39 | 100.0 | 21.6 | 67.2 | 10.7 | 0.4 |
| Aged 40 to 44 | 100.0 | 15.6 | 71.0 | 13.0 | 0.5 |
| Aged 45 to 54 | 100.0 | 8.9 | 76.3 | 13.9 | 0.9 |
| Aged 55 to 64 | 100.0 | 5.4 | 80.2 | 11.9 | 2.6 |
| Aged 65 to 74 | 100.0 | 4.1 | 79.2 | 7.8 | 8.8 |
| Aged 75 to 84 | 100.0 | 3.2 | 73.5 | 3.7 | 19.6 |
| Aged 85 or older | 100.0 | 4.5 | 49.9 | 3.6 | 42.0 |

*Note: (–) means sample is too small to make a reliable estimate.*
*Source: Bureau of the Census,* Marital Status and Living Arrangements: March 1998, *Current Population Reports, P20-514, 1998*

# Marital Status of Women by Age, 1998

*(number and percent distribution of women aged 15 or older by age and marital status, 1998; numbers in thousands)*

| | total women | never married | married | divorced | widowed |
|---|---|---|---|---|---|
| **Total number** | **108,168** | **26,713** | **59,333** | **11,093** | **11,029** |
| Aged 15 to 19 | 9,545 | 9,235 | 289 | 20 | 2 |
| Aged 20 to 24 | 8,788 | 6,178 | 2,372 | 222 | 17 |
| Aged 25 to 20 | 9,546 | 3,689 | 5,298 | 525 | 35 |
| Aged 30 to 34 | 10,282 | 2,219 | 7,044 | 964 | 55 |
| Aged 35 to 39 | 11,392 | 1,626 | 8,145 | 1,484 | 138 |
| Aged 40 to 44 | 11,015 | 1,095 | 8,016 | 1,738 | 166 |
| Aged 45 to 54 | 17,459 | 1,263 | 12,345 | 3,154 | 697 |
| Aged 55 to 64 | 11,582 | 538 | 7,847 | 1,671 | 1,526 |
| Aged 65 to 74 | 9,882 | 425 | 5,420 | 882 | 3,155 |
| Aged 75 to 84 | 6,754 | 340 | 2,300 | 362 | 3,752 |
| Aged 85 or older | 1,923 | 106 | 258 | 71 | 1,487 |
| **Total percent** | **100.0%** | **24.7%** | **54.9%** | **10.3%** | **10.2%** |
| Aged 15 to 19 | 100.0 | 96.8 | 3.0 | 0.2 | 0.0 |
| Aged 20 to 24 | 100.0 | 70.3 | 27.0 | 2.5 | 0.2 |
| Aged 25 to 20 | 100.0 | 38.6 | 55.5 | 5.5 | 0.4 |
| Aged 30 to 34 | 100.0 | 21.6 | 68.5 | 9.4 | 0.5 |
| Aged 35 to 39 | 100.0 | 14.3 | 71.5 | 13.0 | 1.2 |
| Aged 40 to 44 | 100.0 | 9.9 | 72.8 | 15.8 | 1.5 |
| Aged 45 to 54 | 100.0 | 7.2 | 70.7 | 18.1 | 4.0 |
| Aged 55 to 64 | 100.0 | 4.6 | 67.8 | 14.4 | 13.2 |
| Aged 65 to 74 | 100.0 | 4.3 | 54.8 | 8.9 | 31.9 |
| Aged 75 to 84 | 100.0 | 5.0 | 34.1 | 5.4 | 55.6 |
| Aged 85 or older | 100.0 | 5.5 | 13.4 | 3.7 | 77.3 |

*Source: Bureau of the Census,* Marital Status and Living Arrangements: March 1998, *Current Population Reports, P20-514, 1998*

# Most Blacks Are Not Married

**Only 39 percent of blacks are currently married, compared with 59 percent of non-Hispanic whites and 55 percent of Hispanics.**

Most non-Hispanic whites and Hispanics are married by the time they reach their late twenties. But for blacks, marriage does not claim the majority until the 40-to-44 age group. Blacks are less likely to be married than whites or Hispanics because they postpone marriage until a much later age. Among non-Hispanic whites aged 25 to 29 in 1998, only 41 percent had never married. But 62 percent of their black counterparts were still single. In the 30-to-34 age group, only 22 percent of whites but 45 percent of blacks had never married.

Blacks are more likely to be divorced than whites or Hispanics, particularly in the 45-to-54 age group. They are also more likely to be widowed in middle-age than whites or Hispanics. Fifteen percent of blacks aged 55 to 64 are widowed, compared with only 7 percent of non-Hispanic whites and Hispanics in the age group.

♦ Blacks are less likely to marry than whites because many black men have difficulty finding jobs that pay enough to support a family.

# Marital Status by Race, Hispanic Origin, and Age, 1998

*(total number of persons aged 15 or older and percent distribution by marital status, by race and Hispanic origin, and by age, 1998; numbers in thousands)*

| | total | | never married | married | divorced | widowed |
|---|---|---|---|---|---|---|
| | number | percent | | | | |
| **White** | **174,708** | **100.0%** | **25.4%** | **58.8%** | **9.2%** | **6.6%** |
| Under age 20 | 15,462 | 100.0 | 97.5 | 2.3 | 0.2 | 0.0 |
| Aged 20 to 24 | 14,168 | 100.0 | 74.5 | 23.1 | 2.4 | 0.1 |
| Aged 25 to 29 | 15,298 | 100.0 | 41.1 | 53.4 | 5.2 | 0.3 |
| Aged 30 to 34 | 16,481 | 100.0 | 21.9 | 68.0 | 8.7 | 0.4 |
| Aged 35 to 39 | 18,697 | 100.0 | 15.1 | 72.3 | 11.9 | 0.7 |
| Aged 40 to 44 | 18,039 | 100.0 | 10.6 | 74.1 | 14.4 | 0.8 |
| Aged 45 to 54 | 28,871 | 100.0 | 7.3 | 75.1 | 15.5 | 2.2 |
| Aged 55 to 64 | 19,140 | 100.0 | 4.4 | 75.7 | 12.7 | 7.3 |
| Aged 65 to 74 | 15,760 | 100.0 | 4.0 | 67.6 | 8.0 | 20.4 |
| Aged 75 to 84 | 10,211 | 100.0 | 4.1 | 50.8 | 4.5 | 40.6 |
| Aged 85 or older | 2,582 | 100.0 | 5.3 | 26.4 | 3.5 | 64.8 |
| **Black** | **24,998** | **100.0** | **43.5** | **38.6** | **10.8** | **7.0** |
| Under age 20 | 3,058 | 100.0 | 98.5 | 1.3 | 0.3 | – |
| Aged 20 to 24 | 2,563 | 100.0 | 88.2 | 11.2 | 0.5 | 0.1 |
| Aged 25 to 29 | 2,603 | 100.0 | 61.7 | 34.8 | 3.5 | 0.1 |
| Aged 30 to 34 | 2,697 | 100.0 | 45.4 | 45.4 | 8.6 | 0.5 |
| Aged 35 to 39 | 2,851 | 100.0 | 36.8 | 49.2 | 12.6 | 1.4 |
| Aged 40 to 44 | 2,648 | 100.0 | 28.5 | 52.6 | 16.8 | 2.0 |
| Aged 45 to 54 | 3,663 | 100.0 | 15.3 | 57.3 | 22.0 | 4.4 |
| Aged 55 to 64 | 2,224 | 100.0 | 10.8 | 54.9 | 19.3 | 15.0 |
| Aged 65 to 74 | 1,613 | 100.0 | 6.1 | 47.3 | 13.0 | 33.5 |
| Aged 75 to 84 | 789 | 100.0 | 7.7 | 34.9 | 7.9 | 49.6 |
| Aged 85 or older | 289 | 100.0 | 3.5 | 15.9 | 5.5 | 74.7 |

*(continued)*

*(continued from previous page)*

| | total | | never married | married | divorced | widowed |
|---|---|---|---|---|---|---|
| | number | percent | | | | |
| **Hispanic** | **21,430** | **100.0%** | **34.7%** | **54.6%** | **7.2%** | **3.5%** |
| Under age 20 | 2,722 | 100.0 | 95.0 | 4.7 | 0.2 | 0.1 |
| Aged 20 to 24 | 2,663 | 100.0 | 69.3 | 29.4 | 1.1 | 0.2 |
| Aged 25 to 29 | 2,795 | 100.0 | 41.9 | 55.2 | 2.6 | 0.3 |
| Aged 30 to 34 | 2,693 | 100.0 | 23.7 | 69.4 | 6.5 | 0.4 |
| Aged 35 to 39 | 2,505 | 100.0 | 20.4 | 68.5 | 10.1 | 0.9 |
| Aged 40 to 44 | 2,101 | 100.0 | 10.5 | 75.3 | 13.3 | 0.0 |
| Aged 45 to 54 | 2,700 | 100.0 | 10.0 | 73.7 | 13.2 | 3.1 |
| Aged 55 to 64 | 1,633 | 100.0 | 7.3 | 73.2 | 12.9 | 6.7 |
| Aged 65 to 74 | 1,015 | 100.0 | 5.7 | 61.9 | 10.8 | 21.5 |
| Aged 75 to 84 | 480 | 100.0 | 3.1 | 50.0 | 7.5 | 39.6 |
| Aged 85 or older | 123 | 100.0 | 7.3 | 27.6 | 0.8 | 63.4 |
| **Non-Hispanic white** | **154,205** | **100.0** | **24.2** | **59.3** | **9.5** | **6.0** |
| Under age 20 | 12,864 | 100.0 | 97.0 | 1.8 | 0.2 | 0.0 |
| Aged 20 to 24 | 11,631 | 100.0 | 75.7 | 21.5 | 2.6 | 0.1 |
| Aged 25 to 29 | 12,607 | 100.0 | 41.0 | 52.9 | 5.8 | 0.2 |
| Aged 30 to 34 | 13,905 | 100.0 | 21.8 | 68.8 | 9.1 | 0.3 |
| Aged 35 to 39 | 16,318 | 100.0 | 14.3 | 72.7 | 12.2 | 0.7 |
| Aged 40 to 44 | 16,028 | 100.0 | 10.7 | 73.8 | 14.6 | 0.8 |
| Aged 45 to 54 | 26,298 | 100.0 | 6.0 | 75.2 | 15.8 | 2.1 |
| Aged 55 to 64 | 17,560 | 100.0 | 4.1 | 75.9 | 12.7 | 7.3 |
| Aged 65 to 74 | 14,789 | 100.0 | 3.9 | 67.9 | 7.8 | 20.3 |
| Aged 75 to 84 | 9,743 | 100.0 | 4.2 | 50.8 | 4.3 | 40.7 |
| Aged 85 or older | 2,463 | 100.0 | 5.3 | 26.2 | 3.7 | 64.8 |

*Note: (–) means sample is too small to make a reliable estimate.*
*Source: Bureau of the Census,* Marital Status and Living Arrangements: March 1998, *Current Population Reports, P20-514, 1998; calculations by New Strategist*

# 6

# Population Trends

◆ **Older boomers will inflate the number of fiftysomethings between 1999 and 2005.**
Rapid growth in this population—the nation's biggest spenders—will force businesses to rethink the older market.

◆ **The minority share of the American population will rise to 30 percent by 2005.**
The number of Asians is projected to climb 22 percent between 1999 and 2005, while Hispanics will grow 18 percent, blacks 7 percent, and non-Hispanic whites just 2 percent.

◆ **The mountain states should grow faster than any other area of the U.S. between 1999 and 2005.**
The population of the mountain states should grow 11 percent between 1999 and 2005, while the Pacific states are projected to grow 7 percent—slightly faster than the national average of 5 percent.

◆ **Las Vegas is the fastest-growing large metropolitan area.**
Three out of four Americans lived in one of the nation's metropolitan areas in 1990. In 1950, barely half of Americans were metropolitan residents.

◆ **Mobility rates have fallen over the past few decades.**
As the enormous baby-boom generation enters its fifties, the mobility rate may continue to decline because the middle-aged move infrequently.

◆ **Barely half the public voted in the 1996 presidential election.**
The most common excuse for not going to the polls: 22 percent claimed to have no time off or to be too busy.

◆ **Religious diversity is growing.**
Only 47 percent of Americans under age 30 are Protestants compared to about 69 percent of people aged 50 or older.

# More Women Than Men

**American women outnumber men by 6 million.**

Although there are more women than men in the population, women do not begin to outnumber men until the 30-to-34 age group. By ages 85 and older, there are only 40 men for every 100 women. Men slightly outnumber women at younger ages because boys outnumber girls at birth. Women outnumber men at older ages because throughout life men have higher death rates than women. Research has shown that men's death rate is higher primarily because of biological factors rather than lifestyle differences.

In 1999, the largest five-year age group were the 35-to-39-year-olds, at 22.5 million. Most of the people in this age group are the youngest members of the baby-boom generation, born between 1960 and 1964. The baby-boom generation, aged 35 to 53 in 1999, is moving up through the age distribution, changing America as it does.

◆ Because death rates are higher for men than for women, women will continue to outnumber men at older ages.

## Women increasingly outnumber men with age

*(number of males per 100 females, selected ages, 1999)*

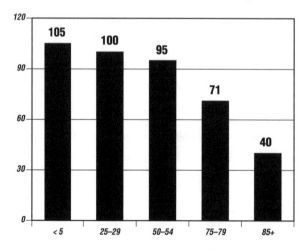

# Population by Age and Sex, 1999

*(number of people by age and sex, and sex ratio by age, 1999; numbers in thousands)*

| | total | male | female | sex ratio |
|---|---|---|---|---|
| **Total people** | **272,330** | **133,039** | **139,291** | **96** |
| Under age 5 | 19,042 | 9,740 | 9,302 | 105 |
| Aged 5 to 9 | 20,059 | 10,270 | 9,789 | 105 |
| Aged 10 to 14 | 19,697 | 10,088 | 9,609 | 105 |
| Aged 15 to 19 | 19,660 | 10,074 | 9,586 | 105 |
| Aged 20 to 24 | 17,801 | 9,028 | 8,773 | 103 |
| Aged 25 to 29 | 18,154 | 9,063 | 9,091 | 100 |
| Aged 30 to 34 | 19,722 | 9,807 | 9,915 | 99 |
| Aged 35 to 39 | 22,492 | 11,204 | 11,289 | 99 |
| Aged 40 to 44 | 22,168 | 10,981 | 11,188 | 98 |
| Aged 45 to 49 | 19,295 | 9,464 | 9,832 | 96 |
| Aged 50 to 54 | 16,422 | 7,983 | 8,439 | 95 |
| Aged 55 to 59 | 12,870 | 6,183 | 6,687 | 92 |
| Aged 60 to 64 | 10,508 | 4,967 | 5,541 | 90 |
| Aged 65 to 69 | 9,429 | 4,323 | 5,106 | 85 |
| Aged 70 to 74 | 8,758 | 3,849 | 4,910 | 78 |
| Aged 75 to 79 | 7,323 | 3,045 | 4,278 | 71 |
| Aged 80 to 84 | 4,806 | 1,794 | 3,012 | 60 |
| Aged 85 or older | 4,124 | 1,179 | 2,945 | 40 |
| Aged 18 to 24 | 25,708 | 13,062 | 12,646 | 103 |
| Aged 18 or older | 201,781 | 96,902 | 104,879 | 92 |
| Aged 65 or older | 34,439 | 14,189 | 20,250 | 70 |
| Median age | 35.5 | 34.3 | 36.6 | – |

*Note: Sex ratio is the number of males per 100 females.*
*Source: Bureau of the Census, Population Projections of the United States by Age, Sex, Race, and Hispanic Origin: 1995 to 2050, Current Population Reports, P25–1130, 1996; calculations by New Strategist*

# Biggest Gainer Will Be the 55-to-59 Age Group

## Older boomers will inflate the number of fiftysomethings between 1999 and 2005.

The United States population is projected to grow 5 percent between 1999 and 2005, according to the Census Bureau. But some age groups will expand rapidly while others will shrink.

The fastest-growing age group will be 55-to-59-year-olds, projected to increase 31 percent between 1999 and 2005 as the oldest boomers enter their late fifties. In contrast, the number of people in their thirties will fall 12 percent as the small baby-bust generation (or Generation X) matures.

The children of baby boomers will boost the number of teens and young adults after years of decline. The number of people aged 20 to 24 should expand 12 percent between 1999 and 2005.

♦ Rapid growth in the fiftysomething population—the nation's biggest spenders—will force businesses to rethink their strategies as the baby-boom generation creates a vibrant mid-life market.

♦ Because of the growth of the teen population, both the youth and mid-life markets will provide expanding opportunities for businesses during the next 10 years.

# Population by Age, 1999 to 2005

*(number of people by age, 1999 to 2005; percent change, 1999–2005; numbers in thousands)*

|  | 1999 | 2000 | 2005 | percent change 1999-2005 |
|---|---|---|---|---|
| Total people | 272,330 | 274,634 | 285,981 | 5.0% |
| Under age 5 | 19,042 | 18,987 | 19,127 | 0.4 |
| Aged 5 to 9 | 20,059 | 19,920 | 19,338 | -3.6 |
| Aged 10 to 14 | 19,697 | 20,057 | 20,809 | 5.6 |
| Aged 15 to 19 | 19,660 | 19,820 | 20,997 | 6.8 |
| Aged 20 to 24 | 17,801 | 18,257 | 19,960 | 12.1 |
| Aged 25 to 29 | 18,154 | 17,722 | 18,057 | -0.5 |
| Aged 30 to 34 | 19,722 | 19,511 | 18,249 | -7.5 |
| Aged 35 to 39 | 22,493 | 22,180 | 19,802 | -12.0 |
| Aged 40 to 44 | 22,169 | 22,479 | 22,363 | 0.9 |
| Aged 45 to 49 | 19,296 | 19,806 | 21,988 | 14.0 |
| Aged 50 to 54 | 16,422 | 17,224 | 19,518 | 18.9 |
| Aged 55 to 59 | 12,870 | 13,307 | 16,798 | 30.5 |
| Aged 60 to 64 | 10,508 | 10,654 | 12,807 | 21.9 |
| Aged 65 to 69 | 9,429 | 9,410 | 10,037 | 6.4 |
| Aged 70 to 74 | 8,759 | 8,726 | 8,332 | -4.9 |
| Aged 75 to 79 | 7,323 | 7,415 | 7,393 | 1.0 |
| Aged 80 to 84 | 4,806 | 4,900 | 5,505 | 14.5 |
| Aged 85 or older | 4,124 | 4,259 | 4,899 | 18.8 |
| Aged 18 to 24 | 25,708 | 26,258 | 28,268 | 10.0 |
| Aged 18 or older | 201,781 | 203,852 | 214,017 | 6.1 |
| Aged 65 or older | 34,439 | 34,709 | 36,166 | 5.0 |

*Source: Bureau of the Census,* Population Projections of the United States by Age, Sex, Race, and Hispanic Origin: 1995 to 2050; *Current Population Reports, P25-1130, 1996; calculations by New Strategist*

# Diversity on the Rise

**The minority share of the American population will rise to 30 percent by 2005.**

The non-Hispanic white share of the U.S. population will fall below 70 percent by 2005, down from 72 percent today.

Between 1999 and 2005, the fastest-growing minority will be non-Hispanic Asians, according to the Census Bureau. The number of Asians is projected to climb 22 percent between 1999 and 2005. The number of Hispanics will grow 18 percent, while non-Hispanic blacks will increase 7 percent. The number of non-Hispanic whites will grow only 2 percent between 1999 and 2005.

Hispanics will be the largest minority in the United States by 2005. Their numbers will rise to 36 million, surpassing the 35 million non-Hispanic blacks projected for that year. In 2005, 13 percent of Americans will be Hispanic, 12 percent will be non-Hispanic black, 4 percent will be non-Hispanic Asian, and fewer than 1 percent will be non-Hispanic Native Americans.

◆ Our multicultural society is here to stay. Businesses must reflect this diversity in their leadership, workforce, products, and services or lose customers to those that more closely mirror America.

## Asians to grow fastest

*(percent change in number of people by race and ethnicity, 1999–2005)*

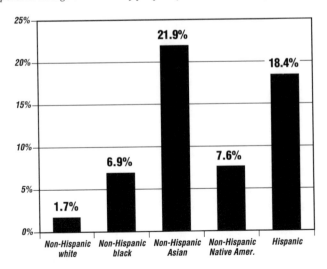

# Population by Race and Hispanic Origin, 1999 to 2005

*(number and percent distribution of people by race and Hispanic origin, 1999 to 2005; percent change in number and percentage point change in share, 1999–2005; numbers in thousands)*

| | 1999 | 2000 | 2005 | percent change 1999–2005 |
|---|---|---|---|---|
| **Total people** | **272,330** | **274,634** | **285,981** | **5.0%** |
| White, non-Hispanic | 196,441 | 197,061 | 199,802 | 1.7 |
| Black, non-Hispanic | 33,180 | 33,568 | 35,485 | 6.9 |
| Asian, non-Hispanic | 10,219 | 10,584 | 12,454 | 21.9 |
| Native American, non-Hispanic | 2,209 | 2,054 | 2,183 | 7.6 |
| Hispanic | 30,461 | 31,366 | 36,057 | 18.4 |
| | | | | percentage point change, 1999–2005 |
| **Total people** | **100.0%** | **100.0%** | **100.0%** | – |
| White, non-Hispanic | 72.1 | 71.8 | 69.9 | −2.3 |
| Black, non-Hispanic | 12.2 | 12.2 | 12.4 | 0.2 |
| Asian, non-Hispanic | 3.8 | 3.9 | 4.4 | 0.6 |
| Native American, non-Hispanic | 0.8 | 0.7 | 0.8 | 0.0 |
| Hispanic | 11.2 | 11.4 | 12.6 | 1.4 |

*Source: Bureau of the Census,* Population Projections of the United States by Age, Sex, Race, and Hispanic Origin: 1995 to 2050*; Current Population Reports P25-1130, 1996; calculations by New Strategist*

# Aging Boomers Will Boost Fiftysomethings in Every Racial and Ethnic Group

**The aging of the baby-boom generation will inflate the number of Asian, black, Hispanic, Native American, and white 50-to-59-year-olds.**

The number of non-Hispanic whites will grow just 2 percent from 1999 to 2005, according to Bureau of the Census projections. But the number of whites aged 55 to 59 will grow 28 percent because of the aging of the baby-boom generation. The number of non-Hispanic blacks will grow 7 percent overall during those same years, while the number of those aged 55 to 59 will grow 34 percent. Among both non-Hispanic whites and non-Hispanic blacks, the fiftysomething age group will grow faster than any other.

Among Hispanics and non-Hispanic Asians, rapid growth in fiftysomethings will be overshadowed by even faster growth among the older population. The number of Hispanics aged 55 to 59 will grow 44 percent between 1999 and 2005, but the number of Hispanics aged 80 to 84 will grow 52 percent. The number of non-Hispanic Asians aged 55 to 59 will grow 50 percent between 1999 and 2005, but the number of those aged 80 or older will grow more than 60 percent.

◆ By 2005, only 61 percent of Americans under age 18 will be non-Hispanic whites, compared with 82 percent of people aged 65 or older. The difference in racial and ethnic composition between the nation's youth and the elderly could lead to political conflict in determining the distribution of the nation's economic resources.

# Non-Hispanic Asians by Age, 1999 to 2005

*(number of non-Hispanic Asians by age, 1999 to 2005; percent change 1999–2005; numbers in thousands)*

|  | 1999 | 2000 | 2005 | percent change 1999–2005 |
|---|---|---|---|---|
| **Total people** | **10,219** | **10,584** | **12,454** | **21.9%** |
| Under age 5 | 846 | 867 | 973 | 15.0 |
| Aged 5 to 9 | 827 | 859 | 960 | 16.1 |
| Aged 10 to 14 | 805 | 834 | 1,043 | 29.6 |
| Aged 15 to 19 | 805 | 835 | 955 | 18.6 |
| Aged 20 to 24 | 724 | 756 | 944 | 30.4 |
| Aged 25 to 29 | 837 | 836 | 900 | 7.5 |
| Aged 30 to 34 | 880 | 907 | 987 | 12.2 |
| Aged 35 to 39 | 903 | 921 | 1,004 | 11.2 |
| Aged 40 to 44 | 844 | 873 | 994 | 17.8 |
| Aged 45 to 49 | 713 | 742 | 893 | 25.2 |
| Aged 50 to 54 | 562 | 602 | 751 | 33.6 |
| Aged 55 to 59 | 403 | 428 | 604 | 49.9 |
| Aged 60 to 64 | 325 | 342 | 442 | 36.0 |
| Aged 65 to 69 | 268 | 278 | 347 | 29.5 |
| Aged 70 to 74 | 212 | 222 | 268 | 26.4 |
| Aged 75 to 79 | 143 | 152 | 195 | 36.4 |
| Aged 80 to 84 | 73 | 79 | 117 | 60.3 |
| Aged 85 or older | 47 | 51 | 78 | 66.0 |
| Aged 18 to 24 | 1,033 | 1,080 | 1,312 | 27.0 |
| Aged 18 or older | 7,244 | 7,514 | 8,891 | 22.7 |
| Aged 65 or older | 744 | 783 | 1,004 | 34.9 |

*Source: Bureau of the Census,* Population Projections of the United States by Age, Sex, Race, and Hispanic Origin: 1995 to 2050; *Current Population Reports, P25-1130, 1996; calculations by New Strategist*

# Non-Hispanic Blacks by Age, 1999 to 2005

*(number of non-Hispanic blacks by age, 1999 to 2005; percent change 1999–2005; numbers in thousands)*

| | *1999* | *2000* | *2005* | *percent change 1999–2005* |
|---|---|---|---|---|
| **Total people** | **33,180** | **33,568** | **35,485** | **6.9%** |
| Under age 5 | 2,920 | 2,929 | 3,016 | 3.3 |
| Aged 5 to 9 | 2,982 | 2,966 | 2,967 | −0.5 |
| Aged 10 to 14 | 2,922 | 2,997 | 3,103 | 6.2 |
| Aged 15 to 19 | 2,868 | 2,872 | 3,140 | 9.5 |
| Aged 20 to 24 | 2,516 | 2,592 | 2,762 | 9.8 |
| Aged 25 to 29 | 2,435 | 2,405 | 2,472 | 1.5 |
| Aged 30 to 34 | 2,489 | 2,458 | 2,411 | −3.1 |
| Aged 35 to 39 | 2,725 | 2,706 | 2,478 | −9.1 |
| Aged 40 to 44 | 2,592 | 2,641 | 2,675 | 3.2 |
| Aged 45 to 49 | 2,128 | 2,199 | 2,530 | 18.9 |
| Aged 50 to 54 | 1,612 | 1,723 | 2,124 | 31.8 |
| Aged 55 to 59 | 1,231 | 1,267 | 1,650 | 34.0 |
| Aged 60 to 64 | 1,010 | 1,034 | 1,200 | 18.8 |
| Aged 65 to 69 | 890 | 894 | 974 | 9.4 |
| Aged 70 to 74 | 706 | 714 | 720 | 2.0 |
| Aged 75 to 79 | 534 | 536 | 566 | 6.0 |
| Aged 80 to 84 | 319 | 327 | 353 | 10.7 |
| Aged 85 or older | 303 | 310 | 344 | 13.5 |
| Aged 18 to 24 | 3,676 | 3,752 | 3,975 | 8.1 |
| Aged 18 or older | 22,649 | 22,963 | 24,472 | 8.0 |
| Aged 65 or older | 2,752 | 2,781 | 2,957 | 7.4 |

*Source: Bureau of the Census,* Population Projections of the United States by Age, Sex, Race, and Hispanic Origin: 1995 to 2050; *Current Population Reports, P25-1130, 1996; calculations by New Strategist*

# Hispanics by Age, 1999 to 2005

*(number of Hispanics by age, 1999 to 2005; percent change 1999–2005; numbers in thousands)*

| | *1999* | *2000* | *2005* | *percent change 1999–2005* |
|---|---|---|---|---|
| **Total people** | **30,461** | **31,366** | **36,057** | **18.4%** |
| Under age 5 | 3,138 | 3,203 | 3,580 | 14.1 |
| Aged 5 to 9 | 3,259 | 3,298 | 3,366 | 3.3 |
| Aged 10 to 14 | 2,772 | 2,906 | 3,558 | 28.4 |
| Aged 15 to 19 | 2,659 | 2,732 | 3,221 | 21.1 |
| Aged 20 to 24 | 2,488 | 2,574 | 3,012 | 21.1 |
| Aged 25 to 29 | 2,512 | 2,510 | 2,734 | 8.8 |
| Aged 30 to 34 | 2,659 | 2,671 | 2,681 | 0.8 |
| Aged 35 to 39 | 2,545 | 2,618 | 2,751 | 8.1 |
| Aged 40 to 44 | 2,121 | 2,218 | 2,670 | 25.9 |
| Aged 45 to 49 | 1,634 | 1,727 | 2,200 | 34.6 |
| Aged 50 to 54 | 1,240 | 1,322 | 1,727 | 39.3 |
| Aged 55 to 59 | 914 | 962 | 1,312 | 43.5 |
| Aged 60 to 64 | 732 | 755 | 948 | 29.5 |
| Aged 65 to 69 | 599 | 618 | 734 | 22.5 |
| Aged 70 to 74 | 482 | 502 | 574 | 19.1 |
| Aged 75 to 79 | 342 | 362 | 453 | 32.5 |
| Aged 80 to 84 | 194 | 206 | 295 | 52.1 |
| Aged 85 or older | 172 | 183 | 242 | 40.7 |
| Aged 18 to 24 | 3,560 | 3,679 | 4,270 | 19.9 |
| Aged 18 or older | 19,705 | 20,332 | 23,590 | 19.7 |
| Aged 65 or older | 1,790 | 1,872 | 2,298 | 28.4 |

*Source: Bureau of the Census,* Population Projections of the United States by Age, Sex, Race, and Hispanic Origin: 1995 to 2050; *Current Population Reports, P25-1130, 1996; calculations by New Strategist*

# Non-Hispanic Native Americans by Age, 1999 to 2005

*(number of non-Hispanic Native Americans by age, 1999 to 2005; percent change 1999–2005; numbers in thousands)*

|  | *1999* | *2000* | *2005* | *percent change 1999–2005* |
|---|---|---|---|---|
| **Total people** | **2,029** | **2,054** | **2,183** | **7.6%** |
| Under age 5 | 179 | 180 | 192 | 7.3 |
| Aged 5 to 9 | 186 | 182 | 186 | 0.0 |
| Aged 10 to 14 | 208 | 212 | 202 | –2.9 |
| Aged 15 to 19 | 194 | 197 | 211 | 8.8 |
| Aged 20 to 24 | 159 | 164 | 190 | 19.5 |
| Aged 25 to 29 | 157 | 156 | 163 | 3.8 |
| Aged 30 to 34 | 146 | 147 | 153 | 4.8 |
| Aged 35 to 39 | 154 | 152 | 143 | –7.1 |
| Aged 40 to 44 | 146 | 149 | 149 | 2.1 |
| Aged 45 to 49 | 124 | 127 | 140 | 12.9 |
| Aged 50 to 54 | 99 | 104 | 119 | 20.2 |
| Aged 55 to 59 | 74 | 77 | 95 | 28.4 |
| Aged 60 to 64 | 58 | 59 | 70 | 20.7 |
| Aged 65 to 69 | 45 | 46 | 52 | 15.6 |
| Aged 70 to 74 | 36 | 36 | 40 | 11.1 |
| Aged 75 to 79 | 28 | 28 | 30 | 7.1 |
| Aged 80 to 84 | 17 | 18 | 22 | 29.4 |
| Aged 85 or older | 19 | 21 | 27 | 42.1 |
| Aged 18 to 24 | 232 | 238 | 268 | 15.5 |
| Aged 18 or older | 1,336 | 1,358 | 1,470 | 10.0 |
| Aged 65 or older | 145 | 149 | 170 | 17.2 |

*Source: Bureau of the Census,* Population Projections of the United States by Age, Sex, Race, and Hispanic Origin: 1995 to 2050; *Current Population Reports, P25-1130, 1996; calculations by New Strategist*

# Non-Hispanic Whites by Age, 1999 to 2005

*(number of non-Hispanic whites by age, 1999 to 2005; percent change 1999–2005; numbers in thousands)*

|  | 1999 | 2000 | 2005 | percent change 1999–2005 |
|---|---|---|---|---|
| **Total people** | **196,441** | **197,061** | **199,802** | **1.7%** |
| Under age 5 | 11,959 | 11,807 | 11,367 | –5.0 |
| Aged 5 to 9 | 12,805 | 12,615 | 11,859 | –7.4 |
| Aged 10 to 14 | 12,990 | 13,109 | 12,903 | –0.7 |
| Aged 15 to 19 | 13,133 | 13,184 | 13,469 | 2.6 |
| Aged 20 to 24 | 11,915 | 12,171 | 13,052 | 9.5 |
| Aged 25 to 29 | 12,213 | 11,816 | 11,789 | –3.5 |
| Aged 30 to 34 | 13,548 | 13,328 | 12,017 | –11.3 |
| Aged 35 to 39 | 16,165 | 15,783 | 13,426 | –16.9 |
| Aged 40 to 44 | 16,466 | 16,599 | 15,874 | –3.6 |
| Aged 45 to 49 | 14,696 | 15,012 | 16,225 | 10.4 |
| Aged 50 to 54 | 12,910 | 13,473 | 14,798 | 14.6 |
| Aged 55 to 59 | 10,249 | 10,574 | 13,137 | 28.2 |
| Aged 60 to 64 | 8,383 | 8,465 | 10,148 | 21.1 |
| Aged 65 to 69 | 7,626 | 7,574 | 7,929 | 4.0 |
| Aged 70 to 74 | 7,323 | 7,251 | 6,731 | –8.1 |
| Aged 75 to 79 | 6,276 | 6,336 | 6,150 | –2.0 |
| Aged 80 to 84 | 4,202 | 4,271 | 4,718 | 12.3 |
| Aged 85 or older | 3,582 | 3,694 | 4,209 | 17.5 |
| Aged 18 to 24 | 17,209 | 17,510 | 18,443 | 7.2 |
| Aged 18 or older | 150,847 | 151,685 | 155,594 | 3.1 |
| Aged 65 or older | 29,009 | 29,126 | 29,737 | 2.5 |

*Source: Bureau of the Census,* Population Projections of the United States by Age, Sex, Race, and Hispanic Origin: 1995 to 2050; *Current Population Reports, P25–1130, 1996; calculations by New Strategist*

# West to Grow Fastest

## The population of the mountain states should grow faster than that of any other area of the U.S. between 1999 and 2005.

While the U.S. population overall is projected to grow 5 percent between 1999 and 2005, the population of the West is projected to grow 8 percent. The mountain states should gain an even more robust 11 percent, while the population of the Pacific states is projected to grow 7 percent—slightly faster than the national average.

The Middle Atlantic division, which includes New Jersey, New York, and Pennsylvania, will have the slowest population growth in the United States during the next few years. Between 1999 and 2005, the population of the Middle Atlantic division is projected to rise just 1.2 percent. Overall, the Northeast should grow 1.5 percent, the Midwest 3 percent, and the South by 6.5 percent between 1999 and 2005.

◆ By 2005, the West will surpass the Midwest in population. Together, the South and West will be home to 59 percent of Americans in that year—increasing the political and economic clout of the Sunbelt states.

### Northeast will be growing slowly

*(percent change in population by region, 1999–2005)*

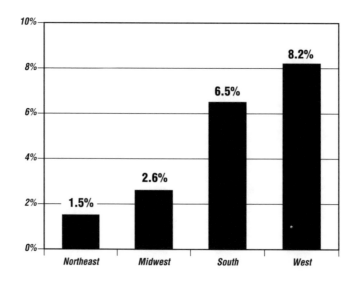

# Population by Region and Division, 1999 to 2005

*(number of people by region and division, 1999 to 2005; percent change, 1999–2005; numbers in thousands)*

| | 1999 | 2000 | 2005 | percent change 1999–2005 |
|---|---|---|---|---|
| **Total people** | **272,330** | **274,634** | **285,981** | **5.0%** |
| **Northeast** | 51,986 | 52,107 | 52,767 | 1.5 |
| New England | 13,531 | 13,581 | 13,843 | 2.3 |
| Middle Atlantic | 38,455 | 38,526 | 38,923 | 1.2 |
| **Midwest** | 63,193 | 63,502 | 64,825 | 2.6 |
| East North Central | 44,247 | 44,419 | 45,151 | 2.0 |
| West North Central | 18,946 | 19,082 | 19,673 | 3.8 |
| **South** | 96,512 | 97,613 | 102,788 | 6.5 |
| South Atlantic | 49,546 | 50,147 | 52,921 | 6.8 |
| East South Central | 16,758 | 16,918 | 17,604 | 5.0 |
| West South Central | 30,207 | 30,548 | 32,263 | 6.8 |
| **West** | 60,640 | 61,413 | 65,603 | 8.2 |
| Mountain | 17,342 | 17,725 | 19,249 | 11.0 |
| Pacific | 43,297 | 43,687 | 46,354 | 7.1 |

*Source: Bureau of the Census,* Projections of the Total Population of States: 1995 to 2025; *PPL-47, 1996; calculations by New Strategist*

# Minority Populations Are Larger in the South and West

**In 2005, one in five Southerners will be non-Hispanic black, while one in four Westerners will be Hispanic.**

Minorities are unevenly distributed across the country, and the South and West are home to the largest share. The minority populations in the South and West will continue to grow during the next few years. By 2005, minorities will account for one-third of people living in the South and 42 percent of those in the West.

The non-Hispanic white share of the population is projected to decline in every region between now and 2005. In the West, only 58 percent of residents in 2005 will be non-Hispanic white.

More than half of non-Hispanic blacks live in the South, a proportion that will climb to 56 percent by 2005. In that year, the West will be home to 53 percent of non-Hispanic Asians, 47 percent of Native Americans, and 46 percent of Hispanics.

◆ The uneven distribution of minorities creates regional tensions as some states and metropolitan areas encounter racial and ethnic diversity on a daily basis, while others only rarely address diversity issues.

### West has smallest share of non-Hispanic whites

*(percent of people who are non-Hispanic white by region, 2000)*

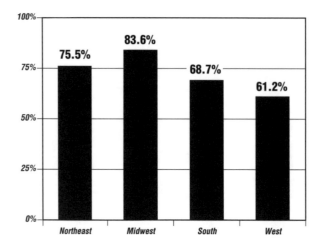

# Population by Region, Race, and Hispanic Origin, 2000

*(number and percent distribution of people by region, race, and Hispanic origin, 2000; numbers in thousands)*

| | total | non-Hispanic white | black | Asian | Native American | Hispanic |
|---|---|---|---|---|---|---|
| **Number** | | | | | | |
| **Total people** | **274,637** | **197,062** | **33,569** | **10,585** | **2,055** | **31,366** |
| Northeast | 52,107 | 39,327 | 5,634 | 2,017 | 113 | 5,016 |
| Midwest | 63,502 | 53,096 | 6,430 | 1,164 | 372 | 2,438 |
| South | 97,613 | 67,080 | 18,553 | 1,771 | 599 | 9,610 |
| West | 61,413 | 37,558 | 2,952 | 5,631 | 971 | 14,300 |
| **Percent distribution by race and Hispanic origin** | | | | | | |
| **Total people** | **100.0%** | **71.8%** | **12.2%** | **3.9%** | **0.7%** | **11.4%** |
| Northeast | 100.0 | 75.5 | 10.8 | 3.9 | 0.2 | 9.6 |
| Midwest | 100.0 | 83.6 | 10.1 | 1.8 | 0.6 | 3.8 |
| South | 100.0 | 68.7 | 19.0 | 1.8 | 0.6 | 9.8 |
| West | 100.0 | 61.2 | 4.8 | 9.2 | 1.6 | 23.3 |
| **Percent distribution by region** | | | | | | |
| **Total people** | **100.0%** | **100.0%** | **100.0%** | **100.0%** | **100.0%** | **100.0%** |
| Northeast | 19.0 | 20.0 | 16.8 | 19.1 | 5.5 | 16.0 |
| Midwest | 23.1 | 26.9 | 19.2 | 11.0 | 18.1 | 7.8 |
| South | 35.5 | 34.0 | 55.3 | 16.7 | 29.1 | 30.6 |
| West | 22.4 | 19.1 | 8.8 | 53.2 | 47.3 | 45.6 |

*Source: Bureau of the Census,* Population Projections for States by Age, Sex, Race, and Hispanic Origin: 1995 to 2025, *PPL-47, 1996; calculations by New Strategist*

# Population by Region, Race, and Hispanic Origin, 2005

*(number and percent distribution of people by region, race, and Hispanic origin, 2005; numbers in thousands)*

| | | non-Hispanic | | | | |
| | total | white | black | Asian | Native American | Hispanic |
|---|---|---|---|---|---|---|
| **Number** | | | | | | |
| **Total people** | **285,962** | **199,802** | **35,485** | **12,454** | **2,184** | **36,057** |
| Northeast | 52,767 | 38,769 | 5,840 | 2,398 | 117 | 5,644 |
| Midwest | 64,825 | 53,521 | 6,734 | 1,369 | 404 | 2,797 |
| South | 102,788 | 69,168 | 19,855 | 2,083 | 632 | 11,049 |
| West | 65,603 | 38,344 | 3,057 | 6,604 | 1,030 | 16,568 |
| **Percent distribution by race and Hispanic origin** | | | | | | |
| **Total people** | **100.0%** | **69.9%** | **12.4%** | **4.4%** | **0.8%** | **12.6%** |
| Northeast | 100.0 | 73.5 | 11.1 | 4.5 | 0.2 | 10.7 |
| Midwest | 100.0 | 82.6 | 10.4 | 2.1 | 0.6 | 4.3 |
| South | 100.0 | 67.3 | 19.3 | 2.0 | 0.6 | 10.7 |
| West | 100.0 | 58.4 | 4.7 | 10.1 | 1.6 | 25.3 |
| **Percent distribution by region** | | | | | | |
| **Total people** | **100.0%** | **100.0%** | **100.0%** | **100.0%** | **100.0%** | **100.0%** |
| Northeast | 18.5 | 19.4 | 16.5 | 19.2 | 5.4 | 15.7 |
| Midwest | 22.7 | 26.8 | 19.0 | 11.0 | 18.5 | 7.8 |
| South | 35.9 | 34.6 | 56.0 | 16.7 | 28.9 | 30.6 |
| West | 22.9 | 19.2 | 8.6 | 53.0 | 47.2 | 45.9 |

*Source: Bureau of the Census,* Population Projections for States by Age, Sex, Race, and Hispanic Origin: 1995 to 2025, *PPL-47, 1996; calculations by New Strategist*

# Nevada to Grow Fastest

## Nevada's population is projected to grow 14 percent between 1999 and 2005.

Other mountain states are also projected to grow rapidly in the next few years. The population of Idaho should grow 13 percent between 1999 and 2005, those of Utah and Arizona 12 percent, and those of New Mexico and Wyoming 10 percent. Overall, the mountain states should have the fastest-growing population of the United States during the next few years.

Many state populations are projected to grow slowly from 1999 to 2005, but no state is projected to lose population. The states whose populations should grow less than 1 percent between 1999 and 2005 include New York, Pennsylvania, West Virginia, and the District of Columbia. The nation's most populous state, California, should grow 7 percent—just slightly higher than the 5 percent national rate.

◆ Political and economic clout will continue to shift from the slow-growing Northeast and Midwest to the fast-growing South and West.

### West has fastest-growing states

*(five states projected to grow the fastest, 1999–2005)*

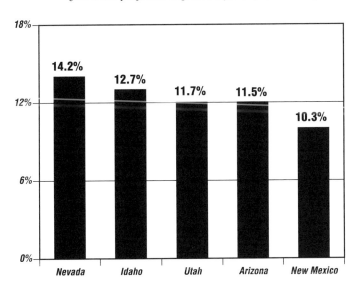

# State Populations, 1999 to 2005

*(number of persons by state, 1999 to 2005; percent change, 1999–2005; numbers in thousands)*

| | 1999 | 2000 | 2005 | percent change 1999–2005 |
|---|---|---|---|---|
| **Total people** | **272,330** | **274,634** | **285,981** | **5.0%** |
| Alabama | 4,412 | 4,451 | 4,631 | 5.0 |
| Alaska | 644 | 653 | 700 | 8.7 |
| Arizona | 4,690 | 4,798 | 5,230 | 11.5 |
| Arkansas | 2,604 | 2,631 | 2,750 | 5.6 |
| California | 32,286 | 32,521 | 34,441 | 6.7 |
| Colorado | 4,092 | 4,168 | 4,468 | 9.2 |
| Connecticut | 3,282 | 3,284 | 3,317 | 1.1 |
| Delaware | 759 | 768 | 800 | 5.4 |
| District of Columbia | 526 | 523 | 529 | 0.6 |
| Florida | 15,023 | 15,233 | 16,279 | 8.4 |
| Georgia | 7,749 | 7,875 | 8,413 | 8.6 |
| Hawaii | 1,242 | 1,257 | 1,342 | 8.1 |
| Idaho | 1,313 | 1,347 | 1,480 | 12.7 |
| Illinois | 12,008 | 12,051 | 12,266 | 2.1 |
| Indiana | 6,001 | 6,045 | 6,215 | 3.6 |
| Iowa | 2,889 | 2,900 | 2,941 | 1.8 |
| Kansas | 2,649 | 2,668 | 2,761 | 4.2 |
| Kentucky | 3,970 | 3,995 | 4,098 | 3.2 |
| Louisiana | 4,407 | 4,425 | 4,535 | 2.9 |
| Maine | 1,256 | 1,259 | 1,285 | 2.3 |
| Maryland | 5,233 | 5,275 | 5,467 | 4.5 |
| Massachusetts | 6,175 | 6,199 | 6,310 | 2.2 |
| Michigan | 9,658 | 9,679 | 9,763 | 1.1 |
| Minnesota | 4,789 | 4,830 | 5,005 | 4.5 |
| Mississippi | 2,793 | 2,816 | 2,908 | 4.1 |
| Missouri | 5,500 | 5,540 | 5,718 | 4.0 |
| Montana | 935 | 950 | 1,006 | 7.6 |
| Nebraska | 1,693 | 1,705 | 1,761 | 4.0 |
| Nevada | 1,812 | 1,871 | 2,070 | 14.2 |
| New Hampshire | 1,211 | 1,224 | 1,281 | 5.8 |
| New Jersey | 8,135 | 8,178 | 8,392 | 3.2 |
| New Mexico | 1,827 | 1,860 | 2,016 | 10.3 |
| New York | 18,139 | 18,146 | 18,250 | 0.6 |

*(continued)*

*(continued from previous page)*

| | 1999 | 2000 | 2005 | percent change 1999–2005 |
|---|---|---|---|---|
| North Carolina | 7,669 | 7,777 | 8,227 | 7.3% |
| North Dakota | 658 | 662 | 677 | 2.9 |
| Ohio | 11,291 | 11,319 | 11,428 | 1.2 |
| Oklahoma | 3,353 | 3,373 | 3,491 | 4.1 |
| Oregon | 3,349 | 3,397 | 3,613 | 7.9 |
| Pennsylvania | 12,181 | 12,202 | 12,281 | 0.8 |
| Rhode Island | 996 | 998 | 1,012 | 1.6 |
| South Carolina | 3,822 | 3,858 | 4,033 | 5.5 |
| South Dakota | 768 | 777 | 810 | 5.5 |
| Tennessee | 5,583 | 5,657 | 5,966 | 6.9 |
| Texas | 19,844 | 20,119 | 21,487 | 8.3 |
| Utah | 2,158 | 2,207 | 2,411 | 11.7 |
| Vermont | 611 | 617 | 638 | 4.4 |
| Virginia | 6,927 | 6,997 | 7,324 | 5.7 |
| Washington | 5,777 | 5,858 | 6,258 | 8.3 |
| West Virginia | 1,839 | 1,841 | 1,849 | 0.5 |
| Wisconsin | 5,289 | 5,326 | 5,479 | 3.6 |
| Wyoming | 516 | 525 | 568 | 10.1 |

*Source: Bureau of the Census, Population Projections for States by Age, Sex, Race, and Hispanic Origin: 1995 to 2025, PPL-47, 1996; calculations by New Strategist*

# Each State Has a Different Racial and Ethnic Mix

**Each of the nation's 50 states has a unique mix of people, but all are affected by the same trends.**

By 2005, 17 states will have more than 1 million blacks, while seven states will have more than 1 million Hispanics. Two states will have more than 1 million Asians in that year. The largest number of Native Americans in any one state will be Oklahoma's 289,000.

Every state is becoming increasingly diverse, but some do so much faster than others. Non-Hispanic whites will account for only 44 percent of California residents in 2005 and will be a minority of New Mexico residents as well. In Texas, non-Hispanic whites will barely account for the majority (54 percent) of the population in just a few years. In contrast, in 2005, 98 percent of the residents of Maine will be non-Hispanic whites, as will 96 percent of people in New Hampshire, 95 percent in West Virginia, and 94 percent in Iowa.

♦ Because some states are far ahead of others in the transition to a multicultural society, expect to see political conflict at the federal level as pioneering states ask for more resources to help them accommodate diversity. States with small minority populations may wonder what all the fuss is about.

# Population by State, Race, and Hispanic Origin, 2000

*(number of people by state, race, and Hispanic origin, 2000; numbers in thousands)*

| | total | non-Hispanic white | black | Asian | Native American | Hispanic |
|---|---|---|---|---|---|---|
| **Total people** | **274,634** | **197,062** | **33,569** | **10,585** | **2,055** | **31,366** |
| Alabama | 4,451 | 3,231 | 1,133 | 32 | 18 | 37 |
| Alaska | 653 | 461 | 27 | 44 | 91 | 31 |
| Arizona | 4,798 | 3,254 | 150 | 91 | 232 | 1,071 |
| Arkansas | 2,631 | 2,155 | 407 | 19 | 15 | 33 |
| California | 32,521 | 15,562 | 2,138 | 4,006 | 170 | 10,647 |
| Colorado | 4,168 | 3,268 | 178 | 98 | 30 | 594 |
| Connecticut | 3,284 | 2,622 | 293 | 76 | 6 | 288 |
| Delaware | 768 | 582 | 143 | 15 | 2 | 25 |
| District of Columbia | 523 | 152 | 315 | 13 | – | 40 |
| Florida | 15,233 | 10,405 | 2,159 | 239 | 39 | 2,390 |
| Georgia | 7,875 | 5,270 | 2,262 | 138 | 15 | 189 |
| Hawaii | 1,257 | 363 | 27 | 755 | 4 | 107 |
| Idaho | 1,347 | 1,211 | 6 | 15 | 18 | 96 |
| Illinois | 12,051 | 8,553 | 1,813 | 399 | 18 | 1,267 |
| Indiana | 6,045 | 5,338 | 494 | 58 | 14 | 140 |
| Iowa | 2,900 | 2,737 | 60 | 41 | 8 | 54 |
| Kansas | 2,668 | 2,293 | 167 | 48 | 23 | 138 |
| Kentucky | 3,995 | 3,643 | 285 | 27 | 6 | 32 |
| Louisiana | 4,425 | 2,792 | 1,438 | 58 | 18 | 119 |
| Maine | 1,259 | 1,230 | 5 | 9 | 6 | 8 |
| Maryland | 5,275 | 3,371 | 1,462 | 213 | 14 | 214 |
| Massachusetts | 6,199 | 5,182 | 332 | 239 | 10 | 437 |
| Michigan | 9,679 | 7,790 | 1,417 | 157 | 55 | 261 |
| Minnesota | 4,830 | 4,387 | 152 | 135 | 61 | 95 |
| Mississippi | 2,816 | 1,755 | 1,010 | 19 | 8 | 21 |
| Missouri | 5,540 | 4,745 | 622 | 61 | 22 | 90 |
| Montana | 950 | 861 | 3 | 7 | 59 | 20 |
| Nebraska | 1,705 | 1,540 | 70 | 21 | 14 | 61 |
| Nevada | 1,871 | 1,366 | 128 | 77 | 25 | 277 |
| New Hampshire | 1,224 | 1,184 | 7 | 14 | 2 | 17 |
| New Jersey | 8,178 | 5,558 | 1,104 | 456 | 14 | 1,044 |
| New Mexico | 1,860 | 912 | 34 | 22 | 157 | 736 |
| New York | 18,146 | 11,640 | 2,668 | 981 | 53 | 2,805 |

*(continued)*

*(continued from previous page)*

| | total | non-Hispanic white | non-Hispanic black | non-Hispanic Asian | non-Hispanic Native American | Hispanic |
|---|---|---|---|---|---|---|
| North Carolina | 7,777 | 5,748 | 1,726 | 92 | 92 | 121 |
| North Dakota | 662 | 611 | 5 | 6 | 32 | 6 |
| Ohio | 11,319 | 9,672 | 1,306 | 136 | 20 | 183 |
| Oklahoma | 3,373 | 2,653 | 276 | 47 | 273 | 124 |
| Oregon | 3,397 | 2,990 | 59 | 110 | 45 | 195 |
| Pennsylvania | 12,202 | 10,460 | 1,181 | 210 | 16 | 334 |
| Rhode Island | 998 | 851 | 40 | 26 | 4 | 76 |
| South Carolina | 3,858 | 2,624 | 1,152 | 31 | 8 | 42 |
| South Dakota | 777 | 698 | 5 | 5 | 60 | 8 |
| Tennessee | 5,657 | 4,607 | 925 | 55 | 12 | 57 |
| Texas | 20,119 | 11,273 | 2,406 | 506 | 60 | 5,875 |
| Utah | 2,207 | 1,961 | 18 | 58 | 33 | 138 |
| Vermont | 617 | 600 | 2 | 6 | 2 | 6 |
| Virginia | 6,997 | 5,061 | 1,394 | 257 | 16 | 269 |
| Washington | 5,858 | 4,881 | 179 | 342 | 95 | 360 |
| West Virginia | 1,841 | 1,758 | 58 | 11 | 2 | 11 |
| Wisconsin | 5,326 | 4,732 | 318 | 97 | 45 | 136 |
| Wyoming | 525 | 469 | 4 | 4 | 12 | 35 |

*Note: (–) means sample is too small to make a reliable estimate.*
*Source: Bureau of the Census,* Population Projections for States by Age, Sex, Race, and Hispanic Origin: 1995 to 2025, *PPL-47, 1996*

# Distribution of State Populations
# by Race and Hispanic Origin, 2000

*(percent distribution of people by state, race, and Hispanic origin, 2000; numbers in thousands)*

| | total | non-Hispanic | | | | Hispanic |
| --- | --- | --- | --- | --- | --- | --- |
| | | white | black | Asian | Native American | |
| **Total people** | **100.0%** | **71.8%** | **12.2%** | **3.9%** | **0.7%** | **11.4%** |
| Alabama | 100.0 | 72.6 | 25.5 | 0.7 | 0.4 | 0.8 |
| Alaska | 100.0 | 70.5 | 4.1 | 6.7 | 13.9 | 4.7 |
| Arizona | 100.0 | 67.8 | 3.1 | 1.9 | 4.8 | 22.3 |
| Arkansas | 100.0 | 82.0 | 15.5 | 0.7 | 0.6 | 1.3 |
| California | 100.0 | 47.8 | 6.6 | 12.3 | 0.5 | 32.7 |
| Colorado | 100.0 | 78.4 | 4.3 | 2.4 | 0.7 | 14.3 |
| Connecticut | 100.0 | 79.8 | 8.9 | 2.3 | 0.2 | 8.8 |
| Delaware | 100.0 | 75.9 | 18.6 | 2.0 | 0.3 | 3.3 |
| District of Columbia | 100.0 | 29.2 | 60.6 | 2.5 | – | 7.7 |
| Florida | 100.0 | 68.3 | 14.2 | 1.6 | 0.3 | 15.7 |
| Georgia | 100.0 | 66.9 | 28.7 | 1.8 | 0.2 | 2.4 |
| Hawaii | 100.0 | 28.9 | 2.1 | 60.1 | 0.3 | 8.5 |
| Idaho | 100.0 | 90.0 | 0.4 | 1.1 | 1.3 | 7.1 |
| Illinois | 100.0 | 71.0 | 15.0 | 3.3 | 0.1 | 10.5 |
| Indiana | 100.0 | 88.3 | 8.2 | 1.0 | 0.2 | 2.3 |
| Iowa | 100.0 | 94.4 | 2.1 | 1.4 | 0.3 | 1.9 |
| Kansas | 100.0 | 85.9 | 6.3 | 1.8 | 0.9 | 5.2 |
| Kentucky | 100.0 | 91.2 | 7.1 | 0.7 | 0.2 | 0.8 |
| Louisiana | 100.0 | 63.1 | 32.5 | 1.3 | 0.4 | 2.7 |
| Maine | 100.0 | 97.8 | 0.4 | 0.7 | 0.5 | 0.6 |
| Maryland | 100.0 | 63.9 | 27.7 | 4.0 | 0.3 | 4.1 |
| Massachusetts | 100.0 | 83.6 | 5.4 | 3.9 | 0.2 | 7.0 |
| Michigan | 100.0 | 80.5 | 14.6 | 1.6 | 0.6 | 2.7 |
| Minnesota | 100.0 | 90.8 | 3.1 | 2.8 | 1.3 | 2.0 |
| Mississippi | 100.0 | 62.4 | 35.9 | 0.7 | 0.3 | 0.7 |
| Missouri | 100.0 | 85.6 | 11.2 | 1.1 | 0.4 | 1.6 |
| Montana | 100.0 | 90.6 | 0.3 | 0.7 | 6.2 | 2.1 |
| Nebraska | 100.0 | 90.3 | 4.1 | 1.2 | 0.8 | 3.6 |
| Nevada | 100.0 | 72.9 | 6.8 | 4.1 | 1.3 | 14.8 |
| New Hampshire | 100.0 | 96.7 | 0.6 | 1.1 | 0.2 | 1.4 |
| New Jersey | 100.0 | 68.0 | 13.5 | 5.6 | 0.2 | 12.8 |
| New Mexico | 100.0 | 49.0 | 1.8 | 1.2 | 8.4 | 39.5 |
| New York | 100.0 | 64.1 | 14.7 | 5.4 | 0.3 | 15.5 |

*(continued)*

*(continued from previous page)*

| | total | non-Hispanic | | | | Hispanic |
| | | white | black | Asian | Native American | |
|---|---|---|---|---|---|---|
| North Carolina | 100.0% | 73.9% | 22.2% | 1.2% | 1.2% | 1.6% |
| North Dakota | 100.0 | 92.6 | 0.8 | 0.9 | 4.8 | 0.9 |
| Ohio | 100.0 | 85.5 | 11.5 | 1.2 | 0.2 | 1.6 |
| Oklahoma | 100.0 | 78.7 | 8.2 | 1.4 | 8.1 | 3.7 |
| Oregon | 100.0 | 88.0 | 1.7 | 3.2 | 1.3 | 5.7 |
| Pennsylvania | 100.0 | 85.7 | 9.7 | 1.7 | 0.1 | 2.7 |
| Rhode Island | 100.0 | 85.4 | 4.0 | 2.6 | 0.4 | 7.6 |
| South Carolina | 100.0 | 68.0 | 29.9 | 0.8 | 0.2 | 1.1 |
| South Dakota | 100.0 | 89.9 | 0.6 | 0.6 | 7.7 | 1.0 |
| Tennessee | 100.0 | 81.5 | 16.4 | 1.0 | 0.2 | 1.0 |
| Texas | 100.0 | 56.0 | 12.0 | 2.5 | 0.3 | 29.2 |
| Utah | 100.0 | 88.8 | 0.8 | 2.6 | 1.5 | 6.3 |
| Vermont | 100.0 | 97.4 | 0.3 | 1.0 | 0.3 | 1.0 |
| Virginia | 100.0 | 72.3 | 19.9 | 3.7 | 0.2 | 3.8 |
| Washington | 100.0 | 83.3 | 3.1 | 5.8 | 1.6 | 6.1 |
| West Virginia | 100.0 | 95.5 | 3.2 | 0.6 | 0.1 | 0.6 |
| Wisconsin | 100.0 | 88.8 | 6.0 | 1.8 | 0.8 | 2.6 |
| Wyoming | 100.0 | 89.5 | 0.8 | 0.8 | 2.3 | 6.7 |

*Note: (–) means sample is too small to make a reliable estimate.*
*Source: Bureau of the Census,* Population Projections for States by Age, Sex, Race, and Hispanic Origin: 1995 to 2025, *PPL-47, 1996; calculations by New Strategist*

# Population by State, Race, and Hispanic Origin, 2005

*(number of people by state, race, and Hispanic origin, 2005; numbers in thousands)*

| | total | non-Hispanic | | | | Hispanic |
| | | white | black | Asian | Native American | |
|---|---|---|---|---|---|---|
| **Total people** | **285,982** | **199,802** | **35,485** | **12,454** | **2,184** | **36,057** |
| Alabama | 4,632 | 3,355 | 1,179 | 38 | 18 | 42 |
| Alaska | 700 | 476 | 29 | 67 | 91 | 37 |
| Arizona | 5,232 | 3,441 | 168 | 109 | 245 | 1,269 |
| Arkansas | 2,747 | 2,249 | 421 | 21 | 16 | 40 |
| California | 34,441 | 15,123 | 2,158 | 4,731 | 161 | 12,268 |
| Colorado | 4,467 | 3,434 | 200 | 117 | 34 | 682 |
| Connecticut | 3,316 | 2,574 | 313 | 91 | 6 | 332 |
| Delaware | 798 | 596 | 154 | 17 | 2 | 29 |
| District of Columbia | 528 | 156 | 310 | 16 | – | 46 |
| Florida | 16,279 | 10,764 | 2,349 | 279 | 42 | 2,845 |
| Georgia | 8,414 | 5,515 | 2,495 | 162 | 16 | 226 |
| Hawaii | 1,341 | 372 | 28 | 818 | 4 | 119 |
| Idaho | 1,480 | 1,314 | 7 | 17 | 21 | 121 |
| Illinois | 12,265 | 8,487 | 1,853 | 457 | 18 | 1,450 |
| Indiana | 6,217 | 5,453 | 520 | 68 | 14 | 162 |
| Iowa | 2,942 | 2,755 | 67 | 50 | 9 | 61 |
| Kansas | 2,763 | 2,337 | 180 | 55 | 25 | 166 |
| Kentucky | 4,097 | 3,727 | 295 | 31 | 6 | 38 |
| Louisiana | 4,536 | 2,803 | 1,509 | 68 | 18 | 138 |
| Maine | 1,283 | 1,251 | 5 | 11 | 6 | 10 |
| Maryland | 5,465 | 3,368 | 1,577 | 248 | 14 | 258 |
| Massachusetts | 6,312 | 5,123 | 361 | 294 | 10 | 524 |
| Michigan | 9,763 | 7,767 | 1,466 | 184 | 57 | 289 |
| Minnesota | 5,006 | 4,480 | 178 | 166 | 68 | 114 |
| Mississippi | 2,906 | 1,804 | 1,047 | 23 | 8 | 24 |
| Missouri | 5,717 | 4,863 | 656 | 69 | 24 | 105 |
| Montana | 1,008 | 904 | 4 | 9 | 65 | 26 |
| Nebraska | 1,765 | 1,572 | 78 | 27 | 16 | 72 |
| Nevada | 2,071 | 1,456 | 146 | 93 | 26 | 350 |
| New Hampshire | 1,280 | 1,233 | 8 | 17 | 2 | 20 |
| New Jersey | 8,394 | 5,462 | 1,165 | 556 | 15 | 1,196 |
| New Mexico | 2,014 | 958 | 36 | 25 | 174 | 821 |
| New York | 18,250 | 11,271 | 2,714 | 1,140 | 54 | 3,071 |

*(continued)*

*(continued from previous page)*

| | total | non-Hispanic | | | | Hispanic |
| | | white | black | Asian | Native American | |
|---|---|---|---|---|---|---|
| North Carolina | 8,228 | 6,040 | 1,844 | 109 | 96 | 139 |
| North Dakota | 676 | 620 | 5 | 6 | 37 | 8 |
| Ohio | 11,428 | 9,669 | 1,370 | 161 | 22 | 206 |
| Oklahoma | 3,489 | 2,700 | 303 | 54 | 289 | 143 |
| Oregon | 3,614 | 3,133 | 66 | 129 | 49 | 237 |
| Pennsylvania | 12,284 | 10,398 | 1,228 | 249 | 18 | 391 |
| Rhode Island | 1,012 | 838 | 44 | 33 | 5 | 92 |
| South Carolina | 4,032 | 2,738 | 1,200 | 36 | 8 | 50 |
| South Dakota | 807 | 721 | 5 | 6 | 66 | 9 |
| Tennessee | 5,966 | 4,828 | 993 | 64 | 14 | 67 |
| Texas | 21,487 | 11,587 | 2,620 | 593 | 63 | 6,624 |
| Utah | 2,412 | 2,117 | 21 | 71 | 39 | 164 |
| Vermont | 638 | 619 | 4 | 7 | 2 | 6 |
| Virginia | 7,322 | 5,175 | 1,500 | 309 | 16 | 322 |
| Washington | 6,256 | 5,115 | 191 | 410 | 103 | 437 |
| West Virginia | 1,849 | 1,761 | 58 | 13 | 2 | 15 |
| Wisconsin | 5,481 | 4,799 | 356 | 122 | 48 | 156 |
| Wyoming | 568 | 501 | 5 | 6 | 14 | 42 |

*Note: (–) means sample is too small to make a reliable estimate.*
*Source: Bureau of the Census,* Population Projections for States by Age, Sex, Race, and Hispanic Origin: 1995 to 2025, *PPL-47, 1996*

# Distribution of State Populations
# by Race and Hispanic Origin, 2005

*(percent distribution of people by state, race, and Hispanic origin, 2005; numbers in thousands)*

| | total | non-Hispanic | | | | Hispanic |
|---|---|---|---|---|---|---|
| | | white | black | Asian | Native American | |
| **Total people** | **100.0%** | **69.9%** | **12.4%** | **4.4%** | **0.8%** | **12.6%** |
| Alabama | 100.0 | 72.4 | 25.5 | 0.8 | 0.4 | 0.9 |
| Alaska | 100.0 | 68.0 | 4.1 | 9.6 | 13.0 | 5.3 |
| Arizona | 100.0 | 65.8 | 3.2 | 2.1 | 4.7 | 24.3 |
| Arkansas | 100.0 | 81.9 | 15.3 | 0.8 | 0.6 | 1.5 |
| California | 100.0 | 43.9 | 6.3 | 13.7 | 0.5 | 35.6 |
| Colorado | 100.0 | 76.9 | 4.5 | 2.6 | 0.8 | 15.3 |
| Connecticut | 100.0 | 77.6 | 9.4 | 2.7 | 0.2 | 10.0 |
| Delaware | 100.0 | 74.7 | 19.3 | 2.1 | 0.3 | 3.6 |
| District of Columbia | 100.0 | 29.5 | 58.7 | 3.0 | – | 8.7 |
| Florida | 100.0 | 66.1 | 14.4 | 1.7 | 0.3 | 17.5 |
| Georgia | 100.0 | 65.5 | 29.7 | 1.9 | 0.2 | 2.7 |
| Hawaii | 100.0 | 27.7 | 2.1 | 61.0 | 0.3 | 8.9 |
| Idaho | 100.0 | 88.8 | 0.5 | 1.1 | 1.4 | 8.2 |
| Illinois | 100.0 | 69.2 | 15.1 | 3.7 | 0.1 | 11.8 |
| Indiana | 100.0 | 87.7 | 8.4 | 1.1 | 0.2 | 2.6 |
| Iowa | 100.0 | 93.6 | 2.3 | 1.7 | 0.3 | 2.1 |
| Kansas | 100.0 | 84.6 | 6.5 | 2.0 | 0.9 | 6.0 |
| Kentucky | 100.0 | 91.0 | 7.2 | 0.8 | 0.1 | 0.9 |
| Louisiana | 100.0 | 61.8 | 33.3 | 1.5 | 0.4 | 3.0 |
| Maine | 100.0 | 97.5 | 0.4 | 0.9 | 0.5 | 0.8 |
| Maryland | 100.0 | 61.6 | 28.9 | 4.5 | 0.3 | 4.7 |
| Massachusetts | 100.0 | 81.2 | 5.7 | 4.7 | 0.2 | 8.3 |
| Michigan | 100.0 | 79.6 | 15.0 | 1.9 | 0.6 | 3.0 |
| Minnesota | 100.0 | 89.5 | 3.6 | 3.3 | 1.4 | 2.3 |
| Mississippi | 100.0 | 62.1 | 36.0 | 0.8 | 0.3 | 0.8 |
| Missouri | 100.0 | 85.1 | 11.5 | 1.2 | 0.4 | 1.8 |
| Montana | 100.0 | 89.7 | 0.4 | 0.9 | 6.4 | 2.6 |
| Nebraska | 100.0 | 89.1 | 4.4 | 1.5 | 0.9 | 4.1 |
| Nevada | 100.0 | 70.3 | 7.0 | 4.5 | 1.3 | 16.9 |
| New Hampshire | 100.0 | 96.3 | 0.6 | 1.3 | 0.2 | 1.6 |
| New Jersey | 100.0 | 65.1 | 13.9 | 6.6 | 0.2 | 14.2 |
| New Mexico | 100.0 | 47.6 | 1.8 | 1.2 | 8.6 | 40.8 |
| New York | 100.0 | 61.8 | 14.9 | 6.2 | 0.3 | 16.8 |

*(continued)*

*(continued from previous page)*

| | total | non-Hispanic | | | | Hispanic |
| | | white | black | Asian | Native American | |
|---|---|---|---|---|---|---|
| North Carolina | 100.0% | 73.4% | 22.4% | 1.3% | 1.2% | 1.7% |
| North Dakota | 100.0 | 91.7 | 0.7 | 0.9 | 5.5 | 1.2 |
| Ohio | 100.0 | 84.6 | 12.0 | 1.4 | 0.2 | 1.8 |
| Oklahoma | 100.0 | 77.4 | 8.7 | 1.5 | 8.3 | 4.1 |
| Oregon | 100.0 | 86.7 | 1.8 | 3.6 | 1.4 | 6.6 |
| Pennsylvania | 100.0 | 84.6 | 10.0 | 2.0 | 0.1 | 3.2 |
| Rhode Island | 100.0 | 82.8 | 4.3 | 3.3 | 0.5 | 9.1 |
| South Carolina | 100.0 | 67.9 | 29.8 | 0.9 | 0.2 | 1.2 |
| South Dakota | 100.0 | 89.3 | 0.6 | 0.7 | 8.2 | 1.1 |
| Tennessee | 100.0 | 80.9 | 16.6 | 1.1 | 0.2 | 1.1 |
| Texas | 100.0 | 53.9 | 12.2 | 2.8 | 0.3 | 30.8 |
| Utah | 100.0 | 87.8 | 0.9 | 2.9 | 1.6 | 6.8 |
| Vermont | 100.0 | 97.0 | 0.6 | 1.1 | 0.3 | 0.9 |
| Virginia | 100.0 | 70.7 | 20.5 | 4.2 | 0.2 | 4.4 |
| Washington | 100.0 | 81.8 | 3.1 | 6.6 | 1.6 | 7.0 |
| West Virginia | 100.0 | 95.2 | 3.1 | 0.7 | 0.1 | 0.8 |
| Wisconsin | 100.0 | 87.6 | 6.5 | 2.2 | 0.9 | 2.8 |
| Wyoming | 100.0 | 88.2 | 0.9 | 1.1 | 2.5 | 7.4 |

*Note: (–) means sample is too small to make a reliable estimate.*
*Source: Bureau of the Census,* Population Projections for States by Age, Sex, Race, and Hispanic Origin: 1995 to 2025, *PPL-47, 1996; calculations by New Strategist*

# A Metropolitan Nation

## Las Vegas is the fastest-growing large metropolitan area.

Three of four Americans lived in one of the nation's metropolitan areas in 1990. In 1950, barely one-half of Americans were metropolitan residents. Within metropolitan areas, the population distribution has changed dramatically as well. The suburbs are now home to 46 percent of Americans, up from just 23 percent in 1950. About one-third of Americans live in the nation's central cities, a figure that has barely changed over the past 40 years. The proportion of Americans living in the nation's nonmetropolitan areas has fallen sharply, from 44 percent in 1950 to just 23 percent in 1990.

The fastest-growing among the nation's 50 largest metropolitan areas is Las Vegas, projected to grow 69 percent between 1990 and 2000. Other rapidly growing metropolitan areas include Phoenix–Mesa, Arizona; Atlanta, Georgia; and Raleigh–Durham–Chapel Hill, North Carolina. Pittsburgh is the only large metropolitan area projected to lose population between 1990 and 2000.

♦ Metropolitan areas in the South and West will continue to grow faster than those in the Northeast and Midwest as Americans flock to warm climates and plentiful jobs.

♦ Metropolitan areas in the mountain states, such as Las Vegas and Phoenix, will grow rapidly along with their states—which are projected to be among the biggest gainers in population during the next few years.

# Population by Metropolitan Status, 1950 to 1990

*(percent distribution of people by metropolitan status, 1950 to 1990; metropolitan areas as defined at each census)*

|  | *1990* | *1980* | *1970* | *1960* | *1950* |
|---|---|---|---|---|---|
| **Total people** | **100.0%** | **100.0%** | **100.0%** | **100.0%** | **100.0%** |
| **Metropolitan areas** | **77.5** | **74.8** | **69.0** | **63.3** | **56.1** |
| Central cities | 31.3 | 30.0 | 31.4 | 32.3 | 32.8 |
| Suburbs | 46.2 | 44.8 | 37.6 | 30.9 | 23.3 |
| **Nonmetropolitan** | **22.5** | **25.2** | **31.0** | **36.7** | **43.9** |

*Note: The suburbs are the portion of a metropolitan area that is outside the central city.*

*(percent distribution of people by metropolitan status and size of metropolitan area, 1950 to 1990; metropolitan areas as defined at each census)*

|  | *1990* | *1980* | *1970* | *1960* | *1950* |
|---|---|---|---|---|---|
| **Total people** | **100.0%** | **100.0%** | **100.0%** | **100.0%** | **100.0%** |
| **Metropolitan areas** | **77.5** | **74.8** | **69.0** | **63.3** | **56.1** |
| More than 5 million | 21.1 | 20.4 | 15.2 | 15.8 | 12.2 |
| 1 million to 5 million | 28.9 | 25.2 | 25.5 | 19.5 | 17.2 |
| 250,000 to 1 million | 18.7 | 19.4 | 19.9 | 18.9 | 18.1 |
| Fewer than 250,000 | 8.6 | 9.9 | 8.4 | 9.1 | 8.6 |
| **Nonmetropolitan** | **22.5** | **25.2** | **31.0** | **36.7** | **43.9** |

*Source: Bureau of the Census,* Metropolitan Areas and Cities, *1990 Census Profile, No. 3, 1991; calculations by New Strategist*

# Populations of the Top 50 Metropolitan Areas, 1990 and 2000

*(number of people in the 50 most populous metropolitan areas, 1990 and 2000; percent change, 1990–2000; ranked by population in 2000; numbers in thousands; metropolitan areas as defined by the Office of Management and Budget as of June 30, 1997)*

|     |     | 1990 | 2000 | percent change 1990–2000 |
| --- | --- | --- | --- | --- |
| 1. | Los Angeles–Long Beach, CA PMSA | 8,875,882 | 9,170,556 | 3.3% |
| 2. | New York, NY PMSA | 8,547,307 | 8,806,432 | 3.0 |
| 3. | Chicago, IL PMSA | 7,424,644 | 7,959,512 | 7.2 |
| 4. | Boston–Worcester–Lawrence–Lowell–Brockton, MA–NH NECMA | 5,688,301 | 5,992,945 | 5.4 |
| 5. | Philadelphia, PA–NJ PMSA | 4,925,373 | 4,963,247 | 0.8 |
| 6. | Washington, DC–MD–VA–WV PMSA | 4,237,360 | 4,796,068 | 13.2 |
| 7. | Detroit, MI PMSA | 4,269,297 | 4,363,415 | 2.2 |
| 8. | Houston, TX PMSA | 3,342,687 | 4,052,446 | 21.2 |
| 9. | Atlanta, GA MSA | 2,977,832 | 4,016,548 | 34.9 |
| 10. | Dallas, TX PMSA | 2,690,111 | 3,359,550 | 24.9 |
| 11. | Phoenix–Mesa, AZ MSA | 2,246,023 | 3,205,112 | 42.7 |
| 12. | Riverside–San Bernardino, CA PMSA | 2,631,234 | 3,118,599 | 18.5 |
| 13. | Minneapolis–St. Paul, MN–WI MSA | 2,548,262 | 2,913,004 | 14.3 |
| 14. | Orange County, CA PMSA | 2,418,718 | 2,794,084 | 15.5 |
| 15. | San Diego, CA MSA | 2,513,581 | 2,708,874 | 7.8 |
| 16. | Nassau–Suffolk, NY PMSA | 2,608,488 | 2,680,691 | 2.8 |
| 17. | St. Louis, MO–IL MSA | 2,496,041 | 2,578,501 | 3.3 |
| 18. | Baltimore, MD PMSA | 2,389,232 | 2,500,150 | 4.6 |
| 19. | Seattle–Bellevue–Everett, WA PMSA | 2,047,820 | 2,342,105 | 14.4 |
| 20. | Pittsburgh, PA MSA | 2,395,128 | 2,308,991 | –3.6 |
| 21. | Tampa–St. Petersburg–Clearwater, FL MSA | 2,075,595 | 2,280,318 | 9.9 |
| 22. | Oakland, CA PMSA | 2,087,499 | 2,276,509 | 9.1 |
| 23. | Miami, FL PMSA | 1,942,135 | 2,253,896 | 16.1 |
| 24. | Cleveland–Lorain–Elyria, OH PMSA | 2,203,406 | 2,228,591 | 1.1 |
| 25. | Denver, CO PMSA | 1,628,382 | 2,006,726 | 23.2 |
| 26. | Newark, NJ PMSA | 1,915,923 | 1,968,156 | 2.7 |
| 27. | Portland–Vancouver, OR–WA PMSA | 1,526,705 | 1,908,088 | 25.0 |
| 28. | Kansas City, MO–KS MSA | 1,587,096 | 1,759,672 | 10.9 |
| 29. | San Jose, CA PMSA | 1,497,905 | 1,711,607 | 14.3 |
| 30. | San Francisco, CA PMSA | 1,602,932 | 1,708,573 | 6.6 |
| 31. | Fort Worth–Arlington, TX PMSA | 1,367,839 | 1,653,521 | 20.9 |
| 32. | New Haven–Bridgeport–Stamford–Waterbury–Danbury, CT NECMA | 1,632,466 | 1,635,506 | 0.2 |

*(continued)*

*(continued from previous page)*

| | | 1990 | 2000 | percent change 1990–2000 |
|---|---|---|---|---|
| 33. | Cincinnati, OH–KY–IN PMSA | 1,529,231 | 1,624,595 | 6.2% |
| 34. | San Antonio, TX MSA | 1,327,466 | 1,610,124 | 21.3 |
| 35. | Fort Lauderdale, FL PMSA | 1,262,082 | 1,563,118 | 23.9 |
| 36. | Indianapolis, IN MSA | 1,385,395 | 1,555,173 | 12.3 |
| 37. | Norfolk–Virginia Beach–Newport News, VA–NC MSA | 1,450,863 | 1,554,883 | 7.2 |
| 38. | Sacramento, CA PMSA | 1,353,507 | 1,542,980 | 14.0 |
| 39. | Orlando, FL MSA | 1,239,093 | 1,530,204 | 23.5 |
| 40. | Columbus, OH MSA | 1,350,373 | 1,494,252 | 10.7 |
| 41. | Las Vegas, NV–AZ MSA | 867,853 | 1,464,229 | 68.7 |
| 42. | Milwaukee–Waukesha, WI PMSA | 1,434,366 | 1,458,923 | 1.7 |
| 43. | Charlotte–Gastonia–Rock Hill, NC–SC MSA | 1,168,616 | 1,453,103 | 24.3 |
| 44. | Bergen–Passaic, NJ PMSA | 1,278,847 | 1,344,270 | 5.1 |
| 45. | New Orleans, LA MSA | 1,284,037 | 1,319,172 | 2.7 |
| 46. | Salt Lake City–Ogden, UT MSA | 1,076,650 | 1,298,955 | 20.6 |
| 47. | Nashville, TN MSA | 988,716 | 1,225,002 | 23.9 |
| 48. | Greensboro–Winston-Salem–High Point, NC MSA | 1,053,657 | 1,213,980 | 15.2 |
| 49. | Austin–San Marcos, TX MSA | 850,650 | 1,204,818 | 41.6 |
| 50. | Raleigh–Durham–Chapel Hill, NC MSA | 864,222 | 1,154,456 | 33.6 |

*Note: For definitions of the terms MSA, NECMA, and PMSA, see glossary.*
*Source: TGE Demographics, Inc., Honeoye Falls, New York*

# Americans Are Moving Less

## The mobility rate has fallen over the past few decades.

Between March 1996 and March 1997, only 16.5 percent of Americans moved to a different house. This figure is far below the 21.2 percent of Americans who moved between 1950 and 1951. Most movers remain in their local area, which indicates that most moves are related to housing needs rather than job relocation. Only 5.5 percent of people moved to a different county between 1996 and 1997, and only 2 percent moved to a different state. Many long-distance moves are job related.

Overall, 43 million Americans moved between 1996 and 1997, 38 percent more than in 1950–51 because of population growth. Those most likely to move are young adults, many of them seeking jobs. Many college students, for example, move from their college community to a job site after graduation.

More than one-third of renters moved between 1996 and 1997, compared with just 8 percent of homeowners. Only 12 percent of people who are not in the labor force moved, compared with 27 percent of the unemployed—many of whom moved looking for jobs.

◆ The rise of the two-income couple is one factor behind the decline in mobility rates over the past four decades. When both husband and wife are employed, it is more difficult for families to relocate.

### Mobility is down

*(percent of people aged 1 or older who moved in a 12-month period, selected years, 1950–51 to 1996–97)*

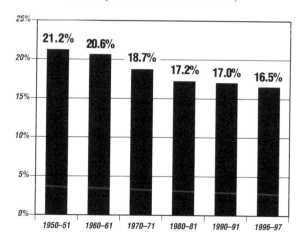

# Geographic Mobility of the Population, 1950 to 1997

*(total number of people aged 1 or older, and number and percent moving by type of move; selected years 1950–97; numbers in thousands)*

| | | | living in the U.S. at the beginning of the year | | | | | |
| | | | | different house, same county | different county | | | not living in U.S. at beginning of year |
| | total | total movers | total | | total | same state | different state | |
| **Number** | | | | | | | | |
| 1996–97 | 262,976 | 43,391 | 42,088 | 27,740 | 14,348 | 7,960 | 6,389 | 1,303 |
| 1995–96 | 260,406 | 42,537 | 41,176 | 26,696 | 14,480 | 8,009 | 6,471 | 1,361 |
| 1994–95 | 258,248 | 42,317 | 41,539 | 27,908 | 13,631 | 7,888 | 5,743 | 778 |
| 1993–94 | 255,774 | 42,835 | 41,590 | 26,638 | 14,952 | 8,226 | 6,726 | 1,245 |
| 1992–93 | 252,799 | 43,099 | 41,704 | 26,932 | 14,772 | 7,855 | 6,916 | 1,395 |
| 1991–92 | 247,380 | 42,800 | 41,545 | 26,587 | 14,957 | 7,853 | 7,105 | 1,255 |
| 1990–91 | 244,884 | 41,539 | 40,154 | 25,151 | 15,003 | 7,881 | 7,122 | 1,385 |
| 1989–90 | 242,208 | 43,381 | 41,821 | 25,726 | 16,094 | 8,061 | 8,033 | 1,560 |
| 1985–86 | 232,998 | 43,237 | 42,037 | 26,401 | 15,636 | 8,665 | 6,971 | 1,200 |
| 1980–81 | 221,641 | 38,200 | 36,887 | 23,097 | 13,789 | 7,614 | 6,175 | 1,313 |
| 1970–71 | 201,506 | 37,705 | 36,161 | 23,018 | 13,143 | 6,197 | 6,946 | 1,544 |
| 1960–61 | 177,354 | 36,533 | 35,535 | 24,289 | 11,246 | 5,493 | 5,753 | 998 |
| 1950–51 | 148,400 | 31,464 | 31,158 | 20,694 | 10,464 | 5,276 | 5,188 | 306 |
| **Percent** | | | | | | | | |
| 1996–97 | 100.0% | 16.5% | 16.0% | 10.5% | 5.5% | 3.0% | 2.4% | 0.5% |
| 1995–96 | 100.0 | 16.3 | 15.8 | 10.3 | 5.6 | 3.1 | 2.5 | 0.5 |
| 1994–95 | 100.0 | 16.4 | 16.1 | 10.8 | 5.3 | 3.1 | 2.2 | 0.3 |
| 1993–94 | 100.0 | 16.7 | 16.3 | 10.4 | 5.8 | 3.2 | 2.6 | 0.5 |
| 1992–93 | 100.0 | 17.0 | 16.5 | 10.7 | 5.8 | 3.1 | 2.7 | 0.6 |
| 1991–92 | 100.0 | 17.3 | 16.8 | 10.7 | 6.0 | 3.2 | 2.9 | 0.5 |
| 1990–91 | 100.0 | 17.0 | 16.4 | 10.3 | 6.1 | 3.2 | 2.9 | 0.6 |
| 1989–90 | 100.0 | 17.9 | 17.3 | 10.6 | 6.6 | 3.3 | 3.3 | 0.6 |
| 1985–86 | 100.0 | 18.6 | 18.0 | 11.3 | 6.7 | 3.7 | 3.0 | 0.5 |
| 1980–81 | 100.0 | 17.2 | 16.6 | 10.4 | 6.2 | 3.4 | 2.8 | 0.6 |
| 1970–71 | 100.0 | 18.7 | 17.9 | 11.4 | 6.5 | 3.1 | 3.4 | 0.8 |
| 1960–61 | 100.0 | 20.6 | 20.0 | 13.7 | 6.3 | 3.1 | 3.2 | 0.6 |
| 1950–51 | 100.0 | 21.2 | 21.0 | 13.9 | 7.1 | 3.6 | 3.5 | 0.2 |

*Source: Bureau of the Census,* Geographical Mobility: March 1996 to March 1997, *Current Population Reports, P20-510, 1998; calculations by New Strategist*

# Number of Movers by Age, Housing Tenure, and Employment Status, 1996–97

*(number of people aged 1 or older moving between March 1996 and March 1997, by age, housing tenure, employment status, and type of move; numbers in thousands)*

| | *total* | *total movers* | *total* | local move (same county) | long distance (different county) total | same state | different state | movers from abroad |
|---|---|---|---|---|---|---|---|---|
| | | | | | different house in the U.S. | | | |
| **Total people** | **262,976** | **43,391** | **42,088** | **27,740** | **14,348** | **7,960** | **6,389** | **1,303** |
| Aged 1 to 4 | 15,965 | 3,762 | 3,667 | 2,559 | 1,108 | 657 | 451 | 95 |
| Aged 5 to 9 | 20,271 | 3,871 | 3,794 | 2,598 | 1,196 | 672 | 524 | 77 |
| Aged 10 to 14 | 19,505 | 3,001 | 2,930 | 2,047 | 883 | 452 | 431 | 71 |
| Aged 15 to 19 | 19,164 | 3,167 | 3,065 | 2,030 | 1,035 | 593 | 442 | 102 |
| Aged 20 to 24 | 17,489 | 5,822 | 5,614 | 3,626 | 1,988 | 1,076 | 912 | 208 |
| Aged 25 to 29 | 19,260 | 6,280 | 6,065 | 3,972 | 2,093 | 1,198 | 895 | 215 |
| Aged 30 to 34 | 20,996 | 4,664 | 4,481 | 2,888 | 1,593 | 884 | 708 | 183 |
| Aged 35 to 44 | 43,960 | 6,443 | 6,238 | 4,109 | 2,128 | 1,170 | 958 | 205 |
| Aged 45 to 54 | 33,013 | 3,200 | 3,118 | 2,058 | 1,060 | 574 | 485 | 82 |
| Aged 55 to 64 | 21,475 | 1,666 | 1,631 | 959 | 673 | 375 | 297 | 35 |
| Aged 65 to 74 | 18,015 | 819 | 806 | 495 | 312 | 167 | 144 | 13 |
| Aged 75 to 84 | 10,954 | 513 | 501 | 307 | 193 | 84 | 109 | 12 |
| Aged 85 or older | 2,909 | 186 | 179 | 91 | 88 | 56 | 32 | 7 |
| **Housing tenure** | | | | | | | | |
| Owner | 179,918 | 15,061 | 14,777 | 9,413 | 5,363 | 3,220 | 2,143 | 284 |
| Renter | 83,058 | 28,331 | 27,311 | 18,327 | 8,985 | 4,740 | 4,245 | 1,020 |
| **Employment status** | | | | | | | | |
| Civilian labor force | 135,227 | 23,985 | 23,375 | 15,307 | 8,068 | 4,585 | 3,483 | 610 |
| Employed | 127,680 | 21,965 | 21,424 | 14,075 | 7,348 | 4,234 | 3,114 | 541 |
| Unemployed | 7,547 | 2,020 | 1,951 | 1,232 | 720 | 351 | 369 | 69 |
| Armed forces | 800 | 294 | 252 | 95 | 157 | 43 | 115 | 42 |
| Not in labor force | 67,288 | 7,898 | 7,496 | 4,756 | 2,740 | 1,443 | 1,297 | 402 |

*Source: Bureau of the Census,* Geographical Mobility: March 1996 to March 1997, *Current Population Reports, P20-510, 1998*

# Distribution of the Population by Mobility Status, 1996–97

*(percent of people aged 1 or older moving between March 1996 and March 1997, by age, housing tenure, employment status, and type of move)*

| | total | total movers | different house in the U.S. | | | | | movers from abroad |
|---|---|---|---|---|---|---|---|---|
| | | | total | local move (same county) | long distance (different county) | | | |
| | | | | | total | same state | different state | |
| **Total people** | 100.0% | 16.5% | 16.0% | 10.5% | 5.5% | 3.0% | 2.4% | 0.5% |
| Aged 1 to 4 | 100.0 | 23.6 | 23.0 | 16.0 | 6.9 | 4.1 | 2.8 | 0.6 |
| Aged 5 to 9 | 100.0 | 19.1 | 18.7 | 12.8 | 5.9 | 3.3 | 2.6 | 0.4 |
| Aged 10 to 14 | 100.0 | 15.4 | 15.0 | 10.5 | 4.5 | 2.3 | 2.2 | 0.4 |
| Aged 15 to 19 | 100.0 | 16.5 | 16.0 | 10.6 | 5.4 | 3.1 | 2.3 | 0.5 |
| Aged 20 to 24 | 100.0 | 33.3 | 32.1 | 20.7 | 11.4 | 6.2 | 5.2 | 1.2 |
| Aged 25 to 29 | 100.0 | 32.6 | 31.5 | 20.6 | 10.9 | 6.2 | 4.6 | 1.1 |
| Aged 30 to 34 | 100.0 | 22.2 | 21.3 | 13.8 | 7.6 | 4.2 | 3.4 | 0.9 |
| Aged 35 to 44 | 100.0 | 14.7 | 14.2 | 9.3 | 4.8 | 2.7 | 2.2 | 0.5 |
| Aged 45 to 54 | 100.0 | 9.7 | 9.4 | 6.2 | 3.2 | 1.7 | 1.5 | 0.2 |
| Aged 55 to 64 | 100.0 | 7.8 | 7.6 | 4.5 | 3.1 | 1.7 | 1.4 | 0.2 |
| Aged 65 to 74 | 100.0 | 4.5 | 4.5 | 2.7 | 1.7 | 0.9 | 0.8 | 0.1 |
| Aged 75 to 84 | 100.0 | 4.7 | 4.6 | 2.8 | 1.8 | 0.8 | 1.0 | 0.1 |
| Aged 85 or older | 100.0 | 6.4 | 6.2 | 3.1 | 3.0 | 1.9 | 1.1 | 0.2 |
| **Housing tenure** | | | | | | | | |
| Owner | 100.0 | 8.4 | 8.2 | 5.2 | 3.0 | 1.8 | 1.2 | 0.2 |
| Renter | 100.0 | 34.1 | 32.9 | 22.1 | 10.8 | 5.7 | 5.1 | 1.2 |
| **Employment status** | | | | | | | | |
| Civilian labor force | 100.0 | 17.7 | 17.3 | 11.3 | 6.0 | 3.4 | 2.6 | 0.5 |
| Employed | 100.0 | 17.2 | 16.8 | 11.0 | 5.8 | 3.3 | 2.4 | 0.4 |
| Unemployed | 100.0 | 26.8 | 25.9 | 16.3 | 9.5 | 4.7 | 4.9 | 0.9 |
| Armed forces | 100.0 | 36.8 | 31.5 | 11.9 | 19.6 | 5.4 | 14.4 | 5.3 |
| Not in labor force | 100.0 | 11.7 | 11.1 | 7.1 | 4.1 | 2.1 | 1.9 | 0.6 |

*Source: Bureau of the Census,* Geographical Mobility: March 1996 to March 1997, *Current Population Reports, P20-510, 1998; calculations by New Strategist*

# Immigration Boosts Nation's Growth

## More than 6 million immigrants came to the United States between 1991 and 1996.

The United States gained more immigrants during the 1980s than in any 10-year period since the first decade of the century. More than 7 million immigrants were granted permanent resident status during the 1980s, a number that was surpassed only by the 8.8 million immigrants who came to the U.S. between 1901 and 1910.

A new record may be set in the 1990s. The number of immigrants that came to the United States between 1991 and 1996 is 70 percent of the present record. Since immigrants are a much smaller share of our population today than they were at the beginning of the 20th century, however, their impact on American society is far less noticeable.

♦ A slowing of immigration would sharply reduce U.S. population growth because immigration accounts for a large share of the nation's population gain each year.

♦ Since most immigrants are of working age, many people worry that immigrants take jobs away from Americans—particularly minorities. With millions of immigrants coming to the U.S. in the 1990s, this issue is likely to be hotly debated among citizens and politicians alike.

# Immigration to the U.S., 1901 to 1996

*(number of immigrants granted permanent residence in the U.S. by decade, 1901–1996; and by single year, 1981–96)*

| year | immigrants |
|------|-----------|
| 1996 | 915,900 |
| 1995 | 720,461 |
| 1994 | 804,416 |
| 1993 | 904,292 |
| 1992 | 973,977 |
| 1991 | 1,827,167 |
| 1990 | 1,536,483 |
| 1989 | 1,090,924 |
| 1988 | 643,025 |
| 1987 | 601,516 |
| 1986 | 601,708 |
| 1985 | 570,009 |
| 1984 | 543,903 |
| 1983 | 559,763 |
| 1982 | 594,131 |
| 1981 | 596,600 |
| | |
| 1991–96 | 6,146,213 |
| 1981–90 | 7,338,062 |
| 1971–80 | 4,493,314 |
| 1961–70 | 3,321,677 |
| 1951–60 | 2,515,479 |
| 1941–50 | 1,035,039 |
| 1931–40 | 528,431 |
| 1921–30 | 4,107,209 |
| 1911–20 | 5,735,811 |
| 1901–10 | 8,795,386 |

*Note: Immigrants are people granted legal permanent residence in the United States. They either arrive in the U.S. with immigrant visas issued abroad or adjust their status in the United States from temporary to permanent residence.*
*Source: Immigration and Naturalization Service, 1996 Statistical Yearbook of the Immigration and Naturalization Service, 1997; and Internet web site <http://www.usdoj.gov/ins>*

# Immigrants Head to California

## The impact of immigration varies dramatically across the country. Some states are overwhelmed with immigrants, while others rarely see any.

Two-thirds of the more than 900,000 immigrants admitted to the United States in 1996 planned to live in just five states: California, New York, Texas, Florida, and New Jersey.

Among immigrants from Mexico, 39 percent planned to live in California, while another 28 percent intended to settle in Texas. Forty-two percent of immigrants from the Philippines intended to live in California. Fifty-two percent of immigrants from the Dominican Republic and 44 percent of those from the Ukraine planned to live in New York.

Of all immigrants settling in Texas, 56 percent are from Mexico. Among immigrants moving to Florida, 28 percent are from Cuba, while 13 percent of immigrants to New York state are from the Dominican Republic.

♦ The influx of non-English-speaking immigrants who need jobs, schools, and health care creates severe problems for some states. There are no easy political answers to their problems, since only a few states are strongly affected while others are untouched.

### California is the top state for immigration

*(percent of immigrants by state of intended residence for the top five states, 1996)*

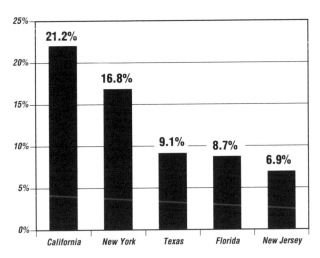

# Immigrants by Country of Birth and State of Intended Residence, 1996

*(number and percent distribution of immigrants admitted to the U.S. from the ten leading countries of birth and percent distribution by intended state of residence, 1996; for the five states receiving the largest total number of immigrants)*

| | total | total for top five states | California | New York | Texas | Florida | New Jersey |
|---|---|---|---|---|---|---|---|
| **Total immigrants** | **915,900** | **581,773** | **201,529** | **154,095** | **83,385** | **79,461** | **63,303** |
| Mexico | 163,572 | 116,474 | 64,238 | 1,553 | 46,403 | 3,155 | 1,125 |
| Philippines | 55,876 | 34,561 | 23,438 | 3,719 | 2,064 | 1,796 | 3,544 |
| India | 44,859 | 24,241 | 7,757 | 5,611 | 3,295 | 1,393 | 6,185 |
| Vietnam | 42,067 | 21,920 | 13,549 | 971 | 5,793 | 977 | 630 |
| China | 41,728 | 26,887 | 10,864 | 11,409 | 1,701 | 773 | 2,140 |
| Dominican Republic | 39,604 | 27,826 | 83 | 20,579 | 108 | 2,050 | 5,006 |
| Cuba | 26,466 | 24,866 | 346 | 452 | 258 | 22,217 | 1,593 |
| Ukraine | 21,079 | 13,238 | 2,630 | 9,185 | 257 | 327 | 839 |
| Russia | 19,668 | 10,330 | 2,377 | 5,854 | 586 | 380 | 1,133 |

**Percent distribution by country of origin**

| | | | | | | | |
|---|---|---|---|---|---|---|---|
| **Total immigrants** | **100.0%** | **100.0%** | **100.0%** | **100.0%** | **100.0%** | **100.0%** | **100.0%** |
| Mexico | 17.9 | 20.0 | 31.9 | 1.0 | 55.6 | 4.0 | 1.8 |
| Philippines | 6.1 | 5.9 | 11.6 | 2.4 | 2.5 | 2.3 | 5.6 |
| India | 4.9 | 4.2 | 3.8 | 3.6 | 4.0 | 1.8 | 9.8 |
| Vietnam | 4.6 | 3.8 | 6.7 | 0.6 | 6.9 | 1.2 | 1.0 |
| China | 4.6 | 4.6 | 5.4 | 7.4 | 2.0 | 1.0 | 3.4 |
| Dominican Republic | 4.3 | 4.8 | 0.0 | 13.4 | 0.1 | 2.6 | 7.9 |
| Cuba | 2.9 | 4.3 | 0.2 | 0.3 | 0.3 | 28.0 | 2.5 |
| Ukraine | 2.3 | 2.3 | 1.3 | 6.0 | 0.3 | 0.4 | 1.3 |
| Russia | 2.1 | 1.8 | 1.2 | 3.8 | 0.7 | 0.5 | 1.8 |

**Percent distribution by state of intended residence**

| | | | | | | | |
|---|---|---|---|---|---|---|---|
| **Total immigrants** | **100.0%** | **63.5%** | **22.0%** | **16.8%** | **9.1%** | **8.7%** | **6.9%** |
| Mexico | 100.0 | 71.2 | 39.3 | 0.9 | 28.4 | 1.9 | 0.7 |
| Philippines | 100.0 | 61.9 | 41.9 | 6.7 | 3.7 | 3.2 | 6.3 |
| India | 100.0 | 54.0 | 17.3 | 12.5 | 7.3 | 3.1 | 13.8 |
| Vietnam | 100.0 | 52.1 | 32.2 | 2.3 | 13.8 | 2.3 | 1.5 |
| China | 100.0 | 64.4 | 26.0 | 27.3 | 4.1 | 1.9 | 5.1 |
| Dominican Republic | 100.0 | 70.3 | 0.2 | 52.0 | 0.3 | 5.2 | 12.6 |
| Cuba | 100.0 | 94.0 | 1.3 | 1.7 | 1.0 | 83.9 | 6.0 |
| Ukraine | 100.0 | 62.8 | 12.5 | 43.6 | 1.2 | 1.6 | 4.0 |
| Russia | 100.0 | 52.5 | 12.1 | 29.8 | 3.0 | 1.9 | 5.8 |

*Note: Total includes immigrants from other countries not shown separately. Immigrants are persons granted legal permanent residence in the United States. They either arrive in the U.S. with immigrant visas issued abroad or adjust their status in the United States from temporary to permanent residence.*
*Source: Immigration and Naturalization Service, 1996 Statistical Yearbook of the Immigration and Naturalization Service, 1997; and Internet web site <http://www.usdoj.gov/ins>; calculations by New Strategist*

# Foreign-Born Americans Are Diverse

## More than 26 million people who live in the United States—or 10 percent of the population—are foreign-born.

The largest share of the foreign-born are from Mexico (27 percent). No other country accounts for more than 5 percent of the nation's foreign-born population. Only 68 percent of the foreign-born are white, compared with 84 percent of native-born Americans. Fully 44 percent of the foreign-born are Hispanic, compared with just 8 percent of native-born Americans.

The foreign-born are more likely to be high school dropouts than native-born Americans, and they are also more likely to be college graduates. This diversity in education stems from the diversity of the foreign-born. Some immigrants have very little education, while others are highly educated professionals. Thirty-five percent of the foreign-born did not graduate from high school, compared with only 16 percent of native-born Americans. Twenty-five percent of the foreign-born have at least a bachelor's degree, compared with 24 percent of native-born Americans.

The unemployment rate of the foreign-born is not much greater than that of the native-born population, but poverty is more widespread among them. Thirty-five percent of the foreign-born have incomes below $10,000, compared with 30 percent of native-born Americans.

◆ The number of foreign-born people living in the U.S. will continue to expand as long as immigration remains high, creating a dynamic multicultural market.

# Foreign-Born Population by Country of Birth, 1998

*(number and percent distribution of foreign-born people by country of birth and year of entry, for the 10 largest foreign-born populations in the United States ranked by size, 1998; numbers in thousands)*

|  | number | percent |
|---|---|---|
| **Total foreign-born** | **26,281** | **100.0%** |
| **Total, top 10 countries** | **14,542** | **55.3** |
| Mexico | 7,119 | 27.1 |
| Philippines | 1,207 | 4.6 |
| China and Hong Kong | 1,022 | 3.9 |
| Vietnam | 989 | 3.8 |
| Cuba | 914 | 3.5 |
| El Salvador | 723 | 2.8 |
| India | 722 | 2.7 |
| Dominican Republic | 635 | 2.4 |
| Great Britain | 622 | 2.4 |
| Korea | 589 | 2.2 |
| Elsewhere | 11,739 | 44.7 |
| **Year of entry** | | |
| **Total foreign-born** | **26,281** | **100.0** |
| Since 1990 | 8,628 | 32.8 |
| 1980 to 1989 | 8,236 | 31.3 |
| 1970 to 1979 | 4,605 | 17.5 |
| Before 1970 | 4,812 | 18.3 |

*Source: Bureau of the Census, Internet web site <www.census.gov/population/socdemo/foreign/98/>*

# Characteristics of the Foreign-Born Population, 1997

*(number and percent distribution of native- and foreign-born people by selected characteristics, and the foreign-born as percentage of the total population, 1997; numbers in thousands)*

| | total population | native-born number | native-born percent | foreign-born number | foreign-born percent | percent of total |
|---|---|---|---|---|---|---|
| **Total people** | **266,792** | **241,014** | **100.0%** | **25,778** | **100.0%** | **9.7%** |
| Under age 5 | 19,781 | 19,482 | 8.1 | 299 | 1.2 | 1.5 |
| Aged 5 to 17 | 43,630 | 41,798 | 17.3 | 1,832 | 7.1 | 4.2 |
| Aged 16 or 17 | 7,813 | 7,326 | 3.0 | 487 | 1.9 | 6.2 |
| Aged 18 to 24 | 24,987 | 22,047 | 9.1 | 2,940 | 11.4 | 11.8 |
| Aged 25 to 29 | 19,260 | 16,489 | 6.8 | 2,771 | 10.7 | 14.4 |
| Aged 30 to 34 | 20,996 | 17,843 | 7.4 | 3,153 | 12.2 | 15.0 |
| Aged 35 to 44 | 43,960 | 38,664 | 16.0 | 5,296 | 20.5 | 12.0 |
| Aged 45 to 64 | 54,488 | 48,276 | 20.0 | 6,212 | 24.1 | 11.4 |
| Aged 65 or older | 31,877 | 29,088 | 12.1 | 2,789 | 10.8 | 8.7 |
| **Sex** | | | | | | |
| Male | 130,636 | 117,690 | 48.8 | 12,946 | 50.2 | 9.9 |
| Female | 136,156 | 123,324 | 51.2 | 12,832 | 49.8 | 9.4 |
| **Race** | | | | | | |
| White | 220,070 | 202,566 | 84.0 | 17,504 | 67.9 | 8.0 |
| Black | 34,218 | 32,190 | 13.4 | 2,028 | 7.9 | 5.9 |
| Native American | 2,433 | 2,291 | 1.0 | 142 | 0.6 | 5.8 |
| Asian | 10,071 | 3,967 | 1.6 | 6,104 | 23.7 | 60.6 |
| **Hispanic origin** | | | | | | |
| Non-Hispanic | 237,089 | 222,703 | 92.4 | 14,386 | 55.8 | 6.1 |
| Hispanic | 29,703 | 18,311 | 7.6 | 11,392 | 44.2 | 38.4 |
| **Educational attainment** | | | | | | |
| **Persons aged 25 or older** | **170,582** | **150,361** | **100.0** | **20,221** | **100.0** | **11.9** |
| Not high school graduate | 30,524 | 23,515 | 15.6 | 7,009 | 34.7 | 23.0 |
| High school graduate, some college | 99,360 | 91,098 | 60.6 | 8,262 | 40.9 | 8.3 |
| Bachelor's degree | 27,357 | 24,185 | 16.1 | 3,172 | 15.7 | 11.6 |
| Graduate or professional degree | 13,341 | 11,563 | 7.7 | 1,778 | 8.8 | 13.3 |

*(continued)*

*(continued from previous page)*

|  | total population | native-born | | foreign-born | | |
|---|---|---|---|---|---|---|
|  |  | number | percent | number | percent | percent of total |
| **Labor force status** |  |  |  |  |  |  |
| **Persons aged 16 or older** | **203,381** | **179,733** | **100.0%** | **23,648** | **100.0%** | **11.6%** |
| Employed | 127,680 | 113,156 | 63.0 | 14,524 | 61.4 | 11.4 |
| Unemployed | 7,547 | 6,479 | 3.6 | 1,068 | 4.5 | 14.2 |
| Armed forces | 866 | 823 | 0.5 | 43 | 0.2 | 5.0 |
| Not in labor force | 67,288 | 59,275 | 33.0 | 8,013 | 33.9 | 11.9 |
| **Income in 1996** |  |  |  |  |  |  |
| **Persons with income** | **188,696** | **168,424** | **100.0** | **20,272** | **100.0** | **10.7** |
| $1 to $9,999 or loss | 57,505 | 50,469 | 30.0 | 7,036 | 34.7 | 12.2 |
| $10,000 to $19,999 | 44,633 | 39,068 | 23.2 | 5,565 | 27.5 | 12.5 |
| $20,000 to $34,999 | 43,403 | 39,380 | 23.4 | 4,023 | 19.8 | 9.3 |
| $35,000 to $49,999 | 21,501 | 19,773 | 11.7 | 1,728 | 8.5 | 8.0 |
| $50,000 or more | 21,654 | 19,733 | 11.7 | 1,921 | 9.5 | 8.9 |

*Source: Bureau of the Census, Internet web site <www.census.gov/population/socdemo/foreign/97/ppltab1 .txt>; calculations by New Strategist*

# Voting Rate Has Declined

## Barely half the public voted in the presidential election of 1996.

Fifty-four percent of Americans aged 18 or older voted in the 1996 presidential election. Not only is the public increasingly disenchanted with politicians, but the election of an incumbent—Bill Clinton—kept many Americans away from the polls.

Older Americans are far more likely to vote than young adults. About two out of three people aged 45 or older voted in the 1996 election, versus just one-third of those aged 18 to 24. When asked why they didn't vote, the largest share of nonvoters claimed they were too busy. More than one in four nonvoters under age 45 said they had no time to vote. Among people aged 65 or older who did not vote, the most common reason was illness, cited by 45 percent.

♦ With so many Americans feeling rushed, it's little wonder many claim to be too busy to vote. Increasingly, elections are won by those who can convince their supporters to go to the polls on election day.

### Young adults are less likely to vote

*(percent of people who voted in presidential election by age, 1996)*

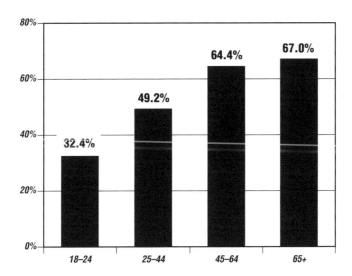

# Voting Rates by Age, 1972 to 1996

*(number of people of voting age and percent who reported voting in presidential elections by age, 1972 to 1996; numbers in thousands)*

|  | total of voting age | percent voting | | | | |
|---|---|---|---|---|---|---|
|  |  | total | 18–24 | 25–44 | 45–64 | 65 or older |
| 1996 | 193,651 | 54.2% | 32.4% | 49.2% | 64.4% | 67.0% |
| 1992 | 185,684 | 61.3 | 42.8 | 58.3 | 70.0 | 70.1 |
| 1988 | 178,098 | 57.4 | 36.2 | 54.0 | 67.9 | 68.8 |
| 1984 | 169,963 | 59.9 | 40.8 | 58.4 | 69.8 | 67.7 |
| 1980 | 157,085 | 59.2 | 39.9 | 58.7 | 69.3 | 65.1 |
| 1976 | 146,548 | 59.2 | 42.2 | 58.7 | 68.7 | 62.2 |
| 1972 | 136,203 | 63.0 | 49.6 | 62.7 | 70.8 | 63.5 |

*Source: U.S. Bureau of the Census,* Voting and Registration in the Election of November 1996, *Current Population Reports, P20-504, 1998*

# Reasons for Not Voting by Age, 1996

*(percent distribution of people who reported registering to vote but not voting, by reason for not voting and age, 1996; numbers in thousands)*

| | total | 18–24 | 25–44 | 45–64 | 65 or older |
|---|---|---|---|---|---|
| **Total number** | **21,340** | **3,587** | **9,990** | **4,640** | **3,123** |
| **Total percent** | **100.0%** | **100.0%** | **100.0%** | **100.0%** | **100.0%** |
| No time off, too busy | 21.5 | 25.8 | 27.3 | 18.6 | 2.0 |
| Not interested | 16.6 | 16.5 | 18.0 | 15.9 | 13.1 |
| Ill, disabled, emergency | 14.9 | 3.5 | 8.7 | 16.7 | 45.1 |
| Didn't like candidates | 13.0 | 9.4 | 13.1 | 17.0 | 11.0 |
| Out of town | 11.1 | 13.4 | 10.5 | 12.8 | 8.3 |
| No transportation | 4.3 | 4.3 | 3.1 | 3.7 | 9.5 |
| Forgot | 4.4 | 6.4 | 4.2 | 4.0 | 3.3 |
| Lines too long | 1.2 | 0.5 | 1.2 | 1.7 | 0.8 |
| Other* | 13.0 | 20.1 | 13.9 | 9.7 | 6.8 |

* Includes "don't know" and refused.
*Source: U.S. Bureau of the Census,* Voting and Registration in the Election of November 1996, *Current Population Reports, P20-504, 1998*

# Most Americans Have a Religion

## Only 12 percent have no religious preference.

The 57 percent majority of Americans are Protestant, while 24 percent are Catholic. People of other religions, such as Muslims, Hindus, and Buddhists, make up 5 percent of the population, while Jews represent 2 percent.

The religious makeup of America is changing. There were fewer Protestants in 1996 than in 1976. The proportion of those who say they have no religious preference rose from 8 to 12 percent during those years.

The religious makeup of the population will change even more as younger generations replace older ones. Among people aged 50 or older, nearly 7 out of 10 are Protestant, but among people under 30, fewer than half are Protestant. Seven percent of the youngest adults are of "other" religion, and 20 percent say they have no religious preference. Some of these young people will identify with a particular religion as they age, but many will continue to seek spiritual fulfillment apart from organized religion. Among people in their forties, 14 percent say they have no religious preference.

◆ As younger generations with diverse religious preferences replace older, heavily Protestant generations, tolerance for religious diversity will grow in the nation's schools and workplaces.

# Religious Preference, 1976 to 1996

## "What is your religious preference? Is it Protestant, Catholic, Jewish, some other religion, or no religion?"

*(percent of people aged 18 or older responding by sex, race, age, and education, 1976–96)*

| | Protestant | | Catholic | | Jewish | | other | | none | |
|---|---|---|---|---|---|---|---|---|---|---|
| | *1996* | *1976* | *1996* | *1976* | *1996* | *1976* | *1996* | *1976* | *1996* | *1976* |
| **Total people** | **57%** | **63%** | **24%** | **26%** | **2%** | **2%** | **5%** | **1%** | **12%** | **8%** |
| Men | 52 | 61 | 26 | 25 | 2 | 2 | 5 | 2 | 15 | 10 |
| Women | 62 | 65 | 21 | 27 | 3 | 2 | 5 | 0 | 9 | 6 |
| Black | 81 | 84 | 8 | 12 | 0 | 0 | 2 | 0 | 8 | 5 |
| White | 55 | 62 | 25 | 27 | 3 | 2 | 4 | 1 | 12 | 8 |
| Aged 18 to 29 | 47 | 53 | 25 | 28 | 2 | 1 | 7 | 2 | 20 | 15 |
| Aged 30 to 39 | 54 | 63 | 26 | 25 | 2 | 1 | 7 | 1 | 11 | 9 |
| Aged 40 to 49 | 53 | 61 | 24 | 31 | 3 | 1 | 6 | 2 | 14 | 5 |
| Aged 50 to 59 | 69 | 71 | 19 | 25 | 3 | 2 | 3 | 0 | 7 | 2 |
| Aged 60 to 69 | 68 | 73 | 24 | 21 | 0 | 2 | 1 | 0 | 5 | 3 |
| Aged 70 or older | 69 | 70 | 20 | 23 | 5 | 4 | 2 | 0 | 5 | 3 |
| Not a high school graduate | 63 | 68 | 20 | 27 | 1 | 1 | 4 | 0 | 12 | 4 |
| High school graduate | 60 | 61 | 24 | 27 | 1 | 2 | 4 | 1 | 11 | 8 |
| Bachelor's degree | 51 | 58 | 24 | 26 | 6 | 1 | 5 | 3 | 13 | 13 |
| Graduate degree | 47 | 61 | 26 | 16 | 6 | 5 | 10 | 3 | 11 | 15 |

*Note: Numbers may not add to 100 because "don't know" and no answer is not included.*
*Source: General Social Surveys, National Opinion Research Center, University of Chicago; calculations by New Strategist*

# Attendance at Art Events Soars with Education

## Arts participation is less affected by educational attainment.

Attendance at art events rises sharply with education. People with no more than a high school diploma are less likely than the average person to attend all types of arts programs. Those with at least some college education have above-average attendance rates. College graduates—especially those who have been to graduate school—are much more likely than average to be seen at arts events. People with graduate degrees are two to three times more likely to attend some events than is the average person. Fully 70 percent of those with graduate-level education visited an art museum in the past 12 months, for example, compared with just 35 percent of all adults.

Education is not as influential in determining participation in art activities. The best educated people, in fact, are less likely than average to participate in weaving and pottery. Those who went no further than high school have above-average participation rates in these activities.

♦ As the educational level of the population increases, attendance at art events will rise, crowding museums and concert halls.

# Attendance at Art Events, 1997

*(percent of people aged 18 or older attending art event or reading literature at least once in the past 12 months, by educational attainment, 1997)*

|  | total | high school graduate | some college | college graduate | graduate school |
|---|---|---|---|---|---|
| Read literature* | 63.1% | 57.6% | 72.1% | 79.5% | 86.3% |
| Visited art/craft fair | 47.5 | 42.9 | 57.8 | 65.2 | 69.3 |
| Visited historic park | 46.9 | 40.5 | 56.3 | 66.6 | 72.7 |
| Visited art museum | 34.9 | 24.6 | 43.2 | 57.7 | 69.8 |
| Musical play | 24.5 | 15.7 | 28.4 | 43.6 | 50.3 |
| Non-musical play | 15.8 | 9.1 | 18.9 | 27.7 | 37.2 |
| Classical music | 15.6 | 8.3 | 18.1 | 28.0 | 44.5 |
| Dance, except ballet | 12.4 | 9.2 | 13.7 | 17.8 | 24.7 |
| Jazz performance | 11.9 | 6.8 | 15.4 | 21.3 | 27.7 |
| Ballet | 5.8 | 3.6 | 6.5 | 10.8 | 14.4 |
| Opera | 4.7 | 1.7 | 5.2 | 10.2 | 14.3 |

*Literature is defined as plays, poetry, novels, or short stories.*
*Source: National Endowment for the Arts, 1997 Survey of Public Participation in the Arts, Summary Report, Internet web site <http://arts.endow.gov/pub/Survey/SurveyPDF.html>*

# Participation in the Arts, 1997

*(percent of people aged 18 or older participating in art activity at least once in the past 12 months, by educational attainment, 1997)*

| | total | high school graduate | some college | college graduate | graduate school |
|---|---|---|---|---|---|
| Buying art | 35.1% | 30.9% | 34.6% | 40.6% | 40.5% |
| Weaving | 27.6 | 28.2 | 31.9 | 32.0 | 25.8 |
| Photography | 16.9 | 13.1 | 21.5 | 23.1 | 21.8 |
| Drawing | 15.9 | 15.0 | 20.3 | 18.0 | 18.2 |
| Pottery | 15.1 | 16.0 | 18.1 | 13.3 | 13.0 |
| Dance, except ballet | 12.6 | 12.3 | 15.7 | 10.3 | 15.2 |
| Writing | 12.1 | 9.2 | 17.0 | 13.9 | 19.4 |
| Classical music | 11.0 | 8.0 | 14.2 | 18.2 | 19.8 |
| Singing in groups | 10.4 | 8.7 | 12.6 | 9.0 | 11.8 |
| Musical play | 7.7 | 5.0 | 10.9 | 11.8 | 15.1 |
| Non-musical play | 2.7 | 1.8 | 3.9 | 3.7 | 2.7 |
| Jazz | 2.2 | 1.5 | 2.6 | 3.3 | 4.3 |
| Opera | 1.8 | 1.2 | 2.6 | 2.4 | 5.1 |
| Ballet | 0.5 | 0.1 | 1.1 | 0.2 | 0.5 |

*Source: National Endowment for the Arts, 1997 Survey of Public Participation in the Arts, Summary Report, Internet web site <http://arts.endow.gov/pub/Survey/SurveyPDF.html>*

# 7

# Spending Trends

♦ **Average household spending rose slightly between 1987 and 1997, from $34,493 to $34,819.**

After adjusting for inflation, spending for many discretionary items is still below 1987 level.

♦ **Households headed by 45-to-54-year-olds spend the most.**

They spent 30 percent more than the average household, or $45,239 in 1997.

♦ **Not surprisingly, households that spend the most have the highest incomes.**

The 29 percent of households with incomes of $50,000 or more account for fully 48 percent of all household spending.

♦ **Married couples with children spend much more than average.**

They account for more than 37 percent of household spending, although they are just 27 percent of households.

♦ **Whites spend more than blacks and Hispanics, but not in every category.**

Blacks spend more than the average household on meat, telephone services, and footwear. Hispanics spend above average on cleaning supplies and baby clothes.

♦ **Income and spending are highest in the West and lowest in the South.**

Because climate has a lot to do with spending, regional spending patterns are not expected to change much in the years ahead.

♦ **College graduates spend like yuppies.**

They spend well above average on alcohol, restaurant meals, and fees and admissions to entertainment events.

# Little Change in Household Spending

## Household spending rose less than 1 percent between 1987 and 1997, after adjusting for inflation.

Although consumer spending has been rising in the past few years because of the booming economy, spending in 1997 barely surpassed the level of 1987. The average household spent $34,819 in 1997, only a few hundred dollars more than the $34,493 of 1987. The recession of the early 1990s cut consumer spending so sharply that it has taken years to regain the spending level of a decade ago. In many categories spending is still below 1987 levels, according to the Bureau of Labor Statistics' Consumer Expenditure Survey. This survey collects household spending data on nearly 1,000 product and service categories.

Spending on food away from home in 1997 was still 13 percent below the level of 1987, after adjusting for inflation. Spending on other discretionary items has fallen even more. Spending on alcoholic beverages was 24 percent below the 1987 level. Spending on major appliances was down 25 percent, apparel spending was 15 percent lower, and spending on reading materials had shrunk 18 percent.

Spending has grown in some categories—many of them nondiscretionary. Spending on property taxes rose 48 percent. Spending on water and other public services rose 32 percent. Out-of-pocket spending on health care rose 15 percent. Some discretionary items also saw a spending rise, however. Spending on entertainment was up 8 percent, spending on personal care products and services rose 13 percent, and spending on leased vehicles grew fully 122 percent.

♦ While Americans have achieved a record level of affluence in recent years, the extra income is not burning a hole in their pocket. With the baby-boom generation now entering its fifties, people are curtailing their spending as they pay off debt and save for retirement.

# Spending Trends, 1987 to 1997

*(average annual spending of consumer units by product and service category, 1987 to 1997; percent change, 1987–97 and 1990–97; in 1997 dollars)*

| | 1997 | 1990 | 1987 | percent change 1990–97 | 1987–97 |
|---|---|---|---|---|---|
| Number of consumer units (in 000s) | 105,576 | 96,968 | 94,150 | – | – |
| Average before-tax income | $39,926 | $39,160 | $38,608 | 2.0% | 3.4% |
| Average annual spending | 34,819 | 34,852 | 34,493 | –0.1 | 0.9 |
| **FOOD** | **$4,801** | **$5,275** | **$5,177** | **–9.0%** | **–7.3%** |
| **FOOD AT HOME** | **2,880** | **3,052** | **2,966** | **–5.6** | **–2.9** |
| **Cereals and bakery products** | **453** | **452** | **422** | **0.2** | **7.2** |
| Cereals and cereal products | 161 | 158 | 147 | 1.6 | 9.6 |
| Bakery products | 292 | 295 | 274 | –0.9 | 6.5 |
| **Meats, poultry, fish, and eggs** | **743** | **820** | **808** | **–9.4** | **–8.1** |
| Beef | 224 | 268 | 270 | –16.3 | –17.0 |
| Pork | 157 | 162 | 164 | –3.1 | –4.2 |
| Other meats | 96 | 122 | 117 | –21.0 | –18.1 |
| Poultry | 145 | 133 | 123 | 9.3 | 18.0 |
| Fish and seafood | 89 | 101 | 93 | –11.6 | –4.6 |
| Eggs | 33 | 37 | 40 | –10.4 | –16.6 |
| **Dairy products** | **314** | **362** | **387** | **–13.3** | **–18.9** |
| Fresh milk and cream | 128 | 172 | 186 | –25.5 | –31.4 |
| Other dairy products | 186 | 190 | 201 | –2.3 | –7.3 |
| **Fruits and vegetables** | **476** | **501** | **503** | **–5.0** | **–5.4** |
| Fresh fruits | 150 | 156 | 160 | –3.8 | –6.0 |
| Fresh vegetables | 143 | 145 | 155 | –1.3 | –8.0 |
| Processed fruits | 102 | 114 | 110 | –10.7 | –7.4 |
| Processed vegetables | 80 | 86 | 78 | –6.9 | 3.0 |
| **Other food at home** | **895** | **916** | **801** | **–2.3** | **11.7** |
| Sugar and other sweets | 114 | 115 | 105 | –1.2 | 9.0 |
| Fats and oils | 81 | 84 | 72 | –3.0 | 12.4 |
| Miscellaneous foods | 403 | 413 | 350 | –2.3 | 15.0 |
| Nonalcoholic beverages | 245 | 262 | 274 | –6.3 | –10.6 |
| Food prepared by household on trips | 52 | 43 | 44 | 21.0 | 18.7 |
| **FOOD AWAY FROM HOME** | **1,921** | **2,224** | **2,211** | **–13.6** | **–13.1** |
| **ALCOHOLIC BEVERAGES** | **$309** | **$360** | **$408** | **–14.1%** | **–24.3%** |
| **HOUSING** | **$11,272** | **$10,687** | **$10,694** | **5.5%** | **5.4%** |

*(continued from previous page)*

| | 1997 | 1990 | 1987 | percent change 1990–97 | percent change 1987–97 |
|---|---|---|---|---|---|
| **SHELTER** | **$6,344** | **$5,939** | **$5,869** | **6.8%** | **8.1%** |
| **Owned dwellings** | **3,935** | **3,626** | **3,356** | **8.5** | **17.3** |
| Mortgage interest and charges | 2,225 | 2,231 | 2,064 | –0.3 | 7.8 |
| Property taxes | 971 | 733 | 656 | 32.4 | 48.1 |
| Maintenance, repairs, insurance, other | 738 | 663 | 634 | 11.3 | 16.3 |
| **Rented dwellings** | **1,983** | **1,883** | **1,900** | **5.3** | **4.4** |
| **Other lodging** | **426** | **429** | **613** | **–0.6** | **–30.5** |
| **UTILITIES, FUELS, PUBLIC SERVICES** | **2,412** | **2,321** | **2,361** | **3.9** | **2.2** |
| Natural gas | 301 | 302 | 328 | –0.4 | –8.2 |
| Electricity | 909 | 931 | 978 | –2.3 | –7.0 |
| Fuel oil and other fuels | 108 | 123 | 133 | –12.1 | –18.7 |
| Telephone services | 809 | 727 | 705 | 11.3 | 14.7 |
| Water and other public services | 286 | 237 | 216 | 20.7 | 32.3 |
| **HOUSEHOLD SERVICES** | **548** | **548** | **524** | **0.1** | **4.5** |
| Personal services | 263 | 269 | 240 | –2.2 | 9.5 |
| Other household expenses | 285 | 279 | 284 | 2.2 | 0.4 |
| **HOUSEKEEPING SUPPLIES** | **455** | **499** | **482** | **–8.7** | **–5.6** |
| Laundry and cleaning supplies | 116 | 139 | 137 | –16.4 | –15.4 |
| Other household products | 210 | 210 | 196 | 0.0 | 6.9 |
| Postage and stationery | 129 | 150 | 148 | –13.9 | –13.0 |
| **HOUSEHOLD FURNISHINGS AND EQUIPMENT** | **1,512** | **1,382** | **1,458** | **9.4** | **3.7** |
| Household textiles | 79 | 122 | 129 | –35.0 | –38.6 |
| Furniture | 387 | 381 | 445 | 1.7 | –13.0 |
| Floor coverings | 78 | 113 | 97 | –31.0 | –20.0 |
| Major appliances | 169 | 181 | 226 | –6.4 | –25.2 |
| Small appliances, misc. housewares | 92 | 92 | 81 | –0.1 | 14.2 |
| Miscellaneous household equipment | 707 | 494 | 480 | 43.2 | 47.2 |
| **APPAREL AND SERVICES** | **$1,729** | **$1,987** | **$2,043** | **–13.0%** | **–15.4%** |
| **Men and boys** | **407** | **483** | **510** | **–15.7** | **–20.2** |
| Men, 16 and over | 323 | 398 | 417 | –18.8 | –22.5 |
| Boys, 2 to 15 | 84 | 86 | 93 | –2.3 | –9.9 |
| **Women and girls** | **680** | **826** | **835** | **–17.7** | **–18.6** |
| Women, 16 and over | 574 | 720 | 721 | –20.2 | –20.3 |
| Girls, 2 to 15 | 106 | 107 | 114 | –0.8 | –7.4 |
| **Children under 2** | **77** | **86** | **82** | **–10.4** | **–6.0** |
| **Footwear** | **315** | **276** | **260** | **14.0** | **21.2** |

*(continued)*

*(continued from previous page)*

|  | 1997 | 1990 | 1987 | percent change 1990–97 | percent change 1987–97 |
|---|---|---|---|---|---|
| Other apparel products, services | $250 | $317 | $355 | –21.1% | –29.5% |
| **TRANSPORTATION** | **$6,457** | **$6,287** | **$6,499** | **2.7%** | **–0.6%** |
| **Vehicle purchases** | **2,736** | **2,614** | **2,857** | **4.7** | **–4.2** |
| Cars and trucks, new | 1,229 | 1,423 | 1,615 | –13.6 | –23.9 |
| Cars and trucks, used | 1,464 | 1,164 | 1,215 | 25.8 | 20.5 |
| Other vehicles | 43 | 27 | 25 | 59.2 | 69.1 |
| **Gasoline and motor oil** | **1,098** | **1,286** | **1,255** | **–14.6** | **–12.5** |
| **Other vehicle expenses** | **2,230** | **2,016** | **2,002** | **10.6** | **11.4** |
| Vehicle finance charges | 293 | 368 | 396 | –20.5 | –25.9 |
| Maintenance and repairs | 682 | 723 | 726 | –5.7 | –6.1 |
| Vehicle insurance | 755 | 691 | 653 | 9.2 | 15.7 |
| Vehicle rental, leases, licenses, other | 501 | 233 | 226 | 114.7 | 121.6 |
| **Public transportation** | **393** | **371** | **386** | **6.0** | **1.9** |
| **HEALTH CARE** | **$1,841** | **$1,817** | **$1,604** | **1.3%** | **14.8%** |
| Health insurance | 881 | 713 | 554 | 23.5 | 59.1 |
| Medical services | 531 | 690 | 660 | –23.1 | –19.5 |
| Drugs | 320 | 309 | 287 | 3.4 | 11.6 |
| Medical supplies | 108 | 104 | 103 | 3.5 | 4.7 |
| **ENTERTAINMENT** | **$1,813** | **$1,746** | **$1,686** | **3.8** | **7.6** |
| Fees and admissions | 471 | 456 | 456 | 3.4 | 3.2 |
| Television, radio, sound equipment | 577 | 558 | 535 | 3.5 | 7.8 |
| Pets, toys, playground equipment | 327 | 339 | 308 | –3.5 | 6.2 |
| Other entertainment supplies, equip., services | 439 | 394 | 386 | 11.4 | 13.8 |
| **PERSONAL CARE PRODUCTS & SERVICES** | **$528** | **$447** | **$466** | **18.1%** | **13.2%** |
| **READING** | **$164** | **$188** | **$201** | **–12.7%** | **–18.3%** |
| **EDUCATION** | **$571** | **$499** | **$476** | **14.5%** | **19.9%** |
| **TOBACCO PRODUCTS & SMOKING SUPPLIES** | **$264** | **$336** | **$328** | **–21.5%** | **–19.5%** |
| **MISCELLANEOUS** | **$847** | **$1,034** | **$794** | **–18.1%** | **6.7%** |
| Cash contributions | 1,001 | 1,002 | 1,047 | –0.1 | –4.4 |
| Personal insurance and pensions | 3,223 | 3,183 | 3,073 | 1.3 | 4.9 |
| Life and other personal insurance | 379 | 424 | 415 | –10.5 | –8.8 |
| Pensions and Social Security | 2,844 | 2,761 | 2,658 | 3.0 | 7.0 |

*Note: The Bureau of Labor Statistics uses consumer units rather than households as the sampling unit. For definition of consumer unit, see the Glossary.*
*Source: Bureau of Labor Statistics, 1987, 1990, and 1997 Consumer Expenditure Surveys; calculations by New Strategist*

# Older Householders Spend the Most

## Spending peaks among householders aged 45 to 54.

Households headed by people aged 45 to 54 spent an average of $45,239 in 1997—30 percent more than the average household. In second place are householders aged 35 to 44, who spent an average of $40,413, according to the Bureau of Labor Statistics' Consumer Expenditure Survey. Householders aged 35 to 54 spend more than younger and older householders not only because they have higher incomes, but also because their households are likely to include children.

After chasing the youth market for years, many businesses may be surprised to discover that young adults are not the nation's big spenders. Households headed by people under age 25 spend less than those headed by any other age group, just $18,450 in 1997. This figure is below the spending of even the oldest householders—those aged 75 or older, who spent $20,279 in 1997. Similarly, the spending of householders aged 55 to 64 surpasses that of 25-to-34-year-olds on most items, including new cars and trucks, entertainment, women's clothes, and food away from home.

### Spending peaks in middle age

*(average annual spending of households by age of householder, 1997)*

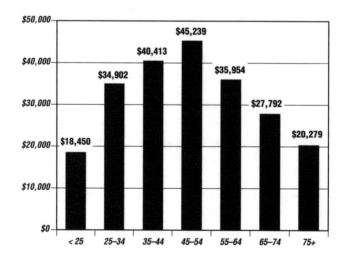

The Indexed Spending table in this section shows spending by age of house-holder in comparison to what the average household spends. An index of 100 means the age group spends the average amount on an item. An index above 100 means households in the age group spend more than average on the item, while an index below 100 reveals below-average spending. A look at the table shows that spending is below average on most items for households headed by people under age 25, close to the average on most items for households headed by 25-to-34-year-olds, and above average in most categories for householders aged 35 to 64. Spending then falls below average again in most categories for householders aged 65 or older.

There are some exceptions, however. Householders under age 25 spend 51 percent more than the average household on rent (with an index of 151). They spend 44 percent more than the average household on baby clothes, and 95 percent more than the average on education (because many are in college). The oldest household-ers spend 18 percent more than the average household on fuel oil and 52 percent more on health care. Householders aged 45 to 54 spend 24 percent less (with an index of 76) than the average household on rent, since most own their homes. They spend 44 percent less than average on personal services—a category that includes day care expenses, which these households no longer have. Householders aged 45 to 54 spend 47 percent more than the average household on new cars and trucks, and nearly three times as much as the average household on gifts of education (their children's college bills).

The Market Share table in this section shows how much of total spending by category is accounted for by three broad age groups of householders. The middle-aged market—households headed by people aged 35 to 54—accounted for 51 percent of all household spending in 1997. Middle-aged householders dominate spending on most items, ranging from furniture to entertainment. Only 23 percent of all household spending is accounted for by young adults, householders under age 35. Young adults dominate only one category—clothes for children under age 2. The remaining 27 percent of spending is controlled by consumers aged 55 or older. Older householders dominate spending only on drugs.

◆ Now that the baby-boom generation has almost entirely filled the big-spending age groups, consumer spending at the aggregate level is surging. But at the level of individual households, spending gains have been modest as boomers save for retirement.

# Spending by Age of Householder, 1997

*(average annual spending of consumer units (cu) by product and service category and age of consumer unit reference person, 1997)*

| | total | under 25 | 25 to 34 | 35 to 44 | 45 to 54 | 55 to 64 | aged 65 or older | | |
| --- | --- | --- | --- | --- | --- | --- | --- | --- | --- |
| | | | | | | | total | 65 to 74 | 75 or older |
| Number of consumer units (in 000s) | 105,576 | 7,501 | 19,918 | 24,560 | 19,343 | 12,316 | 21,936 | 12,109 | 9,827 |
| Average number of persons per cu | 2.5 | 1.8 | 2.8 | 3.2 | 2.7 | 2.2 | 1.7 | 1.9 | 1.5 |
| Average before-tax income | $39,926 | $15,666 | $40,247 | $48,788 | $55,260 | $41,734 | $23,965 | $27,492 | $19,425 |
| Average annual spending | 34,819 | 18,450 | 34,902 | 40,413 | 45,239 | 35,954 | 24,413 | 27,792 | 20,279 |
| **FOOD** | **$4,801** | **$2,838** | **$4,650** | **$5,666** | **$6,028** | **$5,085** | **$3,486** | **$4,066** | **$2,786** |
| FOOD AT HOME | 2,880 | 1,566 | 2,758 | 3,382 | 3,440 | 3,139 | 2,293 | 2,600 | 1,924 |
| **Cereals and bakery products** | **453** | **249** | **432** | **540** | **548** | **470** | **360** | **402** | **309** |
| Cereals and cereal products | 161 | 97 | 168 | 197 | 189 | 160 | 118 | 130 | 103 |
| Bakery products | 292 | 151 | 264 | 344 | 359 | 310 | 242 | 272 | 207 |
| **Meats, poultry, fish, and eggs** | **743** | **385** | **702** | **865** | **915** | **830** | **580** | **676** | **465** |
| Beef | 224 | 125 | 219 | 264 | 284 | 231 | 162 | 190 | 128 |
| Pork | 157 | 75 | 144 | 174 | 193 | 187 | 133 | 148 | 115 |
| Other meats | 96 | 51 | 84 | 120 | 111 | 110 | 77 | 92 | 60 |
| Poultry | 145 | 78 | 146 | 174 | 172 | 150 | 111 | 135 | 81 |
| Fish and seafood | 89 | 37 | 80 | 97 | 117 | 114 | 67 | 77 | 54 |
| Eggs | 33 | 20 | 28 | 35 | 38 | 37 | 30 | 33 | 27 |
| **Dairy products** | **314** | **169** | **303** | **387** | **359** | **325** | **252** | **284** | **212** |
| Fresh milk and cream | 128 | 79 | 125 | 164 | 138 | 122 | 106 | 118 | 91 |
| Other dairy products | 186 | 90 | 177 | 224 | 221 | 203 | 146 | 167 | 121 |

*(continued)*

*(continued from previous page)*

| | total | under 25 | 25 to 34 | 35 to 44 | 45 to 54 | 55 to 64 | aged 65 or older | | |
| --- | --- | --- | --- | --- | --- | --- | --- | --- | --- |
| | | | | | | | total | 65 to 74 | 75 or older |
| **Fruits and vegetables** | $476 | $242 | $434 | $525 | $558 | $549 | $433 | $472 | $386 |
| Fresh fruits | 150 | 77 | 137 | 161 | 174 | 169 | 147 | 151 | 143 |
| Fresh vegetables | 143 | 64 | 124 | 151 | 174 | 185 | 128 | 143 | 109 |
| Processed fruits | 102 | 55 | 97 | 117 | 117 | 108 | 92 | 101 | 82 |
| Processed vegetables | 80 | 46 | 76 | 95 | 93 | 87 | 65 | 76 | 52 |
| **Other food at home** | 895 | 520 | 887 | 1,066 | 1,060 | 965 | 668 | 766 | 550 |
| Sugar and other sweets | 114 | 53 | 106 | 130 | 139 | 131 | 96 | 111 | 79 |
| Fats and oils | 81 | 39 | 72 | 88 | 94 | 99 | 76 | 82 | 68 |
| Miscellaneous foods | 403 | 240 | 434 | 501 | 462 | 403 | 278 | 299 | 252 |
| Nonalcoholic beverages | 245 | 160 | 232 | 294 | 292 | 267 | 178 | 217 | 130 |
| Food prepared by household on trips | 52 | 28 | 43 | 52 | 73 | 65 | 41 | 57 | 21 |
| **FOOD AWAY FROM HOME** | 1,921 | 1,272 | 1,893 | 2,283 | 2,588 | 1,946 | 1,193 | 1,466 | 863 |
| **ALCOHOLIC BEVERAGES** | $309 | $253 | $380 | $348 | $358 | $283 | $197 | $268 | $111 |
| **HOUSING** | $11,272 | $5,860 | $11,774 | $13,415 | $13,892 | $11,090 | $8,082 | $8,876 | $7,107 |
| **SHELTER** | 6,344 | 3,656 | 6,964 | 7,864 | 7,829 | 5,783 | 4,003 | 4,365 | 3,557 |
| **Owned dwellings** | 3,935 | 381 | 3,435 | 5,244 | 5,586 | 4,059 | 2,612 | 3,021 | 2,109 |
| Mortgage interest and charges | 2,225 | 224 | 2,368 | 3,448 | 3,396 | 1,927 | 547 | 779 | 260 |
| Property taxes | 971 | 101 | 639 | 1,054 | 1,303 | 1,195 | 1,060 | 1,197 | 891 |
| Maintenance, repairs, insurance, other | 738 | 57 | 429 | 743 | 887 | 936 | 1,006 | 1,045 | 957 |
| **Rented dwellings** | 1,983 | 3,002 | 3,291 | 2,234 | 1,515 | 1,145 | 1,051 | 911 | 1,223 |
| **Other lodging** | 426 | 273 | 238 | 386 | 729 | 579 | 340 | 432 | 226 |

*(continued)*

*(continued from previous page)*

|  | total | under 25 | 25 to 34 | 35 to 44 | 45 to 54 | 55 to 64 | aged 65 or older total | 65 to 74 | 75 or older |
|---|---|---|---|---|---|---|---|---|---|
| **UTILITIES, FUELS, PUBLIC SERVICES** | **$2,412** | **$1,092** | **$2,229** | **$2,694** | **$2,890** | **$2,654** | **$2,157** | **$2,321** | **$1,954** |
| Natural gas | 301 | 88 | 264 | 327 | 321 | 342 | 338 | 341 | 334 |
| Electricity | 909 | 390 | 785 | 1,015 | 1,114 | 1,013 | 839 | 911 | 751 |
| Fuel oil and other fuels | 108 | 11 | 69 | 108 | 147 | 126 | 131 | 134 | 127 |
| Telephone services | 809 | 550 | 893 | 921 | 952 | 842 | 551 | 627 | 458 |
| Water and other public services | 286 | 55 | 218 | 323 | 357 | 331 | 297 | 309 | 283 |
| **HOUSEHOLD SERVICES** | **548** | **191** | **659** | **724** | **554** | **402** | **452** | **392** | **526** |
| Personal services | 263 | 132 | 493 | 450 | 146 | 59 | 108 | 75 | 149 |
| Other household expenses | 285 | 58 | 167 | 274 | 409 | 343 | 343 | 317 | 377 |
| **HOUSEKEEPING SUPPLIES** | **455** | **163** | **403** | **524** | **552** | **523** | **412** | **449** | **368** |
| Laundry and cleaning supplies | 116 | 56 | 112 | 139 | 137 | 130 | 90 | 105 | 73 |
| Other household products | 210 | 60 | 179 | 249 | 258 | 245 | 190 | 207 | 170 |
| Postage and stationery | 129 | 47 | 112 | 136 | 157 | 148 | 132 | 138 | 124 |
| **HOUSEHOLD FURNISHINGS AND EQUIPMENT** | **1,512** | **759** | **1,518** | **1,609** | **2,066** | **1,728** | **1,059** | **1,349** | **703** |
| Household textiles | 79 | 45 | 70 | 80 | 116 | 100 | 54 | 72 | 33 |
| Furniture | 387 | 257 | 475 | 430 | 515 | 390 | 190 | 268 | 95 |
| Floor coverings | 78 | 18 | 69 | 57 | 70 | 101 | 124 | 142 | 102 |
| Major appliances | 169 | 76 | 149 | 181 | 193 | 246 | 141 | 167 | 109 |
| Small appliances, misc. housewares | 92 | 46 | 76 | 97 | 131 | 123 | 65 | 79 | 49 |
| Miscellaneous household equipment | 707 | 317 | 678 | 764 | 1,041 | 768 | 484 | 622 | 316 |

*(continued)*

*(continued from previous page)*

| | total | under 25 | 25 to 34 | 35 to 44 | 45 to 54 | 55 to 64 | aged 65 or older | | |
| --- | --- | --- | --- | --- | --- | --- | --- | --- | --- |
| | | | | | | | total | 65 to 74 | 75 or older |
| **APPAREL** | **$1,729** | **$1,247** | **$1,957** | **$2,062** | **$2,107** | **$1,656** | **$1,045** | **$1,302** | **$735** |
| **Men and boys** | **407** | **269** | **453** | **496** | **550** | **357** | **219** | **295** | **128** |
| Men, 16 and over | 323 | 247 | 355 | 333 | 457 | 318 | 197 | 262 | 120 |
| Boys, 2 to 15 | 84 | 22 | 98 | 163 | 93 | 39 | 22 | 33 | 8 |
| **Women and girls** | **680** | **466** | **700** | **793** | **834** | **684** | **480** | **552** | **393** |
| Women, 16 and over | 574 | 434 | 580 | 578 | 719 | 633 | 458 | 521 | 381 |
| Girls, 2 to 15 | 106 | 33 | 120 | 215 | 115 | 51 | 23 | 31 | 12 |
| **Children under 2** | **77** | **111** | **163** | **90** | **51** | **34** | **22** | **25** | **18** |
| **Footwear** | **315** | **250** | **342** | **390** | **347** | **337** | **189** | **232** | **138** |
| **Other apparel products, services** | **250** | **151** | **300** | **293** | **325** | **243** | **135** | **199** | **58** |
| **TRANSPORTATION** | **$6,457** | **$3,734** | **$7,051** | **$7,254** | **$8,734** | **$6,708** | **$3,812** | **$4,645** | **$2,785** |
| **Vehicle purchases** | **2,736** | **1,737** | **3,238** | **3,038** | **3,704** | **2,641** | **1,482** | **1,826** | **1,059** |
| Cars and trucks, new | 1,229 | 513 | 1,159 | 1,378 | 1,808 | 1,374 | 777 | 942 | 574 |
| Cars and trucks, used | 1,464 | 1,196 | 2,007 | 1,594 | 1,849 | 1,267 | 686 | 850 | 485 |
| Other vehicles | 43 | 27 | 71 | 67 | 47 | – | 19 | 34 | – |
| **Gasoline and motor oil** | **1,098** | **693** | **1,123** | **1,294** | **1,430** | **1,188** | **648** | **801** | **461** |
| Other vehicle expenses | 2,230 | 1,087 | 2,295 | 2,556 | 3,079 | 2,369 | 1,376 | 1,641 | 1,050 |
| Vehicle finance charges | 293 | 162 | 418 | 349 | 388 | 260 | 95 | 137 | 43 |
| Maintenance and repairs | 682 | 324 | 598 | 788 | 942 | 760 | 491 | 571 | 393 |
| Vehicle insurance | 755 | 341 | 746 | 837 | 994 | 851 | 549 | 661 | 411 |
| Vehicle rental, leases, licenses, other | 501 | 260 | 533 | 582 | 755 | 499 | 241 | 272 | 202 |
| **Public transportation** | **393** | **217** | **395** | **365** | **522** | **509** | **305** | **378** | **216** |

*(continued)*

(continued from previous page)

| | total | under 25 | 25 to 34 | 35 to 44 | 45 to 54 | 55 to 64 | aged 65 or older | | |
| | | | | | | | total | 65 to 74 | 75 or older |
|---|---|---|---|---|---|---|---|---|---|
| **HEALTH CARE** | **$1,841** | **$425** | **$1,236** | **$1,605** | **$1,945** | **$2,187** | **$2,855** | **$2,900** | **$2,799** |
| Health insurance | 881 | 200 | 577 | 748 | 845 | 965 | 1,523 | 1,547 | 1,494 |
| Medical services | 531 | 128 | 422 | 547 | 658 | 664 | 564 | 636 | 475 |
| Drugs | 320 | 65 | 169 | 210 | 303 | 407 | 637 | 594 | 691 |
| Medical supplies | 108 | 31 | 67 | 100 | 139 | 151 | 130 | 123 | 138 |
| **ENTERTAINMENT** | **$1,813** | **$1,051** | **$1,865** | **$2,129** | **$2,416** | **$1,900** | **$1,103** | **$1,300** | **$861** |
| Fees and admissions | 471 | 263 | 424 | 574 | 679 | 451 | 296 | 390 | 180 |
| Television, radio, sound equipment | 577 | 437 | 618 | 671 | 683 | 561 | 400 | 470 | 314 |
| Pets, toys, playground equipment | 327 | 188 | 345 | 403 | 395 | 376 | 188 | 237 | 128 |
| Other entertainment supplies, equipment, services | 439 | 162 | 477 | 481 | 659 | 512 | 219 | 203 | 239 |
| **PERSONAL CARE PRODUCTS & SERVICES** | **$528** | **$292** | **$530** | **$586** | **$637** | **$541** | **$441** | **$494** | **$376** |
| **READING** | **$164** | **$64** | **$132** | **$160** | **$205** | **$198** | **$174** | **$195** | **$148** |
| **EDUCATION** | **$571** | **$1,114** | **$483** | **$604** | **$1,068** | **$281** | **$153** | **$227** | **$61** |
| **TOBACCO PRODUCTS & SMOKING SUPPLIES** | **$264** | **$200** | **$261** | **$329** | **$312** | **$292** | **$156** | **$213** | **$87** |
| **MISCELLANEOUS** | **$847** | **$275** | **$757** | **$989** | **$1,106** | **$1,061** | **$619** | **$745** | **$463** |
| Cash contributions | 1,001 | 157 | 484 | 945 | 1,431 | 1,208 | 1,326 | 1,196 | 1,485 |
| Personal insurance and pensions | 3,223 | 940 | 3,341 | 4,322 | 4,998 | 3,466 | 964 | 1,362 | 473 |
| Life and other personal insurance | 379 | 47 | 239 | 383 | 604 | 523 | 334 | 406 | 244 |
| Pensions and Social Security | 2,844 | 893 | 3,102 | 3,939 | 4,394 | 2,943 | 630 | 956 | 229 |

(continued)

(*continued from previous page*)

| | total | under 25 | 25 to 34 | 35 to 44 | 45 to 54 | 55 to 64 | aged 65 or older | | |
| --- | --- | --- | --- | --- | --- | --- | --- | --- | --- |
| | | | | | | | total | 65 to 74 | 75 or older |
| **PERSONAL TAXES** | **$3,241** | **$660** | **$3,376** | **$4,278** | **$4,863** | **$3,500** | **$1,325** | **$1,706** | **$835** |
| Federal income taxes | 2,468 | 516 | 2,567 | 3,244 | 3,757 | 2,663 | 977 | 1,257 | 617 |
| State and local income taxes | 645 | 143 | 752 | 897 | 941 | 669 | 173 | 245 | 79 |
| Other taxes | 129 | 1 | 56 | 137 | 164 | 169 | 175 | 204 | 139 |
| **GIFTS** | **$1,059** | **$629** | **$762** | **$910** | **$1,789** | **$1,272** | **$889** | **$1,083** | **$652** |
| **Food** | **68** | **48** | **30** | **74** | **130** | **77** | **42** | **47** | **36** |
| **Housing** | **273** | **180** | **250** | **246** | **426** | **328** | **193** | **215** | **166** |
| Housekeeping supplies | 37 | 13 | 32 | 46 | 39 | 44 | 33 | 41 | 24 |
| Household textiles | 8 | 3 | 5 | 6 | 12 | 15 | 9 | 11 | 7 |
| Appliances and misc. housewares | 27 | 12 | 22 | 18 | 42 | 55 | 19 | 25 | 12 |
| Major appliances | 6 | 3 | 5 | 3 | 10 | 13 | 5 | 8 | 2 |
| Small appliances, miscellaneous housewares | 21 | 9 | 17 | 15 | 31 | 41 | 14 | 17 | 10 |
| Miscellaneous household equipment | 66 | 31 | 55 | 60 | 105 | 95 | 45 | 58 | 29 |
| Other housing | 135 | 121 | 136 | 115 | 229 | 119 | 86 | 80 | 94 |
| **Apparel and services** | **252** | **135** | **210** | **229** | **379** | **332** | **202** | **260** | **132** |
| Males, 2 and over | 61 | 15 | 53 | 44 | 95 | 87 | 61 | 73 | 46 |
| Females, 2 and over | 81 | 51 | 57 | 83 | 110 | 101 | 76 | 99 | 48 |
| Children under 2 | 33 | 22 | 44 | 33 | 39 | 32 | 20 | 23 | 17 |
| Other apparel products, services | 77 | 48 | 56 | 69 | 136 | 112 | 45 | 64 | 22 |
| Jewelry and watches | 49 | 42 | 33 | 40 | 96 | 56 | 29 | 45 | 10 |
| All other apparel products, services | 29 | 5 | 23 | 29 | 40 | 55 | 16 | 19 | 12 |

(*continued*)

(continued from previous page)

| | total | under 25 | 25 to 34 | 35 to 44 | 45 to 54 | 55 to 64 | aged 65 or older | | |
| --- | --- | --- | --- | --- | --- | --- | --- | --- | --- |
| | | | | | | | total | 65 to 74 | 75 or older |
| **Transportation** | $57 | $42 | $22 | $29 | $84 | $56 | $101 | $119 | $78 |
| **Health care** | 30 | 7 | 9 | 19 | 48 | 60 | 39 | 27 | 53 |
| **Entertainment** | 99 | 37 | 86 | 84 | 147 | 138 | 85 | 114 | 49 |
| Toys, games, hobbies, tricycles | 41 | 10 | 48 | 35 | 44 | 65 | 36 | 40 | 31 |
| Other entertainment | 58 | 28 | 38 | 49 | 103 | 74 | 49 | 74 | 18 |
| **Education** | 155 | 142 | 28 | 101 | 446 | 98 | 113 | 163 | 50 |
| **All other gifts** | 125 | 37 | 127 | 127 | 129 | 183 | 115 | 138 | 88 |

Note: The Bureau of Labor Statistics uses consumer units rather than households as the sampling unit in the Consumer Expenditure Survey. For the definition of consumer unit, see the Glossary. Gift spending is also included in the preceding product and service categories. (–) means sample is too small to make a reliable estimate.
Source: Bureau of Labor Statistics, 1997 Consumer Expenditure Survey

# Indexed Spending by Age of Householder, 1997

*(indexed average annual spending of consumer units by product and service category and age of consumer unit reference person, 1997)*

| | total | under 25 | 25 to 34 | 35 to 44 | 45 to 54 | 55 to 64 | aged 65 or older | | |
| --- | --- | --- | --- | --- | --- | --- | --- | --- | --- |
| | | | | | | | total | 65 to 74 | 75 or older |
| Number of consumer units (in 000s) | 105,576 | 7,501 | 19,918 | 24,560 | 19,343 | 12,316 | 21,936 | 12,109 | 9,827 |
| Indexed average before-tax income | 100 | 39 | 101 | 122 | 138 | 105 | 60 | 69 | 49 |
| Indexed average annual spending | 100 | 53 | 100 | 116 | 130 | 103 | 70 | 80 | 58 |
| **FOOD** | **100** | **59** | **97** | **118** | **126** | **106** | **73** | **85** | **58** |
| **FOOD AT HOME** | **100** | **54** | **96** | **117** | **119** | **109** | **80** | **90** | **67** |
| **Cereals and bakery products** | **100** | **55** | **95** | **119** | **121** | **104** | **79** | **89** | **68** |
| Cereals and cereal products | 100 | 60 | 104 | 122 | 117 | 99 | 73 | 81 | 64 |
| Bakery products | 100 | 52 | 90 | 118 | 123 | 106 | 83 | 93 | 71 |
| **Meats, poultry, fish, and eggs** | **100** | **52** | **94** | **116** | **123** | **112** | **78** | **91** | **63** |
| Beef | 100 | 56 | 98 | 118 | 127 | 103 | 72 | 85 | 57 |
| Pork | 100 | 48 | 92 | 111 | 123 | 119 | 85 | 94 | 73 |
| Other meats | 100 | 53 | 88 | 125 | 116 | 115 | 80 | 96 | 63 |
| Poultry | 100 | 54 | 101 | 120 | 119 | 103 | 77 | 93 | 56 |
| Fish and seafood | 100 | 42 | 90 | 109 | 131 | 128 | 75 | 87 | 61 |
| Eggs | 100 | 61 | 85 | 106 | 115 | 112 | 91 | 100 | 82 |
| **Dairy products** | **100** | **54** | **96** | **123** | **114** | **104** | **80** | **90** | **68** |
| Fresh milk and cream | 100 | 62 | 98 | 128 | 108 | 95 | 83 | 92 | 71 |
| Other dairy products | 100 | 48 | 95 | 120 | 119 | 109 | 78 | 90 | 65 |

*(continued)*

(continued from previous page)

|  | total | under 25 | 25 to 34 | 35 to 44 | 45 to 54 | 55 to 64 | aged 65 or older | | |
|---|---|---|---|---|---|---|---|---|---|
|  |  |  |  |  |  |  | total | 65 to 74 | 75 or older |
| **Fruits and vegetables** | **100** | **51** | **91** | **110** | **117** | **115** | **91** | **99** | **81** |
| Fresh fruits | 100 | 51 | 91 | 107 | 116 | 113 | 98 | 101 | 95 |
| Fresh vegetables | 100 | 45 | 87 | 106 | 122 | 129 | 90 | 100 | 76 |
| Processed fruits | 100 | 54 | 95 | 115 | 115 | 106 | 90 | 99 | 80 |
| Processed vegetables | 100 | 58 | 95 | 119 | 116 | 109 | 81 | 95 | 65 |
| **Other food at home** | **100** | **58** | **99** | **119** | **118** | **108** | **75** | **86** | **61** |
| Sugar and other sweets | 100 | 46 | 93 | 114 | 122 | 115 | 84 | 97 | 69 |
| Fats and oils | 100 | 48 | 89 | 109 | 116 | 122 | 94 | 101 | 84 |
| Miscellaneous foods | 100 | 60 | 108 | 124 | 115 | 100 | 69 | 74 | 63 |
| Nonalcoholic beverages | 100 | 65 | 95 | 120 | 119 | 109 | 73 | 89 | 53 |
| Food prepared by household on trips | 100 | 54 | 83 | 100 | 140 | 125 | 79 | 110 | 40 |
| **FOOD AWAY FROM HOME** | **100** | **66** | **99** | **119** | **135** | **101** | **62** | **76** | **45** |
| **ALCOHOLIC BEVERAGES** | **100** | **82** | **123** | **113** | **116** | **92** | **64** | **87** | **36** |
| **HOUSING** | **100** | **52** | **104** | **119** | **123** | **98** | **72** | **79** | **63** |
| **SHELTER** | **100** | **58** | **110** | **124** | **123** | **91** | **63** | **69** | **56** |
| **Owned dwellings** | **100** | **10** | **87** | **133** | **142** | **103** | **66** | **77** | **54** |
| Mortgage interest and charges | 100 | 10 | 106 | 155 | 153 | 87 | 25 | 35 | 12 |
| Property taxes | 100 | 10 | 66 | 109 | 134 | 123 | 109 | 123 | 92 |
| Maintenance, repairs, insurance, other | 100 | 8 | 58 | 101 | 120 | 127 | 136 | 142 | 130 |
| **Rented dwellings** | **100** | **151** | **166** | **113** | **76** | **58** | **53** | **46** | **62** |
| **Other lodging** | **100** | **64** | **56** | **91** | **171** | **136** | **80** | **101** | **53** |

(continued)

(continued from previous page)

| | total | under 25 | 25 to 34 | 35 to 44 | 45 to 54 | 55 to 64 | aged 65 or older | | |
| --- | --- | --- | --- | --- | --- | --- | --- | --- | --- |
| | | | | | | | total | 65 to 74 | 75 or older |
| **UTILITIES, FUELS, PUBLIC SERVICES** | **100** | **45** | **92** | **112** | **120** | **110** | **89** | **96** | **81** |
| Natural gas | 100 | 29 | 88 | 109 | 107 | 114 | 112 | 113 | 111 |
| Electricity | 100 | 43 | 86 | 112 | 123 | 111 | 92 | 100 | 83 |
| Fuel oil and other fuels | 100 | 10 | 64 | 100 | 136 | 117 | 121 | 124 | 118 |
| Telephone services | 100 | 68 | 110 | 114 | 118 | 104 | 68 | 78 | 57 |
| Water and other public services | 100 | 19 | 76 | 113 | 125 | 116 | 104 | 108 | 99 |
| **HOUSEHOLD SERVICES** | **100** | **35** | **120** | **132** | **101** | **73** | **82** | **72** | **96** |
| Personal services | 100 | 50 | 187 | 171 | 56 | 22 | 41 | 29 | 57 |
| Other household expenses | 100 | 20 | 59 | 96 | 144 | 120 | 120 | 111 | 132 |
| **HOUSEKEEPING SUPPLIES** | **100** | **36** | **89** | **115** | **121** | **115** | **91** | **99** | **81** |
| Laundry and cleaning supplies | 100 | 48 | 97 | 120 | 118 | 112 | 78 | 91 | 63 |
| Other household products | 100 | 29 | 85 | 119 | 123 | 117 | 90 | 99 | 81 |
| Postage and stationery | 100 | 36 | 87 | 105 | 122 | 115 | 102 | 107 | 96 |
| **HOUSEHOLD FURNISHINGS AND EQUIPMENT** | **100** | **50** | **100** | **106** | **137** | **114** | **70** | **89** | **46** |
| Household textiles | 100 | 57 | 89 | 101 | 147 | 127 | 68 | 91 | 42 |
| Furniture | 100 | 66 | 123 | 111 | 133 | 101 | 49 | 69 | 25 |
| Floor coverings | 100 | 23 | 88 | 73 | 90 | 129 | 159 | 182 | 131 |
| Major appliances | 100 | 45 | 88 | 107 | 114 | 146 | 83 | 99 | 64 |
| Small appliances, misc. housewares | 100 | 50 | 83 | 105 | 142 | 134 | 71 | 86 | 53 |
| Miscellaneous household equipment | 100 | 45 | 96 | 108 | 147 | 109 | 68 | 88 | 45 |

(continued)

*(continued from previous page)*

| | total | under 25 | 25 to 34 | 35 to 44 | 45 to 54 | 55 to 64 | aged 65 or older | | |
| --- | --- | --- | --- | --- | --- | --- | --- | --- | --- |
| | | | | | | | total | 65 to 74 | 75 or older |
| **APPAREL AND SERVICES** | **100** | **72** | **113** | **119** | **122** | **96** | **60** | **75** | **43** |
| **Men and boys** | **100** | **66** | **111** | **122** | **135** | **88** | **54** | **72** | **31** |
| Men, 16 and over | 100 | 76 | 110 | 103 | 141 | 98 | 61 | 81 | 37 |
| Boys, 2 to 15 | 100 | 26 | 117 | 194 | 111 | 46 | 26 | 39 | 10 |
| **Women and girls** | **100** | **69** | **103** | **117** | **123** | **101** | **71** | **81** | **58** |
| Women, 16 and over | 100 | 76 | 101 | 101 | 125 | 110 | 80 | 91 | 66 |
| Girls, 2 to 15 | 100 | 31 | 113 | 203 | 108 | 48 | 22 | 29 | 11 |
| **Children under 2** | **100** | **144** | **212** | **117** | **66** | **44** | **29** | **32** | **23** |
| **Footwear** | **100** | **79** | **109** | **124** | **110** | **107** | **60** | **74** | **44** |
| **Other apparel products, services** | **100** | **60** | **120** | **117** | **130** | **97** | **54** | **80** | **23** |
| **TRANSPORTATION** | **100** | **58** | **109** | **112** | **135** | **104** | **59** | **72** | **43** |
| **Vehicle purchases** | **100** | **63** | **118** | **111** | **135** | **97** | **54** | **67** | **39** |
| Cars and trucks, new | 100 | 42 | 94 | 112 | 147 | 112 | 63 | 77 | 47 |
| Cars and trucks, used | 100 | 82 | 137 | 109 | 126 | 87 | 47 | 58 | 33 |
| Other vehicles | 100 | 63 | 165 | 156 | 109 | – | 44 | 79 | – |
| **Gasoline and motor oil** | **100** | **63** | **102** | **118** | **130** | **108** | **59** | **73** | **42** |
| Other vehicle expenses | 100 | 49 | 103 | 115 | 138 | 106 | 62 | 74 | 47 |
| Vehicle finance charges | 100 | 55 | 143 | 119 | 132 | 89 | 32 | 47 | 15 |
| Maintenance and repairs | 100 | 48 | 88 | 116 | 138 | 111 | 72 | 84 | 58 |
| Vehicle insurance | 100 | 45 | 99 | 111 | 132 | 113 | 73 | 88 | 54 |
| Vehicle rental, leases, licenses, other | 100 | 52 | 106 | 116 | 151 | 100 | 48 | 54 | 40 |
| **Public transportation** | **100** | **55** | **101** | **93** | **133** | **130** | **78** | **96** | **55** |

*(continued)*

*(continued from previous page)*

| | total | under 25 | 25 to 34 | 35 to 44 | 45 to 54 | 55 to 64 | total | aged 65 or older 65 to 74 | 75 or older |
|---|---|---|---|---|---|---|---|---|---|
| **HEALTH CARE** | **100** | **23** | **67** | **87** | **106** | **119** | **155** | **158** | **152** |
| Health insurance | 100 | 23 | 65 | 85 | 96 | 110 | 173 | 176 | 170 |
| Medical services | 100 | 24 | 79 | 103 | 124 | 125 | 106 | 120 | 89 |
| Drugs | 100 | 20 | 53 | 66 | 95 | 127 | 199 | 186 | 216 |
| Medical supplies | 100 | 29 | 62 | 93 | 129 | 140 | 120 | 114 | 128 |
| **ENTERTAINMENT** | **100** | **58** | **103** | **117** | **133** | **105** | **61** | **72** | **47** |
| Fees and admissions | 100 | 56 | 90 | 122 | 144 | 96 | 63 | 83 | 38 |
| Television, radio, sound equipment | 100 | 76 | 107 | 116 | 118 | 97 | 69 | 81 | 54 |
| Pets, toys, playground equipment | 100 | 57 | 106 | 123 | 121 | 115 | 57 | 72 | 39 |
| Other entertainment supplies, equipment, services | 100 | 37 | 109 | 110 | 150 | 117 | 50 | 46 | 54 |
| **PERSONAL CARE PRODUCTS & SERVICES** | **100** | **55** | **100** | **111** | **121** | **102** | **84** | **94** | **71** |
| **READING** | **100** | **39** | **80** | **98** | **125** | **121** | **106** | **119** | **90** |
| **EDUCATION** | **100** | **195** | **85** | **106** | **187** | **49** | **27** | **40** | **11** |
| **TOBACCO PRODUCTS & SMOKING SUPPLIES** | **100** | **76** | **99** | **125** | **118** | **111** | **59** | **81** | **33** |
| **MISCELLANEOUS** | **100** | **32** | **89** | **117** | **131** | **125** | **73** | **88** | **55** |
| Cash contributions | 100 | 16 | 48 | 94 | 143 | 121 | 132 | 119 | 148 |
| Personal insurance and pensions | 100 | 29 | 104 | 134 | 155 | 108 | 30 | 42 | 15 |
| Life and other personal insurance | 100 | 12 | 63 | 101 | 159 | 138 | 88 | 107 | 64 |
| Pensions and Social Security | 100 | 31 | 109 | 139 | 155 | 103 | 22 | 34 | 8 |

*(continued)*

(continued from previous page)

|  | total | under 25 | 25 to 34 | 35 to 44 | 45 to 54 | 55 to 64 | aged 65 or older | | |
|---|---|---|---|---|---|---|---|---|---|
|  |  |  |  |  |  |  | total | 65 to 74 | 75 or older |
| **PERSONAL TAXES** | **100** | **20** | **104** | **132** | **150** | **108** | **41** | **53** | **26** |
| Federal income taxes | 100 | 21 | 104 | 131 | 152 | 108 | 40 | 51 | 25 |
| State and local income taxes | 100 | 22 | 117 | 139 | 146 | 104 | 27 | 38 | 12 |
| Other taxes | 100 | 1 | 43 | 106 | 127 | 131 | 136 | 158 | 108 |
| **GIFTS** | **100** | **59** | **72** | **86** | **169** | **120** | **84** | **102** | **62** |
| **Food** | **100** | **71** | **44** | **109** | **191** | **113** | **62** | **69** | **53** |
| **Housing** | **100** | **66** | **92** | **90** | **156** | **120** | **71** | **79** | **61** |
| Housekeeping supplies | 100 | 35 | 86 | 124 | 105 | 119 | 89 | 111 | 65 |
| Household textiles | 100 | 38 | 63 | 75 | 150 | 188 | 113 | 138 | 88 |
| Appliances and miscellaneous housewares | 100 | 44 | 81 | 67 | 156 | 204 | 70 | 93 | 44 |
| Major appliances | 100 | 50 | 83 | 50 | 167 | 217 | 83 | 133 | 33 |
| Small appliances, misc. housewares | 100 | 43 | 81 | 71 | 148 | 195 | 67 | 81 | 48 |
| Miscellaneous household equipment | 100 | 47 | 83 | 91 | 159 | 144 | 68 | 88 | 44 |
| Other housing | 100 | 90 | 101 | 85 | 170 | 88 | 64 | 59 | 70 |
| **Apparel and services** | **100** | **54** | **83** | **91** | **150** | **132** | **80** | **103** | **52** |
| Males, 2 and over | 100 | 25 | 87 | 72 | 156 | 143 | 100 | 120 | 75 |
| Females, 2 and over | 100 | 63 | 70 | 102 | 136 | 125 | 94 | 122 | 59 |
| Children under 2 | 100 | 67 | 133 | 100 | 118 | 97 | 61 | 70 | 52 |
| Other apparel products, services | 100 | 62 | 73 | 90 | 177 | 145 | 58 | 83 | 29 |
| Jewelry and watches | 100 | 86 | 67 | 82 | 196 | 114 | 59 | 92 | 20 |
| All other apparel products, services | 100 | 17 | 79 | 100 | 138 | 190 | 55 | 66 | 41 |

(continued)

(continued from previous page)

| | total | under 25 | 25 to 34 | 35 to 44 | 45 to 54 | 55 to 64 | aged 65 or older | | |
| --- | --- | --- | --- | --- | --- | --- | --- | --- | --- |
| | | | | | | | total | 65 to 74 | 75 or older |
| **Transportation** | **100** | **74** | **39** | **51** | **147** | **98** | **177** | **209** | **137** |
| **Health care** | **100** | **23** | **30** | **63** | **160** | **200** | **130** | **90** | **177** |
| **Entertainment** | **100** | **37** | **87** | **85** | **148** | **139** | **86** | **115** | **49** |
| Toys, games, hobbies, tricycles | 100 | 24 | 117 | 85 | 107 | 159 | 88 | 98 | 76 |
| Other entertainment | 100 | 48 | 66 | 84 | 178 | 128 | 84 | 128 | 31 |
| **Education** | **100** | **92** | **18** | **65** | **288** | **63** | **73** | **105** | **32** |
| **All other gifts** | **100** | **30** | **102** | **102** | **103** | **146** | **92** | **110** | **70** |

*Note: The Bureau of Labor Statistics uses consumer units rather than households as the sampling unit in the Consumer Expenditure Survey. For the definition of consumer unit, see the Glossary. An index of 100 is the average for all households. An index of 132 means households in the age group spend 32 percent more than the average household. An index of 75 means households in the age group spend 25 percent less than the average household. (–) means sample is too small to make a reliable estimate.*
*Source: Calculations by New Strategist based on the Bureau of Labor Statistics' 1997 Consumer Expenditure Survey*

# Market Shares by Age of Householder, 1997

*(share of total annual spending accounted for by consumer unit age group, 1997)*

| | total | under age 35 | 35 to 54 | 55 or older |
|---|---|---|---|---|
| **Share of total consumer units** | 100.0% | 26.0% | 41.6% | 32.4% |
| **Share of total annual spending** | 100.0 | 22.7 | 50.8 | 26.6 |
| **FOOD** | **100.0%** | **22.5%** | **50.5%** | **27.4%** |
| **FOOD AT HOME** | 100.0 | 21.9 | 49.2 | 29.3 |
| **Cereals and bakery products** | 100.0 | 21.9 | 49.9 | 28.6 |
| Cereals and cereal products | 100.0 | 24.0 | 50.0 | 26.8 |
| Bakery products | 100.0 | 20.7 | 49.9 | 29.6 |
| **Meats, poultry, fish, and eggs** | 100.0 | 21.5 | 49.6 | 29.3 |
| Beef | 100.0 | 22.4 | 50.6 | 27.1 |
| Pork | 100.0 | 20.7 | 48.3 | 31.5 |
| Other meats | 100.0 | 20.3 | 50.3 | 30.0 |
| Poultry | 100.0 | 22.8 | 49.6 | 28.0 |
| Fish and seafood | 100.0 | 19.9 | 49.4 | 30.6 |
| Eggs | 100.0 | 20.3 | 45.8 | 32.0 |
| **Dairy products** | 100.0 | 22.0 | 49.6 | 28.7 |
| Fresh milk and cream | 100.0 | 22.8 | 49.6 | 28.3 |
| Other dairy products | 100.0 | 21.4 | 49.8 | 29.0 |
| **Fruits and vegetables** | 100.0 | 20.8 | 47.1 | 32.4 |
| Fresh fruits | 100.0 | 20.9 | 46.2 | 33.5 |
| Fresh vegetables | 100.0 | 19.5 | 46.9 | 33.7 |
| Processed fruits | 100.0 | 21.8 | 47.7 | 31.1 |
| Processed vegetables | 100.0 | 22.0 | 48.9 | 29.6 |
| **Other food at home** | 100.0 | 22.8 | 49.4 | 28.1 |
| Sugar and other sweets | 100.0 | 20.8 | 48.9 | 30.9 |
| Fats and oils | 100.0 | 20.2 | 46.5 | 33.8 |
| Miscellaneous foods | 100.0 | 24.5 | 49.9 | 26.0 |
| Nonalcoholic beverages | 100.0 | 22.5 | 49.8 | 27.8 |
| Food prepared by household on trips | 100.0 | 19.4 | 49.0 | 31.0 |
| **FOOD AWAY FROM HOME** | 100.0 | 23.3 | 52.3 | 24.7 |
| **ALCOHOLIC BEVERAGES** | **100.0%** | **29.0%** | **47.4%** | **23.9%** |
| **HOUSING** | **100.0%** | **23.4%** | **50.3%** | **26.4%** |
| **SHELTER** | 100.0 | 24.8 | 51.4 | 23.7 |
| **Owned dwellings** | 100.0 | 17.2 | 57.0 | 25.8 |
| Mortgage interest and charges | 100.0 | 20.8 | 64.0 | 15.2 |

*(continued)*

*(continued from previous page)*

| | total | under age 35 | 35 to 54 | 55 or older |
|---|---|---|---|---|
| Property taxes | 100.0% | 13.2% | 49.8% | 37.0% |
| Maintenance, repairs, insurance, other | 100.0 | 11.5 | 45.4 | 43.1 |
| **Rented dwellings** | **100.0** | **42.1** | **40.2** | **17.7** |
| **Other lodging** | **100.0** | **15.1** | **52.4** | **32.4** |
| **UTILITIES, FUELS,** | | | | |
| **PUBLIC SERVICES** | **100.0** | **20.7** | **47.9** | **31.4** |
| Natural gas | 100.0 | 18.6 | 44.8 | 36.6 |
| Electricity | 100.0 | 19.3 | 48.4 | 32.2 |
| Fuel oil and other fuels | 100.0 | 12.8 | 48.2 | 38.8 |
| Telephone services | 100.0 | 25.7 | 48.0 | 26.3 |
| Water and other public services | 100.0 | 15.7 | 49.1 | 35.1 |
| **HOUSEHOLD SERVICES** | **100.0** | **25.2** | **49.3** | **25.7** |
| Personal services | 100.0 | 38.9 | 50.0 | 11.1 |
| Other household expenses | 100.0 | 12.5 | 48.7 | 39.0 |
| **HOUSEKEEPING SUPPLIES** | **100.0** | **19.3** | **49.0** | **32.2** |
| Laundry and cleaning supplies | 100.0 | 21.6 | 49.5 | 29.2 |
| Other household products | 100.0 | 18.1 | 50.1 | 32.4 |
| Postage and stationery | 100.0 | 19.0 | 46.8 | 34.6 |
| **HOUSEHOLD FURNISHINGS** | | | | |
| **AND EQUIPMENT** | **100.0** | **22.5** | **49.8** | **27.9** |
| Household textiles | 100.0 | 20.8 | 50.5 | 29.0 |
| Furniture | 100.0 | 27.9 | 50.2 | 22.0 |
| Floor coverings | 100.0 | 18.3 | 33.4 | 48.1 |
| Major appliances | 100.0 | 19.8 | 45.8 | 34.3 |
| Small appliances, misc. housewares | 100.0 | 19.1 | 50.6 | 30.3 |
| Miscellaneous household equipment | 100.0 | 21.3 | 52.1 | 26.9 |
| **APPAREL AND SERVICES** | **100.0%** | **26.5%** | **50.1%** | **23.7%** |
| **Men and boys** | **100.0** | **25.7** | **53.1** | **21.4** |
| Men, 16 and over | 100.0 | 26.2 | 49.9 | 24.2 |
| Boys, 2 to 15 | 100.0 | 23.9 | 65.4 | 10.9 |
| **Women and girls** | **100.0** | **24.3** | **49.6** | **26.4** |
| Women, 16 and over | 100.0 | 24.4 | 46.4 | 29.4 |
| Girls, 2 to 15 | 100.0 | 23.6 | 67.1 | 10.1 |
| **Children under 2** | **100.0** | **50.2** | **39.3** | **11.1** |
| **Footwear** | **100.0** | **26.1** | **49.0** | **24.9** |
| **Other apparel products, services** | **100.0** | **26.9** | **51.1** | **22.6** |
| **TRANSPORTATION** | **100.0%** | **24.7%** | **50.9%** | **24.4%** |
| **Vehicle purchases** | **100.0** | **26.8** | **50.6** | **22.5** |

*(continued)*

*(continued from previous page)*

| | total | under age 35 | 35 to 54 | 55 or older |
|---|---|---|---|---|
| Cars and trucks, new | 100.0% | 20.8% | 53.0% | 26.2% |
| Cars and trucks, used | 100.0 | 31.7 | 48.5 | 19.8 |
| Other vehicles | 100.0 | 33.6 | 54.3 | 12.3 |
| **Gasoline and motor oil** | **100.0** | **23.8** | **51.3** | **24.9** |
| **Other vehicle expenses** | **100.0** | **22.9** | **52.0** | **25.2** |
| Vehicle finance charges | 100.0 | 30.8 | 52.0 | 17.1 |
| Maintenance and repairs | 100.0 | 19.9 | 52.2 | 28.0 |
| Vehicle insurance | 100.0 | 21.9 | 49.9 | 28.3 |
| Vehicle rental, leases, licenses, other | 100.0 | 23.8 | 54.6 | 21.6 |
| **Public transportation** | **100.0** | **22.9** | **45.9** | **31.2** |
| **HEALTH CARE** | **100.0%** | **14.3%** | **39.6%** | **46.1%** |
| Health insurance | 100.0 | 14.0 | 37.3 | 48.7 |
| Medical services | 100.0 | 16.7 | 46.7 | 36.7 |
| Drugs | 100.0 | 11.4 | 32.6 | 56.2 |
| Medical supplies | 100.0 | 13.7 | 45.1 | 41.3 |
| **ENTERTAINMENT** | **100.0%** | **23.5%** | **51.7%** | **24.9%** |
| Fees and admissions | 100.0 | 21.0 | 54.8 | 24.2 |
| Television, radio, sound equipment | 100.0 | 25.6 | 48.7 | 25.7 |
| Pets, toys, playground equipment | 100.0 | 24.0 | 50.8 | 25.4 |
| Other entertainment supplies, equipment, services | 100.0 | 23.1 | 53.0 | 24.0 |
| **PERSONAL CARE PRODUCTS & SERVICES** | **100.0%** | **22.9%** | **47.9%** | **29.3%** |
| **READING** | **100.0%** | **18.0%** | **45.6%** | **36.1%** |
| **EDUCATION** | **100.0%** | **29.8%** | **58.9%** | **11.3%** |
| **TOBACCO PRODUCTS & SMOKING SUPPLIES** | **100.0%** | **24.0%** | **50.6%** | **25.2%** |
| **MISCELLANEOUS** | **100.0%** | **19.2%** | **51.1%** | **29.8%** |
| Cash contributions | 100.0 | 10.2 | 48.2 | 41.6 |
| Personal insurance and pensions | 100.0 | 21.6 | 59.6 | 18.8 |
| Life and other personal insurance | 100.0 | 12.8 | 52.7 | 34.4 |
| Pensions and Social Security | 100.0 | 22.8 | 60.5 | 16.7 |
| **PERSONAL TAXES** | **100.0%** | **21.1%** | **58.2%** | **21.1%** |
| Federal income taxes | 100.0 | 21.1 | 58.5 | 20.8 |
| State and local income taxes | 100.0 | 23.6 | 59.1 | 17.7 |
| Other taxes | 100.0 | 8.2 | 48.0 | 43.5 |

*(continued)*

*(continued from previous page)*

| GIFTS | total<br>100.0% | under age 35<br>17.8% | 35 to 54<br>50.9% | 55 or older<br>31.5% |
|---|---|---|---|---|
| **Food** | **100.0** | **13.3** | **60.3** | **26.0** |
| **Housing** | **100.0** | **22.0** | **49.6** | **28.7** |
| Housekeeping supplies | 100.0 | 18.8 | 48.2 | 32.4 |
| Household textiles | 100.0 | 14.5 | 44.9 | 45.2 |
| Appliances and miscellaneous housewares | 100.0 | 18.5 | 44.0 | 38.4 |
| Major appliances | 100.0 | 19.3 | 42.2 | 42.6 |
| Small appliances, miscellaneous housewares | 100.0 | 18.3 | 43.7 | 36.6 |
| Miscellaneous household equipment | 100.0 | 19.1 | 50.3 | 31.0 |
| Other housing | 100.0 | 25.4 | 50.9 | 23.5 |
| **Apparel and services** | **100.0** | **19.5** | **48.7** | **32.0** |
| Males, 2 and over | 100.0 | 18.1 | 45.3 | 37.4 |
| Females, 2 and over | 100.0 | 17.7 | 48.7 | 34.0 |
| Children under 2 | 100.0 | 29.9 | 44.9 | 23.9 |
| Other apparel products, services | 100.0 | 18.1 | 53.2 | 29.1 |
| Jewelry and watches | 100.0 | 18.8 | 54.9 | 25.6 |
| All other apparel products, services | 100.0 | 16.2 | 48.5 | 33.6 |
| **Transportation** | **100.0** | **12.5** | **38.8** | **48.3** |
| **Health care** | **100.0** | **7.3** | **44.0** | **50.3** |
| **Entertainment** | **100.0** | **19.0** | **46.9** | **34.1** |
| Toys, games, hobbies, tricycles | 100.0 | 23.8 | 39.5 | 36.7 |
| Other entertainment | 100.0 | 15.8 | 52.2 | 32.4 |
| **Education** | **100.0** | **9.9** | **67.9** | **22.5** |
| **All other gifts** | **100.0** | **21.3** | **42.5** | **36.2** |

*Note: The Bureau of Labor Statistics uses consumer units rather than households as the sampling unit in the Consumer Expenditure Survey. For the definition of consumer unit, see the Glossary. Numbers may not add to total due to rounding.*
*Source: Calculations by New Strategist based on the Bureau of Labor Statistics' 1997 Consumer Expenditure Survey*

# Spending Rises with Income

**Households with incomes of $70,000 or more spend nearly twice as much as the average household.**

The most affluent households are also the largest, housing an average of 3.1 people according to the Bureau of Labor Statistics' Consumer Expenditure Survey. High-income households spend more than average on nearly every category of goods and services, with few exceptions.

The Indexed Spending table in this section shows spending by household income groups in comparison to what the average household spends. An index of 100 means households in the income group spend the average amount on an item. An index above 100 means households in the income group spend more than average on the item, while an index below 100 signifies below-average spending. A look at the table reveals that households with incomes below $30,000 spend well below average on most items, households with incomes of $30,000 to $40,000 spend close to average on most items, and households with incomes of $40,000 or more spend above average on most items. For households with incomes of $70,000 or more, spending is two to three times above average on many items.

### Nearly one-half of spending is done by the most affluent households

*(share of household spending accounted for by household income group, 1997)*

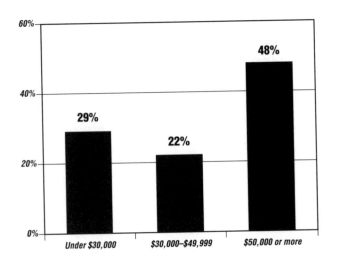

There are some notable exceptions, however. Households with incomes below $30,000 spend close to or more than average on rent, drugs, and tobacco. Households with incomes of $70,000 or more spend 36 percent less than average on rent (with an index of 64), and 3 percent less than average on tobacco. The most affluent households spend at least twice as much as the average household on a variety of items such as food away from home, alcohol, new cars and trucks, entertainment, education, life and other personal insurance, and gifts.

The Market Share table in this section shows how much of total household spending by category is accounted for by three broad income groups: households with annual incomes below $30,000, between $30,000 to $50,000, and $50,000 or more. Forty-nine percent of the nation's households have annual incomes below $30,000, but these households accounted for just 29 percent of all household spending in 1997. The 22 percent of households with incomes between $30,000 and $50,000 accounted for 22 percent of spending. The remaining 29 percent of households, those with incomes of $50,000 or more, accounted for fully 48 percent of all household spending in 1997.

The share of spending accounted for by high-income households is above 50 percent on a variety of categories such as other lodging, which includes hotel and motel expenses; new cars and trucks; fees and admissions to entertainment events; cash contributions; and personal insurance. The share of spending accounted for by low-income households is 50 percent or greater for only two items: rent and drugs. Many low-income households are headed by elderly retirees, which accounts for their above-average spending on drugs.

◆ Spending patterns by income group will remain stable during the next 10 years because the demographic characteristics of those with low or high incomes will not change much. Low-income households will continue to be dominated by young adults and the elderly. High-income households will continue to be dominated by middle-aged two-earner couples.

# Spending by Household Income, 1997

*(average annual spending of consumer units (cu) by product and service category and household income, 1997; data shown for complete income reporters only)*

| | total income reporters | under $10,000 | $10,000–$19,999 | $20,000–$29,999 | $30,000–$39,999 | $40,000–$49,999 | $50,000–$69,999 | $70,000 or more |
|---|---|---|---|---|---|---|---|---|
| Number of consumer units in (000s) | 84,991 | 13,082 | 16,520 | 12,415 | 10,392 | 7,949 | 11,930 | 12,705 |
| Average number of persons per cu | 2.5 | 1.7 | 2.2 | 2.4 | 2.6 | 2.8 | 3 | 3.1 |
| Average before-tax income | $39,926 | $5,901 | $14,649 | $24,599 | $34,583 | $44,396 | $58,249 | $107,170 |
| Average annual spending | 36,146 | 15,598 | 21,075 | 27,836 | 34,376 | 40,779 | 48,417 | 71,656 |
| **FOOD** | **$4,902** | **$2,636** | **$3,347** | **$4,109** | **$4,888** | **$5,429** | **$6,220** | **$8,279** |
| FOOD AT HOME | 2,970 | 1,809 | 2,370 | 2,701 | 3,062 | 3,221 | 3,556 | 4,315 |
| **Cereals and bakery products** | **465** | **276** | **362** | **421** | **489** | **506** | **549** | **691** |
| Cereals and cereal products | 166 | 98 | 141 | 142 | 184 | 168 | 196 | 237 |
| Bakery products | 299 | 177 | 221 | 278 | 305 | 338 | 353 | 453 |
| **Meats, poultry, fish, and eggs** | **756** | **483** | **659** | **728** | **774** | **774** | **880** | **1,024** |
| Beef | 226 | 130 | 193 | 219 | 238 | 238 | 291 | 292 |
| Pork | 161 | 107 | 159 | 161 | 164 | 160 | 171 | 203 |
| Other meats | 99 | 63 | 81 | 92 | 100 | 115 | 114 | 135 |
| Poultry | 146 | 94 | 126 | 132 | 147 | 152 | 169 | 207 |
| Fish and seafood | 91 | 65 | 68 | 88 | 88 | 76 | 99 | 150 |
| Eggs | 34 | 25 | 32 | 36 | 37 | 33 | 36 | 38 |
| **Dairy products** | **329** | **193** | **260** | **295** | **332** | **374** | **395** | **487** |
| Fresh milk and cream | 134 | 84 | 114 | 132 | 143 | 153 | 154 | 173 |
| Other dairy products | 195 | 109 | 146 | 163 | 189 | 221 | 242 | 314 |

*(continued)*

*(continued from previous page)*

| | total income reporters | under $10,000 | $10,000– $19,999 | $20,000– $29,999 | $30,000– $39,999 | $40,000– $49,999 | $50,000– $69,999 | $70,000 more |
|---|---|---|---|---|---|---|---|---|
| **Fruits and vegetables** | $485 | $308 | $393 | $444 | $479 | $496 | $565 | $735 |
| Fresh fruits | 154 | 94 | 118 | 147 | 154 | 153 | 197 | 226 |
| Fresh vegetables | 145 | 92 | 120 | 139 | 138 | 135 | 159 | 231 |
| Processed fruits | 105 | 68 | 86 | 83 | 103 | 112 | 122 | 164 |
| Processed vegetables | 82 | 54 | 70 | 74 | 84 | 96 | 88 | 113 |
| **Other food at home** | 935 | 549 | 696 | 813 | 987 | 1,072 | 1,167 | 1,378 |
| Sugar and other sweets | 118 | 77 | 88 | 100 | 127 | 127 | 152 | 170 |
| Fats and oils | 83 | 56 | 76 | 76 | 92 | 84 | 96 | 105 |
| Miscellaneous foods | 425 | 236 | 306 | 373 | 451 | 501 | 532 | 633 |
| Nonalcoholic beverages | 254 | 159 | 196 | 232 | 267 | 302 | 310 | 347 |
| Food prepared by household on trips | 55 | 22 | 30 | 32 | 50 | 59 | 77 | 123 |
| **FOOD AWAY FROM HOME** | 1,932 | 828 | 976 | 1,408 | 1,826 | 2,208 | 2,664 | 3,964 |
| **ALCOHOLIC BEVERAGES** | **$330** | **$156** | **$156** | **$256** | **$319** | **$363** | **$417** | **$699** |
| **HOUSING** | **$11,348** | **$5,717** | **$7,403** | **$8,782** | **$10,653** | **$12,359** | **$14,380** | **$21,816** |
| **SHELTER** | 6,339 | 3,129 | 4,040 | 4,832 | 6,004 | 6,969 | 7,827 | 12,590 |
| **Owned dwellings** | 3,933 | 1,065 | 1,720 | 2,253 | 3,243 | 4,454 | 5,793 | 9,898 |
| Mortgage interest and charges | 2,235 | 402 | 600 | 1,059 | 1,770 | 2,657 | 3,643 | 6,193 |
| Property taxes | 947 | 343 | 585 | 640 | 734 | 990 | 1,251 | 2,199 |
| Maintenance, repairs, insurance, other | 751 | 320 | 536 | 554 | 739 | 808 | 899 | 1,506 |
| **Rented dwellings** | 1,980 | 1,940 | 2,158 | 2,371 | 2,536 | 2,137 | 1,540 | 1,266 |
| **Other lodging** | 426 | 124 | 162 | 208 | 225 | 378 | 494 | 1,425 |

*(continued)*

(continued from previous page)

| | total income reporters | under $10,000 | $10,000–$19,999 | $20,000–$29,999 | $30,000–$39,999 | $40,000–$49,999 | $50,000–$69,999 | $70,000 more |
|---|---|---|---|---|---|---|---|---|
| **UTILITIES, FUELS, PUBLIC SERVICES** | **$2,408** | **$1,510** | **$1,970** | **$2,218** | **$2,403** | **$2,599** | **$2,933** | **$3,478** |
| Natural gas | 298 | 180 | 244 | 279 | 300 | 337 | 348 | 437 |
| Electricity | 900 | 583 | 776 | 842 | 891 | 973 | 1,080 | 1,235 |
| Fuel oil and other fuels | 109 | 76 | 90 | 98 | 107 | 111 | 126 | 163 |
| Telephone services | 809 | 514 | 640 | 742 | 834 | 859 | 1,001 | 1,168 |
| Water and other public services | 292 | 157 | 221 | 258 | 271 | 319 | 378 | 475 |
| **HOUSEHOLD SERVICES** | **562** | **193** | **310** | **354** | **359** | **500** | **754** | **1,496** |
| Personal services | 273 | 77 | 138 | 174 | 179 | 271 | 433 | 674 |
| Other household expenses | 289 | 116 | 172 | 180 | 180 | 228 | 320 | 822 |
| **HOUSEKEEPING SUPPLIES** | **485** | **247** | **322** | **394** | **482** | **524** | **651** | **833** |
| Laundry and cleaning supplies | 125 | 73 | 94 | 109 | 128 | 145 | 162 | 179 |
| Other household products | 222 | 110 | 145 | 160 | 207 | 238 | 326 | 399 |
| Postage and stationery | 138 | 64 | 83 | 125 | 146 | 141 | 164 | 254 |
| **HOUSEHOLD FURNISHINGS AND EQUIPMENT** | **1,554** | **637** | **762** | **985** | **1,405** | **1,767** | **2,214** | **3,420** |
| Household textiles | 82 | 33 | 44 | 54 | 64 | 80 | 113 | 196 |
| Furniture | 380 | 138 | 184 | 203 | 310 | 373 | 580 | 935 |
| Floor coverings | 83 | 21 | 20 | 26 | 129 | 137 | 96 | 190 |
| Major appliances | 174 | 88 | 116 | 136 | 220 | 167 | 225 | 292 |
| Small appliances, misc. housewares | 100 | 78 | 57 | 69 | 95 | 77 | 137 | 197 |
| Miscellaneous household equipment | 735 | 279 | 341 | 497 | 588 | 932 | 1,064 | 1,610 |

(continued)

(continued from previous page)

| | total income reporters | under $10,000 | $10,000– $19,999 | $20,000– $29,999 | $30,000– $39,999 | $40,000– $49,999 | $50,000– $69,999 | $70,000 more |
|---|---|---|---|---|---|---|---|---|
| **APPAREL** | **$1,786** | **$826** | **$957** | **$1,363** | **$1,772** | **$1,778** | **$2,614** | **$3,442** |
| **Men and boys** | **423** | **164** | **208** | **294** | **414** | **471** | **616** | **874** |
| Men, 16 and over | 338 | 131 | 153 | 214 | 343 | 359 | 506 | 724 |
| Boys, 2 to 15 | 85 | 33 | 56 | 80 | 72 | 112 | 111 | 150 |
| **Women and girls** | **699** | **316** | **369** | **558** | **682** | **672** | **1,051** | **1,336** |
| Women, 16 and over | 591 | 278 | 310 | 485 | 560 | 528 | 903 | 1,134 |
| Girls, 2 to 15 | 108 | 38 | 59 | 73 | 122 | 144 | 148 | 202 |
| **Children under 2** | **84** | **36** | **50** | **78** | **92** | **93** | **120** | **129** |
| **Footwear** | **326** | **206** | **226** | **261** | **339** | **343** | **450** | **494** |
| **Other apparel products, services** | **255** | **105** | **102** | **173** | **246** | **199** | **377** | **609** |
| **TRANSPORTATION** | **$6,669** | **$2,321** | **$3,635** | **$5,249** | **$7,139** | **$8,444** | **$9,436** | **$12,387** |
| **Vehicle purchases** | **2,856** | **895** | **1,470** | **2,276** | **3,382** | **4,074** | **4,085** | **4,900** |
| Cars and trucks, new | 1,310 | 172 | 483 | 976 | 1,579 | 1,682 | 1,915 | 2,865 |
| Cars and trucks, used | 1,500 | 716 | 977 | 1,256 | 1,779 | 2,328 | 2,115 | 1,901 |
| Other vehicles | 47 | 7 | 9 | 44 | 25 | 64 | 55 | 134 |
| **Gasoline and motor oil** | **1,110** | **508** | **734** | **963** | **1,181** | **1,331** | **1,547** | **1,758** |
| Other vehicle expenses | 2,312 | 758 | 1,251 | 1,753 | 2,288 | 2,681 | 3,319 | 4,683 |
| Vehicle finance charges | 305 | 68 | 122 | 234 | 360 | 447 | 510 | 530 |
| Maintenance and repairs | 720 | 273 | 480 | 600 | 699 | 739 | 981 | 1,369 |
| Vehicle insurance | 779 | 259 | 469 | 666 | 849 | 915 | 1,114 | 1,374 |
| Vehicle rental, leases, licenses, other | 508 | 157 | 180 | 253 | 381 | 581 | 714 | 1,410 |
| **Public transportation** | **390** | **160** | **180** | **257** | **288** | **358** | **485** | **1,046** |

(continued)

| | total income reporters | under $10,000 | $10,000–$19,999 | $20,000–$29,999 | $30,000–$39,999 | $40,000–$49,999 | $50,000–$69,999 | $70,000 more |
|---|---|---|---|---|---|---|---|---|
| **HEALTH CARE** | **$1,898** | **$1,099** | **$1,683** | **$1,918** | **$1,820** | **$2,052** | **$2,214** | **$2,642** |
| Health insurance | 900 | 516 | 826 | 918 | 859 | 981 | 1,133 | 1,137 |
| Medical services | 544 | 254 | 389 | 494 | 496 | 625 | 650 | 981 |
| Drugs | 342 | 266 | 383 | 400 | 346 | 322 | 309 | 342 |
| Medical supplies | 113 | 63 | 86 | 106 | 118 | 125 | 123 | 183 |
| **ENTERTAINMENT** | **$1,868** | **$681** | **$935** | **$1,274** | **$1,514** | **$2,054** | **$2,654** | **$4,300** |
| Fees and admissions | 490 | 152 | 181 | 274 | 366 | 496 | 668 | 1,382 |
| Television, radio, sound equipment | 596 | 299 | 424 | 512 | 591 | 681 | 768 | 996 |
| Pets, toys, playground equipment | 339 | 135 | 176 | 257 | 309 | 360 | 539 | 654 |
| Other entertainment supplies, equipment, services | 442 | 96 | 153 | 231 | 248 | 517 | 678 | 1,268 |
| **PERSONAL CARE PRODUCTS & SERVICES** | **$551** | **$243** | **$362** | **$497** | **$594** | **$571** | **$708** | **$957** |
| **READING** | **$171** | **$71** | **$102** | **$141** | **$159** | **$170** | **$233** | **$346** |
| **EDUCATION** | **$548** | **$478** | **$290** | **$354** | **$398** | **$499** | **$722** | **$1,131** |
| **TOBACCO PRODUCTS & SMOKING SUPPLIES** | **$271** | **$213** | **$259** | **$263** | **$321** | **$286** | **$316** | **$262** |
| **MISCELLANEOUS** | **$888** | **$496** | **$540** | **$705** | **$881** | **$1,207** | **$1,170** | **$1,456** |
| Cash contributions | 1,085 | 339 | 582 | 999 | 841 | 1,176 | 1,188 | 2,635 |
| Personal insurance and pensions | 3,830 | 322 | 825 | 1,926 | 3,077 | 4,390 | 6,145 | 11,304 |
| Life and other personal insurance | 387 | 114 | 189 | 295 | 306 | 360 | 571 | 921 |
| Pensions and Social Security | 3,444 | 208 | 636 | 1,630 | 2,770 | 4,030 | 5,574 | 10,382 |

*(continued)*

*(continued from previous page)*

| | total income reporters | under $10,000 | $10,000–$19,999 | $20,000–$29,999 | $30,000–$39,999 | $40,000–$49,999 | $50,000–$69,999 | $70,000 more |
|---|---|---|---|---|---|---|---|---|
| **PERSONAL TAXES** | **$3,241** | **$38** | **$254** | **$1,061** | **$2,460** | **$3,741** | **$5,104** | **$11,133** |
| Federal income taxes | 2,468 | 22 | 93 | 728 | 1,837 | 2,820 | 3,963 | 8,710 |
| State and local income taxes | 645 | 13 | 82 | 233 | 511 | 762 | 978 | 2,153 |
| Other taxes | 129 | 47 | 78 | 100 | 112 | 159 | 163 | 270 |
| **GIFTS** | **$1,069** | **$566** | **$595** | **$764** | **$1,007** | **$907** | **$1,536** | **$2,198** |
| **Food** | **65** | **24** | **32** | **44** | **49** | **60** | **99** | **152** |
| **Housing** | **277** | **172** | **171** | **181** | **224** | **258** | **343** | **609** |
| Housekeeping supplies | 40 | 20 | 23 | 31 | 39 | 42 | 46 | 83 |
| Household textiles | 9 | 6 | 4 | 6 | 6 | 10 | 13 | 19 |
| Appliances and miscellaneous housewares | 30 | 14 | 15 | 21 | 27 | 23 | 40 | 72 |
| Major appliances | 7 | 2 | 6 | 2 | 7 | 6 | 12 | 13 |
| Small appliances, misc. housewares | 23 | 13 | 10 | 19 | 20 | 17 | 28 | 59 |
| Miscellaneous household equipment | 69 | 33 | 29 | 52 | 54 | 59 | 111 | 154 |
| Other housing | 129 | 98 | 99 | 72 | 99 | 123 | 133 | 281 |
| **Apparel and services** | **258** | **111** | **128** | **199** | **279** | **229** | **425** | **474** |
| Males, 2 and over | 61 | 27 | 34 | 52 | 58 | 63 | 61 | 135 |
| Females, 2 and over | 82 | 48 | 40 | 64 | 94 | 83 | 123 | 141 |
| Children under 2 | 33 | 14 | 22 | 27 | 38 | 40 | 45 | 53 |
| Other apparel products, services | 81 | 22 | 32 | 56 | 88 | 42 | 196 | 145 |
| Jewelry and watches | 50 | 11 | 3 | 20 | 60 | 22 | 154 | 97 |
| All other apparel products, services | 31 | 10 | 29 | 36 | 28 | 20 | 43 | 48 |

*(continued)*

(continued from previous page)

| | total income reporters | under $10,000 | $10,000–$19,999 | $20,000–$29,999 | $30,000–$39,999 | $40,000–$49,999 | $50,000–$69,999 | $70,000 more |
|---|---|---|---|---|---|---|---|---|
| **Transportation** | $62 | $19 | $40 | $93 | $28 | $40 | $138 | $76 |
| **Health care** | 31 | 16 | 31 | 17 | 22 | 40 | 26 | 68 |
| **Entertainment** | 102 | 50 | 54 | 78 | 133 | 89 | 136 | 190 |
| Toys, games, hobbies, tricycles | 42 | 15 | 20 | 32 | 50 | 39 | 78 | 65 |
| Other entertainment | 60 | 34 | 34 | 46 | 83 | 50 | 58 | 125 |
| **Education** | 141 | 102 | 73 | 47 | 49 | 94 | 224 | 388 |
| **All other gifts** | 133 | 72 | 65 | 104 | 223 | 99 | 147 | 241 |

*Note: The Bureau of Labor Statistics uses consumer units rather than households as the sampling unit in the Consumer Expenditure Survey. For the definition of consumer unit, see the Glossary. Gift spending is also included in the preceding product and service categories.*
*Source: Bureau of Labor Statistics, 1997 Consumer Expenditure Survey; calculations by New Strategist*

# Indexed Spending by Household Income, 1997

*(indexed average annual spending of consumer units by product and service category and household income of consumer unit, 1997)*

| | total income reporters | under $10,000 | $10,000–$19,999 | $20,000–$29,999 | $30,000–$39,999 | $40,000–$49,999 | $50,000–$69,999 | $70,000 more |
|---|---|---|---|---|---|---|---|---|
| Number of consumer units (in 000s) | 84,991 | 13,082 | 16,520 | 12,415 | 10,392 | 7,949 | 11,930 | 12,705 |
| Indexed average before-tax income | 100 | 15 | 37 | 62 | 87 | 111 | 146 | 268 |
| Indexed average annual spending | 100 | 43 | 58 | 77 | 95 | 113 | 134 | 198 |
| **FOOD** | **100** | **54** | **68** | **84** | **100** | **111** | **127** | **169** |
| **FOOD AT HOME** | **100** | **61** | **80** | **91** | **103** | **108** | **120** | **145** |
| **Cereals and bakery products** | **100** | **59** | **78** | **91** | **105** | **109** | **118** | **149** |
| Cereals and cereal products | 100 | 59 | 85 | 86 | 111 | 101 | 118 | 143 |
| Bakery products | 100 | 59 | 74 | 93 | 102 | 113 | 118 | 152 |
| **Meats, poultry, fish, and eggs** | **100** | **64** | **87** | **96** | **102** | **102** | **116** | **135** |
| Beef | 100 | 57 | 86 | 97 | 105 | 105 | 129 | 129 |
| Pork | 100 | 66 | 99 | 100 | 102 | 99 | 106 | 126 |
| Other meats | 100 | 63 | 82 | 93 | 101 | 116 | 115 | 136 |
| Poultry | 100 | 64 | 86 | 90 | 101 | 104 | 116 | 142 |
| Fish and seafood | 100 | 71 | 75 | 97 | 97 | 84 | 109 | 165 |
| Eggs | 100 | 73 | 93 | 106 | 109 | 97 | 106 | 112 |
| **Dairy products** | **100** | **59** | **79** | **90** | **101** | **114** | **120** | **148** |
| Fresh milk and cream | 100 | 62 | 85 | 99 | 107 | 114 | 115 | 129 |
| Other dairy products | 100 | 56 | 75 | 84 | 97 | 113 | 124 | 161 |

*(continued)*

| | total income reporters | under $10,000 | $10,000–$19,999 | $20,000–$29,999 | $30,000–$39,999 | $40,000–$49,999 | $50,000–$69,999 | $70,000 more |
|---|---|---|---|---|---|---|---|---|
| **Fruits and vegetables** | **100** | **64** | **81** | **92** | **99** | **102** | **116** | **152** |
| Fresh fruits | 100 | 61 | 77 | 95 | 100 | 99 | 128 | 147 |
| Fresh vegetables | 100 | 63 | 83 | 96 | 95 | 93 | 110 | 159 |
| Processed fruits | 100 | 65 | 82 | 79 | 98 | 107 | 116 | 156 |
| Processed vegetables | 100 | 66 | 85 | 90 | 102 | 117 | 107 | 138 |
| **Other food at home** | **100** | **59** | **74** | **87** | **106** | **115** | **125** | **147** |
| Sugar and other sweets | 100 | 65 | 74 | 85 | 108 | 108 | 129 | 144 |
| Fats and oils | 100 | 68 | 92 | 92 | 111 | 101 | 116 | 127 |
| Miscellaneous foods | 100 | 55 | 72 | 88 | 106 | 118 | 125 | 149 |
| Nonalcoholic beverages | 100 | 62 | 77 | 91 | 105 | 119 | 122 | 137 |
| Food prepared by household on trips | 100 | 40 | 55 | 58 | 91 | 107 | 140 | 224 |
| **FOOD AWAY FROM HOME** | **100** | **43** | **51** | **73** | **95** | **114** | **138** | **205** |
| **ALCOHOLIC BEVERAGES** | **100** | **47** | **47** | **78** | **97** | **110** | **126** | **212** |
| **HOUSING** | **100** | **50** | **65** | **77** | **94** | **109** | **127** | **192** |
| **SHELTER** | **100** | **49** | **64** | **76** | **95** | **110** | **123** | **199** |
| **Owned dwellings** | **100** | **27** | **44** | **57** | **82** | **113** | **147** | **252** |
| Mortgage interest and charges | 100 | 18 | 27 | 47 | 79 | 119 | 163 | 277 |
| Property taxes | 100 | 36 | 62 | 68 | 78 | 105 | 132 | 232 |
| Maintenance, repairs, insurance, other | 100 | 43 | 71 | 74 | 98 | 108 | 120 | 201 |
| **Rented dwellings** | **100** | **98** | **109** | **120** | **128** | **108** | **78** | **64** |
| **Other lodging** | **100** | **29** | **38** | **49** | **53** | **89** | **116** | **335** |

(continued)

*(continued from previous page)*

| | total income reporters | under $10,000 | $10,000–$19,999 | $20,000–$29,999 | $30,000–$39,999 | $40,000–$49,999 | $50,000–$69,999 | $70,000 more |
|---|---|---|---|---|---|---|---|---|
| **UTILITIES, FUELS, PUBLIC SERVICES** | **100** | **63** | **82** | **92** | **100** | **108** | **122** | **144** |
| Natural gas | 100 | 60 | 82 | 94 | 101 | 113 | 117 | 147 |
| Electricity | 100 | 65 | 86 | 94 | 99 | 108 | 120 | 137 |
| Fuel oil and other fuels | 100 | 70 | 83 | 90 | 98 | 102 | 116 | 150 |
| Telephone services | 100 | 64 | 79 | 92 | 103 | 106 | 124 | 144 |
| Water and other public services | 100 | 54 | 76 | 88 | 93 | 109 | 129 | 163 |
| **HOUSEHOLD SERVICES** | **100** | **34** | **55** | **63** | **64** | **89** | **134** | **266** |
| Personal services | 100 | 28 | 50 | 64 | 66 | 99 | 159 | 247 |
| Other household expenses | 100 | 40 | 59 | 62 | 62 | 79 | 111 | 284 |
| **HOUSEKEEPING SUPPLIES** | **100** | **51** | **66** | **81** | **99** | **108** | **134** | **172** |
| Laundry and cleaning supplies | 100 | 59 | 75 | 87 | 102 | 116 | 130 | 143 |
| Other household products | 100 | 50 | 65 | 72 | 93 | 107 | 147 | 180 |
| Postage and stationery | 100 | 47 | 60 | 91 | 106 | 102 | 119 | 184 |
| **HOUSEHOLD FURNISHINGS AND EQUIPMENT** | **100** | **41** | **49** | **63** | **90** | **114** | **142** | **220** |
| Household textiles | 100 | 40 | 54 | 66 | 78 | 98 | 138 | 239 |
| Furniture | 100 | 36 | 48 | 53 | 82 | 98 | 153 | 246 |
| Floor coverings | 100 | 25 | 24 | 31 | 155 | 165 | 116 | 229 |
| Major appliances | 100 | 51 | 67 | 78 | 126 | 96 | 129 | 168 |
| Small appliances, misc. housewares | 100 | 78 | 57 | 69 | 95 | 77 | 137 | 197 |
| Miscellaneous household equipment | 100 | 38 | 46 | 68 | 80 | 127 | 145 | 219 |

*(continued)*

(continued from previous page)

| | total income reporters | under $10,000 | $10,000–$19,999 | $20,000–$29,999 | $30,000–$39,999 | $40,000–$49,999 | $50,000–$69,999 | $70,000 more |
|---|---|---|---|---|---|---|---|---|
| **APPAREL AND SERVICES** | **100** | **46** | **54** | **76** | **99** | **100** | **146** | **193** |
| **Men and boys** | **100** | **39** | **49** | **70** | **98** | **111** | **146** | **207** |
| Men, 16 and over | 100 | 39 | 45 | 63 | 101 | 106 | 150 | 214 |
| Boys, 2 to 15 | 100 | 39 | 66 | 94 | 85 | 132 | 131 | 176 |
| **Women and girls** | **100** | **45** | **53** | **80** | **98** | **96** | **150** | **191** |
| Women, 16 and over | 100 | 47 | 52 | 82 | 95 | 89 | 153 | 192 |
| Girls, 2 to 15 | 100 | 35 | 55 | 68 | 113 | 133 | 137 | 187 |
| **Children under 2** | **100** | **43** | **60** | **93** | **110** | **111** | **143** | **154** |
| **Footwear** | **100** | **63** | **69** | **80** | **104** | **105** | **138** | **152** |
| **Other apparel products, services** | **100** | **41** | **40** | **68** | **96** | **78** | **148** | **239** |
| **TRANSPORTATION** | **100** | **35** | **55** | **79** | **107** | **127** | **141** | **186** |
| **Vehicle purchases** | **100** | **31** | **51** | **80** | **118** | **143** | **143** | **172** |
| Cars and trucks, new | 100 | 13 | 37 | 75 | 121 | 128 | 146 | 219 |
| Cars and trucks, used | 100 | 48 | 65 | 84 | 119 | 155 | 141 | 127 |
| Other vehicles | 100 | 15 | 18 | 94 | 53 | 136 | 117 | 285 |
| **Gasoline and motor oil** | **100** | **46** | **66** | **87** | **106** | **120** | **139** | **158** |
| Other vehicle expenses | 100 | 33 | 54 | 76 | 99 | 116 | 144 | 203 |
| Vehicle finance charges | 100 | 22 | 40 | 77 | 118 | 147 | 167 | 174 |
| Maintenance and repairs | 100 | 38 | 67 | 83 | 97 | 103 | 136 | 190 |
| Vehicle insurance | 100 | 33 | 60 | 85 | 109 | 117 | 143 | 176 |
| Vehicle rental, leases, licenses, other | 100 | 31 | 36 | 50 | 75 | 114 | 141 | 278 |
| **Public transportation** | **100** | **41** | **46** | **66** | **74** | **92** | **124** | **268** |

(continued)

*(continued from previous page)*

| | total income reporters | under $10,000 | $10,000–$19,999 | $20,000–$29,999 | $30,000–$39,999 | $40,000–$49,999 | $50,000–$69,999 | $70,000 more |
|---|---|---|---|---|---|---|---|---|
| **HEALTH CARE** | **100** | **58** | **89** | **101** | **96** | **108** | **117** | **139** |
| Health insurance | 100 | 57 | 92 | 102 | 95 | 109 | 126 | 126 |
| Medical services | 100 | 47 | 71 | 91 | 91 | 115 | 119 | 180 |
| Drugs | 100 | 78 | 112 | 117 | 101 | 94 | 90 | 100 |
| Medical supplies | 100 | 56 | 76 | 94 | 104 | 111 | 109 | 162 |
| **ENTERTAINMENT** | **100** | **36** | **50** | **68** | **81** | **110** | **142** | **230** |
| Fees and admissions | 100 | 31 | 37 | 56 | 75 | 101 | 136 | 282 |
| Television, radio, sound equipment | 100 | 50 | 71 | 86 | 99 | 114 | 129 | 167 |
| Pets, toys, playground equipment | 100 | 40 | 52 | 76 | 91 | 106 | 159 | 193 |
| Other entertainment supplies, equipment, services | 100 | 22 | 35 | 52 | 56 | 117 | 153 | 287 |
| **PERSONAL CARE PRODUCTS & SERVICES** | **100** | **44** | **66** | **90** | **108** | **104** | **128** | **174** |
| **READING** | **100** | **42** | **60** | **82** | **93** | **99** | **136** | **202** |
| **EDUCATION** | **100** | **87** | **53** | **65** | **73** | **91** | **132** | **206** |
| **TOBACCO PRODUCTS & SMOKING SUPPLIES** | **100** | **79** | **95** | **97** | **118** | **106** | **117** | **97** |
| **MISCELLANEOUS** | **100** | **56** | **61** | **79** | **99** | **136** | **132** | **164** |
| Cash contributions | 100 | 31 | 54 | 92 | 78 | 108 | 109 | 243 |
| Personal insurance and pensions | 100 | 8 | 22 | 50 | 80 | 115 | 160 | 295 |
| Life and other personal insurance | 100 | 30 | 49 | 76 | 79 | 93 | 148 | 238 |
| Pensions and Social Security | 100 | 6 | 18 | 47 | 80 | 117 | 162 | 301 |

*(continued)*

| | total income reporters | under $10,000 | $10,000–$19,999 | $20,000–$29,999 | $30,000–$39,999 | $40,000–$49,999 | $50,000–$69,999 | $70,000 more |
|---|---|---|---|---|---|---|---|---|
| **PERSONAL TAXES** | **100** | **1** | **8** | **33** | **76** | **115** | **157** | **344** |
| Federal income taxes | 100 | – | 4 | 29 | 74 | 114 | 161 | 353 |
| State and local income taxes | 100 | 2 | 13 | 36 | 79 | 118 | 152 | 334 |
| Other taxes | 100 | 37 | 60 | 78 | 87 | 123 | 126 | 209 |
| **GIFTS** | **100** | **53** | **56** | **71** | **94** | **85** | **144** | **206** |
| **Food** | **100** | **37** | **49** | **68** | **75** | **92** | **152** | **234** |
| **Housing** | **100** | **62** | **62** | **65** | **81** | **93** | **124** | **220** |
| Housekeeping supplies | 100 | 49 | 58 | 78 | 98 | 105 | 115 | 208 |
| Household textiles | 100 | 70 | 44 | 67 | 67 | 111 | 144 | 211 |
| Appliances and miscellaneous housewares | 100 | 47 | 52 | 70 | 90 | 77 | 133 | 240 |
| Major appliances | 100 | 29 | 88 | 29 | 100 | 86 | 171 | 186 |
| Small appliances, misc. housewares | 100 | 56 | 43 | 83 | 87 | 74 | 122 | 257 |
| Miscellaneous household equipment | 100 | 48 | 41 | 75 | 78 | 86 | 161 | 223 |
| Other housing | 100 | 76 | 77 | 56 | 77 | 95 | 103 | 218 |
| **Apparel and services** | **100** | **43** | **50** | **77** | **108** | **89** | **165** | **184** |
| Males, 2 and over | 100 | 44 | 56 | 85 | 95 | 103 | 100 | 221 |
| Females, 2 and over | 100 | 59 | 49 | 78 | 115 | 101 | 150 | 172 |
| Children under 2 | 100 | 43 | 66 | 82 | 115 | 121 | 136 | 161 |
| Other apparel products, services | 100 | 27 | 40 | 69 | 109 | 52 | 242 | 179 |
| Jewelry and watches | 100 | 23 | 7 | 40 | 120 | 44 | 308 | 194 |
| All other apparel products, services | 100 | 32 | 93 | 116 | 90 | 65 | 139 | 155 |

*(continued)*

(continued from previous page)

| | total income reporters | under $10,000 | $10,000–$19,999 | $20,000–$29,999 | $30,000–$39,999 | $40,000–$49,999 | $50,000–$69,999 | $70,000 more |
|---|---|---|---|---|---|---|---|---|
| **Transportation** | 100 | 30 | 65 | 150 | 45 | 65 | 223 | 123 |
| **Health care** | 100 | 53 | 99 | 55 | 71 | 129 | 84 | 219 |
| **Entertainment** | 100 | 49 | 53 | 76 | 130 | 87 | 133 | 186 |
| Toys, games, hobbies, tricycles | 100 | 36 | 48 | 76 | 119 | 93 | 186 | 155 |
| Other entertainment | 100 | 57 | 56 | 77 | 138 | 83 | 97 | 208 |
| **Education** | 100 | 72 | 52 | 33 | 35 | 67 | 159 | 275 |
| **All other gifts** | 100 | 54 | 49 | 78 | 168 | 74 | 111 | 181 |

*Note: The Bureau of Labor Statistics uses consumer units rather than households as the sampling unit in the Consumer Expenditure Survey. For the definition of consumer unit, see the Glossary. And index of 100 is the average for all households. An index of 132 means households in the income group spend 32 percent more than the average household. An index of 75 means households in the income group spend 25 percent less than the average household. (–) means sample is too small to make a reliable estimate.*
*Source: Calculations by New Strategist based on data from the Bureau of Labor Statistics' 1997 Consumer Expenditure Survey*

# Market Shares by Household Income, 1997

*(share of total household spending accounted for by income group, 1997)*

| | total complete reporters | under $30,000 | $30,000–$49,999 | $50,000 or more |
|---|---|---|---|---|
| **Share of total consumer units** | 100.0% | 49.4% | 21.6% | 29.0% |
| **Share of total annual spending** | 100.0 | 29.2 | 22.2 | 48.4 |
| **FOOD** | **100.0%** | **33.8%** | **22.6%** | **43.1%** |
| **FOOD AT HOME** | 100.0 | 38.2 | 22.7 | 38.5 |
| **Cereals and bakery products** | 100.0 | 37.5 | 23.0 | 38.8 |
| Cereals and cereal products | 100.0 | 38.1 | 23.0 | 37.9 |
| Bakery products | 100.0 | 37.1 | 23.0 | 39.2 |
| **Meats, poultry, fish, and eggs** | 100.0 | 40.8 | 22.1 | 36.6 |
| Beef | 100.0 | 39.6 | 22.7 | 37.4 |
| Pork | 100.0 | 44.1 | 21.7 | 33.8 |
| Other meats | 100.0 | 39.3 | 23.2 | 36.5 |
| Poultry | 100.0 | 39.9 | 22.0 | 37.4 |
| Fish and seafood | 100.0 | 39.7 | 19.6 | 39.9 |
| Eggs | 100.0 | 44.8 | 22.4 | 31.6 |
| **Dairy products** | 100.0 | 37.5 | 23.0 | 39.0 |
| Fresh milk and cream | 100.0 | 40.5 | 23.7 | 35.4 |
| Other dairy products | 100.0 | 35.3 | 22.5 | 41.5 |
| **Fruits and vegetables** | 100.0 | 38.9 | 21.6 | 39.0 |
| Fresh fruits | 100.0 | 38.3 | 21.5 | 39.9 |
| Fresh vegetables | 100.0 | 39.8 | 20.3 | 39.2 |
| Processed fruits | 100.0 | 37.4 | 22.0 | 39.7 |
| Processed vegetables | 100.0 | 39.8 | 23.5 | 35.7 |
| **Other food at home** | 100.0 | 36.2 | 23.6 | 39.6 |
| Sugar and other sweets | 100.0 | 36.9 | 23.2 | 39.6 |
| Fats and oils | 100.0 | 41.7 | 23.0 | 35.1 |
| Miscellaneous foods | 100.0 | 35.3 | 24.0 | 39.8 |
| Nonalcoholic beverages | 100.0 | 37.9 | 24.0 | 37.6 |
| Food prepared by household on trips | 100.0 | 25.5 | 21.1 | 53.1 |
| **FOOD AWAY FROM HOME** | 100.0 | 27.1 | 22.2 | 50.0 |
| **ALCOHOLIC BEVERAGES** | **100.0%** | **27.8%** | **22.1%** | **49.4%** |
| **HOUSING** | **100.0%** | **31.7%** | **21.7%** | **46.5%** |

*(continued)*

*(continued from previous page)*

| | total complete reporters | under $30,000 | $30,000–$49,999 | $50,000 or more |
|---|---|---|---|---|
| **SHELTER** | **100.0%** | **31.1%** | **21.9%** | **47.0%** |
| **Owned dwellings** | **100.0** | **21.0** | **20.7** | **58.3** |
| Mortgage interest and charges | 100.0 | 14.9 | 20.8 | 64.3 |
| Property taxes | 100.0 | 27.5 | 19.3 | 53.3 |
| Maintenance, repairs, insurance, other | 100.0 | 31.2 | 22.1 | 46.8 |
| **Rented dwellings** | **100.0** | **53.8** | **25.8** | **20.5** |
| **Other lodging** | **100.0** | **19.0** | **14.8** | **66.3** |
| **UTILITIES, FUELS, PUBLIC SERVICES** | **100.0** | **39.0** | **22.3** | **38.7** |
| Natural gas | 100.0 | 38.9 | 22.9 | 38.3 |
| Electricity | 100.0 | 40.4 | 22.2 | 37.4 |
| Fuel oil and other fuels | 100.0 | 40.0 | 21.5 | 38.6 |
| Telephone services | 100.0 | 38.6 | 22.5 | 39.0 |
| Water and other public services | 100.0 | 35.9 | 21.6 | 42.5 |
| **HOUSEHOLD SERVICES** | **100.0** | **25.2** | **16.1** | **58.6** |
| Personal services | 100.0 | 23.5 | 17.3 | 59.2 |
| Other household expenses | 100.0 | 26.8 | 15.0 | 58.1 |
| **HOUSEKEEPING SUPPLIES** | **100.0** | **32.6** | **22.3** | **44.5** |
| Laundry and cleaning supplies | 100.0 | 36.4 | 23.4 | 39.6 |
| Other household products | 100.0 | 30.8 | 21.4 | 47.5 |
| Postage and stationery | 100.0 | 32.1 | 22.5 | 44.2 |
| **HOUSEHOLD FURNISHINGS AND EQUIPMENT** | **100.0** | **25.1** | **21.7** | **52.9** |
| Household textiles | 100.0 | 26.2 | 18.7 | 55.1 |
| Furniture | 100.0 | 22.8 | 19.2 | 58.2 |
| Floor coverings | 100.0 | 13.1 | 34.4 | 50.5 |
| Major appliances | 100.0 | 32.2 | 24.4 | 43.2 |
| Small appliances, misc. housewares | 100.0 | 33.3 | 18.8 | 48.7 |
| Miscellaneous household equipment | 100.0 | 24.8 | 21.6 | 53.1 |
| **APPAREL AND SERVICES** | **100.0%** | **28.7%** | **21.4%** | **49.4%** |
| **Men and boys** | **100.0** | **25.7** | **22.4** | **51.3** |
| Men, 16 and over | 100.0 | 24.0 | 22.3 | 53.0 |
| Boys, 2 to 15 | 100.0 | 32.5 | 22.7 | 44.7 |
| **Women and girls** | **100.0** | **28.9** | **20.9** | **49.7** |
| Women, 16 and over | 100.0 | 29.4 | 19.9 | 50.1 |
| Girls, 2 to 15 | 100.0 | 26.0 | 26.3 | 47.2 |
| **Children under 2** | **100.0** | **31.9** | **23.7** | **43.0** |
| **Footwear** | **100.0** | **34.9** | **22.6** | **42.0** |
| **Other apparel products, services** | **100.0** | **24.0** | **19.1** | **56.5** |

*(continued)*

*(continued from previous page)*

| | total complete reporters | under $30,000 | $30,000– $49,999 | $50,000 or more |
|---|---|---|---|---|
| **TRANSPORTATION** | **100.0%** | **27.4%** | **24.9%** | **47.6%** |
| **Vehicle purchases** | **100.0** | **26.5** | **27.8** | **45.7** |
| Cars and trucks, new | 100.0 | 20.1 | 26.7 | 53.2 |
| Cars and trucks, used | 100.0 | 32.2 | 29.0 | 38.7 |
| Other vehicles | 100.0 | 19.5 | 19.2 | 59.0 |
| **Gasoline and motor oil** | **100.0** | **32.6** | **24.2** | **43.2** |
| **Other vehicle expenses** | **100.0** | **26.6** | **22.9** | **50.4** |
| Vehicle finance charges | 100.0 | 22.4 | 28.1 | 49.4 |
| Maintenance and repairs | 100.0 | 31.0 | 21.5 | 47.5 |
| Vehicle insurance | 100.0 | 29.3 | 24.3 | 46.4 |
| Vehicle rental, leases, licenses, other | 100.0 | 18.9 | 19.9 | 61.2 |
| **Public transportation** | **100.0** | **24.9** | **17.6** | **57.5** |
| **HEALTH CARE** | **100.0%** | **40.9%** | **21.8%** | **37.2%** |
| Health insurance | 100.0 | 41.6 | 21.9 | 36.6 |
| Medical services | 100.0 | 34.3 | 21.9 | 43.7 |
| Drugs | 100.0 | 50.8 | 21.2 | 27.6 |
| Medical supplies | 100.0 | 37.0 | 23.1 | 39.5 |
| **ENTERTAINMENT** | **100.0%** | **25.3%** | **20.2%** | **54.4%** |
| Fees and admissions | 100.0 | 20.1 | 18.6 | 61.3 |
| Television, radio, sound equipment | 100.0 | 34.1 | 22.8 | 43.1 |
| Pets, toys, playground equipment | 100.0 | 27.3 | 21.1 | 51.2 |
| Other entertainment supplies, equip., services | 100.0 | 17.7 | 17.8 | 64.4 |
| **PERSONAL CARE PRODUCTS & SERVICES** | **100.0%** | **32.7%** | **22.9%** | **44.0%** |
| **READING** | **100.0%** | **30.1%** | **20.7%** | **49.4%** |
| **EDUCATION** | **100.0%** | **33.2%** | **17.4%** | **49.3%** |
| **TOBACCO PRODUCTS & SMOKING SUPPLIES** | **100.0%** | **44.9%** | **24.4%** | **30.8%** |
| **MISCELLANEOUS** | **100.0%** | **32.0%** | **24.8%** | **43.0%** |
| Cash contributions | 100.0 | 28.7 | 19.6 | 51.7 |
| Personal insurance and pensions | 100.0 | 12.8 | 20.5 | 66.6 |
| Life and other personal insurance | 100.0 | 25.2 | 18.4 | 56.3 |
| Pensions and Social Security | 100.0 | 11.4 | 20.8 | 67.8 |
| **PERSONAL TAXES** | **100.0%** | **6.5%** | **20.1%** | **73.5%** |
| Federal income taxes | 100.0 | 4.9 | 19.8 | 75.3 |

*(continued)*

*(continued from previous page)*

| | total complete reporters | under $30,000 | $30,000–$49,999 | $50,000 or more |
|---|---|---|---|---|
| State and local income taxes | 100.0% | 8.1% | 20.7% | 71.2% |
| Other taxes | 100.0 | 28.7 | 22.1 | 49.0 |
| **GIFTS** | **100.0%** | **29.4%** | **19.5%** | **50.9%** |
| **Food** | **100.0** | **25.1** | **17.9** | **56.3** |
| **Housing** | **100.0** | **31.1** | **18.6** | **50.2** |
| Housekeeping supplies | 100.0 | 30.1 | 21.7 | 47.2 |
| Household textiles | 100.0 | 29.2 | 18.5 | 51.8 |
| Appliances and miscellaneous housewares | 100.0 | 27.6 | 18.2 | 54.6 |
| Major appliances | 100.0 | 25.6 | 20.2 | 51.8 |
| Small appliances, miscellaneous housewares | 100.0 | 29.0 | 17.5 | 55.4 |
| Miscellaneous household equipment | 100.0 | 26.5 | 17.6 | 55.9 |
| Other housing | 100.0 | 34.8 | 18.3 | 47.0 |
| **Apparel and services** | **100.0** | **27.5** | **21.5** | **50.6** |
| Males, 2 and over | 100.0 | 30.0 | 21.3 | 47.1 |
| Females, 2 and over | 100.0 | 30.0 | 23.5 | 46.8 |
| Children under 2 | 100.0 | 31.5 | 25.4 | 43.1 |
| Other apparel products, services | 100.0 | 22.0 | 18.1 | 60.7 |
| Jewelry and watches | 100.0 | 10.7 | 18.8 | 72.2 |
| All other apparel products, services | 100.0 | 40.0 | 17.1 | 42.6 |
| **Transportation** | **100.0** | **39.2** | **11.6** | **49.6** |
| **Health care** | **100.0** | **35.5** | **20.7** | **44.6** |
| **Entertainment** | **100.0** | **28.9** | **24.1** | **46.6** |
| Toys, games, hobbies, tricycles | 100.0 | 26.1 | 23.2 | 49.2 |
| Other entertainment | 100.0 | 30.8 | 24.7 | 44.7 |
| **Education** | **100.0** | **26.1** | **10.5** | **63.4** |
| **All other gifts** | **100.0** | **29.3** | **27.5** | **42.6** |

*Note: The Bureau of Labor Statistics uses consumer units rather than households as the sampling unit in the Consumer Expenditure Survey. For the definition of consumer unit, see the glossary. Numbers may not add to total due to rounding.*
*Source: Calculations by New Strategist based on the Bureau of Labor Statistics' 1997 Consumer Expenditure Survey*

# Couples with Children Spend the Most

## Married couples with children spend 37 percent more than the average household.

Married couples with children spend much more than average because they have the highest incomes and the largest households. In 1997, couples with kids spent an average of $47,716 compared with $34,819 spent by the average household.

Married couples without children at home spend 13 percent more than average. Most are empty nesters with grown children living elsewhere or young couples who have not yet had children. Single-person households spend the least among the household types shown in these tables, just $20,923 in 1997.

The Indexed Spending table in this section shows spending by household type in comparison to what the average household spends. An index of 100 means the household type spends the average amount on an item. An index above 100 means the household type spends more than average on the item, while an index below 100 signifies below-average spending. A look at the table reveals that spending is well below average for single-parent and single-person households, although single-parent households spend close to the average on most foods. Single-parent house-

### Spending is below average for single parents

*(indexed average annual spending of consumer units by type, 1997)*

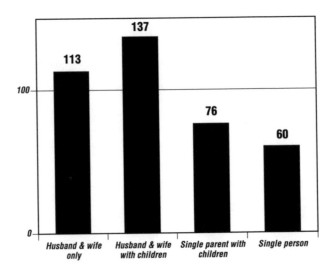

holds spend 88 percent more than the average household (with an index of 188) on household personal services, much of which is day care expenses.

Married couples without children at home spend more than average on many items. But these households spend much less than average on products and services for children such as household personal services (day care), children's clothing, and education.

The Market Share table in this section shows how much of total household spending is accounted for by each household type. More than one-third of all spending is accounted for by married couples with children, although they are just 27 percent of all households. Married couples without children at home spend slightly more than their share of households. Both single-parent and single-person households account for a smaller share of spending than their share of households.

Within categories, market shares vary sharply by household type. Married couples with children account for more than half of all spending on some items, such as household personal services (day care) and children's clothing. Married couples without children at home account for more than 50 percent of all spending on floor coverings. Single-parent households account for less than 10 percent of spending in all categories except household personal services (day care) and children's clothing. Single-person householders account for a disproportionately large share of spending on rent.

♦ The spending of married couples without children may grow faster than average in the years ahead as two-income baby-boom couples enter the empty-nest years.

# Spending by Household Type, 1997

*(average annual spending of consumer units (cu) by product and service category and type of consumer unit, 1997)*

| | | married couples | | | | |
|---|---|---|---|---|---|---|
| | total consumer units | total | husband and wife only | husband and wife with children | single parent, w/ children < age 18 | single person |
| Number of consumer units (in 000s) | 105,576 | 55,205 | 22,531 | 28,382 | 6,626 | 30,330 |
| Average number of persons per cu | 2.5 | 3.2 | 2.0 | 4.0 | 3.0 | 1.0 |
| Average before-tax income | $39,926 | $52,981 | $47,475 | $57,598 | $24,185 | $22,174 |
| Average annual spending | 34,819 | 44,101 | 39,515 | 47,716 | 26,352 | 20,923 |
| **FOOD** | **$4,801** | **$6,102** | **$5,266** | **$6,634** | **$4,055** | **$2,579** |
| FOOD AT HOME | 2,880 | 3,692 | 2,994 | 4,099 | 2,765 | 1,354 |
| **Cereals and bakery products** | 453 | 583 | 454 | 660 | 412 | 218 |
| Cereals and cereal products | 161 | 205 | 144 | 241 | 175 | 72 |
| Bakery products | 292 | 379 | 310 | 420 | 237 | 146 |
| **Meats, poultry, fish, and eggs** | 743 | 946 | 755 | 1,039 | 772 | 309 |
| Beef | 224 | 286 | 222 | 320 | 237 | 88 |
| Pork | 157 | 202 | 167 | 212 | 151 | 65 |
| Other meats | 96 | 122 | 92 | 139 | 93 | 42 |
| Poultry | 145 | 182 | 140 | 208 | 171 | 61 |
| Fish and seafood | 89 | 114 | 100 | 119 | 84 | 37 |
| Eggs | 33 | 40 | 34 | 41 | 36 | 15 |
| **Dairy products** | 314 | 404 | 314 | 465 | 300 | 152 |
| Fresh milk and cream | 128 | 164 | 120 | 191 | 132 | 60 |
| Other dairy products | 186 | 240 | 194 | 275 | 167 | 92 |
| **Fruits and vegetables** | 476 | 601 | 533 | 631 | 457 | 245 |
| Fresh fruits | 150 | 189 | 179 | 194 | 131 | 83 |
| Fresh vegetables | 143 | 179 | 165 | 180 | 163 | 72 |
| Processed fruits | 102 | 130 | 105 | 145 | 90 | 56 |
| Processed vegetables | 80 | 103 | 85 | 112 | 72 | 34 |
| **Other food at home** | 895 | 1,158 | 939 | 1,302 | 825 | 430 |
| Sugar and other sweets | 114 | 152 | 133 | 163 | 103 | 52 |
| Fats and oils | 81 | 103 | 91 | 107 | 75 | 37 |
| Miscellaneous foods | 403 | 523 | 392 | 615 | 371 | 194 |
| Nonalcoholic beverages | 245 | 309 | 253 | 343 | 248 | 120 |
| Food prepared by household on trips | 52 | 71 | 70 | 73 | 28 | 26 |
| FOOD AWAY FROM HOME | 1,921 | 2,411 | 2,271 | 2,536 | 1,291 | 1,225 |
| **ALCOHOLIC BEVERAGES** | **$309** | **$343** | **$406** | **$296** | **$131** | **$246** |

*(continued)*

*(continued from previous page)*

| | total consumer units | married couples | | | single parent, w/ children < age 18 | single person |
|---|---|---|---|---|---|---|
| | | total | husband and wife only | husband and wife with children | | |
| **HOUSING** | **$11,272** | **$13,718** | **$12,241** | **$14,885** | **$9,833** | **$7,586** |
| **SHELTER** | **6,344** | **7,485** | **6,511** | **8,339** | **5,514** | **4,742** |
| **Owned dwellings** | **3,935** | **5,505** | **4,691** | **6,290** | **2,349** | **2,003** |
| Mortgage interest and charges | 2,225 | 3,221 | 2,311 | 3,995 | 1,533 | 941 |
| Property taxes | 971 | 1,333 | 1,325 | 1,383 | 507 | 550 |
| Maintenance, repairs, insurance, other | 738 | 951 | 1,055 | 911 | 310 | 512 |
| **Rented dwellings** | **1,983** | **1,364** | **1,147** | **1,453** | **2,974** | **2,512** |
| **Other lodging** | **426** | **616** | **672** | **596** | **190** | **227** |
| **UTILITIES, FUELS, PUBLIC SERVICES** | **2,412** | **2,887** | **2,575** | **3,067** | **2,265** | **1,563** |
| Natural gas | 301 | 355 | 332 | 375 | 278 | 197 |
| Electricity | 909 | 1,105 | 1,001 | 1,159 | 889 | 555 |
| Fuel oil and other fuels | 108 | 139 | 134 | 146 | 59 | 66 |
| Telephone services | 809 | 919 | 781 | 997 | 818 | 583 |
| Water and other public services | 286 | 367 | 328 | 390 | 221 | 161 |
| **HOUSEHOLD SERVICES** | **548** | **722** | **438** | **950** | **666** | **265** |
| Personal services | 263 | 368 | 39 | 620 | 494 | 57 |
| Other household expenses | 285 | 354 | 399 | 331 | 172 | 208 |
| **HOUSEKEEPING SUPPLIES** | **455** | **603** | **561** | **639** | **333** | **222** |
| Laundry and cleaning supplies | 116 | 151 | 125 | 167 | 121 | 48 |
| Other household products | 210 | 289 | 269 | 311 | 139 | 96 |
| Postage and stationery | 129 | 162 | 167 | 161 | 73 | 78 |
| **HOUSEHOLD FURNISHINGS AND EQUIPMENT** | **1,512** | **2,021** | **2,156** | **1,890** | **1,056** | **794** |
| Household textiles | 79 | 105 | 116 | 96 | 56 | 44 |
| Furniture | 387 | 515 | 539 | 480 | 293 | 220 |
| Floor coverings | 78 | 119 | 191 | 67 | 48 | 29 |
| Major appliances | 169 | 218 | 240 | 202 | 98 | 84 |
| Small appliances, misc. housewares | 92 | 117 | 108 | 124 | 64 | 56 |
| Miscellaneous household equipment | 707 | 946 | 961 | 921 | 497 | 361 |
| **APPAREL AND SERVICES** | **$1,729** | **$2,224** | **$1,801** | **$2,550** | **$1,519** | **$866** |
| **Men and boys** | **407** | **540** | **381** | **661** | **293** | **197** |
| Men, 16 and over | 323 | 425 | 358 | 481 | 93 | 185 |
| Boys, 2 to 15 | 84 | 115 | 24 | 179 | 200 | 12 |
| **Women and girls** | **680** | **856** | **749** | **938** | **638** | **382** |
| Women, 16 and over | 574 | 704 | 718 | 688 | 436 | 366 |
| Girls, 2 to 15 | 106 | 152 | 31 | 250 | 202 | 16 |

*(continued)*

| | total consumer units | married couples | | | single parent, w/ children < age 18 | single person |
|---|---|---|---|---|---|---|
| | | total | husband and wife only | husband and wife with children | | |
| Children under 2 | $77 | $112 | $41 | $161 | $117 | $11 |
| Footwear | 315 | 394 | 314 | 463 | 320 | 162 |
| Other apparel products, services | 250 | 323 | 316 | 327 | 150 | 113 |
| **TRANSPORTATION** | **$6,457** | **$8,461** | **$7,353** | **$9,318** | **$4,200** | **$3,239** |
| **Vehicle purchases** | **2,736** | **3,593** | **3,168** | **3,948** | **1,743** | **1,244** |
| Cars and trucks, new | 1,229 | 1,662 | 1,709 | 1,703 | 697 | 650 |
| Cars and trucks, used | 1,464 | 1,887 | 1,403 | 2,215 | 994 | 578 |
| Other vehicles | 43 | 44 | 56 | 29 | 52 | 17 |
| **Gasoline and motor oil** | **1,098** | **1,431** | **1,185** | **1,595** | **760** | **567** |
| **Other vehicle expenses** | **2,230** | **2,943** | **2,468** | **3,300** | **1,468** | **1,148** |
| Vehicle finance charges | 293 | 402 | 306 | 471 | 200 | 100 |
| Maintenance and repairs | 682 | 880 | 743 | 980 | 510 | 391 |
| Vehicle insurance | 755 | 974 | 837 | 1,066 | 478 | 417 |
| Vehicle rental, leases, licenses, other | 501 | 687 | 582 | 783 | 280 | 239 |
| **Public transportation** | **393** | **494** | **531** | **475** | **229** | **280** |
| **HEALTH CARE** | **$1,841** | **$2,358** | **$2,687** | **$2,093** | **$1,096** | **$1,249** |
| Health insurance | 881 | 1,149 | 1,366 | 977 | 461 | 575 |
| Medical services | 531 | 674 | 620 | 720 | 365 | 369 |
| Drugs | 320 | 394 | 547 | 262 | 181 | 240 |
| Medical supplies | 108 | 141 | 154 | 134 | 89 | 65 |
| **ENTERTAINMENT** | **$1,813** | **$2,405** | **$2,225** | **$2,596** | **$1,248** | **$1,011** |
| Fees and admissions | 471 | 623 | 526 | 723 | 311 | 296 |
| Television, radio, sound equipment | 577 | 688 | 582 | 758 | 553 | 394 |
| Pets, toys, playground equipment | 327 | 439 | 391 | 472 | 201 | 166 |
| Other entertainment supplies, equip., services | 439 | 655 | 726 | 643 | 184 | 155 |
| **PERSONAL CARE PRODUCTS & SERVICES** | **$528** | **$653** | **$605** | **$683** | **$477** | **$305** |
| **READING** | **$164** | **$204** | **$228** | **$194** | **$84** | **$125** |
| **EDUCATION** | **$571** | **$684** | **$397** | **$930** | **$591** | **$447** |
| **TOBACCO PRODUCTS & SMOKING SUPPLIES** | **$264** | **$293** | **$249** | **$304** | **$188** | **$169** |
| **MISCELLANEOUS** | **$847** | **$967** | **$916** | **$1,010** | **$818** | **$694** |
| Cash contributions | 1,001 | 1,216 | 1,388 | 1,112 | 416 | 811 |
| Personal insurance and pensions | 3,223 | 4,472 | 3,754 | 5,111 | 1,696 | 1,597 |
| Life and other personal insurance | 379 | 544 | 519 | 568 | 176 | 170 |
| Pensions and Social Security | 2,844 | 3,927 | 3,234 | 4,543 | 1,520 | 1,427 |

*(continued)*

*(continued from previous page)*

| | total consumer units | married couples | | | single parent, w/children < age 18 | single person |
|---|---|---|---|---|---|---|
| | | total | husband and wife only | husband and wife with children | | |
| **PERSONAL TAXES** | **$3,241** | **$4,362** | **$4,480** | **$4,423** | **$1,533** | **$2,011** |
| Federal income taxes | 2,468 | 3,325 | 3,520 | 3,297 | 1,141 | 1,537 |
| State and local income taxes | 645 | 859 | 761 | 959 | 324 | 400 |
| Other taxes | 129 | 178 | 199 | 167 | 68 | 74 |
| **GIFTS** | **$1,059** | **$1,303** | **$1,503** | **$1,192** | **$601** | **$837** |
| **Food** | **68** | **95** | **111** | **83** | **18** | **42** |
| **Housing** | **273** | **333** | **341** | **331** | **198** | **209** |
| Housekeeping supplies | 37 | 46 | 53 | 44 | 21 | 29 |
| Household textiles | 8 | 10 | 14 | 8 | 2 | 8 |
| Appliances and miscellaneous housewares | 27 | 34 | 41 | 29 | 11 | 23 |
| Major appliances | 6 | 7 | 8 | 5 | 4 | 6 |
| Small appliances, miscellaneous housewares | 21 | 28 | 33 | 24 | 7 | 17 |
| Miscellaneous household equipment | 66 | 81 | 95 | 76 | 52 | 45 |
| Other housing | 135 | 161 | 137 | 174 | 112 | 104 |
| **Apparel and services** | **252** | **323** | **362** | **298** | **138** | **158** |
| Males, 2 and over | 61 | 78 | 90 | 68 | 34 | 39 |
| Females, 2 and over | 81 | 105 | 130 | 85 | 40 | 56 |
| Children under 2 | 33 | 44 | 41 | 48 | 33 | 11 |
| Other apparel products, services | 77 | 96 | 102 | 98 | 32 | 52 |
| Jewelry and watches | 49 | 63 | 52 | 76 | 15 | 27 |
| All other apparel products, services | 29 | 33 | 49 | 21 | 17 | 24 |
| **Transportation** | **57** | **73** | **104** | **53** | **17** | **45** |
| **Health care** | **30** | **29** | **39** | **23** | **45** | **36** |
| **Entertainment** | **99** | **118** | **141** | **104** | **53** | **91** |
| Toys, games, hobbies, tricycles | 41 | 54 | 63 | 48 | 18 | 27 |
| Other entertainment | 58 | 64 | 78 | 55 | 36 | 64 |
| **Education** | **155** | **211** | **233** | **214** | **64** | **114** |
| **All other gifts** | **125** | **121** | **171** | **85** | **67** | **142** |

*Note: The Bureau of Labor Statistics uses consumer units rather than households as the sampling unit in the Consumer Expenditure Survey. For the definition of consumer unit, see the Glossary. Spending on gifts is also included in the preceding product and service categories.*
*Source: Bureau of Labor Statistics, 1997 Consumer Expenditure Survey; calculations by New Strategist*

# Indexed Spending by Household Type, 1997

*(indexed average annual spending of consumer units by product and service category and type of consumer unit, 1997)*

| | total consumer units | married couples total | husband and wife only | husband and wife with children | single parent, w/ children < age 18 | single person |
|---|---|---|---|---|---|---|
| Number of consumer units (in 000s) | 105,576 | 55,205 | 22,531 | 28,382 | 6,626 | 30,330 |
| Indexed average before-tax income | 100 | 133 | 119 | 144 | 61 | 56 |
| Indexed average annual spending | 100 | 127 | 113 | 137 | 76 | 60 |
| **FOOD** | **100** | **127** | **110** | **138** | **84** | **54** |
| FOOD AT HOME | 100 | 128 | 104 | 142 | 96 | 47 |
| **Cereals and bakery products** | **100** | **129** | **100** | **146** | **91** | **48** |
| Cereals and cereal products | 100 | 127 | 89 | 150 | 109 | 45 |
| Bakery products | 100 | 130 | 106 | 144 | 81 | 50 |
| **Meats, poultry, fish, and eggs** | **100** | **127** | **102** | **140** | **104** | **42** |
| Beef | 100 | 128 | 99 | 143 | 106 | 39 |
| Pork | 100 | 129 | 106 | 135 | 96 | 41 |
| Other meats | 100 | 127 | 96 | 145 | 97 | 44 |
| Poultry | 100 | 126 | 97 | 143 | 118 | 42 |
| Fish and seafood | 100 | 128 | 112 | 134 | 94 | 42 |
| Eggs | 100 | 121 | 103 | 124 | 109 | 45 |
| **Dairy products** | **100** | **129** | **100** | **148** | **96** | **48** |
| Fresh milk and cream | 100 | 128 | 94 | 149 | 103 | 47 |
| Other dairy products | 100 | 129 | 104 | 148 | 90 | 49 |
| **Fruits and vegetables** | **100** | **126** | **112** | **133** | **96** | **51** |
| Fresh fruits | 100 | 126 | 119 | 129 | 87 | 55 |
| Fresh vegetables | 100 | 125 | 115 | 126 | 114 | 50 |
| Processed fruits | 100 | 127 | 103 | 142 | 88 | 55 |
| Processed vegetables | 100 | 129 | 106 | 140 | 90 | 43 |
| **Other food at home** | **100** | **129** | **105** | **145** | **92** | **48** |
| Sugar and other sweets | 100 | 133 | 117 | 143 | 90 | 46 |
| Fats and oils | 100 | 127 | 112 | 132 | 93 | 46 |
| Miscellaneous foods | 100 | 130 | 97 | 153 | 92 | 48 |
| Nonalcoholic beverages | 100 | 126 | 103 | 140 | 101 | 49 |
| Food prepared by household on trips | 100 | 137 | 135 | 140 | 54 | 50 |
| FOOD AWAY FROM HOME | 100 | 126 | 118 | 132 | 67 | 64 |
| **ALCOHOLIC BEVERAGES** | **100** | **111** | **131** | **96** | **42** | **80** |

*(continued)*

*(continued from previous page)*

| | total consumer units | married couples | | husband and wife with children | single parent, w/ children < age 18 | single person |
|---|---|---|---|---|---|---|
| | | total | husband and wife only | | | |
| **HOUSING** | **100** | **122** | **109** | **132** | **87** | **67** |
| **SHELTER** | **100** | **118** | **103** | **131** | **87** | **75** |
| **Owned dwellings** | **100** | **140** | **119** | **160** | **60** | **51** |
| Mortgage interest and charges | 100 | 145 | 104 | 180 | 69 | 42 |
| Property taxes | 100 | 137 | 136 | 142 | 52 | 57 |
| Maintenance, repairs, insurance, other | 100 | 129 | 143 | 123 | 42 | 69 |
| **Rented dwellings** | **100** | **69** | **58** | **73** | **150** | **127** |
| **Other lodging** | **100** | **145** | **158** | **140** | **45** | **53** |
| **UTILITIES, FUELS, PUBLIC SERVICES** | **100** | **120** | **107** | **127** | **94** | **65** |
| Natural gas | 100 | 118 | 110 | 125 | 92 | 65 |
| Electricity | 100 | 122 | 110 | 128 | 98 | 61 |
| Fuel oil and other fuels | 100 | 129 | 124 | 135 | 55 | 61 |
| Telephone services | 100 | 114 | 97 | 123 | 101 | 72 |
| Water and other public services | 100 | 128 | 115 | 136 | 77 | 56 |
| **HOUSEHOLD SERVICES** | **100** | **132** | **80** | **173** | **122** | **48** |
| Personal services | 100 | 140 | 15 | 236 | 188 | 22 |
| Other household expenses | 100 | 124 | 140 | 116 | 60 | 73 |
| **HOUSEKEEPING SUPPLIES** | **100** | **133** | **123** | **140** | **73** | **49** |
| Laundry and cleaning supplies | 100 | 130 | 108 | 144 | 104 | 41 |
| Other household products | 100 | 138 | 128 | 148 | 66 | 46 |
| Postage and stationery | 100 | 126 | 129 | 125 | 57 | 60 |
| **HOUSEHOLD FURNISHINGS** | | | | | | |
| **AND EQUIPMENT** | **100** | **134** | **143** | **125** | **70** | **53** |
| Household textiles | 100 | 133 | 147 | 122 | 71 | 56 |
| Furniture | 100 | 133 | 139 | 124 | 76 | 57 |
| Floor coverings | 100 | 153 | 245 | 86 | 62 | 37 |
| Major appliances | 100 | 129 | 142 | 120 | 58 | 50 |
| Small appliances, misc. housewares | 100 | 127 | 117 | 135 | 70 | 61 |
| Miscellaneous household equipment | 100 | 134 | 136 | 130 | 70 | 51 |
| **APPAREL AND SERVICES** | **100** | **129** | **104** | **147** | **88** | **50** |
| **Men and boys** | **100** | **133** | **94** | **162** | **72** | **48** |
| Men, 16 and over | 100 | 132 | 111 | 149 | 29 | 57 |
| Boys, 2 to 15 | 100 | 137 | 29 | 213 | 238 | 14 |
| **Women and girls** | **100** | **126** | **110** | **138** | **94** | **56** |
| Women, 16 and over | 100 | 123 | 125 | 120 | 76 | 64 |
| Girls, 2 to 15 | 100 | 143 | 29 | 236 | 191 | 15 |

*(continued)*

*(continued from previous page)*

| | total consumer units | married couples | | | single parent, w/ children < age 18 | single person |
|---|---|---|---|---|---|---|
| | | total | husband and wife only | husband and wife with children | | |
| Children under 2 | 100 | 145 | 53 | 209 | 152 | 14 |
| Footwear | 100 | 125 | 100 | 147 | 102 | 51 |
| Other apparel products, services | 100 | 129 | 126 | 131 | 60 | 45 |
| **TRANSPORTATION** | **100** | **131** | **114** | **144** | **65** | **50** |
| **Vehicle purchases** | **100** | **131** | **116** | **144** | **64** | **45** |
| Cars and trucks, new | 100 | 135 | 139 | 139 | 57 | 53 |
| Cars and trucks, used | 100 | 129 | 96 | 151 | 68 | 39 |
| Other vehicles | 100 | 102 | 130 | 67 | 121 | 40 |
| **Gasoline and motor oil** | **100** | **130** | **108** | **145** | **69** | **52** |
| **Other vehicle expenses** | **100** | **132** | **111** | **148** | **66** | **51** |
| Vehicle finance charges | 100 | 137 | 104 | 161 | 68 | 34 |
| Maintenance and repairs | 100 | 129 | 109 | 144 | 75 | 57 |
| Vehicle insurance | 100 | 129 | 111 | 141 | 63 | 55 |
| Vehicle rental, leases, licenses, other | 100 | 137 | 116 | 156 | 56 | 48 |
| **Public transportation** | **100** | **126** | **135** | **121** | **58** | **71** |
| **HEALTH CARE** | **100** | **128** | **146** | **114** | **60** | **68** |
| Health insurance | 100 | 130 | 155 | 111 | 52 | 65 |
| Medical services | 100 | 127 | 117 | 136 | 69 | 69 |
| Drugs | 100 | 123 | 171 | 82 | 57 | 75 |
| Medical supplies | 100 | 131 | 143 | 124 | 82 | 60 |
| **ENTERTAINMENT** | **100** | **133** | **123** | **143** | **69** | **56** |
| Fees and admissions | 100 | 132 | 112 | 154 | 66 | 63 |
| Television, radio, sound equipment | 100 | 119 | 101 | 131 | 96 | 68 |
| Pets, toys, playground equipment | 100 | 134 | 120 | 144 | 61 | 51 |
| Other entertainment supplies, equip., services | 100 | 149 | 165 | 146 | 42 | 35 |
| **PERSONAL CARE PRODUCTS & SERVICES** | **100** | **124** | **115** | **129** | **90** | **58** |
| **READING** | **100** | **124** | **139** | **118** | **51** | **76** |
| **EDUCATION** | **100** | **120** | **70** | **163** | **104** | **78** |
| **TOBACCO PRODUCTS & SMOKING SUPPLIES** | **100** | **111** | **94** | **115** | **71** | **64** |
| **MISCELLANEOUS** | **100** | **114** | **108** | **119** | **97** | **82** |
| Cash contributions | 100 | 121 | 139 | 111 | 42 | 81 |
| Personal insurance and pensions | 100 | 139 | 116 | 159 | 53 | 50 |
| Life and other personal insurance | 100 | 144 | 137 | 150 | 46 | 45 |
| Pensions and Social Security | 100 | 138 | 114 | 160 | 53 | 50 |

*(continued)*

*(continued from previous page)*

| | total consumer units | married couples total | married couples husband and wife only | married couples husband and wife with children | single parent, w/ children < age 18 | single person |
|---|---|---|---|---|---|---|
| **PERSONAL TAXES** | 100 | 135 | 138 | 136 | 47 | 62 |
| Federal income taxes | 100 | 135 | 143 | 134 | 46 | 62 |
| State and local income taxes | 100 | 133 | 118 | 149 | 50 | 62 |
| Other taxes | 100 | 138 | 154 | 129 | 53 | 57 |
| **GIFTS** | **100** | **123** | **142** | **113** | **57** | **79** |
| **Food** | 100 | 140 | 163 | 122 | 26 | 62 |
| **Housing** | 100 | 122 | 125 | 121 | 73 | 77 |
| Housekeeping supplies | 100 | 124 | 143 | 119 | 57 | 78 |
| Household textiles | 100 | 125 | 175 | 100 | 25 | 100 |
| Appliances and miscellaneous housewares | 100 | 126 | 152 | 107 | 41 | 85 |
| Major appliances | 100 | 117 | 133 | 83 | 67 | 100 |
| Small appliances, miscellaneous housewares | 100 | 133 | 157 | 114 | 33 | 81 |
| Miscellaneous household equipment | 100 | 123 | 144 | 115 | 79 | 68 |
| Other housing | 100 | 119 | 101 | 129 | 83 | 77 |
| **Apparel and services** | **100** | **128** | **144** | **118** | **55** | **63** |
| Males, 2 and over | 100 | 128 | 148 | 111 | 56 | 64 |
| Females, 2 and over | 100 | 130 | 160 | 105 | 49 | 69 |
| Children under 2 | 100 | 133 | 124 | 145 | 100 | 33 |
| Other apparel products, services | 100 | 125 | 132 | 127 | 42 | 68 |
| Jewelry and watches | 100 | 129 | 106 | 155 | 31 | 55 |
| All other apparel products, services | 100 | 114 | 169 | 72 | 59 | 83 |
| **Transportation** | **100** | **128** | **182** | **93** | **30** | **79** |
| **Health care** | **100** | **97** | **130** | **77** | **150** | **120** |
| **Entertainment** | **100** | **119** | **142** | **105** | **54** | **92** |
| Toys, games, hobbies, tricycles | 100 | 132 | 154 | 117 | 44 | 66 |
| Other entertainment | 100 | 110 | 134 | 95 | 62 | 110 |
| **Education** | **100** | **136** | **150** | **138** | **41** | **74** |
| **All other gifts** | **100** | **97** | **137** | **68** | **54** | **114** |

*Note: The Bureau of Labor Statistics uses consumer units rather than households as the sampling unit in the Consumer Expenditure Survey. For the definition of consumer unit, see the Glossary. An index of 100 is the average for all households. An index of 132 means households of that type spend 32 percent more than the average household. An index of 75 means households of that type spend 25 percent less than the average household.*

*Source: Calculations by New Strategist based on the Bureau of Labor Statistics' 1997 Consumer Expenditure Survey*

# Market Shares by Household Type, 1997

*(share of total household spending accounted for by type of consumer unit, 1997)*

| | total consumer units | married couples | | | single parent, w/ children < age 18 | single person |
|---|---|---|---|---|---|---|
| | | total | husband and wife only | husband and wife with children | | |
| Share of total consumer units | 100.0% | 52.3% | 21.3% | 26.9% | 6.3% | 28.7% |
| Share of total annual spending | 100.0 | 66.2 | 24.2 | 36.8 | 4.7 | 17.3 |
| **FOOD** | **100.0%** | **66.5%** | **23.4%** | **37.1%** | **5.3%** | **15.4%** |
| **FOOD AT HOME** | **100.0** | **67.0** | **22.2** | **38.3** | **6.0** | **13.5** |
| **Cereals and bakery products** | **100.0** | **67.3** | **21.4** | **39.2** | **5.7** | **13.8** |
| Cereals and cereal products | 100.0 | 66.6 | 19.1 | 40.2 | 6.8 | 12.8 |
| Bakery products | 100.0 | 67.9 | 22.7 | 38.7 | 5.1 | 14.4 |
| **Meats, poultry, fish, and eggs** | **100.0** | **66.6** | **21.7** | **37.6** | **6.5** | **11.9** |
| Beef | 100.0 | 66.8 | 21.2 | 38.4 | 6.6 | 11.3 |
| Pork | 100.0 | 67.3 | 22.7 | 36.3 | 6.0 | 11.9 |
| Other meats | 100.0 | 66.5 | 20.5 | 38.9 | 6.1 | 12.6 |
| Poultry | 100.0 | 65.6 | 20.6 | 38.6 | 7.4 | 12.1 |
| Fish and seafood | 100.0 | 67.0 | 24.0 | 35.9 | 5.9 | 11.9 |
| Eggs | 100.0 | 63.4 | 22.0 | 33.4 | 6.8 | 13.1 |
| **Dairy products** | **100.0** | **67.3** | **21.3** | **39.8** | **6.0** | **13.9** |
| Fresh milk and cream | 100.0 | 67.0 | 20.0 | 40.1 | 6.5 | 13.5 |
| Other dairy products | 100.0 | 67.5 | 22.3 | 39.7 | 5.6 | 14.2 |
| **Fruits and vegetables** | **100.0** | **66.0** | **23.9** | **35.6** | **6.0** | **14.8** |
| Fresh fruits | 100.0 | 65.9 | 25.5 | 34.8 | 5.5 | 15.9 |
| Fresh vegetables | 100.0 | 65.5 | 24.6 | 33.8 | 7.2 | 14.5 |
| Processed fruits | 100.0 | 66.6 | 22.0 | 38.2 | 5.5 | 15.8 |
| Processed vegetables | 100.0 | 67.3 | 22.7 | 37.6 | 5.6 | 12.2 |
| **Other food at home** | **100.0** | **67.7** | **22.4** | **39.1** | **5.8** | **13.8** |
| Sugar and other sweets | 100.0 | 69.7 | 24.9 | 38.4 | 5.7 | 13.1 |
| Fats and oils | 100.0 | 66.5 | 24.0 | 35.5 | 5.8 | 13.1 |
| Miscellaneous foods | 100.0 | 67.9 | 20.8 | 41.0 | 5.8 | 13.8 |
| Nonalcoholic beverages | 100.0 | 65.9 | 22.0 | 37.6 | 6.4 | 14.1 |
| Food prepared by household on trips | 100.0 | 71.4 | 28.7 | 37.7 | 3.4 | 14.4 |
| **FOOD AWAY FROM HOME** | **100.0** | **65.6** | **25.2** | **35.5** | **4.2** | **18.3** |
| **ALCOHOLIC BEVERAGES** | **100.0%** | **58.0%** | **28.0%** | **25.8%** | **2.7%** | **22.9%** |

*(continued)*

*(continued from previous page)*

| | total consumer units | married couples | | | single parent, w/ children < age 18 | single person |
|---|---|---|---|---|---|---|
| | | total | husband and wife only | husband and wife with children | | |
| **HOUSING** | **100.0%** | **63.6%** | **23.2%** | **35.5%** | **5.5%** | **19.3%** |
| **SHELTER** | **100.0** | **61.7** | **21.9** | **35.3** | **5.5** | **21.5** |
| **Owned dwellings** | **100.0** | **73.2** | **25.4** | **43.0** | **3.7** | **14.6** |
| Mortgage interest and charges | 100.0 | 75.7 | 22.2 | 48.3 | 4.3 | 12.1 |
| Property taxes | 100.0 | 71.8 | 29.1 | 38.3 | 3.3 | 16.3 |
| Maintenance, repairs, insurance, other | 100.0 | 67.4 | 30.5 | 33.2 | 2.6 | 19.9 |
| **Rented dwellings** | **100.0** | **36.0** | **12.3** | **19.7** | **9.4** | **36.4** |
| **Other lodging** | **100.0** | **75.6** | **33.7** | **37.6** | **2.8** | **15.3** |
| **UTILITIES, FUELS, PUBLIC SERVICES** | **100.0** | **62.6** | **22.8** | **34.2** | **5.9** | **18.6** |
| Natural gas | 100.0 | 61.7 | 23.5 | 33.5 | 5.8 | 18.8 |
| Electricity | 100.0 | 63.6 | 23.5 | 34.3 | 6.1 | 17.5 |
| Fuel oil and other fuels | 100.0 | 67.3 | 26.5 | 36.3 | 3.4 | 17.6 |
| Telephone services | 100.0 | 59.4 | 20.6 | 33.1 | 6.3 | 20.7 |
| Water and other public services | 100.0 | 67.1 | 24.5 | 36.7 | 4.8 | 16.2 |
| **HOUSEHOLD SERVICES** | **100.0** | **68.9** | **17.1** | **46.6** | **7.6** | **13.9** |
| Personal services | 100.0 | 73.2 | 3.2 | 63.4 | 11.8 | 6.2 |
| Other household expenses | 100.0 | 64.9 | 29.9 | 31.2 | 3.8 | 21.0 |
| **HOUSEKEEPING SUPPLIES** | **100.0** | **69.3** | **26.3** | **37.8** | **4.6** | **14.0** |
| Laundry and cleaning supplies | 100.0 | 68.1 | 23.0 | 38.7 | 6.5 | 11.9 |
| Other household products | 100.0 | 72.0 | 27.3 | 39.8 | 4.2 | 13.1 |
| Postage and stationery | 100.0 | 65.7 | 27.6 | 33.6 | 3.6 | 17.4 |
| **HOUSEHOLD FURNISHINGS** | | | | | | |
| **AND EQUIPMENT** | **100.0** | **69.9** | **30.4** | **33.6** | **4.4** | **15.1** |
| Household textiles | 100.0 | 69.5 | 31.3 | 32.7 | 4.4 | 16.0 |
| Furniture | 100.0 | 69.6 | 29.7 | 33.3 | 4.8 | 16.3 |
| Floor coverings | 100.0 | 79.8 | 52.3 | 23.1 | 3.9 | 10.7 |
| Major appliances | 100.0 | 67.5 | 30.3 | 32.1 | 3.6 | 14.3 |
| Small appliances, misc. housewares | 100.0 | 66.5 | 25.1 | 36.2 | 4.4 | 17.5 |
| Miscellaneous household equipment | 100.0 | 70.0 | 29.0 | 35.0 | 4.4 | 14.7 |
| **APPAREL AND SERVICES** | **100.0%** | **67.3%** | **22.2%** | **39.6%** | **5.5%** | **14.4%** |
| **Men and boys** | **100.0** | **69.4** | **20.0** | **43.7** | **4.5** | **13.9** |
| Men, 16 and over | 100.0 | 68.8 | 23.7 | 40.0 | 1.8 | 16.5 |
| Boys, 2 to 15 | 100.0 | 71.6 | 6.1 | 57.3 | 14.9 | 4.1 |
| **Women and girls** | **100.0** | **65.8** | **23.5** | **37.1** | **5.9** | **16.1** |
| Women, 16 and over | 100.0 | 64.1 | 26.7 | 32.2 | 4.8 | 18.3 |
| Girls, 2 to 15 | 100.0 | 75.0 | 6.2 | 63.4 | 12.0 | 4.3 |

*(continued)*

| | total consumer units | married couples | | | single parent, w/ children < age 18 | single person |
|---|---|---|---|---|---|---|
| | | total | husband and wife only | husband and wife with children | | |
| Children under 2 | 100.0% | 76.1% | 11.4% | 56.2% | 9.5% | 4.1% |
| Footwear | 100.0 | 65.4 | 21.3 | 39.5 | 6.4 | 14.8 |
| Other apparel products, services | 100.0 | 67.6 | 27.0 | 35.2 | 3.8 | 13.0 |
| **TRANSPORTATION** | **100.0%** | **68.5%** | **24.3%** | **38.8%** | **4.1%** | **14.4%** |
| **Vehicle purchases** | 100.0 | 68.7 | 24.7 | 38.8 | 4.0 | 13.1 |
| Cars and trucks, new | 100.0 | 70.7 | 29.7 | 37.3 | 3.6 | 15.2 |
| Cars and trucks, used | 100.0 | 67.4 | 20.5 | 40.7 | 4.3 | 11.3 |
| Other vehicles | 100.0 | 53.5 | 27.8 | 18.1 | 7.6 | 11.4 |
| **Gasoline and motor oil** | **100.0** | **68.1** | **23.0** | **39.1** | **4.3** | **14.8** |
| **Other vehicle expenses** | **100.0** | **69.0** | **23.6** | **39.8** | **4.1** | **14.8** |
| Vehicle finance charges | 100.0 | 71.7 | 22.3 | 43.2 | 4.3 | 9.8 |
| Maintenance and repairs | 100.0 | 67.5 | 23.2 | 38.6 | 4.7 | 16.5 |
| Vehicle insurance | 100.0 | 67.5 | 23.7 | 38.0 | 4.0 | 15.9 |
| Vehicle rental, leases, licenses, other | 100.0 | 71.7 | 24.8 | 42.0 | 3.5 | 13.7 |
| **Public transportation** | **100.0** | **65.7** | **28.8** | **32.5** | **3.7** | **20.5** |
| **HEALTH CARE** | **100.0%** | **67.0%** | **31.1%** | **30.6%** | **3.7%** | **19.5%** |
| Health insurance | 100.0 | 68.2 | 33.1 | 29.8 | 3.3 | 18.7 |
| Medical services | 100.0 | 66.4 | 24.9 | 36.5 | 4.3 | 20.0 |
| Drugs | 100.0 | 64.4 | 36.5 | 22.0 | 3.5 | 21.5 |
| Medical supplies | 100.0 | 68.3 | 30.4 | 33.4 | 5.2 | 17.3 |
| **ENTERTAINMENT** | **100.0%** | **69.4%** | **26.2%** | **38.5%** | **4.3%** | **16.0%** |
| Fees and admissions | 100.0 | 69.2 | 23.8 | 41.3 | 4.1 | 18.1 |
| Television, radio, sound equipment | 100.0 | 62.3 | 21.5 | 35.3 | 6.0 | 19.6 |
| Pets, toys, playground equipment | 100.0 | 70.2 | 25.5 | 38.8 | 3.9 | 14.6 |
| Other entertainment supplies, equip., services | 100.0 | 78.0 | 35.3 | 39.4 | 2.6 | 10.1 |
| **PERSONAL CARE PRODUCTS & SERVICES** | **100.0%** | **64.7%** | **24.5%** | **34.8%** | **5.7%** | **16.6%** |
| **READING** | **100.0%** | **65.0%** | **29.7%** | **31.8%** | **3.2%** | **21.9%** |
| **EDUCATION** | **100.0%** | **62.6%** | **14.8%** | **43.8%** | **6.5%** | **22.5%** |
| **TOBACCO PRODUCTS & SMOKING SUPPLIES** | **100.0%** | **58.0%** | **20.1%** | **31.0%** | **4.5%** | **18.4%** |
| **MISCELLANEOUS** | **100.0%** | **59.7%** | **23.1%** | **32.1%** | **6.1%** | **23.5%** |
| Cash contributions | 100.0 | 63.5 | 29.6 | 29.9 | 2.6 | 23.3 |
| Personal insurance and pensions | 100.0 | 72.6 | 24.9 | 42.6 | 3.3 | 14.2 |
| Life and other personal insurance | 100.0 | 75.1 | 29.2 | 40.3 | 2.9 | 12.9 |
| Pensions and Social Security | 100.0 | 72.2 | 24.3 | 42.9 | 3.4 | 14.4 |

*(continued)*

*(continued from previous page)*

| | total consumer units | married couples total | husband and wife only | husband and wife with children | single parent, w/ children < age 18 | single person |
|---|---|---|---|---|---|---|
| **PERSONAL TAXES** | **100.0%** | **70.4%** | **29.5%** | **36.7%** | **3.0%** | **17.8%** |
| Federal income taxes | 100.0 | 70.4 | 30.4 | 35.9 | 2.9 | 17.9 |
| State and local income taxes | 100.0 | 69.6 | 25.2 | 40.0 | 3.2 | 17.8 |
| Other taxes | 100.0 | 72.2 | 32.9 | 34.8 | 3.3 | 16.5 |
| **GIFTS** | **100.0%** | **64.3%** | **30.3%** | **30.3%** | **3.6%** | **22.7%** |
| **Food** | **100.0** | **73.1** | **34.8** | **32.8** | **1.7** | **17.7** |
| **Housing** | **100.0** | **63.8** | **26.7** | **32.6** | **4.6** | **22.0** |
| Housekeeping supplies | 100.0 | 65.0 | 30.6 | 32.0 | 3.6 | 22.5 |
| Household textiles | 100.0 | 65.4 | 37.3 | 26.9 | 1.6 | 28.7 |
| Appliances and miscellaneous housewares | 100.0 | 65.8 | 32.4 | 28.9 | 2.6 | 24.5 |
| Major appliances | 100.0 | 61.0 | 28.5 | 22.4 | 4.2 | 28.7 |
| Small appliances, miscellaneous housewares | 100.0 | 69.7 | 33.5 | 30.7 | 2.1 | 23.3 |
| Miscellaneous household equipment | 100.0 | 64.2 | 30.7 | 31.0 | 4.9 | 19.6 |
| Other housing | 100.0 | 62.4 | 21.7 | 34.6 | 5.2 | 22.1 |
| **Apparel and services** | **100.0** | **67.0** | **30.7** | **31.8** | **3.4** | **18.0** |
| Males, 2 and over | 100.0 | 66.9 | 31.5 | 30.0 | 3.5 | 18.4 |
| Females, 2 and over | 100.0 | 67.8 | 34.3 | 28.2 | 3.1 | 19.9 |
| Children under 2 | 100.0 | 69.7 | 26.5 | 39.1 | 6.3 | 9.6 |
| Other apparel products, services | 100.0 | 65.2 | 28.3 | 34.2 | 2.6 | 19.4 |
| Jewelry and watches | 100.0 | 67.2 | 22.6 | 41.7 | 1.9 | 15.8 |
| All other apparel products, services | 100.0 | 59.5 | 36.1 | 19.5 | 3.7 | 23.8 |
| **Transportation** | **100.0** | **67.0** | **38.9** | **25.0** | **1.9** | **22.7** |
| **Health care** | **100.0** | **50.5** | **27.7** | **20.6** | **9.4** | **34.5** |
| **Entertainment** | **100.0** | **62.3** | **30.4** | **28.2** | **3.4** | **26.4** |
| Toys, games, hobbies, tricycles | 100.0 | 68.9 | 32.8 | 31.5 | 2.8 | 18.9 |
| Other entertainment | 100.0 | 57.7 | 28.7 | 25.5 | 3.9 | 31.7 |
| **Education** | **100.0** | **71.2** | **32.1** | **37.1** | **2.6** | **21.1** |
| All other gifts | 100.0 | 50.6 | 29.2 | 18.3 | 3.4 | 32.6 |

*Note: The Bureau of Labor Statistics uses consumer units rather than households as the sampling unit in the Consumer Expenditure Survey. For the definition of consumer unit, see the Glossary. Numbers will not add to total because not all consumer types are shown.*
*Source: Calculations by New Strategist based on the Bureau of Labor Statistics' 1997 Consumer Expenditure Survey*

# Spending of Blacks and Hispanics Is above Average on Many Items

**Hispanics are big spenders on food, while blacks spend big on personal care products and services.**

Spending patterns by race and ethnicity are more complex than total spending figures would suggest. Overall, white (and "other") households spent an average of $36,076 in 1997, compared with the $25,509 spent by blacks. Non-Hispanic households spent an average of $35,325, while Hispanic households spent $29,333. But an examination of the Indexed Spending table in this section shows that both blacks and Hispanics spend more than the average household on a number of items.

The Indexed Spending table in this section shows the household spending of each racial and ethnic group relative to what the average household spends. An index of 100 means the racial or ethnic group spends the average amount on an item. An index above 100 means the racial or ethnic group spends more than average on the item, while an index below 100 signifies below-average spending. A look at the table reveals below-average spending by black and Hispanic households on most items and average spending by white and non-Hispanic households.

### Blacks and Hispanics spend much more than average on meats, poultry, fish, and eggs

*(indexed average annual spending of consumer units on meat, poultry, fish, and eggs, by race and Hispanic origin of consumer unit reference person, 1997)*

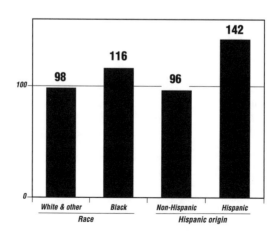

There are some important exceptions, however. Black households spend much more than average on meat, poultry, fish, and eggs. They spend 17 percent more than average on telephone service, 36 percent more on boys' clothes, and 13 percent more on shoes. Black households also spend 20 percent more on personal care products and services, and twice as much as the average household on gifts of jewelry and watches.

Hispanic households spend more than average on many foods, probably because their households are above average in size—3.4 people compared with 2.5 people in the average household. Hispanic households spend 50 percent more than the average household on rented dwellings, 27 percent more on laundry and cleaning supplies, 82 percent more on baby clothes, and 32 percent more on footwear. They also spend 30 percent more on gifts of baby clothes.

Because black and Hispanic households account for a minority of all households, and because their spending is below average as well, they account for a small share of the overall household market in most product and service categories.

◆ Black households have lower incomes and spending than white households because so many are headed by single parents rather than married couples. The spending of black households will remain below average as long as these differences in household composition persist.

◆ The spending of Hispanics is likely to remain below average because many are recent immigrants with low incomes.

# Spending by Race and Hispanic Origin, 1997

*(average annual spending of consumer units (cu) by product and service category and race and Hispanic origin of consumer unit reference person, 1997)*

| | total consumer units | race white/other | race black | Hispanic origin non-Hispanic | Hispanic origin Hispanic |
|---|---|---|---|---|---|
| Number of consumer units (in 000s) | 105,576 | 93,004 | 12,572 | 96,670 | 8,905 |
| Average number of persons per cu | 2.5 | 2.5 | 2.8 | 2.4 | 3.4 |
| Average before-tax income | $39,926 | $41,382 | $28,678 | $40,907 | $29,976 |
| Average annual spending | 34,819 | 36,076 | 25,509 | 35,325 | 29,333 |
| **FOOD** | **$4,801** | **$4,967** | **$3,571** | **$4,796** | **$4,869** |
| FOOD AT HOME | 2,880 | 2,929 | 2,515 | 2,839 | 3,363 |
| **Cereals and bakery products** | **453** | **463** | **376** | **452** | **468** |
| Cereals and cereal products | 161 | 163 | 148 | 159 | 190 |
| Bakery products | 292 | 300 | 228 | 293 | 279 |
| **Meats, poultry, fish, and eggs** | **743** | **727** | **861** | **716** | **1,057** |
| Beef | 224 | 221 | 244 | 215 | 326 |
| Pork | 157 | 152 | 194 | 151 | 225 |
| Other meats | 96 | 96 | 97 | 95 | 114 |
| Poultry | 145 | 140 | 185 | 141 | 189 |
| Fish and seafood | 89 | 86 | 106 | 84 | 144 |
| Eggs | 33 | 32 | 35 | 30 | 58 |
| **Dairy products** | **314** | **328** | **210** | **311** | **346** |
| Fresh milk and cream | 128 | 134 | 87 | 125 | 169 |
| Other dairy products | 186 | 194 | 123 | 186 | 178 |
| **Fruits and vegetables** | **476** | **485** | **402** | **464** | **607** |
| Fresh fruits | 150 | 156 | 113 | 146 | 199 |
| Fresh vegetables | 143 | 148 | 107 | 137 | 208 |
| Processed fruits | 102 | 103 | 99 | 101 | 114 |
| Processed vegetables | 80 | 80 | 84 | 80 | 87 |
| **Other food at home** | **895** | **925** | **666** | **896** | **884** |
| Sugar and other sweets | 114 | 117 | 93 | 115 | 103 |
| Fats and oils | 81 | 81 | 80 | 80 | 92 |
| Miscellaneous foods | 403 | 420 | 278 | 404 | 388 |
| Nonalcoholic beverages | 245 | 251 | 194 | 243 | 263 |
| Food prepared by household on trips | 52 | 56 | 20 | 53 | 38 |
| FOOD AWAY FROM HOME | 1,921 | 2,038 | 1,056 | 1,958 | 1,506 |
| **ALCOHOLIC BEVERAGES** | **$309** | **$332** | **$137** | **$318** | **$206** |

*(continued)*

*(continued from previous page)*

| | total consumer units | race | | Hispanic origin | |
|---|---|---|---|---|---|
| | | white/other | black | non-Hispanic | Hispanic |
| **HOUSING** | **$11,272** | **$11,573** | **$9,044** | **$11,397** | **$9,907** |
| **SHELTER** | **6,344** | **6,512** | **5,098** | **6,394** | **5,797** |
| **Owned dwellings** | **3,935** | **4,165** | **2,235** | **4,051** | **2,672** |
| Mortgage interest and charges | 2,225 | 2,341 | 1,369 | 2,269 | 1,750 |
| Property taxes | 971 | 1,039 | 469 | 1,012 | 527 |
| Maintenance, repairs, insurance, other | 738 | 785 | 397 | 770 | 395 |
| **Rented dwellings** | **1,983** | **1,883** | **2,721** | **1,892** | **2,972** |
| **Other lodging** | **426** | **464** | **143** | **451** | **153** |
| **UTILITIES, FUELS,** | | | | | |
| **PUBLIC SERVICES** | **2,412** | **2,406** | **2,461** | **2,435** | **2,169** |
| Natural gas | 301 | 298 | 324 | 304 | 265 |
| Electricity | 909 | 909 | 909 | 922 | 761 |
| Fuel oil and other fuels | 108 | 117 | 41 | 113 | 55 |
| Telephone services | 809 | 791 | 945 | 807 | 833 |
| Water and other public services | 286 | 292 | 241 | 289 | 256 |
| **HOUSEHOLD SERVICES** | **548** | **571** | **379** | **569** | **322** |
| Personal services | 263 | 266 | 245 | 269 | 202 |
| Other household expenses | 285 | 306 | 134 | 301 | 120 |
| **HOUSEKEEPING SUPPLIES** | **455** | **477** | **289** | **460** | **398** |
| Laundry and cleaning supplies | 116 | 117 | 108 | 113 | 147 |
| Other household products | 210 | 222 | 123 | 214 | 168 |
| Postage and stationery | 129 | 138 | 58 | 133 | 82 |
| **HOUSEHOLD FURNISHINGS** | | | | | |
| **AND EQUIPMENT** | **1,512** | **1,606** | **818** | **1,539** | **1,220** |
| Household textiles | 79 | 83 | 53 | 81 | 63 |
| Furniture | 387 | 402 | 277 | 389 | 368 |
| Floor coverings | 78 | 83 | 37 | 82 | 26 |
| Major appliances | 169 | 178 | 105 | 172 | 144 |
| Small appliances, misc. housewares | 92 | 100 | 30 | 94 | 73 |
| Miscellaneous household equipment | 707 | 760 | 316 | 722 | 547 |
| **APPAREL AND SERVICES** | **$1,729** | **$1,742** | **$1,631** | **$1,709** | **$1,958** |
| **Men and boys** | **407** | **417** | **332** | **400** | **490** |
| Men, 16 and over | 323 | 337 | 218 | 320 | 362 |
| Boys, 2 to 15 | 84 | 80 | 114 | 80 | 128 |
| **Women and girls** | **680** | **698** | **550** | **681** | **668** |
| Women, 16 and over | 574 | 590 | 459 | 578 | 528 |
| Girls, 2 to 15 | 106 | 108 | 91 | 103 | 139 |

*(continued)*

(continued from previous page)

| | total consumer units | race | | Hispanic origin | |
|---|---|---|---|---|---|
| | | white/other | black | non-Hispanic | Hispanic |
| Children under 2 | $77 | $77 | $78 | $72 | $140 |
| Footwear | 315 | 309 | 357 | 306 | 417 |
| Other apparel products, services | 250 | 242 | 314 | 251 | 243 |
| **TRANSPORTATION** | **6,457** | **6,687** | **4,754** | **6,537** | **5,585** |
| **Vehicle purchases** | **2,736** | **2,830** | **2,036** | **2,770** | **2,367** |
| Cars and trucks, new | 1,229 | 1,299 | 712 | 1,271 | 772 |
| Cars and trucks, used | 1,464 | 1,485 | 1,307 | 1,451 | 1,594 |
| Other vehicles | 43 | 47 | 18 | 47 | – |
| **Gasoline and motor oil** | **1,098** | **1,138** | **798** | **1,098** | **1,095** |
| **Other vehicle expenses** | **2,230** | **2,310** | **1,640** | **2,271** | **1,785** |
| Vehicle finance charges | 293 | 291 | 307 | 296 | 254 |
| Maintenance and repairs | 682 | 712 | 454 | 694 | 548 |
| Vehicle insurance | 755 | 776 | 596 | 762 | 675 |
| Vehicle rental, leases, licenses, other | 501 | 531 | 282 | 519 | 308 |
| **Public transportation** | **393** | **408** | **280** | **398** | **339** |
| **HEALTH CARE** | **$1,841** | **$1,950** | **$1,035** | **$1,903** | **$1,167** |
| Health insurance | 881 | 922 | 579 | 912 | 546 |
| Medical services | 531 | 572 | 229 | 548 | 352 |
| Drugs | 320 | 340 | 179 | 331 | 202 |
| Medical supplies | 108 | 116 | 49 | 112 | 67 |
| **ENTERTAINMENT** | **$1,813** | **$1,940** | **$872** | **$1,875** | **$1,137** |
| Fees and admissions | 471 | 509 | 191 | 492 | 237 |
| Television, radio, sound equipment | 577 | 587 | 507 | 587 | 474 |
| Pets, toys, playground equipment | 327 | 357 | 98 | 335 | 228 |
| Other entertainment supplies, equipment, services | 439 | 488 | 76 | 461 | 198 |
| **PERSONAL CARE PRODUCTS & SERVICES** | **$528** | **$514** | **$631** | **$532** | **$479** |
| **READING** | **$164** | **$175** | **$77** | **$173** | **$66** |
| **EDUCATION** | **$571** | **$612** | **$269** | **$581** | **$456** |
| **TOBACCO PRODUCTS & SMOKING SUPPLIES** | **$264** | **$276** | **$170** | **$278** | **$111** |
| **MISCELLANEOUS** | **$847** | **$886** | **$563** | **$862** | **$694** |
| Cash contributions | 1,001 | 1,046 | 669 | 1,056 | 398 |

(continued)

*(continued from previous page)*

| | total consumer units | race | | Hispanic origin | |
|---|---|---|---|---|---|
| | | white/other | black | non-Hispanic | Hispanic |
| Personal insurance and pensions | $3,223 | $3,377 | $2,086 | $3,308 | $2,299 |
| Life and other personal insurance | 379 | 386 | 321 | 395 | 205 |
| Pensions and Social Security | 2,844 | 2,990 | 1,765 | 2,913 | 2,095 |
| **PERSONAL TAXES** | **$3,241** | **$3,461** | **$1,548** | **$3,371** | **$1,929** |
| Federal income taxes | 2,468 | 2,645 | 1,101 | 2,561 | 1,525 |
| State and local income taxes | 645 | 677 | 396 | 672 | 369 |
| Other taxes | 129 | 139 | 51 | 138 | 34 |
| **GIFTS** | **$1,059** | **$1,113** | **$660** | **$1,087** | **$758** |
| **Food** | **68** | **73** | **25** | **69** | **59** |
| **Housing** | **273** | **290** | **149** | **282** | **180** |
| Housekeeping supplies | 37 | 41 | 8 | 37 | 31 |
| Household textiles | 8 | 9 | 3 | 9 | 4 |
| Appliances and miscellaneous housewares | 27 | 30 | 5 | 28 | 24 |
| Major appliances | 6 | 7 | 2 | 6 | 11 |
| Small appliances, miscellaneous housewares | 21 | 23 | 3 | 22 | 13 |
| Miscellaneous household equipment | 66 | 73 | 14 | 69 | 34 |
| Other housing | 135 | 137 | 119 | 139 | 87 |
| **Apparel and services** | **252** | **250** | **269** | **255** | **223** |
| Males, 2 and over | 61 | 64 | 38 | 61 | 64 |
| Females, 2 and over | 81 | 84 | 61 | 82 | 72 |
| Children under 2 | 33 | 34 | 25 | 32 | 43 |
| Other apparel products, services | 77 | 68 | 145 | 80 | 44 |
| Jewelry and watches | 49 | 40 | 112 | 51 | 16 |
| All other apparel products, services | 29 | 28 | 34 | 29 | 28 |
| **Transportation** | **57** | **62** | **15** | **58** | **38** |
| **Health care** | **30** | **33** | **8** | **32** | **17** |
| **Entertainment** | **99** | **105** | **55** | **103** | **47** |
| Toys, games, hobbies, tricycles | 41 | 44 | 20 | 43 | 17 |
| Other entertainment | 58 | 61 | 35 | 60 | 31 |
| **Education** | **155** | **171** | **38** | **159** | **118** |
| **All other gifts** | **125** | **128** | **102** | **129** | **77** |

*Note: The Bureau of Labor Statistics uses consumer units rather than households as the sampling unit in the Consumer Expenditure Survey. For the definition of consumer unit, see the Glossary. Hispanics may be of any race. Gift spending is also included in the preceding product and service categories. (–) means sample is too small to make a reliable estimate.*
*Source: Bureau of Labor Statistics, 1997 Consumer Expenditure Survey*

# Indexed Spending by Race and Hispanic Origin, 1997

*(indexed average annual spending of consumer units by product and service category and race and Hispanic origin of consumer unit reference person, 1997)*

| | total consumer units | race | | Hispanic origin | |
|---|---|---|---|---|---|
| | | white/other | black | non-Hispanic | Hispanic |
| Number of consumer units (in 000s) | 105,576 | 93,004 | 12,572 | 96,670 | 8,905 |
| Indexed average before-tax income | 100 | 104 | 72 | 102 | 75 |
| Indexed average annual spending | 100 | 104 | 73 | 101 | 84 |
| **FOOD** | **100** | **103** | **74** | **100** | **101** |
| **FOOD AT HOME** | **100** | **102** | **87** | **99** | **117** |
| **Cereals and bakery products** | **100** | **102** | **83** | **100** | **103** |
| Cereals and cereal products | 100 | 101 | 92 | 99 | 118 |
| Bakery products | 100 | 103 | 78 | 100 | 96 |
| **Meats, poultry, fish, and eggs** | **100** | **98** | **116** | **96** | **142** |
| Beef | 100 | 99 | 109 | 96 | 146 |
| Pork | 100 | 97 | 124 | 96 | 143 |
| Other meats | 100 | 100 | 101 | 99 | 119 |
| Poultry | 100 | 97 | 128 | 97 | 130 |
| Fish and seafood | 100 | 97 | 119 | 94 | 162 |
| Eggs | 100 | 97 | 106 | 91 | 176 |
| **Dairy products** | **100** | **104** | **67** | **99** | **110** |
| Fresh milk and cream | 100 | 105 | 68 | 98 | 132 |
| Other dairy products | 100 | 104 | 66 | 100 | 96 |
| **Fruits and vegetables** | **100** | **102** | **84** | **97** | **128** |
| Fresh fruits | 100 | 104 | 75 | 97 | 133 |
| Fresh vegetables | 100 | 103 | 75 | 96 | 145 |
| Processed fruits | 100 | 101 | 97 | 99 | 112 |
| Processed vegetables | 100 | 100 | 105 | 100 | 109 |
| **Other food at home** | **100** | **103** | **74** | **100** | **99** |
| Sugar and other sweets | 100 | 103 | 82 | 101 | 90 |
| Fats and oils | 100 | 100 | 99 | 99 | 114 |
| Miscellaneous foods | 100 | 104 | 69 | 100 | 96 |
| Nonalcoholic beverages | 100 | 102 | 79 | 99 | 107 |
| Food prepared by household on trips | 100 | 108 | 38 | 102 | 73 |
| **FOOD AWAY FROM HOME** | **100** | **106** | **55** | **102** | **78** |
| **ALCOHOLIC BEVERAGES** | **100** | **107** | **44** | **103** | **67** |

*(continued)*

*(continued from previous page)*

| | total consumer units | race | | Hispanic origin | |
|---|---|---|---|---|---|
| | | white/other | black | non-Hispanic | Hispanic |
| **HOUSING** | **100** | **103** | **80** | **101** | **88** |
| **SHELTER** | **100** | **103** | **80** | **101** | **91** |
| **Owned dwellings** | **100** | **106** | **57** | **103** | **68** |
| Mortgage interest and charges | 100 | 105 | 62 | 102 | 79 |
| Property taxes | 100 | 107 | 48 | 104 | 54 |
| Maintenance, repairs, insurance, other | 100 | 106 | 54 | 104 | 54 |
| **Rented dwellings** | **100** | **95** | **137** | **95** | **150** |
| **Other lodging** | **100** | **109** | **34** | **106** | **36** |
| **UTILITIES, FUELS, PUBLIC SERVICES** | **100** | **100** | **102** | **101** | **90** |
| Natural gas | 100 | 99 | 108 | 101 | 88 |
| Electricity | 100 | 100 | 100 | 101 | 84 |
| Fuel oil and other fuels | 100 | 108 | 38 | 105 | 51 |
| Telephone services | 100 | 98 | 117 | 100 | 103 |
| Water and other public services | 100 | 102 | 84 | 101 | 90 |
| **HOUSEHOLD SERVICES** | **100** | **104** | **69** | **104** | **59** |
| Personal services | 100 | 101 | 93 | 102 | 77 |
| Other household expenses | 100 | 107 | 47 | 106 | 42 |
| **HOUSEKEEPING SUPPLIES** | **100** | **105** | **64** | **101** | **87** |
| Laundry and cleaning supplies | 100 | 101 | 93 | 97 | 127 |
| Other household products | 100 | 106 | 59 | 102 | 80 |
| Postage and stationery | 100 | 107 | 45 | 103 | 64 |
| **HOUSEHOLD FURNISHINGS AND EQUIPMENT** | **100** | **106** | **54** | **102** | **81** |
| Household textiles | 100 | 105 | 67 | 103 | 80 |
| Furniture | 100 | 104 | 72 | 101 | 95 |
| Floor coverings | 100 | 106 | 47 | 105 | 33 |
| Major appliances | 100 | 105 | 62 | 102 | 85 |
| Small appliances, misc. housewares | 100 | 109 | 33 | 102 | 79 |
| Miscellaneous household equipment | 100 | 107 | 45 | 102 | 77 |
| **APPAREL AND SERVICES** | **100** | **101** | **94** | **99** | **113** |
| **Men and boys** | **100** | **102** | **82** | **98** | **120** |
| Men, 16 and over | 100 | 104 | 67 | 99 | 112 |
| Boys, 2 to 15 | 100 | 95 | 136 | 95 | 152 |
| **Women and girls** | **100** | **103** | **81** | **100** | **98** |
| Women, 16 and over | 100 | 103 | 80 | 101 | 92 |
| Girls, 2 to 15 | 100 | 102 | 86 | 97 | 131 |

*(continued)*

*(continued from previous page)*

| | total consumer units | race | | Hispanic origin | |
|---|---|---|---|---|---|
| | | white/other | black | non-Hispanic | Hispanic |
| Children under 2 | 100 | 100 | 101 | 94 | 182 |
| Footwear | 100 | 98 | 113 | 97 | 132 |
| Other apparel products, services | 100 | 97 | 126 | 100 | 97 |
| **TRANSPORTATION** | **100** | **104** | **74** | **101** | **86** |
| Vehicle purchases | **100** | **103** | **74** | **101** | **87** |
| Cars and trucks, new | 100 | 106 | 58 | 103 | 63 |
| Cars and trucks, used | 100 | 101 | 89 | 99 | 109 |
| Other vehicles | 100 | 109 | 42 | 109 | – |
| **Gasoline and motor oil** | **100** | **104** | **73** | **100** | **100** |
| **Other vehicle expenses** | **100** | **104** | **74** | **102** | **80** |
| Vehicle finance charges | 100 | 99 | 105 | 101 | 87 |
| Maintenance and repairs | 100 | 104 | 67 | 102 | 80 |
| Vehicle insurance | 100 | 103 | 79 | 101 | 89 |
| Vehicle rental, leases, licenses, other | 100 | 106 | 56 | 104 | 61 |
| **Public transportation** | **100** | **104** | **71** | **101** | **86** |
| **HEALTH CARE** | **100** | **106** | **56** | **103** | **63** |
| Health insurance | 100 | 105 | 66 | 104 | 62 |
| Medical services | 100 | 108 | 43 | 103 | 66 |
| Drugs | 100 | 106 | 56 | 103 | 63 |
| Medical supplies | 100 | 107 | 45 | 104 | 62 |
| **ENTERTAINMENT** | **100** | **107** | **48** | **103** | **63** |
| Fees and admissions | 100 | 108 | 41 | 104 | 50 |
| Television, radio, sound equipment | 100 | 102 | 88 | 102 | 82 |
| Pets, toys, playground equipment | 100 | 109 | 30 | 102 | 70 |
| Other entertainment supplies, equipment, services | 100 | 111 | 17 | 105 | 45 |
| **PERSONAL CARE PRODUCTS & SERVICES** | **100** | **97** | **120** | **101** | **91** |
| **READING** | **100** | **107** | **47** | **105** | **40** |
| **EDUCATION** | **100** | **107** | **47** | **102** | **80** |
| **TOBACCO PRODUCTS & SMOKING SUPPLIES** | **100** | **105** | **64** | **105** | **42** |
| **MISCELLANEOUS** | **100** | **105** | **66** | **102** | **82** |
| Cash contributions | 100 | 104 | 67 | 105 | 40 |

*(continued)*

*(continued from previous page)*

| | total consumer units | race | | Hispanic origin | |
|---|---|---|---|---|---|
| | | white/other | black | non-Hispanic | Hispanic |
| Personal insurance and pensions | 100 | 105 | 65 | 103 | 71 |
| Life and other personal insurance | 100 | 102 | 85 | 104 | 54 |
| Pensions and Social Security | 100 | 105 | 62 | 102 | 74 |
| **PERSONAL TAXES** | **100** | **107** | **48** | **104** | **60** |
| Federal income taxes | 100 | 107 | 45 | 104 | 62 |
| State and local income taxes | 100 | 105 | 61 | 104 | 57 |
| Other taxes | 100 | 108 | 40 | 107 | 26 |
| **GIFTS** | **100** | **105** | **62** | **103** | **72** |
| **Food** | **100** | **107** | **37** | **101** | **87** |
| **Housing** | **100** | **106** | **55** | **103** | **66** |
| Housekeeping supplies | 100 | 111 | 22 | 100 | 84 |
| Household textiles | 100 | 113 | 38 | 113 | 50 |
| Appliances and miscellaneous housewares | 100 | 111 | 19 | 104 | 89 |
| Major appliances | 100 | 117 | 33 | 100 | 183 |
| Small appliances, miscellaneous housewares | 100 | 110 | 14 | 105 | 62 |
| Miscellaneous household equipment | 100 | 111 | 21 | 105 | 52 |
| Other housing | 100 | 101 | 88 | 103 | 64 |
| **Apparel and services** | **100** | **99** | **107** | **101** | **88** |
| Males, 2 and over | 100 | 105 | 62 | 100 | 105 |
| Females, 2 and over | 100 | 104 | 75 | 101 | 89 |
| Children under 2 | 100 | 103 | 76 | 97 | 130 |
| Other apparel products, services | 100 | 88 | 188 | 104 | 57 |
| Jewelry and watches | 100 | 82 | 229 | 104 | 33 |
| All other apparel products, services | 100 | 97 | 117 | 100 | 97 |
| **Transportation** | **100** | **109** | **26** | **102** | **67** |
| **Health care** | **100** | **110** | **27** | **107** | **57** |
| **Entertainment** | **100** | **106** | **56** | **104** | **47** |
| Toys, games, hobbies, tricycles | 100 | 107 | 49 | 105 | 41 |
| Other entertainment | 100 | 105 | 60 | 103 | 53 |
| **Education** | **100** | **110** | **25** | **103** | **76** |
| **All other gifts** | **100** | **102** | **82** | **103** | **62** |

*Note: The Bureau of Labor Statistics uses consumer units rather than households as the sampling unit in the Consumer Expenditure Survey. For the definition of consumer unit, see the Glossary. An index of 100 is the average for all households. An index of 132 means households in the race or Hispanic origin group spend 32 percent more than the average household. An index of 75 means households in the race or Hispanic origin group spend 25 percent less than the average household. Hispanics may be of any race. (–) means sample is too small to make a reliable estimate.*
*Source: Calculations by New Strategist based on the Bureau of Labor Statistics' 1997 Consumer Expenditure Survey*

# Market Shares by Race and Hispanic Origin, 1997

*(share of total annual spending accounted for by race and Hispanic origin group, 1997)*

| | total consumer units | race white/other | race black | Hispanic origin non-Hispanic | Hispanic origin Hispanic |
|---|---|---|---|---|---|
| **Share of total consumer units** | 100.0% | 88.1% | 11.9% | 91.6% | 8.4% |
| **Share of total annual spending** | 100.0 | 91.3 | 8.7 | 92.9 | 7.1 |
| **FOOD** | **100.0%** | **91.1%** | **8.9%** | **91.5%** | **8.6%** |
| **FOOD AT HOME** | 100.0 | 89.6 | 10.4 | 90.3 | 9.8 |
| **Cereals and bakery products** | 100.0 | 90.0 | 9.9 | 91.4 | 8.7 |
| Cereals and cereal products | 100.0 | 89.2 | 10.9 | 90.4 | 10.0 |
| Bakery products | 100.0 | 90.5 | 9.3 | 91.9 | 8.1 |
| **Meats, poultry, fish, and eggs** | 100.0 | 86.2 | 13.8 | 88.2 | 12.0 |
| Beef | 100.0 | 86.9 | 13.0 | 87.9 | 12.3 |
| Pork | 100.0 | 85.3 | 14.7 | 88.1 | 12.1 |
| Other meats | 100.0 | 88.1 | 12.0 | 90.6 | 10.0 |
| Poultry | 100.0 | 85.1 | 15.2 | 89.0 | 11.0 |
| Fish and seafood | 100.0 | 85.1 | 14.2 | 86.4 | 13.6 |
| Eggs | 100.0 | 85.4 | 12.6 | 83.2 | 14.8 |
| **Dairy products** | 100.0 | 92.0 | 8.0 | 90.7 | 9.3 |
| Fresh milk and cream | 100.0 | 92.2 | 8.1 | 89.4 | 11.1 |
| Other dairy products | 100.0 | 91.9 | 7.9 | 91.6 | 8.1 |
| **Fruits and vegetables** | 100.0 | 89.8 | 10.1 | 89.3 | 10.8 |
| Fresh fruits | 100.0 | 91.6 | 9.0 | 89.1 | 11.2 |
| Fresh vegetables | 100.0 | 91.2 | 8.9 | 87.7 | 12.3 |
| Processed fruits | 100.0 | 89.0 | 11.6 | 90.7 | 9.4 |
| Processed vegetables | 100.0 | 88.1 | 12.5 | 91.6 | 9.2 |
| **Other food at home** | 100.0 | 91.0 | 8.9 | 91.7 | 8.3 |
| Sugar and other sweets | 100.0 | 90.4 | 9.7 | 92.4 | 7.6 |
| Fats and oils | 100.0 | 88.1 | 11.8 | 90.4 | 9.6 |
| Miscellaneous foods | 100.0 | 91.8 | 8.2 | 91.8 | 8.1 |
| Nonalcoholic beverages | 100.0 | 90.2 | 9.4 | 90.8 | 9.1 |
| Food prepared by household on trips | 100.0 | 94.9 | 4.6 | 93.3 | 6.2 |
| **FOOD AWAY FROM HOME** | 100.0 | 93.5 | 6.5 | 93.3 | 6.6 |
| **ALCOHOLIC BEVERAGES** | **100.0%** | **94.6%** | **5.3%** | **94.2%** | **5.6%** |

*(continued)*

*(continued from previous page)*

| | total consumer units | race | | Hispanic origin | |
|---|---|---|---|---|---|
| | | white/other | black | non-Hispanic | Hispanic |
| **HOUSING** | **100.0%** | **90.4%** | **9.6%** | **92.6%** | **7.4%** |
| **SHELTER** | **100.0** | **90.4** | **9.6** | **92.3** | **7.7** |
| **Owned dwellings** | **100.0** | **93.2** | **6.8** | **94.3** | **5.7** |
| Mortgage interest and charges | 100.0 | 92.7 | 7.3 | 93.4 | 6.6 |
| Property taxes | 100.0 | 94.3 | 5.8 | 95.4 | 4.6 |
| Maintenance, repairs, insurance, other | 100.0 | 93.7 | 6.4 | 95.5 | 4.5 |
| **Rented dwellings** | **100.0** | **83.6** | **16.3** | **87.4** | **12.6** |
| **Other lodging** | **100.0** | **95.9** | **4.0** | **96.9** | **3.0** |
| **UTILITIES, FUELS,** | | | | | |
| **PUBLIC SERVICES** | **100.0** | **87.9** | **12.1** | **92.4** | **7.6** |
| Natural gas | 100.0 | 87.2 | 12.8 | 92.5 | 7.4 |
| Electricity | 100.0 | 88.1 | 11.9 | 92.9 | 7.1 |
| Fuel oil and other fuels | 100.0 | 95.4 | 4.5 | 95.8 | 4.3 |
| Telephone services | 100.0 | 86.1 | 13.9 | 91.3 | 8.7 |
| Water and other public services | 100.0 | 89.9 | 10.0 | 92.5 | 7.5 |
| **HOUSEHOLD SERVICES** | **100.0** | **91.8** | **8.2** | **95.1** | **5.0** |
| Personal services | 100.0 | 89.1 | 11.1 | 93.7 | 6.5 |
| Other household expenses | 100.0 | 94.6 | 5.6 | 96.7 | 3.6 |
| **HOUSEKEEPING SUPPLIES** | **100.0** | **92.4** | **7.6** | **92.6** | **7.4** |
| Laundry and cleaning supplies | 100.0 | 88.9 | 11.1 | 89.2 | 10.7 |
| Other household products | 100.0 | 93.1 | 7.0 | 93.3 | 6.7 |
| Postage and stationery | 100.0 | 94.2 | 5.4 | 94.4 | 5.4 |
| **HOUSEHOLD FURNISHINGS** | | | | | |
| **AND EQUIPMENT** | **100.0** | **93.6** | **6.4** | **93.2** | **6.8** |
| Household textiles | 100.0 | 92.6 | 8.0 | 93.9 | 6.7 |
| Furniture | 100.0 | 91.5 | 8.5 | 92.0 | 8.0 |
| Floor coverings | 100.0 | 93.7 | 5.6 | 96.3 | 2.8 |
| Major appliances | 100.0 | 92.8 | 7.4 | 93.2 | 7.2 |
| Small appliances, misc. housewares | 100.0 | 95.8 | 3.9 | 93.6 | 6.7 |
| Miscellaneous household equipment | 100.0 | 94.7 | 5.3 | 93.5 | 6.5 |
| **APPAREL AND SERVICES** | **100.0%** | **88.8%** | **11.2%** | **90.5%** | **9.6%** |
| **Men and boys** | **100.0** | **90.3** | **9.7** | **90.0** | **10.2** |
| Men, 16 and over | 100.0 | 91.9 | 8.0 | 90.7 | 9.5 |
| Boys, 2 to 15 | 100.0 | 83.9 | 16.2 | 87.2 | 12.9 |
| **Women and girls** | **100.0** | **90.4** | **9.6** | **91.7** | **8.3** |
| Women, 16 and over | 100.0 | 90.5 | 9.5 | 92.2 | 7.8 |
| Girls, 2 to 15 | 100.0 | 89.8 | 10.2 | 89.0 | 11.1 |

*(continued)*

| | total consumer units | race | | Hispanic origin | |
|---|---|---|---|---|---|
| | | white/other | black | non-Hispanic | Hispanic |
| Children under 2 | 100.0% | 88.1% | 12.1% | 85.6% | 15.3% |
| Footwear | 100.0 | 86.4 | 13.5 | 88.9 | 11.2 |
| Other apparel products, services | 100.0 | 85.3 | 15.0 | 91.9 | 8.2 |
| **TRANSPORTATION** | **100.0%** | **91.2%** | **8.8%** | **92.7%** | **7.3%** |
| **Vehicle purchases** | **100.0** | **91.1** | **8.9** | **92.7** | **7.3** |
| Cars and trucks, new | 100.0 | 93.1 | 6.9 | 94.7 | 5.3 |
| Cars and trucks, used | 100.0 | 89.4 | 10.6 | 90.8 | 9.2 |
| Other vehicles | 100.0 | 96.3 | 5.0 | 100.1 | – |
| **Gasoline and motor oil** | **100.0** | **91.3** | **8.7** | **91.6** | **8.4** |
| **Other vehicle expenses** | **100.0** | **91.3** | **8.8** | **93.2** | **6.8** |
| Vehicle finance charges | 100.0 | 87.5 | 12.5 | 92.5 | 7.3 |
| Maintenance and repairs | 100.0 | 92.0 | 7.9 | 93.2 | 6.8 |
| Vehicle insurance | 100.0 | 90.5 | 9.4 | 92.4 | 7.5 |
| Vehicle rental, leases, licenses, other | 100.0 | 93.4 | 6.7 | 94.9 | 5.2 |
| **Public transportation** | **100.0** | **91.5** | **8.5** | **92.7** | **7.3** |
| **HEALTH CARE** | **100.0%** | **93.3%** | **6.7%** | **94.6%** | **5.3%** |
| Health insurance | 100.0 | 92.2 | 7.8 | 94.8 | 5.2 |
| Medical services | 100.0 | 94.9 | 5.1 | 94.5 | 5.6 |
| Drugs | 100.0 | 93.6 | 6.7 | 94.7 | 5.3 |
| Medical supplies | 100.0 | 94.6 | 5.4 | 95.0 | 5.2 |
| **ENTERTAINMENT** | **100.0%** | **94.3%** | **5.7%** | **94.7%** | **5.3%** |
| Fees and admissions | 100.0 | 95.2 | 4.8 | 95.6 | 4.2 |
| Television, radio, sound equipment | 100.0 | 89.6 | 10.5 | 93.2 | 6.9 |
| Pets, toys, playground equipment | 100.0 | 96.2 | 3.6 | 93.8 | 5.9 |
| Other entertainment supplies, equipment, services | 100.0 | 97.9 | 2.1 | 96.2 | 3.8 |
| **PERSONAL CARE PRODUCTS & SERVICES** | **100.0%** | **85.8%** | **14.2%** | **92.3%** | **7.7%** |
| **READING** | **100.0%** | **94.0%** | **5.6%** | **96.6%** | **3.4%** |
| **EDUCATION** | **100.0%** | **94.4%** | **5.6%** | **93.2%** | **6.7%** |
| **TOBACCO PRODUCTS & SMOKING SUPPLIES** | **100.0%** | **92.1%** | **7.7%** | **96.4%** | **3.5%** |
| **MISCELLANEOUS** | **100.0%** | **92.1%** | **7.9%** | **93.2%** | **6.9%** |
| Cash contributions | 100.0 | 92.1 | 8.0 | 96.6 | 3.4 |

*(continued)*

*(continued from previous page)*

| | total consumer units | race white/other | black | Hispanic origin non-Hispanic | Hispanic |
|---|---|---|---|---|---|
| Personal insurance and pensions | 100.0% | 92.3% | 7.7% | 94.0% | 6.0% |
| Life and other personal insurance | 100.0 | 89.7 | 10.1 | 95.4 | 4.6 |
| Pensions and Social Security | 100.0 | 92.6 | 7.4 | 93.8 | 6.2 |
| **PERSONAL TAXES** | **100.0%** | **94.1%** | **5.7%** | **95.2%** | **5.0%** |
| Federal income taxes | 100.0 | 94.4 | 5.3 | 95.0 | 5.2 |
| State and local income taxes | 100.0 | 92.5 | 7.3 | 95.4 | 4.8 |
| Other taxes | 100.0 | 94.9 | 4.7 | 98.0 | 2.2 |
| **GIFTS** | **100.0%** | **92.6%** | **7.4%** | **94.0%** | **6.0%** |
| **Food** | **100.0** | **94.6** | **4.4** | **92.9** | **7.3** |
| **Housing** | **100.0** | **93.6** | **6.5** | **94.6** | **5.6** |
| Housekeeping supplies | 100.0 | 97.6 | 2.6 | 91.6 | 7.1 |
| Household textiles | 100.0 | 95.5 | 4.5 | 95.8 | 4.2 |
| Appliances and miscellaneous housewares | 100.0 | 97.9 | 2.2 | 92.5 | 7.5 |
| Major appliances | 100.0 | 96.0 | 4.0 | 84.5 | 15.5 |
| Small appliances, misc. housewares | 100.0 | 96.5 | 1.7 | 95.9 | 5.2 |
| Miscellaneous household equipment | 100.0 | 97.4 | 2.5 | 95.7 | 4.3 |
| Other housing | 100.0 | 89.4 | 10.5 | 94.3 | 5.4 |
| **Apparel and services** | **100.0** | **87.4** | **12.7** | **92.7** | **7.5** |
| Males, 2 and over | 100.0 | 92.4 | 7.4 | 91.6 | 8.8 |
| Females, 2 and over | 100.0 | 91.4 | 9.0 | 92.7 | 7.5 |
| Children under 2 | 100.0 | 90.8 | 9.0 | 88.8 | 11.0 |
| Other apparel products, services | 100.0 | 77.8 | 22.4 | 95.1 | 4.8 |
| Jewelry and watches | 100.0 | 71.9 | 27.2 | 95.3 | 2.8 |
| All other apparel products, services | 100.0 | 85.1 | 14.0 | 91.6 | 8.1 |
| **Transportation** | **100.0** | **95.8** | **3.1** | **93.2** | **5.6** |
| **Health care** | **100.0** | **96.9** | **3.2** | **97.7** | **4.8** |
| **Entertainment** | **100.0** | **93.4** | **6.6** | **95.3** | **4.0** |
| Toys, games, hobbies, tricycles | 100.0 | 94.5 | 5.8 | 96.0 | 3.5 |
| Other entertainment | 100.0 | 92.6 | 7.2 | 94.7 | 4.5 |
| **Education** | **100.0** | **97.2** | **2.9** | **93.9** | **6.4** |
| **All other gifts** | **100.0** | **90.2** | **9.7** | **94.5** | **5.2** |

*Note: The Bureau of Labor Statistics uses consumer units rather than households as the sampling unit in the Consumer Expenditure Survey. For the definition of consumer unit, see the Glossary. Hispanics may be of any race. (–) means sample is too small to make a reliable estimate. Numbers may not add to total due to rounding.*
*Source: Calculations by New Strategist based on the Bureau of Labor Statistics' 1997 Consumer Expenditure Survey*

# Spending Is Highest in the West

## Households in the South spend the least.

Spending closely parallels income. Both income and spending are highest in the West, where average household income was $44,368 in 1997 and average household spending was $39,037. Income and spending are lowest in the South, where average household income was $35,691 and average household spending was $32,226. By product and service category, however, spending varies by region.

The Indexed Spending table in this section compares the spending of households by region with average household spending. An index of 100 means households in the region spend the average amount on an item. An index above 100 means households in the region spend more than average on the item, while an index below 100 signifies below-average spending.

Households in the West spend 14 percent less than the average household on property taxes (with an index of 86), although they spend 40 percent more than average on mortgage interest. Households in the South spend 10 percent more than average on pork, and also more than average on electricity, major appliances, new cars and trucks, and drugs. Households in the Midwest spend much less than average on fish and seafood but more on property taxes, drugs, and entertainment. In the Northeast, spending is above average for many items including gifts, education, fuel oil, and alcohol.

The Market Share table in this section shows how much of total household spending by category is accounted for by households in each region. In most categories, spending closely matches each region's share of total households. The South, which is home to 35 percent of the nation's households, accounts for 32 percent of all household spending. With 21 percent of all households located in the West, the region accounts for 24 percent of household spending. There are some exceptions, however. Households in the South, for example, account for a disproportionately large share of spending on electricity (42 percent), while those in the West account for only 18 percent of spending on this item.

♦ Because regional spending patterns are partly determined by climate, spending by region is not likely to change much in the years ahead.

# Spending by Region, 1997

*(average annual spending of consumer units (cu) by product and service category and region of residence, 1997)*

| | total | Northeast | Midwest | South | West |
|---|---|---|---|---|---|
| Number of consumer units (in 000s) | 105,576 | 21,090 | 25,228 | 36,832 | 22,426 |
| Average number of persons per cu | 2.5 | 2.5 | 2.5 | 2.5 | 2.7 |
| Average before-tax income | $39,926 | $43,336 | $39,222 | $35,691 | $44,368 |
| Average annual spending | 34,819 | 36,070 | 33,791 | 32,226 | 39,037 |
| **FOOD** | **$4,801** | **$5,358** | **$4,631** | **$4,426** | **$5,077** |
| **FOOD AT HOME** | **2,880** | **2,970** | **2,739** | **2,771** | **3,125** |
| **Cereals and bakery products** | **453** | **504** | **446** | **415** | **474** |
| Cereals and cereal products | 161 | 177 | 154 | 149 | 175 |
| Bakery products | 292 | 326 | 292 | 266 | 299 |
| **Meats, poultry, fish, and eggs** | **743** | **789** | **663** | **753** | **774** |
| Beef | 224 | 214 | 207 | 235 | 233 |
| Pork | 157 | 141 | 153 | 173 | 150 |
| Other meats | 96 | 112 | 101 | 88 | 90 |
| Poultry | 145 | 177 | 119 | 141 | 151 |
| Fish and seafood | 89 | 108 | 58 | 85 | 110 |
| Eggs | 33 | 36 | 25 | 31 | 41 |
| **Dairy products** | **314** | **327** | **308** | **290** | **345** |
| Fresh milk and cream | 128 | 130 | 129 | 119 | 140 |
| Other dairy products | 186 | 198 | 179 | 171 | 205 |
| **Fruits and vegetables** | **476** | **525** | **430** | **438** | **541** |
| Fresh fruits | 150 | 169 | 146 | 131 | 170 |
| Fresh vegetables | 143 | 162 | 122 | 125 | 176 |
| Processed fruits | 102 | 115 | 92 | 93 | 116 |
| Processed vegetables | 80 | 79 | 70 | 89 | 79 |
| **Other food at home** | **895** | **825** | **892** | **876** | **991** |
| Sugar and other sweets | 114 | 109 | 116 | 115 | 117 |
| Fats and oils | 81 | 85 | 73 | 81 | 86 |
| Miscellaneous foods | 403 | 346 | 408 | 387 | 476 |
| Nonalcoholic beverages | 245 | 228 | 240 | 253 | 251 |
| Food prepared by household on trips | 52 | 57 | 55 | 40 | 62 |
| **FOOD AWAY FROM HOME** | **1,921** | **2,388** | **1,892** | **1,655** | **1,952** |
| **ALCOHOLIC BEVERAGES** | **$309** | **$379** | **$306** | **$229** | **$377** |

*(continued)*

*(continued from previous page)*

| | total | Northeast | Midwest | South | West |
|---|---|---|---|---|---|
| **HOUSING** | **$11,272** | **$12,480** | **$10,532** | **$9,877** | **$13,255** |
| **SHELTER** | **6,344** | **7,539** | **5,653** | **5,070** | **8,089** |
| **Owned dwellings** | **3,935** | **4,704** | **3,785** | **3,059** | **4,818** |
| Mortgage interest and charges | 2,225 | 2,351 | 1,955 | 1,779 | 3,143 |
| Property taxes | 971 | 1,569 | 1,088 | 630 | 838 |
| Maintenance, repairs, insurance, other | 738 | 784 | 742 | 650 | 836 |
| **Rented dwellings** | **1,983** | **2,298** | **1,477** | **1,694** | **2,731** |
| **Other lodging** | **426** | **536** | **391** | **317** | **541** |
| **UTILITIES, FUELS,** | | | | | |
| **PUBLIC SERVICES** | **2,412** | **2,480** | **2,452** | **2,463** | **2,220** |
| Natural gas | 301 | 396 | 446 | 185 | 238 |
| Electricity | 909 | 830 | 834 | 1,094 | 762 |
| Fuel oil and other fuels | 108 | 255 | 115 | 55 | 48 |
| Telephone services | 809 | 785 | 778 | 839 | 817 |
| Water and other public services | 286 | 215 | 279 | 290 | 355 |
| **HOUSEHOLD SERVICES** | **548** | **473** | **458** | **534** | **745** |
| Personal services | 263 | 219 | 248 | 249 | 346 |
| Other household expenses | 285 | 254 | 210 | 286 | 399 |
| **HOUSEKEEPING SUPPLIES** | **455** | **418** | **485** | **427** | **501** |
| Laundry and cleaning supplies | 116 | 111 | 112 | 117 | 122 |
| Other household products | 210 | 187 | 224 | 204 | 226 |
| Postage and stationery | 129 | 119 | 149 | 106 | 152 |
| **HOUSEHOLD FURNISHINGS** | | | | | |
| **AND EQUIPMENT** | **1,512** | **1,570** | **1,484** | **1,383** | **1,699** |
| Household textiles | 79 | 86 | 78 | 64 | 99 |
| Furniture | 387 | 424 | 354 | 386 | 392 |
| Floor coverings | 78 | 102 | 85 | 63 | 72 |
| Major appliances | 169 | 145 | 160 | 187 | 173 |
| Small appliances, misc. housewares | 92 | 91 | 95 | 75 | 117 |
| Miscellaneous household equipment | 707 | 723 | 711 | 608 | 847 |
| **APPAREL AND SERVICES** | **$1,729** | **$1,916** | **$1,707** | **$1,620** | **$1,755** |
| **Men and boys** | **407** | **432** | **446** | **350** | **432** |
| Men, 16 and over | 323 | 347 | 353 | 271 | 351 |
| Boys, 2 to 15 | 84 | 85 | 93 | 79 | 80 |
| **Women and girls** | **680** | **722** | **713** | **648** | **657** |
| Women, 16 and over | 574 | 624 | 592 | 547 | 552 |
| Girls, 2 to 15 | 106 | 98 | 121 | 101 | 105 |

*(continued)*

*(continued from previous page)*

| | total | Northeast | Midwest | South | West |
|---|---|---|---|---|---|
| **Children under 2** | $77 | $80 | $63 | $69 | $103 |
| **Footwear** | 315 | 339 | 298 | 323 | 298 |
| **Other apparel products, services** | 250 | 343 | 186 | 231 | 266 |
| **TRANSPORTATION** | **$6,457** | **$5,830** | **$6,367** | **$6,473** | **$7,120** |
| **Vehicle purchases** | 2,736 | 2,040 | 2,784 | 3,055 | 2,811 |
| Cars and trucks, new | 1,229 | 973 | 1,216 | 1,486 | 1,062 |
| Cars and trucks, used | 1,464 | 1,052 | 1,544 | 1,541 | 1,633 |
| Other vehicles | 43 | 15 | 24 | 29 | 115 |
| **Gasoline and motor oil** | 1,098 | 979 | 1,107 | 1,112 | 1,174 |
| **Other vehicle expenses** | 2,230 | 2,223 | 2,131 | 2,062 | 2,624 |
| Vehicle finance charges | 293 | 214 | 307 | 335 | 281 |
| Maintenance and repairs | 682 | 584 | 659 | 657 | 838 |
| Vehicle insurance | 755 | 808 | 684 | 727 | 831 |
| Vehicle rental, leases, licenses, other | 501 | 617 | 480 | 343 | 674 |
| **Public transportation** | 393 | 587 | 345 | 243 | 511 |
| **HEALTH CARE** | **$1,841** | **$1,709** | **$1,903** | **$1,902** | **$1,793** |
| Health insurance | 881 | 871 | 912 | 931 | 775 |
| Medical services | 531 | 480 | 521 | 502 | 638 |
| Drugs | 320 | 240 | 357 | 367 | 277 |
| Medical supplies | 108 | 119 | 113 | 102 | 102 |
| **ENTERTAINMENT** | **$1,813** | **$1,769** | **$1,915** | **$1,561** | **$2,153** |
| Fees and admissions | 471 | 528 | 468 | 358 | 604 |
| Television, radio, sound equipment | 577 | 581 | 560 | 570 | 605 |
| Pets, toys, playground equipment | 327 | 320 | 325 | 299 | 378 |
| Other entertainment supplies, equipment, services | 439 | 340 | 561 | 334 | 565 |
| **PERSONAL CARE PRODUCTS & SERVICES** | **$528** | **$521** | **$506** | **$544** | **$530** |
| **READING** | **$164** | **$192** | **$170** | **$130** | **$186** |
| **EDUCATION** | **$571** | **$772** | **$512** | **$449** | **$647** |
| **TOBACCO PRODUCTS & SMOKING SUPPLIES** | **$264** | **$260** | **$302** | **$268** | **$217** |
| **MISCELLANEOUS** | **$847** | **$821** | **$824** | **$806** | **$965** |
| Cash contributions | 1,001 | 765 | 989 | 1,057 | 1,145 |
| Personal insurance and pensions | 3,223 | 3,298 | 3,128 | 2,883 | 3,819 |

*(continued)*

*(continued from previous page)*

| | total | Northeast | Midwest | South | West |
|---|---|---|---|---|---|
| Life and other personal insurance | $379 | $386 | $361 | $421 | $322 |
| Pensions and Social Security | 2,844 | 2,912 | 2,767 | 2,461 | 3,497 |
| **PERSONAL TAXES** | **$3,241** | **$3,170** | **$3,318** | **$2,399** | **$4,529** |
| Federal income taxes | 2,468 | 2,280 | 2,405 | 1,918 | 3,538 |
| State and local income taxes | 645 | 719 | 768 | 379 | 872 |
| Other taxes | 129 | 172 | 145 | 102 | 119 |
| **GIFTS** | **$1,059** | **$1,188** | **$1,063** | **$953** | **$1,110** |
| **Food** | **68** | **78** | **68** | **62** | **68** |
| **Housing** | **273** | **297** | **288** | **245** | **280** |
| Housekeeping supplies | 37 | 39 | 48 | 30 | 32 |
| Household textiles | 8 | 10 | 8 | 7 | 9 |
| Appliances and miscellaneous housewares | 27 | 31 | 33 | 24 | 23 |
| Major appliances | 6 | 8 | 6 | 6 | 7 |
| Small appliances, misc. housewares | 21 | 23 | 28 | 18 | 16 |
| Miscellaneous household equipment | 66 | 65 | 74 | 57 | 73 |
| Other housing | 135 | 152 | 124 | 128 | 142 |
| **Apparel and services** | **252** | **272** | **242** | **252** | **246** |
| Males, 2 and over | 61 | 62 | 71 | 54 | 61 |
| Females, 2 and over | 81 | 88 | 91 | 73 | 78 |
| Children under 2 | 33 | 35 | 27 | 30 | 40 |
| Other apparel products, services | 77 | 86 | 53 | 96 | 66 |
| Jewelry and watches | 49 | 51 | 31 | 64 | 42 |
| All other apparel products, services | 29 | 35 | 22 | 32 | 24 |
| **Transportation** | **57** | **44** | **52** | **52** | **82** |
| **Health care** | **30** | **22** | **22** | **20** | **64** |
| **Entertainment** | **99** | **96** | **114** | **88** | **103** |
| Toys, games, hobbies, tricycles | 41 | 33 | 51 | 39 | 40 |
| Other entertainment | 58 | 63 | 62 | 49 | 63 |
| **Education** | **155** | **257** | **152** | **114** | **132** |
| **All other gifts** | **125** | **122** | **125** | **119** | **136** |

*Note: The Bureau of Labor Statistics uses consumer units rather than households as the sampling unit in the Consumer Expenditure Survey. For the definition of consumer unit, see the Glossary. Spending on gifts is also included in the preceding product and service categories.*
*Source: Bureau of Labor Statistics, 1997 Consumer Expenditure Survey*

# Indexed Spending by Region, 1997

*(average annual spending of consumer units by product and service category and region of residence, 1997)*

| | total | Northeast | Midwest | South | West |
|---|---|---|---|---|---|
| Number of consumer units (in 000s) | 105,576 | 21,090 | 25,228 | 36,832 | 22,426 |
| Indexed before-tax income | 100 | 109 | 98 | 89 | 111 |
| Indexed average annual spending | 100 | 104 | 97 | 93 | 112 |
| **FOOD** | **100** | **112** | **96** | **92** | **106** |
| **FOOD AT HOME** | **100** | **103** | **95** | **96** | **109** |
| **Cereals and bakery products** | **100** | **111** | **98** | **92** | **105** |
| Cereals and cereal products | 100 | 110 | 96 | 93 | 109 |
| Bakery products | 100 | 112 | 100 | 91 | 102 |
| **Meats, poultry, fish, and eggs** | **100** | **106** | **89** | **101** | **104** |
| Beef | 100 | 96 | 92 | 105 | 104 |
| Pork | 100 | 90 | 97 | 110 | 96 |
| Other meats | 100 | 117 | 105 | 92 | 94 |
| Poultry | 100 | 122 | 82 | 97 | 104 |
| Fish and seafood | 100 | 121 | 65 | 96 | 124 |
| Eggs | 100 | 109 | 76 | 94 | 124 |
| **Dairy products** | **100** | **104** | **98** | **92** | **110** |
| Fresh milk and cream | 100 | 102 | 101 | 93 | 109 |
| Other dairy products | 100 | 106 | 96 | 92 | 110 |
| **Fruits and vegetables** | **100** | **110** | **90** | **92** | **114** |
| Fresh fruits | 100 | 113 | 97 | 87 | 113 |
| Fresh vegetables | 100 | 113 | 85 | 87 | 123 |
| Processed fruits | 100 | 113 | 90 | 91 | 114 |
| Processed vegetables | 100 | 99 | 88 | 111 | 99 |
| **Other food at home** | **100** | **92** | **100** | **98** | **111** |
| Sugar and other sweets | 100 | 96 | 102 | 101 | 103 |
| Fats and oils | 100 | 105 | 90 | 100 | 106 |
| Miscellaneous foods | 100 | 86 | 101 | 96 | 118 |
| Nonalcoholic beverages | 100 | 93 | 98 | 103 | 102 |
| Food prepared by household on trips | 100 | 110 | 106 | 77 | 119 |
| **FOOD AWAY FROM HOME** | **100** | **124** | **98** | **86** | **102** |
| **ALCOHOLIC BEVERAGES** | **100** | **123** | **99** | **74** | **122** |

*(continued)*

*(continued from previous page)*

| | total | Northeast | Midwest | South | West |
|---|---|---|---|---|---|
| **HOUSING** | **100** | **111** | **93** | **88** | **118** |
| **SHELTER** | **100** | **119** | **89** | **80** | **128** |
| **Owned dwellings** | **100** | **120** | **96** | **78** | **122** |
| Mortgage interest and charges | 100 | 106 | 88 | 80 | 141 |
| Property taxes | 100 | 162 | 112 | 65 | 86 |
| Maintenance, repairs, insurance, other | 100 | 106 | 101 | 88 | 113 |
| **Rented dwellings** | **100** | **116** | **74** | **85** | **138** |
| **Other lodging** | **100** | **126** | **92** | **74** | **127** |
| **UTILITIES, FUELS,** | | | | | |
| **PUBLIC SERVICES** | **100** | **103** | **102** | **102** | **92** |
| Natural gas | 100 | 132 | 148 | 61 | 79 |
| Electricity | 100 | 91 | 92 | 120 | 84 |
| Fuel oil and other fuels | 100 | 236 | 106 | 51 | 44 |
| Telephone services | 100 | 97 | 96 | 104 | 101 |
| Water and other public services | 100 | 75 | 98 | 101 | 124 |
| **HOUSEHOLD SERVICES** | **100** | **86** | **84** | **97** | **136** |
| Personal services | 100 | 83 | 94 | 95 | 132 |
| Other household expenses | 100 | 89 | 74 | 100 | 140 |
| **HOUSEKEEPING SUPPLIES** | **100** | **92** | **107** | **94** | **110** |
| Laundry and cleaning supplies | 100 | 96 | 97 | 101 | 105 |
| Other household products | 100 | 89 | 107 | 97 | 108 |
| Postage and stationery | 100 | 92 | 116 | 82 | 118 |
| **HOUSEHOLD FURNISHINGS** | | | | | |
| **AND EQUIPMENT** | **100** | **104** | **98** | **91** | **112** |
| Household textiles | 100 | 109 | 99 | 81 | 125 |
| Furniture | 100 | 110 | 91 | 100 | 101 |
| Floor coverings | 100 | 131 | 109 | 81 | 92 |
| Major appliances | 100 | 86 | 95 | 111 | 102 |
| Small appliances, misc. housewares | 100 | 99 | 103 | 82 | 127 |
| Miscellaneous household equipment | 100 | 102 | 101 | 86 | 120 |
| **APPAREL AND SERVICES** | **100** | **111** | **99** | **94** | **102** |
| **Men and boys** | **100** | **106** | **110** | **86** | **106** |
| Men, 16 and over | 100 | 107 | 109 | 84 | 109 |
| Boys, 2 to 15 | 100 | 101 | 111 | 94 | 95 |
| **Women and girls** | **100** | **106** | **105** | **95** | **97** |
| Women, 16 and over | 100 | 109 | 103 | 95 | 96 |
| Girls, 2 to 15 | 100 | 92 | 114 | 95 | 99 |

*(continued)*

*(continued from previous page)*

| | total | Northeast | Midwest | South | West |
|---|---|---|---|---|---|
| Children under 2 | 100 | 104 | 82 | 90 | 134 |
| Footwear | 100 | 108 | 95 | 103 | 95 |
| Other apparel products, services | 100 | 137 | 74 | 92 | 106 |
| **TRANSPORTATION** | **100** | **90** | **99** | **100** | **110** |
| **Vehicle purchases** | **100** | **75** | **102** | **112** | **103** |
| Cars and trucks, new | 100 | 79 | 99 | 121 | 86 |
| Cars and trucks, used | 100 | 72 | 105 | 105 | 112 |
| Other vehicles | 100 | 35 | 56 | 67 | 267 |
| **Gasoline and motor oil** | **100** | **89** | **101** | **101** | **107** |
| **Other vehicle expenses** | **100** | **100** | **96** | **92** | **118** |
| Vehicle finance charges | 100 | 73 | 105 | 114 | 96 |
| Maintenance and repairs | 100 | 86 | 97 | 96 | 123 |
| Vehicle insurance | 100 | 107 | 91 | 96 | 110 |
| Vehicle rental, leases, licenses, other | 100 | 123 | 96 | 68 | 135 |
| **Public transportation** | **100** | **149** | **88** | **62** | **130** |
| **HEALTH CARE** | **100** | **93** | **103** | **103** | **97** |
| Health insurance | 100 | 99 | 104 | 106 | 88 |
| Medical services | 100 | 90 | 98 | 95 | 120 |
| Drugs | 100 | 75 | 112 | 115 | 87 |
| Medical supplies | 100 | 110 | 105 | 94 | 94 |
| **ENTERTAINMENT** | **100** | **98** | **106** | **86** | **119** |
| Fees and admissions | 100 | 112 | 99 | 76 | 128 |
| Television, radio, sound equipment | 100 | 101 | 97 | 99 | 105 |
| Pets, toys, playground equipment | 100 | 98 | 99 | 91 | 116 |
| Other entertainment supplies, equipment, services | 100 | 77 | 128 | 76 | 129 |
| **PERSONAL CARE PRODUCTS & SERVICES** | **100** | **99** | **96** | **103** | **100** |
| **READING** | **100** | **117** | **104** | **79** | **113** |
| **EDUCATION** | **100** | **135** | **90** | **79** | **113** |
| **TOBACCO PRODUCTS & SMOKING SUPPLIES** | **100** | **98** | **114** | **102** | **82** |
| **MISCELLANEOUS** | **100** | **97** | **97** | **95** | **114** |
| Cash contributions | 100 | 76 | 99 | 106 | 114 |
| Personal insurance and pensions | 100 | 102 | 97 | 89 | 118 |

*(continued)*

*(continued from previous page)*

| | total | Northeast | Midwest | South | West |
|---|---|---|---|---|---|
| Life and other personal insurance | 100 | 102 | 95 | 111 | 85 |
| Pensions and Social Security | 100 | 102 | 97 | 87 | 123 |
| **PERSONAL TAXES** | **100** | **98** | **102** | **74** | **140** |
| Federal income taxes | 100 | 92 | 97 | 78 | 143 |
| State and local income taxes | 100 | 111 | 119 | 59 | 135 |
| Other taxes | 100 | 133 | 112 | 79 | 92 |
| **GIFTS** | **100** | **112** | **100** | **90** | **105** |
| **Food** | **100** | **115** | **100** | **91** | **100** |
| **Housing** | **100** | **109** | **105** | **90** | **103** |
| Housekeeping supplies | 100 | 105 | 130 | 81 | 86 |
| Household textiles | 100 | 125 | 100 | 88 | 113 |
| Appliances and miscellaneous housewares | 100 | 115 | 122 | 89 | 85 |
| Major appliances | 100 | 133 | 100 | 100 | 117 |
| Small appliances, misc. housewares | 100 | 110 | 133 | 86 | 76 |
| Miscellaneous household equipment | 100 | 98 | 112 | 86 | 111 |
| Other housing | 100 | 113 | 92 | 95 | 105 |
| **Apparel and services** | **100** | **108** | **96** | **100** | **98** |
| Males, 2 and over | 100 | 102 | 116 | 89 | 100 |
| Females, 2 and over | 100 | 109 | 112 | 90 | 96 |
| Children under 2 | 100 | 106 | 82 | 91 | 121 |
| Other apparel products, services | 100 | 112 | 69 | 125 | 86 |
| Jewelry and watches | 100 | 104 | 63 | 131 | 86 |
| All other apparel products, services | 100 | 121 | 76 | 110 | 83 |
| **Transportation** | **100** | **77** | **91** | **91** | **144** |
| **Health care** | **100** | **73** | **73** | **67** | **213** |
| **Entertainment** | **100** | **97** | **115** | **89** | **104** |
| Toys, games, hobbies, tricycles | 100 | 80 | 124 | 95 | 98 |
| Other entertainment | 100 | 109 | 107 | 84 | 109 |
| **Education** | **100** | **166** | **98** | **74** | **85** |
| **All other gifts** | **100** | **98** | **100** | **95** | **109** |

*Note: The Bureau of Labor Statistics uses consumer units rather than households as the sampling unit in the Consumer Expenditure Survey. For the definition of consumer unit, see the Glossary. An index of 100 is the average for all households. An index of 132 means households in the region spend 32 percent more than the average household. An index of 75 means households in the region spend 25 percent less than the average household. Source: Calculations by New Strategist based on the Bureau of Labor Statistics' 1997 Consumer Expenditure Survey*

# Market Shares by Region, 1997

*(share of total household spending accounted for by consumer units in region, 1997)*

|  | total | Northeast | Midwest | South | West |
|---|---|---|---|---|---|
| Share of total consumer units | 100.0% | 20.0% | 23.9% | 34.9% | 21.2% |
| Share of total annual spending | 100.0 | 20.7 | 23.2 | 32.3 | 23.8 |
| **FOOD** | **100.0%** | **22.3%** | **23.0%** | **32.2%** | **22.5%** |
| FOOD AT HOME | 100.0 | 20.6 | 22.7 | 33.6 | 23.0 |
| **Cereals and bakery products** | **100.0** | **22.2** | **23.5** | **32.0** | **22.2** |
| Cereals and cereal products | 100.0 | 22.0 | 22.9 | 32.3 | 23.1 |
| Bakery products | 100.0 | 22.3 | 23.9 | 31.8 | 21.8 |
| **Meats, poultry, fish, and eggs** | **100.0** | **21.2** | **21.3** | **35.4** | **22.1** |
| Beef | 100.0 | 19.1 | 22.1 | 36.6 | 22.1 |
| Pork | 100.0 | 17.9 | 23.3 | 38.4 | 20.3 |
| Other meats | 100.0 | 23.3 | 25.1 | 32.0 | 19.9 |
| Poultry | 100.0 | 24.4 | 19.6 | 33.9 | 22.1 |
| Fish and seafood | 100.0 | 24.2 | 15.6 | 33.3 | 26.3 |
| Eggs | 100.0 | 21.8 | 18.1 | 32.8 | 26.4 |
| **Dairy products** | **100.0** | **20.8** | **23.4** | **32.2** | **23.3** |
| Fresh milk and cream | 100.0 | 20.3 | 24.1 | 32.4 | 23.2 |
| Other dairy products | 100.0 | 21.3 | 23.0 | 32.1 | 23.4 |
| **Fruits and vegetables** | **100.0** | **22.0** | **21.6** | **32.1** | **24.1** |
| Fresh fruits | 100.0 | 22.5 | 23.3 | 30.5 | 24.1 |
| Fresh vegetables | 100.0 | 22.6 | 20.4 | 30.5 | 26.1 |
| Processed fruits | 100.0 | 22.5 | 21.6 | 31.8 | 24.2 |
| Processed vegetables | 100.0 | 19.7 | 20.9 | 38.8 | 21.0 |
| **Other food at home** | **100.0** | **18.4** | **23.8** | **34.1** | **23.5** |
| Sugar and other sweets | 100.0 | 19.1 | 24.3 | 35.2 | 21.8 |
| Fats and oils | 100.0 | 21.0 | 21.5 | 34.9 | 22.6 |
| Miscellaneous foods | 100.0 | 17.2 | 24.2 | 33.5 | 25.1 |
| Nonalcoholic beverages | 100.0 | 18.6 | 23.4 | 36.0 | 21.8 |
| Food prepared by household on trips | 100.0 | 21.9 | 25.3 | 26.8 | 25.3 |
| FOOD AWAY FROM HOME | 100.0 | 24.8 | 23.5 | 30.1 | 21.6 |
| **ALCOHOLIC BEVERAGES** | **100.0%** | **24.5%** | **23.7%** | **25.9%** | **25.9%** |

*(continued)*

*(continued from previous page)*

| | total | Northeast | Midwest | South | West |
|---|---|---|---|---|---|
| **HOUSING** | **100.0%** | **22.1%** | **22.3%** | **30.6%** | **25.0%** |
| **SHELTER** | **100.0** | **23.7** | **21.3** | **27.9** | **27.1** |
| **Owned dwellings** | **100.0** | **23.9** | **23.0** | **27.1** | **26.0** |
| Mortgage interest and charges | 100.0 | 21.1 | 21.0 | 27.9 | 30.0 |
| Property taxes | 100.0 | 32.3 | 26.8 | 22.6 | 18.3 |
| Maintenance, repairs, insurance, other | 100.0 | 21.2 | 24.0 | 30.7 | 24.1 |
| **Rented dwellings** | **100.0** | **23.1** | **17.8** | **29.8** | **29.3** |
| **Other lodging** | **100.0** | **25.1** | **21.9** | **26.0** | **27.0** |
| **UTILITIES, FUELS,** | | | | | |
| **PUBLIC SERVICES** | **100.0** | **20.5** | **24.3** | **35.6** | **19.6** |
| Natural gas | 100.0 | 26.3 | 35.4 | 21.4 | 16.8 |
| Electricity | 100.0 | 18.2 | 21.9 | 42.0 | 17.8 |
| Fuel oil and other fuels | 100.0 | 47.2 | 25.4 | 17.8 | 9.4 |
| Telephone services | 100.0 | 19.4 | 23.0 | 36.2 | 21.5 |
| Water and other public services | 100.0 | 15.0 | 23.3 | 35.4 | 26.4 |
| **HOUSEHOLD SERVICES** | **100.0** | **17.2** | **20.0** | **34.0** | **28.9** |
| Personal services | 100.0 | 16.6 | 22.5 | 33.0 | 27.9 |
| Other household expenses | 100.0 | 17.8 | 17.6 | 35.0 | 29.7 |
| **HOUSEKEEPING SUPPLIES** | **100.0** | **18.4** | **25.5** | **32.7** | **23.4** |
| Laundry and cleaning supplies | 100.0 | 19.1 | 23.1 | 35.2 | 22.3 |
| Other household products | 100.0 | 17.8 | 25.5 | 33.9 | 22.9 |
| Postage and stationery | 100.0 | 18.4 | 27.6 | 28.7 | 25.0 |
| **HOUSEHOLD FURNISHINGS** | | | | | |
| **AND EQUIPMENT** | **100.0** | **20.7** | **23.5** | **31.9** | **23.9** |
| Household textiles | 100.0 | 21.7 | 23.6 | 28.3 | 26.6 |
| Furniture | 100.0 | 21.9 | 21.9 | 34.8 | 21.5 |
| Floor coverings | 100.0 | 26.1 | 26.0 | 28.2 | 19.6 |
| Major appliances | 100.0 | 17.1 | 22.6 | 38.6 | 21.7 |
| Small appliances, misc. housewares | 100.0 | 19.8 | 24.7 | 28.4 | 27.0 |
| Miscellaneous household equipment | 100.0 | 20.4 | 24.0 | 30.0 | 25.4 |
| **APPAREL AND SERVICES** | **100.0%** | **22.1%** | **23.6%** | **32.7%** | **21.6%** |
| **Men and boys** | **100.0** | **21.2** | **26.2** | **30.0** | **22.5** |
| Men, 16 and over | 100.0 | 21.5 | 26.1 | 29.3 | 23.1 |
| Boys, 2 to 15 | 100.0 | 20.2 | 26.5 | 32.8 | 20.2 |
| **Women and girls** | **100.0** | **21.2** | **25.1** | **33.2** | **20.5** |
| Women, 16 and over | 100.0 | 21.7 | 24.6 | 33.2 | 20.4 |
| Girls, 2 to 15 | 100.0 | 18.5 | 27.3 | 33.2 | 21.0 |

*(continued)*

*(continued from previous page)*

| | total | Northeast | Midwest | South | West |
|---|---|---|---|---|---|
| Children under 2 | 100.0% | 20.8% | 19.6% | 31.3% | 28.4% |
| Footwear | 100.0 | 21.5 | 22.6 | 35.8 | 20.1 |
| Other apparel products, services | 100.0 | 27.4 | 17.8 | 32.2 | 22.6 |
| **TRANSPORTATION** | **100.0%** | **18.0%** | **23.6%** | **35.0%** | **23.4%** |
| **Vehicle purchases** | **100.0** | **14.9** | **24.3** | **39.0** | **21.8** |
| Cars and trucks, new | 100.0 | 15.8 | 23.6 | 42.2 | 18.4 |
| Cars and trucks, used | 100.0 | 14.4 | 25.2 | 36.7 | 23.7 |
| Other vehicles | 100.0 | 7.0 | 13.3 | 23.5 | 56.8 |
| **Gasoline and motor oil** | **100.0** | **17.8** | **24.1** | **35.3** | **22.7** |
| **Other vehicle expenses** | **100.0** | **19.9** | **22.8** | **32.3** | **25.0** |
| Vehicle finance charges | 100.0 | 14.6 | 25.0 | 39.9 | 20.4 |
| Maintenance and repairs | 100.0 | 17.1 | 23.1 | 33.6 | 26.1 |
| Vehicle insurance | 100.0 | 21.4 | 21.6 | 33.6 | 23.4 |
| Vehicle rental, leases, licenses, other | 100.0 | 24.6 | 22.9 | 23.9 | 28.6 |
| **Public transportation** | **100.0** | **29.8** | **21.0** | **21.6** | **27.6** |
| **HEALTH CARE** | **100.0%** | **18.5%** | **24.7%** | **36.0%** | **20.7%** |
| Health insurance | 100.0 | 19.7 | 24.7 | 36.9 | 18.7 |
| Medical services | 100.0 | 18.1 | 23.4 | 33.0 | 25.5 |
| Drugs | 100.0 | 15.0 | 26.7 | 40.0 | 18.4 |
| Medical supplies | 100.0 | 22.0 | 25.0 | 32.9 | 20.1 |
| **ENTERTAINMENT** | **100.0%** | **19.5%** | **25.2%** | **30.0%** | **25.2%** |
| Fees and admissions | 100.0 | 22.4 | 23.7 | 26.5 | 27.2 |
| Television, radio, sound equipment | 100.0 | 20.1 | 23.2 | 34.5 | 22.3 |
| Pets, toys, playground equipment | 100.0 | 19.5 | 23.7 | 31.9 | 24.6 |
| Other entertainment supplies, equipment, services | 100.0 | 15.5 | 30.5 | 26.5 | 27.3 |
| **PERSONAL CARE PRODUCTS & SERVICES** | **100.0%** | **19.7%** | **22.9%** | **35.9%** | **21.3%** |
| **READING** | **100.0%** | **23.4%** | **24.8%** | **27.7%** | **24.1%** |
| **EDUCATION** | **100.0%** | **27.0%** | **21.4%** | **27.4%** | **24.1%** |
| **TOBACCO PRODUCTS & SMOKING SUPPLIES** | **100.0%** | **19.7%** | **27.3%** | **35.4%** | **17.5%** |
| **MISCELLANEOUS** | **100.0%** | **19.4%** | **23.2%** | **33.2%** | **24.2%** |
| Cash contributions | 100.0 | 15.3 | 23.6 | 36.8 | 24.3 |
| Personal insurance and pensions | 100.0 | 20.4 | 23.2 | 31.2 | 25.2 |

*(continued)*

(continued from previous page)

| | total | Northeast | Midwest | South | West |
|---|---|---|---|---|---|
| Life and other personal insurance | 100.0% | 20.3% | 22.8% | 38.8% | 18.0% |
| Pensions and Social Security | 100.0 | 20.5 | 23.2 | 30.2 | 26.1 |
| **PERSONAL TAXES** | **100.0%** | **19.5%** | **24.5%** | **25.8%** | **29.7%** |
| Federal income taxes | 100.0 | 18.5 | 23.3 | 27.1 | 30.5 |
| State and local income taxes | 100.0 | 22.3 | 28.5 | 20.5 | 28.7 |
| Other taxes | 100.0 | 26.6 | 26.9 | 27.6 | 19.6 |
| **GIFTS** | **100.0%** | **22.4%** | **24.0%** | **31.4%** | **22.3%** |
| **Food** | **100.0** | **22.9** | **23.9** | **31.8** | **21.2** |
| **Housing** | **100.0** | **21.7** | **25.2** | **31.3** | **21.8** |
| Housekeeping supplies | 100.0 | 21.1 | 31.0 | 28.3 | 18.4 |
| Household textiles | 100.0 | 25.0 | 23.9 | 30.5 | 23.9 |
| Appliances and miscellaneous housewares | 100.0 | 22.9 | 29.2 | 31.0 | 18.1 |
| Major appliances | 100.0 | 26.6 | 23.9 | 34.9 | 24.8 |
| Small appliances, misc. housewares | 100.0 | 21.9 | 31.9 | 29.9 | 16.2 |
| Miscellaneous household equipment | 100.0 | 19.7 | 26.8 | 30.1 | 23.5 |
| Other housing | 100.0 | 22.5 | 21.9 | 33.1 | 22.3 |
| **Apparel and services** | **100.0** | **21.6** | **22.9** | **34.9** | **20.7** |
| Males, 2 and over | 100.0 | 20.3 | 27.8 | 30.9 | 21.2 |
| Females, 2 and over | 100.0 | 21.7 | 26.8 | 31.4 | 20.5 |
| Children under 2 | 100.0 | 21.2 | 19.6 | 31.7 | 25.7 |
| Other apparel products, services | 100.0 | 22.3 | 16.4 | 43.5 | 18.2 |
| Jewelry and watches | 100.0 | 20.8 | 15.1 | 45.6 | 18.2 |
| All other apparel products, services | 100.0 | 24.1 | 18.1 | 38.5 | 17.6 |
| **Transportation** | **100.0** | **15.4** | **21.8** | **31.8** | **30.6** |
| **Health care** | **100.0** | **14.6** | **17.5** | **23.3** | **45.3** |
| **Entertainment** | **100.0** | **19.4** | **27.5** | **31.0** | **22.1** |
| Toys, games, hobbies, tricycles | 100.0 | 16.1 | 29.7 | 33.2 | 20.7 |
| Other entertainment | 100.0 | 21.7 | 25.5 | 29.5 | 23.1 |
| **Education** | **100.0** | **33.1** | **23.4** | **25.7** | **18.1** |
| **All other gifts** | **100.0** | **19.5** | **23.9** | **33.2** | **23.1** |

*Note: The Bureau of Labor Statistics uses consumer units rather than households as the sampling unit in the Consumer Expenditure Survey. For the definition of consumer unit, see the Glossary. Numbers may not add to total due to rounding.*
*Source: Calculations by New Strategist based on the Bureau of Labor Statistics' 1997 Consumer Expenditure Survey*

# College Graduates Spend More

## Because college graduates earn more, they spend more, too.

College graduates have much higher incomes than those who did not graduate from college. Consequently, they spend more. In 1997, households headed by college graduates spent $50,324—45 percent more than the $34,819 spent by the average household.

The Indexed Spending table in this section compares the spending of households by education with average household spending. An index of 100 means households in the educational group spend the average amount on an item. An index above 100 means households in the educational group spend more than average on the item, while an index below 100 signifies below-average spending.

Households headed by college graduates spend like the yuppies many of them are. Their spending on beef, pork, and eggs is below average, but they spend well above average on fish and seafood, fresh fruits and vegetables, restaurant meals, and alcoholic beverages. They spend only an average amount on laundry and cleaning supplies, but much more than average on household textiles (bedroom and bathroom linens, for example). They spend twice as much as the average household on

## College graduates spend like yuppies

*(indexed average annual spending of college graduates on selected products and services)*

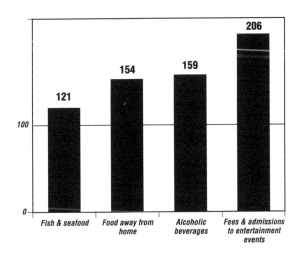

fees and admissions to entertainment events, but only about half the average on tobacco.

The Market Share table in this section shows how much of total household spending by category is accounted for by households in each educational group. College graduates spend disproportionately more than their share of households while those who did not graduate from college spend less.

College graduates head 25 percent of households, but account for 35 percent of household spending. On some items their spending is even higher. They account for 52 percent of spending on other lodging, which includes hotel and motel expenses. They account for 43 percent of spending on leased vehicles and 50 percent of spending on public transportation (including airline fares). They account for 51 percent of spending on fees and admission to entertainment events and for 50 percent of all education spending. They also account for over half the spending on gifts of jewelry and watches.

◆ As the proportion of older adults with a college degree rises, the spending of college graduates on products purchased by older consumers—such as drugs—will rise.

# Spending by Education of Householder, 1997

*(average annual spending of consumer units by product and service category and educational attainment of consumer unit (cu) reference person, 1997)*

|  | total consumer units | not a high school graduate | high school graduate | some college or associate's degree | college degree or more |
|---|---|---|---|---|---|
| Number of consumer units (in 000s) | 105,576 | 18,920 | 30,782 | 30,010 | 25,863 |
| Average number of persons per cu | 2.5 | 2.7 | 2.6 | 2.5 | 2.5 |
| Average before-tax income | $39,926 | $21,413 | $33,461 | $38,276 | $62,721 |
| Average annual expenditures | 34,819 | 22,026 | 29,726 | 34,438 | 50,324 |
| **FOOD** | **$4,801** | **$3,744** | **$4,399** | **$4,547** | **$6,202** |
| FOOD AT HOME | 2,880 | 2,773 | 2,822 | 2,666 | 3,241 |
| **Cereals and bakery products** | 453 | 421 | 440 | 418 | 524 |
| Cereals and cereal products | 161 | 156 | 150 | 152 | 188 |
| Bakery products | 292 | 266 | 290 | 267 | 336 |
| **Meats, poultry, fish, and eggs** | 743 | 838 | 758 | 685 | 730 |
| Beef | 224 | 247 | 231 | 217 | 207 |
| Pork | 157 | 199 | 173 | 138 | 134 |
| Other meats | 96 | 107 | 98 | 93 | 92 |
| Poultry | 145 | 151 | 141 | 131 | 160 |
| Fish and seafood | 89 | 93 | 79 | 77 | 108 |
| Eggs | 33 | 40 | 35 | 30 | 28 |
| **Dairy products** | 314 | 281 | 308 | 292 | 363 |
| Fresh milk and cream | 128 | 135 | 131 | 119 | 131 |
| Other dairy products | 186 | 146 | 178 | 173 | 231 |
| **Fruits and vegetables** | 476 | 454 | 434 | 422 | 590 |
| Fresh fruits | 150 | 142 | 135 | 132 | 191 |
| Fresh vegetables | 143 | 141 | 124 | 124 | 184 |
| Processed fruits | 102 | 88 | 92 | 93 | 133 |
| Processed vegetables | 80 | 83 | 83 | 73 | 82 |
| **Other food at home** | 895 | 779 | 881 | 848 | 1,034 |
| Sugar and other sweets | 114 | 105 | 113 | 108 | 128 |
| Fats and oils | 81 | 88 | 82 | 76 | 82 |
| Miscellaneous foods | 403 | 329 | 393 | 387 | 478 |
| Nonalcoholic beverages | 245 | 233 | 251 | 228 | 263 |
| Food prepared by household on trips | 52 | 24 | 43 | 50 | 83 |
| FOOD AWAY FROM HOME | 1,921 | 971 | 1,578 | 1,881 | 2,961 |
| **ALCOHOLIC BEVERAGES** | **$309** | **$144** | **$244** | **$304** | **$490** |

*(continued)*

(continued from previous page)

| | total consumer units | not a high school graduate | high school graduate | some college or associate's degree | college degree or more |
|---|---|---|---|---|---|
| **HOUSING** | **$11,272** | **$7,247** | **$9,502** | **$11,267** | **$16,278** |
| **SHELTER** | **6,344** | **3,831** | **5,128** | **6,369** | **9,600** |
| **Owned dwellings** | **3,935** | **1,903** | **3,064** | **3,874** | **6,528** |
| Mortgage interest and charges | 2,225 | 879 | 1,587 | 2,298 | 3,885 |
| Property taxes | 971 | 546 | 828 | 859 | 1,582 |
| Maintenance, repairs, insurance, other | 738 | 478 | 648 | 717 | 1,061 |
| **Rented dwellings** | **1,983** | **1,825** | **1,805** | **2,110** | **2,164** |
| **Other lodging** | **426** | **102** | **259** | **385** | **908** |
| **UTILITIES, FUELS,** | | | | | |
| **PUBLIC SERVICES** | **2,412** | **2,098** | **2,346** | **2,360** | **2,782** |
| Natural gas | 301 | 269 | 285 | 286 | 360 |
| Electricity | 909 | 837 | 934 | 880 | 965 |
| Fuel oil and other fuels | 108 | 102 | 129 | 90 | 107 |
| Telephone services | 809 | 651 | 728 | 826 | 1,001 |
| Water and other public services | 286 | 239 | 270 | 279 | 348 |
| **HOUSEHOLD SERVICES** | **548** | **199** | **380** | **535** | **1,018** |
| Personal services | 263 | 90 | 216 | 272 | 435 |
| Other household expenses | 285 | 109 | 165 | 263 | 583 |
| **HOUSEKEEPING SUPPLIES** | **455** | **326** | **407** | **454** | **587** |
| Laundry and cleaning supplies | 116 | 116 | 115 | 113 | 119 |
| Other household products | 210 | 143 | 183 | 208 | 283 |
| Postage and stationery | 129 | 68 | 109 | 133 | 185 |
| **HOUSEHOLD FURNISHINGS** | | | | | |
| **AND EQUIPMENT** | **1,512** | **793** | **1,241** | **1,549** | **2,290** |
| Household textiles | 79 | 38 | 65 | 78 | 127 |
| Furniture | 387 | 201 | 321 | 377 | 614 |
| Floor coverings | 78 | 21 | 79 | 82 | 110 |
| Major appliances | 169 | 128 | 153 | 173 | 214 |
| Small appliances, misc. housewares | 92 | 63 | 76 | 83 | 139 |
| Miscellaneous household equipment | 707 | 342 | 546 | 756 | 1,086 |
| **APPAREL AND SERVICES** | **$1,729** | **$1,086** | **$1,465** | **$1,658** | **$2,507** |
| **Men and boys** | **407** | **268** | **345** | **397** | **579** |
| Men, 16 and over | 323 | 205 | 261 | 311 | 483 |
| Boys, 2 to 15 | 84 | 63 | 84 | 86 | 95 |
| **Women and girls** | **680** | **408** | **581** | **647** | **998** |
| Women, 16 and over | 574 | 327 | 489 | 536 | 866 |
| Girls, 2 to 15 | 106 | 82 | 92 | 111 | 132 |

(continued)

*(continued from previous page)*

| | total consumer units | not a high school graduate | high school graduate | some college or associate's degree | college degree or more |
|---|---|---|---|---|---|
| Children under 2 | $77 | $53 | $82 | $75 | $91 |
| Footwear | 315 | 228 | 279 | 324 | 396 |
| Other apparel products, services | 250 | 130 | 178 | 215 | 443 |
| **TRANSPORTATION** | **$6,457** | **$4,131** | **$5,780** | **$6,714** | **$8,657** |
| **Vehicle purchases** | **2,736** | **1,906** | **2,479** | **2,918** | **3,437** |
| Cars and trucks, new | 1,229 | 340 | 1,124 | 1,333 | 1,884 |
| Cars and trucks, used | 1,464 | 1,557 | 1,323 | 1,531 | 1,485 |
| Other vehicles | 43 | 9 | 32 | 54 | 68 |
| **Gasoline and motor oil** | **1,098** | **791** | **1,102** | **1,128** | **1,280** |
| **Other vehicle expenses** | **2,230** | **1,252** | **1,956** | **2,341** | **3,136** |
| Vehicle finance charges | 293 | 188 | 310 | 336 | 299 |
| Maintenance and repairs | 682 | 416 | 566 | 705 | 981 |
| Vehicle insurance | 755 | 484 | 714 | 769 | 986 |
| Vehicle rental, leases, licenses, other | 501 | 165 | 367 | 531 | 870 |
| **Public transportation** | **393** | **182** | **243** | **327** | **804** |
| **HEALTH CARE** | **$1,841** | **$1,589** | **$1,719** | **$1,689** | **$2,343** |
| Health insurance | 881 | 796 | 857 | 794 | 1,074 |
| Medical services | 531 | 339 | 443 | 520 | 788 |
| Drugs | 320 | 367 | 334 | 268 | 329 |
| Medical supplies | 108 | 88 | 85 | 106 | 151 |
| **ENTERTAINMENT** | **$1,813** | **$843** | **$1,499** | **$1,854** | **$2,827** |
| Fees and admissions | 471 | 112 | 286 | 456 | 970 |
| Television, radio, sound equipment | 577 | 383 | 550 | 624 | 698 |
| Pets, toys, playground equipment | 327 | 176 | 292 | 337 | 453 |
| Other entertainment supplies, equipment, services | 439 | 173 | 370 | 436 | 706 |
| **PERSONAL CARE PRODUCTS & SERVICES** | **$528** | **$342** | **$471** | **$563** | **$681** |
| **READING** | **$164** | **$75** | **$121** | **$153** | **$290** |
| **EDUCATION** | **$571** | **$125** | **$286** | **$627** | **$1,166** |
| **TOBACCO PRODUCTS & SMOKING SUPPLIES** | **$264** | **$308** | **$333** | **$270** | **$141** |
| **MISCELLANEOUS** | **$847** | **$532** | **$796** | **$824** | **$1,165** |
| Cash contributions | 1,001 | 546 | 674 | 831 | 1,921 |
| Personal insurance and pensions | 3,223 | 1,312 | 2,438 | 3,137 | 5,656 |

*(continued)*

(continued from previous page)

| | total consumer units | not a high school graduate | high school graduate | some college or associate's degree | college degree or more |
|---|---|---|---|---|---|
| Life and other personal insurance | $379 | $242 | $316 | $360 | $575 |
| Pensions and Social Security | 2,844 | 1,069 | 2,122 | 2,777 | 5,081 |
| **PERSONAL TAXES** | **$3,241** | **$929** | **$2,049** | **$3,227** | **$6,313** |
| Federal income taxes | 2,468 | 652 | 1,503 | 2,471 | 4,898 |
| State and local income taxes | 645 | 213 | 426 | 651 | 1,203 |
| Other taxes | 129 | 63 | 121 | 105 | 213 |
| **GIFTS** | **$1,059** | **$502** | **$857** | **$1,016** | **$1,728** |
| **Food** | **68** | **17** | **47** | **66** | **127** |
| **Housing** | **273** | **138** | **235** | **260** | **425** |
| Housekeeping supplies | 37 | 18 | 32 | 32 | 59 |
| Household textiles | 8 | 4 | 8 | 8 | 12 |
| Appliances and miscellaneous housewares | 27 | 11 | 26 | 21 | 46 |
| Major appliances | 6 | 4 | 7 | 6 | 8 |
| Small appliances, misc. housewares | 21 | 7 | 20 | 15 | 38 |
| Miscellaneous household equipment | 66 | 29 | 55 | 66 | 104 |
| Other housing | 135 | 77 | 113 | 133 | 205 |
| **Apparel and services** | **252** | **165** | **211** | **250** | **354** |
| Males, 2 and over | 61 | 41 | 53 | 62 | 82 |
| Females, 2 and over | 81 | 65 | 74 | 81 | 99 |
| Children under 2 | 33 | 21 | 37 | 33 | 35 |
| Other apparel products, services | 77 | 38 | 47 | 75 | 137 |
| Jewelry and watches | 49 | 9 | 26 | 45 | 101 |
| All other apparel products, services | 29 | 29 | 20 | 29 | 36 |
| **Transportation** | **57** | **24** | **50** | **55** | **91** |
| **Health care** | **30** | **14** | **19** | **30** | **57** |
| **Entertainment** | **99** | **49** | **90** | **101** | **141** |
| Toys, games, hobbies, tricycles | 41 | 25 | 45 | 31 | 57 |
| Other entertainment | 58 | 24 | 45 | 70 | 84 |
| **Education** | **155** | **37** | **102** | **107** | **361** |
| **All other gifts** | **125** | **59** | **103** | **147** | **172** |

*Note: The Bureau of Labor Statistics uses consumer units rather than households as the sampling unit in the Consumer Expenditure Survey. For the definition of consumer unit, see the Glossary. Spending on gifts is also included in the preceding product and service categories.*
*Source: Bureau of Labor Statistics, 1997 Consumer Expenditure Survey*

# Indexed Spending by Education of Householder, 1997

*(indexed average annual spending of consumer units by product and service category and educational attainment of consumer unit reference person, 1997)*

| | total consumer units | not a high school graduate | high school graduate | some college or associate's degree | college degree or more |
|---|---|---|---|---|---|
| Number of consumer units (in 000s) | 105,576 | 18,920 | 30,782 | 30,010 | 25,863 |
| Indexed average before-tax income | 100 | 54 | 84 | 96 | 157 |
| Indexed average annual expenditures | 100 | 63 | 85 | 99 | 145 |
| **FOOD** | **100** | **78** | **92** | **95** | **129** |
| **FOOD AT HOME** | **100** | **96** | **98** | **93** | **113** |
| **Cereals and bakery products** | **100** | **93** | **97** | **92** | **116** |
| Cereals and cereal products | 100 | 97 | 93 | 94 | 117 |
| Bakery products | 100 | 91 | 99 | 91 | 115 |
| **Meats, poultry, fish, and eggs** | **100** | **113** | **102** | **92** | **98** |
| Beef | 100 | 110 | 103 | 97 | 92 |
| Pork | 100 | 127 | 110 | 88 | 85 |
| Other meats | 100 | 111 | 102 | 97 | 96 |
| Poultry | 100 | 104 | 97 | 90 | 110 |
| Fish and seafood | 100 | 104 | 89 | 86 | 121 |
| Eggs | 100 | 121 | 106 | 90 | 85 |
| **Dairy products** | **100** | **89** | **98** | **93** | **116** |
| Fresh milk and cream | 100 | 105 | 102 | 93 | 102 |
| Other dairy products | 100 | 78 | 96 | 93 | 124 |
| **Fruits and vegetables** | **100** | **95** | **91** | **89** | **124** |
| Fresh fruits | 100 | 95 | 90 | 88 | 127 |
| Fresh vegetables | 100 | 99 | 87 | 86 | 129 |
| Processed fruits | 100 | 86 | 90 | 92 | 130 |
| Processed vegetables | 100 | 104 | 104 | 92 | 103 |
| **Other food at home** | **100** | **87** | **98** | **95** | **116** |
| Sugar and other sweets | 100 | 92 | 99 | 95 | 112 |
| Fats and oils | 100 | 109 | 101 | 94 | 101 |
| Miscellaneous foods | 100 | 82 | 98 | 96 | 119 |
| Nonalcoholic beverages | 100 | 95 | 102 | 93 | 107 |
| Food prepared by household on trips | 100 | 46 | 83 | 96 | 160 |
| **FOOD AWAY FROM HOME** | **100** | **51** | **82** | **98** | **154** |
| **ALCOHOLIC BEVERAGES** | **100** | **47** | **79** | **98** | **159** |

*(continued)*

*(continued from previous page)*

| | total consumer units | not a high school graduate | high school graduate | some college or associate's degree | college degree or more |
|---|---|---|---|---|---|
| **HOUSING** | **100** | **64** | **84** | **100** | **144** |
| **SHELTER** | **100** | **60** | **81** | **100** | **151** |
| **Owned dwellings** | **100** | **48** | **78** | **98** | **166** |
| Mortgage interest and charges | 100 | 40 | 71 | 103 | 175 |
| Property taxes | 100 | 56 | 85 | 88 | 163 |
| Maintenance, repairs, insurance, other | 100 | 65 | 88 | 97 | 144 |
| **Rented dwellings** | **100** | **92** | **91** | **106** | **109** |
| **Other lodging** | **100** | **24** | **61** | **90** | **213** |
| **UTILITIES, FUELS,** | | | | | |
| **PUBLIC SERVICES** | **100** | **87** | **97** | **98** | **115** |
| Natural gas | 100 | 89 | 95 | 95 | 120 |
| Electricity | 100 | 92 | 103 | 97 | 106 |
| Fuel oil and other fuels | 100 | 94 | 119 | 83 | 99 |
| Telephone services | 100 | 80 | 90 | 102 | 124 |
| Water and other public services | 100 | 84 | 94 | 97 | 122 |
| **HOUSEHOLD SERVICES** | **100** | **36** | **69** | **98** | **186** |
| Personal services | 100 | 34 | 82 | 103 | 165 |
| Other household expenses | 100 | 38 | 58 | 92 | 205 |
| **HOUSEKEEPING SUPPLIES** | **100** | **72** | **89** | **100** | **129** |
| Laundry and cleaning supplies | 100 | 100 | 99 | 98 | 103 |
| Other household products | 100 | 68 | 87 | 99 | 135 |
| Postage and stationery | 100 | 53 | 84 | 103 | 143 |
| **HOUSEHOLD FURNISHINGS** | | | | | |
| **AND EQUIPMENT** | **100** | **52** | **82** | **102** | **151** |
| Household textiles | 100 | 48 | 82 | 98 | 161 |
| Furniture | 100 | 52 | 83 | 97 | 159 |
| Floor coverings | 100 | 27 | 101 | 105 | 141 |
| Major appliances | 100 | 76 | 91 | 102 | 127 |
| Small appliances, misc. housewares | 100 | 68 | 83 | 90 | 151 |
| Miscellaneous household equipment | 100 | 48 | 77 | 107 | 154 |
| **APPAREL AND SERVICES** | **100** | **63** | **85** | **96** | **145** |
| **Men and boys** | **100** | **66** | **85** | **98** | **142** |
| Men, 16 and over | 100 | 63 | 81 | 96 | 150 |
| Boys, 2 to 15 | 100 | 75 | 100 | 102 | 113 |
| **Women and girls** | **100** | **60** | **85** | **95** | **147** |
| Women, 16 and over | 100 | 57 | 85 | 93 | 151 |
| Girls, 2 to 15 | 100 | 77 | 87 | 105 | 125 |

*(continued)*

*(continued from previous page)*

| | total consumer units | not a high school graduate | high school graduate | some college or associate's degree | college degree or more |
|---|---|---|---|---|---|
| Children under 2 | 100 | 69 | 106 | 97 | 118 |
| Footwear | 100 | 72 | 89 | 103 | 126 |
| Other apparel products, services | 100 | 52 | 71 | 86 | 177 |
| **TRANSPORTATION** | **100** | **64** | **90** | **104** | **134** |
| **Vehicle purchases** | **100** | **70** | **91** | **107** | **126** |
| Cars and trucks, new | 100 | 28 | 91 | 108 | 153 |
| Cars and trucks, used | 100 | 106 | 90 | 105 | 101 |
| Other vehicles | 100 | 21 | 74 | 126 | 158 |
| **Gasoline and motor oil** | **100** | **72** | **100** | **103** | **117** |
| **Other vehicle expenses** | **100** | **56** | **88** | **105** | **141** |
| Vehicle finance charges | 100 | 64 | 106 | 115 | 102 |
| Maintenance and repairs | 100 | 61 | 83 | 103 | 144 |
| Vehicle insurance | 100 | 64 | 95 | 102 | 131 |
| Vehicle rental, leases, licenses, other | 100 | 33 | 73 | 106 | 174 |
| **Public transportation** | **100** | **46** | **62** | **83** | **205** |
| **HEALTH CARE** | **100** | **86** | **93** | **92** | **127** |
| Health insurance | 100 | 90 | 97 | 90 | 122 |
| Medical services | 100 | 64 | 83 | 98 | 148 |
| Drugs | 100 | 115 | 104 | 84 | 103 |
| Medical supplies | 100 | 81 | 79 | 99 | 140 |
| **ENTERTAINMENT** | **100** | **46** | **83** | **102** | **156** |
| Fees and admissions | 100 | 24 | 61 | 97 | 206 |
| Television, radio, sound equipment | 100 | 66 | 95 | 108 | 121 |
| Pets, toys, playground equipment | 100 | 54 | 89 | 103 | 139 |
| Other entertainment supplies, equipment, services | 100 | 39 | 84 | 99 | 161 |
| **PERSONAL CARE PRODUCTS & SERVICES** | **100** | **65** | **89** | **107** | **129** |
| **READING** | **100** | **46** | **74** | **93** | **177** |
| **EDUCATION** | **100** | **22** | **50** | **110** | **204** |
| **TOBACCO PRODUCTS & SMOKING SUPPLIES** | **100** | **117** | **126** | **102** | **53** |
| **MISCELLANEOUS** | **100** | **63** | **94** | **97** | **138** |
| Cash contributions | 100 | 55 | 67 | 83 | 192 |
| Personal insurance and pensions | 100 | 41 | 76 | 97 | 175 |

*(continued)*

*(continued from previous page)*

| | total consumer units | not a high school graduate | high school graduate | some college or associate's degree | college degree or more |
|---|---|---|---|---|---|
| Life and other personal insurance | 100 | 64 | 83 | 95 | 152 |
| Pensions and Social Security | 100 | 38 | 75 | 98 | 179 |
| **PERSONAL TAXES** | **100** | **29** | **63** | **100** | **195** |
| Federal income taxes | 100 | 26 | 61 | 100 | 198 |
| State and local income taxes | 100 | 33 | 66 | 101 | 187 |
| Other taxes | 100 | 49 | 94 | 81 | 165 |
| **GIFTS** | **100** | **47** | **81** | **96** | **163** |
| **Food** | **100** | **25** | **69** | **97** | **187** |
| **Housing** | **100** | **51** | **86** | **95** | **156** |
| Housekeeping supplies | 100 | 49 | 86 | 85 | 159 |
| Household textiles | 100 | 50 | 100 | 102 | 150 |
| Appliances and miscellaneous housewares | 100 | 41 | 96 | 79 | 170 |
| Major appliances | 100 | 67 | 117 | 105 | 133 |
| Small appliances, misc. housewares | 100 | 33 | 95 | 71 | 181 |
| Miscellaneous household equipment | 100 | 44 | 83 | 99 | 158 |
| Other housing | 100 | 57 | 84 | 99 | 152 |
| **Apparel and services** | **100** | **65** | **84** | **99** | **140** |
| Males, 2 and over | 100 | 67 | 87 | 102 | 134 |
| Females, 2 and over | 100 | 80 | 91 | 100 | 122 |
| Children under 2 | 100 | 64 | 112 | 99 | 106 |
| Other apparel products, services | 100 | 49 | 61 | 97 | 178 |
| Jewelry and watches | 100 | 18 | 53 | 93 | 206 |
| All other apparel products, services | 100 | 100 | 69 | 100 | 124 |
| **Transportation** | **100** | **42** | **88** | **96** | **160** |
| **Health care** | **100** | **47** | **63** | **99** | **190** |
| **Entertainment** | **100** | **49** | **91** | **102** | **142** |
| Toys, games, hobbies, tricycles | 100 | 61 | 110 | 76 | 139 |
| Other entertainment | 100 | 41 | 78 | 120 | 145 |
| **Education** | **100** | **24** | **66** | **69** | **233** |
| **All other gifts** | **100** | **47** | **82** | **118** | **138** |

*Note: The Bureau of Labor Statistics uses consumer units rather than households as the sampling unit in the Consumer Expenditure Survey. For the definition of consumer unit, see the Glossary. An index of 100 is the average for all households. An index of 132 means households at that educational level spend 32 percent more than the average household. An index of 75 means households at that educational level spend 25 percent less than the average household.*

*Source: Calculations by New Strategist based on the Bureau of Labor Statistics' 1997 Consumer Expenditure Survey*

# Market Shares by Education, 1997

*(share of total household spending accounted for by educational group, 1997)*

| | total consumer units | not a college graduate | college graduates |
|---|---|---|---|
| Share of total consumer units | 100.0% | 75.5% | 24.5% |
| Share of total annual spending | 100.0 | 64.3 | 35.4 |
| **FOOD** | **100.0%** | **67.6%** | **31.6%** |
| **FOOD AT HOME** | 100.0 | 72.1 | 27.6 |
| **Cereals and bakery products** | 100.0 | 71.2 | 28.3 |
| Cereals and cereal products | 100.0 | 71.4 | 28.6 |
| Bakery products | 100.0 | 71.2 | 28.2 |
| **Meats, poultry, fish, and eggs** | 100.0 | 76.2 | 24.1 |
| Beef | 100.0 | 77.4 | 22.6 |
| Pork | 100.0 | 79.9 | 20.9 |
| Other meats | 100.0 | 77.2 | 23.5 |
| Poultry | 100.0 | 72.7 | 27.0 |
| Fish and seafood | 100.0 | 69.1 | 29.7 |
| Eggs | 100.0 | 78.1 | 20.8 |
| **Dairy products** | 100.0 | 71.1 | 28.3 |
| Fresh milk and cream | 100.0 | 75.1 | 25.1 |
| Other dairy products | 100.0 | 68.5 | 30.4 |
| **Fruits and vegetables** | 100.0 | 68.9 | 30.4 |
| Fresh fruits | 100.0 | 68.2 | 31.2 |
| Fresh vegetables | 100.0 | 67.5 | 31.5 |
| Processed fruits | 100.0 | 67.8 | 31.9 |
| Processed vegetables | 100.0 | 74.9 | 25.1 |
| **Other food at home** | 100.0 | 71.2 | 28.3 |
| Sugar and other sweets | 100.0 | 72.4 | 27.5 |
| Fats and oils | 100.0 | 75.6 | 24.8 |
| Miscellaneous foods | 100.0 | 70.4 | 29.1 |
| Nonalcoholic beverages | 100.0 | 73.4 | 26.3 |
| Food prepared by household on trips | 100.0 | 59.8 | 39.1 |
| **FOOD AWAY FROM HOME** | 100.0 | 60.8 | 37.8 |
| **ALCOHOLIC BEVERAGES** | **100.0%** | **59.4%** | **38.8%** |

*(continued)*

(continued from previous page)

| | total consumer units | not a college graduate | college graduates |
|---|---|---|---|
| **HOUSING** | **100.0%** | **64.5%** | **35.4%** |
| **SHELTER** | **100.0** | **62.9** | **37.1** |
| **Owned dwellings** | **100.0** | **59.4** | **40.6** |
| Mortgage interest and charges | 100.0 | 57.2 | 42.8 |
| Property taxes | 100.0 | 60.1 | 39.9 |
| Maintenance, repairs, insurance, other | 100.0 | 64.8 | 35.2 |
| **Rented dwellings** | **100.0** | **73.3** | **26.7** |
| **Other lodging** | **100.0** | **47.7** | **52.2** |
| **UTILITIES, FUELS, PUBLIC SERVICES** | **100.0** | **71.8** | **28.3** |
| Natural gas | 100.0 | 70.7 | 29.3 |
| Electricity | 100.0 | 74.0 | 26.0 |
| Fuel oil and other fuels | 100.0 | 75.4 | 24.3 |
| Telephone services | 100.0 | 69.7 | 30.3 |
| Water and other public services | 100.0 | 70.2 | 29.8 |
| **HOUSEHOLD SERVICES** | **100.0** | **54.5** | **45.5** |
| Personal services | 100.0 | 59.5 | 40.5 |
| Other household expenses | 100.0 | 49.9 | 50.1 |
| **HOUSEKEEPING SUPPLIES** | **100.0** | **67.3** | **31.6** |
| Laundry and cleaning supplies | 100.0 | 74.6 | 25.1 |
| Other household products | 100.0 | 65.8 | 33.0 |
| Postage and stationery | 100.0 | 63.4 | 35.1 |
| **HOUSEHOLD FURNISHINGS AND EQUIPMENT** | **100.0** | **62.5** | **37.1** |
| Household textiles | 100.0 | 60.6 | 39.4 |
| Furniture | 100.0 | 61.2 | 38.9 |
| Floor coverings | 100.0 | 64.2 | 34.5 |
| Major appliances | 100.0 | 69.1 | 31.0 |
| Small appliances, misc. housewares | 100.0 | 62.0 | 37.0 |
| Miscellaneous household equipment | 100.0 | 61.6 | 37.6 |
| **APPAREL AND SERVICES** | **100.0%** | **63.2%** | **35.5%** |
| **Men and boys** | **100.0** | **64.2** | **34.8** |
| Men, 16 and over | 100.0 | 62.3 | 36.6 |
| Boys, 2 to 15 | 100.0 | 71.7 | 27.7 |
| **Women and girls** | **100.0** | **62.7** | **36.0** |
| Women, 16 and over | 100.0 | 61.6 | 37.0 |
| Girls, 2 to 15 | 100.0 | 68.9 | 30.5 |

(continued)

*(continued from previous page)*

| | total consumer units | not a college graduate | college graduates |
|---|---|---|---|
| Children under 2 | 100.0% | 70.9% | 29.0% |
| Footwear | 100.0 | 68.0 | 30.8 |
| Other apparel products, services | 100.0 | 54.5 | 43.4 |
| **TRANSPORTATION** | **100.0%** | **67.1%** | **32.8%** |
| **Vehicle purchases** | **100.0** | **69.2** | **30.8** |
| Cars and trucks, new | 100.0 | 62.4 | 37.6 |
| Cars and trucks, used | 100.0 | 75.1 | 24.8 |
| Other vehicles | 100.0 | 61.3 | 38.7 |
| **Gasoline and motor oil** | **100.0** | **71.4** | **28.6** |
| **Other vehicle expenses** | **100.0** | **65.5** | **34.4** |
| Vehicle finance charges | 100.0 | 74.9 | 25.0 |
| Maintenance and repairs | 100.0 | 64.5 | 35.2 |
| Vehicle insurance | 100.0 | 68.0 | 32.0 |
| Vehicle rental, leases, licenses, other | 100.0 | 57.4 | 42.5 |
| **Public transportation** | **100.0** | **50.0** | **50.1** |
| **HEALTH CARE** | **100.0%** | **68.8%** | **31.2%** |
| Health insurance | 100.0 | 70.2 | 29.9 |
| Medical services | 100.0 | 63.6 | 36.4 |
| Drugs | 100.0 | 74.8 | 25.2 |
| Medical supplies | 100.0 | 65.6 | 34.3 |
| **ENTERTAINMENT** | **100.0%** | **61.5%** | **38.2%** |
| Fees and admissions | 100.0 | 49.5 | 50.5 |
| Television, radio, sound equipment | 100.0 | 70.4 | 29.6 |
| Pets, toys, playground equipment | 100.0 | 64.9 | 33.9 |
| Other entertainment supplies, equip., services | 100.0 | 59.9 | 39.4 |
| **PERSONAL CARE PRODUCTS & SERVICES** | **100.0%** | **67.9%** | **31.6%** |
| **READING** | **100.0%** | **56.3%** | **43.3%** |
| **EDUCATION** | **100.0%** | **49.7%** | **50.0%** |
| **TOBACCO PRODUCTS & SMOKING SUPPLIES** | **100.0%** | **86.7%** | **13.1%** |
| **MISCELLANEOUS** | **100.0%** | **66.3%** | **33.7%** |
| Cash contributions | 100.0 | 53.0 | 47.0 |
| Personal insurance and pensions | 100.0 | 57.0 | 43.0 |

*(continued)*

*(continued from previous page)*

| | total consumer units | not a college graduate | college graduates |
|---|---|---|---|
| Life and other personal insurance | 100.0% | 62.7% | 37.2% |
| Pensions and Social Security | 100.0 | 56.2 | 43.8 |
| **PERSONAL TAXES** | **100.0%** | **51.9%** | **47.7%** |
| Federal income taxes | 100.0 | 50.9 | 48.6 |
| State and local income taxes | 100.0 | 53.9 | 45.7 |
| Other taxes | 100.0 | 59.2 | 40.4 |
| **GIFTS** | **100.0%** | **59.4%** | **40.0%** |
| **Food** | **100.0** | **52.2** | **45.8** |
| **Housing** | **100.0** | **61.2** | **38.1** |
| Housekeeping supplies | 100.0 | 58.2 | 39.1 |
| Household textiles | 100.0 | 63.3 | 36.7 |
| Appliances and miscellaneous housewares | 100.0 | 57.9 | 41.7 |
| Major appliances | 100.0 | 67.3 | 32.7 |
| Small appliances, miscellaneous housewares | 100.0 | 53.9 | 44.3 |
| Miscellaneous household equipment | 100.0 | 60.4 | 38.6 |
| Other housing | 100.0 | 62.7 | 37.2 |
| **Apparel and services** | **100.0** | **64.4** | **34.4** |
| Males, 2 and over | 100.0 | 66.4 | 32.9 |
| Females, 2 and over | 100.0 | 69.5 | 29.9 |
| Children under 2 | 100.0 | 72.2 | 26.0 |
| Other apparel products, services | 100.0 | 54.2 | 43.6 |
| Jewelry and watches | 100.0 | 45.1 | 50.5 |
| All other apparel products, services | 100.0 | 66.6 | 30.4 |
| **Transportation** | **100.0** | **60.4** | **39.1** |
| **Health care** | **100.0** | **54.9** | **46.5** |
| **Entertainment** | **100.0** | **64.3** | **34.9** |
| Toys, games, hobbies, tricycles | 100.0 | 64.4 | 34.1 |
| Other entertainment | 100.0 | 64.3 | 35.5 |
| **Education** | **100.0** | **43.1** | **57.1** |
| **All other gifts** | **100.0** | **66.0** | **33.7** |

*Note: The Bureau of Labor Statistics uses consumer units rather than households as the sampling unit in the Consumer Expenditure Survey. For the definition of consumer unit, see the Glossary. Numbers may not add to total due to rounding.*
*Source: Calculations by New Strategist based on the Bureau of Labor Statistics' 1997 Consumer Expenditure Survey*

# 8

# Wealth Trends

♦ **Most households have little wealth.**

The median net worth of the average household stood at $56,400 in 1995.

♦ **The median value of the financial assets owned by the average household amounted to just $13,000 in 1995.**

Nine out of 10 households own financial assets, which peak at $32,000 in median value for householders aged 55 to 64.

♦ **The median value of the nonfinancial assets owned by the average household stood at $83,000 in 1995.**

Owned homes are the biggest nonfinancial asset of most households.

♦ **Two-thirds of American households have debts.**

Median debt was $22,500 in 1995. Credit card debt is most common, held by 48 percent of households.

♦ **Homeownership is at a record high, reaching 66.2 percent in 1998.**

Homeownership has yet to reach record levels among young adults, however.

♦ **Forty-two percent of workers are covered by pensions.**

Among workers, women are almost as likely as men to have pension coverage.

# Net Worth Rises with Age

**In 1995, the median net worth of the average household stood at $56,400.**

Median net worth peaks in the 55-to-64 age group at $110,800. It is lowest among householders under age 35, at $11,400 in 1995 (the latest data available).

Net worth is defined as assets—both financial and nonfinancial—minus debts. Not surprisingly, net worth is greatest for households with incomes of $100,000 or more, which had a median of fully $486,000 in 1995. Households with incomes between $50,000 and $100,000 also have a median net worth of more than $100,000. But households with incomes below $50,000 have a smaller-than-average net worth.

Net worth also rises with education, but the correlation with education is not as strong as the correlation with age or income. This is because older people have the highest net worth, yet they are the least-educated Americans. As well-educated baby boomers age, the correlation between education and net worth will become much stronger.

The median net worth of non-Hispanic whites stood at $73,900 in 1995, compared with just $16,500 for nonwhites and Hispanics. One reason for this gap is the far lower homeownership rate among blacks and Hispanics.

◆ As boomers save for retirement, net worth should grow—particularly for the college educated and for people aged 45 to 64.

## Median net worth peaks in 55-to-64 age group

*(median net worth of households by age of householder, 1995)*

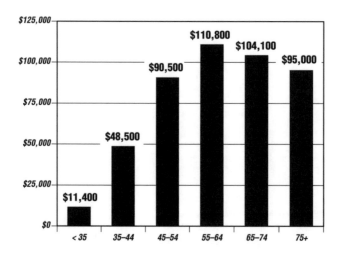

# Net Worth of Households, 1995

*(median net worth of households by selected characteristics of householders, 1995*

|  | *median net worth* |
|---|---|
| **Total households** | **$56,400** |
| **Income** | |
| Under $10,000 | 4,800 |
| $10,000 to $24,999 | 30,000 |
| $25,000 to $49,999 | 54,900 |
| $50,000 to $99,999 | 121,100 |
| $100,000 or more | 485,900 |
| **Age of householder** | |
| Under age 35 | 11,400 |
| Aged 35 to 44 | 48,500 |
| Aged 45 to 54 | 90,500 |
| Aged 55 to 64 | 110,800 |
| Aged 65 to 74 | 104,100 |
| Aged 75 or older | 95,000 |
| **Education of householder** | |
| No high school diploma | 26,300 |
| High school diploma | 50,000 |
| Some college | 43,200 |
| College degree | 104,100 |
| **Race or ethnicity of householder** | |
| Non-Hispanic white | 73,900 |
| Nonwhite or Hispanic | 16,500 |

*Source: Federal Reserve Board,* Family Finances in the U.S.: Recent Evidence from the Survey of Consumer Finances, *Federal Reserve Bulletin, January 1997*

# Americans Have Few Financial Assets

**The median value of the financial assets owned by the average household stood at $13,000 in 1995.**

For most Americans, the value of their financial assets—such as checking and savings accounts, retirement accounts, stocks, mutual funds, and the cash value of life insurance policies—does not add up to much. Even among householders aged 55 to 64—who supposedly are saving for retirement—financial assets amounted to only about $32,300 in 1995 (the latest data available).

Nine out of 10 households own some kind of financial asset, with the most common being transaction accounts such as checking and savings accounts. Forty-three percent of households own retirement accounts, and 31 percent own life insurance policies. All other financial assets are owned by fewer than one in four households.

The only households with considerable financial assets are those with incomes of $100,000 or more. These households had a median of $214,500 in financial assets in 1995, with a median of $85,000 in retirement accounts.

◆ With millions of Americans saving for retirement, the financial assets of households should expand considerably in the years ahead.

## Nonfinancial assets are greater than financial assets

*(median value of financial and nonfinancial assets for the average household, 1995)*

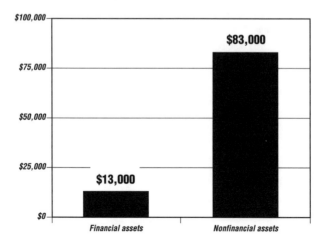

# Ownership of Financial Assets, 1995

*(percent of households owning financial assets, and median value of asset for owners, by selected characteristics of households and type of asset, 1995)*

| | any financial asset | transaction accounts | CDs | savings bonds | bonds | stocks | mutual funds | retirement accounts | life insurance | other managed | other financial |
|---|---|---|---|---|---|---|---|---|---|---|---|
| **PERCENT OWNING ASSET** | | | | | | | | | | | |
| **Total households** | 90.8% | 87.1% | 14.1% | 22.9% | 3.0% | 15.3% | 12.0% | 43.0% | 31.4% | 3.8% | 11.0% |
| **Income** | | | | | | | | | | | |
| Under $10,000 | 68.1 | 61.1 | 7.2 | 5.9 | – | 2.5 | 1.8 | 5.9 | 15.8 | – | 8.9 |
| $10,000 to $24,999 | 87.6 | 82.3 | 16.0 | 11.8 | – | 9.2 | 4.9 | 24.2 | 25.2 | 3.2 | 8.6 |
| $25,000 to $49,999 | 97.8 | 94.7 | 13.7 | 27.4 | 3.2 | 14.3 | 12.4 | 52.6 | 33.1 | 4.2 | 13.2 |
| $50,000 to $99,999 | 99.5 | 98.6 | 15.6 | 39.9 | 4.8 | 26.0 | 20.9 | 69.8 | 42.5 | 5.3 | 11.3 |
| $100,000 or more | 100.0 | 100.0 | 21.1 | 36.3 | 14.5 | 45.2 | 38.0 | 84.6 | 54.1 | 8.0 | 15.2 |
| **Age of householder** | | | | | | | | | | | |
| Under age 35 | 87.0 | 80.8 | 7.1 | 21.1 | 0.5 | 11.1 | 8.8 | 39.2 | 22.3 | 1.6 | 13.5 |
| Aged 35 to 44 | 92.0 | 87.4 | 8.2 | 31.0 | 1.6 | 14.5 | 10.5 | 51.5 | 28.9 | 3.4 | 10.5 |
| Aged 45 to 54 | 92.4 | 88.9 | 12.5 | 25.1 | 4.6 | 17.5 | 16.0 | 54.3 | 37.5 | 2.9 | 13.0 |
| Aged 55 to 64 | 90.5 | 88.2 | 16.2 | 19.6 | 2.9 | 14.9 | 15.2 | 47.2 | 37.5 | 7.1 | 9.0 |
| Aged 65 to 74 | 92.0 | 91.1 | 23.9 | 17.0 | 5.1 | 18.0 | 13.7 | 35.0 | 37.0 | 5.6 | 10.4 |
| Aged 75 or older | 93.8 | 93.0 | 34.1 | 15.3 | 7.0 | 21.3 | 10.4 | 16.5 | 35.1 | 5.7 | 5.3 |
| **Race and ethnicity of householder** | | | | | | | | | | | |
| Non-Hispanic white | 94.7 | 92.4 | 16.5 | 26.2 | 3.7 | 18.2 | 14.5 | 47.0 | 33.5 | 4.7 | 11.7 |
| Nonwhite or Hispanic | 77.4 | 69.1 | 5.9 | 11.3 | 0.6 | 5.5 | 3.5 | 29.2 | 24.4 | 1.0 | 8.5 |

*(continued)*

(continued from previous page)

## MEDIAN VALUE OF ASSET FOR OWNERS

| | any financial asset | transaction accounts | CDs | savings bonds | bonds | stocks | mutual funds | retirement accounts | life insurance | other managed | other financial |
|---|---|---|---|---|---|---|---|---|---|---|---|
| **Total households** | $13,000 | $2,100 | $10,000 | $1,000 | $26,200 | $8,000 | $19,000 | $15,600 | $5,000 | $30,000 | $3,000 |
| **Income** | | | | | | | | | | | |
| Under $10,000 | 1,200 | 700 | 7,000 | 400 | – | 2,000 | 25,000 | 3,500 | 1,500 | – | 2,000 |
| $10,000 to $24,999 | 5,400 | 1,400 | 10,000 | 800 | – | 5,700 | 8,000 | 6,000 | 3,000 | 19,700 | 2,000 |
| $25,000 to $49,999 | 12,100 | 2,000 | 10,000 | 700 | 29,000 | 6,900 | 12,500 | 10,000 | 5,000 | 25,000 | 2,500 |
| $50,000 to $99,999 | 40,700 | 4,500 | 13,000 | 1,200 | 9,400 | 5,700 | 15,000 | 23,000 | 7,000 | 35,000 | 3,000 |
| $100,000 or more | 214,500 | 15,800 | 15,600 | 1,500 | 58,000 | 30,000 | 48,000 | 85,000 | 12,000 | 62,500 | 23,000 |
| **Age of householder** | | | | | | | | | | | |
| Under age 35 | 5,300 | 1,200 | 6,000 | 500 | 2,000 | 3,700 | 5,000 | 5,200 | 3,400 | 3,800 | 1,000 |
| Aged 35 to 44 | 11,600 | 2,000 | 6,000 | 1,000 | 11,000 | 4,000 | 10,000 | 12,000 | 5,000 | 10,800 | 2,000 |
| Aged 45 to 54 | 24,800 | 2,700 | 12,000 | 1,000 | 17,000 | 10,000 | 17,500 | 25,000 | 6,500 | 43,000 | 5,000 |
| Aged 55 to 64 | 32,300 | 3,000 | 14,000 | 1,100 | 10,000 | 17,000 | 55,000 | 32,800 | 6,000 | 42,000 | 9,000 |
| Aged 65 to 74 | 19,100 | 3,000 | 17,000 | 1,500 | 58,000 | 15,000 | 50,000 | 28,500 | 5,000 | 26,000 | 9,000 |
| Aged 75 or older | 20,900 | 5,000 | 11,000 | 4,000 | 40,000 | 25,000 | 50,000 | 17,500 | 5,000 | 100,000 | 35,000 |
| **Race and ethnicity of householder** | | | | | | | | | | | |
| Non-Hispanic white | 16,900 | 2,500 | 10,000 | 1,000 | 26,200 | 8,600 | 20,000 | 17,500 | 5,000 | 30,000 | 4,000 |
| Nonwhite or Hispanic | 5,200 | 1,500 | 10,000 | 500 | 27,000 | 5,000 | 7,800 | 9,600 | 5,000 | 1,800 | 1,500 |

*Note: (–) means sample is too small to make a reliable estimate.*
*Source: Federal Reserve Board, Family Finances in the U.S.: Recent Evidence from the Survey of Consumer Finances, Federal Reserve Bulletin, January 1997*

# Homes Are the Biggest Nonfinancial Asset

## The primary residence accounts for 65 percent of the average household's nonfinancial assets.

The median value of the average American home was $90,000 in 1995. Although a greater percentage of households own a vehicle (84 percent) than own a home (65 percent), the median value of vehicles was just $10,000.

Not surprisingly, ownership of nonfinancial assets rises with income, as does the median value of those assets. Ownership of nonfinancial assets also rises with age, peaking at 94 percent in the 55-to-64 age group. The median value of nonfinancial assets peaks in the 45-to-64 age group.

Whites and non-Hispanics are much more likely to own nonfinancial assets than nonwhites and Hispanics. The asset most likely to be owned by all racial and ethnic groups is a vehicle, owned by 71 percent of nonwhites and Hispanics and by 88 percent of non-Hispanic whites. The median value of the nonfinancial assets owned by nonwhites and Hispanics is far lower than that for non-Hispanic whites, $42,100 versus $93,000. Behind this difference is homeownership. Sixty-nine percent of non-Hispanic whites owned a home in 1995, compared with just 48 percent of nonwhites and Hispanics.

♦ Because nonfinancial assets account for the largest share of household wealth, and because homes account for the largest share of nonfinancial assets, trends in homeownership and home values have a major impact on Americans' wealth.

# Value of Nonfinancial Assets, 1995

*(percent of households owning nonfinancial assets, and median value of assets for owners, by selected characteristics of households and type of asset, 1995)*

| | any nonfinancial asset | vehicles | primary residence | investment real estate | business | other non-financial |
|---|---|---|---|---|---|---|
| **PERCENT OWNING ASSET** | | | | | | |
| **Total households** | **91.1%** | **84.2%** | **64.7%** | **17.5%** | **11.0%** | **9.0%** |
| **Income** | | | | | | |
| Under $10,000 | 69.8 | 57.7 | 37.6 | 6.9 | 4.8 | 3.8 |
| $10,000 to $24,999 | 89.4 | 82.7 | 55.4 | 11.5 | 6.2 | 6.2 |
| $25,000 to $49,999 | 96.6 | 92.2 | 68.4 | 16.5 | 9.8 | 9.6 |
| $50,000 to $99,999 | 99.1 | 93.3 | 84.4 | 24.9 | 17.5 | 11.5 |
| $100,000 or more | 99.4 | 90.2 | 91.1 | 52.3 | 32.1 | 22.6 |
| **Age of householder** | | | | | | |
| Under age 35 | 87.6 | 83.9 | 37.9 | 7.2 | 9.3 | 7.6 |
| Aged 35 to 44 | 90.9 | 85.1 | 64.6 | 14.4 | 13.9 | 10.2 |
| Aged 45 to 54 | 93.7 | 88.2 | 75.4 | 23.9 | 14.8 | 10.7 |
| Aged 55 to 64 | 94.0 | 88.7 | 82.1 | 26.9 | 11.7 | 9.8 |
| Aged 65 to 74 | 92.5 | 82.0 | 79.0 | 26.5 | 7.9 | 8.9 |
| Aged 75 or older | 90.2 | 72.8 | 73.0 | 16.6 | 3.8 | 5.4 |
| **Race and ethnicity of householder** | | | | | | |
| Non-Hispanic white | 94.9 | 88.1 | 69.4 | 19.7 | 12.6 | 10.5 |
| Nonwhite or Hispanic | 78.1 | 71.1 | 48.2 | 10.2 | 5.4 | 3.5 |

*(continued)*

*(continued from previous page)*

| MEDIAN VALUE OF | any nonfinancial asset | vehicles | primary residence | investment real estate | business | other non-financial |
|---|---|---|---|---|---|---|
| **ASSET FOR OWNERS** | | | | | | |
| **Total households** | **$83,000** | **$10,000** | **$90,000** | **$50,000** | **$41,000** | **$10,000** |
| **Income** | | | | | | |
| Under $10,000 | 13,100 | 3,600 | 40,000 | 16,200 | 50,600 | 2,500 |
| $10,000 to $24,999 | 44,500 | 6,100 | 65,000 | 30,000 | 30,000 | 8,000 |
| $25,000 to $49,999 | 81,500 | 11,100 | 80,000 | 40,000 | 26,300 | 6,000 |
| $50,000 to $99,999 | 145,200 | 16,200 | 120,000 | 57,300 | 30,000 | 14,000 |
| $100,000 or more | 319,300 | 22,800 | 200,000 | 130,000 | 300,000 | 20,000 |
| **Age of householder** | | | | | | |
| Under age 35 | 21,500 | 9,000 | 80,000 | 33,500 | 20,000 | 5,000 |
| Aged 35 to 44 | 95,600 | 10,700 | 95,000 | 45,000 | 35,000 | 9,000 |
| Aged 45 to 54 | 111,700 | 12,400 | 100,000 | 55,000 | 60,000 | 12,000 |
| Aged 55 to 64 | 107,000 | 11,900 | 85,000 | 82,500 | 75,000 | 10,000 |
| Aged 65 to 74 | 93,500 | 8,000 | 80,000 | 55,000 | 100,000 | 16,000 |
| Aged 75 or older | 79,000 | 5,300 | 80,000 | 20,000 | 30,000 | 15,000 |
| **Race and ethnicity of householder** | | | | | | |
| Non-Hispanic white | 93,000 | 10,800 | 92,000 | 50,000 | 45,000 | 10,000 |
| Nonwhite or Hispanic | 42,100 | 7,700 | 70,000 | 33,500 | 26,300 | 8,000 |

*Source: Federal Reserve Board,* Family Finances in the U.S.: Recent Evidence from the Survey of Consumer Finances, *Federal Reserve Bulletin, January 1997*

# Seventy-Five Percent of American Households Have Debt

## The median amount of debt stood at $22,500 in 1995.

Three-quarters of American households have debts, owing a median of $22,500 in 1995. Credit card debt is most common, with almost half of all households (48 percent) holding this form of debt. The biggest debts are for mortgages and home equity loans, with a median value of $51,000.

The percentage of American households with debt rises with income. In contrast, debt levels decline with age after peaking in the 35-to-54 age group. The expenses of buying a home and raising children explain why 87 percent of 35-to-54-year-olds are in debt. The proportion is a smaller 75 percent among 55-to-64-year-olds, then falls to 54 percent among 65-to-74-year-olds. Among householders aged 75 or older, a 30 percent minority have any debt.

The proportion of households with debt does not vary much by race or ethnicity. But the median amount of debt is much greater for non-Hispanic whites ($27,000) than for nonwhites and Hispanics ($12,200).

♦ Although the average American household is not deeply in debt, the total debt load carried by Americans is substantial because the enormous baby-boom generation is in the most debt-prone age group, 35 to 54.

### Credit card debt is most common

*(percent of households with debt by type, 1995)*

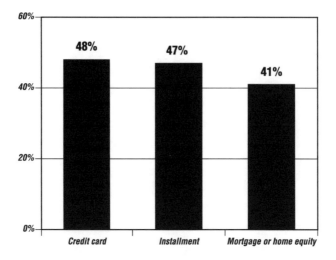

# Households with Debt, 1995

*(percent of households with debt, and median value of debt for those with debt, by selected characteristics of households and type of debt, 1995)*

| | any debt | mortgage and home equity | installment | other lines of credit | credit card | investment real estate | other debt |
|---|---|---|---|---|---|---|---|
| **PERCENT WITH DEBT** | | | | | | | |
| **Total households** | **75.2%** | **41.1%** | **46.5%** | **1.9%** | **47.8%** | **6.3%** | **9.0%** |
| **Income** | | | | | | | |
| Under $10,000 | 48.5 | 8.9 | 25.9 | – | 25.4 | 1.6 | 6.6 |
| $10,000 to $24,999 | 67.3 | 24.8 | 41.3 | 1.4 | 41.9 | 2.5 | 8.7 |
| $25,000 to $49,999 | 83.9 | 47.3 | 54.3 | 2.0 | 56.7 | 5.8 | 8.5 |
| $50,000 to $99,999 | 89.9 | 68.7 | 60.7 | 3.2 | 62.8 | 9.5 | 10.0 |
| $100,000 or more | 86.4 | 73.6 | 37.0 | 4.0 | 37.0 | 27.9 | 15.8 |
| **Age of householder** | | | | | | | |
| Under age 35 | 83.8 | 32.9 | 62.2 | 2.6 | 55.4 | 2.6 | 7.8 |
| Aged 35 to 44 | 87.2 | 54.1 | 60.7 | 2.2 | 55.8 | 6.5 | 11.1 |
| Aged 45 to 54 | 86.5 | 61.9 | 54.0 | 2.3 | 57.3 | 10.4 | 14.1 |
| Aged 55 to 64 | 75.2 | 45.8 | 36.0 | 1.4 | 43.4 | 12.5 | 7.5 |
| Aged 65 to 74 | 54.2 | 24.8 | 16.7 | 1.3 | 31.3 | 5.0 | 5.5 |
| Aged 75 or older | 30.1 | 7.1 | 9.6 | – | 18.3 | 1.5 | 3.6 |
| **Race and ethnicity of householder** | | | | | | | |
| Non-Hispanic white | 75.8 | 43.5 | 46.4 | 2.1 | 47.5 | 6.9 | 9.1 |
| Nonwhite or Hispanic | 73.1 | 32.7 | 46.9 | 1.3 | 48.8 | 4.4 | 8.5 |

*(continued)*

*(continued from previous page)*

| | any debt | mortgage and home equity | installment | other lines of credit | credit card | investment real estate | other debt |
|---|---|---|---|---|---|---|---|
| **MEDIAN VALUE OF DEBT** | | | | | | | |
| **FOR DEBTOR HOUSEHOLDS** | | | | | | | |
| **Total households** | **$22,500** | **$51,000** | **$6,100** | **$3,500** | **$1,500** | **$28,000** | **$2,000** |
| **Income** | | | | | | | |
| Under $10,000 | 2,600 | 14,000 | 2,900 | – | 600 | 15,000 | 2,000 |
| $10,000 to $24,999 | 9,200 | 26,000 | 3,900 | 3,000 | 1,200 | 18,300 | 1,200 |
| $25,000 to $49,999 | 23,400 | 46,000 | 6,600 | 3,000 | 1,400 | 25,000 | 1,500 |
| $50,000 to $99,999 | 65,000 | 68,000 | 9,000 | 2,200 | 2,200 | 34,000 | 2,500 |
| $100,000 or more | 112,200 | 103,400 | 8,500 | 19,500 | 3,000 | 36,800 | 7,000 |
| **Age of householder** | | | | | | | |
| Under age 35 | 15,200 | 63,000 | 7,000 | 1,400 | 1,400 | 22,800 | 1,500 |
| Aged 35 to 44 | 37,600 | 60,000 | 5,600 | 2,000 | 1,800 | 30,000 | 1,700 |
| Aged 45 to 54 | 41,000 | 48,000 | 7,000 | 5,700 | 2,000 | 28,100 | 2,500 |
| Aged 55 to 64 | 25,800 | 36,000 | 5,900 | 3,500 | 1,300 | 26,000 | 4,000 |
| Aged 65 to 74 | 7,700 | 19,000 | 4,900 | 3,800 | 800 | 36,000 | 2,000 |
| Aged 75 or older | 2,000 | 15,900 | 3,900 | – | 400 | 8,000 | 3,000 |
| **Race and ethnicity of householder** | | | | | | | |
| Non-Hispanic white | 27,200 | 54,000 | 6,400 | 3,500 | 1,500 | 29,000 | 2,000 |
| Nonwhite or Hispanic | 12,200 | 36,500 | 5,000 | 800 | 1,200 | 25,000 | 1,500 |

*Note: (–) means sample is too small to make a reliable estimate.*
*Source: Federal Reserve Board,* Family Finances in the U.S.: Recent Evidence from the Survey of Consumer Finances, *Federal Reserve Bulletin, January 1997*

# Homeownership Is at Record High

## Two out of three householders own their home.

Homeownership reached a record high in 1997 and continued to rise—to 66.2 percent in 1998. Of the nation's 103 million households, 68 million own their home.

Those most likely to own their home are householders aged 55 to 64, with a homeownership rate of 80 percent. Among household types, married couples are most likely to be homeowners, with an ownership rate of 81 percent. While white households are more likely to be homeowners than black and Hispanic households, the ownership rate among blacks and Hispanics is close to 50 percent, at 46 and 45 percent respectively.

The nation's homeownership rate is at a record high because married couples and older Americans are more likely to own a home than ever before. In contrast, the ownership rate among young adults is still below the level of the early 1980s. Similarly, male- and female-headed families are less likely to own a home today than they were in the early 1980s, whereas men and women who live alone are much more likely to be homeowners.

◆ The homeownership rate will continue to rise as the baby-boom generation plays catch-up in the housing market.

## Homeownership rate peaks in 55-to-64 age group

*(percent of householders who own their home, by age, 1998)*

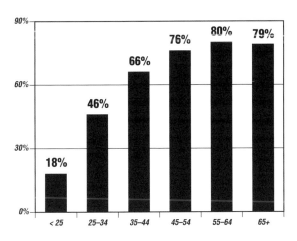

# Homeownership, 1998

*(number and percent of householders who own their home, by selected characteristics, 1998; numbers in thousands)*

| | number | owners number | owners percent |
|---|---|---|---|
| **Total households** | **102,528** | **67,873** | **66.2%** |
| **Age of householder** | | | |
| Under age 25 | 5,435 | 965 | 17.8 |
| Aged 25 to 34 | 19,033 | 8,743 | 45.9 |
| Aged 35 to 44 | 23,943 | 15,909 | 66.4 |
| Aged 45 to 54 | 19,547 | 14,762 | 75.5 |
| Aged 55 to 64 | 13,072 | 10,493 | 80.3 |
| Aged 65 or older | 21,497 | 16,999 | 79.1 |
| **Type of household** | | | |
| **Family households** | **70,880** | **52,109** | **73.5** |
| Married couples | 54,317 | 43,964 | 80.9 |
| Female householder, no spouse present | 12,652 | 5,940 | 46.9 |
| Male householder, no spouse present | 3,911 | 2,204 | 56.4 |
| **Nonfamily households** | **31,648** | **15,765** | **49.8** |
| Female householder | 17,516 | 9,552 | 54.5 |
| Living alone | 15,317 | 8,650 | 56.5 |
| Male householder | 14,133 | 6,212 | 44.0 |
| Living alone | 11,010 | 5,019 | 45.6 |
| **Race and Hispanic origin of householder** | | | |
| White | 86,106 | 60,050 | 69.7 |
| Black | 12,474 | 5,735 | 46.0 |
| Hispanic | 8,590 | 3,857 | 44.9 |

*Source: Bureau of the Census, detailed tables from* Household and Family Characteristics: March 1998, *Current Population Reports, P20-515, 1998; calculations by New Strategist*

# Homeownership, 1982 to 1997

*(percent of householders who own their home by age and household type, 1982, 1990, and 1997; percentage point change, 1982–97 and 1990–97)*

| | 1997 | 1990 | 1982 | percentage point change | |
| --- | --- | --- | --- | --- | --- |
| | | | | 1982–97 | 1990–97 |
| **Total households** | **65.7%** | **63.9%** | **64.8%** | **0.9** | **1.8** |
| **Age of householder** | | | | | |
| Under age 35 | 38.7 | 38.5 | 41.2 | –2.5 | 0.2 |
| Aged 35 to 44 | 66.1 | 66.3 | 70.0 | –3.9 | –0.2 |
| Aged 45 to 54 | 75.8 | 75.2 | 77.4 | –1.6 | 0.6 |
| Aged 55 to 64 | 80.1 | 79.3 | 80.0 | 0.1 | 0.8 |
| Aged 65 or older | 79.1 | 76.3 | 74.4 | 4.7 | 2.8 |
| **Type of household** | | | | | |
| Married couples | 80.8 | 78.1 | 78.5 | 2.3 | 2.7 |
| Female householder, no spouse present | 46.1 | 44.0 | 47.1 | –1.0 | 2.1 |
| Male householder, no spouse present | 54.0 | 55.2 | 59.3 | –5.3 | –1.2 |
| Women living alone | 56.7 | 53.6 | 51.2 | 5.5 | 3.1 |
| Men living alone | 45.2 | 42.4 | 38.0 | 7.2 | 2.8 |

*Source: Bureau of the Census, unpublished data from the Housing Vacancy Surveys, Internet web site <http:// www.census.gov/hhes/www/housing/hvs/annual97/ann97t15.html>; calculations by New Strategist*

# Forty-Two Percent of Workers Are Covered by a Pension

## Women are almost as likely to have pension coverage as men.

Among workers with earnings in 1996, 44 percent of men and 40 percent of women were covered by pensions. Pension coverage peaks among workers aged 45 to 64, at 57 percent for men and 50 percent for women.

Pension coverage is almost as high among black workers as among whites. Forty-one percent of black workers had pension coverage in 1997 compared with 42 percent of whites. Among black women aged 45 to 64, 56 percent were covered by a pension—a substantially higher share than the 50 percent of white women with coverage.

Hispanic workers are much less likely to have pension coverage than both white and black workers. In 1997, only 28 percent of Hispanic workers were covered by pensions.

◆ A large share of baby-boom women will have pension coverage in old age because of their propensity to work. Consequently, many of today's dual-income couples will be dual-pension couples in retirement.

# Pension Coverage, 1997

*(number and percent of workers with earnings in 1996 covered by pensions, by sex, age, race, and Hispanic origin, 1997; numbers in thousands)*

| | total | | white | | black | | Hispanic | |
|---|---|---|---|---|---|---|---|---|
| | number | percent | number | percent | number | percent | number | percent |
| **Total workers with coverage** | **59,923** | **41.9%** | **51,168** | **42.3%** | **6,351** | **40.5%** | **3,835** | **28.0%** |
| **Men with coverage** | **33,363** | **43.8** | **29,023** | **44.3** | **3,004** | **40.9** | **2,236** | **27.4** |
| Aged 15 to 24 | 1,501 | 12.0 | 1,277 | 12.0 | 166 | 12.6 | 170 | 9.8 |
| Aged 25 to 44 | 18,768 | 48.4 | 16,147 | 49.2 | 1,773 | 43.7 | 1,427 | 30.4 |
| Aged 45 to 64 | 12,456 | 56.5 | 11,034 | 56.9 | 1,013 | 55.9 | 612 | 37.9 |
| Aged 65 or older | 639 | 22.5 | 564 | 22.0 | 51 | 31.6 | 27 | 23.2 |
| **Women with coverage** | **26,560** | **39.8** | **22,145** | **40.0** | **3,347** | **40.1** | **1,599** | **28.9** |
| Aged 15 to 24 | 1,176 | 10.3 | 969 | 10.3 | 164 | 10.6 | 98 | 8.7 |
| Aged 25 to 44 | 15,091 | 45.0 | 12,436 | 45.4 | 1,976 | 43.5 | 1,002 | 32.1 |
| Aged 45 to 64 | 9,815 | 50.0 | 8,320 | 49.8 | 1,172 | 56.1 | 474 | 39.6 |
| Aged 65 or older | 478 | 22.4 | 420 | 22.0 | 35 | 21.5 | 25 | 29.8 |

*Note: Numbers will not add to total because not all races are shown and Hispanics may be of any race.*
*Source: Bureau of the Census, Statistical Abstract of the United States: 1998*

# For More Information

*The federal government is a rich source of accurate and reliable data about almost every aspect of American life. Below are the web site addresses of the federal agencies collecting the data analyzed in this book, as well as the web site addresses of other organizations whose data appear here. Also listed are the phone numbers of organizations mentioned in this book, as well as government subject specialists, arranged alphabetically by topic. A list of State Data Centers and Small Business Development Centers appears here as well. Researchers can contact these centers for help in tracking down demographic and economic information.*

## Web Site Addresses

Bureau of the Census ................................................................ http://www.census.gov
Bureau of Labor Statistics ............................................................. http://www.bls.gov
Current Population Survey home page .............................. http://www.bls.census.gov/cps
Consumer Expenditure Survey home page ................... http://www.bls.gov/csxhome.htm
Immigration and Naturalization Service ..................... http://www.usdoj.gov/ins
National Center For Education Statistics ....................................... http://nces.ed.gov
National Center For Health Statistics .................................. http://www.cdc.gov/nchswww
National Endowment for the Arts .......................................... http://arts.endow.gov
National Opinion Research Center ....................................... http://www.norc.uchicago.edu

## Telephone Numbers of Subject Specialists and Organizations

Absences from work, Staff ................................................................ 202-606-6378
Aging population, Staff ................................................................... 301-457-2422
Ancestry, Staff .............................................................................. 301-457-2403
Apportionment, Ed Byerly ............................................................... 301-457-2381
Census, 1990 tabulations, Staff ......................................................... 301-457-2422
Census, 2000 plans, Arthur Cresce/John Stuart ........................................ 301-457-3947/3949
Census Bureau Customer Services ....................................................... 301-457-4100
Child care, Martin O'Connell/Lynne Casper .......................................... 301-457-2416
Children, Staff ............................................................................. 301-457-2465
Citizenship, Staff .......................................................................... 301-457-2403
College graduate job outlook, Mark Mittelhauser ..................................... 202-606-5707
Commuting, Phil Salopek/Celia Boertlein .............................................. 301-457-2454
Consumer Expenditure Survey, Staff .................................................... 202-606-6900
Contingent workers, Sharon Cohany ..................................................... 202-606-6378
County population, Staff .................................................................. 301-457-2422
Crime, Kathleen Creighton ............................................................... 301-457-3925
Current employment analysis, Philip Rones ............................................ 202-606-6378
Current Population Survey (general information), Staff ............................... 301-457-4100
Demographic surveys (general information), Staff ..................................... 301-457-3773
Disability, Jack McNeil/Bob Bennefield ................................................ 301-763-8300/8213
Discouraged workers, Staff ............................................................... 202-606-6378

Displaced workers, Steve Hipple ............................................................................ 202-606-6378

Economic Census, 1997

- Accommodations, Fay Dorsett ........................................................................ 301-457-2687
- Census promotions, Herb Gerardi ................................................................. 301-457-2989
- Communications industry, Jack Moody ....................................................... 301-457-2689
- Construction, Pat Horning ............................................................................. 301-457-4680
- Financial and insurance, Laurie Torene ...................................................... 301-457-2824
- Food services, Fay Dorsett ............................................................................. 301-457-2687
- General information, Robert Marske ............................................................ 301-457-2547
- Internet dissemination, Paul Zeisset ........................................................... 301-457-4151
- Manufacturing, durable goods, Kenneth Hansen ...................................... 301-457-4755
- Manufacturing, nondurable goods, Michael Zampogna ........................... 301-457-4810
- Mining, Pat Horning ....................................................................................... 301-457-4680
- Minority/women-owned businesses, Valerie Strang ................................. 301-457-3316
- North American Industry Class. Sys., Bruce Goldhirsch ......................... 301-457-2589
- Puerto Rico, outlying areas, territories, Eddie Salyers ............................ 301-457-3318
- Real estate and rental/leasing, Steve Roman ............................................. 301-457-2824
- Retail trade and accomodations, Fay Dorsett ............................................. 301-457-2687
- Services, Jack Moody ....................................................................................... 301-457-2689
- Transportation and utilities, establishments, Jim Poyer ......................... 301-457-2786
- Vehicle Inventory and Use Survey, Kim Moore ........................................ 301-457-2797
- Wholesale trade, John Trimble ...................................................................... 301-457-2725

Education, training statistics, Alan Eck ................................................................. 202-606-5705

Education surveys, Steve Tourkin ......................................................................... 301-457-3791

Educational attainment, Staff ................................................................................ 301-457-2464

Emigration/illegal immigrants, Staff ................................................................... 301-457-2403

Employee Benefit Research Institute, Staff ......................................................... 202-659-0670

Employee benefits, Staff .......................................................................................... 202-606-6222

Employee tenure, Jennifer Martel .......................................................................... 202-606-6378

Employment and unemployment , Staff ............................................................... 301-457-3242

Employment and Earnings periodical, Gloria P. Green ............................. 202-606-6373 x255

Employment and unemployment trends, Staff ................................................... 202-606-6378

Employment Situation News Release, Staff ......................................................... 202-606-6378

Equal employment opportunity data, Staff ......................................................... 301-457-3242

Fertility, Amara Bachu ............................................................................................ 301-457-2449

Flexitime and shift work, Thomas Beers .............................................................. 202-606-6378

Foreign born, Staff ................................................................................................... 301-457-2403

General Social Survey, National Opinion Research Center ............................... 773-753-7500

Group quarters population, Denise Smith ............................................................ 301-457-2378

Health surveys, Adrienne Quasney ....................................................................... 301-457-3879

Hispanic statistics, Staff ......................................................................................... 301-457-2403

Home-based work, Staff .......................................................................................... 202-606-6378

Homeless, Annetta Clark Smith ............................................................................. 301-457-2378

Household wealth, Staff ........................................................................... 301-457-3242

Households and families, Staff ............................................................... 301-457-2465

Housing

• Affordability, Peter Fronczek/Howard Savage ............................... 301-457-3199

• American Housing Survey, Edward Montfort ................................ 301-457-3235

• Census, Staff ...................................................................................... 301-457-3237

• Components of inventory change, Barbara Williams .................... 301-457-3235

• Market absorption, Alan Friedman ................................................ 301-457-3199

• Residential finance, Howard Savage .............................................. 301-457-3199

• Vacancy data, Alan Friedman/Robert Callis ................................. 301-457-3199

Immigrants, Jay Meisenheimer ............................................................. 202-606-6378

Immigration, (general information), Staff ............................................ 301-457-2422

Income and poverty statistics, Staff ..................................................... 301-457-3242

Industry

• Business expenditures, Sheldon Ziman ......................................... 301-457-3315

• Business investment, Charles Funk ................................................ 301-457-3331

• Characteristics of business owners, Valerie Strang ...................... 301-457-3316

• County Business Patterns, Dennis Wagner .................................... 301-457-2580

• Economic studies, Arnold Reznek .................................................. 301-457-1856

• Enterprise statistics, Eddie Salyers ................................................ 301-457-3318

• Industry and commodity classification, James Kristoff ............... 301-457-2813

• Mineral industries, Pat Horning ..................................................... 301-457-4680

• Minority/women-owned businesses, Valerie Strang .................... 301-457-3316

• North American Industry Class. Sys., Bruce Goldhirsch .............. 301-457-2589

• Puerto Rico and outlying areas, Irma Harahush ........................... 301-457-3314

• Quarterly Financial Report, Ronald Lee ........................................ 301-457-3343

• Statistics of U.S. Businesses, Mike Mashburn .............................. 301-457-8641

Job mobility and tenure, Alan Eck ....................................................... 202-606-5705

Journey to work, Phil Salopek/Gloria Swieczkowski ......................... 301-457-2454

Labor force concepts, Staff .................................................................... 202-606-6378

Labor force demographics, Howard Fullerton ..................................... 202-606-5711

Language, Staff ....................................................................................... 301-457-2464

Longitudinal surveys, Sarah Higgins .................................................... 301-457-3801

Marital and family characteristics of workers, Staff ........................... 202-606-6378

Marital status and living arrangements, Lynne Casper ...................... 301-457-2416

Metropolitan areas, Staff ....................................................................... 301-457-2422

Migration, Kristin Hansen/Carol Faber ............................................... 301-457-2454

Minimum wage data, Steven Haugen ................................................... 202-606-6378

Minority workers, Staff .......................................................................... 202-606-6378

Multiple jobholders, John Stinson ........................................... 202-606-6373 x263

National Alliance for Caregiving, Staff ................................................. 301-718-8444

National Opinion Research Center ....................................................... 773-753-7500

National estimates and projections, Staff ............................................ 301-457-2422

Occupation (general information), Doug Braddock ............................ 202-606-5695

Occupational data, Staff ........................................................................ 202-606-6378

Occupational Outlook Quarterly, Kathleen Green ................................................ 202-606-5717
Occupational projections
- Computer, Carolyn Veneri ................................................................................ 202-606-5714
- Construction, Hall Dillon ................................................................................ 202-606-5704
- Education, Chad Fleetwood ............................................................................. 202-606-5690
- Engineering, Erik Savisaar .............................................................................. 202-606-5698
- Food and lodging, Gary Steinberg .................................................................. 202-606-5694
- Health, Theresa Coscaq .................................................................................. 202-606-5712
- Legal, Jill Silver ............................................................................................... 202-606-5696
- Mechanics and repairers, Sean Kirby ............................................................ 202-606-5719
- Sales, Andrew Nelson ..................................................................................... 202-606-5718
- Scientific, Tina Shelley ................................................................................... 202-606-5726
Older workers, Diane Herz .................................................................................. 202-606-6378
Outlying areas, Michael Levin ............................................................................ 301-457-1444
Part-time workers, Staff ....................................................................................... 202-606-6378
Place of birth, Kristin Hansen/Carol Faber ....................................................... 301-457-2454
Population information, Staff ............................................................................... 301-457-2422
Prisoner surveys, Kathleen Creighton ................................................................ 301-457-3925
Puerto Rico, Lourdes Flaim ................................................................................. 301-457-4041
Race statistics, Staff ............................................................................................. 301-457-2422
Reapportionment and redistricting, Marshall Turner, Jr. ................................... 301-457-4015
Sampling methods, census, Ann Vacca ............................................................... 301-457-4304
School Districts, 1990 census, NCES ................................................................... 202-219-1627
School enrollment, Staff ....................................................................................... 301-457-2464
Seasonal adjustment methodology, Robert McIntire ......................................... 202-606-6345
Special censuses, Elaine Csellar .......................................................................... 301-457-1429
Special surveys, Sarah Higgins ........................................................................... 301-457-3801
Special tabulations, Marie Pees .......................................................................... 301-457-2447
State population and projections, Staff ................................................................ 301-457-2422
Survey of Income & Program Participation (SIPP), Staff ................................... 301-457-3242
Undercount, demographic analysis, Gregg Robinson ....................................... 301-457-2103
Union membership , Timothy Consedine ............................................................ 202-606-6378
Urban/rural, Michael Ratcliff/Rodger Johnson ................................................ 301-457-2419
Veterans in the labor force, Staff ........................................................................ 202-606-6378
Veterans' status, Staff .......................................................................................... 301-457-3242
Voters, characteristics, Lynne Casper ................................................................. 301-457-2445
Voting age population, Staff ................................................................................ 301-457-2422
Weekly earnings, Staff ......................................................................................... 202-606-6378
Women, Staff ........................................................................................................ 301-457-2378
Women in the labor force, Staff .......................................................................... 202-606-6378
Work experience, Staff ......................................................................................... 202-606-6378
Working poor, Staff .............................................................................................. 202-606-6378
Youth, students, and dropouts, Tiffany Stringer ................................................ 202-606-6378

## Census Regional Offices

| | |
|---|---|
| Atlanta, GA | 404-730-3833/3964 |
| Boston, MA | 617-424-0510/0565 |
| Charlotte, NC | 704-344-6144/6548 |
| Chicago, IL | 708-562-1740/1791 |
| Dallas, TX | 214-640-4470/4434 |
| Denver, CO | 303-969-7750/6769 |
| Detroit, MI | 313-259-1875/5169 |
| Kansas City, KS | 913-551-6711/5839 |
| Los Angeles, CA | 818-904-6339/6249 |
| New York, NY | 212-264-4730/3863 |
| Philadelphia, PA | 215-656-7578/7550 |
| Seattle, WA | 206-553-5835/5859 |

## State Data Centers And Business/Industry Data Centers

*Below are listed the State Data Center and Business/Industry Data Center (BIDC) lead agency contacts only. Lead data centers are usually state government agencies, universities, or libraries that head up a network of affiliate centers. Every state has a State Data Center. The asterisks (\*) identify states that also have Business/Industry Data Centers. In some states, one agency serves as the lead for both the State Data Centers and the Business/Industry Data Centers. The Business/Industry Data Center is listed separately if there is a separate agency serving as the lead.*

| | |
|---|---|
| Alabama, Annette Watters, University of Alabama | 205-348-6191 |
| Alaska, Kathryn Lizik, Department of Labor | 907-465-2437 |
| *Arizona, Betty Jeffries, Department of Security | 602-542-5984 |
| Arkansas, Sarah Breshears, University of Arkansas at Little Rock | 501-569-8530 |
| California, Linda Gage, Department of Finance | 916-323-4086 |
| Colorado, Rebecca Picaso, Department of Local Affairs | 303-866-2156 |
| Connecticut, Bill Kraynak, Office of Policy & Management | 860-418-6230 |
| *Delaware, Mike Mahaffie, Development Office | 302-739-4271 |
| District of Columbia, Herb Bixhorn, Mayor's Office of Planning | 202-727-6533 |
| *Florida, Pam Schenker, Dept. of Labor & Employment Security | 850-488-1048 |
| Georgia, Robert Giacomini, Georgia Institute of Technology | 404-894-9416 |
| Guam, Rose Deaver, Department of Commerce | 011-671-475-0325/6 |
| Hawaii, Jan Nakamoto, Dept. of Business, Econ. Dev., & Tourism | 808-586-2493 |
| Idaho, Alan Porter, Department of Commerce | 208-334-2470 |
| Illinois, Suzanne Ebetsch, Bureau of the Budget | 217-782-1381 |
| *Indiana, Sylvia Andrews, State Library | 317-232-3733 |
| Indiana BIDC, Carol Rogers, Business Research Center | 317-274-2205 |
| Iowa, Beth Henning, State Library | 515-281-4350 |
| Kansas, Marc Galbraith, State Library | 913-296-3296 |
| *Kentucky, Ron Crouch, University of Louisville | 502-852-7990 |
| Louisiana, Karen Paterson, Office of Planning & Budget | 504-342-7410 |

*Maine .................................................................................. [Currently being reorganized]
*Maryland, Jane Traynham, Office of Planning ..................................................... 410-767-4450
*Massachusetts, John Gaviglio, Mass. Inst. for Social and Econ. Res ................. 413-545-3460
Michigan, Carolyn Lauer, Dept. of Management & Budget ............................. 517-373-7910
*Minnesota, David Birkholz, State Demographer's Office .................................. 612-296-2557
Minnesota BIDC, David Rademacher, State Dem. Office .................................. 612-297-3255
*Mississippi, Rachael McNeely, University of Mississippi ................................. 601-232-7288
Mississippi BIDC, Deloise Tate, Dept. of Econ. & Comm. Dev ........................ 601-359-3593
*Missouri, Debra Pitts, State Library ................................................................. 573-526-7648
Missouri BIDC, Steve Garrotto, Small Business Dev. Centers .......................... 573-882-0344
*Montana, Patricia Roberts, Department of Commerce ................................... 406-444-2896
Nebraska, Jerome Deichert, University of Nebraska-Omaha ........................... 402-595-2311
Nevada, Linda Nary, State Library & Archives ................................................ 702-687-8326
New Hampshire, Thomas Duffy, Office of State Planning ............................... 603-271-2155
*New Jersey, David Joye, Department of Labor ................................................ 609-984-2595
*New Mexico, Kevin Kargacin, University of New Mexico ............................. 505-277-6626
*New York, Staff, Department of Economic Development ................................ 518-474-1141
*North Carolina, Staff, State Library ............................................................... 919-733-6418
North Dakota, Richard Rathge, State University .............................................. 701-231-8621
Northern Mariana Islands, Juan Borja, Dept. of Commerce ...................... 011-670-664-3034
*Ohio, Barry Bennett, Department of Development ......................................... 614-466-2115
*Oklahoma, Jeff Wallace, Department of Commerce ....................................... 405-815-5184
Oregon, George Hough, Portland State Univ. ............... 503-725-5159 / 1-800-547-8887x5159
*Pennsylvania, Diane Shoop, Penns. State Univ. at Harrisburg ......................... 717-948-6336
Puerto Rico, Lillian Torres Aguirre, Planning Bd. ................... 787-728-4430 / 723-6200x2502
Rhode Island, Paul Egan, Department of Administration ................................ 401-277-6493
South Carolina, Mike MacFarlane, Budget & Control Board ........................... 803-734-3780
South Dakota, Theresa Bendert, Univ. of South Dakota .................................. 605-677-5287
Tennessee, Don Walli, State Planning Office .................................................... 615-741-1676
Texas, Steve Murdock, Texas A&M University ........................................ 409-845-5115 / 5332
*Utah, David Abel, Office of Planning & Budget ............................................. 801-538-1036
Vermont, Sybil McShane, Department of Libraries ........................................... 802-828-3261
*Virginia, Don Lillywhite, Virginia Employment Commission ........................ 804-786-8026
Virgin Islands, Frank Mills, Univ. of the Virgin Islands .................................. 340-693-1027
*Washington, Yi Zhao, Office of Financial Management ................................... 360-902-0599
*West Virginia, Delphine Coffey, Office of Comm. & Industrial Dev. .............. 304-558-4010
West Virginia BIDC, Randy Childs, Center for Econ. Research ...................... 304-293-7832
*Wisconsin, Robert Naylor, Department of Administration .............................. 608-266-1927
Wisconsin BIDC, David Mohn, Univ. of Wisconsin-Madison .......................... 608-262-3097
Wyoming, Wenlin Liu, Dept. of Administration & Fiscal Control .................. 307-777-7504

# Glossary

**adjusted for inflation** Incomes or changes in income have been adjusted for the rise in the cost of living, or the consumer price index (CPI-U-XI). In this book, any year-to-year changes in income or spending are shown in inflation-adjusted dollars.

**Asian** In this book, the term "Asian" includes both Asians and Pacific Islanders.

**baby boom** Americans born between 1946 and 1964.

**baby bust** Americans born between 1965 and 1976; also known as Generation X.

**central city** The largest city in a metropolitan area is called the central city. The balance of the metropolitan area outside the central city is regarded as the "suburbs."

**complete income reporters** (on spending tables only) Survey respondents who told government interviewers how much money they received from major sources of income, such as wages and salaries, self-employment income, and Social Security income.

**consumer unit** (on spending tables only) For convenience, the terms consumer unit and household are used interchangeably in the spending section of this book, although consumer units are somewhat different from the Census Bureau's households. A consumer unit comprises all related members of a household or a financially independent member of a household. A household may include more than one consumer unit.

**dual-earner couple** A married couple in which both the householder and the householder's spouse are in the labor force.

**earnings** One type of income. *See also* Income.

**employed** All civilians who did any work as paid employees or farmers/self-employed workers, or who worked 15 hours or more as unpaid farm workers or in a family-owned business, during the reference period. All those who have jobs but are temporarily absent from their jobs due to illness, bad weather, vacation, labor management dispute, or personal reasons are considered employed.

**expenditure** The transaction cost including excise and sales taxes of goods and services acquired during the survey period. The full cost of each purchase is recorded even though full payment may not have been made at the date of purchase. Average expenditure figures may be artificially low for infrequently purchased items such as cars because figures are calculated using all consumer units within a demographic segment rather than just purchasers. Expenditure estimates include money spent on gifts for others.

**family** A group of two or more people (one of whom is the householder) related by birth, marriage, or adoption and living in the same household.

**family household** A household maintained by a householder who lives with one or more people related to him or her by blood, marriage, or adoption.

**female/male householder** A woman/man who maintains a household without a spouse present. May head family or nonfamily household.

**full-time employment** Full-time employment is 35 or more hours of work per week during a majority of the weeks worked.

**full-time, year-round** Indicates 50 or more weeks of full-time employment during the previous calendar year.

**geographic regions** The four major regions and nine census divisions of the United States are the state groupings as shown below:

*Northeast:*
—New England: Connecticut, Maine, Massachusetts, New Hampshire, Rhode Island, and Vermont
—Middle Atlantic: New Jersey, New York, and Pennsylvania

*Midwest:*
—East North Central: Illinois, Indiana, Michigan, Ohio, and Wisconsin
—West North Central: Iowa, Kansas, Minnesota, Missouri, Nebraska, North Dakota, and South Dakota

*South:*
—South Atlantic: Delaware, District of Columbia, Florida, Georgia, Maryland, North Carolina, South Carolina, Virginia, and West Virginia
—East South Central: Alabama, Kentucky, Mississippi, and Tennessee
—West South Central: Arkansas, Louisiana, Oklahoma, and Texas

*West:*
—Mountain: Arizona, Colorado, Idaho, Montana, Nevada, New Mexico, Utah, and Wyoming
—Pacific: Alaska, California, Hawaii, Oregon, and Washington

**Generation X** Americans born between 1965 and 1976; also known as the baby-bust generation.

**Hispanic** Persons who identify their origin as Mexican, Puerto Rican, Central or South American, or some other Hispanic origin. Persons of Hispanic origin may be of any race. In other words, there are black Hispanics, white Hispanics, Asian Hispanics, and Native American Hispanics.

**household** All the persons who occupy a housing unit. A household includes the related family members and all the unrelated persons, if any, such as lodgers, foster children, wards, or employees who share the housing unit. A person living alone is counted as a household. A group of unrelated people who share a housing unit as roommates or unmarried partners is also counted as a household. Households do not include group quarters such as college dormitories, prisons, or nursing homes.

**household, race/ethnicity of** Households are categorized according to the race or ethnicity of the householder only.

**householder** The householder is the person (or one of the persons) in whose name the housing unit is owned or rented or, if there is no such person, any adult member. With married couples, the householder may be either the husband or the wife. The householder is the reference person for the household.

**householder, age of** The age of the householder is used to categorize households into age groups. Married couples, for example, are classified according to the age of either the husband or the wife, depending on which one identified him- or herself as the householder.

**income** Money received in the preceding calendar year by a person aged 15 or older from any of the following sources: (1) earnings from longest job (or self-employment); (2) earnings from jobs other than longest job; (3) unemployment compensation; (4) workers' compensation; (5) Social Security; (6) Supplemental Security income; (7) public assistance; (8) veterans' payments; (9)

survivor benefits; (10) disability benefits; (11) retirement pensions; (12) interest; (13) dividends; (14) rents and royalties or estates and trusts; (15) educational assistance; (16) alimony; (17) child support; (18) financial assistance from outside the household, and other periodic income. Income is reported in several ways in this book. Household income is the combined income of all household members. Income of a person is all income accruing to the person from all sources. Earnings is the amount of money a person receives from his or her job.

**income fifths or quintiles**  A useful way to compare the characteristics of households by dividing the total number of households into fifths based on household income. One-fifth of households fall into the lowest income quintile, one-fifth into the second income quintile, and so on.

**industry**  Refers to the industry in which a person worked longest in the preceding calendar year.

**job tenure**  The length of time a person has been employed continuously by the same employer.

**labor force**  The labor force tables in this book are for the civilian labor force, which includes both the employed and the unemployed—people who are looking for work.

**labor force participation rate**  The percentage of the civilian noninstitutional population that is in the civilian labor force, which includes both the employed and the unemployed.

**married couples with/without children under age 18**  Refers to married couples with/without own children under age 18 living in the same household. Couples without children under age 18 may be parents of grown children who live elsewhere, or they could be childless couples.

**median**  The median is the value that divides the population or households into two equal portions: one below and one above the median. Medians can be calculated for income, age, and many other characteristics.

**median income**  The amount that divides the income distribution into two equal groups, one-half having incomes above the median, one-half having incomes below the median. The median for households or families is based on all households or families. The median for persons is based on all persons aged 15 or older with income.

**metropolitan statistical area**  To be defined as a metropolitan statistical area (or MSA), an area must include a city with 50,000 or more inhabitants, or a Census Bureau-defined urbanized area of at least 50,000 inhabitants and a total metropolitan population of at least 100,000 (75,000 in New England). The county (or counties) with the largest city becomes the "central county" (counties), along with any adjacent counties that have at least 50 percent of their population in the urbanized area surrounding the largest city. Additional counties are included in the MSA if they meet specified requirements of commuting to the central county (or counties) and other selected requirements of metropolitan character such as population density and percent urban. In New England, MSAs are defined in terms of cities and towns rather than counties. For this reason, the concept of NECMA is used to define metropolitan areas in the New England division.

PMSAs, or primary metropolitan statistical areas, are MSAs with populations of 12 million or more.

NECMAs, or New England county metropolitan areas, are county-based alternatives to the city- and town-based New England MSAs. NECMAs are defined as the county containing the first-named city in the MSA title (this county may include the first-named cities of other MSAs as well), and each additional county having at least half its population in the MSA whose first-named cities are in the previously identified county. Central cities of NECMAs are those cities in the NECMA that qualify as central cities of an MSA.

**Millennial generation**  Americans born between 1997 and 1994.

**MSA**  *See* Metropolitan statistical area.

**NECMA**  *See* Metropolitan statistical area.

**nonfamily household**  A household maintained by a householder who lives alone or with people to whom he or she is not related.

**nonfamily householder**  A householder who lives alone or with nonrelatives.

**non-Hispanic**  People who did not identify themselves as Hispanic on the Current Population Survey or the 1990 Census are classified as non-Hispanic. Non-Hispanics may be of any race.

**nonmetropolitan area**  Counties that are not classified as metropolitan areas.

**occupation**  Occupational classification is based on the kind of work a person did at his or her job during the previous calendar year. If a person changed jobs during the year, the data refer to the occupation of the job held the longest during that year.

**outside central city**  The portion of a metropolitan county or counties that falls outside of the central city or cities; generally regarded as the suburbs.

**own children**  Own children in a family are sons and daughters, including stepchildren and adopted children, of the householder. The totals include never-married children

living away from home in college dormitories.

**owner occupied**  A housing unit is owner occupied if the owner lives in the unit, even if it is mortgaged or not fully paid for. A cooperative or condominium unit is owner occupied only if the owner lives in it. All other occupied units are classified as renter occupied.

**part-time employment**  Part-time employment is less than 35 hours of work per week in a majority of the weeks worked during the year.

**percent change**  The change (either positive or negative) in a measure expressed as a proportion of the starting measure. When median income changes from $20,000 to $25,000, for example, this is a 25 percent increase.

**percentage point change**  The change (either positive or negative) in a value which is already expressed as a percentage. When the labor force participation rate changes from 70 percent to 75 percent, for example, this is a 5 percentage point increase.

**PMSA**  *See* Metropolitan statistical area.

**poverty level**  The official income threshold below which families and persons are classified as living in poverty. The threshold rises each year with inflation and varies depending on family size and age of householder. In 1997, the poverty threshold for a family of four was $16,400.

**proportion or share**  The value of a part expressed as a percentage of the whole. If there are 4 million people aged 25 and 3 million of them are white, then the white proportion is 75 percent.

**race**  Race is self-reported and appears in four categories in this book: white, black, Native American, and Asian. A household is assigned the race of the householder.

**rounding** Percentages are rounded to the nearest one-tenth of a percent; therefore, the percentages in a distribution do not always add exactly to 100.0 percent, although totals are always shown as 100.0. Moreover, individual figures are rounded to the nearest 1,000 without being adjusted to group totals, which are independently rounded; percentages are based on the unrounded numbers.

**self-employment** A person is categorized as self-employed if he or she was self-employed in the job held longest during the reference period. People who report self-employment from a second job are excluded, but those who report wage-and-salary income from a second job are included. Unpaid workers in family businesses are excluded. Self-employment statistics include only nonagricultural workers and exclude people who work for themselves in incorporated businesses.

**sex ratio** The number of men per 100 women.

**suburbs** *See* Outside central city.

**unemployed** Unemployed people are those who, during the survey period, had no employment but were available and looking for work. Those who were laid off from their jobs and were waiting to be recalled are also classified as unemployed.

# Bibliography

Bureau of the Census

    Internet web site, http://www.census.gov

    ——1998 Current Population Survey, unpublished data

    ——*Educational Attainment in the United States: March 1998*, detailed tables from Current Population Reports, P20-513, 1998

    ——*Geographic Mobility: March 1996 to March 1997*, Current Population Reports, P20-510, 1998

    ——*Household and Family Characteristics: March 1998*, detailed tables from Current Population Reports, P20-515, 1998

    ——Housing Vacancy Surveys, unpublished data

    ——*Marital Status and Living Arrangements: March 1998*, Current Population Reports, P20-514, 1998

    ——*Metropolitan Areas and Cities*, 1990 Census Profile, No. 3, 1991

    ——*Money Income in the United States: 1997*, Current Population Reports, P60-200, 1998

    ——*Population Projections of the United States by Age, Sex, Race, and Hispanic Origin: 1995 to 2050*, Current Population Reports, P25-1130, 1996

    ——*Poverty in the United States: 1997*, Current Population Reports, P60-201, 1998

    ——*Projections of the Total Population of States: 1995 to 2025*, PPL-47, 1996

    ——*School Enrollment—Social and Economic Characteristics of Students: October 1996*, Current Population Reports, P20-500, 1998

    ——*Statistical Abstract of the United States: 1996* (116th edition) Washington, DC 1996

    ——*Statistical Abstract of the United States: 1998* (118th edition) Washington, DC 1998

    ——*U.S. Population Estimates, by Age, Sex, Race, and Hispanic Origin: 1980 to 1991*, Current Population Reports, P25-1095, 1993

    ——*Voting and Registration in the Election of November 1996*, Current Population Reports, P20-504, 1998

Bureau of Labor Statistics

    Internet web site, http://www.bls.gov

    ——1997 Consumer Expenditure Survey, unpublished data

    ——*Contingent and Alternative Employment Arrangements*, February 1997

    ——*Employee Benefits in Medium and Large Private Establishments*, 1997

    ——*Employee Benefits in Small Private Establishments*, 1996

    ——*Employment and Earnings*, January 1991

    ——*Employment and Earnings*, January 1999

*——Handbook of Labor Statistics*, Bulletin 2340, 1989

*——Monthly Labor Review*, November 1997

*——Work at Home in 1997*, USDL 98-93

Federal Reserve Board

*——Family Finances in the U.S.: Recent Evidence from the Survey of Consumer Finances*, Federal Reserve Bulletin, January 1997

Immigration and Naturalization Service

Internet web site, http://www.usdoj.gov/ins

*——1996 Statistical Yearbook of the Immigration and Naturalization Service*, 1997

National Center for Education Statistics

Internet web site, http://nces.ed.gov

*——Degrees and Other Awards Conferred by Degree-granting Institutions: 1995—96*, NCES 98-256, 1998

*——Digest of Education Statistics: 1997*, NCES 98-015, 1997

*——Projections of Education Statistics to 2008*, NCES 98-016, 1998

National Center for Health Statistics

Internet web site, http://www.cdc.gov/nchswww

*——An Overview of Home Health and Hospice Care Patients: 1996 National Home and Hospice Care Survey*, Advance Data, No. 297, 1998

*——Births and Deaths: Preliminary Data for 1997*, National Vital Statistics Report, Vol. 47, No. 4, 1998

*——Current Estimates from the National Health Interview Survey, 1995*, Series 10, No. 199, 1998

*——Health, United States, 1996-97*

*——Health, United States, 1998*

*——National Ambulatory Medical Care Survey: 1996 Summary*, Advance Data, No. 295, 1997

*——Report of Final Natality Statistics, 1996*, Monthly Vital Statistics Report, Vol. 46, No. 11 Supplement, 1998

National Endowment for the Arts

Internet web site, http://arts.endow.gov

*——1997 Survey of Public Participation in the Arts, Summary Report*, 1998

National Opinion Research Center

Internet web site, http://www.norc.uchicago.edu

*——1994 General Social Survey, unpublished data*

*——1996 General Social Survey, unpublished data*

TGE Demographics, Inc.

1244 Pittsford-Mendon Center Road, Honeoye Falls, New York, 14472, 716-624-7390

——Population of the top 50 metropolitan areas, 1990 and 2000

U.S. Department of Agriculture

Internet web site http://www.barc.usda.gov

——1994–95 National Survey on Recreation and the Environment, Forest Service

——ARS Food Surveys Research Group, *1994 and 1995 Continuing Survey of Food Intakes by Individuals*

——ARS Food Surveys Research Group, *1994 and 1995 Diet and Health Knowledge Survey*

U.S. Substance Abuse and Mental Health Services Administration

Internet wet site http://www.samhsa.gov

——*National Household Survey on Drug Abuse, 1997*

# Index

accidents, as cause of death, 96–97

acute conditions, 78–79

adult education, 53–54

affluence. *See* Income

age:

  acute conditions by, 78–79;

  AIDS cases by, 93–94;

  alcoholic beverage consumption by, 74, 76;

  alternative workers by, 197–98;

  chronic conditions by, 78, 80–81;

  college enrollment by, 27–28, 44–45;

  debt by, 424–26;

  disabled by, 82–84;

  drugs, illicit use by, 74, 77;

  dual-income couples by, 177–78;

  educational attainment by, 4–8;

  employment status by, 168–73;

  exercise, frequency of, 68–69;

  female-headed families with children by, 249–50;

  financial assets by, 418–20;

  foreign born by, 303–06;

  health insurance coverage by, 72–73;

  health status by, 56–57;

  home health care by, 90–91;

  homeownership by, 427–29;

  hospice care by, 90, 92;

  hospital care by, 87–89;

  householders by, 219, 222–26, 230–31;

  job tenure by, 193–94;

  labor force participation by, 166–73, 204–05;

  living alone by, 234–35;

  male-headed families with children by, 249–50;

  marital status by, 253, 255–59;

  married couples with children by, 246–48;

  mobility by, 295, 297–98;

  net worth by, 416–17;

  non-financial assets by, 421–23;

  of cohabitors, 251–52;

  of householders by income, 106–07, 112–17, 122–28, 134–36;

  of men by income, 139–40, 145–46;

  of women by income, 139, 141, 145, 147;

  of women giving birth, 65–67;

  pension coverage by, 430–31;

  physician visits by, 85–86;

  population by, 261–65, 268–73;

  poverty rate by, 161–62;

  religious preference by, 261, 310–11;

  school enrollment by, 11, 13, 53–54;

  self-employment by, 195–96;

  smoking behavior by, 74–75;

  sources of income by, 159–60;

  spending by, 315, 320–39;

  vitamin consumption by, 61–62;

  voters by, 307–08

AIDS:

  cumulative cases by race and Hispanic origin, 93, 95;

  cumulative cases by sex and age, 93–94

alcoholic beverages, consumption of, 60, 74, 76

arthritis, 78, 80

arts:

  attendance at events, 312–13;

  participation in, 312, 314

Asian Americans:

  AIDS cases, 95;

  births, 65–66;

  by age, 269;

  by Hispanic origin, 266–69, 276–78, 282–90;

  by region, 276–78;

  by state, 282–90;

  college enrollment by degree level, 29–30;

  degrees earned by level of degree, 32–33;

  foreign born, 305;

  labor force projections, 206–08;

  population, 261, 266–69, 276–90;

  SAT scores, 20–21

assets:

  financial, 415, 418–20;

  non-financial, 415, 421–23

associate's degrees. *See under* Degrees earned

bachelor's degrees. *See under* Degrees earned

bank accounts, 418–20

bicycling, 55, 68, 70

births:

  by age, race and Hispanic origin, 65–66;

  by marital status, 65, 67;

  number of, 55, 63–67

Black American men:

  AIDS cases, 93, 95;

  educational attainment, 7–8;

  employment status, 170–71;

  high school drop-outs, 16–17;

  income, 101, 142–43;

  labor force participation, 170–71;

  labor force projections, 206, 208;

  living arrangements, 227–29;

  pension coverage, 430–31

Black American women:

  AIDS cases, 93, 95;

  births to, 65–67;

  educational attainment, 7–8;

  employment status, 170–71;

  high school drop–outs, 16–17;

  income, 142, 144;

  labor force participation, 170–71;

  labor force projections, 206, 208;

  living arrangements, 227–29;

  pension coverage, 430–31

Black Americans:

  AIDS cases, 93, 95;

  births to, 65–67;

  by age, 270;

  by Hispanic origin, 266–68, 270, 276–78, 282–90;

  by region, 276–78;

  by state, 282–90;

  children's living arrangements, 240–41;

  college enrollment by degree level, 29–30;

  college enrollment rate, 24, 26;

  degrees earned by level of degree, 29, 32–33;

  educational attainment, 7–8;

  employment status, 170–71;

  foreign born, 305;

  health status of, 56–57;

  households, 227–29, 230–31;

  income, 101, 110–11, 114–15, 118–19, 142–44;

  labor force participation, 165, 170–71;

  labor force projections, 206–08;

  living arrangements, 219, 227–29;

  marital status, 257–58;

  occupation of, 165, 185–92;

  pension coverage, 430–31;

  population, 261, 266–68, 270, 276–78, 282–90;

  poverty rate, 161–63;

  religious preferences of, 310–11;

  SAT scores, 3, 20–21;

  spending by, 315, 374–87;

  working at home, 199–200

blood conditions, 81

boating, 68, 70

bonds, 419–20

businesses, privately held, as non-financial asset, 422–23

cancer, as cause of death, 96–97

cerebrovascular diseases, as cause of death, 97

certificates of deposit, 419–20

child-bearing. *See* Births

children:

  AIDS cases, 93–95;

  by race and Hispanic origin, 268–73;

  disabled, 83;

  drug use of, 77;

  foreign born, 305;

  health insurance coverage of, 73;

  hospital care of, 87–89;

  living arrangements of, 219, 240–41;

  mobility of, 296–97;

  physician visits by, 85–86;

  population, 262–65, 268–73;

  poverty of, 101, 161–63;

  presence of in households, 129–33, 220–21;

  school enrollment of, 11, 13

chronic conditions, 78, 80–81

cigarette smoking, 55, 74–75

circulatory conditions, 78, 81

cities. *See* Metropolitan

cocaine use, 74, 77

cohabitation, 219, 251–52

college enrollment:
 by attendance status, 27–28;
 by degree level, race, and Hispanic origin,
  29–30;
 by family income, 22–23;
 projections, 44–49;
 rate by race and Hispanic origin, 24, 26;
 rate by sex, 24–25

consumer spending. *See* Spending

contractors. *See* Independent contractors

credit card debt, 424–26

death, causes of, 96–97

debt, personal, 415, 424–26

deformity, 80

degrees earned:
 associate's, 32, 34–36, 44, 50;
 bachelor's, 32, 34, 37–38; 50;
 by race and Hispanic origin, 29–32;
 by sex, 34–44, 50;
 doctoral, 32, 34, 41–42; 50;
 first professional, 33, 43; 44, 50;
 master's, 32, 34, 39–40; 50

diabetes, as cause of death, 97

digestive system conditions:
 acute, 79;
 chronic, 80–81

disability:
 by age, 82–83;
 by type and age, 82, 84;
 income, percent receiving, 160

doctoral degrees. *See under* Degrees earned

drugs, illicit use, by age group, 55, 74, 77

dual-income couples, 129–31

earnings:
 by educational attainment, 150–52;
 by occupation, 153–55;
 percent receiving, 159–60

education:
 adult, 53–54;
 art attendance and participation by,
  312–14;
 effect on income, 101, 137–38, 150–52;
 funding, percent receiving, 160;
 health status by, 56–57;
 net worth by, 416–171;
 of workers, 165, 216–17;
 religious preferences by, 310–11;
 spending by, 315, 401–14

educational attainment, 3–10:
 by degree, 4–6;
 by race and Hispanic origin, 3, 7–8;
 by sex, 3, 4–6;
 by state, 9–10;
 of foreign born, 303, 305;
 of married couples, 51–52

employee benefits, 201–03

employment status:
 by race and Hispanic origin, 170–73;
 by sex, 168–73;
 mobility by, 295, 297–98;
 of foreign born, 303, 306

endocrine conditions, 81

exercise, participation in, 55, 68–71

eye and ear conditions, 79, 80

families, with children in college, 3, 22–23.
 *See also* Households

female-headed household. *See under*
 Households

financial assets, 415, 418–20

first-professional degrees. *See under* Degrees
 earned

fishing, 55, 68, 70

food, consumption by type, 56, 58–60

foreign born, 303–06. *See also* Immigration

fruits, consumption of, 59–60

full-time workers, 174–75, 179–80, 201–03

genitourinary conditions, 81

geographic mobility. *See* Immigration *and*
 mobility, geographic

golfing, 68, 70

headache, 79, 81

health care visits, 85–86

health insurance coverage, 55, 72–73

health issues, 55–99

health problems by type, 78–81

health status, 56–57

hearing impairments, 78, 80

heart disease:
  as cause of death, 96–97;
  chronic condition, 78, 81

high blood pressure, 78, 81

high school:
  drop-outs, 16–17;
  projections of enrollment by public and
      private, 14–15;
  projections of graduates, 18–19

Hispanic American men:
  AIDS cases, 95;
  educational attainment, 7–8;
  employment status, 170, 172;
  high school drop-outs, 16–17;
  income, 142–43;
  labor force participation, 170, 172;
  labor force projections, 206, 208;
  living arrangements, 227–29;
  pension coverage, 430–31

Hispanic American women:
  AIDS cases, 95;
  births to, 65–67;
  educational attainment, 7–8;
  employment status, 170, 172;
  high school drop-outs, 16–17;
  income, 142, 144,
  labor force participation, 170, 172;
  labor force projections, 206, 208;
  living arrangements, 227–29;
  pension coverage, 430–31

Hispanic Americans:
  AIDS cases, 95;
  births to, 65–67;
  by age, 271;
  by region, 276–78;
  by state, 282–90;
  children's living arrangements, 240–41;
  college enrollment by degree level, 29–30;

college enrollment rate, 24, 26;
  degrees earned by level of degree, 29,
      32–33;
  educational attainment, 7–8;
  employment status, 170, 172;
  foreign born, 303, 305;
  high school drop-outs, 16–17;
  households, 227–29, 230–31;
  income, 110–11, 114, 116, 118–19, 142–44;
  labor force participation, 165, 170, 172;
  labor force projections, 206–08;
  living arrangements, 219, 227–29;
  marital status, 257, 259;
  occupation of, 165, 185–92;
  pension coverage, 430–31;
  population, 261, 266–68, 271, 276–78,
      282–90;
  poverty rate, 161–63;
  SAT scores, 20–21;
  spending by, 315, 374–87;
  working at home, 199–200

home health care, 90–91

homeownership, 415, 427–29, 295, 297–98,
    421–22

homes, as non-financial assets, 415, 421–23,
    427–29

homosexual couples. *See* Cohabitation

hospice care, 90, 92

hospital care, 87–89

households:
  by age, 219, 222–26, 230–31, 246–50;
  by income, 101–38; 156–58;
  by metropolitan status, 238–39;
  by race and Hispanic origin of householder,
      219, 227–31;
  by region, 236–37;
  by size, 219, 232–33;
  by type, 219–21, 224–29;
  debt of, 415, 424–26;
  financial assets of, 415, 418–20;
  homeownership of, 427–29;
  net worth of, 415–17;
  non-financial assets of, 415, 421–23;
  spending by, 315–414; 360–73;
  with children, 129–33, 219–21, 246–50

households, female-headed:
  by age, 123–28, 134, 136, 224–25, 249–50;
  employment status of, 174, 176;
  family, 220–21, 224–29, 249–50;
  homeownership of, 427–29;
  in poverty, 161, 163;
  income, 108–09, 118–28, 132–36;
  living alone, 134, 136, 220–21, 224–29;
  non-family, 220–21, 224–29
households, male-headed:
  by age, 123–28, 134–35, 249–50;
  employment status of, 174, 176;
  family, 220–21, 224–29, 249–50;
  homeownership of, 427–29;
  in poverty, 161, 163;
  income, 108–09, 118–28, 132–36;
  living alone, 134–35, 220–21, 224–29;
  non-family, 220–21, 224–29
households, married-couple, 219–21, 224–29:
  by age, 123–28, 224–29, 246–48;
  by education of husband and wife, 51–52;
  by race and Hispanic origin, 227–29;
  dual-income, 129–31, 177–78;
  employment status of, 174, 176;
  homeownership of, 427–29;
  in poverty, 161, 163;
  income, 101, 108–09, 118–31;
  spending by, 315, 360–73;
  with children, 129–31, 219–21, 246–48
human immunodeficiency disease (HIV),
      93–96. *See also* AIDS

immigration, 299–306
impairments, physical, 80, 82–84
income, 101–63:
  by age, 106–107, 112–17, 122–36, 139–41,
      145–47;
  by education, 137–38, 150–52;
  by household type, 101, 108–09, 118–38;
  by metropolitan status, 156–57;
  by occupation and sex, 153–55;
  by race and Hispanic origin, 110–11,
      114–19, 142–44;
  by region, 156–57;
  by state, 156, 158;
  debt by, 424–26;

distribution, 102–05;
  financial assets by, 418–20;
  net worth by, 416–17;
  non-financial assets by, 421–23;
  of foreign born, 303, 306;
  of households, 101–38, 156–58;
  of men, 101, 139–40, 142–43, 145–46, 148–51,
      153–55;
  of women, 101, 139, 141–42, 144–45, 147–50,
      152–55;
  sources of, 159–60;
  spending by, 315, 340–60
independent contractors, 197–98
industry of employment, 190–92, 199–200,
      213–15
infective and parasitic diseases, 79
injuries, 79
installment debt, 424–26
insurance. *See* Life insurance, health
      insurance
investment real estate, 422–23

job tenure, 165, 193–94

labor force, 165–217:
  alternative workers in, 197–98;
  by age, 166–73;
  by education, projected, 216–17;
  by full- and part-time status, 179–80;
  by industry, 190–92; 213–15;
  by occupation, 181–192, 209–12;
  by race and Hispanic origin, 165, 170–73,
      185–89;
  by sex, 165–73, 181–84;
  employee benefits, 201–03;
  foreign born in, 303, 306;
  job tenure of, 193–94;
  mobility of, 295, 297–98;
  parents in by presence of children, 174, 176;
  projections of, 165; 204–17;
  self-employed, 195–96;
  status of married couples, 177–78;
  unemployed, 169–73;
  women in by presence of children, 174–75;
  working at home, 199–200
life expectancy, 55, 98–99

life insurance, 418–20

living alone:

  by income, 108–09, 118–28, 134–36;

  by sex, 220–21, 224–29, 234–35, 244–45;

  homeowners, 427–29;

  spending of householders, 360–73

living arrangements, 219–59

male-headed households. *See under* Households

marijuana use, 74, 77

marital status:

  by race and Hispanic origin, 257–59;

  by sex, 219, 253–56;

  home health care by, 90–91;

  hospice care by, 90, 92;

  median age at first marriage, 253–54

married-couple households. *See under* Households

master's degrees. *See under* Degrees earned

meat, poultry, and fish consumption, 58–59

medical conditions:

  acute, 78–79;

  chronic, 78, 80–81

men:

  AIDS cases, 93–95;

  cohabiting by age, 251–52;

  college enrollment rate, 24–25;

  college enrollment projections, 44–49;

  degrees earned, 34–43; 44, 50;

  disabled, 83;

  educational attainment, 3–5, 7–8;

  employment status, 168–73;

  foreign born, 305;

  frequency of exercise, 68–69;

  full-time workers, 179–80;

  health status of, 56–57;

  high school drop-outs, 16–17;

  home health care recipients, 90–91;

  hospice care, 90, 92;

  hospital care, 87–89;

  income, 101, 139–140, 142–43, 145–46, 148–51, 153–55;

  labor force participation, 165–73;

  labor force projections, 204–05, 208;

  life expectancy, 98–99;

living alone, 221, 234–35;

living alone, by income, 108–09, 118–28, 134–35;

living arrangements, 219, 242–45; 251–52;

marital status, 219, 253–55;

occupation of, 181–84, 190–91;

part-time workers, 179–80;

pension coverage, 430–31;

physician visits by, 85–86;

population, 262–63;

religious preferences of, 310–11;

school enrollment, 44–49;

smoking behavior, 55, 74–75;

vitamin consumption, 61–62;

working at home, 199–200

mental disability, 82, 84

metabolic conditions, 81

metropolitan:

  households by size of area, 238–39;

  income by size of area, 156–57;

  population, 261, 291–94

migration. *See* Immigration *and* mobility, geographic

milk and milk products, consumption by sex, 58–59

mobility, geographic, 261, 295–98. *See also* Immigration

mortgage debt, 424–26

musculoskeletal conditions:

  acute, 79;

  chronic, 80–81

mutual funds, 418–20

Native Americans:

  AIDS cases, 95;

  births to, 65–66;

  by age, 272;

  by Hispanic origin, 266–68, 272, 276–78, 282–90;

  by region, 276–78;

  by state, 282–90;

  college enrollment by degree level, 29–30;

  degrees earned by level of degree, 32–33;

  foreign born, 306;

  population, 266–68, 272, 276–78, 282–90;

  SAT scores, 20–21

nervous conditions, 81
net worth, personal, 415–17
non-financial assets, 415, 421–23

occupation:
  by race and Hispanic origin, 165; 185–92;
  by sex, 153–55, 165, 181–84;
  by work at home status, 199–200;
  projections, 165, 209–12
outdoor recreational activities, 68, 70–71

part-time workers, 174–75, 179–80, 201–03
pensions, percent receiving, 160, 430–31
physician office visits, 85–86
picnicking, 68, 70
pneumonia, 79, 97
political behavior, by age, 261, 307–09. *See*
    *also* Voters
population, 261–314:
  by age, 261–65, 268–73;
  by metropolitan area, 261, 291–94;
  by race and Hispanic origin, 261, 266–73,
      276–78, 282–290;
  by region, 261, 274–78;
  by sex, 262–65;
  by state, 261, 279–90;
  foreign born, 303–06;
  immigrants in, 299–306;
  mobility of, 261, 296–99;
  projections, 264–76, 278–282, 287–290;
poverty rate, 101, 161–63

recreational activities, 68, 70–71
region:
  hospital care by, 87–89;
  households in, 236–37;
  income by, 156–57;
  population of, 261, 274–78;
  spending by, 315, 388–400
religious preference, by age, 261, 310–11
respiratory conditions:
  acute, 78–79;
  chronic, 81
retirement accounts, 418–20

SAT scores, 3, 20–21
savings bonds, 419–20
school enrollment, 3:
  by age, 11, 13;
  by grade, 11–12;
  college, 27–31;
  projections of college, 44–49;
  projections of high school, 14–15
self-employment:
  at home, 199–200;
  by age, 195–96;
  income, percent receiving, 160
sightseeing, 68, 70
single parent. *See* Households, male-headed
    *and* female-headed
single-person households. *See* Living alone
sinus problems, 78, 81
skin conditions, 79, 80
smoking behavior, by age, 74–75
snowboarding, 68, 71
spending, 315–414:
  by age, 320–39;
  by education, 401–14;
  by household type, 360–73;
  by income, 340–60;
  by race and Hispanic origin, 374–87;
  by region, 388–400;
  trends, 315–19
sport events, attendance at outdoor, 68, 70
state:
  as destination of immigrants, 301–302;
  educational attainment by, 9–10;
  income by, 156, 158;
  population of, 279–90
stocks, 418–20
suburbs. *See* Metropolitan
suicide, as cause of death, 97;
swimming, 55, 68, 70

tennis, 68, 70

unemployment. *See* Employment status
unmarried couples. *See* Cohabitation
urinary conditions, 81

vegetables, consumption of, 60
vehicles, as non-financial assets, 421–23
visual impairments, 80
vitamin consumption, 61–62
voters:
  by age, 261, 307–08;
  reasons for not voting, 261, 307, 309

walking for exercise, 55, 68, 60
wealth, personal, 415–31
wheelchair use, 84
White American men:
  educational attainment, 7–8;
  employment status, 170, 173;
  income, 142–43;
  labor force participation, 170, 173;
  labor force projections, 206, 208
  living arrangements, 227–29
  pension coverage, 430–31
White American women:
  births to, 65–67;
  educational attainment, 7–8;
  employment status, 170, 173;
  income, 142, 144;
  labor force participation, 170, 173;
  labor force projections, 206, 208;
  living arrangements, 227–29;
  pension coverage, 430–31
White Americans. *See also* White
     non-Hispanic Americans:
  births to, 65–67;
  children's living arrangements, 240–41;
  college enrollment rate, 24, 26;
  educational attainment, 7–8;
  employment status, 170, 173;
  foreign born, 303, 305;
  health status of, 56–57;
  households, 227–29, 230–31;
  income, 110–11, 114, 117–19, 142–44;
  labor force participation, 170, 173;
  labor force projections, 206–08;
  living arrangements, 219, 227–29;
  marital status, 257–58;
  occupation of, 185–92;
  pension coverage, 430–31;
  poverty rate, 161–63;

  religious preferences of, 310–11;
  SAT scores, 20–21;
  spending by, 315, 374–87;
  working at home, 199–200
White, non-Hispanic Americans:
  AIDS cases, 93, 95;
  births to, 65–66;
  by age, 273;
  by region, 276–78;
  by state, 282–90;
  college enrollment by degree level, 29–30;
  debt, 424–26;
  degrees earned by level of degree, 29,
    32–33;
  financial assets, 418–20;
  foreign born, 303, 305;
  income, 101, 110–11, 142–44;
  high school drop-outs, 16–17;
  labor force projections, 165, 206–08;
  marital status, 257, 259;
  net worth, 416–17;
  non-financial assets, 421–23;
  population, 261, 266–68, 273, 276–78,
    282–90
  women:
    AIDS cases, 93–95;
    births to, 65–67;
    cohabiting by age, 251–52;
    college enrollment rate, 24–25;
    college enrollment projections, 44–49;
    degrees earned, 34–43; 44, 50;
    disabled, 83;
    educational attainment, 3–4, 6, 8;
    employment status, 168–73;
    foreign born, 305;
    frequency of exercise by, 68–69;
    full-time workers, 174–75, 179–80;
    health status of, 56–57;
    high school drop-outs, 16–17;
    home health care recipients, 90–91;
    hospice care, 90, 92;
    hospital care, 87–89;
    income, 101, 139, 141–42, 144–45, 147–50,
     152–55;
    labor force participation, 165–73, 174–76;
    labor force projections, 204–05, 208;

life expectancy, 98–99;

living alone, 221, 234–35;

living alone, by income, 108–09, 118–28, 134, 136;

living arrangements, 219, 242–45, 251–52;

marital status, 219, 253–54, 256;

occupation of, 181–84, 190, 192;

part-time workers, 174–75, 179–80;

pension coverage, 430–31;

physician visits by, 85–86;

population, 262–63;

religious preferences of, 310–11;

school enrollment, 44–49;

smoking behavior, 74–75;

vitamin consumption of, 61–62;

with children, in labor force, 174–76;

working at home, 199–200

work arrangements, alternative, 197–98

workers:

at home, 199–200;

by education, 216–17;

by industry, 190–92, 213–15;

by occupation, 165, 181–92; 209–12;

full-time, 174–75, 179–80, 201–03;

independent contract, 197–98;

on call, 197–98;

part-time, 174–75, 179–80, 201–03;

projections of, 204–17;

self-employed, 195–96, 199–200;

temporary, 197–98;

with children, 174–76

young adults, living arrangements, 242-43